ENGLISH DRAMA
1660–1700

ENGLISH DRAMA
1660–1700

DEREK HUGHES

CLARENDON PRESS · OXFORD
1996

Oxford University Press, Walton Street, Oxford OX2 6DP

Oxford New York

Athens Auckland Bangkok Bombay
Calcutta Cape Town Dar es Salaam Delhi
Florence Hong Kong Istanbul Karachi
Kuala Lumpur Madras Madrid Melbourne
Mexico City Nairobi Paris Singapore
Taipei Tokyo Toronto

and associated companies in
Berlin Ibadan

Oxford is a trade mark of Oxford University Press

Published in the United States
by Oxford University Press Inc. New York

British Library Cataloging in Publication Data
Data available

Library of Congress Cataloguing-in-Publication Data
Hughes, Derek, 1944–
English drama, 1660–1700 / Derek Hughes.
Includes bibliographical references and indexes.
1. English drama—Restoration, 1660–1700—History and criticism.
I. Title.
PR691.H75 1995
822'.409–dc20 95–40292
ISBN 0–19–811974–7

1 3 5 7 9 10 8 6 4 2

Typeset by Alliance Phototypesetters
Printed in Great Britain
on acid-free paper by
Biddles Ltd,
Guildford and King's Lynn

FOR KATHERINE

Preface

This book is a critical study of all the surviving plays which were professionally premièred in England between 1660 and 1700: it analyses individual texts, often in detail, but tries to avoid the perils of isolated close reading by seeing each play in relation to the whole span of theatrical activity. It also attempts, on a more modest scale, to extend understanding of the social, political, and philosophical influences which shaped the dramatists' work. In setting particular texts within the total field, I try to achieve something like a close reading of the entire corpus, tracing recurrent and interacting motifs which often elude the eye when texts are viewed in isolation: examples are the stranger, or the woman falsified by history. My focus thus differs from that of Robert D. Hume's *The Development of English Drama in the Late Seventeenth Century*, but my intention is to complement rather than to challenge that indispensable work.

I discuss plays which received professional performance, though in this and other matters I have tried to place common sense above rigid consistency. It would, for example, be perverse to omit *The Country Gentleman* and *The State of Innocence*, and in some cases it is not clear whether a play was performed or not; here, I have generally given it the benefit of the doubt. A few manifestly unperformable plays have been mentioned because they throw some light on the performed repertoire. Perhaps three other pragmatic inconsistencies should be mentioned: I have given subtitles in my text only when they have some particular significance to my argument, and I have discussed *The Rehearsal* and *The Female Wits* in chapters on tragedy, in order to see them in conjunction with the plays which they parody. And, after experimenting with the consistent non-modernization of all play titles, I decided that the path of least inconvenience and anomaly would be to follow the form given in the copy-text.

In conformity with current scholarly practice, I use 'Caroline' to mean 'of Charles I' and 'Carolean' to mean 'of Charles II'. Because of the very large number of play-texts cited, I have not given an individual footnote citation for each, but have instead followed the example of Hume's *The Development of English Drama in the Late Seventeenth Century* in documenting copy-texts by means of a separate index of plays. The index is preceded by a bibliography of all dramatic texts cited, other than original quartos, and index entries are accompanied by a parenthetical indication of the text used, a simple parenthetical date being that of a quarto.

Clearly, the fundamental work of reference for a project such as this is Part i of *The London Stage*, but since its publication there has been further signif-icant work on the dating of premières, the most extensive being Judith Milhous and Robert D. Hume's 'Dating Play Premières from Publication Data, 1660–1700' and Pierre Danchin's *The Prologues and Epilogues of the Restoration 1660–1700*. I have generally followed the most recent authority, which is normally Danchin when a prologue or epilogue survives for the play. It must be emphasized, however, that definite external evidence for première dates is often lacking, and that the brief, parenthetical datings which I supply cannot capture all the nuances of probability or uncertainty. Marked uncer-tainty has been registered, but I have not distinguished certain dates from highly probable ones.

I should like this book to appeal to as wide a readership as possible, and have therefore briefly explained some things with which specialists will be well acquainted, such as the history of the companies and their theatres. I have tried to indicate all specific points of contact with other scholars, and to make pertinent suggestions for further reading, but I have been very sparing in the explicit expression of disagreement, and considerations of space have made it impossible to rehearse the existing state of critical opinion on every topic. To three scholars, however, I have intellectual debts which cannot ade-quately be expressed in a curt series of bibliographical references. They are Robert D. Hume, Judith Milhous, and Susan Staves.

Paul Hammond and Rob Hume have, respectively, read part and all of the manuscript, and I am most grateful for their labour and their constructive and detailed comments, on which I have acted to the best of my ability. Nadia Rigaud's invitation to participate on a colloquium on the Stranger in English Literature opened up a line of enquiry whose influence is evident throughout this book. My colleagues Bernard Capp and Robin Clifton have responded patiently to years of questioning about seventeenth-century history, and Sir Brooke Boothby and Michael Hodgetts have given painstaking help in my so far uncompleted research into the identity of Frances Boothby.

My discussion of the Dryden–Davenant *Tempest* appeared, in different form, as 'The Dryden–Davenant *Tempest* and some seventeenth-century images of the stranger', in *L'Étranger dans la littérature et la Pensée Anglaises*, ed. Nadia J. Rigaud, Centre Aixois de Recherches Anglaises 9 (Aix-en-Provence, 1989), 83–108. Material from the following articles has also been reworked, in abbreviated or selective form: 'Play and Passion in *The Man of Mode*', *Comparative Drama*, 15 (1981), 231–57; 'Dryden's *Don Sebastian* and the Literature of Heroism', *Yearbook of English Studies*, 12 (1982), 72–90; 'The Unity of Dryden's *Marriage A-la-Mode*', *Philological Quarterly*, 61 (1982), 125–42; 'The *Plain-Dealer*: A Reappraisal', *Modern Language Quarterly*, 43 (1982), 315–36; 'Art and Life in *All for Love*', *Studies in Philology*, 80 (1983), 84–107; 'Otway's *The Orphan*: An Interpretation', *Durham University Journal*, 75 (1983), 45–54; 'Cibber and Vanbrugh:

Language, Place, and Social Order in *Love's Last Shift*', *Comparative Drama*, 20 (1986), 287–304; 'Vanbrugh and Cibber: Language, Place, and Social Order in *The Relapse*', *Comparative Drama*, 21 (1987), 62–83; 'Naming and Entitlement in Wycherley, Etherege, and Dryden', *Comparative Drama*, 21 (1987), 259–89. In all cases, I am grateful to the original publishers for permission to reuse material.

Contents

1. 'To call every thing into question': Influences on the Drama   1

2. Astraea Redux? Drama, 1660–1668   30

3. 'Where is Astrea fled?': Tragedy, 1668–1676   78

4. 'The freedoms of the present': Comedy, 1668–1676   113

5. 'A Song expressing the Change of their Condition': Tragicomedy and Opera, 1668–1676   162

6. 'Senseless Riot, Neronian Gambols': Comedy, 1676–1682   185

7. 'Not one mark of former Majesty': Tragedy, 1676–1682   240

8. 'Dire is the Dearth and Famine on the Stage': Drama, 1682–1688   307

9. 'The surprising success of the Baudy Batchelour': Comedy, 1688–1695   331

10. 'A Cause like yours would summon the Just Gods': Tragedy, 1688–1695   358

11. 'Madam, You have done Exemplary Justice': Comedy, 1695–1700   377

12. 'Scarce a good One Play'd': Tragedy, 1695–1700   424

    Conclusion   450

BIBLIOGRAPHY OF NON-DRAMATIC TEXTS   459

INDEX OF PLAYS   473

GENERAL INDEX   477

CHAPTER ONE

'To call every thing into question': Influences on the Drama

'It proceeds from the same mind not to be pleas'd with Princes on the Stage, and not to affect them in the Throne.'[1] The stage and the monarchy were inseparably suppressed and inseparably restored, and for much of the 1660s the twin restorations remained ostentatiously linked, as play after play re-enacted and reconsecrated the miracle of 29 May. Shortly after the Restoration, the right to perform plays in London was vested by royal patent in two companies, the King's and the Duke's, managed respectively by Thomas Killigrew and Sir William Davenant, though discontented competitors remained active for some years.[2] During the previous reign both Killigrew and Davenant had been dramatists strongly associated with the court (Davenant being the more professional of the pair),[3] and both had shared Charles II's exile, though Davenant had perforce reconciled himself to the usurping regime after his capture en route to take up the lieutenant-governorship of Maryland in 1650. Whereas Killigrew turned out two-part closet dramas on the Continent, Davenant was keeping up his links with live theatre, finding loopholes in the ban on plays by staging a series of musical shows, sometimes with tactfully implicit royalist messages. The most substantial of these was *The Siege of Rhodes* (1656, with a second part in 1659), whose embattled hero and heroine seem to represent Charles I and Henrietta Maria in conflict with a foe more merciful than the one they had in fact found,[4] and with this Davenant achieved an impressive number of firsts: it was the first English opera, and made the first use of changeable scenery on the public stage; when,

Epigraph: *The Works of the Most Reverend Dr. John Tillotson* (12 vols., London, 1757), i. 95.

[1] Davenant, *The Siege of Rhodes*, dedication, ll. 32–4.

[2] The fullest account of theatrical operations in the early Restoration, and of illicit theatre during the Interregnum, is Leslie Hotson, *The Commonwealth and Restoration Stage* (Cambridge, Mass., 1928; repr. New York, 1962). Important later studies include Gunnar Sorelius, 'The Rights of the Restoration Theatrical Companies in the Older Drama', *Studia Neophilologica*, 37 (1965), 174–89; John Freehafer, 'The Formation of the London Patent Companies in 1660', *Theatre Notebook*, 20 (1965–6), 6–30; Judith Milhous and Robert D. Hume, 'New Light on English Acting Companies in 1646, 1648, and 1660', *Review of English Studies*, NS 42 (1991), 487–509.

[3] For sharp criticism of even Davenant's professionalism, see Deborah C. Payne, 'Patronage and the Dramatic Marketplace under Charles I and II', *Yearbook of English Studies*, 21 (1991), 137–52 (p. 143).

[4] Davenant, *The Siege of Rhodes*, pp. li–liii; Curtis A. Price, 'Political Allegory in Late-seventeenth-century Opera', in *Music and Theatre: Essays in Honour of Winton Dean*, ed. Nigel Fortune (Cambridge, 1987), 1–29 (pp. 4–5).

in 1661, Davenant opened his Lincoln's Inn Fields theatre, making changeable scenery a regular and indispensable part of professional theatre, he did so with a revised version of *The Siege of Rhodes*; and, when Dryden discussed the genesis of the heroic play in the preface to *The Conquest of Granada*, he named *The Siege of Rhodes* as the pioneering work of the genre. If, at this stage, it was sheer chance which had favoured Davenant's wily professionalism and confined Killigrew to the role of doodling amateur, the future was to show that chance had chosen wisely.

The Duke's Company moved to Lincoln's Inn Fields (a converted tennis-court) after a brief period at the Salisbury Court theatre, and after a longer initial stay in makeshift premises the King's Company moved in 1663 from Gibbons's Tennis Court in Vere Street to Bridges Street, Drury Lane. In 1671, three years after Davenant's death, the Duke's Company moved once more, to the new Dorset Garden theatre, which was the best equipped of all Restoration theatres for mounting scenically spectacular productions. The competitive advantage which the Duke's gained with Dorset Garden was cruelly augmented when, within weeks of its opening, the Bridges Street theatre was destroyed by fire, and for over two years Killigrew's company had the humiliating task of competing with its rival's novel technological splendour from the very theatre which the Duke's Company had just vacated. Nor could the King's Company afford to rebuild on a scale comparable to that of Dorset Garden, and when the new Drury Lane theatre opened in 1674 it was, in Dryden's apologetic words, 'A Plain Built House'[5]—though one which proved more satisfactory for straight drama.

Davenant from the outset had created the more innovative and enterprising company. It was he, for example, who had taken the lead in the field of scenery. Even Killigrew's assets were mixed blessings: he had the lion's share of old plays and experienced actors, but Davenant was in consequence obliged to take the plunge with new plays and to build a vigorous young company.[6] The King's Company had Dryden and, among its players, the star turn of Charles Hart and Nell Gwyn, whose talent for scenes of *risqué*, bantering courtship materially shaped the character and development of comedy, and by the end of the first decade the King's Company could boast the more adventurous and accomplished body of plays. But, from 1668, most new playwrights with any pretensions to status—Shadwell, Behn, Otway, Ravenscroft, Settle, Crowne, Durfey, Payne—wrote primarily or exclusively for the Duke's. The only significant writers to join Dryden at the King's were Lee and Wycherley (though the latter's *The Gentleman Dancing-Master* went to the Duke's because of

---

[5] 'Prologue . . . Spoken at the Opening of the New House', l. 1, in *The Works of John Dryden* (20 vols.; 1956–   ), i, ed. Edward Niles Hooker *et al.* (Berkeley and Los Angeles, 1956), 148.

[6] See Robert D. Hume, 'Securing a Repertory: Plays on the London Stage 1660–5', in *Poetry and Drama 1570–1700: Essays in Honour of Harold F. Brooks*, ed. Antony Coleman and Antony Hammond (London, 1981), 156–72.

the Bridges Street fire). But, by 1678, Wycherley's career was over, and the company was in such managerial disarray that Dryden and Lee defected; and, in 1682, it eventually merged with the Duke's. The disappearance of competition inhibited the risky venture of putting on new plays, and there was a slump in the staging of untried work, which somewhat eased after the Glorious Revolution, but was only completely reversed when theatrical competition resumed in 1695. Until the recent, very welcome, revivals of Behn's *The Lucky Chance* (1685), the popular 'Restoration' comedies dated either from the mid-1670s or from the period after 1695: from periods twenty to thirty years apart, separated by decisive domestic political change and an exhausting European war, and with almost no writers in common. Before rushing to huddle these plays under a single label, we might consider that the same is true of *Murder in the Cathedral* (1935) and *The Birthday Party* (1960), except that here the continuity of writers is greater.

The introduction of changeable scenery was one of a number of obvious changes in the practicalities of theatre. Apart from a few performances at the old Red Bull early in the Restoration, theatre moved completely indoors, though not yet behind the proscenium arch: scenery was behind the arch, but in most cases the acting was done on a substantial forestage, facilitating the complex and intimate dialogue of the best Restoration comedy. Admission charges were more expensive than to the old outdoor theatres,[7] but the idea that the Restoration audience was an upper-class coterie has long been discredited.[8] Actresses quickly appeared at both companies. And it became normal for plays to be published shortly after performance, though successful performance was by far the greater source of profit.[9] Inevitably, novel visual effects were indulged in moderation, with most plays using stock scenery and costumes: the main purveyor of lavish productions was the Dorset Garden theatre, with shows such as the operatic *Tempest* and *Psyche*, but these represented a major and special investment.[10] Nevertheless, the new scenic resources clearly influenced the character of drama. In comedy, they provided the possibility of recognizable representation of fashionable London locales, such as the New Exchange, the Mall, or the Mulberry Garden, and of visually

[7] The range of seat prices for ordinary performances was 1s., 1s. 6d., 2s. 6d., and 4s. (Judith Milhous, 'Company Management', in *The London Theatre World, 1660–1800*, ed. Robert D. Hume (Carbondale and Edwardsville, 1980), 1–34 (p. 17)).

[8] Harold Love, 'Who Were the Restoration Audience?', *Yearbook of English Studies*, 10 (1980), 21–44; Allan Richard Botica, 'Audience, Playhouse and Play in Restoration Theatre, 1660–1710', D.Phil. thesis (Oxford, 1985).

[9] Shirley Strum Kenny, 'The Publication of Plays', in *The London Theatre World*, ed. Hume, 309–36; Judith Milhous and Robert D. Hume, 'Dating Play Premières from Publication Data, 1660–1700', *Harvard Library Bulletin*, 22 (1974), 374–405. For the movement towards publication before the Restoration, see Richard Levin, 'Performance-Critics vs. Close Readers in the Study of English Renaissance Drama', *Modern Language Review*, 81 (1986), 545–59.

[10] See Judith Milhous, 'The Multimedia Spectacular on the Restoration Stage', in *British Theatre and the Other Arts, 1660–1800*, ed. Shirley Strum Kenny (Washington, London, and Toronto, 1984), 41–66.

rendering the clash between public and private that is central to so many London-based comedies: in *The Man of Mode*, for example, Dorimant's chief discomfitures occur, or originate, outdoors. Alternations between contrasting kinds of significant space have always been a fundamental theatrical resource, but they now have a new precision and new range of nuance. When Pinchwife loses Margery in the New Exchange and dashes around in panicky insecurity, as helplessly disorientated as one of the lovers in *A Midsummer Night's Dream*, or in Wycherley's own *Love in a Wood*, there is a vivid sense of the familiar becoming the unfamiliar, the city becoming forest. In *The Man of Mode*, similarly, when Dorimant starts to lose control of his emotions and lifestyle in the familiar but threateningly public setting of the Mall, the known civic locale quite explicitly becomes a pathless waste: 'Snatched from myself, how far behind | Already I behold the shore!' (III. iii. 125–6).[11]

This sudden dissolution of the familiar prepares us for Dorimant's journey into the desert which he believes to exist beyond Hyde Park; for here, momentarily, it has already swallowed the park up. Shadwell's operatic version of *The Tempest* renders the wilderness more literally, its shifts between '*Wild Island*' and the more regular landscape of '*Cypress Trees and Cave*'[12] emphasizing its alternation between the polarities of anarchy and ordering power, though these are not simply unsubtle visual tautologies: the most shocking failure of civilization occurs when Ferdinand apparently kills Hippolito (a non-Shakespearian character) in a duel, and it is appropriately ironic that this failure should occur amidst the more tamed landscape of the Cypress walks (IV, pp. 251–2). And in Shadwell's *Psyche* the same fundamental conflict is represented through a lavish variety of particular images: a wood, a temple, a palace, a garden, which turns into a desert, hell, a heaven containing the palace of Jupiter. Again, however, visual imagery can be ironically discredited, the temple being the setting for one of Shadwell's characteristic attacks on priestcraft and revealed religion.

In tragedy, perhaps the most positive consequence of spectacular scenery was to invest the action with the grandeur of a Le Brun historical painting, as in the battle for the Temple Mount which climaxes the second part of Crowne's *The Destruction of Jerusalem*. If scenic resources enabled writers of comedy to represent the familiar, and at times to defamiliarize it, they seduced tragedians into over-indulgence in the strange: exotic localities and supernatural effects, the latter often combining spectacle with music, as in the incantation scenes in Dryden's first three heroic plays. Yet, more often than not, such spectacle had little point. Dramatists laboured the exotic at a time

---

[11] Dorimant is quoting Waller, 'Of Loving at First Sight', ll. 3–4 (*The Poems of Edmund Waller*, ed. G. Thorn Drury (2 vols., London, 1893)), i. 100).

[12] As Judith Milhous points out, however, the stage directions in the Dryden–Davenant *Tempest* are often too perfunctory to permit full comparison between the stagings of the two versions ('The Multimedia Spectacular', 46).

when, as will be argued below, the strange was singularly lacking in symbolic potency, and they could be patently sceptical of the supernatural effects which they called for: Shadwell's *The Lancashire Witches* portrays the magical cavortings of witches, and yet denies their existence. The pre-eminent use of scenery as a sign-system articulating social and moral values had been in the ordering spectacle of the masque, but the ideology which had informed the masque was now in decline,[13] and indeed, far from seeing visible forms as expressing structural analogies between the various hierarchical levels of creation, many dramatists actively questioned whether they even corresponded to the nature of the specific thing seen. Elaborate visible spectacle became available at the very point at which the visual was losing much of its traditional weight of signification.

One dramatist, Nathaniel Lee, regularly used scenic spectacle to portray the extinction of the old signs, but others hankered for significance without achieving it, as Elkanah Settle did in *The Empress of Morocco*: '*The Scene open'd, is represented a Prospect of a Clouded Sky, with a Rain-bow. After a shower of Hail, enter from within the Scenes* Muly Hamet, *and* Abdelcador' (IV, p. 141). The play is suspended while the audience admires the unpopulated vista (unprecedentedly, the play was published with illustrations of its scenic effects). The hail-shower is then justified as an omen of disaster, validated by the analogy between the political and natural orders: 'When my King frowns, 'tis just that Heaven frown too' (IV, p. 141). But the analogy is invoked to make possible the spectacle, not vice versa, for the omen proves illusory. It is noteworthy that Settle feels compelled to justify the scenic spectacle by representing it as a sign, but in reality it signifies nothing.[14] In general, however, the subtlest visual signifiers were not specific scenic representations but—as in the past—neutral objects with multiple functions: when Horner, the apparently liberating lover, shuts Margery Pinchwife behind a door, he must obviously use the same proscenium door behind which her oppressive husband has already repeatedly locked her, and which has come to symbolize the oppressive restrictions of her marriage.

Information about casts of new plays is incomplete during the first decade, but thereafter a cast list often accompanies the published text, though our knowledge of casting is very sketchy for revivals and performances of old plays. Casting can be a useful guide to interpretation. On the few occasions on which the stereotypically virtuous Anne Bracegirdle is cast in an unchaste

<hr />

[13] See Nancy Klein Maguire, *Regicide and Restoration: English Tragicomedy, 1660–1671* (Cambridge, 1992); Paul Hammond, 'Dryden's *Albion and Albanius*: The Apotheosis of Charles II', in *The Court Masque*, ed. David Lindley (Manchester, 1984), 169–83.

[14] As so often with Settle, however, it is not entirely clear where the boundary between incompetence and subtlety lies. Shortly afterwards, a villain disguised as a priest assists his disguise by falsely interpreting the hail as a divine sign (IV, pp. 143–4). Perhaps Settle is, after all, making a statement about the death of the old signs. But the false interpretation quickly turns out to be dramatically irrelevant, since Muly Hamet is scornfully sceptical of it, and is captured by mere force.

role, the casting helps to defamiliarize and reassess the character of the transgressor, and the whole character of *All for Love* derives from the unusual assignment of the chief female roles (perhaps necessitated by depletion of King's Company personnel), with Cleopatra being written for the small, baby-faced Elizabeth Bowtell and Octavia for the bulky, domineering Katherine Corey.[15] Sir Fopling Flutter, played by the forceful and versatile leading actor William Smith, obviously stands in a relationship to his society quite different from that of Sparkish in *The Country-Wife*, who was played by a specialist fool, the buffoonish Jo Haynes.[16] Charles Hart, the leading actor of the King's Company, generally played engaging comic scallywags and dignified or flamboyant tragic heroes, with only occasional forays into villainy (for example, in Fletcher's Rollo, Jonson's Catiline, and Lee's Nero). He is unlikely to have given a darkly sadistic rendering of the part of Horner. But Betterton, the leading Duke's Company actor, had a far wider range and more menacing register. Although he did play roles like Hart's (such as Ramble in Crowne's *The Countrey Wit*), his repertoire also included such darkly sadistic characters as Bosola and Sir Salomon Single (Arnolphe) in John Caryll's conflation of Molière's *École* plays, and this range and register was fully exploited in his first great sex comedy role, as Dorimant in *The Man of Mode*: a part and a play that utterly altered the direction of comedy. After this decisive turning-point, there are a couple of parts which significantly expand Hart's range: Thomas Frollick in Durfey's *Trick for Trick*, and Manly in Wycherley's *The Plain-Dealer*. In the early Restoration, the gifts of Charles Hart and Nell Gwyn for bantering, outrageous courtship encouraged the exploitation of a particular duo of character types, which John Harrington Smith in 1948 christened the gay couple.[17] The influence of Betterton was altogether of a different order, consisting not in the creation of a particular character type but in encouraging the complexity and frequent darkness of post-1676 comedy.

Of course, much was restored in 1660 besides the King and the theatre. The royalist gentry returned to power, intent on restoring hierarchy and deference, as did a church in which the advocates of accommodation with moderate dissenters were outnumbered by those who favoured the repressive enforcement of orthodoxy. Many of the earliest Restoration plays were written by members of the nobility or the higher gentry, such as the Earl of Orrery and the

---

[15] See Michael A. Yots, 'Dryden's *All for Love* on the Restoration Stage', *Restoration and 18th Century Theatre Research*, 16/1 (1977), 1–10.

[16] When Betterton recast Octavia in 1684, the two actresses he considered, Charlotte Butler (who got the part) and Sarah Cooke, were both beauties (*The Letters of John Dryden*, ed. Charles E. Ward (Durham, NC, 1942), 24 (letter 11)). This casting would have created a quite different balance of sympathy between the two ladies. Similarly, William Mountfort's Sparkish would have created a different set of tensions than Haynes's.

[17] John Harrington Smith, *The Gay Couple in Restoration Comedy* (Cambridge, Mass., 1948).

Howard brothers (sons of the Earl of Berkshire), who celebrated the restitution of hierarchical normality after its prolonged and perplexing suspension. The sense of normality restored was spoiled by the plight of loyal cavaliers who could not recover estates which they had sold to pay fines, and by the continuing good fortune of many who had prospered under the rebels. But, whatever the rise and fall of individuals, the hierarchy itself was safe for a very long time. As late as 1738, Nicholas Brady marked the anniversary of the Restoration with a sermon lamenting that, in the Interregnum, 'The ancient Nobility were levelled with their Vassals, and the Peerage invaded by a Race of Upstarts'.[18] The social outlook here is indistinguishable from that of the earliest Restoration comedies, such as Sir Robert Howard's satire of Puritan upstarts, *The Committee* (1662). Yet the intellectual foundations of power may start to decay long before the power itself. Among late seventeenth-century writers, even those of a markedly conservative outlook, there is wide-spread recognition that women and men are differentiated in capabilities only by their difference in education—that one much cherished form of hierarchy was culturally rather than naturally determined—though the practical benefits of this recognition were long delayed. Christianity, though solidly and securely entrenched, was for the first time subjected to open sceptical critique. And, although the aristocracy was still secure, there was some recognition that it was a feudal archaism whose original rationale had vanished. 'The fashion of the age', lamented John Tillotson, 'is to call every thing into question.'[19]

The questioning which most troubled Tillotson and his fellows was that of Christian doctrine, and recent scholarship has concluded that the late seventeenth century witnessed an 'explosion' of upper-class atheism which exceeded anything in the following century.[20] The Earl of Rochester and Charles Gildon, both figures with theatrical connections, confessed to contact with atheistic circles (both had links with Charles Blount, a vigorous disseminator of anti-Christian argument),[21] and there are other slighter but still suggestive

---

[18] Nic[h]olas Brady, *A Sermon Preach'd . . . at the Cathedral Church of St. Paul on Monday the Twenty Ninth Day of May, 1738* (London, 1738), p. 12.

[19] Tillotson, *Works*, i. 95.

[20] David Berman, *A History of Atheism in Britain: From Hobbes to Russell* (London, New York, and Sydney, 1988), 48; id., 'Deism, Immortality, and the Art of Theological Lying', in *Deism, Masonry, and the Enlightenment: Essays Honoring Alfred Owen Aldridge*, ed. J. A. Leo Lemay (Newark, London, and Toronto, 1987), 61–78. See also *Atheism from the Reformation to the Enlightenment*, ed. Michael Hunter and David Wootton (Oxford, 1992); John Redwood, *Reason, Ridicule and Religion: The Age of Enlightenment in England 1660–1750* (London, 1976).

[21] Robert Parsons, *A Sermon Preached at the Funeral of the Right Honourable John Earl of Rochester*, in Gilbert Burnet, *Some Passages in the Life and Death of John, Earl of Rochester* (London, 1810), 107–44 (pp. 122, 125); C[harles] Gildon, *The Deist's Manual; or, a Rational Enquiry into the Christian Religion* (London, 1705), sigs. [A5^{r-v}]. Well-known martyrs to the cause of irreligion are Daniel Scargill (expelled from a Cambridge fellowship in 1669 and reduced to extreme poverty), Thomas Aikenhead (executed in 1697), and John Frazer (imprisoned in the previous year). See Samuel I. Mintz, *The Hunting of Leviathan: Seventeenth-Century Reactions to the Materialism*

links between theatre and the culture of free thought: Aphra Behn translated Fontenelle's *The History of Oracles and the Cheats of the Pagan Priests*, which adopts the common procedure (also used by Blount) of mocking paganism in ways which implicitly reflected upon Christianity,[22] Congreve corresponded warmly (though not on religious questions) with the republican free-thinker Walter Moyle, and both Sir Robert Howard and John Dennis published polemics against priestcraft. Here the intention is possibly to purify rather than to subvert Christianity, though among the baggage which Howard discards is belief in Christ's divinity.[23]

What is unclear, however, is the ratio of tip to iceberg, and the nature and extremity of opinions that were privately voiced, away from the evasive circumspection of print. The overwhelming impression created by churchmen is of an all-engulfing tide of scepticism, amoralism, and atheism, associated primarily with the materialism of Hobbes and his forerunner Epicurus, who described a universe of randomly moving material particles, with no governing providential design (a doctrine explicitly endorsed in Shadwell's plays). Deism was also beginning to attract notice in the early years of the Restoration: Stillingfleet and Boyle expressed concern in the 1660s, and according to the *Dictionary of National Biography* Edmund Hickeringill had experimented with it during the previous decade.[24] Indeed, although recent scholarship has generally seen Dryden as a lifelong Christian, *The State of Innocence* (1674) is, as Verrall noticed many years ago, clearly deist in its outlook:[25] Dryden was not inexplicably fabricating an intellectually misspent past when he confessed in *The Hind and the Panther* to a 'manhood, long misled by

and Moral Philosophy of Thomas Hobbes* (Cambridge, 1962), 50–2; Michael Hunter, ' "Aikenhead the Atheist": The Context and Consequences of Articulate Irreligion in the Late Seventeenth Century', in *Atheism from the Reformation to the Enlightenment*, ed. Hunter and Wootton, 221–54.

[22] [Bernard Le Bovier de Fontenelle], *The History of Oracles and the Cheats of the Pagan Priests*, [trans. Aphra Behn] (London, 1688).

[23] [Sir Robert Howard], *The History of Religion* (London, 1694); [John Dennis], *The Danger of Priestcraft to Religion and Government* (London, 1702); id., *Priestcraft Distinguish'd from Christianity* (London, 1715). Howard's work is attacked in [Charles Leslie], *The Charge of Socinianism against Dr. Tillotson Considered* (Edinburgh, 1695), 25–33.

[24] Edward Stillingfleet, *Six Sermons* (London, 1669), sig. A3ᵛ, pp. 99–101. In 1677 Stillingfleet published his *A Letter to a Deist*. In *A Free Enquiry into the Vulgarly Receiv'd Notion of Nature* (London, 1685/6), which he states to have been written *c.* 1666 (sig. [A8]), R[obert] B[oyle] observes that 'there is lately sprung up a Sect of Men . . . who . . . talk much indeed of God, but mean such a One, as is not really distinct from the Animated and Intelligent Universe' (p. 98). Phillip Harth provides a good account of seventeenth-century British deism (*Contexts of Dryden's Thought* (Chicago and London, 1968), 56–94).

[25] A. W. Verrall, *Lectures on Dryden*, ed. Margaret de G. Verrall (Cambridge, 1914; repr. New York, 1963), 150. Scott argued that Dryden was a religious sceptic until shortly before his conversion to Catholicism (*The Life of John Dryden*, in *The Works of John Dryden*, ed. Walter Scott (18 vols., London, 1808), i. 305–14). In the preface to *Tyrannick Love* Dryden mentions that he has been charged with '*Prophaneness and Irreligion*', and his rejection of atheism seems to me to avoid any specific commitment to Christianity (p. 110). The case for Dryden's deism has recently been revived in two capricious articles by William Empson, 'Dryden's Apparent Scepticism', *Essays in Criticism*, 20 (1970), 172–81, and 'A Deist Tract by Dryden', *Essays in Criticism*, 25 (1975), 74–100.

wandring fires'.²⁶ Atheism is in the eye of the beholder, and any challenge to the polemicist's system of belief could be construed as a repudiation of God himself: even Tillotson was charged with being 'own'd by the *Atheistical* Wits of all *England*, as their true *Primate* and *Apostle*'.²⁷ But the evidence strongly suggests that there was a small but flourishing sub-culture of fashionable atheism, particularly among young men about town, and that even deism could involve frivolous and unconstructive derision of Christianity.

The aggressive discourtesy of unbelievers was a frequent subject of comment: Samuel Parker entertainingly portrays a youth culture of bumptious ignorance, in which sciolists with '*no other stock of Learning, but a few shavings of Wit gathered out of Plays and Comedies . . . can scarce meet with a Clergy-man, but they must be pelting him with Oaths, or Ribaldry*, or *Atheistical Drollery*', and a specific encounter with mocking unbelief is commemorated in William Assheton's *A Discourse against Blasphemy*, addressed to one M. S., a blaspheming deist in the household of the Duke of Ormonde.²⁸ Nor was Assheton's encounter with M. S. an isolated indignity: 'ever after', records Assheton's biographer, '(instead of disputing with such) he tender'd them these little Two-penny books'.²⁹ Predominantly, atheism was seen as a genteel vice, though the shoe-maker in *The Man of Mode* has picked it up from his betters, and there is some evidence that tradesmen did likewise in real life. In a close echo of Samuel Parker, John Scott, canon of St Paul's, complained of '*little Pretenders* to Atheism,' with 'a few *shavings* of Wit gathered out of *Plays* and *Romances*'. But he then went on to complain that the malaise had spread from the gentry to the whole of society: 'for now adays to *scorn* and *despise* Religion is no longer the Prerogative of *Wits* and *Vertuosoes*, but the Infection is spread and propagated into *Shops* and *Stalls*, and the *Rabble* are become *Professors* of *Atheism*'.³⁰

We cannot know how common men such as Mr M. S. were; nor can we know how far John Scott was transmitting personally verified information and how far he was reproducing and improving what he had read in Samuel Parker. But the Christian polemicists themselves acknowledge that they are combating an oral culture with a disproportionately small number of published texts, and although moral scares can easily lead to exaggeration, we have no grounds to suspect the churchmen of wholescale misrepresentation. In a well-known letter, Richard Bentley wrote to an Oxford friend, Edward

---

²⁶ I. 73, in *The Works of John Dryden* (20 vols., 1956–), iii, ed. Earl Miner *et al.* (Berkeley and Los Angeles, 1969). The passage is cited by Verrall (*Lectures on Dryden*, 150).

²⁷ Leslie, *The Charge of Socinianism against Dr. Tillotson Considered*, 13–14.

²⁸ [Samuel Parker], *A Discourse of Ecclesiastical Politie*, 3rd edn. (London, 1671), pp. xxi, xxxii; William Assheton, *A Discourse against Blasphemy*, 3rd edn. (London, 1694). Parker's reference to '*Plays and Comedies*' is not an early attack on Restoration comedy, but a lament for the way in which impious drolls pervert the chaste wit of Fletcher and Jonson.

²⁹ Thomas Watts, *The Christian Indeed, and Faithful Pastor* (London, 1714), 60.

³⁰ John Scott, *The Christian Life*, pt. ii, 2nd edn. (London, 1686), i. 102, 109.

Bernard, assuring him on his personal experience that the paucity of atheistic books did not guarantee a paucity of atheists. There were many English atheists, all inspired by a single atheistic writer, Hobbes: 'I know it to be true by the conversation I have had with them'.[31] But Hobbes was not in fact alone, especially by the 1690s. Throughout the period, a more diffused and varied stimulus to heterodoxy came from Montaigne, whose work in a few respects foreshadows that of Hobbes.[32] Particularly influential were his denial of the possibility of certain knowledge, his moral relativism, and his emphasis on the vulnerability of reason to convulsive change as a result of trivial physical stimuli. This promoted a belief in the incoherence of human identity, already to be found in Shakespeare and prominent in plays such as *Marriage A-la-Mode* and *Venice Preserv'd*, and his denial of values validated by universal consent was even more influential. In words which many dramatists took to heart, he wrote: 'Thou seest but the order and policie of this little little Cell wherein thou art placed. . . . This law thou aleagest is but a municipall law, and thou knowest not what the universall is'.[33] The little cell and the municipal law provide the fundamental images of many late seventeenth-century plays, right up to Congreve's *The Way of the World* (1700), whose very title paradoxically links the ideas of universality (world) and idiosyncratic fashion (way).

Montaigne's denial of universal consent in morality prepared the way for denial of universal consent about the existence of God. It also encouraged a critical comparison of Christianity and other religions, and promoted a mode of covert attack upon Christianity through mockery of absurdities in non-Christian religions which were patently shared by Christianity itself. Scepticism about Vespasian's healing of a blind and a lame man,[34] for example, is a coded way of expressing scepticism about the miracles of Christ.

---

[31] *The Correspondence of Richard Bentley, D. D.* [ed. Christopher Wordsworth] (2 vols., London, 1842), i. 39. The disparity between the numbers of atheistic books and of atheists is also noted in Simon Patrick, *A Sermon Preached . . . Novemb. 13.* (London, 1678), 21.

[32] The seminal account of Montaigne's influence on Restoration literature is in Louis I. Bredvold, *The Intellectual Milieu of John Dryden: Studies in Some Aspects of Seventeenth-Century Thought* (Ann Arbor, 1934), 29–34, 117–19, and *passim*. While stressing Montaigne's influence on French unbelief, Bredvold accepts his claim to be diminishing reason in order to exalt faith, and also accepts the similar claims of Montaigne's successors Charron and La Mothe Le Vayer. Richard H. Popkin regards the genuineness of Montaigne's faith as undecidable, but accepts the Christian professions of Charron and La Mothe Le Vayer (*The History of Scepticism from Erasmus to Spinoza* (Berkeley, Los Angeles, and London, 1979), 55–6, 62, 90–3). La Mothe Le Vayer's insincerity seems to me to be quite transparent, and recent scholarship has made a strong case for Charron's unbelief: Tullio Gregory, 'Pierre Charron's "Scandalous Book" ', in *Atheism from the Reformation to the Enlightenment*, ed. Hunter and Wootton, 87–109. The monumental study of educated unbelief in seventeenth-century France is René Pintard, *Le Libertinage érudit dans la première moitié du XVIIe siècle* (Paris, 1943). According to Pintard, Montaigne was 'naturaliste ou épicurien . . . et toujours se disant et se voulant chrétien' (p. 60).

[33] *Montaigne's Essays*, tr. John Florio, Everyman's Library (3 vols., London and New York, 1910), ii. 229 (ch. xii).

[34] Suetonius, *De Vita Caesarum* viii, 'Divus Vespasianus', 7; [Charles Blount], *Great is Diana of the Ephesians* (London, 1680), 26. The incident is mentioned in Montaigne, iii. 182 (ch. 8).

This is probably the import of La Mothe Le Vayer's 'Dialogue sur le sujet de la divinité', a work much influenced by Montaigne, and it is certainly the import of Charles Blount's commentary on the first two books of Philostratus' life of the Neopythagorean miracle-worker Apollonius of Tyana, who provides a vehicle for the covert mockery of Christ. Noting that Apollonius' parents were too well known for him to pretend to be the son of Jupiter, Blount observes that 'nothing is so great an assistant to a Divine Birth, as obscure and mean Parents'.35

Interest in the diversity of cultural values raised the possibility that the subordination of the female to the male might be a local cultural convention, not a universal natural law.36 It also emphasized the absence of any fixed and universally agreed sexual morality. Diversity of sexual codes is documented in Sextus Empiricus (Montaigne's philosophical master), Montaigne himself, Charron, and more extensively in La Mothe Le Vayer. It is also the subject of Louis de Gaya's *Ceremonies Nuptiales* (1680), a study of exotic matrimonial customs, such as the Cuban habit of permitting all the wedding guests to sleep with the bride.37 A more explicitly subversive work was William Lawrence's extraordinary *Marriage by the Morall Law of God Vindicated*, which John Moore, Bishop of Norwich, regarded as being comparable in perniciousness with *Leviathan* itself.38 Despite its disarmingly orthodox title, this is a polemic denial of the proposition that religious ceremony can have any role in validating a marriage: the only foundation of marriage is copulation (so that, by implication, the Duke of Monmouth is legitimate heir to the throne).39 Lawrence lists some wonderfully absurd customs for solemnizing marriage, with the insinuation that no ceremony, however venerable and revered, can bind more effectively, and Mosaic Law is subjected to the mocking scrutiny of cultural relativism, being judged less humane in its treatment of non-virgin brides than the customs of some American Indian tribes (pp. 6–8).

Cruder attacks on the ceremonial containment of sexuality were mounted by libertine poetasters such as Thomas Sawyer, who denounces marriage as a 'religious Cheat, | By which man kind their freedome loose',40 and there was

---

35 Charles Blount, *The Two First Books, of Philostratus. Concerning the Life of Apollonius Tyanaeus* (London, 1680), 16.

36 See e.g. Oratius Tubero [François de La Mothe Le Vayer], 'Dialogue sur le mariage', in *Cincq dialogues, faits à l'imitation des Anciens* (2 vols., Frankfurt am Main, 1716), ii, *Quatre autres dialogues du mesme auteur. Faits comme les precedens à l'imitation des Anciens*, 361–466 (pp. 374–82).

37 [Louis de Gaya], *Matrimonial Customs; or, the Various Ceremonies, and Divers Ways of Celebrating Weddings, Practised amongst all the Nations, in the whole World* (London, 1687), 96–7.

38 [William Lawrence], *Marriage by the Morall Law of God Vindicated against All Ceremonial Laws* ([London], 1680); John Moore, *A Sermon Preach'd . . . 28th of May, 1682* (London, 1682), 5–6.

39 This conclusion is spelt out clearly in Lawrence's *The Right of Primogeniture, in Succession to the Kingdoms of England, Scotland, and Ireland* (London, 1681).

40 [Thomas Sawyer], *Antigamus; or, A Satyr against Marriage* (Oxford, [1681]), 1. The offensive against marriage is discussed in Maximillian E. Novak, 'Margery Pinchwife's "London Disease": Restoration Comedy and the Libertine Offensive of the 1670's', *Studies in the Literary Imagination*, 10 (1977), 1–23.

an alarmist sense that marriage itself was under threat. Men, complained Robert Boyle, have always drunk and whored, but in the past they knew that they were doing wrong; now, they regard their actions as having impeccable intellectual justification.[41] The modest sex, complained Robert South, 'are come to brave it in theatres and taverns; where virtue and modesty are drunk down, and honour left behind to pay the reckoning;'[42] and, alluding to a notorious publication of the Blount circle, he noted that 'Some have dared to argue for their debauchery from principles (some call them oracles) of reason' (p. 86).[43] In a far earlier work than *The Oracles of Reason*, *Great is Diana of the Ephesians* (1680), Blount quoted the Chorus Sacerdotum from Fulke Greville's *Mustapha*, treating it as sheer testimony to the claims of appetite:

> *Oh wearisom condition of Humanity!*
> *   Born under one Law, to another bound . . .*
> *If Nature did not take delight in blood,*
> *She would have made more easie way to good.*

Quoting the same passage in the same year, in a sermon preached on 2 April, Tillotson noted that it is 'frequently in the mouths of many who are thought to bear no good-will to religion'.[44]

Marriage was not superseded by an anarchy of philosophic lust, and the theatre itself never took up the callow libertinism of a Sawyer: for all their scepticism, the best Restoration comedies portray not the joys and freedoms of the new sexual outlook but its psychological and practical problems, though they do frequently suggest that unhappy marriages should be subject to easy dissolution. But the image of morality as municipal rather than universal law was profoundly influential, and dramatists often push it to extremes, portraying even the single city of London as a Babel of absurdly localized codes, articulated in diverse languages that approach and even attain the condition of idiolects. And here the influence of Montaigne is certainly reinforced by that of Hobbes: a writer whose influence on the drama has repeatedly been discussed, yet discussed in very limited terms. Critics have on the whole concentrated on Hobbes's materialistic interpretation of human nature, his consequent denial of free will, his portrayal of man as an appetitive creature who in the state of nature was at war with all other men, and his moral relativism (which was more vigorously developed than Montaigne's):

---

[41] [Rober]T [Boyl]E, *Some Considerations about the Reconcileableness of Reason and Religion* (London, 1675), pp. i–ii.

[42] Robert South, *Sermons Preached upon Several Occasions* (7 vols., Oxford, 1823), iii. 82. For similar sentiments, again associating the general malaise with the stage, see ii. 36; iii. 382; vii. 159, 167. See also Tillotson, *Works*, iv. 12, 63; vi. 291; xi. 72, 110 (a particularly long and well-known denunciation).

[43] Char[les] Blount, [Charles] Gildon, *et al.*, *The Oracles of Reason* (London, 1693) was a collection of deistic and free-thinking essays.

[44] [Blount], *Great is Diana of the Ephesians*, 4–5; *Mustapha*, Chorus Sacerdotum [concluding chorus], ll. 1–2, 17–18 (Blount quotes the entire chorus). Tillotson, *Works*, ii. 272.

right and wrong had no meaning in the state of nature, and the arbiter of morality was the sovereign, to whom Hobbes eventually gave the authority even to determine which books of the Bible were canonical.[45] Yet even these well-covered topics deserve some further attention. Hobbes's materialism, for example, helped to formulate the problems of human identity that recur throughout Carolean drama. Like Montaigne's less methodical subjection of reason to material influence, his reduction of human life and consciousness to processes of matter in motion implies that human identity is essentially unstable, and indeed he specifically addresses the question of identity, citing the problem of whether the ship of Theseus remains the same object when a gradual sequence of repairs has replaced all the original material.[46] It does, but only because identity consists in an unbroken sequence of movements: 'that man will always be the same, whose actions and thoughts proceed all from the same beginning of motion' (p. 137). Sameness of personality is simply an unbroken continuum of change. 'But,' the Cambridge Platonist John Smith objected, 'if our *Souls* were nothing else but *a Complex of fluid Atomes*, how should we be continually roving and sliding from our selves, and soon forget what we once were?'[47] This could well be a description of Jaffeir in *Venice Preserv'd*.

Social identity is as problematic as personal identity. To escape from the horror of the state of nature, men formed societies, surrendering the dangerous freedom of anarchy for subjection to a protective authority, the most stable protection being offered by an absolute monarch, to whom men contracted away their natural rights in return for security (but who could not himself be reciprocally bound by the contract). Hobbes's conception of society is thus grounded upon a paradox. Aristotle had taught in his *Politics* that man was a social animal who fulfils his natural potential within a civilized community, but this is a view which Hobbes explicitly rejects,[48] since for him society is necessitated specifically by the appetitive, antisocial savagery of the human race. Humanity creates societies not to fulfil its nature but to escape it. The paradox of a civilization created by and inseparable from the intrinsic savagery of its members recurs throughout the drama of Charles II's reign, being equally fundamental to (for example) the comedy of *The Country-Wife* and the tragedy of *The Orphan*. It is a prime postulate of such plays that man is in equal measure both savage and citizen: he can neither reconcile these

45 Thomas Hobbes, *Leviathan*, ed. C. B. Macpherson (Harmondsworth, 1968), ch. xxxiii, 415. Richard Tuck notes that Hobbes's earlier *De Cive* and the *Elements of Law* were not offensive to Christians ('The "Christian Atheism" of Thomas Hobbes', in *Atheism from the Reformation to the Enlightenment*, ed. Hunter and Wootton, 111–30 (p. 113)).

46 *Elements of Philosophy*, in *The English Works of Thomas Hobbes of Malmesbury*, ed. Sir William Molesworth (11 vols., London, 1839–45; repr. Aalen, 1966), i. 136–8. The problem is also cited in Robert Boyle, *Some Physico-Theological Considerations about the Possibility of the Resurrection* (London, 1675), 6.

47 John Smith, *Select Discourses*, 2nd edn. (Cambridge, 1673), 78.

48 *Philosophical Rudiments Concerning Government and Society*, in *English Works*, ii. 2–3.

elements of his nature nor cultivate one to the exclusion of the other; they remain eternally conflicting, yet eternally inseparable.

Social hierarchy is no more grounded upon innate principles of order than society itself. Aristotle's belief that men are naturally differentiated for pre-eminence or subordination was as groundless as his belief in man's natural sociability, and Hobbes repeatedly derides it.[49] Pre-eminence and subordination were necessary, but their allocation did not correspond with innate distinctions of worth, and the claims of certain classes or castes to congenital pre-eminence (claims which figured largely in the early drama of restoration) were preposterous. The hierarchical superiority of the male to the female was also called into question.[50] But Hobbes dissolved the universal, natural character not only of traditional hierarchy but of traditional morality. Beyond the nucleus of natural laws essential for social stability, moral values were decided by political authority: for right and wrong had no meaning in the state of nature. In an analogy which finds strong echoes in *The Man of Mode*, Hobbes even likened social codes to the rules of a game: 'It is in the Lawes of a Commonwealth, as in the Lawes of Gaming; whatsoever the Gamesters all agree on, is Injustice to none of them'; 'as men in playing turn up trump, and as in playing their game their morality consisteth in not renouncing, so in our civil conversation our morality is all contained in not disobeying of the laws.'[51]

Hobbes's work is a sustained attempt to contain and limit the possibilities of scepticism:[52] to link doctrine to authority and (a constant preoccupation) to determine the signs by which probabilities may be determined and by which social stability may be maintained. There should, for example, be 'manifest signs' that the law expresses the ruler's will (*Leviathan*, ch. xxvi, 319), and signs by which one may interpret events, or the possibly hostile intentions of one's fellows. He shared the widespread horror of confusing words with 'things', believing that the insubordination of the sects and the intellectual stagnation of scholasticism were alike sustained by a corruption of language in which insignificant expressions (among which he included the '*incorporeall substance*' of the soul (*Leviathan*, ch. iv, 108)) were held to correspond to real entities. Linguistic signs have no essential significance, for

---

49 Ibid. 38–9; *De Corpore Politico; or, The Elements of Law, Moral and Politic*, in *English Works*, iv. 102–3; *Leviathan*, ch. xv, 211; cf. *Behemoth: the History of the Causes of the Civil Wars of England*, in *English Works*, vi. 251.

50 In *De Corpore Politico* Hobbes claims that in general, and with exceptions, women are less apt for government than men (p. 160), but in *Leviathan* he questions whether man is 'of the more excellent Sex' (ch. xx, 253).

51 *Leviathan*, ch. xxx, 388; *The Questions concerning Liberty, Necessity, and Chance*, in *English Works*, v. 194.

52 In his Boyle lectures, John Harris unfairly but half-truthfully links him with Sextus Empiricus (*A Defence of Natural and Revealed Religion: Being a Collection of the Sermons Preached at the Lecture Founded by the Honourable Robert Boyle, Esq; (From the Year 1691 to the Year 1732)* [ed. Sampson Letsome and John Nicholl] (3 vols., London, 1739), i. 370, 407).

language originates in arbitrary compact, as consequence of the need to establish signs for the conducting of social intercourse. The Neoplatonic view that Adam's original language had been a system of natural signs, genuinely corresponding to the things expressed, was in decline, and Hobbes trenchantly rejects it: God taught Adam a few words to introduce him to the principles of language, but even God could not invent the natural verbal sign; and, in any case, language was reinvented afresh after Babel (*Leviathan*, ch. iv, 100–1). 'That is a true sign, which by the consent of men becomes a sign' (*Philosophical Rudiments*, 221). The linguistic compact is potentially unstable, and it is perpetually necessary to establish agreed meanings and careful definitions. But communal contracts about the meanings of signs necessarily confine them to denoting the shared experiences of the contractors. Language cannot describe the sacred, and the terms which we apply to God simply have their origin in agreed social convention: 'And because words (and consequently the Attributes of God) have their signification by agreement, and constitution of men; those Attributes are to be held significative of Honour, that men intend shall so be' (*Leviathan*, ch. xxxi, 405–6). Verbal contact the other way, between God and man, is also a problem. To give the monarch authority to determine the biblical canon is, obviously, to diminish its status as direct divine utterance, and Hobbes himself treated Holy Writ with lordly idiosyncrasy, for example identifying the Trinity as Moses, Christ, and the Apostles (*Leviathan*, ch. lxii, 522–3). When the Bible records instances of divine speech to men, Hobbes does his best to explain them away, and his radical reinterpretation of the biblical text turns it into a history of material events whose divine authorship cannot be verified: 'Christian men doe not know, but onely beleeve the Scripture to be the Word of God' (*Leviathan*, ch. xliii, 614). The oath, too, a verbal commitment which was traditionally inscribed in the Book of God, was no more effective than an ordinary civil contract (*Leviathan*, ch. xiv, 201).

The divine exceeds human expressibility because it lies outside the shared, communicable experience proper to conventional signs. Even if God spoke directly to a man, the recipient could not authenticate his experience to other men. But the intentions and passions of the individual are also on, or beyond, the margins of shared experience. Man reads another's passions from his own, but constitutions and priorities differ, and 'the characters of mans heart, blotted and confounded as they are, with dissembling, lying, counterfeiting, and erroneous doctrines, are legible onely to him that searcheth hearts' (*Leviathan*, Introduction, 83). Speech cannot provide 'certain signes' of the passions (*Leviathan*, ch. vi, 129). Nor can individuals easily correlate their private intentions with the public currency of meaning, or be sure of the externally received meanings of the words with which they express them: it is '*difficult* to recover those conceptions for which the name was ordained; and that not only in the language of other men . . . but also in our discourse, which being derived from the custom and common use of speech, representeth unto us not our own conceptions'.[53]

When characters in Carolean drama experience problems with language, they are generally Hobbesian problems. Dryden loved to trace language back to its psychological or social beginnings, and created several dramatic moments which encapsulate or re-enact some linguistic moment of origin. In *The Indian Emperour* Guyomar, inhabiting a society without metaphor, spontaneously invents it as he struggles to use the shared signs of his culture to describe something that lies outside their shared cultural experience: European sailing ships. And in *Marriage A-la-Mode* there is a very literal scene of language acquisition, in which the scatter-brained Melantha gains her day's supply of French words from her maid, who has scoured French romances for them, Melantha exchanging an item of her wardrobe for each word. This is an extreme case of the Hobbesian view of language as an externally originating and imperfectly understood sign-system which 'representeth unto us not our own conceptions'. Yet the imperfect, incomplete medium of language can exercise a paralysing power by supplanting the reality which it so inadequately signifies. Character after character in drama of the 1670s re-lives the errors of Hobbes's schoolmen, mistaking systems of words for the actual substance of experience. Many of Dryden's characters flagrantly treat words as things, and Lee's are mesmerized by incantatory patterns whose power is exclusively that of linguistic structure. Yet more insidiously, characters can only envisage the order of experience in terms of the structure of language. For example, the age-old question of whether the loved one is true or false remains as obsessive as ever, but it becomes a question that is not only tormenting but meaningless, since it seeks in experience for qualities that can only be found in discourse: as Hobbes wrote, '*True* and *False* are attributes of Speech, not of Things' (*Leviathan*, ch. iv, 105). For Hobbes, according to a recent editor, 'Language is the expression or reflection of thought, not reality. To know the basic structure of language is to know the basic structure of our thought; this may or may not coincide with the basic structure of reality.'[54] For many, it plainly did not. Dramatists were far more fascinated by the perception of an essential and insuperable incompatibility between the orders of language and experience than by what is nowadays the best known area of seventeenth-century linguistics: the Royal Society's aim 'to return back to the primitive purity, and shortness, when men deliver'd so many *things*, almost in an equal number of *words*',[55] and John Wilkins's associated attempt to circumvent the snares of language by producing a system of signs whose

---

[53] *Human Nature; or, The Fundamental Elements of Policy*, in *English Works*, iv. 23.

[54] Thomas Hobbes, *Computatio sive Logica*, translation and commentary by Aloysius Martinich, ed. and introd. by Isabel C. Hungerland and George R. Vick (New York, 1981), 363.

[55] Thomas Sprat, *History of the Royal Society*, ed. Jackson I. Cope and Harold Whitmore Jones (St Louis and London, 1959), 113.

hierarchies and interrelationships would mimic those of the world of things, and which, like numerals, could be understood by speakers of different languages.56

Hobbes appears to be the chief inspiration of the conspicuous disjunction of language and the sacred that characterizes so much leading drama in the late seventeenth century, though there was some interest (on the part, for example, of Charles Blount) in the still more drastic approach of Spinoza's *Tractatus Theologico-Politicus* (1670), which describes both Testaments as 'a fortuitous collection of the works of men',57 and regards Scripture as sacred only 'so long as it stirs mankind to devotion towards God;' otherwise, 'it becomes nothing but paper and ink' (p. 168). Spinoza constantly combats the status of the Scriptures as a unique and exclusive record of divine law. His deconsecration of the biblical text necessarily involves rationalistic explanations of direct utterances from God to man, and even the Mosaic Law becomes one of Montaigne's municipal laws: the Hebrews were chosen only to inhabit 'a certain strip of territory', and the Law of Moses was only for them (p. 8). But it is also possible to find more simply whimsical and mischievous redefinitions of the idea of a sacred text. Deriding the idea that marriage is in any way dependent upon verbal ceremony, that great marital revisionist William Lawrence startlingly redefined one of the most archetypal images of divine writing: 'The Paps therefore wonderfully prepared to overflow with Milk, just against the time the Child is to be born, are External Tables, wherein God hath written to Innocents, in letters white as Snow; that the Mother ought to aliment them with the Milks of her Breasts'.58 The word is here made flesh in a new sense.

Differences of religious belief are differences in the imaginative apprehension and representation of the cosmos. For the sceptics and Hobbes, humanity lived amidst doubtful appearances and signs, but for the Christian the cosmos, though full of enigma, was adequately legible. Against Hobbes's belief that 'the characters of man's heart' are 'blotted' almost beyond recognition may be set the adherence of Charles Hickman, Bishop of Derry, to the old maxim of *Loquere ut te videam*:

And to make Society more safe and easie to us, he [God] has endow'd us with faculties fit and proper for this use; a wonderful Talent of Language, to communicate unto one another the secret resentments of our Soul; and an open countenance, like Windows into our heart, thro' which our passions and inclinations may be plainly read.59

---

56 John Wilkins, *An Essay towards a Real Character, and a Philosophical Language* (London, 1668).

57 *The Chief Works of Benedict de Spinoza*, tr. R. H. M. Elwes (2 vols., London, 1883; repr. New York, 1951), i. 170.

58 [Lawrence], *Marriage by the Morall Law of God*, 132.

59 Charles Hickman, *Fourteen Sermons Preach'd, at St. James's Church in Westminster* (London, 1700), 133.

It was, certainly, possible to attain a state of illegibility, though this was an unnatural and often impermanent condition:

Every Action of Man has an indelible Character stamp'd upon it, by which its value is easie to be known.

'Tis true, that this Evidence also may be stifled for a time; and there are those who, with much adoe, wear out these Characters of Good and Evil, which Nature has imprinted in their Souls.[60]

As Ben Jonson more crisply phrased it, '*Language* most shewes a man: speake that I may see thee.'[61] *Loquere ut te videam* was also cited by South.[62] But when Dryden cited it, in *An Evening's Love*, he did so ironically, in the midst of a frenzied non-conversation, and in the context of a play in which heaven itself was mute: 'all eyes and no tongue'.[63] Nevertheless, for many, as for Hickman, man remained a morally legible creature in a morally legible universe, and images of writing abound in Restoration sermons. Extraordinary acts of Providence, such as the Restoration, provided visible characters and signatures of divine design. God's law was still legibly inscribed in the human heart, and, for many, in what Thomas Jekyll termed the 'visible Sermon' of the Creation.[64] Human acts are still legibly recorded in celestial books. Language is a divine gift to man, which is perverted from its intrinsic purpose if used as an instrument of deception or malice; and the greatest perversion of language, perjury, is liable to 'all the *Curses* in Gods Book' and 'the *flying Roll* loaded with the Curses of God'.[65] The book thus remained a fundamental Christian image of the divine and natural order, and the celebrants of cosmic legibility far outnumbered the sceptics and Hobbists. Yet it is striking how little their outlook is reflected in the work of the leading dramatists. For example, one notable feature of the Restoration adaptations of Shakespeare is their uninterest in the symbolically potent book. In the Dryden–Davenant *Tempest* Prospero no longer exercises power through the book; in Durfey's adaptation of *Cymbeline* Jupiter does not descend to lay an inscribed tablet in the breast of the sleeping hero; and in Cibber's adaptation

---

60 Charles Hickman, *A Sermon Preached . . . Octob. 2. 1692* (London, 1692), 7.

61 *Discoveries*, ll. 2031–2, in *Ben Jonson*, ed. C. H. Herford, Percy and Evelyn Simpson (11 vols., Oxford, 1925–52), viii.

62 South, *Sermons Preached upon Several Occasions*, iii. 37.

63 III. i. 360; IV. i. 115.

64 Tho[mas] Jekill [*for* Jekyll], *A Sermon Preach'd . . . June 27. 1698* (London, 1698), 27.

65 Thomas Comber, *The Nature and Usefulness of Solemn Judicial Swearing* (London, 1682), 36; Richard Lucas, *Sixteen Sermons, The Eight Last of which were Preach'd upon Particular Occasions* (London, 1716), 277. The roll of curses (an allusion to Zech. 5: 2–3) is also mentioned in *The Theological Works of William Beveridge, D. D.*, Library of Anglo-Catholic Theology (12 vols., Oxford, 1842–8), v. 421–2. Susan Staves argues that the numinous power of oaths declined in the late seventeenth century, though she also emphasizes that 'elements of earlier thinking survived' (*Players' Scepters: Fictions of Authority in the Restoration* (Lincoln, Nebr. and London, 1979), 201, 231). John Spurr has recently documented the continuing power of the oath throughout and beyond the late seventeenth century ('Perjury, Profanity and Politics', *The Seventeenth Century*, 8 (1993), 29–50).

of *Richard III* Forrest is not briefly deterred from the murder of the Princes by the sight of a prayer book.

The legible universe is one which demonstrates fixed and inviolable principles of rational order. For the royalist divines Robert South and Richard Allestree, as for Shakespeare's Ulysses, the providential wisdom which gave order to the universe also gave hierarchy to society:

And God, who has ordained both society and order, accounts himself so much served by each man's diligent pursuit, though of the meanest trade, that his stepping out of the bounds of it to some other work (as he presumes) more excellent, is but a bold and thankless presumption, by which the man puts himself out of the common way and guard of Providence.[66]

[Man,] as well as the rest of the creation, has his particular station assign'd him; and that not only in reference to other creatures, but himself; [God] has put a difference between one man and another, ordained several ranks and Classes of men, and endowed them with special and appropriate qualifications for those stations wherein he has set them.[67]

Such views are easy to parallel, especially among diehard royalists such as Sir George ('Bluidy') Mackenzie, the fearsome Lord Advocate of Scotland.[68] Yet they were also open to intellectual challenge, and they clashed with the actual and perceived dynamism of late seventeenth-century society, with its striking rise in the fortunes both of middling tradesmen and of the great merchants and financiers, the blurring of boundaries between gentry and non-gentry, and the multiplication of great tycoons most of whom had no interest in acquiring the trappings of gentility.[69] The republican Henry Neville saw with perfect clarity that he was living in the transition from feudalism to capitalism: that the established hierarchies of social degree were the dead relics of a system whose workings and rationale had long since passed away. With the disappearance of villeinage, he argued, titular power was now at variance with actual,[70] and the imbalance between the economic power of the commons and the constitutional power of the nobility was a fundamental source of political tension: 'I cannot say that the greater part of the people do know this their condition, but they find very plainly that they want something which they ought to have' (p. 145).

In drama, Neville's thesis is most obviously paralleled in Mary Pix's *The Beau Defeated*, whose closing speech distinguishes titular from economic

---

[66] South, *Sermons Preached upon Several Occasions*, v. 38.

[67] [Richard Allestree], *The Art of Contentment. By the Author of The Whole Duty of Man* (Oxford, 1675), 108. [68] Sir George Mackenzie, *Moral Gallantry* (Edinburgh, 1667), 24–5.

[69] Richard Ashcraft, *Revolutionary Politics & Locke's 'Two Treatises of Government'* (Princeton, 1986), 146; J. R. Jones, *Country and Court: England, 1658–1714* (Cambridge, Mass., 1978), 86; Lawrence Stone and Jeanne C. Fawtier Stone, *An Open Elite? England 1540–1880* (Oxford, 1984), 8, 217–19.

[70] Henry Neville, *Plato Redivivus; or, A Dialogue Concerning Government*, in *Two English Republican Tracts*, ed. Caroline Robbins (Cambridge, 1969), 133–4.

power, but the same theory is more carefully sustained and explored by that most radical of Carolean dramatists, Thomas Shadwell. Like several contemporaries, Shadwell habitually uses parodic imagery of knightly romance, but whereas the others simply create a quixotic disparity between outmoded ideal and quotidian reality, Shadwell treats knightly romance (and its offspring, the heroic play) as recording a social code of irrational power and violence: a residual feudal archaism in a society plagued by feudal archaisms. ('Your *Hero's* in Plays beat five times as many,' says the gentleman Don John in *The Libertine*, as he beats off the menials who attempt to apprehend him for murder and rape, I, p. 37). For Shadwell, the prime role of the seventeenth-century aristocracy ought to be as an intellectual élite of scholars and patrons, and in dedicating *The Woman-Captain* to Lord Ogle, a grandson of the first Duke of Newcastle, he expressed the hope his dedicatee's family might produce '*a race of true, and not Romantick Heroes*' (p. 13). But Shadwell was concerned to limit the role of the aristocracy as well as to define it: in his adaptation of *Timon of Athens* he locates Alcibiades in the historical context which Shakespeare ignores, concluding the play with the deposition of the Four Hundred—of an aristocratic oligarchy—and the restoration of democracy. He views the landed classes with a curious mixture of radicalism and conservatism, hostility towards thuggish and over-powerful noblemen combining with a nostalgia for the vanishing ideals of the country gentleman that is unique among important Carolean dramatists. He perhaps distinguishes the gentry from the nobility, with their greater entrenched power and privilege: Apemantus in *Timon* delivers a lengthy denunciation of the aristocracy (III, p. 231), and Isabella in *A True Widow* rejects the prospect of a noble lover with a more succinct indictment: 'A Lord? a Beast' (II, p. 303). His radicalism and nostalgia, however, combine to depict a social order which has lost its original justification: outmoded forms of privilege and oppression survive, while genuine ideals of gentlemanly responsibility are now mere memories.

The ideal of the learned, cultivated gentleman was obviously not new, but Shadwell highlights an important historical point: that the aristocracy was no longer a warrior caste, and that it was necessary for the best of its number to find new areas of expertise, such as scholarship and patronage.[71] The most influential handbook of gentlemanly accomplishment in seventeenth-century England was Henry Peacham's *The Compleat Gentleman*, which lovingly describes many areas of social and intellectual accomplishment. Education is completed by travel, but travel abroad equips the gentleman to fulfil his place at home: 'for if it be the common Law of Nature, that the learned should haue rule ouer and instruct the ignorant, the experienced, the vnexperienced, what concearneth more Nobility, taking place aboue other, then to be learned and wise?'[72] Shadwell's monument of mindless and useless

---

71 See Lawrence Stone, *The Crisis of the Aristocracy 1558–1641* (Oxford, 1965), 239, 715–22.

72 [Henry Peacham], *Peacham's Compleat Gentleman 1634*, ed. G. S. Gordon (Oxford, 1906), 235.

learning, Sir Nicholas Gimcrack, is a detailed negation of the Peacham ideal, travelling merely in order to study and instruct spiders and disregarding the obligations of his 'place' by neglecting his country estate, with its concomitant responsibilities to tenants. Even his experiments in blood transfusion compromise the essence of nobility: 'the Honour of blood in a Race or Linage [*sic*]' (Peacham, p. 2).

The degeneracy of the gentry was a perennial topic, generally more associated with a desire to revivify the old order than to change it: Peacham himself complains that 'to be drunke, sweare, wench, follow the fashion and to do just nothing, are the attributes and markes now adayes of a great part of our Gentry' (p. 10). Edward Panton even regretted the passing of feudalism, urging that the nobleman's proper area of activity is war.[73] For Richard Allestree, the inversion of order in the great rebellion had been a punishment for the atheism of the gentry, and he urged that the gentleman's privileged position within the social Chain of Being carried with it a divinely sanctioned vocation to assist and set an improving example to his inferiors.[74] The gentleman, that is, should fulfil his place. 'The heavens themselves, the planets, and this centre', Shakespeare's Ulysses famously declared, 'Observe degree, priority, and place;'[75] 'taking place aboue other,' argued Peacham (p. 235), the nobility require a commensurate superiority of training and talent. Despite the jeremiads about corrupt gentry, there was the usual qualified but strong belief that differences of hereditary social place corresponded to differences of innate and hereditary virtue, with much citation of the key text of the heredity school, Horace's

> fortes creantur fortibus et bonis;
> est in iuvencis, est in equis patrum
> virtus, neque inbellem feroces
> progenerant aquilae columbam.[76]

Yet there was also acknowledgement, sometimes within the same writers, that great abilities might lie, uneducated and undiscovered, at the bottom of the hierarchy. Jean Gailhard cited Horace,[77] but did not believe that the genetic principle was universally true, and wrote of the untutored abilities of the obscure peasant in terms which anticipate Gray's 'Elegy': nature makes us all alike, but education creates great differences, and 'For want of this, a poor Country-man's Son will be fit only to handle a Plough . . . though perhaps

---

73 Edw[ard] Panton, *Speculum Juventutis; or, a True Mirror; where Errors in Breeding Noble and Generous Youth . . . are clearly made manifest* (London, 1671), fo. [7ʳ⁻ᵛ], pp. 32–4, 214.

74 [Richard Allestree], *The Gentlemans Calling* (London, 1660), 1–4, 10, 132–8.

75 *Troilus and Cressida*, I. iii. 85–6.

76 *Odes*, IV. iv. 29–32, in *Q. Horati Flacci Opera*, ed. Thomas Ethelbert Page, Arthur Palmer, and A. S. Wilkins (London, 1910). ('The strong are created from the strong and good. Horses and bullocks have the strength of their fathers, and fierce eagles do not beget the feeble dove.')

77 J[ean] Gailhard, *The Compleat Gentleman; or, Directions for the Education of Youth* (London, 1678), pt. i, p. 61; pt. ii, pp. 109–10.

he has within him dispositions to learn great things' (Part i, p. 3). Less ambivalently, William Ramesay writes slightingly of 'the empty Title of a 𝕲entleman, which duely considered in its Rise, Progress, and End, is but a *Non ens*,' asserts that many noble families begin in bawdry and that the gentleman's true father might turn out to be a family servant, and (as even Henry Peacham had done) lists virtuous plebeians and bastards who have achieved eminence.[78]

According to J. E. Mason, such ambivalence about the origins of nobility remains a constant feature of courtesy literature from the sixteenth century to the eighteenth.[79] But belief in hereditary nobility of character, though tenacious among those whom it benefited, was losing credibility as a serious intellectual basis for social philosophy, appealing neither to Locke, the Whig radical, nor to the absolutist Hobbes, to whom the hierarchies of command and subordination were arbitrary. Nor does belief in natural hierarchy feature much in the drama. Sir Robert Howard's *The Committee* contains a heroine whose inherited nobility of character survives a base upbringing, and portrays the master–servant relationship as paternalistic protection of a vulnerable inferior, but this was an early and backward-looking play, expressing the gentry's desire to reinstate the old order, and after the early 1660s few other plays reproduced its outlook. Indeed, in *The Twin-Rivals* (1702) Farquhar specifically re-created the figure of Teague, Howard's bungling and helpless servant, changing his relationship to established order from one of dependency to one of critical scepticism. There are, similarly, few unqualified examples of the displaced child whose inherited nobility survives a base upbringing. When Durfey adapted *Cymbeline*, he cut not only Jupiter's book but also Belarius' paraphrase of 'fortes creantur fortibus': 'Cowards father cowards, and base things sire base' (IV. ii. 26).

Peacham's denunciation of an idle, pleasure-loving gentry is repeatedly echoed in Shadwell, but in general the heroes of the well-known Carolean comedies confirm Peacham's worst nightmares, and A. M. of the Church of England warned young gentlemen against attending the theatre.[80] If Sir Nicholas Gimcrack is a comprehensive violation of the courtesy book ideal, Etherege's heroes are comprehensive repudiations of it: Dorimant violates conventional precept in his stubbornly urban lifestyle, his easy and familiar relationships with servants, his disdain for the traditions of the past, and above all, in his insouciance about oaths. 'It is a common saying amongst us,' wrote Richard Brathwait, '*That a Gentleman will doe like a Gentleman*; hee scornes to doe unlike himself, for his word is his gage, and his promise such a

---

[78] [William Ramesay], *The Gentlemans Companion; or, A Character of True Nobility, and Gentility* (London, 1672), 1–6.

[79] John E. Mason, *Gentlefolk in the Making: Studies in the History of English Courtesy Literature and Related Topics from 1531 to 1774* (Philadelphia, 1935; repr. New York, 1971), 293–4.

[80] A. M., *The Reformed Gentleman; or, The Old English Morals Rescued from the Immoralities of the Present Age* (London, 1693), 84.

tie as his reputation will not suffer him to dispence with.'[81] But Dorimant prefers the opposite principle, epigrammatically stated by his predecessor Courtall in *She Would If She Could*: 'the keeping of one's word is a thing below the honor of a gentleman' (II. ii. 201–2).

What is particularly noticeable after the earliest stages of Carolean drama, as exemplified in plays such as *The Committee*, is that *place* is deprived of its value as the shared term which binds the social order to the moral order. If Durfey cut 'Cowards father cowards' when adapting *Cymbeline*, Dryden drastically cut Ulysses' speech when adapting *Troilus and Cressida*. Shadwell portrayed a society whose system of place had lost its original rationale, but other leading Carolean dramatists questioned the rationale itself, portraying life as a condition of essential and inescapable dislocation. For Etherege, for example, the governing principle of existence is the random movement of the Epicurean atom, which is obviously incompatible with providential placing and design, and the widespread Hobbism encouraged the portrayal of hier-archies of wit and power which often conflicted with the nominal hierarchies of precedence. One benign parallel to the weakening theoretical credit of hereditary hierarchy was a growing interest in the rights and potentialities of women; and, of course, the stage itself gave women a new forum, both as writers and actresses, at a time when some traditional areas of commercial activity were becoming closed to them.[82] From the prolix fantasies of the Duchess of Newcastle onwards, there was a sequence of works combating the enforced ignorance and marital servitude to which many women were con-demned by ossified social practice: 'I'le have Women say and do what they will,' says Hillaria in Ravenscroft's *The Careless Lovers*: 'Have not we Ra-tional Souls as well as Men; what made Women Mopes in former Ages, but being rul'd by a company of old Men and Women[?]' (III, p. '33' [25]).

Even some men of very conservative temperament took for granted the essential intellectual equality of the sexes, though without drawing any radi-cal social conclusions from their belief. In 1670–1 Edward Howard, a man of severely hierarchical outlook, brought out two plays in which experiments in gynocracy fizzle out, but contribute to the civilizing of the male. One of these, *The Six Days Adventure*, appeared with commendatory verses by Aphra Behn and Edward Ravenscroft, and in the preface Howard admitted that the play had upheld a socially conventional view of women as 'the weaker Sex' which might misrepresent their actual capacities:

and perhaps it is more the authority of usage and manners, than the law of nature, which does generally incapacitate the Rule of women, there being not seldome to be

[81] Richard Brathwait, *The English Gentleman; and the English Gentlewoman*, 3rd edn. (London, 1641), 148.

[82] Katharine Eisaman Maus, ' "Playhouse Flesh and Blood": Sexual Ideology and the Restoration Actress', *ELH* 46 (1979), 595–617 (p. 600); Laura Brown, 'The Defenseless Woman and the Development of English Tragedy', *Studies in English Literature*, 22 (1982), 429–43 (pp. 438–9).

found as great abilities in them (allowing for the disadvantage they have in not being suitably educated to letters,) as are to be observ'd in men of greatest comprehensions. (sig. A3^v)

But, Howard patronizingly concluded, women do not need political power, since they command by their beauty.

Another man of conservative and hierarchical views, Richard Graham (later Viscount Preston, and later still a Jacobite conspirator), regarded women as having been tricked into subordination by men: man,

fearing lest they should Rival him in his Government, imposeth on them, by per-swading them that their faculties are not receptive of Arts, and rough Virtues; and by this stratagem confineth them by the administration of a narrow Province . . . when it is clear that their inclinations are better than this, and their resolutions greater.[83]

Graham suggests, and Behn would have agreed, that women have co-operated in their own subjection and internalized the processes of oppression, seeming 'to have made a Salique Law to bind themselves' (p. 75). Nevertheless, these enormous concessions inspired only qualified proposals for reform: 'I offer this, not to encourage them to rebel against Man, whom God hath made their head; but to advise them to serve the World under some other Noble Char-acter, and not onely to devote themselves to the uses of Generation' (p. 76).

This is feminism of a very diluted and embryonic kind, and it is not un-common to find men giving with one hand and taking away with the other. Another future Jacobite, George Hickes, who championed female education, wrote eloquently of the powers of the female mind, arguing that 'there is no natural difference between their understandings and ours, nor any defects in their knowledge of things, but what Education makes'.[84] Yet the aim of this eloquence was to discredit the intellectual basis of democracy: since women are the equals of men, democrats cannot reasonably exclude them from suf-frage; and the prospect of female suffrage makes democracy itself absurd. This is a disconcerting, imaginatively irrecoverable, combination of ideas, and it should warn us against rushing to embrace any Restoration writer as our contemporary. Virtually all important dramatists vigorously support some liberation of women, yet it is a liberation which, magically, fails to threaten or erode any socially acceptable male privilege. Nevertheless, con-cern about the social inequality suffered by women is an important feature of a drama which has too often been misconstrued as being crassly macho in its outlook. *The Country-Wife* plainly advocates neither female suffrage nor female education, but it does show women claiming a variety of unconven-tional social and sexual liberties. It associates the oppression or patronizing

---

[83] [Richard Graham, Viscount Preston], *Angliæ Speculum Morale: The Moral State of England* (London, 1670), 74.

[84] George Hickes, *A Discourse of the Soveraign Power, in a Sermon Preached at St. Mary Le Bow, Nov. 28. 1682* (London, 1682), 22. This sermon is also discussed in Staves, *Players' Scepters*, 117.

of women with fools, and it thoroughly demolishes the accepted social fictions of sexual identity, not only by portraying a compulsive seducer operating in the guise of a eunuch but also by showing the frail and modest sex to be stronger in both desire and intellect than their overlords: time and again, it is the woman who dreams up the excuse which prevents embarrassment or exposure. When one reads the play, Alithea's quest for social liberty may seem duller than the prevailing pursuit of liberty in the bedroom, but a recent Stratford production showed how compellingly central could be her attempt not only to secure freedom but to understand its meaning.[85]

In the above pages I have tried to establish some context for the range of social attitudes and philosophical ideas which we find in the drama, and to give due emphasis to ways in which the more experimental dramatists were at odds with the received ideas of their culture. (I do not, of course, imagine that the mere availability of any idea of itself guarantees its presence in drama, or that we may construe Restoration plays as irreligious on the mere *ipsi dixerunt* of outraged clerics.) In discussing the drama, I shall not give primary emphasis to monolithic and all-embracing patterns of 'evolution'. Important shifts and transformations can, of course, be detected in the large body of particulars, but they take the form of competing and serpentine cross-currents, not parallel and linear advances towards the future; there is a constant tension between innovation and reaction, and there are also very local and transient patterns, and indeed some downright anomalies. Nor does each stage in the process arise from the same kinds of factor as its predecessor, and in consequence we are not always comparing like with like. Certainly, drama in the late seventeenth century shifts from an aristocratic outlook, in which individuals are part of a greater hierarchy, to one which sees the separate individual as the primary point of interest. But the simply hierarchical outlook of early Restoration drama arises from very special circumstances, of both politics and authorial personnel. Its sudden banishment to the margins in favour of a more sceptical and heterodox drama does not signal a transformation of social outlook but the passing of authorship to a different but co-existing segment in a diverse culture. The decline of the aristocratic world-view remains an important feature of drama, but one magnifies and over-simplifies the process by treating the Earl of Orrery and his like as evolutionary starting-points rather than transitory blips: at what other point in the seventeenth century, before or after the 1660s, did so many members of great noble families write for the public stage?

Nevertheless, dominant shifts and trends are clearly visible. As already mentioned, the early drama of hierarchy was followed by a drama of dislocation,

---

[85] This is a production emphasis which Judith Milhous and Robert D. Hume pronounced to be impossible (*Producible Interpretation: Eight English Plays 1675–1707* (Carbondale and Edwardsville, 1985), 91–4).

in which social roles and responsibilities are no longer tied to ideas of place. This shift brings a number of associated changes. For example, although dramatists in the Carolean period remain fascinated with the figure of the stranger, the literal outsider—Tamora, Shylock, Sir Giles Overreach—almost entirely disappears; for, where social systems are no longer conceived as hierarchies of place, there is no point in associating violation of social norms with alienness of place. Obviously, barbarians such as Tamora show that the alien is already latent within the city, but (like Shakespeare in *Coriolanus*) Carolean dramatists dispensed with the external catalyst and concentrated on the stranger within: the Dryden–Davenant *Tempest* provides a particularly clear example of the shift, constantly portraying potential fellow citizens as aliens to each other yet never applying the term *strange* to Caliban.

The idea of fixed social place implies that an individual's identity is properly defined by and fully integrated with his or her social function. When, at the end of Jonson's *Poetaster*, Augustus finds in his court the alien presence of socially climbing citizens engaged in amateur theatricals, his insistent question is not who but *what* they are: 'I aske not, what you play? but, what you are?' (IV. vi. 26). And, forthwith, they are returned to the place appropriate to what they are: 'they are rid *home* i' the coach, as fast as the wheeles can runne' (IV. vii. 3–4; italics added). 'What are you?' is also the question directed at Edgar in *King Lear* when he appears at the trial by combat to reclaim the name and social identity lost during his period as poor Tom, a placeless and almost languageless vagabond (V. iii. 119). At this stage, the still dislocated Edgar cannot identify himself—his 'name is lost' (V. iii. 121)—and he is able to recover his name only when his defeat of Edmund restores him to his social and familial place. Here the ritual remarriage of language, identity, and society is momentary, but we can see a more stable version of the same configuration in the purging of social disarray at the end of Chapman's *The Gentleman Usher*, which is again accomplished by an act of renaming, when the counterfeit nobleman Medice is exposed as the appropriately named vagabond Mendice: he is literally placeless, being 'Of no country . . . | But born upon the seas' (V. iv. 249–50) and having been brought up by gypsies, and even his 'real' name is spurious, since he 'was never christen'd' (V. iv. 252). Finally, he is expelled into the unfixed vagrancy in which he originated.

In the tragedies of the Earl of Orrery, the first successful tragedian after the Restoration, the name continues to denote the essentially social character of the individual, and, at the other end of the period, one feature of Cibber's in many ways backward-looking *Love's Last Shift* (1696) is its reinstatement of the ritual of naming as the point at which the proper relationship between personal character and social place is re-established: the errant hero's moral and literal homecoming is completed by his recognition of his name on his estranged wife's arm. But, especially in the Carolean period, drama predominantly stresses the separateness, incommensurateness, or irreconcilability of the interior self and the roles necessitated by social existence. In its most positive and optimistic form, the separateness can imply the primacy and integrity of the individual: 'What are you?' is virtually wiped out by 'Who are you?' But more common was a pessimistic sense that the self was isolated and inexpressible. Doubt about the possibility of verifiable knowledge necessarily implies a segregated self, denied any objective reception of the external or communication of the internal, and such isolation can be implied even without total scepticism: for example, by the widespread belief (shared by Gassendi, Descartes, Hobbes, Locke, and scientists such as Robert Boyle) that sensory qualities were not present in the objects, but arose from the way in which the mind registered the motions of intrinsically silent, colourless, and odourless atoms. In a memorable analogy, Descartes suggests that the sensory qualities of objects bear no more essential relationship to the objects themselves than words do to things.[86] For Addison, the sensory neutrality of matter was to inspire wondering gratitude for the divine gift of imagination,[87] but it could also suggest that the mind was insulated by an unbridgeable divide from the outward elements of its experience: for Almanzor in Dryden's *The Conquest of Granada*, and probably for Dryden himself in the early part of his career, man was 'like a Captive in an Isle confin'd, | . . . a Pris'ner of the Mind' (Part II, IV. iii. 147–8). The universe of scentless, colourless atoms raised problems for a poet that were less pressing for an empirical philosopher or scientist: how can one idealize love if all the beauties of the loved one exist solely in internal mental phantasms excited by the movements of featureless atoms? The impossibility of escaping from love of a phantasm into love of a person is, for example, a recurrent problem in *Marriage A-la-Mode*.

If humanity is confined to the limits and phantasms of its own consciousness, it is difficult to assert a seamless integrity between the self and the fabric of social existence. In Dryden, the name is not the bond between the essential self and its social manifestations but an arbitrary token whereby the closed, invisible essence of a particular self is registered in the closed, invisible area of another consciousness: the single, infinitesimal, point at which the two separate circles meet. And it is a regular feature of the mind's inability to escape its own interior phantasms that, for Dryden's characters, the name becomes indistinguishable from the person. The name is no longer the bridge between the personal and social, but a fragmentary and unrevealing marker of an invisible totality.

But naming is only one of the problematic ways of signifying the self. Perhaps the most obvious symptom of difficulties in self-representation is the frequency with which characters in Carolean drama split into two: in *The Country-Wife*, for example, Harcourt disguises himself as his own (fictitious)

---

[86] *Le Monde: traité de la lumière*, in *Œuvres de Descartes*, ed. Charles Adam and Paul Tannery (11 vols., Paris, 1897–1909; repr. 1964–74), xi. 3–4; *La Dioptrique* (*Œuvres*, vi. 112).

[87] *Spectator*, no. 413.

twin brother, and Margery disguises herself as her real younger brother. The splitting often expresses the duality of human nature, reflecting the Hobbesian paradox that human beings are citizens because they are savages, and emphasizing the simultaneous interdependence and irreconcilability of their social and antisocial impulses, and two particular forms of divided identity proved especially popular. One was the bedroom trick, whereby a man or woman sleeps with a desired partner by impersonating someone else (Otway uses attempted or accomplished bedroom tricks in four plays, and Behn and Southerne were similarly fascinated by them). The other, structurally similar, ruse is known as the Invisible Mistress trick, from the 'Histoire de l'amante invisible' in Scarron's *Le Roman comique* (pt. i, ch. ix): in this ruse, a woman appears to her lover in the guise of a second (and sometimes also a third) woman, thereby testing his fidelity to her original manifestation. Both tricks liberate the deceiver's sexual motives from the constraints of publicly perceived identity, and the two may merge, with the Invisible Mistress using a bedroom trick as part of her test. Both have the potential to reconcile wayward desire with the moral standards of society: in the bedroom trick, a wife may reclaim her husband by disguising herself as a new conquest, so that an apparently illicit copulation turns out to be consummation or reconsummation of a marriage, as happens with somewhat equivocal results in *All's Well that Ends Well* and *Measure for Measure*, and with perfect success (at least until the première of *The Relapse*) in *Love's Last Shift*; and in the Invisible Mistress trick a lover may discover with delight that his divided desires (for, say, a beauty and an intelligent masked woman, as in Scarron) are in fact harmoniously directed towards a single object.[88] Yet the deceptions may also expose insoluble conflicts between desire and civic existence. In the bedroom tricks in *The Plain-Dealer* and *The Orphan*, for example, a man contrives the cheat in an impossible attempt to escape from civilization and its verbal codes into pure and inarticulate instinct, outside social character and the signs that sustain it. In their frequent occurrence throughout Restoration drama, the two tricks are used with considerable diversity of nuance and effect, and they usefully differentiate the manifold and shifting ways in which the dramatists interpreted the social capacities and limitations of humanity.

Another useful index is the treatment of justice: of the rituals, officers, and terminology of formal judicial ritual. The early celebrations of restoration, such as Dryden's poem *Astraea Redux*, depict the return of justice to a world distracted by anarchy and subverted degree, but the treatment of justice rapidly becomes more critical, as a result both of rapid reassessment of the new regime and of growing interest in those aspects of life which are not socially assimilable. On the one hand, there are encounters between the ministers of justice and the forces of the flesh (carnival, festivity, saturnalia), the bal-

<hr />

[88] See e.g. 'The History of Timantes and Parthenia' in [Georges (i.e. Madeleine)] de Scudéry, *Artamenes; or, the Grand Cyrus*, tr. F. G. (London, 1653), vi/i, pp. 17–68.

ance between authority and licence undergoing several revealing shifts during the period. On the other hand, interest in the perceptual and epistemological isolation of the individual consciousness leads to emphasis on the imprecision and even meaninglessness of legal judgement: on the inevitable mismatch between publicly formulated judicial categories (such as guilt and innocence) and the invisible individual consciousness to which they are applied.

Perhaps the fundamental difference in outlook—the difference present in all the other differences—concerns the relationship assumed between the interior constitution and consciousness of the individual and the world beyond the limits of the self, and there are many positions between and besides the epistemological solitude of Dryden's early characters and the relentless self-transcendence of Orrery's totally social heroes. It is implicit in many of the problems sketched above, of language, of perception, of alienness within the community. Although this book does not attempt to impose a grand plan upon the sequence of almost four hundred plays which it covers, it will trace patterns of diversity which gradually shift in their composition and proportions, and a number of interlinked motifs will become evident, the chief of which have been introduced in the foregoing paragraphs. After the predominant Carolean emphasis on dislocation, for example, it is noteworthy that, after 1688, contented Whigs such as Shadwell and Cibber resurrect fixity of place as an important moral and social symbol, and that, partly in consequence, the stranger once more becomes a dramatically potent figure. It is equally noteworthy, however, that it was not only melancholy Jacobites such as Dryden who continued the portrayal of human dislocation: it is a fundamental state in the plays of Congreve and Vanbrugh, and Congreve more than anyone else inherits the youthful Dryden's interest in the isolated consciousness, though this is now interpreted, optimistically, as a source of individual independence from the tyranny of social demands. This is not a book on the diverse and changing relationship between consciousness and the exterior world in Restoration drama, but it does assume that the dramatists' creative personalities are fundamentally influenced by their interpretation of this relationship, in all its multitude of implications.

CHAPTER TWO

Astraea Redux? Drama, 1660–1668

In *Astraea Redux*, his first full-scale poetic response to the Restoration of Charles II, Dryden celebrated the return of the goddess of Justice and of the Golden Age, portraying the Civil War as a rebellion of the rabble against their natural masters, during which essentially loyal men had been misled by bad example. Gentlemen, whether seduced or oppressed, were alike victims of the mob, and the restoration of royal authority has also restored plebeian subordination, the incorrigible fanatics now inspiring loyalty in their betters as the drunken Spartan helots had once inspired sobriety in theirs. This pattern, of subverted degree ceding to the revival of an earlier order of justice, recurred in many plays of the 1660s.[1] For, not surprisingly, the first great subject of Restoration drama was the Restoration itself.

In John Tatham's *The Rump*, for example, acted by a scratch company in May/June 1660,[2] the Puritan leaders and their wives are caricatured as foolish and unscrupulous upstarts, finally stripped of their borrowed plumes as a world turned upside-down is set to rights by Monck, here represented, with great moral certitude, under the name of Philagathus (lover of the good). This account, needless to say, oversimplified both the event and its architect, and comedy adjusted itself more quickly than other dramatic genres to the fact that the world remained slightly askew and that loyalty was frequently neither unequivocally triumphant nor unequivocally ideal. But the first professionally acted new comedy, Abraham Cowley's revision of his youthful *The Guardian* as *Cutter of Coleman-Street* (Duke's, December 1661) was slightly premature in its realism. Set in the Interregnum, it features two bogus Cavaliers and a dispossessed royalist, Colonel Jolly, unidealistically portrayed as having been driven by destitution to dishonourable stratagems; namely, marriage to a Puritan soap-boiler's widow, the current owner of his estate, and the attempted swindling of his niece. The play succeeded, but its failure to associate suffering loyalty with '*exemplary virtue*' provoked indignation.[3] Between them, *The Rump* and *Cutter of Coleman-Street* define the range of

---

[1] For celebrations of restored social hierarchy in early Restoration panegyric, see Nicholas Jose, *Ideas of the Restoration in English Literature, 1660–71* (London and Basingstoke, 1984), 18.

[2] Harold Love argues that it was performed by a scratch company ('State Affairs on the Restoration Stage, 1660–1675', *Restoration and 18th Century Theatre Research*, 14/1 (1975), 1–9 (p. 1)). John Freehafer argues that it was performed at Salisbury Court by William Beeston's company in Feb. or Mar. ('The Formation of the London Patent Companies in 1660', 9–11).

[3] See Cowley's preface (sig. A3) and *The London Stage 1660–1800*, (5 parts in 11 vols., Carbondale, Ill., 1960–8), i, ed. William Van Lennep, introd. Emmett L. Avery and Arthur H. Scouten (1965), 44.

early Restoration comedy; but, briefly, the outlook of *The Rump* was in the ascendant.

Sir Robert Howard's early plays, for example, could almost be refutations of Cowley's comedy. In *The Surprisal* (King's, April 1662) the heroic general Cialto recovers his estate from Brancadoro, a rich and cowardly usurer's son who represents commercial forces unrestrained by the obligations of rank. Cialto marries not a soap-boiler's widow but a chaste and loyal heroine, Providence and 'Justice' are vindicated,[4] and aristocratic regard for the word—insistently stressed—triumphs over Brancadoro's belief that sheer wealth entitles him to break 'Writings and Covenants' (I, p. 8). Howard's next play, *The Committee* (King's, November 1662), provides a comic version of the same plot. Like *Cutter of Coleman-Street*, it is set in the late Interregnum, but Howard's Cavaliers (Blunt and Careless) are entirely heroic, rescuing their sequestered estates and their loved ones from venal and hypocritical Puritan bureaucrats, led by Mr and Mrs Day. Puritan rule perverts natural hierarchy: in the '*topsie turvy*' world of the Interregnum (IV, p. 13), former servants are the 'new Gentry' (I, p. 71) and impose '*strange*' (II, p. 92; italics added) systems of justice. Insubordination of class is complemented by insubordination of sex, in Mrs Day's domination of her husband, though the norm which she violates is not meek submissiveness but strong and intelligent co-operativeness: Ruth, the more active of the two heroines, rescues Careless from prison and reforms his sexual character.

The very name Day explicitly marks the upstarts' reign as ephemeral, an intrinsically unstable disturbance of fixed principles of order, and the natural worth of the true gentry remains unimpaired amidst the social chaos: Ruth is really Anne Thorowgood, a Cavalier's daughter brought up by the Days since the age of 2, who like Marina in the brothel preserves the hereditary virtue of her stock (in one of the very few unqualified occurrences of this motif in late seventeenth-century drama).[5] The insubordination of the Days also contrasts with the natural deference of Teague, a good-natured but dim-witted Irishman who attaches himself to the Cavaliers, needing the paternalistic protection of a servant–master relationship in order to survive. This natural, benevolent hierarchy of protection and dependence represents the old world which has been temporarily violated by the rapacious and self-serving reign of parvenus (Clarendon complained that the rebels had dissolved the bond between master and servant).[6] But it is also an archaic ideal which was consistently to be challenged as younger dramatists of less exalted birth came to the fore. Inevitably, the Days are perverters of language, and it is fitting that

[4] III, pp. 39–40; V, pp. 61, 66.

[5] Others are in Sir Robert Stapylton's *The Slighted Maid*, Charles Saunders's *Tamerlane the Great* (Mar. 1681), Durfey's *The Banditti* (*c.* Jan. 1686), and Motteux's *Beauty in Distress* (May 1698).

[6] [Edward Hyde, Earl of Clarendon], *The Life of Edward Earl of Clarendon* (3 vols., Oxford, 1759), ii. 40.

their chief perversion of the word, the Covenant, should exemplify the subjugation of language to commercial imperatives, featuring as an object for sale on a bookseller's stall. They are also forgers, improving upon Brancadoro's disrespect for authentic bonds, and their temporary authority is reflected in temporary control of nomenclature, which enables them to overwrite former social distinctions by naming themselves 'Honorable' and their former masters 'Malignant' (III, p. 104). Mrs Day is in more than one sense a '*translated* Kitchen-maid' (III, p. 96; italics added), and, when Anne Thorowgood is once again free to affirm the glories of her ancestry, she does so by untranslating herself in a triumphant act of self-naming (like that of Shakespeare's Edgar), escaping from the alien name that her captors have imposed on her (V, p. 116).

Usurpation and restoration were also dominant themes in the serious drama of the early 1660s. Their chief exponent was the Earl of Orrery, whose plays constitute a public therapy and atonement for his record of service under the rebellious regime, and at times address, if in stilted and artificial terms, the problems of loyal men trapped by obligations to morally complex usurpers.[7] In 1661 he courted the King's favour with his first play, *The Generall*,[8] in which a virtuous and self-sacrificing general (Monck, here named Clorimun) turns against a usurper he had previously served and restores a rightful monarch. Orrery returned to the defeat of usurpation in his last performed tragedy, *Tryphon* (Duke's, December 1668), where the character of the usurper and the dilemmas of his subjects are treated with greater complexity, though equal artifice. *The History of Henry the Fifth* (Duke's, August 1664) also portrays a king recovering a kingdom to which he has just hereditary right, and in addition highlights the duty of avenging a murdered father (the Duke of Burgundy). And in *Mustapha* (Duke's, April 1665) Solyman's execution of his own heir is contrasted with the restoration to the Hungarian throne of the Queen Mother and infant King. Confidence in manifest providential justice is frequent, except when the death of Mustapha demonstrates 'The dang'rous state even of great vertue' (V. 420).

But Orrery was less concerned to analyse the past than to exorcize it, and the dark labyrinths of civil strife are replaced by symmetrically precise, and easily decipherable, contests of love, friendship, and honour. The usurper in *The Generall* has seized the throne because of his love for the heroine, Altemera, whom he eventually plans to rape, whereas Clorimun triumphs over his unrequited love for her, saving the man she loves and uniting the pair. Lust is socially subversive, and Orrery's characters can only fulfil themselves

---

7 Nancy Klein Maguire, 'Regicide and Reparation: The Autobiographical Drama of Roger Boyle, Earl of Orrery', *English Literary Renaissance*, 21 (1991), 257–82.

8 *The Generall* was first performed in Dublin in 1662, under the title of *Altemera*. The first London production was by the King's Company in Sept. 1664, after Davenant's staging of *The History of Henry the Fifth* the previous month.

by acting as social beings, cultivating an exemplary honour in which the self is exalted and purified by the mastery of those desires that estrange the individual from the shared demands of human culture. Clorimun's noble selflessness in love (which revives an ideal popular in the drama of Charles I's reign)[9] is shared by later Orrery heroes, who actually plead with the loved one to favour a rival friend, convinced that it is nobler to deserve than to possess; that the creation of obligation is more satisfying than the gratification of desire. Similarly, the recognition of obligation can often conquer desire: in *The Black Prince* (King's, October 1667) King John of France is torn between his amorous vows to Valeria and his new passion for Plantagenet, but the vows triumph, and the decision to honour them instantly redirects John's passion from Plantagenet to his former love. The demands of social class equal those of social obligation. Though Henry V and Owen Tudor selflessly seek to unite each other with Princess Katherine, Tudor's inferiority of station means that there is only one possible outcome for their friendly rivalry: as she reflects, 'Since Glory is the Souls most proper Sphear, | It does but wander when it moves not there' (II. 368–9). *Place* is omnipotent: to trangress the demands of degree is to exchange the stability of fixed social identity for a condition of rootless displacement.

As individuals are entirely contained and expressed within the society that orders their existence, so their nature is fully expressible within social signs; for Orrery conspicuously lacks the epistemological *Angst* that was soon to grip the Restoration stage. In *The Black Prince* Plantagenet is briefly suspected of unchastity but is vindicated by irrefutable 'Proofs' (V. 569), and in *Tryphon* Cleopatra unwittingly reveals to her friend Hermione 'By many Proofs' (III. 33) that she is in love. Indeed, the language which enshrines the imperatives of social existence almost becomes what it signifies. In *The Generall* the 'sacred name of freind' exercises compelling power (I. 295), in *Henry the Fifth* 'Angels are Guardians of that Sacred name' (I. 210) of King, and in *The Black Prince* 'Divinity' dwells in the 'Pow'rful Names' of father and king (III. 446–50). To subvert the sign, as Dryden and Wycherley were persistently to do, is here the work of anarchic villains, such as the Vizier Rustan in *Mustapha*, whose success in persuading Solyman to execute his virtuous son is persistently associated with corruption of signs and the bonds which they record: whereas friendship for Mustapha is 'a stronger tye than that of blood' (I. 227), it is for Rustan 'a meer name 'twixt those who covet power' (II. 116).

Orrery's early plays were well received, and *Mustapha* proved a lasting success, but the audience at the première of *Tryphon* finally realized that he was writing the same play time and again,[10] and he is now most significant for his

[9] See Laurens J. Mills, *One Soul in Bodies Twain: Friendship in Tudor Literature and Stuart Drama* (Bloomington, Ind., 1937).

[10] See Pepys, 8 Dec. 1668. All references to Pepys's diary are to *The Diary of Samuel Pepys*, ed. Robert Latham and William Matthews (11 vols., London, 1970–83).

influence upon those, such as Dryden, who reacted against him. But if the formula which he created, and over-exploited, proved sterile, his outlook was representative enough, being much the same as that of Sir Robert Howard and of the many lesser gentleman amateurs who turned to drama in the early Restoration, and much the same as that of Davenant, the chief surviving celebrant of the Caroline order. For example, Davenant's *The Siege of Rhodes* also portrays self-sacrificing magnanimity in love, in that Solyman the Magnificent behaves generously to Alphonso, his antagonist in love and war, and an Admiral on the Christian side similarly copes virtuously with his love for the heroine. When Richard Flecknoe revised his *Love's Dominion* (1654) as *Love's Kingdom* (Duke's, by autumn 1663), one alteration was to increase the emphasis on noble rivalry: in both versions one heroine intercedes with another on behalf of a man she herself loves, but in the later version the man subsequently seeks to die in the place of his more favoured rival.[11] Noble rivalry is also a subsidiary theme in John Caryll's Richard III play *The English Princess* (Duke's, March 1667), and a primary concern in William Killigrew's *Ormasdes* (?1663–4),[12] where Queen Cleandra nobly relinquishes her beloved general Ormasdes to his true love (the monarch's conquest of love perhaps exemplifying the tactful reproof of Charles's conduct that crept very early into the loyalest of drama). But the fundamental topic of this celebratory drama is the triumph of Justice in the restoration of a social hierarchy upheld by clear, uncorrupted language: in Davenant's *The Law against Lovers* (Duke's, February 1662), a conflation of *Measure for Measure* with the Beatrice and Benedick plot of *Much Ado about Nothing*, the Duke's return is a providential response to pious prayer (V, p. 323), whereas devious statesmen abandon language for voiceless signs (II, p. 284), and in *The English Princess* John Caryll's Richard III woos Princess Elizabeth in 'strange Language' (II, p. 20). As in *The Committee*, political subversion is associated with female insubordination: Davenant's Lady Macbeth regrets that her husband did not govern her 'by the Charter of [his] sex' (IV. iv. 63) and reinstated sexual hierarchy is a major theme in the two tragicomedies of Sir Robert Stapylton.

The four adaptations of Shakespearian plays which Davenant produced

---

[11]   The title-page of *Love's Kingdom* states that it incorporates some revisions made since performance (*Not as it was Acted at the Theatre near Lincolns-Inn, but as it was written, and since corrected by Richard Flecknoe*). In both versions, the eccentric immigration laws of Cyprus demand that strangers start to love a native within a fixed deadline or suffer banishment. At decision-time, Bellinda unexpectedly sees her true love in the crowd and says that she loves someone on the island. But, since her lover is not a native, she is initially sentenced to death for perjury, though the confusion is cleared up. In the revised version, Bellinda's favoured and rejected lovers can compete to die in her place. In the original, the rejected suitor switches affections to the woman who loves him after she apparently commits suicide. In the revision, he says his heart is as immovable as Love's Temple—which is promptly shaken by an earthquake. Flecknoe's dedication, to the Marquess of Newcastle, reveals that the play was (unsurprisingly) damned.

[12]   See J. P. Vander Motten, 'Some Unpublished Restoration Prologues and Epilogues: New Light on the Stage History of Sir William Killigrew's Plays', *Modern Philology*, 77 (1979–80), 159–63.

after the Restoration all portray the re-establishment of legitimate rule, and although *The Tempest*, written in collaboration with Dryden, takes a darkly ironic view of its subject, the unaided plays are purely celebratory. In *The Law against Lovers* honest men are seduced into rebellion for mistaken motives, Benedick rebelling because he believes that Claudio's life is really in danger, but the play concludes with comprehension and reconciliation of all jarring elements: Benedick and Lucio are forgiven, Bernardine (*sic*) is penitent, and Angelo, the apparent Puritan, marries Isabella, having revealed that he was only testing her. In *The Rivals* (Duke's, by September 1664), an adaptation of *Two Noble Kinsmen*, the defeat of Creon is turned into the providential deposition of a usurping tyrant, and the climax is again reconciliation, the conflict between the rival friends being resolved not by fighting and death but, in best Caroline fashion, by the convenient transference of one lover's affections to another woman. In *Macbeth* (Duke's, November 1664), the exiled and restored son of the murdered parent gains a significance beyond that of his Shakespearian original, and there is the inevitable final triumph of 'Justice' (v. iii. 45), as there is also in Caryll's *The English Princess*, where the defeat of Richard III's usurpation is explicitly paralleled to the Restoration of Charles II (III, p. 33). William Killigrew's rambling romance *Selindra* (King's, March 1662) restores the heir of Hungary to his throne, and in *The Usurper* (King's, January 1664), a romanticized version of recent events by Sir Robert Howard's brother Edward, Providence and a Monck-like general restore Cleander to the Sicilian throne and (in another unheeded moral hint to Charles) unite him with a beloved queen. In contrast with the usurper in Orrery's *The Generall*, Howard's is a crudely drawn monster, but both men attempt to rape the heroine: in contrast to the younger generation of dramatists, both playwrights see unrestrained sexual desire as a politically subversive yet politically controllable force.

Unheeded praise of royal monogamy also distinguishes Sir Robert Stapylton's *The Slighted Maid* (Duke's, February 1663), where Prince Salerno affects rakishness because of disappointment in love, but eventually settles down with a Bulgarian princess. The marriage reflects a general restoration and relocation of the displaced. The Princess and her sister have been dispossessed but retain their native royalty of character, although reared as the daughters of a Greek 'Impostress', Menanthe; two gentlemen have been impoverished by war, one being reduced to the status of a servant; and the maid of the title, who usurps the guise of masculinity and acts as a tyrannical husband, eventually resumes her natural place, marrying one of the impoverished gentlemen. The slave Vindex, who gains freedom through loyalty, belongs to the same paternalistic social order as Sir Robert Howard's Teague, and although Stapylton is one of the first Restoration dramatists to use the bedroom trick (which Davenant had excluded from *The Law against Lovers*), it is used merely to preserve social place: a sea-captain sleeps with Menanthe in the belief that his partner is one of the princesses. (The bedroom trick had already restored normative moral order in Richard Flecknoe's probably unperformed *Erminia* (1661), uniting a philandering prince with the princess to whom he promised marriage.[13]) Social and sexual hierarchy are also simultaneously restored in Stapylton's *The Step-Mother* (Duke's, October 1663), where a queen repents her usurpation of her husband's power, her reform being emphasized by two masques in which Ovidian metamorphoses are reversed.[14] Social place and personal identity are inseparable, and to pervert the former is to lose the latter.

There is yet more restoration in Edward Howard's *The Change of Crownes* (King's, April 1667), where a queen who has usurped the throne of her elder sister is paralleled with a king who has usurped the throne of his elder brother, pointedly named Carolo, both usurpers repenting and marrying the legitimate ruler of the opposite sex. Parallel pairs of ruling and disloyal siblings also, of course, figure in *The Tempest*, and indeed Howard's two kingdoms are those of Naples and Lombardy (whose chief city is Milan). But here good wombs never bear bad sons, and nobility of rank guarantees nobility of character even in usurpers. Honour 'Does tamely sleepe in course, and Common Bosomes, | And onely wakes in Princes' (II. iii. 4–5), the offspring of kings cannot stoop to the crimes of a Cromwell, and the guilt of subversion is transferred to a surrogate from the non-noble classes, the ambitious turncoat Malvecchio. The Caliban of Howard's world is a bumpkinly country gentleman, Asinello (acted by John Lacy), who represents another attempted invasion of wealth into established allocations of place: he comes to court hoping that money will buy him a place but finally returns 'home' (V. iii. 27), like the upstarts in *Poetaster*, reduced once more to his appointed place. But, in the event, Caliban struck back; for, in the King's presence, Lacy ad libbed such outspoken satire of his court that the play was withdrawn, and in an ensuing altercation with Howard, Lacy breached the proprieties of degree by striking the author—an Earl's son—with a cane, telling him 'that he was more a fool then a poet'.[15] Thus did Howard encounter the vigorous professional self-esteem that was increasingly to challenge his kind of drama and the social vision that it embodied.

A more puzzling representation of restored authority occurs, at a strikingly early date, in *The Mariage Night* (sic) (Duke's, ?spring 1663)[16] by Henry Cary, Viscount Falkland. Here topical elements are infused into a pseudo-Jacobean

[13] For Flecknoe's subsequent revision of this play see J. Douglas Canfield, 'The Authorship of *Emilia*: Richard Flecknoe's Revision of *Erminia*', *Restoration*, 3 (1979), 3–7.

[14] III, pp. 42–4; IV, pp. 59–62. Curtis Alexander Price discusses the quasi-operatic nature of the masques (*Henry Purcell and the London Stage* (Cambridge, 1984), 8–9).

[15] Pepys, 20 Apr. 1667. See also 15, 16 Apr.

[16] No performance is known before Mar. 1667, but the play was published in 1664, having been licensed and advertised in late 1663 (the year of Falkland's death). See Milhous and Hume, 'Dating Play Premières', 380.

portrayal of intrigue and vengeance in a sexually corrupt ducal court, filled with knighted pimps and barbers, and dominated by the Duchess Claudilla, the Duke's manipulative and low-born mistress. Rebellion and attempted regicide (in the Duke's attempt to kill his royal brother) are providentially frustrated, the image of the beheaded father being transferred to the father of two virtuous noblemen, unjustly executed on the Duke's orders. The patrician insistence on degree evident in the mockery of upstart knights is evident also in the treatment of the mob, who prescribe religion to their betters, and demand the destruction of universities (I, p. 1; V, p. 44). Yet the sexually decadent court, the quarrelling royal brothers, and the upstart ducal whore may seem not so much antitheses to the restored monarchy as images of what had been restored. No such interpretation struck Pepys when he saw *The Mariage Night* on 21 March 1667; but, whether intentional or fortuitous, the reversability of the play does highlight the almost instant discrepancy between the dramatic iconography of restoration and the nature of the Restoration itself; and some dramatists were clearly aware of this.

Preoccupation with rebellion and restoration also influenced the translation and staging of Corneille. The Duke's Company's early production of *Le Cid* (December 1662), probably in Joseph Rutter's 1638 translation, seems to cater simply to the incipient fashion for the heroic, but with new translations the case was different, and texts were selected more on the grounds of topicality than merit. There were two versions of *La Mort de Pompée*, a dull play, but one which concerns the murder of a just ruler defeated in a civil war.[17] And the minor Caroline dramatist Lodowick Carlell approached one of the companies (probably the Duke's) with a version of *Héraclius*, only to have it returned on the very day that a rival translation (probably by Sir Thomas Clarges) was staged (March 1664). *Héraclius* is another substandard play, but it had the merit of depicting '*the restoration of a gallant Prince to his just inheritance*' (preface, sig. A3ᵛ). Of Corneille's masterpieces, the only one to be newly translated and staged in the 1660s was *Horace* (by Katherine Philips and John Denham), and this too is topical, for it portrays families divided by what is essentially civil war. This was acted at court (February 1668) by the Duchess of Monmouth, Lady Castlemaine, and others, where the main impression was created by Castlemaine, who was bedecked with jewels (including the crown jewels) worth £200,000. The appearance of an extravagantly adorned royal mistress in a play in which the personal and sexual are savagely sacrificed to national interest is another of the silent incongruities that run through the idealistic drama of this decade. When the translation reached the public stage (King's, January 1669), however, the play was beautified in a quite

---

[17] One, by Katherine Philips, was performed in Dublin in Feb. 1663, and perhaps in London in the late spring. The other (Duke's, Jan. 1664) was by Edmund Waller, Sir Charles Sedley, Edward Filmer, Sidney Godolphin, and Charles Sackville. Nicholas Jose notes the prominence of the word *restore* in Philips's *Pompey* (*Ideas of the Restoration*, 131).

different fashion: with the spectacle of some Dutchmen climbing through the mouth and fundament of a giant sow.[18] The brains behind this improvement were John Lacy's. Since Britain had recently been humiliated in war by the Dutch, it is clearly a gesture of assertive nationalism, but it is difficult to think of a more inspired contrast with that other gesture of assertive nationalism on which the play itself hinges: Horace's killing of his sister, for grieving that he has killed her fiancé in battle. In their different ways, both productions provide an incongruously decadent context for a drama which places its characters at the extremes of commitment and loss. Two months earlier, at the première of *Tryphon*, Orrerian tragedy had died of old age,[19] and the swarming Dutchmen give fresh evidence that the heroics of early Restoration tragedy were beginning to pall. Philips's first translation of Corneille, *Pompey*, had indeed been burlesqued in 1663, in the piece which concludes Davenant's medley *The Play-house to be Let* (August 1663), and Langbaine recalls seeing the parody acted as an afterpiece to the original.[20] But Davenant's parody of Corneille was part of a display of confident jingoism: the piece also included a troupe of French actors performing a translation of Molière's *Sganarelle* in heavy French accents, and it provided the means of reviving two short nationalistic pieces from the Interregnum, *The History of Sir Francis Drake* and *The Cruelty of the Spaniards in Peru*. Now, however, confident jingoism was to be in short supply until the 1690s.

Although uncritical celebrations of restoration dominated tragedy and tragicomedy for much of the decade, *The Rump* and *The Committee* did not establish a comparable fashion in comedy, and indeed Sir Robert Howard himself quickly showed, both in parliament and on the stage, that he had lost his celebratory mood.[21] The only play substantially to follow their lead (and that after an interval of nearly six years) was Sir Charles Sedley's *The Mulberry Garden* (May 1668). Nevertheless, the hierarchical social outlook of *The Committee* remained widespread, and dominates one of the most successful comedies of the early Restoration, Sir Samuel Tuke's *The Adventures of Five Hours* (Duke's, January 1663), an adaptation (at Charles II's suggestion) of a play by Coello, which initiated a durable fashion for Spanish intrigue plays. This does not portray a returning king, but it shares the moral outlook of the

---

[18] Pepys, 19 Jan. 1669.

[19] Orrery's *Herod the Great* was scheduled for production in 1672, but performance was prevented by the Bridges Street fire.

[20] Gerard Langbaine, *An Account of the English Dramatick Poets* (Oxford, 1691; repr. Hildesheim, 1968), 110.

[21] Howard joined Buckingham in securing passage of the Irish Cattle Bill, to which the King was opposed, in leading the attack on Clarendon, and in covert opposition to the Duke of York. See H. J. Oliver, *Sir Robert Howard (1626–1698): A Critical Biography* (Durham, NC, 1963), 131–2; James Anderson Winn, *John Dryden and his World* (New Haven and London, 1987), 178–91. For the Irish Cattle Bill see Ronald Hutton, *The Restoration: A Political and Religious History of England and Wales 1658–1667* (Oxford, 1985), 251–6.

celebratory plays, showing the triumph of justice and reason over barbarous irrationality, one element in Tuke's modifications of his source being an added emphasis on the destructiveness of irrationality and the controlling power of reason and justice (an emphasis still greater in the expanded third edition). A fairly stereotyped jealous brother in Coello, for example, becomes a case study in potentially murderous rage, whose sense of personal honour leads him to despise the precepts of law, ignorant (in the third edition) that 'Honour is Justice, rightly understood' (III, p. 185).[22] By contrast, 'Justice her self holds not the Scales more Even'[23] than the hero, Antonio.

Though Pepys was moved to rapturous wonder by *The Adventures*, deeming *Othello* 'a mean thing' in comparison (20 August 1666), the play is now chiefly interesting as a model which was transformed by abler and less orthodox dramatists (notably Dryden). The story is one of mistaken identity. Antonio has in the past rescued Camilla from enemy soldiers and, although the pair fell in love at first sight, he felt compelled by honour to return to battle without staying to discover her name. At the beginning of the play, he arrives in Seville to enter an arranged marriage with Porcia, whom he has never seen. When he sees his beloved Camilla and joyfully leaps to the conclusion that she is Porcia, Camilla and the real Porcia decide to encourage the mistake in the hope, which events justify, that it will enable them to end up with the partners of their choice. But many confusions precede the happy ending, not least because Antonio's friend Octavio loves the real Porcia, and the two friends are for a while estranged by the belief that they are rivals.

There is a nominal concern with the limits of male authority over the female, the tyranny of Porcia's brother, Henrique, being contrasted with the humanity of Camilla's brother, Carlos, but Tuke's world is nevertheless regulated by masculine values and authority, his main concern being to ensure that this authority protects female interests instead of oppressing them. Protective male authority is shown when Antonio rescues Camilla; oppressive, when the egocentric rage of a Don Henrique divorces power from justice. Even when she flees the private injustice of her brother, Porcia still has no power of self-definition, for she narrowly escapes being arrested as a strumpet by the officers of public justice. At moments of crucial moral choice, the men think first of the duties appropriate to their sex: summoned back to battle, Antonio obeys the call of honour without even staying to discover the name of his new love, and later he alternately duels with Octavio, his imagined rival, and combines with him to drive off the assaults of Henrique, the demands of love here being repeatedly overridden by those of male friendship. One way of categorizing the many imitations of Tuke is to consider how they modified the rigid formula which he bequeathed, allowing characters to be moved by factors

---

[22] *The Adventures of Five Hours*, III, p. 185. Swaen's edition contains Antonio Coello y Ochoa's *Los Empeños de seis horas*, Tuke's first and third editions, and the commendatory poems from the second.   [23] First edition, V, p. 124. Not in Coello.

other than external misunderstanding, so that social values are tested internally, and so that the woman's viewpoint becomes more independent and effectual.

For example, as its title suggests, Thomas Porter's *The Carnival* (King's, ?autumn 1663) is more open-minded about sexual and judicial authority: it includes an unresolved gay couple courtship and a boisterous serenade of a prostitute, and shows two women (one in male disguise) vigorously pursuing and reforming their errant lovers. As in Tuke, marauding males (here bandits) are prominent, but their significance is now different. Tuke had opposed Antonio and the enemy soldiers as embodiments of the just and unjust use of male power, but here the bandits duplicate the hero's own moral inadequacy: captured along with his disguised (and unrecognized) mistress, he realizes that his infidelity debases him below his captors, and promises not to call in judicial authority (III, p. 40). (Similar indulgence towards the female and the criminal appears in T. P.'s (= ?Porter's) *A Witty Combat; or, the Female Victor* (private, ?1662–3) which portrays the frauds, trial, and acquittal of the contemporary confidence trickster Mary Moders, an impostress far more favourably viewed than the Menanthe of the morally earnest Stapylton.)

For some considerable time in *The Carnival*, a ridiculous Spanish patriarch remains ignorant that half his beard, that criterion of manhood, has been shaved off. In Richard Rhodes's *Flora's Vagaries* (King's, *c.* November 1663), similarly, a tyrannical guardian who is outsmarted by his daughter and witty niece at one point loses those insignia of gender, his clothes. Here, as in Tuke, one of the heroes first proves his worth by rescuing his eventual wife from violence, but thereafter the initiative passes to her, for it is her ingenuity that brings about a further meeting, and her persuasiveness that turns him from a prospective fornicator into a husband. Like *The Carnival*, the play modifies Tuke's simple association of the male role with the proper exercise of machismo. (Although it is not an intrigue play, Sir William Killigrew's *The Seege of Urbin* (?King's, ?1664–5) interestingly contributes to this pattern by showing a heroine in male disguise showing perfect expertise—if considerable self-doubt—in accomplishing a sequence of conventionally male actions, one being the rescue of one of the heroes from bandits (I, p. 6).)

Yet another Spanish intrigue play to champion the woman's cause is Thomas St Serfe's *Tarugo's Wiles* (Duke's, October 1667), which (like Crowne's *Sir Courtly Nice*, 1685) is based on Moreto's *No puede ser*. With the aid of an amiable trickster, a woman with 'vast knowledg in Masculine learning' (I, p. 1)[24] converts her suitor Patricio from his tyrannical male chauvinism and enables Patricio's sister to marry the man of her choice. Unsurprisingly, the suitor chosen for his sister by Patricio is another embodiment of male tyranny, abusing feudal relationships by slaking his lusts upon his tenants'

---

[24] See Staves, *Players' Scepters*, 121–2.

daughters (II, p. 15). St Serfe's interest in the heroine's masculine learning is less extensively developed than that of Moreto himself, whose heroine presides over a literary salon, but the emphasis on female initiative nevertheless compares favourably with the treatment of the heroine in *Elvira; or, The Worst Not Always True* (November 1664), the only survivor of three Spanish adaptations by George Digby, Earl of Bristol, the source being Calderón's *No siempre lo peor es cierto*.[25] Here the outlook is more like that of Tuke, and the heroine is entirely passive. Condemned by false appearances (her lover suspects the worst after finding an intruder in her room), Elvira can only wait submissively for vindication, her repeated appeals for providential aid constituting one of Bristol's chief embroideries of his source. In her period of undeserved humiliation, Elvira (like Edgar in *King Lear*) is obliged to relinquish her name and social status, transforming herself from a gentlewoman into the servant Silvia, and entering a state of inverted degree which will only end when 'heaven's justice | Shall her entirely to her self *restore*' (I, p. 9; italics added). Bristol gives a subliminal political resonance to her plight, but the woman has minimal control of her social character or of the 'justice' which determines it.

Of the early responses to Tuke's success, the most intelligent and original was Dryden's second play, *The Rival Ladies* (King's, June 1664), which constitutes a thoroughgoing critique and inversion of its model. Dryden's first play, *The Wild Gallant*, had been swamped by the success of *The Adventures of Five Hours* at the rival house, and accordingly Dryden here challenged Tuke on his own ground, providing a Spanish intrigue play which opens with the situation which had first brought Tuke's hero and heroine together: a gentleman (Gonsalvo) rescues a beautiful woman (Julia) from bandits and falls in love with her. In Dryden's version, however, the lady mistakes her rescuer for the bandit chief, and the false association of ideas induces an irrational aversion from him that remains unconquered at the end of the play, despite repeated acts of nobility on Gonsalvo's part. Whereas Tuke portrays irrational passion as a deformation of man's intrinsically reasonable and social character, Dryden sees human consciousness as the creation of arbitrary and mechanical processes. His associative psychology appears to be derived from Descartes, who stressed the susceptibility of the passions to the power of specific association: he revealed, for example, that he had long been drawn to squinting people, until he realized that the cause of this attraction was a childhood infatuation with a squinting girl.[26]

[25] Bristol had been a leading adviser of Charles I, a royalist exile, and a prominent courtier in the new reign. In 1663, however, political ambition had led him to mount a mistimed and ill-planned attack upon Clarendon, and after its failure he went into hiding to avoid imprisonment in the Tower. Vivid vignettes of his erratic character and career are given throughout Ronald Hutton's *Charles the Second: King of England, Scotland, and Ireland* (Oxford, 1989). Hutton considers him to have been 'one of the most destructive individuals of his age' (p. 17).

[26] *Œuvres de Descartes*, v. 57 (letter 488).

But, in Descartes, rational self-analysis was able to cure the irrational association, whereas the minds of Dryden's characters are enslaved to material sequences of cause and effect: there is no immaterial soul within the body-machine. Indeed, it is in the dedication of this play that Dryden most explicitly reveals a sympathetic interest in Hobbesian determinism. Bringing himself to praise Orrery's skill as a dramatist, he does so by likening his power over his characters to that of a Hobbesian deity over his creation:

They are mov'd (if I may dare to say so) like the Rational Creatures of the Almighty Poet, who walk at Liberty, in their own Opinion, because their Fetters are Invisible; when indeed the Prison of their Will, is the more sure for being large: and instead of an absolute Power over their Actions, they have only a wretched Desire of doing that, which they cannot choose but do. (p. 97)

Scholars have been remarkably reluctant to take this passage at face value. For example, Bredvold properly quotes John Aubrey's famous observation that 'Mr. John Dreyden, Poet Laureat, is his [Hobbes's] great admirer, and often-times makes use of his doctrine in his playes—from Mr. Dreyden himselfe',[27] but Bredvold nevertheless warns that we should not 'rush . . . to the conclusion that Dryden was at this time a disciple of Hobbes,' and will concede no more than that Dryden was 'interested in necessitarianism' (p. 329). But the passage about 'the Almighty Poet' does not reveal merely an interest in necessitarianism: it reveals the thing itself. Dryden never swallowed Hobbesian politics whole, but this is one of several instances in his early work of the direct absorption of Hobbesian ideas, and these have not been adequately addressed.[28]

When the characters in *The Rival Ladies* define the forces which are motivating them, they see themselves as participants in mechanical and material processes of cause and effect. Agreeing to spare Rodorick, his rival for Julia's love, Gonsalvo envisages his honour as a physical encumbrance, complaining that 'Honour sits on me like some heavy Armour' (III. i. 155). Deciding (like an Orrery hero) to hand over his mistress to his rival, he exclaims 'Never was Man so Dragg'd along by Virtue' (IV. iii. 115), and, when he transfers his affections to the woman who has loyally followed him for five acts in male disguise, the imagery is again of mechanical physical process: his heart is 'not

---

[27] John Aubrey, *'Brief Lives', Chiefly of Contemporaries*. ed. Andrew Clark (2 vols., Oxford, 1898), i. 372; Louis I. Bredvold, 'Dryden, Hobbes, and the Royal Society', *Modern Philology*, 25 (1927–8), 417–38, repr. in *Essential Articles for the Study of John Dryden*, ed. H. T. Swedenberg, Jr. (Hamden, Conn., 1966), 314–40 (p. 327).

[28] Louis Teeter and John A. Winterbottom deny that Dryden was substantially committed to Hobbesian ideas: Teeter, 'The Dramatic Use of Hobbes's Political Ideas', *ELH* 3 (1936), 140–69, repr. in *Essential Articles for the Study of John Dryden*, ed. Swedenberg, 341–73; Winterbottom, 'The Place of Hobbesian Ideas in Dryden's Tragedies', *Journal of English and Germanic Philology*, 57 (1958), 665–83, repr. ibid. 374–94. Mildred E. Hartsock argues that Dryden was influenced by Hobbes, but does so by a crude handling of speeches taken out of dramatic context: 'Dryden's Plays: A Study in Ideas', in *Seventeenth Century Studies (Second Series)*, ed. Robert Shafer (Princeton and London, 1937), 69–176.

worn out, but Polish'd by the wearing' (v. iii. 278). Gonsalvo's assistance of a more favoured rival and his transference of affection to a deserving partner both rework favourite situations of Orrery and his Caroline predecessors, which conventionally demonstrate the power of reason to direct passion. Here, however, even magnanimity is represented as the product of unthinking corporeal process, and indeed Gonsalvo's attempt to act as a noble rival has farcical consequences, for Rodorick assumes that Gonsalvo has deflowered Julia and is attempting to dispose of her. When Gonsalvo wounds Rodorick in the resulting duel, his attempts at self-sacrificing service of his beloved turn out to have gone spectacularly and embarrassingly wrong, and the débâcle establishes the treatment of ideal codes that was to characterize Dryden's comic and serious drama for over a decade: human life and nature are too complex, unpredictable, and irrational for the flawless paragon of honour either to exist or to be theoretically desirable.

The Rival Ladies failed, and has attracted little attention since. Yet, along with Dryden's own *The Wild Gallant* and Etherege's hugely successful *The Comical Revenge*, it heralds a growing intellectual challenge to the world-picture of Tuke, Orrery, Stapylton, Davenant, and the Howards. In any case, drama hymning the glories of 1660 could not continue indefinitely amidst the growing public disrepute of the royal brothers' lifestyle, the tensions between the King and the Cavalier Parliament, the grievances of royalists unable to re-cover estates which they had sold to pay fines imposed during the Inter-regnum, and the disasters of plague, fire, and humiliation in the Dutch War. Indeed, even Orrery and Sir Robert Howard did not long retain the pure optimism of *The Generall* and *The Committee*.

Loyal concern about Charles's lifestyle is clear in the anonymous and un-acted tragedy *Irena* (1664), in which a monarch recovers from an infatuation which has endangered his throne,[29] and in Orrery's *The Black Prince*, written in the wake of Louis XIV's declaration of war upon England (January 1666), which portrays a heroic warrior-king recovering from the enfeeblement of love. His infatuation brings him into sexual rivalry with his son: a situation which was to recur several times, generally in far more insoluble form, in tragedy of the mid-1670s. More ambiguous is Orrery's *Mustapha*, where a standard 1660 story (restoration of the infant King of Hungary) is paired with its contrary, in which Solyman the Magnificent is manœuvred by his Vizier and his second wife into executing his own son. The outlines of this plot seem to reflect the perceptions not of 1660 but of 1665: an unscrupulous

---

[29] This is a version of the much told story, later also dramatized by Payne in *The Siege of Constantinople* and Samuel Johnson in *Irene*. In the original history, the Sultan, Mahomet II, demon-strates his conquest of love by beheading his mistress in full view of his court (see Richard Knolles, *The Turkish History*, 6th edn. (London, 1687), 238–40). Here, as later in Payne, the heroine retains both life and honour.

counsellor (?Clarendon), an endangered succession, and an amorous King whose name 'Beauties fair hand' has 'foully blotted in the Book of Fame' (v. 575–6). A more pronounced change can be seen in the work of Sir Robert Howard, starting with the alternative tragic and tragicomic versions of *The Vestal Virgin* (King's, *c.* October 1664), whose dual form (like the contrasting plots of *Mustapha*) constitutes a semi-departure from the tragicomic form which the preoccupation with restoration had made the characteristic mode of serious drama in this period. The play labours the evils of passion, and contains some standard examples of rational magnanimity in love, as when the heroic general Sertorius and the captive Armenian prince Tiridates compete for the beautiful Hersilia with relative fairness. But, if the stranger from Armenia poses no threat, the same is not true of Sertorius's treacherous brother Sulpitius, and throughout the play Howard emphasizes that the true dangers lie within the city and within the home: the most spectacular calamity is a burning house, engineered by Sulpitius with the aid of pro-Caesarean (i.e. royalist) Civil War veterans, who have formerly been lauded as national saviours, but are now starving and anarchic malcontents (I, p. 159). The designs of Providence are no longer visible, and man is a dislocated wanderer in the cosmos:

> The Road unto Religion's misery.
> The ways might have been easier to find out . . .
> To every object we submit our sense,
> And call our accidents their providence.

> (V, p. 183)

The tragic version concludes with a bloodbath, and the tragicomic one (apparently written first)[30] with penitence, reconciliation, and mercy. There is probably no profundity of intention behind the double ending, but the fact that the aftermath of a civil war could interchangeably produce bloody chaos and harmonious reconciliation provides a nice illustration of the tensions that were shaping drama in this period. At about the same time, Sir Robert's brother James gave the same treatment to another play of civil strife, *Romeo and Juliet*, providing a tragicomic version which was acted alternately with the original.[31] In *The Vestal Virgin*, Sir Robert moves away from the preoccupation with disruptive but isolable upstarts such as Brancadoro and the Days and starts to see danger as lurking within established and sanctioned patterns of order. This is a shift of emphasis that continues in his last two plays. In his anti-Clarendon play *The Great Favourite* (King's, February 1668), for example, a weak, manipulable, and amorous king is reformed and

---

[30] See Oliver, *Sir Robert Howard*, 86.

[31] For information about Howard's revision, which is lost, see John Downes, *Roscius Anglicanus*, ed. Judith Milhous and Robert D. Hume (London, 1987), 53. Hume and Milhous (p. 53 n. 143) conjecture that the revision preceded the closing of the theatres (because of plague) in June 1665.

the ambitious and evil Duke of Lerma is finally neutralized, but he remains in triumphant impunity because of his rank as cardinal.

Tragedy, however, remained rare among the new plays produced in the early years of the Restoration. Apart from Dryden's early experiments with the heroic play, only Thomas Porter's popular *The Villain* (Duke's, October 1662) remains to be considered. With its Iago-like villain Malignii, this is the first of many Restoration imitations of *Othello*, and it is noteworthy that *The Vestal Virgin* and *Mustapha* also have a villain who works by abusing trust and slandering innocence. All three plays are linked by a sense of danger within the community, proceeding from the fallaciousness and deceptiveness of social bonds, and indeed *The Villain* is an *Othello* with the figure of the outsider virtually excised, the only candidate for that role being the comic and unimportant usurer Colignii. Although Porter's mind had not yet been concentrated by the example of *The Adventures of Five Hours*, he does (like Shakespeare in *Othello*) depict a social milieu dominated by male codes: a town upon which a regiment has been billeted. As D'orvile, the Governor of the town, asserts,

> For Friendship in Young-men breeds a delight
> In doing great and worthy things, whereby
> They may tie fast the bond of Friendship sworn.
>
> (I, p. 2)

D'orvile also expects his daughter, Charlotte, to comply unquestioningly with his marital plans for her, brusquely insisting that her honour 'is mine' (II, p. 17). By attempting to impose an unloved suitor on his daughter he contributes to the final sequence of calamities, which commences with a fatal duel between his favoured suitor and her own. Indeed, the tragedy is also advanced by the sexually exclusive nature of male friendship. In its coarsest and least consequential form, this appears in the cameraderie of fellow whoremasters: 'Quarrel about a Wench? no *Pilades*, | I thy *Orestes* will be still thy friend' (II, p. 22). But this expression of taproom *bonhomie* is closely and significantly juxtaposed with another and more serious display of exclusive male friendship: Beaupres, one of the heroes, insists on concealing his marriage to Bellmont because of his friendship with her brother (the friendship that D'orvile had praised): 'did he know the passion I have for you, | He then might doubt my freindships perfectness' (II, p. 21).[32] This act of concealment contributes to the unfolding of the tragedy, which culminates in Beaupres's jealous murder of his wife. Although the two heroines somewhat tentatively model their friendship upon the pattern supplied by males—'For friendship in all men grows up by trust, | And sure 'mongst women it is much the same' (III, p. 37)—it is in fact only among the women that trust and loyalty survive.

[32] Pages 3–17 of *The Villain* are misnumbered as 7–21, whereafter the true pagination is resumed. Two sequences of pages are thus numbered 18–21.

Trust, bond, obligation, merit, the word, and service (the key value of *The Committee*) are prominent and recurrent ideas throughout the play, but their power to regulate and restrain is weak. When Malignii persuades Beaupres that Bellmont is unfaithful, Beaupres vows eternal 'service' (V, p. 85) to the deceiver and descends to a state below language, renouncing 'Words' for 'deeds' (V, p. 88), and in this condition murders his wife. Undeceived, he resolves to execute justice, while recognizing that his own status as murderer invests this resolve with considerable irony: 'No, I will first perform one act of justice, | (That I should talk of justice now!)' (V, p. 92). But he lacks more than moral authority for his 'act of justice', for it is explicitly stated that he has no formal judicial authority to organize the concluding impalement of Malignii. We are, presumably, to applaud the punishment, but its unauthorized nature provides continuing testimony that the forms of society have of themselves failed to impose a satisfactory order upon human conduct.

The motive that inspires Malignii to kill is the same motive that inspired the heroes: the sensation of frustrated love (for he, like Beaupres, loves Bellmont). Hence he cannot be an outsider, for he presents a distorted and destructively simplified version of impulses sanctioned by the officer code itself: a group of whoring officers sings a song celebrating rape and plunder (I, p. 10), Malignii attempts to rape Bellmont (IV, p. 60), and the men of principle are driven to tragedy by subtler and more morally complex forms of destructive possessiveness. It would be dangerous to assume that Porter compares and evaluates these various aspects of machismo exactly as Aphra Behn would have done: he had already killed a man, probably in a duel, and was later to kill his best friend in a quarrel still more senseless than that between the friends in his play.[33] Porter too is an insider in the world he portrays, giving an insider's view of the tensions and tragic potentialities of the officer code.

The limitations of heroic codes were, however, most subtly examined in Dryden's heroic plays: *The Indian Queen* (King's, January 1664), written in collaboration with Sir Robert Howard, *The Indian Emperour* (King's, February–March 1665), *Tyrannick Love* (King's, June 1669), the two parts of *The Conquest of Granada* (King's, December 1670, January 1671), and *Aureng-Zebe* (King's, November 1675).[34] Here the intricacy of life and the irrationality of human character forbid the exemplary deeds and characters of Orrery's plays. Dryden's heroes and heroines are obstructed by villainous characters embodying extremes of egocentric and destructive passion, but the passions that reign unchecked in the villainous also infiltrate the motivation of the most principled, and the unpredictable arbitrariness of life means that honourable and villainous actions can be strangely parallel in their outcomes.

---

33 For the first duel, see *DNB*. For the second (an 'emblem of the general complexion of this whole Kingdom'), see Pepys, 29 July 1667.

34 I have discussed these plays extensively in my *Dryden's Heroic Plays* (London and Basingstoke, 1981).

The point is not, of course, that the honourable are no better than the base, but that they are variant manifestations of the same human material, linked by affinities that can never be eradicated. Hence, whereas Orrery's heroes are natural citizens, Montezuma in *The Indian Queen* and Almanzor in *The Conquest of Granada* emerge from a primal state of nature where appetite has been unconstrained, and in the process of emergence inevitably reveal a residual kinship with their villainous antitypes. *The Indian Queen* portrays the restoration of Montezuma to his ancestral throne, but it is the most complex of the early tragicomic representations of restoration, for the king enters civilization not as a natural embodiment of order but as a stranger (the word occurs repeatedly) from the wilderness, who learns the disciplines of civilization with difficulty. (In the sequel, *The Indian Emperour*, the restored hero-king has—as in the sequel on the stage of history—become enfeebled by love, Dryden apparently sharing the concerns evident in other plays of the mid-1660s.) Even when a noble character has no origin in the wilds, Dryden can still create startling symmetries between the noble and base: in *Tyrannick Love*, for example, St Catharine's fierce sense of religious calling makes her unwilling to forgo martyrdom or sanctity in order to save the lives of others, with the result that her celestial ambitions prove oddly parallel in their destructiveness to the earthly ambitions of her persecutor, the tyrant Maximin. 'Plusieurs saincts', observed Charron, 'ont fuy à mourir . . . combien que pour leur particulier ils eussent bien voulu s'en aller. C'est acte de charité vouloir vivre pour autruy'.[35]

In the last case, however, Dryden is not so much emphasizing similarity of motive as indicating that radically opposed codes may tend towards paradoxical similarity of consequence. This is another recurrent feature of his serious drama, perhaps best illustrated in an incident in *The Indian Emperour*, which he adapted from a contemporary epic, Georges de Scudéry's *Alaric*.[36] In *Alaric*, the virtuous Probé successively asks her two noble suitors, Valere and Tiburse, to save the besieged and famine-stricken city of Rome by letting in the enemy. Valere indignantly refuses, whereas Tiburse agrees, only to find that Alaric honourably rejects the offered betrayal. Tiburse then repents his folly, and subsequently redeems himself by a noble death in battle (x. 422). In Dryden, the virtuous Alibech makes the same request in comparable circumstances. Her rival suitors are the two sons of Montezuma, Guyomar and Odmar, the former a man of honour, the latter a villain. Whereas Scudéry presents a shared code of honour which one character briefly misinterprets, Dryden (like Shakespeare in *The Tempest*) portrays the mysterious emergence

---

[35] Pierre Charron, *De la sagesse, trois livres*, ed. Amaury Duval (3 vols., Paris, 1824; repr. Geneva, 1968), bk. ii, ch. xi, p. 271.

[36] See Derek Hughes, 'Dryden's *The Indian Emperour* and Georges de Scudéry's *Alaric*', *Review of English Studies*, NS 33 (1982), 47–51; Georges de Scudéry, *Alaric; ou, Rome vaincue* (Paris, 1654), x. 412–18. The earlier stages of the Probé story (vii. 271–83, viii. 289–92) are also used in *The Indian Emperour*.

of nobility and corruption from the same womb: that of Orazia, the virtuous princess whom Montezuma had wooed and won in *The Indian Queen*. Moreover, he adds a complication in the comparison of the two suitors. When Guyomar has indignantly rejected Alibech's request, he decides to make a secret sortie against the invading Spaniards, but is so preoccupied with gaining personal honour from the venture that he tells no one, not even Alibech. And so, in her ignorance of Guyomar's plan, Alibech approaches Odmar and plants the seed of treason in his mind. Guyomar's sortie succeeds, but its success is promptly counteracted by that of Odmar's betrayal (which, unlike Tiburse's, is gladly accepted by the enemy). The two brothers remain very different in their motives and characters, but the imperatives of Guyomar's sense of honour none the less accidentally assist Odmar's villainy and destroy his own heroic achievement. Fixed codes are of limited value in an arbitrary and unpredictable world, and Guyomar cannot ultimately cope with the real world: whereas several other Dryden heroes enter civilization from the state of nature, Guyomar eventually leaves his devastated country for the desert. The codes of honour do not articulate the actual principles of human coexistence, and the hero is not a natural citizen.

Dryden's concern with the limitations of fixed codes extends to a concern with the limitations of language. Language in Orrery is a stable bond between individual and community, and a mirror of the moral order that sustains society, but in Dryden it is an imperfect system of arbitrary signs, whose inadequacies typify the impossibility of an objective intermediary between individual consciousness and the world outside it: in neither direction can there be a natural and direct transmission of likeness. True community is therefore epistemologically impossible, for each individual is locked in the profound and unbreachable isolation of his own consciousness, 'a Pris'ner', in Almanzor's words, 'of the Mind'.[37] The strained and inappropriate imagery that has proved so troublesome to interpreters of Dryden's heroic plays often seems to reveal the fumblings of the mind as it seeks to apprehend the alien forms beyond its boundaries, and such fumblings are quite clearly portrayed in Guyomar's first speech in *The Indian Emperour*, where the man of honour enters the play not as a paragon of linguistic stability but as a man whose language is plainly insufficient for the tasks confronting it. For Guyomar is struggling to describe his first ever glimpse of ships (the invading Spanish fleet), awkwardly applying words from his acquired stock of experience to an unknown and uncomprehended object (the ships are, for example, 'floating Palaces', I. ii. 111). The incident illustrates a fundamental paradox of language—that words acquired in the context of past experience must be used to define new and possibly unique experiences—and it acts as a demonstration of the psychological origins of metaphor, showing that metaphor is

---

[37] *The Conquest of Granada*, Part II, IV. iii. 148.

both an inevitable and an inevitably distorting constituent in the linguistic communication of new experience. If, indirectly, it communicates knowledge of the object, it also expresses the veil of incomprehension that exists between the mind and the object. (Up to this point, indeed, the language of the Indians—unlike that of the Spaniards—has displayed very little metaphor. Metaphor erupts at the moment when Western artifice enters their world.)

One curious feature of the first four heroic plays is that—in contrast to the split-plot romances—their action rarely involves writing. Even St Catharine never refers to Holy Writ (and there are only fleeting references to books in the Dryden–Davenant *Tempest*). Perhaps the absence of writing focuses attention on pure, unmediated action, released from the contamination of interpretation: unlike Coriolanus, Almanzor has no need to qualify his boasts with 'If you have writ your annals true' (V. vi. 113). Characters are not instantly transformed into texts, and the most that is achieved is an imprecise oral prediction of future narrative: King Ferdinand prophesies that 'All stories, which *Granada*'s Conquest tell, | Shall celebrate the name of *Isabel*' (Part II, V. iii. 228–9), but he is wrong, for Dryden's story suggests that Isabel's role in the conquest of Granada was insignificant in comparison to that of the evil Lyndaraxa; it is a self-negating moment of interpretation. But the absence of writing also means that the written word no longer serves as a reification of constant principles of order, and, when characters do use images of writing to express their conception of a transcendent order, the imagery is patently inadequate, revealing—like Guyomar's description of the ships— the gropings of minds to comprehend things that lie beyond the limits of acquired experience. Fearing that she and her Porphyrius will not recognize each other in heaven, Berenice in *Tyrannick Love* ingenuously longs to 'wear a Scroul, | With this Inscription, *Berenice's Soul*' (V. 492–3). And when, in *The Conquest of Granada*, Almanzor falls in love with Almahide only to discover that she is already betrothed, his response is to demand that Heaven should revise reality into conformity with his expectations: 'Good Heav'n thy book of fate before me lay, | But to tear out the journal of this day' (Part I, III. i. 397–8). Almanzor for a moment genuinely believes that he can cancel the past by tearing tangible pages out of a tangible book of destiny, the book being no more than the crude fiction of a mind which cannot apprehend anything beyond its own material images and impulses: the book of heaven, for so long a written archetype of a moral order originating in the divine word, here becomes a sign of man's mental confinement to the realm of matter. Similarly, when the Koran is revered at the beginning of Almahide's trial by combat, a flawed ritual of justice in which violence becomes the criterion of truth, the wrong book sanctifies an inadequate process of interpretation.

A play that is closely related in subject and outlook to the heroic plays is the revision of *The Tempest* (Duke's, November 1667) which Dryden undertook in collaboration with Davenant. Indeed, it is far more closely related to

Dryden's earlier work than to Davenant's, virtually reversing the approach that Davenant had taken in his unaided adaptations of Shakespeare. As in *The Indian Queen* and *The Conquest of Granada*, there is regression from civilization to the state of nature, and as in *The Indian Queen* there is consistent and purposeful redirection of the term *stranger* to describe characters who are nominally key elements in the social order. There is also a proliferation of literal strangers and outsiders, so that alienness becomes an inescapable dimension of human experience: two monsters for Shakespeare's one, two women to whom the male sex is alien and unknown, and one man similarly ignorant of women.[38] *The Tempest* is, of course, a play of restoration, and the Dryden–Davenant revision was the most ironic serious treatment of the restoration theme yet to have appeared.

In the period of neglectful rule which preceded his deposition, Shakespeare's Prospero 'to my state grew stranger' (I. ii. 76), but Shakespeare emphasizes the reintegration of community through compassion, first introduced when Miranda 'suffered | With those that I saw suffer' (I. ii. 5–6) in the sinking vessel. Shakespeare also portrays responses to shipwrecks in *Pericles* (by compassionate fishermen) and *The Winter's Tale* (by a gawping and uncompassionate clown), and he was perhaps recalling and rejecting the opening of Book ii of Lucretius' *De Rerum Natura*, where the detached calm of the philosopher is compared to the pleasant detachment of the man on the sea-shore watching a sinking ship.[39] As it happens, Dryden was also interested in the Lucretian spectator at about the time of his collaborative revision of *The Tempest*, though he differs from Shakespeare in seeing egocentric detachment as the inevitable condition of the human mind. In particular, the image of the Lucretian spectator dominates his next play, *Tyrannick Love* (1669), where in my view it emphasizes the chilling detachment of St Catharine from the fears and frailties of those who must also die if she is to gain the martyr's crown which is her one, obsessive, ambition.[40]

Dryden and Davenant do retain Miranda's distress at the shipwreck, though they reduce its prominence: as in Shakespeare, the 'spectacle' raises 'the very virtue of compassion' in her (I. ii. 26–7), but there is no 'O, I have suffered | With those that I saw suffer', and Miranda has in fact left the scene of

---

[38] In Samuel Johnson's words, 'The effect produced by the conjunction of these two powerful minds was that to Shakespeare's monster Caliban is added a sister-monster Sicorax; and a woman, who, in the original play, had never seen a man, is in this brought acquainted with a man that had never seen a woman' ('Dryden', in *Lives of the English Poets*, ed. George Birkbeck Hill (3 vols., Oxford, 1905), i. 341).

[39] *De Rerum Natura*, ii. 1–6. My text of Lucretius is *Titi Lucreti Cari, De Rerum Natura Libri Sex*, ed. Cyril Bailey (3 vols., Oxford, 1947). The sentiments of this passage had been discussed by Montaigne: 'in the middest of compassion, we inwardly feele a kinde of bitter-sweet-pricking of malicious delight, to see others suffer' (*Essays*, iii. 8 (ch. i.)).

[40] Hughes, *Dryden's Heroic Plays*, 59–78. Unlike Lucretius, Dryden locates the observer in a 'Cell' (III. i. 48)—perhaps a reminiscence of Montaigne's 'little little Cell'. Cells are also even more prominent in the revised *Tempest* than in the original.

the wreck early, whereas her un-Shakespearian sister, Dorinda, is still watching it. As this detail would lead us to expect, it is Dorinda's reactions to the wreck which receive the most prominence, and these are reactions not of compassion but of uncomprehending curiosity; of Lucretian detachment. Like Guyomar describing the arrival of the Spanish fleet in *The Indian Emperour*, she narrates sensory impressions which she lacks the knowledge to categorize and interpret, and which she must therefore accommodate to the limited store of images acquired in her experience, the ship for example becoming a 'floating Ram' (I. ii. 304). There is no compassion, only a puzzled listing of disjunct sensations by an observer whose confined experience makes understanding or compassionate engagement impossible, and it is in this context that the term *strange* first enters the play, when Miranda—now largely sharing her sister's attitude—promises 'stranger news': 'shortly we may chance to see that thing, | Which you have heard my Father call, a Man' (I. ii. 314–17). To call a person a 'thing' is, of course, to exclude his consciousness and experience, and even the language which defines the 'thing' is uncomprehendingly memorized from external sources (a Hobbesian touch). Dorinda recognizes no community of experience or nature with the strangers whose sufferings she watches, and the absence of such community is everywhere evident.

For the revisers' multiplication of isolated inexperienced figures—Miranda having both a sister and a male counterpart, who has neither seen nor been seen by the sisters—leads to a proliferation of encounters between human beings who do not understand their shared humanity, and it is in this context that the words *strange* and *strangely* chiefly figure in the revision. Shakespeare's concern with the *strange* as the revelatory virtually disappears. Hippolito, the man who has never seen woman, is 'strangely' puzzled by what they may be (II. v. 8). And, when he has seen and fallen in love with Dorinda, discovered that she is not the only being of her kind in the world, and concluded that all women are similarly his property—'found | Within my self, they are all made for me' (IV. i. 268–9), as he later puts it—he inevitably regards Ferdinand as a dangerous sexual rival: 'This Stranger does insult and comes into my | World to take those heavenly beauties from me' (III. vi. 93–4). Like Almanzor (another character reared alone in the state of nature), Hippolito cannot imagine any distinction between the nature of his desires and the nature of the world. The latter must self-evidently be a projection of the former, and it is revealing that he should expect Dorinda to share his elation at there being other beauties for him to enjoy (IV. i. 178–246): he can only see her as an extension of himself, not as an autonomous being who inhabits a sphere of desire different from his own. Dorinda's calm Lucretian detachment from the sufferings of the sinking mariners is typical of the characters' inability to incorporate the sensations of others within their own experience. They are prisoners of the mind.

Among the most important foundations of community in Shakespeare's play are sight and touch (normally hand-holding), which in their fullest and properest exercise are recognitions of shared moral condition. Dryden and Davenant do retain Prospero's praise of Ariel's 'touch' and 'feeling' (III. i. 173) of his prisoners' afflictions, though (as we shall see) its significance is ultimately reversed; and Miranda is 'touch'd' with compassion for the imperilled voyagers (I. ii. 22), though the force of her reaction is counteracted by the prominence given to Dorinda's. But sight and touch cumulatively assume a thematic significance in this play which is quite different from that which they have in Shakespeare's, and which qualifies the meaning of the surviving Shakespearian usages that I have quoted. For they refer merely to corporeal sensation, and frequently to sexual sensation. Both, for instance, are recurrently used to define the purely sensual attraction of Hippolito and Dorinda, as when Dorinda describes their first meeting:

DOR. At first it [an alienating pronoun] star'd upon me and seem'd wild . . .
    Then it drew near, and with amazement askt
    To touch my hand . . .
    He put it to his mouth so eagerly, I was afraid he
    Would have swallow'd it.

(III. i. 104–11)

How different from the moment when Shakespeare's Alonso takes Ferdinand's and Miranda's hands. The touching of hands here signifies not union of understanding but merely a desire for corporeal possession on the part of one whom Dorinda initially sees as an alien predator. Sight and touch in this play are predominantly the media not of understanding but of desire, and desire itself breeds not understanding but the suspicion and conflict of strangers competing for possession in the Hobbesian condition of nature. Sexual passion causes the sisters to deceive Prospero, as fear of their sexual experience has caused him to deceive them. Ferdinand more than once quarrels jealously with Miranda, misinterpreting her request for 'compassion' to the 'stranger' Hippolito (IV. i. 76–7), whom he later nearly kills in a duel, and, when Miranda tends Hippolito's wound, Dorinda also quarrels with her, preferring that Hippolito should die rather than be cured by another woman: 'Y'are very charitable to a Stranger' (V. ii. 89), she says, suspiciously.

In examining humanity in the state of nature, the Restoration *Tempest* (obviously) portrays not the regenerative nature of Shakespeare but the nature of Hobbes. The most common images of nature in the play are of predatory beasts and of poison, and there is no masque of reapers: at the corresponding point in the Dryden–Davenant version an implacably vengeful Prospero has sentenced Ferdinand to death for the murder of Hippolito, and Prospero's conduct at this point constitutes the single most striking reversal of Shakespeare's affirmation that compassion is natural to man because men are creatures of a common 'kind'. In both versions, as I have indicated, Prospero praises Ariel's 'touch' and 'feeling' of the prisoners' afflictions, and in both he goes on to affirm that 'the rarer action is | In virtue than in vengeance'.[41] In Shakespeare, however, the affirmation is in Act V, and is the key to Prospero's final actions. In the revision, it occurs near the beginning of Act III, and is later explicitly disowned. 'No pleasure now is left me but Revenge' (IV. iii. 38), Prospero exclaims on hearing of Hippolito's seeming death, remaining deaf to all appeals for pity: 'I have no room for pity left within me' (IV. iii. 190).

Pity in Shakespeare provides assurance of community, assurance that mankind is not a fortuitous gathering of irremediably isolated strangers, and, from Miranda's response to the sinking vessel onwards, pity and the other civilizing virtues are associated with the enlightened exercise of sight, as understanding (rather than mere observation) of another's condition. In the revision, the assurance vanishes, for the chief embodiment of pity suddenly turns into an embodiment of its reverse, and the transformation of Prospero leads to a shocking reversal of what in Shakespeare is the culmination of the moral exercise of sight, where Prospero rewards Alonso's penitence and completes his enlightenment by inviting him to 'look in' (V. i. 167) on the lovers' chess game. This is where the moment of sight and recognition is sealed by the moment of touch, when Alonso takes the lovers' hands (V. i. 213). But the Restoration Prospero reveals Ferdinand to Alonzo (*sic*) in a very different spectacle:

> I in bitterness have sent for you
> To have the sudden joy of *seeing* him alive,
> And then the greater grief to *see* him dye.
>
> (IV. iii. 151–3; italics added)

The episode closes with Alonzo's despairing plea that Prospero *see* his and Ferdinand's condition: '*Look* on my age, and *look* upon his youth' (IV. iii. 188; italics added); but Prospero does not see, for this is where he has 'no room for pity left' (IV. iii. 190). He has become another Lucretian observer.

When Ariel has restored Hippolito to life, Alonzo does acknowledge the justice of Prospero's action, and of course it is just, though public justice is disturbingly derived—perhaps derived in its very nature—from ugly vengefulness. For Prospero's justice indicates that society is founded upon primarily coercive and repressive principles (the executioner appointed to wield 'the Sword | Of Justice' (V. i. 28–9) is *Caliban*). The natural discovery of community is replaced by the violent containment of man's natural hostility to man, and as a result the experience of confinement loses the potentially educative value which it has in Shakespeare, becoming a mere insurance against the violence of human nature. Hippolito has been a prisoner all his life because Prospero foresees the danger that will ensue when he first sees a woman, and Miranda and Dorinda have similarly spent their lives within prescribed

---

[41] Shakespeare, V. i. 21–8; Dryden–Davenant, III. i. 173–9.

'bounds' (II. iv. 92), to prevent them from seeing Hippolito. Ferdinand's confinement is not, as it is in Shakespeare, that of the nobleman learning service (still a fundamental value in *The Committee*) but of the condemned man awaiting execution. Marriage is not the sanctification of harmonious fruition celebrated in the masque of reapers, but a necessary constraint upon human appetite: 'if you love you must be *ty'd* to one,' Ferdinand says to the sexually voracious Hippolito (III. vi. 57; italics added). There is no innate and inherited nobility of character, as the behaviour of Duke Hippolito and others in the state of nature demonstrates, and external influence and coercion form the primary civilizing process. Hippolito is cured of his rampant sexual appetite not because he apprehends the value of Shakespeare's 'sanctimonious ceremonies . . . | With full and holy rite' (IV. i. 16–17) but for purely material reasons, in that his wound causes great loss of blood, and Ferdinand's greater temperance and responsibility is the product of civilization rather than nature: a product which is imperfect enough for him to challenge the inexperienced Hippolito to a duel which he is certain to lose, though sufficiently moderating for him to be reluctant to kill his opponent.

One consequence of the revisers' shift from innate to imperfectly acquired sociability is that their play creates an entirely new relationship between its noble and base characters, and particularly between the noble characters and Caliban, the monster. Although Caliban is still a monster, he is no longer a stranger: no longer Shakespeare's 'strange fish' or 'strange thing' (II. ii. 27–8; v. i. 289). While the human characters are inexhaustibly 'strange' to each other, the term is entirely removed from the chief outsider of the original version. As we might expect, Stephano, Trincalo, and their companions present a study of man in a condition of natural conflict and savagery, their rivalry for power leading to a constant state of war. They propose to sustain themselves by going one better than the Lucretian spectator and actually plundering shipwrecks (II. iii. 52–4), and they illustrate most explicitly the play's recurrent definition of mankind as a gathering of strangers: while Trincalo is off-stage, Stephano and his companions invent a political community and constitution (II. iii. 51–82), and, when Trincalo appears and protests against the new arrangement, he is dismissed as 'a meer stranger | To the Laws of the Country' (II. iii. 138–9). The forms of society are artificial and mutable, and the companion easily lapses into the stranger. Surprisingly, however, although the unruliness of Stephano and his circle obviously parodies the upheavals of the Civil War, it is less menacing than that of their social superiors (a symptom of the change of emphasis being that they do not attempt to kill Prospero). Caliban's monstrous sister becomes an object of sexual rivalry because it is believed that her consort will rule the island, and her indiscriminate sexual appetite for all the available men—clearly parallel to Hippolito's lust for every woman in the world—provokes a quarrel which is closely and pointedly juxtaposed with the duel of Ferdinand and Hippolito: when both are brought up in the state of nature, a Duke and a monster can display remarkably similar constitution and appetites. But it is the quarrel of the Duke which is the more serious and dangerous.

In Shakespeare, Antonio and Sebastian remain outsiders, participating in Caliban's nature and incapable of assimilation into the community. In the revision, Caliban's nature is universally dispersed throughout the community, as Ariel indicates when, at the end of the fourth act, he describes the chain of discord that links everyone from the ruler to the monster: Hippolito is seemingly dead, Prospero is consumed with vengeful anger, Ferdinand is sentenced to death, Miranda and Dorinda are quarrelling about the fates of their lovers, Alonzo and his associates are bitterly reproaching each other, and the low characters are quarrelling about the power believed to await the man who sleeps with Caliban's sister. Ariel's speech provides a particularly clear example of the characteristic Restoration emphasis on strangeness within proximity: '*Antonio* and *Gonzalo* disagree, | And wou'd, though in one Cave, at distance be' (IV. iii. 264–5). Even a single 'little Cell' may contain irreconcilable diversity of vision. Moreover, Caliban is no longer an external embodiment of the antisocial extreme: 'The Monsters *Sycorax* and *Caliban* | More monstrous grow by passions learn'd from man' (IV. iii. 270–1). As the men are the greater monsters, so the word *strange* and its cognates are removed from Caliban and distributed around the human characters. The figure of the external stranger, his role diminished and qualified (since he does not seek Prospero's death), remains as a projection of the characters' imperfect assimilation into the condition of society, but he does not initiate anything in the way that Tamora, Shylock, or the original Caliban do. The real stranger is the stranger within, and we have a society very different from that postulated in the earliest and rosiest portrayals of restoration: a society whose disciplines are uneasily imposed upon selfish and refractory individuals, and whose justice owes little to Astraea.

Fascination with restoration did not dominate comedy to the same extent as it did tragedy and tragicomedy. As already indicated, *The Rump* and *The Committee* did not establish a fashion, and later comedies (including Sir Robert Howard's own *The Country Gentleman*) portray the post-Restoration order with considerable latitude and irreverence. A clear contrast to *The Committee*, for example, is provided by John Wilson's city comedy *The Cheats* (King's, March 1663), which satirizes the avarice and lechery of Puritan hypocrites, and portrays an impoverished gentleman recovering his fortunes by marrying the daughter of one of them. Unlike Howard, Wilson does not feel obliged to keep his heroine genetically distinct from the Puritans, and indeed Puritan venality and hypocrisy is not a violation of a prevailing disposition to harmonious hierarchy but a particular manifestation of a widespread enthusiasm for fraud, by which even the heroes gain their ends. As the sham astrologer Mopus says, 'there are but 2 Sorts of people in the world—Aut qui Captant aut qui Captantur' (IV. ii. 124–5). Moreover, while Wilson exuberantly portrays corrupted language and ludicrous linguistic theory (Welsh is the primitive tongue, and a new language has been discovered in Ireland), there is no simple opposition between linguistic aberration and social normality. On the contrary, one of the final displays of linguistic chaos is that in which the Nonconformist Scruple decides to comply with the official order by accepting the benefits of an Anglican parsonage: 'I will conforme, reforme, transforme, deforme, any forme—forme—forme—tis but one Syllable and has no very ill Sound, It may be Swallowed' (V. iv. 35–7). In the Ovidian masques in *The Step-Mother*, form is a fixed and unambiguous principle of personal and political integrity. Here, by a nice paradox, the very word *form* symbolizes the absence of the thing itself, dissolved in the infinite fluidity of Scruple's conscience and vocabulary. *The Committee* tentatively suggests the future assimilation of the Days, but *The Cheats* ends with the fanatic cynically surviving and prospering within the restored order. (Wilson provides a more serious, but still only mutedly celebratory, view of the Restoration in his tragedy *Andronicus Comnenius*, one of three probably unperformed plays about the Byzantine usurper, who gained power when nobles opposed to an inadequate king lost control of what they intended to be a limited revolution. There is unusual emphasis on the role of the mob both in revolution and restoration, and the concluding speech is not a celebration of the miraculous but a sober warning that progress will be gradual (V, p. 87).[42]

Still more irreverent than *The Cheats* is John Lacy's excellent Civil War farce *The Old Troop* (King's, *c.* December 1664). There are some conventional elements here: hypocrite upstarts, raised 'from Coblers to Commanders' (IV, p. 27), who briefly delude men of the better sort into following their cause. But we are also shown the milder, but still considerable, flaws of plundering Cavaliers, and throughout the play Lacy reiterates and discredits the moral and social vocabulary associated with idealizing representations of restoration: trust, honour, honesty, truth, troth, faith, service, and friendship.

---

[42] According to the dedication (sig. A3), the play was written some time before publication, but had not been acted in the interval. Nicholas Jose notes the restraint with which this play treats the Restoration (*Ideas of the Restoration*, 126–8). *Andronicus: A Tragedy, Impieties Long Successe, or Heavens Late Revenge* (1661) contributes to the Astraea Redux theme by displaying on its title-page the topical Virgilian motto '*Discite Justitiam moniti, & ne temnite Divos*' (*Aeneid*, vi. 620), which had been used on Charles's first coronation arch. According to the preface, it had been written eighteen years previously. It is a pseudo-classical tragedy with choruses and irrelevant Senecan debates, and seems essentially unperformable. *The Unfortunate Usurper* (1663) draws explicit parallels with recent British history (V, pp. 61–5) and (like *The Cheats*) shows the fanatic adapting effortlessly to the post-Restoration order. Its excessively lengthy speeches make performance unlikely. In the dedication the author is candid enough to refer to '*Readers, who have bespattered with the blackest Obloquy they can, a Piece lately publisht by me*' (sig. [A3]), and one would therefore expect an allusion to the reception of the play, however appalling, had it in fact been performed. Antony Hammond, however, believes that all three plays may have been performed in the early 1660s ('John Wilson and the Andronicus Plays: A Re-consideration', *Yearbook of English Studies*, 4 (1974), 112–19 (p. 118)).

In a reversal of the conventional association between political order and socially regulated sexual instinct, the practical significance of these terms is summed up in the prostitute Dol, who (in an episode crowded with the terms *truth* and *truly*) protests, 'I have been as true and faithful a Woman to the Troop, as ever Wife was to a Husband;' 'this is', the listening Captain Honour concedes, 'some honesty yet' (II, pp. 13–14). As an unscrupulous Lieutenant observes to Dol, 'the general principle of mankind' is not friendship but the desire for others' property (I, p. 7), and even the arrestingly named Tom Tell-Troth exemplifies not a pure ideal of truth and troth but the truth about human motives: he fights 'as all men fight for Kings, partly for Love, partly for my own Ends' (I, p. 4). Although Captain Honour enforces justice by ending the plundering, he readily (with Tom Tell-Troth's approval) limits the value of his name by allowing his Lieutenant to offer the enemy terms of surrender which he himself intends to repudiate; for 'the Captain may with his Honour' break the Lieutenant's word (V, p. 34). Not surprisingly, this play does not promise restoration of Astraea-like absolutes of order. Lacy does evoke an archetypal icon of justice—the Judgement of Solomon—but it figures as an item in the repertoire of a puppeteer, wedged between such undignified images of authority as the King of Spain playing the bagpipes and the Queen of Swiveland showing a leg (IV, p. 29). The absence of simple absolutes is reflected in the fluidity with which Lacy treats the figure of the cultural outsider, Monsieur Raggou, a cook in the Cavalier army who counterbalances the social outsiders in the Roundhead camp. For Raggou is not excluded from and measured against constant norms of national conduct, but is a parasitic shape-shifter who constantly penetrates into the forms of his host nation. At one point, for example, he and an English soldier simultaneously plunder disguised as each other, and mimicking each other's accents. Raggou's career as a shape-shifter reaches its most dazzling heights when he evades capture by pretending to be a wooden post, successfully deceiving even the inevitable man with the pot of paint (V, p. 32): hardly the Royal Oak, but the play pleased the King.

For comedy writers, however, the main alternative to celebrating the return of an old order was to portray the post-Restoration order as one of healthy innovation, dispensing with the moral and social rigidities of the past. One result was some polemically non-moral definitions of gentlemanly conduct, which postulate a social order quite different from the natural moral hierarchy of *The Committee*, or of Richard Allestree's social order as replication of the Great Chain of Being. Bellamy in Dryden's *An Evening's Love* (1668), for example, gives a resolutely secular account of the gentleman's calling: 'I am a Gentleman, a man of the Town, one who wears good Cloathes, Eates, Drinks, and Wenches abundantly; I am a damn'd ignorant, and senceless Fellow' (IV. 363–5). Similarly, Courtall in Etherege's *She Would If She Could* cheerfully abolishes the prime gentlemanly virtue by announcing that 'the keeping of one's word is a thing below the honor of a gentleman' (II. ii. 201–2). But if the precepts of Christian moralists constrain the role of the gentleman, they also justify and protect it; Dryden and Etherege both liberate and endanger him, exposing him to an interrogating irony against which the moral wisdom of the past provides no defence. (At the beginning of *The Comical Revenge*, a gentleman's manners are subjected to systematic critique by the chambermaid of a prostitute.)

Gentility of place and lineage are, indeed, the butts of Dryden's first play, *The Wild Gallant* (King's, February 1663), a challenging play which was eclipsed by Tuke's tamer product at the rival house. Like the contrasting formulation of 'noble Savage', which Dryden coined to describe Almanzor,[43] 'Wild Gallant' expresses Dryden's interest in the persistence of the wilderness within civilization; indeed, one of the heroines satirizes hunting enthusiasts as 'a pack of gentlemen Salvages' (III. i. 240–1). But there are more unexpected forms of gentility even than that of the gentleman savage, for the title of gentleman is bestowed three times upon the Devil, to whom the hero, Loveby, mistakenly attributes some anonymous gifts of money (and consequently undertakes to 'wear a Sword at his *Service*', II. ii. 11–12; italics added).[44] 'The Gentleman in the black Pantaloons' (IV. i. 121) is decidedly not a gentleman whose rank and estate give him moral responsibility in a providential order, and although Loveby's gifts are not actually demonic in origin, they violate the principle of patriarchal inheritance in more prosaic ways, in that the heroine, Lady Constance, has stolen the money from her father, Lord Nonsuch. The irreverence towards established bases of continuity and order also finds expression in a very imperfect agent of Astraea, Justice Trice, who exercises his office amidst carnivalistic inversions of authority, which reach their extreme of absurdity when the noble patriarch Lord Nonsuch is tricked into thinking himself to be pregnant. Indeed, Trice is himself explicitly associated with the indulgence of that flesh which it is his office to regulate: he is 'ever good in a Flesh Market', and his mind is 'ever upon' his 'belly' (II. i. 262, 270). (The flesh, and indeed the Devil, were to be recurrent images in Dryden's early comedies.)

Interesting though the play is, however, it is hard to quantify Dryden's contribution to it, since it is by his own account a greatly altered version of an old (and now lost) play.[45] The published text is of a revised (and again unsuccessful) version prepared in 1667, and the only part which is certainly his is a scene which he states to have been added at this stage, in which Loveby tries to persuade Constance that a bawd and two prostitutes are ladies of quality.[46] This scene obviously contributes to the ironic treatment of gentility,

[43] *The Conquest of Granada*, Part I, I. i. 209.   [44] II. ii. 15, 18; IV. i. 121.
[45] See Dryden's preface. Alfred Harbage argues that the original was by Brome ('Elizabethan–Restoration Palimpsest', *Modern Language Review*, 35 (1940), 287–319 (pp. 304–9)).
[46] 'Prologue to the Wild-Gallant Reviv'd', ll. 19–20.

though we cannot on that account conclude that every instance of such irony was added by Dryden. He does not here imply (as others were soon to do) that prostitutes and fine ladies are virtually indistinguishable, for these women are blatant, garlic-eating impostors who are quickly found out. But the imposture develops other jokes which represent Loveby's relationship to them in parodic images of gentle ancestry, so that the gentleman's commerce with whores satirically reproduces the structure of patrilineal nobility: Lady Dulake, the bawd, claims Loveby as her 'Son' (IV. i. 94) and verifies his lineage, pronouncing him to be like his father and grandfather. Both jokes have many counterparts elsewhere in the play, for emphasis on inheritance is—appropriately enough—accompanied by emphasis on parentage. But the greatest symmetry between the apparent opposites of whoring and patrilineal succession is this: that 'the best Heraldry of a Gentleman is a Clap deriv'd to him, from three Generations' (I. i. 107–8).

Both paternity and inheritance are running jokes. It is Frances Bibber, a tailor's wife, who condemns female adultery on the grounds that it confuses true succession (III. ii. 169–70), but the gentry impose rather different restrictions upon paternity: immediately before Lady Dulake's entrance the bumbling Justice Trice wins Loveby's approval for his severity to a pauper defendant in a paternity suit; for the 'poor lowsie Rascal' has dared 'to intrench upon the Game of Gentlemen!' (IV. i. 58–9). Paternity is most farcically scrutinized when Constance evades her noble father's plan to marry her to an idiotic knight by pretending to be pregnant (and therefore not a fit carrier of her husband's seed), and in the process compromises patriarchy to the extent of persuading her father that he too is with child. In the revised version, the lady's masquerade as a strumpet complements the prostitutes' masquerade as ladies: Constance has become 'a *bona roba*' (IV. ii. 276), using the alternative social order of Lady Dulake in order to escape from the constraints imposed by her father's preoccupation with exalted lineage (a form of escape that was to recur in several later plays). Even after she has married Loveby, however, her father only forgives her because he has no other heirs, and his concern with preservation of the line continues to the end of the play, where he promises Loveby £3,000 per annum for a grandchild.

The courtship of Loveby and Constance was the earliest gay couple courtship on the Restoration stage, though Constance lacks the sexual openness of the parts soon to be written for Nell Gwyn, and the broad farce of illusory male pregnancy was not the stuff of which genteel comedy was to be made in the next few years. More prophetic was another gay couple play, *The English Mounsieur* (King's, by July 1663), by James Howard. Welbred, a mildly rakish compulsive gambler, is tamed and cured by a witty woman (the widowed Lady Wealthy), and Frenchlove and Vaine, respectively a Frenchified fop and a boastful sexual fantasist, are married off to two prostitutes masquerading as gentlewomen. Less conventionally, the gentleman Comely falls in love with the rustic sweetheart of a Wiltshire yokel, but cannot detach her from her amiably clownish first love. Characters here are not placed in the kind of all-comprehending social order that distinguishes *The Committee*. The four principal men are all seized by eccentric and isolating obsessions ('humours'),[47] and the eccentricities of the heroes at times reduce them to parity with the fools: Comely wishes to swap identities with his rival 'Clown' (IV, p. 41), and Welbred is made to 'look like an Ass' by Lady Wealthy (IV, p. 52). The controlling principles here are custom and conditioning, rather than fixed verities of class and order. Vaine's mendacious sexual bragging comes from 'hearing the Orange Wenches talk' (I, p. 4). Frenchlove, the English Monsieur, is entirely possessed by foreign customs, and even Comely resolves to 'try if the Air of another Countrey' can cure him of his love (V, p. 64). While hearty Englishness is preferable to Frenchlove's effeminate Francophilia, the behaviour of class and nation is nevertheless based not on fixed natural principles but on contingent conventions. One function of the rustic couple, William and Elsbeth, is to introduce a viewpoint from which the accepted modes of the fashionable world appear as exotic and slightly absurd wonders: when they stray from Wiltshire into the fashionable London world, they view its manners and artefacts with the sort of incomprehension and misinterpretation with which Dryden's noble savages in *The Indian Emperour* were to view the inventions of civilization. Comely's rivalry with William reaches its climax when they vie for Elsbeth with successive declarations of love, and William's rustic gibberish easily beats Comely's romantic—but equally comic—rhetoric. There is no fixed or normative linguistic decorum, simply a clash of equally customary and equally arbitrary modes of speech.

Etherege's first play, *The Comical Revenge* (Duke's, March 1664), follows and outdoes *The English Mounsieur* in portraying the social power of custom. Its noblest characters ostensibly live by the principles of Orrery's,[48] but, whereas Orrery's social code expresses and fulfils his characters' natures, Etherege's is a restrictive imposition which must ultimately be evaded or compromised. Like *The Committee*, *The Comical Revenge* is set during the Protectorate, but the social change on which it concentrates is not the defeat of Puritanism but the movement from, in Etherege's later words, 'the forms and civility of the last age' to 'the freedoms of the present'.[49] The most socially and morally exalted of the four levels of plot shows a milieu dominated by ideals of self-denying honour. Lovis unimaginatively insists that his sister Graciana marry his heroic friend Bruce (who at the outset is a prisoner of the Protectorate), though she loves the equally heroic Beaufort. But, when Bruce

---

47 I, pp. 4, 7; II, pp. 19, 26; IV, p. 39.

48 Jean Gagen has pointed out that the noble characters continually violate the love and honour code even as they profess adhesion to it ('The Design of the High Plot in Etherege's *The Comical Revenge*', *Restoration and 18th Century Theatre Research*, 2nd ser., 1/2 (1986), 1–15 (p. 3)).

49 *The Man of Mode*, I. 117–20.

dangerously wounds himself after losing a duel with Beaufort, Graciana vows that she will reject Beaufort if Bruce dies, and honour the memory of her dead suitor. Aurelia, who loves Bruce, nobly conceals her affections and strives to unite him with Graciana (her sister). And, finally discovering her nobility, Bruce transfers his affections to her.

As critics have noted,[50] the three other plots transform and vary elements from the heroic plot. In the boisterous courtship of Sir Frederick Frollick and the Widow Rich (Graciana's aunt), the woman can in large measure control the conduct of a courtship whose terms are spontaneously improvised, without reference to the fixed prescriptions of custom, while elements of both genteel plots are reproduced and debased in the low plots. For example, the gulling of the Cromwellian knight Sir Nicholas Cully (the offspring of a dairymaid) involves a fake shepherd, who parodies the pastoral imagery of idealistic heroines, and features a duel scene which parallels that between the heroic males, though this duel is aborted when Sir Nicholas signs away £1,000 to his challenger, the dictates of gentlemanly honour ceding to those of commerce. Whereas Orrery presents a unified world governed by a single, comprehensive set of values, Etherege presents a complex and multivalent society, where adjacent milieux are governed by profoundly different codes and rituals, and where the same images and acts change meaning and value when transposed from one area to another: the heroine Graciana and the wench Grace (a former mistress of Graciana's beloved Beaufort) have variants of a single name, so that Orrery's use of the name as a perfect mirror of social identity disappears. When Bruce finds 'charms in *Graciana*'s Name' (IV. iv. 69), we are aware (as he is not) of languages and values that lie outside the heroic world and challenge his simple belief in stable and univocal signs of value.[51] As Montaigne wrote, 'Thou seest but the order and policie of this little little Cell wherein thou art placed,' and indeed characters are repeatedly and literally placed in little cells, from Bruce's Cromwellian dungeon to the tub in which the valet Dufoy is farcically trapped. These prisons, diverse in form and dignity yet alike in their constraint, correspond to the varieties of custom which separate and inhibit the characters.

Whereas Orrery's heroic characters follow the rational imperatives of nature, Etherege's are oppressed by the arbitrary prescriptions of custom. As Aurelia, reflecting on her suppressed love for Bruce, complains, 'we by Custom, not by Nature led, | Must in the beaten paths of Honour tread' (II. ii. 123–4); and, eventually, she triumphs over her scruples and declares her love

---

[50] See Norman N. Holland, *The First Modern Comedies: The Significance of Etherege, Wycherley and Congreve* (Cambridge, Mass., 1959), 20–7; Virginia Ogden Birdsall, *Wild Civility: The English Comic Spirit on the Restoration Stage* (Bloomington, Ind. and London, 1970), 41–57.

[51] Robert Markley has well argued that the diverse languages in *The Comical Revenge* subvert 'hierarchical distinctions between "low" and "high" forms of dramatic discourse' (*Two-Edg'd Weapons: Style and Ideology in the Comedies of Etherege, Wycherley, and Congreve* (Oxford, 1988), 105).

to Bruce. Similarly, when Bruce and Beaufort duel, with Sir Frederick and Lovis as their seconds, Sir Frederick's festive disrespect for established form overrules Lovis's rigid sense of honour, halting the duel before it becomes a massacre. Even social degree becomes an inhibiting, imprisoning custom. Whereas Orrery's Princess Katherine rightly and naturally loves in conformity with her class, Etherege sympathetically portrays the maid Leticia's hopeless love for a social superior whom she dare not even name. The stress on the unutterable constitutes another difference from Orrery, for, while Orrery's paragons entirely translate themselves into the names that enshrine social duties, Etherege's stultify the self in order to observe social decorums of language which are as arbitrarily constrictive as a dungeon, or a tub. As Leticia suppresses her true love's name, so Aurelia conceals her passion for Bruce; and, after the duel, Graciana feels impelled to deny her continuing love for Beaufort.

The tension between what is felt and what may be expressed is conveyed by frequent emphasis on the act of narration, which (in an early instance of a soon popular theme) primarily indicates that women lack self-representation in a world where men control the forms and processes of narrative. The decision to thrust Bruce upon Graciana originated almost as a conversational stopgap, 'When barren of Discourse one day, and free | With's Friend, my Brother chanc'd to talk of me' (II. ii. 85–6), the narrative here expressing a socially sanctioned and male-determined view of the woman while ignoring her character and desires. Consistently, unsuccessful love is associated with ineffectual narrative. When Aurelia offers Graciana a letter from Bruce, she refuses to 'read the story of his grief' (I. iv. 9), and, when Aurelia and the maid Leticia deplore their hopeless love, they do so by indulging in an impotent secluded narrative whose subject is in turn an impotent act of female narrative: repeating 'The saddest tales we ever learn'd of Love' (II. ii. 152), they tell of a shepherdess whose solitary narration of her love failed 'To ease her pain' (II. ii. 161). The boisterous informality of Sir Frederick Frollick's life frees him from such slavery to form and word, and his characteristic genre is not narrative but the enacted masquerade. The Widow's ability to spar with him, however, is indicated by her ability imaginatively to transpose him from his rowdy play-acting into situations of embarrassing narrative, in which he is subordinated to a woman or a social inferior: he will 'with a tristful look tell a mournful tale to a Lady' (II. ii. 105–6), 'might get a pretty living by reading Mother *Shipton*'s Prophecies' (III. ii. 37–8), and will have his 'woful Tragedy' sung nightly to plebeians (IV. vii. 38).

Clearly, the conflict between what can be said and what can be felt is resolved at the conclusion of the heroic plot, but the resolution does not unite the decorums of society with the claims of individual life: rather, these claims can only be honoured by breaching the decorums, as when Aurelia abandons her maidenly reticence and reveals her love. Leticia, imprisoned in inexpressible love for an unattainable superior, cannot follow her example, but the predominant emphasis is on the relaxation of custom and deference. Though Sir Nicholas Cully's social origin is identical to Mrs Day's, he is treated far more genially, and the buffoonery of the new gentleman at times seems an alternative species of folly to the solemnity of the old. When he is tricked by the threat of a duel into signing away £1,000, his cowardice provides an opposite extreme to Lovis's crass enthusiasm for carnage, and it is noteworthy that Sir Frederick steps in to save both the new and the old gentleman from the consequences of his life-style, restoring Sir Nicholas's money to him and countermanding Lovis's eagerness for blood. The upstart does finally receive a familiar form of comeuppance, marrying Frederick's cast mistress Lucy in the belief that he is advancing himself by marrying Frederick's sister, but the deception is by no means an unqualified humiliation, for the final prospect is of Lucy making him a good wife and passing in the country for 'a virtuous well-bred Lady' (v. v. 115). We should not exaggerate Lucy's or Sir Nicholas's good fortune—certainly, Sir Nicholas is in no mood to do so himself—but Lucy's free sexuality and upward mobility are not self-evidently to be dismissed in favour of Leticia's emotional and social paralysis.

In James Howard's *All Mistaken* (Spring 1665)[52] heroic but constricting principle once again forbids the speaking of love, and once again is opposed by festive carnality. In the heroic plot the Duke and Amphelia conceal their love for each other, because the Duke's villainous kinsman has persuaded each of the other's hate: love, they convince themselves, must be excluded from the tongue (a key word). The constricting power of public forms is reflected and symbolized when Amphelia's defensive pretence of love for another actually leads to her imprisonment and near-execution. To cover up his feelings, the Duke has likewise (with 'Seduceing Tongue', III, p. 29) feigned love for another woman, Artabella. The lovers' misunderstanding is only resolved when Amphelia is on the scaffold, and in her joy she at first believes that she has been beheaded and that the Duke's words of love are the language of heaven. But this moment of linguistic apotheosis is both illusory and inconsequential, and the word still oppresses: the Duke, Amphelia self-denyingly insists, must honour his oath to Artabella. Desire is only reconciled with obligation when Artabella is identified as the Duke's long-lost sister. The result is another linguistic apotheosis, the Duke decreeing that 'no other word but | Sister' shall be pronounced in the Dukedom, and that it shall be the first word uttered by the 'sucking tongues' of infants (v, p. 66). Released by purest accident from the constraint of verbal bonds, the Duke promptly turns the word which liberates him into a grotesque imposition upon his subordinates, constraining utterance even in the first, hesitant, babbling of babies. There is no point at which

[52] See James Sutherland, 'The Date of James Howard's "All Mistaken, or The Mad Couple" ', *Notes and Queries*, 209 (1964), 339–40; and Robert D. Hume, 'Dryden, James Howard, and the Date of *All Mistaken*', *Philological Quarterly*, 51 (1972), 422–9.

language becomes a pure medium of benevolent social order: there is always a concealed trap.

The comic plot features perhaps the earliest exploitation of the talents of Charles Hart and Nell Gwyn in a gay couple courtship (though Buckingham's *The Chances* may be earlier). There are, of course, precedents for this form of courtship in earlier plays, including Howard's own *The English Mounsieur*, and Elizabeth Howe has noted that Hart and Gwyn gave 'a new lease of life' to such plays.[53] But this is the first occasion on which the male has the exuberant promiscuity which was later to characterize Wycherley's Horner (created by Hart) and Etherege's Dorimant. At this stage, however, the promiscuity is recollected rather than enacted. Philidor, a cheerful rake with many bastards to his credit, vies with Mirida in deceiving and hoaxing unwanted lovers, the word chiefly associated with their pranks being to *fool*—a word also associated with the deceptions of the heroic plot. Obviously, the plots are largely antithetical, for, unlike the heroic lovers, Philidor and Mirida are cheerfully unconstrained by publicly sanctioned forms of speech: 'the very name of | Wife, wou'd be a vomit' to Philidor, and Mirida deplores 'that dull, dull | Name of Husband' (v, pp. 67–8). But there are also similarities. The Duke and Philidor, for example, both imprison mistresses, the main difference between the Duke's tortured duplicity and Philidor's cheerful promiscuity being that Philidor imprisons six (in a funeral vault) for the Duke's one. Extremes of ideal integrity and carefree rakishness ironically produce similar results. Like Etherege in *The Comical Revenge*, Howard complicates the apparently unambiguous images of the heroic world by giving them an alternative life in unheroic contexts.

A tame response to the interest in wayward heroes and witty heroines is provided by John Bulteel's *Amorous Orontus*, a translation of Thomas Corneille probably performed by the King's Company by autumn 1664. The fickle, yet chaste, hero is explicitly likened to Hylas, the cheerful inconstant of D'Urfé's *L'Astrée*, and Hylas also provides the model for one of the greatest comic inconstants of the 1660s, Celadon in Dryden's *Secret Love* (King's, January 1667).[54] This is Dryden's first experiment in combining heroic action with a comic sub-plot, after the fashion of *The Comical Revenge* and *All Mistaken*, and he is particularly close to James Howard in juxtaposing a heroic plot of suppressed and unspoken love with a gay couple courtship. In the comic plot Celadon (Hart) is tamed by the witty Florimell (Gwyn), the courtship culminating in a series of marriage provisos that permit the possibility of future infidelity. The heroic plot depicts the entangled passions of

---

53 Elizabeth Howe, *The First English Actresses: Women and Drama 1660–1700* (Cambridge, 1992), 67.

54 The play was probably written during the closure of the theatres because of the plague. For discussion of the première date, see Arthur H. Scouten, 'The Premiere of Dryden's *Secret Love*', *Restoration*, 9 (1985), 9–11.

four characters: the ambitious Lysimantes courts the unnamed Queen of Sicily, who secretly loves Philocles, who loves and is loved by Candiope. The Queen's public role conflicts with her love for Philocles, and the conflict means that language must reflect decorum of role rather than truth of character ('shame stops my mouth', I. iii. 223), it being perhaps for this reason that the Queen is never given a personal name. She does, however, indulge her love to the extent of obstructing Philocles' courtship of Candiope. Whereas the nameless Queen repeatedly experiences difficulty in voicing the claims of the personal life, Florimell rapidly moves from comic reduplication of her sovereign's plight to confident self-assertion: she is unnamed in her first scene and opens her second by pretending to be a dumb woman reduced to sign-language, but as soon as her name is uttered in this scene she gains a control over her life which never falters. The name is thus associated with a specific individual identity, rather than with the individual's socially determined role. As in *The Comical Revenge* and *All Mistaken*, moreover, the claims of the public world are represented in the image of imprisonment: the Queen lacks her subjects' 'freedom' (I. iii. 159) in love, marriage will destroy not only her personal independence but her queenly power, and ambitious love actually leads Lysimantes to rebel and to capture her.

In important respects, however, Dryden differs from Etherege and James Howard. The easy-going sexual loyalties of his comic plot are not as purely playful as those of Philidor and Mirida, for its harmless betrayals are mirrored in the heroic plot by Lysimantes' and Philocles' sexually inspired rebellion against their Queen, the former wishing to marry her, the latter to overturn her ban on his marriage to Candiope. Indeed, Celadon and his fellow-revellers participate in the rebellion: his inconstancy is one manifestation of a general and often irreconcilable conflict between individual desire and the disciplines of society, and it is significant that Celadon's first act of rebellion occurs when he resists some soldiers who have been sent to prevent Philocles' marriage to Candiope, and mistake Celadon for their quarry (IV. i. 184–92). The libertine is confused with the romantic hero, and the distinction between them starts to seem oddly unstable. When Philocles discovers that the Queen's opposition to his marriage was due to her love for him, he switches to her side, carrying Celadon with him. But, at the same time, he starts to experience a troubling division in his affections which introduces a degree of affinity with the constitutionally fickle Celadon: the heroic lover is infected with the waywardness of the comic inconstant, and renewed political loyalty is qualified by incipient emotional disloyalty. As so often in Dryden, the passions of the unideal world both lurk within and threaten its heroic antitype, and the relationship between the two milieux is far more equivocal than the simple conflict between stifling form and liberating exuberance in *The Comical Revenge* and *All Mistaken*. Remarkably, in a period which saw so many crudely optimistic representations of restoration, Dryden links the instinct to rebel to a fundamental and universal incompatibility between public imperatives and personal appetites; for all the heroes of the play are tainted by rebellion. Unlike *The Committee*, *Secret Love* does not confine the guilt of rebellion to easily derided upstarts and outsiders, for the principles of disruption are implicit within the order itself.[55]

Consequently, it offers no easy harmonization of the public and the personal; no reconstruction of the social order to accommodate legitimate private desire. The Queen vows a lifelong spinsterhood, sustained by the thought that Philocles will inherit the crown after her death. Lysimantes also vows celibacy. Philocles reconciles himself to marrying Candiope only because the Queen is sexually out of everyone's reach. And Celadon and Florimell agree on a marriage which may yet stray from accepted patterns of fidelity. Nor is there any final harmonization of language and interior experience. Conventionally enough, the rebellion brings semantic chaos, as when the 'Ruffins' who aid Celadon's uprising are respectfully redefined as 'Gentlemen' (IV. i. 268–75). Knowing that the Queen loves a social inferior, but not yet realizing that it is he, Philocles proposes to 'raze' her unseemly love 'from the Annals of her Reign' (IV. i. 355–6), claiming the power to write the course of his Queen's life and to exclude her love from what is written. Coriolanus' 'If you have writ your annals true' would not be at all out of place here: like Etherege, Dryden displays an incipient interest in the inability of women to control the narrative of their lives. The denouement does restore semantic stability to the heroic world, but there is no final reconciliation between public words and personal essence. In surrendering Philocles to Candiope, the Queen has to 'force my tongue, | To speak words so far distant from my heart!' (V. i. 400–1). Conversely, Celadon and Florimell revel in semantic instability, abolishing 'the names of Husband and Wife' and deciding to marry 'by the more agreeable names of Mistress and Gallant' (V. i. 547–52). Approved sexual nomenclature cannot represent the diversity and anomalousness of individual life.

Buckingham's revision of Fletcher's *The Chances* (King's, ?summer 1664)[56] provides another gay couple courtship by developing the role of the prostitute, the second Constantia (presumably played by Nell Gwyn). At the end of Fletcher's play Constantia faces a whipping unless she repents, whereas Buckingham leaves her in unwedded bliss with the rakish Don John. In both plays, misunderstandings arise when Constantia is confused with a noble namesake, who has been impregnated by a Duke after her family refused to

---

55 Cf. Dryden's extraordinary defence of Philocles in the preface: 'As for that other objection of his joyning in the Queens imprisonment, it is indisputably that which every man, if he examines himself, would have done on the like occasion' (p. 117).

56 The earliest known performance is in Feb. 1667. The earlier dating has been proposed in K. Robinson, 'Two Cast Lists for Buckingham's "The Chances" ', *Notes and Queries*, 224 (1979), 436–7. It is based on a manuscript cast list, in an early nineteenth-century hand, containing the name of Walter Clun (d. 2 Aug. 1664). Some support for Robinson's argument is offered in Scouten, 'The Premiere of Dryden's *Secret Love*', 10.

permit the lovers' marriage, and whose brother now dementedly seeks the satisfaction of honour. By increasing the prominence of the heroine's *doppelgänger*, and giving her a manipulative parent with her own, ludicrous, punctilios of decorum, Buckingham follows Etherege in juxtaposing contrasting yet parallel worlds, where constancy—literally—of name creates ironically inappropriate continuities of sign amidst profound discontinuities of code and outlook. John Lacy's disappointing debasement of *The Taming of the Shrew* into *Sauny the Scot* (King's, April 1667) seems to promise yet another gay couple, with Petruchio's undertaking that he and Peg (Kate) will be a '*Mad Couple well match'd*' (II, p. 11)—the title of Brome's seminal gay couple comedy, to which the subtitle of *All Mistaken* had already alluded. But Lacy primarily invites laughter at a woman overcome by brute, farcical violence. Part of the point, however, may be that male authority has no other basis: there is no ideology of natural hierarchy and, when Peg finally submits (to avoid being entombed alive), Petruchio surrenders authority and accepts her as an equal.[57]

Equally farcical is *Sir Martin Mar-all* (Duke's, August 1667), a lightweight (and very popular) adaptation of Molière and Quinault which Dryden and the Duke of Newcastle wrote for the Duke's Company. Here, however, farce is more clearly used to disturb conventional social and sexual hierarchies. Like *The Committee*, this features a royalist gentleman (Warner) who lost his estate during the Interregnum, but unlike *The Committee* this portrays a post-Restoration world, and the gentleman is still poor, reduced to acting as the servant of the foolish Sir Martin. In his folly, Sir Martin is typical of his rank, for the play's two other titled men (Sir John Swallow and Lord Dartmouth) are also fools. The sexual alliances of the trio increase the sense of social dislocation, Sir Martin mistakenly marrying the maid of his intended bride and Sir John being duped into marrying Lord Dartmouth's whore, who has already spectacularly enriched herself at the lord's expense. Dryden thus goes beyond *The Wild Gallant* in making the prostitute and the lady literally one. Although Warner regains prosperity by marrying the heiress designed for Sir Martin, who inadvertently marries the heroine's maid, the sense of social disarray continues, for in marrying the heroine's maid Sir Martin has made her a lady and given her precedence over her former mistress. The concluding elevation of the servant (and, still more, of the prostitute) institutionalizes what in *The Committee* had been a temporary aberration, and the ruse which allows the heroine to marry the unsuspecting Warner reduces the idea of exalted station to an absurd literalness, the dupes being persuaded to immobilize themselves by standing on high stools in 'the Frolick of the Altitudes' (v. ii. 48).

In *Sir Martin Mar-all* the traditional terminology of social rank survives, but the effective hierarchy is one of wit coupled with aggression, and in this respect—if not in its farcical action—the play looks forward to later and

57 See Eric Rothstein and Frances M. Kavenik, *The Designs of Carolean Comedy* (Carbondale and Edwardsville, 1988), 30; Staves, *Players' Scepters*, 133–4.

better known works by Etherege and Wycherley. It contrasts emphatically, however, with another contemporary play on a similar theme, Davenant's *The Man's The Master* (Duke's, March 1668), adapted from Scarron. This also features a confusion of master–servant roles (a significantly prominent theme in the 1660s), but it depicts a simple case of inverted order restored to normality, and the two men's natural characters constantly shine through their assumed roles. When Davenant returned to writing without Dryden's aid, he reverted to a thoroughly conservative social vision. When left to his own devices, the Duke of Newcastle also wrote in similarly unprophetic vein. His *The Humorous Lovers* (Duke's, March 1667), produced a few months before *Sir Martin Mar-all*, shows some influence of *The English Mounsieur* and *The Comical Revenge* in showing a libertine, Boldman, falling under the spell of a witty widow, and an already reformed libertine persuading his mistress that his reform is genuine. There is a foppish pseudo-wit—one of the earliest in Restoration comedy—but the best feature is an old-fashioned humours character with an obsessive fear of the cold.

If Dryden took the lead in forming the outlook of the new comedy, however, he did not help to fix its dominant social tone and setting, and it was Etherege who provided the prototype for genteel London comedy in *She Would If She Could* (Duke's, February 1668). It is important to remember, however, that this play was not an initial success, whereas the broadly farcical *Sir Martin* was a hit, and that the first clear imitation of *She Would*—Shadwell's *Epsom-Wells* (December 1672)—appeared after an interval of nearly five years. *All Mistaken* and *The Comical Revenge* had employed an obvious clash of competing milieux to imply that received social codes were systems of convention, though in the concluding lines of *The Comical Revenge* Etherege had moved from symptom to cause, providing a more fundamental and explicit vision of the power of the arbitrary in shaping human life: 'Chance, not prudence, makes us fortunate'. Custom still dominates in *She Would If She Could*: for example, the obsessive decorousness that repeatedly frustrates Lady Cockwood's lust is an addictive 'custom' (II. ii. 98). Here, however, Etherege abandons the extreme clash of heroic and libertine for subtler differentiations of code (municipal laws), associated with differences of generation, sex, class, and even dwelling-place: the rules of the country are not those of the town, and men and women are governed by contrasting codes of conduct and honour that obscure their shared biological impulses. He also extends the role of the random: *chance* and its synonyms recur frequently, accidents constantly frustrate the provisions of human contrivance, and, in oblique testimony to the pervasive power of chance, characters repeatedly attempt to disguise their own plots as unpremeditated coincidence.

A random world is obviously not one in which social structures can be grounded upon naturally ordained systems of order, and there is here no natural hierarchy of place and responsibility. Definitions of conduct befitting a gentleman abound, but they are definitions which exalt the actual at the expense of the ideal. Sir Oliver Cockwood's 'to a true-bred gentleman all lawful solace is abomination' (III. iii. 204–5) invites our condemnation only because he is not able to put precept into practice (for Courtall's sexual neglect of Lady Cockwood is not 'altogether like a gentleman', IV. ii. 137). The gentility of Rake-hell the pimp is repeatedly stressed,[58] and he acts as a living courtesy book, instructing Sir Oliver in the manners and dress appropriate to his class. Most outrageously of all, 'the keeping of one's word is', as already noted, 'a thing below the honor of a gentleman' (II. ii. 201–2). Language and rank are morally insignificant, and the old values survive only in the professional ethics of the gentleman-pimp, who is 'a man of his word' (III. iii. 176).

Although the language of citizenship persists, it does so in greatly weakened form. The Cockwoods and the young lovers repeatedly define their relationships in images of political authority, and enquire into the justice, injustice, or even treason of their companions' actions, though they do so in order to enforce standards which they are themselves evading. They also evoke fixed norms of civilized integrity, deploring actions as barbarous, inhuman, and strange. But the norms are in reality parochial and arbitrary. When Sir Oliver is reluctant that 'these *strangers* should know this is my penitential suit' (III. iii. 62–3; italics added), the order to which the outsiders are alien is a preposterous domestic ritual, in which his wife disciplines his drunken insubordination by forcing him to spend the day in unfashionable clothes. This is custom piled upon custom, the extremely localized household ritual given meaning by the wider, but still localized, rituals of fashion. Yet again, images of more objective and universal authority are transferred to the pimp and his circle, Rake-hell being appointed to 'judge' sexual prowess (III. iii. 282), and his women conducting their practice like lawyers (IV. ii. 34–7). Here, most explicitly, the agents of justice are transformed into the agents of desire (it is notable that, when Freeman visits Lady Cockwood, he tells Courtall that he is going to visit a lawyer).

The misappropriation of law culminates in a parodic reconstruction of social order, when Lady Cockwood pardons her husband's excesses (and conceals her own) with an 'Act of Oblivion' (V. i. 525). This satiric allusion to the post-Restoration amnesty implies a recovery of moral and familial order for which the Restoration itself can stand as a fitting model (as it was unproblematically to do in Sir Charles Sedley's *The Mulberry Garden*). Etherege's parallel between domestic and political order is, however, full of problems, for the situation which parallels the triumph and clemency of Charles II is the continued impunity of a domineering and deceitful wife. Human life continues its inglorious and disingenuous ways, untouched by the miraculous archetype of social regeneration that had opened the decade. The analogy between

[58] III. ii. 19, iii. 72, 148.

family and state, one of the most popular arguments for man's natural sociability, here works against its usual implications, highlighting the deceit and compromise that are the elements of human existence.

But, if society fails to embody cosmic and universal principles of moral order, it nevertheless imposes practical and inescapable constraints upon human freedom. Scenes of sexual privacy are repeatedly rendered public through interruption or eavesdropping: in the opening scene, for example, Freeman hides and overhears the sexual proposition from Lady Cockwood which Sentry brings to Courtall, and Sentry in turn hides to overhear the sexual boasts and plans of Sir Oliver. Lady Cockwood may be outstandingly ludicrous in her constant sexual tantalization, but her frustrations are shared by more polished and impressive characters, for deceived sexual expectation is a general condition and affects even the heroes, as when Lady Cockwood tricks them with forged letters into thinking that Ariana and Gatty are ready to sleep with them, or when their eventual proposals of marriage gain them merely a month's probation, their goal remaining tantalizingly on the horizon. The conflict between private desire and the entanglements of social existence is expressed in a frequent division of identity, in that most characters are during the course of the play taken to be two distinct people: Courtall and Freeman take Sir Oliver's nieces and the masked ladies in the Mulberry Garden to be different pairs of women, and, to prevent Lady Cockwood from learning about the meeting with the heroes in the Mulberry Garden, Gatty pretends that she and Ariana had met someone else there (III. i. 242–7); and, disguised as a prostitute, Lady Cockwood is lustfully courted by her own husband. Etherege here introduces an idea that would dominate sex comedy of the following decade: so fully does an intrusive society obstruct the expression of intimate desire that the very representation of the self must be distorted and divided.[59]

In fact, libertine promiscuity is confined to the raucous fantasy of Sir Joslin's songs and Sir Oliver's boasts; whereas festive liberty had guided and transformed events in *The Comical Revenge*, it is here pushed to the margins, surviving only in the delusions of two buffoons,[60] and, when the young lovers move from the pursuit of freedom to the acceptance of responsibility, the transition is associated with a movement from song to actual experience: Ariana goes to the closet for her guitar in order to sing a song, but instead finds Courtall and Freeman hiding there. With this moment of passage from fiction to experience, the men's uncontained sexual instinct begins its truce with the actual demands of life, though full reconciliation remains an unattained

---

59 At the end of *Sir Martin Mar-all*, Warner marries the heroine in the belief that he is marrying her maid. Seeing his veiled bride and the unmasked maid together, he exclaims 'What, is *Rose* split in two?' (V. ii. 92).

60 Henry Harris, who had played Sir Frederick Frollick, here plays Sir Joslin Jolley. In *The Man of Mode* he played another marginal figure, Medley, who is preoccupied with the playful subversion of social decorum, but does so only in linguistic fictions.

and perhaps unattainable goal, for the young lovers end the play in a state of unresolved expectation, not yet assimilated into the social institution of marriage.

In his boisterous *An Evening's Love* (King's, June 1668) Dryden again matched Etherege in outlook, while retaining the still popular format of the Spanish intrigue play. The play juxtaposes customs, cultures, and climates, again highlighting the conventional, localized nature of social codes (more municipal laws). Wildblood (Hart) and Bellamy, gallants from cold England, wander in hot Spain, and actual clashes of cultures and places are complicated by imaginary ones, the beautiful Spaniard Jacinta (Gwyn) testing Wildblood's fidelity by disguising herself as a visitor from Morocco, and the two-timing Don Melchor deceiving his pair of women by pretending to be in transit to Flanders. Since Bellamy has been tricked into posing as an astrologer, Melchor's lover Aurelia asks Bellamy to conjure up the image of her absent suitor, and is not impressed by Bellamy's desperate argument that magic will not work across water: 'I am not so ill a *Geographer*, or to speak more properly, a *Chorographer*, as not to know there is a passage by land from hence to *Flanders*' (III. i. 184–6). Chorography is the delineation of particular regions, and Aurelia's ostentatious precision of terminology highlights an important aspect of the play, for the delineation of human conduct is in many respects a delineation of regional custom. The most fitting image of the moral schemes that shape human life is not a vertical ladder of fixed absolutes extending from heaven to earth, but a horizontal map of different regions with different conventions. Like *The Tempest*, therefore, this is a play—explicitly—about the encounters of strangers,[61] but strangeness is here specifically associated with variations of culture.

An Evening's Love is a carnival play, set in the Madrid Carnival of 1665, and it defiantly frees the flesh from the claims of law, honour, and religion: for Bellamy, 'the world and the flesh' (I. i. 51) are the essentials of life, and he later completes the triad by claiming the power to raise devils; it is hardly surprising that Pepys found the play 'smutty' and Evelyn 'very prophane'.[62] The flesh is the universal constant of human experience, which national customs disguise or oppress in a variety of ways—as we see very literally in Wildblood's complaints about Spanish cuisine: 'I had a mind to eat of a Pheasant, and as soon as I got it into my mouth, I found I was chawing a limb of Cinamon; then I went to cut a piece of Kid, and no sooner it had touch'd my lips, but it turn'd to red Pepper' (I. i. 38–41). Life itself is a continual transformation of the flesh. In a version of the Invisible Mistress plot, Jacinta tests Wildblood by tempting him in two disguises, of Moor and Mulatta, which are specifically

---

[61] For Bellamy and Wildblood as strangers, see I. i. 88, ii. 47; V. i. 445. For other images of the strange, see I. i. 16, 92; II. i. 304.

[62] Pepys, 20 June 1668; *The Diary of John Evelyn*, ed. E. S. de Beer (6 vols., Oxford, 1955), 19 June 1668.

disguises which alter the appearance of the flesh, and on each occasion he falls for the bait (compare the repeated division of identity in *She Would If She Could*). In more idealistic versions of this plot, the divided woman may prove that the man loves her essential self more than her body. Jacinta, however, merely gives Wildblood a choice between different varieties of flesh: and he chooses them all.

Systems that allegedly regulate or transcend the carnal are treated with satiric irreverence. Jacinta's bungled testing of Wildblood is regularly represented as a form of judicial trial, and the play reaches its climax with a still more striking defeat of judicial process and ritual. As the officers of justice approach to prevent the heroes from absconding with their women, Jacinta's father is, on threat of death, induced to send a message to the *corregidor* calling them off: 'tell him it was only a Carnival merriment, which I mistook for a Rape and Robbery' (v. i. 434–5). The author of *Astraea Redux* here stops the goddess's agents in their tracks. Other forms of official code are also treated with scepticism. For example, when Bellamy reduces the definition of a gentleman to that of 'one who wears good Cloathes, Eates, Drinks, and Wenches abundantly,' he describes a mere unthinking sequence of appetites: gentlemanly conduct reflects not a providentially fixed social order but one created by matter in motion. And, again, Dryden reworks Orrery's favourite pattern of human sociability, the noble rival who sacrifices love to friendship: Lopez has sworn to help his friend Melchor in love, and now finds that Melchor is his rival, while courting another woman as well. Lopez, however, is no Clorimun, for he initially tries to displace Melchor while observing the letter of his oath, and when this approach fails he simply breaks his word by revealing Melchor's duplicity, persuaded to do so by the libertine cynicism of Bellamy, for whom Lopez' principles are needless impediments to the free play of natural forces: 'We *English* seldom make such scruples; Women are not compris'd in our Laws of friendship: they are *feræ naturæ*' (iv. i. 419–20). The moral absolutes of Orrery dwindle into the quaint customs of a strange nation.

Oaths are also treated lightly in the volatile relationship of Wildblood and Jacinta (when Jacinta appears in Moorish guise, Wildblood declares love with an oath—by Mahomet, iii. i. 444), and scenes of jargon and noncommunication give more general emphasis to the limitations of language, locating it within the schemes of adventitious and clashing customs whose conflicts permeate the play. '*Loquere ut te videam*' (iii. i. 360) says Alonzo, Jacinta's father, quoting one of the popular definitions of language as a perfect sign of the speaker's mind and character. But he utters the tag amidst a torrent of garrulity that prevents his interlocutor from communicating anything (iii. i. 323–67).[63] In the disregarded oaths, however, what is questioned

---

[63] Dryden is here indebted to Molière's *Dépit amoureux*, ii. vi. 759–76. See California Dryden, x. 439–40.

is not only the communicative power of language but its dependence upon the sacred. The questioning becomes blasphemously explicit when Jacinta, in her role as Mulatta, reminds Wildblood of his promises to his Spanish mistress:

> JAC. I, but Heaven that sees all things.——
> WILD. Heaven that sees all things will say nothing: that is,
> all eyes and *no tongue*.
>
> (IV. i. 113–15; italics added)

The image of a tongueless heaven strikingly separates human discourse from any heavenly original, and a distinctly secular view of the forces controlling human affairs is also implicit in the plot in which Bellamy is tricked by his clever servant, Maskall, into posing as an astrologer. Here Maskall awards Bellamy the written words of power that Dryden and Davenant had taken from Prospero: 'did not I see you an hour ago, turning over a great Folio with *strange* figures in it, and then muttering to your self like any Poet, and then naming *Theodosia*' (II. i. 303–6; first italics added). But the folio is a figment of Maskall's imagination, and Bellamy does not after all command the alien signs of the heavenly realm: 'he has', Maskall eventually confesses, 'been alwayes an utter *stranger* to the Stars: and indeed to any thing that belongs to heaven' (V. i. 445–6; italics added). Bellamy is a stranger both to heaven and Spain: distinctions in the vertical universe have the same status as the divisions of national culture (Bellamy at one point tries to conceal his ignorance by suggesting that the jargon of astrology may be different in England and Spain, II. i. 425–6), and indeed the only spokesman for the traditional vertical gradation of nature (and of linguistic authority) is the foolish patriarch Don Alonzo, who sees any impediment to his torrential verbiage as a total inversion of natural order: 'let the order of all things be turn'd topsy-turvy . . .', he exclaims; 'let the Infants preach to their Great-Grandsires' (III. i. 374–6). And he concludes this almost Ulyssean celebration of degree by affirming what the 'chorography' of the play denies, that the order of human life can be represented as one of fixed and naturally ordained place: if he is not to be heard, 'Let Fishes live upon dry-land, and the Beasts of the Earth inhabit in the Water' (III. i. 378–9).[64] The most remarkable unfixing of a place traditionally fixed, however, is that of hell. For this too becomes a place on a horizontal map, another country with another climate. When Alonzo turns up during the young lovers' elopement, Bellamy for a while manages to persuade him that his companions are devils whom he has summoned up. Discovery seems imminent when Wildblood sneezes, but Bellamy has a convincing explanation: 'One of the Devils I warrant you has got a cold with being so long out of the fire' (V. i. 356–7). The joke plays upon the earlier contrasts between hot Spain and the cold North:[65] as Spain is to England, so hell is to Spain. All is relative.

---

[64] Sir Paul Plyant delivers a similar rant in Congreve's *The Double-Dealer* (II. i. 224–6). Congreve's plays owe a great deal to *An Evening's Love*.   [65] I. i. 47, ii. 14–17.

But not all new voices proclaimed the old codes of social conduct as obsolete fictions. Given the author's notoriety as a rake, Sir Charles Sedley's *The Mulberry Garden* (King's, May 1668) is a surprisingly tame and seemly play. It takes some hints from *She Would If She Could* and a great deal from *The Comical Revenge*, in its Interregnum setting and its combination of exalted heroics and bantering love-comedy. But it lacks Etherege's festive rejection of social discipline. The gay couple courtship of Olivia and Wildish leads to the clear reform of the roving male, and Sedley's unironic representation of Cavalier heroism (loyal young men are rescued from sequestration and imprisonment by the timely restoration of the King) is chiefly indebted to *The Committee*.

Echoing Terence's *Adelphi*, the play opens with two brothers debating how to 'govern' their families (I. i. 1), the lenience of the royalist man about town Sir John Everyoung being opposed by the repressiveness of the Puritan Sir Samuel Forecast, whose despotic rule of his daughters represents the general 'tyranny' (II. ii. 1) to which women are born. The complementary tyrannies of Forecast and the Puritans fall, and benevolent paternalism triumphs in the persons of Everyoung and Charles II (though Forecast will continue to prosper, having gained credit by inadvertently harbouring a royalist fugitive). But, if benevolent paternalism triumphs, the paternalism is as important as the benevolence, and the play chiefly opposes inappropriate hierarchies to more appropriate ones, with little of Etherege's subversive festivity. Sir John is a mildly saturnalian character, dressed (as Sir Samuel complains) in a way that ill becomes 'a reverend justice' (I. i. 9), and he is allowed one flourish of misrule when, in his capacity as Justice, he liberates three riotous apprentices on condition that they cudgel Forecast. But on the whole he represents a tactfully limited authority rather than a carefree abandon. When his daughter Olivia furtively marries the reformed rake Wildish, Sir John's pardon is readily given, but it is morally needed, as that of Dryden's Don Alonzo is not. In general, Sedley's view of male authority recalls Tuke's idealization of benevolent machismo. The fops Modish and Estridge are sexually oppressive, even plotting to kidnap an allegedly rich widow, but the counterbalancing ideal is not female liberation but male protection: Forecast's daughter Althea denounces male tyranny, but observes that only men can fight to vindicate the right, women's role being to approve their efforts (I. iv. 64–73).[66] Another Tuke-like touch is that the royalists Philander and Eugenio have rightly deserted their mistresses to serve their king: in contrast to Etherege, Sedley gives duty, here conceived as bonds between men, a simple priority over natural impulse, and the unqualified primacy of social life means that signs do not deceive and oppress at the point where the public fails the personal. Equivocal signification belongs to Modish and Estridge, but the noble characters seek clarity. To

---

[66] By contrast, the heroine of William Killigrew's *The Seege of Urbin* does wonders in battle. So does Affectionata in the Duchess of Newcastle's *The Second Part of Loves Adventures*.

express is a key word, and indeed provides the final verb of the play, when, exultant at the King's restoration, the characters retire to 'vie who shall express | The highest sense of this great happiness' (V. v. 176–7).[67] Such perfect equilibrium between language, desire, and social existence was to be quite un-attainable in the greatest Carolean comedies.

In general, however, comic dramatists interested in social renewal outgrew pure celebration fairly quickly. For example, an earlier play which combines the restoration motif with that of the reformed rake is William Killigrew's *Pandora* (Duke's, 1662/3), a comedy that was apparently first written as a tragedy,[68] in which the virtuous prince of a usurping line marries his daughter to the true heir. But one of the reformed rakes is the restored prince, so that Killigrew suggests (as perhaps Stapylton more mildly does in *The Slighted Maid*) that political restoration necessitates moral restoration. At the begin-ning, a gentleman open-mindedly allows the royal heir to sleep with his mis-tress by means of a bedroom trick (a debasement of Orrery's favourite subject of noble rivalry), but the two fundamentally good-natured rakes are reformed by the power of love (to their ruler's delight), and the play concludes with an epilogue addressed to the Ladies. The play thus follows a pattern generally thought to be characteristic of the 1690s (down to the prefatory poem lament-ing the corruption of the stage). The difference from the later plays is the ex-plicit presence of court and monarchic values as arbiters of sexual conduct. The virtuous prince becomes the archetype of ideal sexual morality.

But the chief critic of post-1660 public and artistic morality was Thomas Shadwell. Like Sedley, he admired Etherege: in the preface to *The Humorists* (1670) he deplored the poor reception of *She Would If She Could*, praising it as the best comedy since the Restoration (p. 183), and he gave the play the sincerest form of flattery by imitating it in *Epsom-Wells* and *The Virtuoso*. Increasingly, moreover, he came to share Etherege's Epicurean outlook. But he was earnestly concerned, as Etherege was not, with the moral reconstruction of society: in the preface to *The Humorists* he claims to satirize those who, like highwaymen, are guilty of 'a disturbance of Societies in general' (p. 184) and in the preface to *The Sullen Lovers* (Duke's, May 1668) he denounced gay couple comedy (chiefly, one presumes, Dryden's) because it dissociated gentil-ity from morality, representing a 'Swearing, Drinking, Whoring, Ruffian' and an 'ill-bred *tomrig*' as 'fine People' (p. 11). Shadwell's comedies certainly do not portray a miraculously regenerated social order. The gentry have declined from their former moral and intellectual glory, and Shadwell hankers for the ideals of good lordship celebrated (and already portrayed as obsolescent) in Jonson's 'To Penshurst'. But he acknowledged that established systems of rank were worthless if they had ceased to benefit the whole community, and in

---

[67] See also I. iv. 30; III. ii. 35, 42; IV. ii. 118.
[68] J. P. Vander Motten, *Sir William Killigrew (1605–1695): His Life and Dramatic Works* (Ghent, 1980), 161–2.

the preface to *The Humorists* he mocked upper-class philistines as 'the higher sort of Rabble' (p. 185).

In *The Sullen Lovers* the inflexibly principled Stanford (a favourably viewed version of Molière's Alceste) is tormented by a world overrun by disturbers of society: upstarts, hypocrites, and pretentious fools. He finds a soul-mate in the similarly inclined Emilia, and at the conclusion the lovers resolve (like Guyomar and Alibech in *The Indian Emperour*) to leave for '*some distant desart*' (v, p. 91). But the imaginative identification with the desert does not indicate, as it does in Dryden, that the city inevitably contains the wilderness: civilization is simply rejected because it has lost its essential character. One aspect of the loss is that social degree has become insignificant. When Emilia and Stanford deplore upstarts who have risen overnight from 'Linsey Woolsey' to 'Perriwiggs and Lac'd Linnen', they are expressing not so much a Ulyssean concern that degree has been subverted as a belief that it has become a meaningless system of oppression, in which 'almost all mankind flatter the greatest, and oppress the least' and in which gentility means drinking, whoring, and the mistreatment of inferiors (II, pp. 37–8). The recurrent term *son of a whore* constitutes the most common description of ancestry in the play, and indeed the strumpet who masquerades as Lady Vaine ultimately exchanges her false title for a real one by marrying the boastful Sir Positive At-all, ensuring that his exalted progeny will in truth be the sons of a whore.

But, if the basely born covet the trappings of the great, the great have complementary pretensions, and prove similarly inexpert at adapting their lives to their capabilities and station. In Sir Positive and the poet Ninny, Shadwell satirizes two of the play-writing Howard brothers, Sir Robert and Edward, portraying Sir Positive as a monstrous perversion of the widely cultivated aristocrat: a bumptious know-all who claims supremacy in every field, however dishonourable, plebeian, or mindless; for the world can afford no finer pimp, player of trap-ball, or maker of mud pies.[69] What disappears amongst this welter of pseudo-accomplishments is any distinctive, useful pattern of gentlemanly or aristocratic existence, and when his boasts reach their maniacal climax he becomes imaginatively displaced from all social structure: 'I'le undermine all Commonwealths, destroy all Monarchies, and write Heroick Plays' (v, p. 79)—explicit evidence that Shadwell associated the values of the heroic play with a deranged aristocratic arrogance. Even when he claims skills more laudable than pimping, Sir Positive's level of accomplishment can easily be outdone by abler men of humbler birth, such as 'an ordinary Fiddler or Sign-Painter' (III, p. 45). As in Lacy's mockery of Edward Howard, the man of rank is overshadowed by the competent professional. Outdone by inferiors in all his pet pastimes, Sir Positive has only the lustre of lineage to justify his so-

---

[69] II, p. 40; III, pp. 53–4; IV, p. 73. According to Pepys, the Duke of York confirmed Sir Robert's pride in his skill at trap-ball (8 May 1668).

cial position, and this he denies his heirs by marrying a harlot. The satire is directed at a person, but also at a class—at 'the higher sort of Rabble'.

Since Davenant had been the more enterprising manager, it is appropriate that in the year of his death his company should have staged the prophetic *She Would If She Could*. But, despite its lesser adventurousness, it was the King's Company that had so far done most to establish a distinctive house style of drama. Davenant's company had produced no serious drama to equal Dryden's (except when Dryden himself was called in to revise *The Tempest*), and in comedy had achieved nothing as distinctive as the gay couple comedy that Dryden and James Howard creatêd for Charles Hart and Nell Gwyn. The great early successes of the Duke's Company, such as *The Adventures of Five Hours*, *Mustapha*, and *The Villain*, had hardly been trail-blazers, and even *The Comical Revenge* proved to be a dead end. It was only now that drama of some merit and originality was taking hold at both houses.

CHAPTER THREE

'Where is Astrea fled?': Tragedy, 1668–1676

In 1669 Sir William Killigrew published his last play, *The Imperial Tragedy*, a play of regicide and restoration based on *Zeno; sive, Ambitio Infelix* by the English Jesuit Joseph Simons, which opens with the appearance of Astraea on high (I, p. 1). Langbaine believed that the play had been acted at the Barbican Nursery (p. 535), but there is no record of performance at either of the main houses, and by this time its subject and outlook were dated.[1] Indeed, Simons was at the time helping to make it even more dated by converting the Duke of York to Catholicism. Orrery's *Tryphon* (Duke's, December 1668), another play about restoration, had already failed, and when Dryden depicted the deposition of the usurper Maximin in *Tyrannick Love* (King's, June 1669), he portrayed not a return to hereditary monarchy but the election of two Emperors by the Senate.[2] Increasingly, indeed, serious dramatists turned from celebration of restored authority to reflection upon the problems inherent in the exercise and very nature of power.

William Joyner's Senecan tragedy *The Roman Empress* (King's, *c*. August 1670) deals with the topical subject of civil war and usurpation, but disorder is here irremediable, for political upheaval has so obliterated family ties that even the true heir to the Roman Empire is unrecognized, lusted after by his Phaedra-like stepmother, Fulvia, and executed by his father. The play ends not with restoration but with moral chaos: the escape of the evil Fulvia and the suicide of the Emperor and his long-lost first wife, Palladia. An interesting feature of the play is its sympathetic treatment of the oppressed women, whose condition parallels the prevailing civic disarray. A minor, and not entirely admirable, female character makes a nevertheless persuasive attack on the double standard: 'Who made these laws and customs?' she asks; 'did our Sex | Ever give up their voice, and suffrages?' (II, p. 24). Joyner also emphasizes

Epigraph: Nathaniel Lee, *The Tragedy of Nero, Emperour of Rome*, II. iii. 90.

[1] For an account of this play, see Vander Motten, *Sir William Killigrew*, 302–25. The play was published anonymously, but Killigrew's authorship is now certain: see Joseph S. Johnston, Jr., 'Sir William Killigrew's Revised Copy of his *Four New Plays*: Confirmation of His Claim to *The Imperial Tragedy*', *Modern Philology*, 74 (1976–7), 72–4; John Hordern and J. P. Vander Motten, '*Five New Plays*: Sir William Killigrew's Two Annotated Copies', *Library*, 6th ser., 11 (1989), 253–71. Vander Motten points out that a Nursery performance must have occurred after the play's publication, since acting there took place between 1671 and *c*. 1682.

[2] For extended discussion of this play see my *Dryden's Heroic Plays*, 59–78.

the linguistic vindication of the wronged Palladia, who had seemingly been executed years before on a false charge of unchastity. Whereas Fulvia is a corrupter of linguistic signs, Palladia has been falsely incriminated by a misinterpreted letter (v, p. 63), and her death is at least mitigated by the proper telling of her story. Indeed, a loyal follower has embedded brass inscriptions of her story beneath the plaster of the Roman buildings in the confidence that time will quickly bring them to light (I, p. 7). Such linguistic vindication was to be denied to some later tragic heroines (most notably Dryden's Cleopatra), who cannot control the posthumous historical narrative of their lives.

The oppression of women is also the subject of a play clearly set in an era of post-Restoration immorality, Elizabeth Polwhele's 'The Faithfull Virgins', licensed for performance by the Duke's Company *circa* 1670 and surviving in manuscript, with two significant cuts marked by the Master of the Revels, Sir Henry Herbert.[3] In part, this is a standard offshoot of Caroline Platonic drama, featuring female constancy and noble rivalry: two friends watch in perfect concord over the hearse of the man they both loved, while another heroine in male disguise tries to persuade one of them to love the man she herself loves. Unusually, the self-denying idealism ends in tragedy, the agents of destruction being a lustful duke and his jealous, vengeful wife. Act III is dominated by a wedding masque for the pair, in which Virtue banishes Lechery, Drunkenness, and other vices from the court, but life fails to imitate art and shortly afterwards the Duke is planning to rape and the Duchess (more successfully) to murder one of the faithful virgins. The subsequent killing of the Duke (essentially regicide) is portrayed with complete approval, and it provokes a generalization which Herbert found unacceptably provocative: 'for it is fitt | all that so sinn, should punisht be for itt' (v, fo. 76). The other deletion is of a passage in which the future Duchess is sarcastically urged to 'shackle with' the Duke until he tires of her (I, fo. 52ᵛ)—evidently too close for comfort to the home life of the Yorks.

Restored authority is treated with a more qualified and reserved irony in Dryden's two-part heroic play, *The Conquest of Granada* (King's, December–January 1670–1), portraying the recovery by Christian Spain of a Granada torn by the sectarian rivalry of the Abencerrages and the Zegrys, and by the rebellion of King Boabdelin's brother Abdalla. The recovery of Granada had been celebrated in one of the best seventeenth-century epics of warfare against the infidel, Girolamo Graziani's *Il Conquisto di Granata*, but Dryden, characteristically, treats the restoration of true faith and kingship with considerable scepticism. There is no pure antithesis between faction and authority, since King Ferdinand triumphs with the aid of Zegry treachery, and seals his triumph by enthroning the monstrously subversive Lyndaraxa as his client ruler. Even in the decisive battle for Granada, the inspiring presence of Queen Isabella with her company of Spanish beauties is overshadowed by the contribution of the real female agent of victory: Lyndaraxa, with her Zegry troops. As so often in Dryden's work of this period, legitimacy and subversion turn out to be deeply intertwined.

Indeed, when the Duke of Arcos explains to Boabdelin the basis of the Spanish claim (Part I, I. i. 292–356), he quickly abandons the argument of legitimate ancestral right for that of pure military force, and we are reminded in Almanzor's subsequent debate with Arcos that the conquest of Granada coincides with the start of Spain's expansionist designs in the New World (Part I, II. i. 39–40), which had no colour of ancestral right, and which Dryden had already portrayed with some severity in *The Indian Emperour*. Later, when Ferdinand himself states his aims, he reveals a quite strikingly secular and materialistic view of his conquering mission. Unlike Graziani's noble Christian hero, who is an agent of providential design, Dryden's Ferdinand sees himself as an agent of sheer historical inevitability, and conceives the workings of history as a simple process of material cause and effect, likening the decline of empire to the plummeting of a massive object over a cliff:

K. FERD. When from behind, there starts some petty State;
    And pushes on its now unwieldy fate:
    Then, down the precipice of time it goes,
    And sinks in Minutes, which in Ages rose.

                    (Part II, I. i. 13–16)

Immediately, Isabella again sets the enterprise in the larger context of Spanish imperialism, alluding to Columbus's quest for Western gold (Part II, I. i. 17–27),[4] whereupon Ferdinand emphasizes his pragmatic viewpoint by announcing his support for Abdalla's rebellion, because 'He brings a specious title to our side' (Part II, I. i. 39)—a curious desideratum in a champion of divine truth and ancestral right, foreshadowing the symbiosis of Ferdinand and the evil Lyndaraxa.

Disorder is unalterably present at the heart of order: hence the centrality of the 'noble Savage' (Part I, I. i. 209) Almanzor, in whom (as the oxymoronic designation suggests) the norms of civilization and disorders of the wilderness overlap and intermingle. He is a 'Stranger' within the city,[5] but the fortunes of civilization nevertheless depend on him, and the rival causes compete for his necessary aid; and, although an outsider to civilization, he ultimately proves to be of royal blood. Almanzor is not the traditional romance hero who preserves an uncontaminated innate royalty amidst obscurity and deprivation. Although fundamentally magnanimous, he cannot comprehend

---

4 Graziani's laudatory treatment of Columbus (cantos xxii, xxv–xxvi), by contrast, reflects the idealization of Christian exploration prominent in several Renaissance epics (notably the *Lusiads*).

5 For Almanzor as stranger, see Part I, I. i. 198, 235, 239; V. i. 230.

that there is any law, or any reality, beyond his own all-important desires, and he alternately accepts and dishonours political and moral constraints, erratic in his allegiance to Boabdelin and even in his duty to his beloved Almahide, Boabdelin's wife, whom he at one point attempts to seduce. In his lapses into lawless appetite, he reveals a partial yet striking affinity with those creatures of pure appetite, the villainous siblings Lyndaraxa and Zulema, who foment the Zegry rebellion. He is not, of course, their moral equal, for unlike him they make no attempt to accept the disciplines of society, but they embody in extreme form instincts that can never be exorcized from civilization (hence Lyndaraxa's part in Ferdinand's victory). For example, at the same time as Almanzor arrives in Almahide's chamber in order to tempt her, Zulema arrives intent on downright rape.

Almanzor is, indeed, far more readily responsive to Lyndaraxa's voice than to Almahide's. For a long time, Almahide painstakingly attempts to elevate his desire for her into an innocent Platonic love, which will enable him to serve her by serving her husband (in a conquest of self worthy of an Orrery hero). But, at Lyndaraxa's first meeting with him (deferred until the mid-point of Part II so as to emphasize its instant and extraordinary effect), the villainess undoes all Almahide's teaching in a few lines, rekindling his lusts and preparing for his attempted seduction of the heroine. Too confidently, he prefaces their encounter with a close echo of the Orrery hero's claim that it is nobler to deserve than to possess: 'There is this comfort in a noble Fate, | That I deserve to be more fortunate' (Part II, III. iii. 51–2). But his Orrerian principles are demolished in seconds, as Lyndaraxa corners him into admitting the continuing carnality of his desires. Later, she persuades him that Almahide has slept with her own hapless devotee, Abdelmelech, again commanding an instant assent that Almahide can never inspire. But the affinity between Lyndaraxa and Almanzor has been established long before their first meeting, and appears most strikingly at the mid-point of Part I (the structural counterpart to the point at which they first meet in Part II). Here, amidst the insurrection that she has provoked, Lyndaraxa rants in ugly blood-lust at the waning of battle: 'Beat faster, Drums, and mingle Deaths more thick' (Part I, III. i. 260). She then leaves, whereupon Almanzor immediately enters and expresses the same sentiments in acceptably heroic terms: 'I am griev'd the noble sport is done' (Part I, III. i. 271). What particularly emphasizes the connection between the speeches is that Lyndaraxa leaves to wait '*Hero*-like' (Part I, III. i. 263) for her lover Abdalla, the leader of the rebels. She refers, of course, to Hero the mistress of Leander, and grossly departs from this exemplar, but the word is a provocative instruction to compare and contrast the two versions of *Hero*, and what is compared is not only the conduct of Lyndaraxa and Almanzor but the roles of woman and man, for a single word has radically different meanings, which are determined exclusively by the sex of the person to which it is applied. Lyndaraxa is monstrous because her actions, unlike

Almanzor's, are nakedly evil; she is also monstrous because, unlike Almanzor, she is a woman.

As Almanzor's dual role as savage stranger and royal kinsman indicates, he sums up the ambiguities of civilization itself, and these ambiguities are apparent even in the ceremonies with which civilization celebrates itself. On two occasions, the opening sports and the Zambra dance which immediately precedes Abdalla's rebellion, formal ceremony collapses into anarchy. In the first, where the Zegrys attempt to murder Ozmyn by furtively introducing a real javelin into a mock-combat, a civilization which expresses itself in ritual orderings and imitations of violence is threatened when these lose their purely ritual character and verge towards chaos;[6] though he had celebrated carnival in *An Evening's Love*, Dryden here portrays a festivity which implies and produces anarchy. The ambiguities of civilization are also illustrated in the perplexed behaviour of Almahide, who marries Boabdelin in order to save Almanzor's life, but is never as successful as she imagines in sacrificing her private affections to her marital role. For example, having assured Boabdelin that he need 'No more the shadow of *Almanzor* fear,' she quickly admits to herself that 'for *Almanzor* I in secret mourn' (Part II, I. ii. 150, 217). In the tortured, forbidden love of Almanzor and Almahide, we see the impossibility of Orrery's ideal social being: Almanzor cannot act the part of noble rival which Almahide designs for him, and Almahide herself cannot subjugate passion to social ideals.

Their socially unassimilable love leads to one of the many flawed judicial rituals that characterize drama of this period, in marked contrast to the manifestations of Astraea only a few years earlier. Wrongly convinced, through Lyndaraxa's all-pervasive influence, that Almahide is an adulteress, Boabdelin arranges a trial by combat, showing that the ritualized violence central to Granada's ceremonies of order governs even the rituals of justice. Although Almahide is vindicated by Almanzor's muscle-power, he himself believes her guilty while defending her, and she almost immediately falls under renewed suspicion from Boabdelin. But the trial by combat is not only unsatisfactory because it grounds the primary ordering procedures of civilization upon archaic violence, and because it denies the woman a voice, giving wordless machismo the responsibility of defining her character. It is also unsatisfactory because the simple public categories of guilt and innocence are crude and insufficient terms for judging complex personal states such as Almahide's emotional alienation from Boabdelin. (Dryden later returned to this issue in *Aureng-Zebe* and *All for Love*, creating in each a pair of mock trials in which the heroine's innocence is inadequately investigated by her lover.) Human nature is no longer, as it had been in Orrery, perfectly and fully expressible in

---

[6] J. Douglas Canfield sees the ritual combat as 'designed to sublimate the very deadly rivalry it now precipitates' (*Word as Bond in English Literature from the Middle Ages to the Restoration* (Philadelphia, 1989), 32).

social terms, and the intimacies of personal existence cannot fully be translated into the approved language of public morality. This is especially true of
women, who, as Antonia in *The Roman Empress* complains, did not give
'their voice, and suffrages' to the laws by which they are judged.

Dryden, indeed, repeatedly suggests that the mind is unbridgeably separated from the exterior world with which it must communicate. Alien elements
persist within the structures of civilization because the mind and the outward
world are largely alien to each other, and the isolation of the mind means that
the public currency of language is a fallible means of either informing or
representing the individual consciousness: hence the procrustean imprecision
of judicial terms. Almanzor is constantly confined within his own sensations,
confusing his desires with objective reality, and later concluding that man is 'a
Pris'ner of the Mind' (Part II, IV. iii. 148), trapped in an inexorably determined sequence of thought and desire. (In the dedication of *The Rival Ladies*,
Dryden himself had spoken of 'the Prison' of the human will (p. 97).) Even
Almahide becomes 'lost in my own Webb of thought' (Part II, I. ii. 226), her
mind an enveloping prison, like a silkworm's cocoon. Language is part of the
cocoon. In particular, the characters' constant reliance on simile reveals the
perceptual elusiveness of the object, the paradox that objects cannot be defined by circular reference to themselves, but only by reference to that which
they are not. It is a paradox extensively displayed in Guyomar's description of
the Spanish ships in *The Indian Emperour*, or Almanzor's attempt to understand the new experience of love by likening it to the old and only marginally
similar experience of a tarantula bite (Part I, III. i. 328–9), and it is too little
noticed that the far-fetched similes for which the play is notorious are seldom
just ornamentally illustrative, and generally express clear misconstruction or
frank incomprehension of the situations they describe. When, for example,
Boabdelin compares Almahide in some detail to a tulip (Part I, V. i. 298–302),
he is mistakenly suggesting that she is terrified by Almanzor's presence and
will be relieved by his execution; and, when Almahide compares herself and
Boabdelin to two turtle doves (Part II, I. ii. 128–33), her pastoral fantasy
glosses over the actual bitterness of their marriage.[7]

At one point, the mental processes behind the similes are exposed with
particular clarity. Liberating the captive Almahide, yet wishing to establish a
claim on her affections, Almanzor first likens himself to a pirate restoring
merchandise and then legitimately buying it; when Almahide exposes the inadequacy of the simile, Almanzor compares himself to a subject honouring a
queen; and, when Almahide successfully criticizes that simile too, he abandons the search for convincing analogies, deciding to commit suicide and
pursue her as a ghost (Part I, IV. ii. 400–25). The play here lays bare its own
poetic processes and incorporates them into the plot, momentarily turning
one of its central questions—will the hero marry the heroine?—into an

[7] Both similes are mocked in *The Rehearsal* (I. i. 358–63; II. iii. 18–25).

issue of literary criticism. The similes are uttered only to be discredited, and they reveal Almanzor's inability to comprehend the publicly sanctioned categories—Almahide's betrothal to Boabdelin—that make the world other than the one demanded by his will.

At one extreme, the similes actively induce error (they play a prominent role in the sophistries of Lyndaraxa and Zulema), whereas at others they merely express unfulfilled intentions, as in the Zegry patriarch Selin's happily frustrated determination to await death like '*Rome*'s old Senate' (Part II, II. i. 17). But, even when apposite, the similes are often (like Almahide's silkworm simile) expressions of incomprehension or helplessness rather than exercises in controlled rhetorical illustration; for, paradoxically, the similes are at their most precisely and appropriately descriptive when they define the factors that make the mind a prison and entangle the observing consciousness in its 'Webb of thought'. In these cases they evoke a condition either of paralysis or of helpless subjection to material process. The materialism that distinguishes Ferdinand's interpretation of history is universally present in the characters' interpretations of their motives, their mental and linguistic isolation being the isolation of minds locked in separate and discrete cycles of material consequence. Unable to suppress his love for Lyndaraxa, Abdalla finds himself in a living nightmare in which he tries to run but cannot move, and (reducing the operations of mind to those of matter) likens her attraction to that of rubbed amber (Part I, II. i. 180–1). Lyndaraxa herself compares her fluctuating affections to the mobile liquid in a barometer (Part I, IV. ii. 5–6);[8] Almanzor compares his love for Almahide to a fire which refines ore (Part I, III. i. 423–4); and even Abenamar, movingly abandoning his resistance to his son Ozmyn's love for his enemy's daughter, compares his conversion to a material operation: the melting of a frozen river (Part II, IV. i. 130–3). As in *The Rival Ladies*, life and thought are operations of matter in motion, and there are clearly moments when the characters have difficulty in describing anything outside their personal cycle of material process. Almanzor does converse with his mother's ghost, whose voice subsequently dissuades him from the unwitting murder of his father, but even she is confined to the material world, encumbered by gravity and too heavy with unpurged sin to pass the walls of heaven. It is impossible to step outside the material workings of language and history. Even the voice of Providence speaks from the world of matter, and this is the world that shapes human history and civilization, with all their moral, imaginative, and linguistic limitations.

The Conquest of Granada was one of the chief butts of *The Rehearsal* (King's, December 1671), by the Duke of Buckingham and others, in which Mr Bayes (Dryden) supervises the rehearsal of a preposterous heroic play, to the increasing scorn and incredulity of two gentlemen of sense, Smith and

---

[8] Bruce King observes that 'Lyndaraxa has become a mechanical object conditioned in its responses to external stimuli' (*Dryden's Major Plays* (Edinburgh and London, 1966), 76).

Johnson. But the subject of *The Rehearsal* is not merely aesthetic chaos. It is, after all, a mock play of restoration: two kings of Brentford are deposed by two humbly born usurpers (all four indistinguishable from each other),⁹ but return in hyperbolic apotheosis. The finality of the apotheosis is, however, counteracted by further fighting, in which Drawcansir (Almanzor), an enemy of 'justice' (IV. i. 104– 7), indiscriminately annihilates both of the opposing armies, and the play of restoration never reaches any kind of conclusion, since the actors get bored and leave for dinner. A mimic apotheosis gives way to chaos and then peters away inconclusively as the common people follow the more compelling call of the feast (Drawcansir's first act in the play is to disrupt a feast, IV. i. 220–1).¹⁰ The multiple kings divide and discredit the received iconography of authority, and there is a general royal obsession with love that is as indecorous in literature as it is in politics; in these respects, at least, the play is more of a sequel to *The Conquest of Granada* than a satire upon it.

The Rehearsal was a great and lasting success, but it did not, as used to be thought, laugh the heroic play out of existence.¹¹ On the contrary, only in the early 1670s did Dryden's heroic plays start to exercise a substantial influence on the work of other dramatists, when a rising generation of young tragedians (Settle, Crowne, Lee, Otway) took them as starting-points before developing more diverse personal styles. For the most part (though Crowne's early work is an exception) they follow Dryden's lead in rejecting the paeans to just political order that had characterized the first generation of heroic plays. Justice and legitimate authority are flawed and even undiscoverable, and the focus is on the displaced, rootless individual, alienated from society and even family.

The first imitation was the very successful *Cambyses King of Persia* (Duke's, January 1671) by Elkanah Settle, an author whose incompetence in every sphere of dramatic construction and linguistic expression was no bar to a serious and radical interest in problems of authority, though it sometimes makes deliberate complexity hard to distinguish from inadvertent confusion. Unlike Dryden, Settle does portray clearly exemplary characters, and indeed preserves most of the ideals of the early heroic play. Language, for example, is a clear and celestially judged instrument of moral order: when the Sultan Solyman in *Ibrahim* adulterously pursues the mistress of his friend, both of whom he has adopted as his children, he violates 'sacred Vows' (IV, p. 42), the

---

⁹ See Staves, *Players' Scepters*, 70–2.

¹⁰ Margarita Stocker has attractively suggested a dual literary and political reading of the satire, in which Bayes, sharp practiser in the world of poetry, glances at a comparable figure in the world of politics: Charles's chief minister and Buckingham's great rival, Arlington ('Political Allusion in *The Rehearsal*', *Philological Quarterly*, 67 (1988), 11–35). Stocker is greatly refining the identification of Bayes and Arlington made in George McFadden, 'Political Satire in *The Rehearsal*', *Yearbook of English Studies*, 4 (1974), 120–8.

¹¹ See Robert D. Hume, *The Development of English Drama in the Late Seventeenth Century* (Oxford, 1976), 290–1.

'Sacred Name' of father (III, p. 30), and the duty of a monarch to 'speak . . . Sacred things' (III, p. 36). Settle also has generally conservative views on social degree. He is one of the few dramatists of the period to focus on the threat to established order of the unambiguous outsider (such as Joanna Anglica in *The Female Prelate* and Celestina in *The Ambitious Slave*), and he lacks his contemporaries' preoccupation with the stranger within, repeatedly using the term *stranger* to denote his villains' departure from moral and linguistic norms: in *Cambyses*, the virtuous Phedima treats the lustful Smerdis as both morally and linguistically alien ('Stranger, what means this language?', I, p. 11), and the unscrupulous Prexaspes defines his villainy as estrangement from divinely written absolutes: 'Religion, Loyalty, and th'aery scrowl | Of gods, are strangers to a *Scythians* soul' (I, p. 5).[12] The emphasis on moral societies bonded by sacred language leads to an Orrery-like exaltation of friendship and verbal bonds, and magnanimous lovers selflessly help favoured rivals. For example, in *Cambyses* Theramnes endangers his love in order to honour an obligation that verges on being a punctilio: he has sworn not to reveal that a letter was written by his king, and continues to honour his oath even on finding that the letter is a forgery in his own name, making him seem false to the woman he loves.

But Settle rarely follows Orrery in portraying a triumphant moral reconstitution of society. On the contrary, the status of social obligations is often appallingly ambiguous. While Theramnes is inhibited from clearing his name because he is trapped by an oath to his king, the audience knows that the king is an impostor, lacking the authority which Theramnes attributes to him. Traditional patterns of social obligation become empty formulas and, conversely, individual integrity is frequently denied social vindication. Whereas Orrery's noble rivals suppress self to fulfil themselves as social beings, Settle's noble rivals can end up as social outcasts: as martyrs (Tygranes in *The Ambitious Slave*) or exiles (Hametalhaz in *The Empress of Morocco*, Ulama in *Ibrahim*). Hametalhaz, a villain reformed by hopeless love for the heroine, finally retreats from civilization into the desert, exemplifying a very common Restoration motif, and one that is incompatible with Orrery's stress on the essentially social character of the heroic paragon.

Legitimacy and authority are frequently problematic. In *Cambyses*, two rival tyrants (the inspiration for the two usurpers in *The Rehearsal*) contend for control of Persia: Cambyses, who has murdered his younger brother, Smerdis, and an impostor posing as Smerdis. One is the true king and one a usurper, but (as Theramnes' misguided fit of self-denying principle shows) it is not easy for subjects to discover which is which, and indeed the false king is rather less tyrannical than the true. In the end, after both tyrants have been murdered, the succession is (as in *Tyrannick Love*) determined not by

---

12 For parallel imagery of characters as strangers to linguistic or moral absolutes, see *The Conquest of China by the Tartars*, II, p. 22; *Ibrahim*, V, p. 72; *Distress'd Innocence*, IV, p. 42.

inheritance but by worth, the rightful heir insisting that the crown be transferred to Darius, the greater man. The perplexed treatment of authority here contrasts with the simple celebrations of restored legitimacy of a few years before, and it was to be characteristic of Settle throughout his work. Whatever its quality, this play is an important landmark: joy at restoration has finally yielded to worry about succession.

Throughout his plays Settle is mainly interested not simply in the tyrant or usurper but in the enigma of the *criminal* ruler, whether the ruler who commits crimes or the unrecognized ruler who is falsely labelled a criminal. The most troublesome figure is the absolute monarch who performs acts commonly defined as criminal: for, if the king himself is the criterion of justice, by what other criterion can he be termed criminal? Yet what meaning does the term have if he cannot? As so often, justice (a recurrent term throughout Settle's work) becomes ambiguous in nature and application. Settle clearly rejects the identification of justice with power, which he leaves to villains such as Prexaspes in *Cambyses* (v, pp. 67–8), but he seems surer of what to reject than what to affirm, and he delights in paradoxical inversions of judicial role and process. In *Cambyses* a death sentence issued by a criminal ruler is, improbably enough, frustrated when the executioner turns out to be a virtuous hero in disguise, and the same play features two extended scenes of judicial disarray. In the second, the newly enthroned Darius reluctantly finds himself forced by law to sentence the noble Mandana to death for her apparent murder of Cambyses; the judicial process is powerless to save or vindicate her, and she is spared only because the real killer spontaneously exults in his guilt before the court. Earlier, however, the rituals of justice have been complicated to the point of comedy, when King Smerdis performs convolutions of judicial role almost as awkward as the better known contortions of the Lord Chancellor in *Iolanthe*. Unrecognized, he has made lustful advances to the virtuous Phedima, and subsequently contrives that Phedima should appeal to him for justice on the criminal, Phedima not yet realizing that the criminal and judge are one and the same. In the ensuing welter of judicial paradoxes, judge and plaintiff exchange places, and Phedima asserts love and honour as absolutes that transcend the social terminology of justice and entitle her to condemn a king as a criminal:

> Although you Monarchs are exempt from Laws,
> As wanting higher Pow'rs to Judge your cause:
> Yet that you, Smerdis, may have Justice done,
> Since you want Laws, I'le Judge you by my own. . . .
> Honour and Love are but respective things;
> Greater or less in Subjects or in Kings.
> In which if Kings transgress, the more sublime
> Their greatness is, the greater is their Crime.
>
> (II, pp. 19–20)

Settle can only 'solve' the problem by resorting to contradiction and nonsense: as so often in his work, an ideological stance is struck without an ideological rationale. Even his insistence on the sanctity of the word is never imaginatively justified. Perhaps not entirely inadvertently, he presents a world of confused and ambiguous particulars which do not yield general or transcendent principles of order.

The unjust ruler is treated with far more orthodoxy in a play which Settle brought to the stage, Samuel Pordage's *Herod and Mariamne* (?Duke's, *c.* August 1673, but according to the prologue written twelve years earlier). This is a bombastic adaptation of the account in La Calprenède's *Cléopâtre* of the virtuously suppressed love of the heroic warrior Tyridates and Herod's ill-treated queen, which Dryden had already used in portraying Porphyrius' love for the wife of the tyrant Maximin in *Tyrannick Love*. Though later a Whig propagandist during the Exclusion Crisis, Pordage here propounds passive obedience. Perversions of justice provide a heavily emphasized unifying motif, culminating in the elaborate judicial formalities which sanction Mariamne's tragic execution, but subjects must leave tyrants to the justice of heaven. (Tyridates is, however, allowed to kill Herod, since he is a foreign ruler rather than a subject.) There is no progress from tyranny to restoration, and the representation of authority is bleak; yet, at the same time, it is problem-free.

By contrast, John Crowne's *The History of Charles the Eighth of France; or, The Invasion of Naples by the French* (Duke's, November 1671) is a slavish glorification of royal power, perhaps justifying the recent alliance between England and France.[13] The play apes the gestures of *The Conquest of Granada*, but lacks its sense of the inevitable contradictions within civilization: its Almanzor-figure, the haughty and ambitious Prince of Salerne, is a simple case of good qualities misapplied (he is 'mislead by too much bravary [*sic*]', V, p. 72), and his relationship with the unprincipled villain Trivultio is one of sheer alliance and dependence, as opposed to the partial and inadvertent affinities which in Dryden link a hero of noble aspiration to his evil anti-type, Zulema. Charles campaigns to recover his ancestral Neapolitan throne from King Ferdinand, but refuses to profit from dissension against his fellow-monarch; for 'Subjects or Kingdoms are but trifling things, | When laid together in the scale with Kings' (III, p. 30). Ferdinand's love for the Queen of Cyprus is often of more moment to him than the dangers of his kingdom (e.g. II, p. 24), yet there is no obvious indication that his priorities are misplaced; subjects, indeed, are repeatedly described as slaves. In its portrayal of disinterested magnanimity between opposing commanders, *Charles the Eighth* harks back to the conventions of French prose romance and of such first-generation heroic plays as *The Siege of Rhodes*. Dryden's Cortez had

---

[13] Harold Love, 'State Affairs on the Restoration Stage', 4; Beth S. Neman, 'Setting the Record Straight on John Crowne', *Restoration and 18th Century Theatre Research*, 2nd ser., 8/1 (1993), 1–26 (p. 15).

attempted such magnanimity to the Mexicans in *The Indian Emperour* but could not control the violence and avarice of his associates, revealing the failure of ideal codes to restrain the anarchy of desire. But Dryden's Ferdinand (in *The Conquest of Granada*) has no interest in such heroic principle, and eagerly manipulates the dissension against Boabdelin.

More ominous is Thomas Shipman's *Henry the Third of France Stabb'd by a Fryer* (King's, *c.* June 1672), a play of regicide and legitimate succession, but also a crude and early piece of anti-Catholic propaganda, reflecting the atmosphere which a year later produced the Test Act and thereby drove the heir presumptive to the throne into public declaration of his already widely known Catholicism.[14] The play deals with the French Wars of Religion, which Dryden and Lee later portrayed in *The Duke of Guise*, and indeed it includes the murder of Guise. But, whereas Dryden and Lee treat the subversive fanaticism of the Catholic League as a parallel to that of the Protestant Whigs, Shipman makes specific, non-transferable attacks on Catholicism, which is seen as an international force of terror and oppression (witness the Armada and St Bartholomew). There is praise of that future icon of the Whigs, Elizabeth I. And, as England combined with Catholic France for a war against Protestant Holland (declared in March 1672), Shipman recalls the time when England's alliances had been the other way round (I, pp. 2–3). The play was not published until late 1678, and the Popish Plot scare broke while it was in press, whereupon Shipman added a dedicatory poem to Monmouth, praising him as protector against '*Jesuits* rage' (a compliment which was suppressed when the poem was reprinted in Shipman's posthumous *Carolina; or, Loyal Poems*).[15] *Carolina* also contains a poem on the 1679 prorogation, addressed to the Nottinghamshire MP Sir Scrope Howe (pp. 221–2), a close associate of Shaftesbury.[16] These later statements of allegiance were still some years in the future, but the play itself, with its clear signs of discontent from a man of impeccably royalist stock, is a foreshadowing of the storm to come.

Shipman's Elizabeth had demonstrated that 'no Sex is in the soul' (IV, p. 43), and the position of woman is more subtly examined in Henry Neville Payne's domestic tragedy *The Fatal Jealousie* (Duke's, by August 1672). 'Husband's prerogatives are absolute, | Their wills we must obey, and not dispute' (III, p. 49), says the heroine Cælia, blindly justifying the authority of a man who is to contrive her death. This is one of many late seventeenth-century imitations of *Othello* (the first was Thomas Porter's *The Villain*), and,

---

[14] On 10 Mar. 1671 both Houses had presented a petition against the growth of popery, and Charles had required all Jesuit and Roman priests to leave the country before 1 May (David Ogg, *England in the Reign of Charles II*, 2nd edn. (2 vols., Oxford, 1955), i. 350–1).

[15] Tho[mas] Shipman, *Carolina; or, Loyal Poems* (London, 1683), 209. For the complex publishing history of *Henry the Third* see Robert D. Hume and Curt A. Zimansky, 'Thomas Shipman's *Henry the Third of France*: Some Questions of Date, Performance, and Publication', *Philological Quarterly*, 55 (1976), 436–44.

[16] See K. H. D. Haley, *The First Earl of Shaftesbury* (Oxford, 1968), 420, 522, 658.

characteristically, it excises the cultural or social outsider, concentrating entirely on the individual's intrinsic alienation. This results from the imperfection of earthly knowledge and communication (*doubt* is a recurrent word, as in Payne's later *The Siege of Constantinople*), for the mind can never apprehend the essence of objects, as the exemplary Gerardo argues:

> in Terrestrial things there is not one
> But takes its Form and Nature from our fancy;
> Not its own being, and is what we do think it.
>
> (II, p. 28)

Humanity is irremediably dislocated in a maze of false perceptions, and the fatal jealousy of Gerardo's friend Antonio exemplifies this universal displacement:

> Like Nighted Travellers we lose our way;
> Then every *Ignis Fatuus* makes us stray.
> By the false Lights of Reason led about.
>
> (III, p. 36)

Since Antonio's jealousy is a particular form of a general isolation within error, he is not represented as an outsider. Whereas Othello and Iago mirror each other as complementary strangers, Antonio and his Iago (Jasper) mirror each other in a quite contrary fashion, for their origins lie in the very centre of the state. Jasper, the Iago, is the grandson of a disgraced Vice-Admiral of Spain, explicitly inheriting his ancestor's flaws, and Antonio is the present owner of Jasper's ancestral estates, who gradually displays equal unfitness for the ancestral honour.

Language is treacherous. Antonio's jealousy is fuelled by a scene of fraudulent magical incantation, where language possesses a sham power, and on two important occasions ignorance proceeds from unheard speech. A loyal servant observes Antonio talking with Jasper, but his observation 'did signifie but little', for the noise of the wind ensured that the words 'Came so divided they had no connexion' (III, p. 34). Similarly, when (in a recollection of *Much Ado About Nothing*) Antonio is persuaded that Cælia is false by the sight of her sister Eugenia meeting a lover in Cælia's gown, he 'cannot hear their words' (IV, p. 55) and impulsively kills Eugenia. Eugenia suffers in another way from the incompleteness and inadequacy of speech. Having been raped in the past, she is forced through fear of exposure into repeated surrender to the rapist. But, although Gerardo (Eugenia's prospective husband) discovers the truth as she is dying and affirms his confidence in her purity, he too is killed—because Eugenia dies before she can complete a speech warning him of danger—and the tale of Eugenia's unchastity survives her, while the extenuating reasons are forever lost. There are no brass inscriptions (as there are in Joyner's *The Roman Empress*) to carry the woman's story beyond the grave.

The dying Eugenia is preoccupied with her 'story' (IV, p. 55), but women cannot determine the history of their lives, and they repeatedly lack the power of narrative: Jasper 'stopt' the 'Mouth' of his aunt, the pseudo-witch, by killing her (V, p. 72), and Antonio urges the Nurse to 'stop your mouth' when she defends Cælia (V, p. 68). The Nurse does disclose Jasper's villainy, but without the torrent of speech that Shakepeare's Emilia is permitted; for Jasper has already stabbed her, determined to 'prevent' her 'story' (V, p. 71). Unlike Iago, indeed, Jasper controls the narrative to the end, anxious that his 'Tale' and 'story' should survive (V, pp. 71–2), and stabbing himself to avoid society's forms of description in 'a formal Tryal' (V, p. 73). Trials were increasingly to be linked with historical narrative as parallel translations of private deeds and motives into public terminology. But here neither trial nor 'story' gains an ordering and socially integrating function.

Following the failure of his comedy *The Assignation* and the burning of the Theatre Royal, Dryden produced little for the stage for some years. His *Amboyna* (King's, *c.* May 1672), written at the time of the Third Dutch War, is a hack work, 'which,' in his own words, 'tho' it succeeded on the Stage, will scarcely bear a serious Perusal' (dedication, sig. R4ᵛ). The aim was to defend a controversial war and to combat a growing view that England was fighting the wrong enemy: a view later forcibly expressed in Marvell's *An Account of the Growth of Popery and Arbitrary Government in England* (1677). Thus, while Shipman's roughly contemporary *Henry the Third of France* stresses Catholic cruelty, Dryden stresses Dutch cruelty (and portrays a noble Catholic, the Spaniard Perez). Dutch unfitness for alliance or trust is the central theme, and the belief that they are fellow Protestants is an illusion, for their 'Religion . . . is only made up of Interest' (II, p. 415): the noble Englishman Towerson, for example, has a suicidal trust in Dutch gratitude and an ingenuous faith in the heroic gesture, at one point displaying an Almanzor-like impulsiveness in rescuing the outnumbered Harman Junior from two attackers, unaware that the attackers are trying to prevent the villainous Harman from murdering him.

But what is most remarkable about the play is the extent to which Dryden had to desert his normal outlook in order to write it. The East Indian heroine, Ysabinda, is a noble savage of a kind quite different from Almanzor and from the Indians of Dryden's first two heroic plays: an embodiment of a universal natural morality who shows up the refined villainy of the Dutch. Another change lies in Dryden's treatment of language. In their compulsive perjury and treatment of moral values as mere words, the Dutch imply by reverse a natural association between language and ethics that would have won assent from a traditionalist such as Charles Hickman, and indeed on one occasion Dutch villainy is exposed by a victim's natural capacity for signification that is virtually identical to Hickman's 'open countenance, like Windows into our heart': 'Her Heart speaks in her Tongue,' says Ysabinda, 'and were she silent, her Habit and her Face speak for her' (III, p. 425). The sign is most effectually powerful when the Spanish captain Perez comes to murder the sleeping Towerson but is converted to nobility by some writing by the head of his prospective victim. The incident is very similar to the one reported in Shakespeare's *Richard III* (but omitted from Cibber's), in which Forrest is more transiently deterred from murder by the sight of a prayer book by the side of the sleeping princes. Dryden still, however, does not endow language with a sacred or transcendent character. The text which moves Perez is not a holy text; it is an order, signed by Towerson, to pay him £500 (III, p. 417). But it bears his name, and the spectacle of a man being recalled to social virtue by the sight of his name is an archaic touch rare in the drama of this decade.

The possibility of natural and universal signs means that the rituals of justice are no longer grounded upon epistemological impossibility: like many Dryden plays of this period, *Amboyna* features a flawed judicial ritual—a rigged trial, after which the English are agonizingly executed—but justice is here simply corrupt rather than intrinsically inexact. Correspondingly, the claims of the flesh, which had rightly triumphed over formal justice in *The Wild Gallant* and *An Evening's Love*, are here associated with evil and oppression. Young Harman rapes Ysabinda (the most attractive feature of the play is its insistence on the purity of the rape victim), and his fat father's corporeal grossness is repeatedly mentioned. Indeed, in the middle of the corrupt judicial ritual one of the victims rounds on Harman Senior and identifies him with the archetype of obese carnal licence: 'you Sir *John Falstaff* of *Amsterdam*' (V, p. 447). This is by far the best moment in the play. William Cartwright, the actor who created Harman Senior, was a celebrated Falstaff, and the arresting glimpse of festive licence becoming judicial oppression is still more arresting as a reversal of one of the fundamental images of Dryden's earlier work. Almost as arresting is a reversal of one of the most heterodox jokes of *An Evening's Love*: the relativism which makes hell a mere provincial locality on a map scribbled over with provincial localities. This, too, is now the property of the enemy: 'if there be a Hell,' says the Fiscal (the chief judicial officer), ''tis but for those that Sin in *Europe*, not for us in *Asia*; Heathens have no Hell' (IV, p. 433). What is common to all these transient U-turns is an abandonment of relativism in favour of a universal scheme of signification, justice, and morality. These are fixed norms of civilization shared by the English, the noble Indian Ysabinda, and the noble Catholic Perez, but they are incomprehensible to the Dutch: simply (not to say simple-mindedly) portrayed strangers who have little to do with Dryden's more usual figure of the stranger within civilization. Towerson's recurrent mistake is to think that he can establish shared ties of culture with such creatures.

During Dryden's period of relative inactivity, Settle scored his greatest success with his spectacular heroic play *The Empress of Morocco* (Duke's, by July 1673), subsequently published with illustrations of its most extravagant scenic effects. Angered by its success, Dryden collaborated with Shadwell and Crowne in a lengthy and ill-tempered attack on the play, though Settle's reply left him with at least equal honours.[17] Settle again portrays authority as problematic, both in family and state: at the beginning of the play Muly Labas, the rightful heir to the throne, has been imprisoned by his father, and is saved only because his father is murdered (on his mother's orders) while pronouncing his death sentence; but his respite is brief, for he is saved from his father's hatred only to be killed by the agency of his mother and her lover, Crimalhaz. Such dark views of the family, interpreting it as an archetype not of society but of the Hobbesian state of war, were to be strikingly common until 1688, contrasting with the official derivation of royal authority from the natural authority of the father. Authority is equally unsatisfactory in the state, and problems of authority again create problems of justice. During his brief reign Muly Labas is well intentioned but weak, easily deluded by his mother and Crimalhaz into condemning the innocent, and finally destroyed by the agency of the villainous pair. He condemns the innocent Muly Hamet for attempted rape (the victim piously exclaiming that the sentence must be just because a king has passed it), and after Muly Labas's murder his queen, Morena, is tried for the crime by its true author, Crimalhaz.

As in *Cambyses*, the throne passes to the worthiest, when Muly Hamet, now betrothed to Muly Labas's sister, violently ends Crimalhaz' tyranny. As in *Cambyses*, however, it is difficult to arrive at universal and absolute principles that validate seizure of the throne by the worthy and not by the unworthy: in preparing to resist Muly Hamet, Crimalhaz cynically derives authority from success ('I'll try, | Who's the successful Rebel, he, or I', V, p. 167), and although the virtuous Abdelcador declares that true kings go to heaven and usurpers to hell (V, p. 175), his declaration provides no means of distinguishing them in life; as a guide to the temporal, the eternal is mute. As so often, Settle presents life as a concatenation of particular events that rarely support the formula-tion of general laws, and indeed the lives of the three successive rulers of Morocco in themselves present incoherent medleys of discrete events. Muly Labas and Muly Hamet go from prison to throne, while Crimalhaz makes the reverse journey. Muly Labas and Crimalhaz, true and false king, both preside at unjust trials, and Muly Hamet, who proclaims his own false condemnation to be just since uttered by a king, suddenly finds that he himself is the arbiter of justice. Settle quite ostentatiously emphasizes the instability and dis-continuity of the roles of authority.

There is one particularly obvious way in which Settle portrays life as a sequence of discrete concrete events, irreducible to general and immaterial laws, and that is his use of imagery of the hand: imagery that is persistently

---

[17] [John Crowne, John Dryden, and Thomas Shadwell], *Notes and Observations on The Empress of Morocco* (London, 1674); [Elkanah Settle], *Notes and Observations on The Empress of Morocco Revised* (London, '1674' [?1675]).

prominent throughout his plays. Hands are rarely linked, as they are in Shakespeare and Milton, in token of the natural social interdependence of humanity; nor is the human hand contrasted or compared with the beneficently controlling hand of God. Rather, Settle portrays a world of conflicting hands engaged in competing action, and rarely articulates criteria of value beyond them. Only in *Ibrahim* is the repeated stress on manual violence counteracted by something nobler: the hero and heroine defying Solyman's power with a prolonged holding and kissing of hands (V, p. 61), and Solyman's penitent clasp of his dying wife (V, p. 72). But, in *The Empress of Morocco* itself, the hand merely acts. Crimalhaz and the Queen Mother constantly execute evil or fraudulent justice with their hands, the Queen's dying boast being 'Let single murders, common hands suffice' (V, p. 166). But the good, too, live by the hand: Crimalhaz' army is defeated by '*Muly Hamet*'s hand', Crimalhaz then being delivered to '*Muly Hamet*'s hands' and his mistress Mariamne (two lines later) to his 'Hand' (V, pp. 167, 172). Virtue triumphs, but Settle is better at portraying the physical agencies which the good share with the evil than the metaphysical criteria which distinguish them.

The absence of such criteria is implicit in the one incident of real dramatic skill and subtlety in Settle's *œuvre*. When the Queen Mother decides to establish her own power by killing her son, she arranges that he and the Young Queen, Morena, shall star in a masque of Orpheus and Eurydice. Morena is told that Crimalhaz will play Orpheus, and that he plans to abduct her under cover of the masque. And so, at the moment when Eurydice is given to Orpheus' 'hand' (IV, pp. 148, 153), she surprises the audience by stabbing him to death (IV, p. 153), only to find that she has killed her husband: the brief linkage of hands is tragically delusory, and there is laborious stress on the role of Morena's 'hand' in performing the murder. It is equally prominent throughout the aftermath of the murder. She promises herself to the lustful Crimalhaz, provided that his 'hand' avenge the King (IV, p. 160), though she privately resolves to give only her corpse: 'Morena's hand shall wash the stain she wears' (IV, p. 161). She seals the pact by giving him her hand to kiss (IV, p. 160), and honours it by offering him her hand as she dies (V, p. 165).

In contrast with Isabella and Ibrahim's linking of hands, the three occasions on which Morena links hands are all ironic expressions of disharmony and impotence, fitting adjuncts to a masque in which the hands of the good unwittingly enact the dramaturgic designs of the wicked. Appropriately, the masque itself becomes a representation of the entangled obscurity of justice, for Settle here turns from the problem of the criminal ruler to that of the criminal god. Orpheus confronts the voluntaristic ravisher Pluto, daring '*of a Crime* [to] *impeach a Deity*' (IV, p. 151), and repeatedly appears as a dislocated outsider in the cosmos whose rules he challenges: a stranger (twice), a '*wanderer*', and '*a Pilgrim*' (IV, pp. 151–2). He appears, that is, as a noble individual in a cosmos whose order provides no support for or analogy to his nobility. Eurydice is restored, though the atonement of Pluto's crime is curiously described as a relaxation rather than a fulfilment of justice: '*Mercy as well as Justice rules in Hell*' (IV, p. 153), Proserpine sings, with the implication that Pluto's divinity made his crime itself just. But this fictitious and rather grudging display of providential benevolence is promptly counteracted by the actual death of the rightful king.

Settle was a blunderer, but an innovative blunderer. If Dryden provided a model for the spate of Siege, Conquest, and Destruction plays that were to flood the stage in the mid-1670s, *The Empress of Morocco* gives new prominence to the dark and brutal chaos at the heart of the family and state, later more searchingly portrayed by Lee and Otway. The increasing political gloom of drama reflects the national mood. There was growing mistrust of the King's aims in the Third Dutch War and fear of his brother's religion and character, which was to be compounded by James's marriage in September 1673 to the Catholic Princess Mary of Modena: a marriage which, in view of Charles's lack of legitimate issue, raised the possibility of a perpetual Catholic dynasty.[18] 'Looking back,' John Miller writes, 'thoughtful contemporaries saw 1672–3 as a watershed in Charles's reign, in which designs to establish popery and arbitrary government first became apparent.'[19]

Nathaniel Lee's *The Tragedy of Nero, Emperour of Rome* (King's, by May 1674) continues the dissident treatment of authority, celebrating the deposition of a self-deifying tyrant by popular uprising. But *Nero* is not a play of order restored: it contains the elements of earlier plays of restoration, but they are warped and disarranged. There is the customary figure of the true heir (Britannicus)[20] but he is not a triumphant or even potentially regenerative figure, for he quickly goes mad for love, fantasizes (like many later Lee characters) of retreat to a private pastoral landscape (III. i. 87–100),[21] and is killed before Nero's fall, leaving the throne to go to the outsider Galba, with whose apotheosis the play unenthusiastically concludes: although Nero's excesses have provoked the anguished cry of 'where is Astrea fled?' (II. iii. 90), there is now no miraculous return of the goddess.[22] Rather, the heavens become inscrutable. Like other egomaniacs in Lee, Nero sees his language as more potent than that of the gods: his word is 'an Oracle' and 'Fate' (I. i. 93), and the book which orders human existence is his personal recipe book of ingenious and exquisite tortures (V. iii. 172–6). In his dying moments, however, he

---

[18] See J. M. Armistead, *Nathaniel Lee*, Twayne's English Authors Series 270 (Boston, 1979), 41.

[19] John Miller, *Charles II* (London, 1991), 219.

[20] Britannicus was the son of Claudius, Nero his adopted son and heir.

[21] The relationship between the heroic and the pastoral is discussed throughout Eric Rothstein's important *Restoration Tragedy: Form and the Process of Change* (Madison, 1967).

[22] See David Scott Kastan, 'Nero and the Politics of Nathaniel Lee', *Papers on Language and Literature*, 13 (1977), 125–35 (p. 132). The political dissidence of Lee's plays was first recognized in Frances Barbour, 'The Unconventional Heroic Plays of Nathaniel Lee', *University of Texas Studies in English*, 20 (1940), 109–16.

does hear the language of the gods, for when he challenges them to thunder they at once respond, posthumously vindicating the suffering innocents who have demanded divine thunder, but have not lived to hear it.[23] 'If there be Gods,' Nero exclaims, 'sure this must be their voice' (V. iii. 231). But the voice of the gods is an inarticulate noise that requires human interpretation, and its only interpreter is Nero, who quickly concludes that his death is ennobled by divine participation. It is reasonable to assume that Nero is ignoring the obvious message of the thunder, and an articulate supernatural sphere is evidenced in the appearance of two ghosts (IV. iii. 55b; IV. iv. 0), but in later works Lee was to draw out the potential for ambiguity in incidents like that of the thunderclap: the voice of the gods remains inarticulate, but the status of the human interpretation becomes harder to establish. The voice of the gods is also muted in *Piso's Conspiracy* (Duke's, *c.* August 1675), an anonymously pruned version of the *Nero* of 1624 prompted by the success of Lee's play. For, whereas the original concludes with the exhortation 'People depart, and say there is a God' (V. iii. 153), the revision merely subdivides categories of human agency: 'Tyrants by Conquest have their Fall Decreed; | But Traitours should by Execution Bleed' (V, p. 55).

Nero made no use of Racine's *Britannicus*, the first sign of Racine's influence coming in John Crowne's *Andromache* (Duke's, August 1674). Crowne claims simply to have turned into prose the verse translation of a young gentleman, and writes slightingly of Racine's play, claiming that English taste has matured since the 'times, when the *Cid*[,] *Heraclius*, and other *French Playes* met such applause' (sig. [A3]). The chief alterations are mechanical: the breaking up of long speeches, and the staging of Pyrrhus' murder (merely narrated in Racine). The 'parricide' of the original (V. iii. 1534) becomes, still topically, 'regicide' (V, p. 44), and Andromache leaves at the end for a life of wandering exile. In these minor details, we see traces of the great concerns of the early Restoration: the killing of the King, the descent into the wilderness. But they are here merely instinctive tics.

By contrast, Henry Neville Payne's *The Siege of Constantinople* (Duke's, by November 1674) is brimming with detailed topicality, and is the first of many tragedies to respond specifically to the crises that threatened the monarchy in the years following James's public declaration of his Catholicism.[24] A villainous Chancellor (Shaftesbury) undermines a weak king's faith in his loyal brother, and promotes a disastrous war in which he secretly favours the enemy. False allies (Rome in the play, France in actuality) treacherously withhold promised aid, and a foreign general (Justiniano, Schomberg) is called in to no purpose. The play is a *Conquest of Granada* in reverse, with a Christian outpost falling to Islam, its king killed, his brother turned into the client ruler of a foreign, if benevolent, despotism. There is also an equivalent to Almanzor,

---

[23] II. iii. 126; V. i. 15–21. Piso also appeals to thunder in V. iii. 74–5.
[24] See Love, 'State Affairs on the Restoration Stage', 6–8.

the ranting Justiniano, though he is a mere *miles gloriosus*, not a disturbing image of the incompleteness of civilization.

What does vitiate civilization is the imperfection of knowledge. 'By strength of Argument & Reason' (I, p. 1) the Council embarks upon a disastrous war, the populace entertain restless doubt (a recurrent word) about the Emperor's intentions, the Emperor is deceived into thinking his brother Thomazo disloyal (the treason being, according to a villainous Cardinal, 'too evident for any doubt', V, p. 79), and Thomazo himself falls into total scepticism, hurling away a book of philosophy with the exclamation 'Rank mist of words be gone; there's nothing true' (IV, p. 65). Language and the book are divested of authority, revealing man's confused isolation in an enigmatic world.[25] Clear monarchic authority is thus a necessary counterbalance to the obscurities of knowledge, and there is no association of authority with a particular system of belief, for the Turkish Sultan proves to be a better ruler than the Christian Emperor. It is he who executes the treacherous Chancellor (impaled in full view, like Settle's Crimalhaz), demonstrating that 'Severity, not Mercy, strengthens power' (V, p. 87).

But, if power creates certainty in the midst of ambiguity, the ambiguity itself remains. The imperfection of the sign is embodied in Mutantrope, initially a counterfeit and finally a genuine mute, whose condition the reticent heroine Irene explicitly compares to her own ('My Love, like *Mutantrope*, your Highness Boy, | Does now and then make signs, but cannot speak', I, p. 10). This reticence leads to a particularly striking failure of woman to control the posthumous narrative of her life, which perhaps justifies Thomazo's gesture in throwing away the book. Because of her diffidence, Irene becomes confused with Calista, the Chancellor's daughter, who under the name of Irene becomes the Sultan's mistress, and is subsequently executed by him to demonstrate his superiority to passion. In the original form of this famous story, retained in Johnson's tragedy, Irene herself had been the executed mistress. It had already been used, in tactful admonition of the King's sex-life, in the anonymous *Irena* (1664), where the heroine is similarly kept alive through the execution of a substitute. But in his contemptuous 'Satire' of Charles II (1677), John Lacy was directly and abusively to commend the example of Irene's execution.[26] Payne is perhaps also admonishing a pleasure-loving king, but he also uses the story to emphasize that, like Eugenia in *The Fatal Jealousie*, Irene cannot fix her own story. She finds happiness with Thomazo, but at the price of eternal historical opprobrium.

Elkanah Settle's *Love and Revenge* (Duke's, by November 1674), based upon William Heming's *The Fatal Contract*, also portrays quarrelling royal

[25] The pessimistic scepticism of the play is discussed in Gerald D. Parker, ' "History as Nightmare" in Nevil Payne's *The Siege of Constantinople* and Nathaniel Lee's *Lucius Junius Brutus*', *Papers on Language and Literature*, 21 (1985), 3–18.

[26] *Poems on Affairs of State: Augustan Satirical Verse, 1660–1714*, gen. ed. George deF. Lord (7 vols., New Haven and London, 1963–75), i (1963), 428.

brothers, but here the younger (Lewis) is genuinely disloyal, leading a successful rebellion against the violent and lecherous Clotair, who has attempted both to kill him and to rape his beloved Aphelia. Once again, the intrinsic incoherence of the family represents that of the state, and once again (as in *The Empress of Morocco*) a lustful queen murders her husband and plots against her offspring. The central element in the plot, however, is the vengeance of another victim of Clotair's lust, the raped Chlotilda. The rape makes Clotair another of Settle's criminal kings, and he is in addition wildly unstable in the execution of justice, rapidly changing his mind about his decrees and blaming his subordinates for executing them. Institutional justice thus loses all meaning and consistency, and the victims of power repeatedly desire justice of other kinds. As Aphelia's brother argues,

> the Laws
> Of Friendship and of Nature ought to be
> Obey'd before th'unjust commands of Kings. . . .
> The serving of my Friend
> And Sister then, is a design so just,
> That all the Cheats I use, and shapes I take,
> Are pardon'd for their glorious cause sake:
> Moved by the tyes of Friendship and of Blood,
> The means are lawful where the end's so good.

> (IV, p. 56)

But the problem (half-grasped, as usual) is whether justice has any significance when its only criterion is the individualistic resentment of the injured. Is there any real distinction between justice and vengeance? Increasingly, Settle's plays in this period suggest that there is not. At the end of the play, Lewis regrets deposing a 'guiltless' brother, but tells Chlotilda that her 'Rage was just', and resolves henceforth to be 'just' himself (v, p. '73' [83]). Yet the guiltless Clotair was a tyrannical rapist, the new, just, ruler is both usurper and hereditary king, and in her just rage Chlotilda has assisted not only in the deposition of Clotair but in the murder of the old king, and in addition has plotted (unsuccessfully) the rape and murder of Aphelia.[27] Justice in Settle never transcends the Hobbesian battle of warring individualists, and in this respect he reflected half-passively concerns which were more deliberately and expertly developed by his contemporaries.

These problems are more fully examined in Settle's next play, *The Conquest of China by the Tartars* (Duke's, by May 1675), where authority and justice again prove bewilderingly mutable. At the beginning of the play, King Theinmingus of Tartary is invading China to avenge the death of his father in battle, rather unwillingly assisted by his son Zungteus. By the final act, there has been a total change of crowns: the King of China has been deposed by a

---

[27] Settle alters his source, where Aphelia dies through Chrotilda's (*sic*) Iago-like plotting.

usurper, and Zungteus, who now rules Tartary, joins forces with a virtuous Chinese prince to depose the usurper, so that Settle again shows a throne passing to an outsider whose only claim is merit. Amidst all the changes of kingship, definitions of justice proliferate in a virtual Babel; but one constant element is that justice and revenge are synonymous. For Theinmingus, resentful of his father's death, 'Imperial Heads in Blood, and Thrones in Dust, | Are th'only Vengeance that can make Me just' (I, p. 2), and his son's friend Palexus soon afterwards confirms that 'Revenge and Justice' demand the ruin of China (I, p. 6). But, since Settle does not specify the circumstances of the father's death, we cannot arbitrate between Theinmingus' vision of justice and that of the Chinese heroine Amavanga, who 'justifies' the killing (I, p. 3), or of the exemplary Chinese hero Quitazo, who prays for his King's 'just cause' (III, p. 35). Zungteus, Theinmingus' son, is himself troubled about the 'injustice' (I, p. 7) of his father's cause, but only because he spent his youth in China, loves Amavanga, and regrets that these original loyalties should be overridden by 'a Turn of State' (I, p. 6). Political ideals are capricious and transitory, and individual claims alone have substance. The patterns of justice are complicated yet again in the fifth act, when each of the opposing nations has a new king. Theinmingus dies, leaving his throne to Zungteus, the King of China is deposed by the villainous Lycungus, who promptly affronts justice by burning sixteen thousand legal scholars (V, p. 58), and the Chinese hero Quitazo therefore joins the Tartars in a 'just' (V, p. 56) campaign against the usurper.

But, if the usurper's slaughter of the legal scholars mocks codified justice, the system he destroys has not emerged with much credit. Earlier in the play, Quitazo is selected by the King to marry his daughter Orunda (and, consequently, become his heir). By established law, refusal is punishable by death, but Quitazo remains faithful to his beloved Alcinda, and Orunda consequently demands 'Justice' and her 'just right' (III, p. 28) from a father who is only too eager to oblige:

> I'le punish his Affront on his whole Race,
> And from Man-kind his hated Name deface.
> *Alcinda*'s Blood first Expiates her sin . . .
> And to confirm my Rage, I'le pluck out all
> Their Eyes, that shed a Tear to see her fall.
>
> (III, p. 28)

Orunda, more modestly, desires only the 'Revenge and Justice' of Alcinda's death, and persuades the King to delegate his 'Justice' to her (III, p. 29), though it is characteristic of Settle's habitual complication of judicial roles that the Princess should then pursue her justice through the agency of hired criminals, and that she herself should accidentally become their victim. In this strand of the action, vengefulness appears at its ugliest, even though, more than anywhere else, it is allied to formalized law. But, if Orunda's murderous jealousy is marked by the call for 'Revenge and Justice', the very same words vindicate the Tartars' heroic campaign against China (I, p. 6), itself distinguished by spectacular images of violence: 'We burn down Citys till we melt our Way' (I, p. 2). Heroic and base aims are justified with identical terminology and pursued with similar violence. They are all, indeed, pursued with the hand. The vengeful Orunda and lawless Lycungus alike rely on the violent hand (e.g. III, pp. 33–4), and for Amavanga China feels 'an Invaders hand' (I, p. 2); but, for Theinmingus, it feels 'the hand of Justice' (I, p. 4). Though the causes in the play demand to be interpreted and judged with reference to absolutes which transcend the imperatives of individual desire, Settle does not provide them.

Settle's plays frequently dwell on arbitrary, extreme, and meaningless suffering. Overcome by Lycungus, the King of China chooses suicide and commands his wives to do likewise, but the earthly embodiment of justice again proves capricious and tragically inadequate, for—too late—he changes his mind: '*The Scene opens, and is discovered a Number of Murdred Women, some with Daggers in their Breasts, some thrust through with Swords, some strangled, and others Poyson'd; with several other Forms of Death*' (V, p. 60). 'Then their own Murder each bold *hand* performs', adds a witness (V, p. 61; italics added). Scorning 'to fall by a Traitor's Hand,' and confident in Lycungus' ultimate downfall, the King and his entourage fall on their swords, and—in Settle's most aphoristic expression of comprehensive violence—'*Dy Omnes*' (V, p. 61). The King's belief in Lycungus' imminent punishment is belief in Providence, but a Providence shaped by the human will and executed by the human hand:

> I'le Conjure the Higher Pow'rs,
> And choose the Gods for my Executors,
> To see the true Performance of my Will,
> And by [Zungteus'] *Arm* my Just Revenge fulfill.

> ⟨V, p. 61; italics added⟩

Manual action is again the one consistent element in a world of fluctuating principle, since the hand that is to execute the King's 'Just Revenge' had earlier inflicted justice and vengeance *on* him and his subjects. Settle's sensational tableaux, such as that of the slaughtered women with their '*several*' forms of death, are appropriate climaxes to plays which reduce the various categories of life to inexpertly distinguished varieties of violence. As Orunda says to Quitazo, 'If killing is such an Heroick part . . . | Then Plagues and Famines have more worth than you' (II, p. 17).

Similar sentiments pervade Nathaniel Lee's first study of clashing empires, *Sophonisba; or, Hannibal's Overthrow* (King's, April 1675). King Massinissa is particularly afflicted by anti-heroic doubt, asking 'What are we, but the Murd'rers of the Field?' (I. i. 137) and 'What real pleasure can it be to kill?'

(I. i. 314), and it is notable that the vocabulary of heroism is now explicitly the vocabulary of power and domination: although honour remains an import-ant term, ambition and empire gain a new prominence. Throughout the play, Lee reveals an irreconcilable and intolerable conflict between the demands of public life and the needs of the private self: the tragic counterpart to the con-flict between instinct and social existence in contemporary sex comedy. Massinissa has given his nephew Massina a childhood similar to Almanzor's, inuring him to war in the desert and keeping him from the sight of female beauty. Yet, as soon as he sees the beautiful Rosalinda (Hannibal's mistress), he falls into a desperate infatuation which quickly drives him to suicide. Almanzor's eventual reconciliation of love and heroism is now impossible: the disciplines of empire have been unable to quench the natural impulses of individual life, but no accommodation between them can be found. Although Scipio conquers his own love for Rosalinda, the conquest of passion turns him into not a stoic sage but an imaginatively crippled semi-human, for he refuses Hannibal's reasonable peace terms, and the portrayal of his ensuing victory invites us to apply criteria remote from those of heroic machismo. Rosalinda, assuming male garb in order to enter the alien world of glory, is promptly and ingloriously destroyed in an anonymous skirmish. In the aftermath of victory, Scipio drives Massinissa and his beloved Sophonisba to suicide, believing Massinissa's love to be incompatible with the demands of masculinity and empire. Then, in his last speech, he belatedly recognizes the hollowness of the ideals to which he has devoted himself and sacrificed others.

The march of imperial destiny is relentless and oppressive, and there is no visible guiding principle in history. Though Lee habitually used the new scenic resources to portray omens and other spectacular expressions of divine will, the omens declare catastrophe, not justice, and become increasingly ambigu-ous, showing that communication between earth and heaven is tenuous and uncertain. *Sophonisba* contains 'a Heaven of blood, two Suns, Spirits in Battle, Arrows shot to and fro in the Air: Cryes of yielding Persons, &c. Cryes of Carthage is fal'n, Carthage, &c' (II. ii. 87b), where the chaos and inarticu-late clamour of battle are transferred to heaven itself. Later a prophetess gives Hannibal an ambiguous prophecy, seemingly of victory but actually of defeat (IV. i. 60–81). She does, however, clearly foretell the death of Rosalinda, though clarity is significantly associated with the suspension of language, for the prophecy is conveyed through a worldless vision (IV. i. 132b-c). Like many Lee characters, Hannibal wishes to supplant the language of the gods with that of man: 'We'l drown the talking Gods with our last cry, | And Earth shall thunder back upon the sky' (II. ii. 105–6). He fails, but nobility lies with the divided and suffering mortals, and the celestial regime against which he ex-claims never emerges as a source of coherence and meaning.[28]

<hr />

[28] The indifference of the gods is discussed in Peter N. Skrine, 'Blood, Bombast, and Deaf Gods: The Tragedies of Lee and Lohenstein', *German Life and Letters*, 24 (1971), 14–30.

A great deal of ink has been spilt on the supposed discrepancy between the cynical libertinism of Restoration comedy and the exalted idealism of the heroic play. But, in fact, there is no exalted idealism in tragedy of the early 1670s; instead, tragedy antedates comedy in its deep scepticism about the codes and power structures of civilization, with comedy only catching up in 1675. The confluence of comedy and tragedy in this year is to some extent acknowledged in Shadwell's Don Juan play, *The Libertine* (Duke's, May–June 1675), which appeared six months after the première of *The Country-Wife*, and explores the destructive potential of the rake, expressing Shadwell's continuing concern with the debasement of gentility. Profiting all the time from their gentlemanly rank, Don John and his two friends commit seduction, rape, incest, robbery, murder, and parricide, morally overshadowed by the humble peasants who rescue or champion their victims. The rakes are also enemies of justice, here portrayed as an unambiguous norm of order: Don John has 'Laugh'd at old feeble Judges, and weak Laws' (I, p. 25), and one of his nastiest acts is to betray a magistrate (Francisco) who has given him shelter after a shipwreck, seducing his benefactor's daughters and then killing him, thus combining the violation of justice with that of hospitality, Shadwell's favourite social virtue.

Shadwell's unfashionable confidence in the existence of palpable and uncomplicated social norms is illustrated in his handling of the bedroom trick. Otway and Wycherley were to exploit the silence that is almost inevitably associated with this deception in order to portray an insoluble tension between human rationality and sexuality: the bout of speechless sensuality represents a brief, unsustainable flight from articulate social consciousness into bestial oblivion, each a permanent part of human nature, yet each irreconcilable with the other. But, when Don John commits rape by means of the bedroom trick, he does not abandon speech, and Shadwell portrays not a flight from signification but a simple perversion of it: much stress is laid on Don John's need to discover 'the Sign' (I, pp. 33–4) which gains admittance, and when this is discovered he kills his rival and assumes his name and clothes. The bedroom trick confirms that Don John simply negates all the forms that bind individuals into communities: both the forms that differentiate (clothes) and those that unite (words). Indeed, he perpetually delights in obliterating the distinctions that uphold and express civilized values, killing his father and committing a rape upon his tomb: 'All times and places are alike to him,' his servant Jacomo says (I, p. 29).

Shadwell had reworked the Dryden–Davenant *Tempest* as a semi-opera, and his intellectual engagement with the play appears in his reworking of the standard situation of the rakes' shipwreck. As usual, Don John is cast ashore not on a mysterious, remote island but in his native land, but this substitution of the familiar for the alien enables Shadwell to amplify the implication of the first Restoration *Tempest*, that the alien and the monstrous are everywhere endemic in civilization: John and his friends are 'Monsters of the Land' (III, p. 59),[29] the raped Maria laments that 'More savage cruelty reigns in Cities, | Than ever yet in Desarts' (II, p. 48), and the shipwrecked John enters Francisco's hospitable household as a 'Stranger' (III, p. 63) and proceeds to destroy it. The Shakespearian virtue of compassion appears in the hermit who first assists the travellers, and who contemplates their ship with a pity like Miranda's (III, p. 53), reversing the indifference of the Lucretian spectator, and rising above the libertines' selfish appetitiveness. But the compassion proves disastrously misplaced, and on the whole Shadwell portrays a world more susceptible to the methods of the Restoration Prospero than of Shakespeare's; for human capacity for shared moral experience is palpably limited. Shadwell plainly rejects the relativistic juxtaposition of conflicting codes favoured by Etherege and Dryden, but his characters are nevertheless as confined in little cells as theirs are, and indeed the Hermit, who has lived in the same cave for forty years (III, p. 53), is a prime example of such confinement. After the libertines have left him and gone to enjoy the unfortunate Francisco's hospitality, the Hermit rescues two of Don John's pursuing victims, Maria and Leonora, who tell him of their seducer's crimes. Leonora is bound by the 'Chains' (III, p. 58) of passion, but the Hermit is also constricted by his way of life, '*bound* in charity' to help the distressed (III, p. 54; italics added), but also unable to leave the 'small bounds' (III, p. 58) of his cell even to warn Francisco, who consequently learns too late of the danger to his family. Francisco's daughters fall for Don John because they have grown 'wild by confinement' (III, p. 59); and, sadder and wiser, they opt for confinement again, this time in a nunnery. And when, at the end of the play, Don John and his friends sink unmoved into the confinement of the abyss, their calm proceeds not from defiant courage but from the sheer inability to escape their natures. It is necessary for the community to repress the libertines' anarchy, instead of investing them with the impunity of rank. But, while Shadwell differs from his leading contemporaries in affirming an unambiguous set of social rules, the individuals whom they govern are very deficient in their capacity for moral choice or shared moral purpose.

Thomas Otway's first play, *Alcibiades* (Duke's, September 1675), stays far more within established fashions, using a heroic subject to highlight the tension between individualistic aspiration and social order. At the beginning of the play Alcibiades desecrates a statue of Zeus, flees from his native Athens to the enemy state of Sparta, and in the process deserts his mistress, Timandra, who deplores his broken 'Faith' and 'Truth' (I. 19). Thereafter, however, he conducts himself admirably, doing wonders in battle, forming an exemplary friendship with the Spartan hero Patroclus, refusing to betray the King by sleeping with his beautiful and lustful wife, Deidamia, and continuing to love

---

[29] Cf. II, p. 51; III, p. 66.

Timandra—who has followed him into exile—with an exalted rapture. His only miscalculation is courteously to imply to the Queen—with predictable results—that he would love her if Timandra and the King were out of the way. Otherwise, he is as punctilious in love, loyalty, and friendship as an Orrery hero. But all the loyalty and friendship are displayed on the wrong side: values that integrate Orrery's heroes with their native community are here detached from the social setting that originally gave them meaning.

The uprootedness of Alcibiades reflects a general failure of the systems that traditionally express and sustain man's social character. Images of displacement permeate the play. The Queen desires to be 'Free as the Ayr, and boundless as the Wind' (II. 186), and the villainous favourite Tissaphernes broods on his rootless youth ('no dwelling but a Tent', I. 274). The virtuous Patroclus also experiences displacement, becoming increasingly alienated from an evil father (Tissaphernes) with whom he has no bond of nature or culture. Even when he becomes king, the demands of the personal and the public remain irreconcilable, for (in another displacement) his beloved Draxilla has wandered without trace into exile, and Patroclus has to send subordinates in search of her, being prevented by the responsibilities of office from seeking his own loved one. The main elements of Otway's later plays—the displaced protagonist, the collapsing family, the decaying community—dominate his work from the outset.

Otway's first, clumsy, experiment in the heroic play was soon followed by Dryden's last essay in the genre, *Aureng-Zebe* (King's, November 1675), written almost five years after *The Conquest of Granada*. Unsurprisingly, he took few hints from his younger contemporaries, for Otway and Lee had yet to find their voices and Settle was beneath imitation. As he revealed in his prologue, his preferred model was now Shakespeare, but he could not yet move from paralysed awe to creative absorption. As in *The Conquest of Granada*, he pits brother against brother in civil conflict, but it is a sign of the times that the context of the conflict is no longer sectarian strife but a disputed succession. Although he preserves the patriarchal line, he dispenses with primogeniture, showing the crown passing to the worthiest son, the temperate Aureng-Zebe, rather than to the eldest, the noble but unforgiving Darah, or the valiant Sujah, disabled by bigoted adherence to a foreign creed, and reliance on foreign aid. This is not the Dryden of *Absalom and Achitophel*.[30]

When the Crisis came, Dryden opted for primogeniture and Darah–Sujah, and he is here concerned far less with specific political issues than with the philosophical problems that beset the maintenance of civilization: with the isolation imposed on humanity by the very nature of desire and perception, and the consequent fragility of social units. Yet again we see the essential

---

[30] The play was, however, dedicated to the Yorkist Earl of Mulgrave (Winn, *John Dryden and his World*, 254), and, when *The State of Innocence* was published in 1677, it was dedicated to the Duchess of York.

incoherence of the family, for the royal family of India is comprehensively divided by sexual rivalry and the lust for power, three of the Emperor's four sons being in rebellion against him. The Emperor himself falls in love with Indamora, the fiancée of his only loyal son, Aureng-Zebe, who is consequently imprisoned, and displaced in the succession by his younger half-brother Morat, who promptly falls for Indamora himself. Torn between love for Indamora and loyalty to his father, Aureng-Zebe experiences a conflict between social duty and personal desire that he can never internally resolve—resolution only coming when the Emperor repents—and he never equals the socially perfect paragons of early Restoration drama. The courtier Arimant concedes that Aureng-Zebe is ambitious and that, since younger brothers were normally executed after the new king's accession, it is in his interest to gain the succession through loyalty. Aureng-Zebe himself repeatedly confirms Arimant's assessment, combining ostentatious public gestures of magnanimity with complex private calculation of the benefit they will bring him: for example, he resonantly discourages his soldiers from rebelling in his support, only to opine in an aside that his ends can be gained without rebellion (II. 21–30). In his dealings with others, however, and particularly with Indamora, he inflexibly demands unyielding heroic principle, outraged by her decision to save his life by playing upon Morat's affections, by her fear of death, and by the emotional involvement which, in the belief that Aureng-Zebe is dead, she develops with the dying and partially penitent Morat.

Both the survival and ultimate union of Indamora and Aureng-Zebe proceed from her violations of his code: a code that does not even adequately represent the true range of his own aims and motives. Once again, the theoretical disciplines of civilization fail to match the vagaries of human nature, and once again the failure is imaged in a failure of judicial process: the two scenes in which Aureng-Zebe berates Indamora become impromptu trials, full of the language of guilt, crime, and innocence, and although she is in each case pronounced not guilty, the verdict is never reached by rational apprehension of her nature, for in each case the hero drops his accusations not because they are disproved but because Indamora wrong-foots him by ending their betrothal. Mental processes are fundamentally capricious, influenced (as in Montaigne) by incongruous causes, and external objects can never be directly comprehended in their essence. Here Dryden demonstrates with particular clarity what is so often affirmed in drama of this period: that the determination of guilt and innocence, so fundamental to the ritual ordering of community, is a process that can never penetrate into the nature of the individual under examination.

Community is thus unstable not only because of the unruliness of individual appetite but because the individual is a prisoner of the mind, perceiving the world only through mental phantasms which bear no verifiable equivalence to the objects themselves. Most characters become trapped in

Cartesian problems, without finding Cartesian solutions: problems of verifying the existence of the world outside the mind, and of establishing that other human beings also possess a soul and consciousness, instead of being unthinking automata. For Descartes, the answer to the latter problem was that automata could not use articulate language, and his solution had been elaborated in Géraud de Cordemoy's *Discours physique de la parole* (1668), the English translation of which had been bought and praised by Pepys.[31] But this solution does not impress the Empress Nourmahal, who suggests that the Emperor 'onely mov'd, and talk'd, but did not live' (V. 294), and the characters in general repeatedly view the self as centre of the universe and others as possessing a shadowy half-existence. Nourmahal sees Indamora as an empty replica of her own self (V. 280–5), and Aureng-Zebe dismisses Morat as a human form inhabited by a brute soul (III. 304–9), later similarly denouncing Indamora as 'Adorn'd, without; unfinish'd left, within' (IV. 492). Almost all the major characters doubt the independent reality of beings outside the mind, and none attains a satisfactory criterion whereby to settle his doubts, even Aureng-Zebe's renewed faith in Indamora being an unreasoned consequence of a change in the balance of power between them.

Isolated within their mental phantasms, characters are isolated also within the words that represent those phantasms.[32] Words become confused with things, the sign eclipsing an object whose essence is perpetually closed to inspection: Indamora 'printed kisses' on Aureng-Zebe's name (IV. 403); and, when Aureng-Zebe accuses her of infidelity with Morat, he asserts that his very repetition of Morat's name will give her a kind of aural orgasm (IV. 426–32). The characters' isolation within language has a further implication, which was more fully developed in Dryden's later plays, and which indeed had already been extensively explored in Wycherley's *The Country-Wife* (January 1675): that to categorize life in terms of simple polarities such as guilt and innocence is to seek in it pure symmetries to which language naturally tends but which are alien to the tangled nature of experience. Aureng-Zebe's fixation on determining Indamora's innocence or guilt is part of a more widespread failure to distinguish the patterns of language from those of life. Other plays will extend the list of seductive antitheses: truth and falsity, king and usurper, man and woman.

The only other Restoration tragedian so far to have matched Dryden's interest in epistemological enigma was Payne, though Otway and Crowne were to follow him in their mature tragedies, and Wycherley had shown similar preoccupations from his earliest comedy. But in other respects *Aureng-Zebe* addresses problems of widespread concern. For example, Nathaniel

---

[31] [Louis Géraud de Cordemoy], *A Philosophicall Discourse concerning Speech* (London, 1668), 11–20; Pepys, 6 Dec. 1668.

[32] 'Spoken words are the symbols of mental experience' (Aristotle, *De Interpretatione*, tr. E. M. Edghill, 16a, in *The Works of Aristotle*, ed. J. A. Smith and W. D. Ross (12 vols., Oxford, 1908–52), i).

Lee's *Gloriana; or, The Court of Augustus Caesar* (King's, January 1676) also portrays a divided royal family and focuses on disputes about inherited power. Early in the play, Augustus renounces his daughter Julia as a 'Stranger to my blood' (I. i. 161) and curses the tomb of her mother, Scribonia. Caesario, illegitimate son of Julius Caesar (by Cleopatra), vies for power with Augustus, Caesar's adopted son ('I am by birth what you adopted are', IV. i. 217), asserting that Caesar would have written a different will had he known the qualities of his natural son. Heredity is here not a fixed and clear criterion of succession, but one that is arbitrary, contingent, and speculative, and it is repeatedly stressed that Augustus is a cruel and lustful despot, with neither the moral nor the military qualities of a great ruler. He is regularly compared to a beast of prey and, disgusted by the adultery of Julia and Ovid, actually wishes he could be reincarnated as a lion to rule the nobler and simpler world of the beasts (II. i. 369–73). The hierarchies of empire are essentially those of the jungle, and Caesario deplores the absence of providential rationale from the political order:

> Heav'n that can see such Vertue in distress,
> And with exceeding power a Tyrant bless . . .
> Heav'n that allows this parricide a name
> As great and good as the first Sons of Fame.

> (IV. i. 187–92)

But Caesario is scarcely developed as an ideal alternative to Augustus. Both men have illusions of divinity, Caesario believing himself immortal (II. i. 12), Augustus promising to raise the dead (V. i. 108); and Caesario (despite his Almanzor-like bluster and war record) is an erratic blunderer whose foolish mistrust of his beloved Gloriana frustrates her plan to assassinate Augustus and drives her to suicide.

Gloriana (Pompey's daughter) is another offspring of the great, her longing for the lost might of her race accentuated by the disabilities of her sex: she wishes that she too could command 'mighty men' (III. ii. 47). But, being a woman, she is nearly raped by Augustus, and is destroyed by the jealousy of the man she loves. The problems of female descendants of the great are equally emphasized in the portrayal of Augustus' notorious daughter Julia. Lee's would-be rapist is in no position to condemn the lapses of his daughter, who indeed presents a female version of his own characteristics, 'being boundless born, and mark'd for sway' (I. i. 97). But Augustus fails to see the point, concluding simply that she is 'all o're woman' (I. i. 192), while her husband Marcellus wonders what could so 'unman' Augustus as to make him beget such a child (II. i. 236). When Julia eventually reforms, she also—in a significant correlation—dissociates herself from her father's tyranny.

Perhaps the most striking expression of Julia's early unruliness comes in an incident narrated by Tiberius, when she stole thunder and lightning from a statue of Jupiter and brandished the thunder in the god's face (II. i. 242–7). She covets the language of the gods, though, as so often in Lee, divine language is filtered through human mediation: the thunder is mere mimicry and artefact. Nero and Hannibal had also desired to master divine utterance, the latter capping his threat to 'drown the talking Gods' by boasting that 'Earth shall thunder back upon the sky' (II. ii. 105–6), and here a woman trespasses upon the aspirations of the male overreachers. But thundering remains the privilege of the male. Reflecting on Caesar's dalliance with Cleopatra, Augustus declares, in a speech of agreeable absurdity,

> 'Twas God-like, and he imitated Jove,
> Who with excessive thundring tir'd above,
> Comes down for ease, enjoys a Nymph, and then
> Mounts dreadful and to thundring goes again.
>
> (IV. i. 248–51)

In both the cosmic and mundane spheres, women are a recuperative diversion from the male mission of deafening the world with thunder. For the men, the association of women and thunder is monstrous: when Caesario accuses Gloriana of falsity, he accuses her of having 'a heart compos'd of Thunder' (V. ii. 40).

Desire for thunder is desire for linguistic power. We do not see Julia's theft of the thunderbolt, but shortly after it is narrated she enters, provocatively engaged in a shared act of reading with Ovid, and comparing his poetic style with Virgil's. Reading and writing become the manifestations of the sexual and social presumption for which Julia and Ovid are respectively condemned, for this literary discussion brings about Ovid's banishment, and is the only direct glimpse of their relationship, evidence of Julia's sexual excesses coming solely from the rather suspect Tiberius. It is a sign of Julia's failure to acquire the words of power that she is yet another tragic heroine whose tale is never narrated: a victim of history, like Payne's Irene. 'Vainly her thoughts they guess by outward form,' says Mecenas (I. i. 99), and Julia herself tells Marcellus, her husband, that 'What I have done | Shall to no mortal, not to you be known' (IV. i. 48–9). Although she reads on equal terms with a great poet, she is treated by her husband as a mere passive text:

> Disgrace so bold is grav'd upon thy brow,
> That ev'n old age, whose eyes are seldom clear,
> Dim with death's mist, can read thy falshood there.
>
> (IV. i. 2–4)

Indeed, right at the beginning of the play Augustus assumes the power to control the significance of Julia's name—'Of all great evil Julia be the name' (I. i. 89)—and he speaks with the voice of posterity far more than Julia does when she scorns 'the awfull puff of Caesar's name' (I. i. 188). For, as Caesario says,

Julius Caesar's name is inscribed in golden letters 'in Fate's Book' (II. i. 136). In general, men battle for linguistic power while women remain linguistically vulnerable, their vulnerability being especially illustrated in Marcellus' sister Narcissa, 'highly born, yet educated low' (V. i. 157).

The woman's linguistic exclusion reflects a wider subordination of language to power. For the writer, too, is vulnerable. Augustus is the murderer of Cicero (III. ii. 74–6) and banisher of Ovid (II. i. 349), and the first incident in the play is of Augustus hearing a song by Ovid and the praises of his subordinates and then silencing them: 'Ye must not speak since I can hear no more' (I. i. 45). There is, however, one point at which Ovid asserts his own claims. Caught reading with Julia, he reveals the professional's sense of his own worth by physically defending himself against Marcellus, the poet (in a politically telling gesture) assuming the right of self-defence against the heir presumptive to the crown (II. i. 315–16). Indignant, Caesario—the conventional warrior-hero—crudely asserts the inferiority of the writer to the soldier: 'in Fields we should our Standards raise, | And make this Writer but our drudge to praise' (II. i. 324–5). Caesario elsewhere shows a violent mistrust of language (he later repudiates vows as 'Smoak' and 'air', III. i. 20), and his arrogant outburst here invites dissent, opening the old question of how far the glory of the deed derives from the doer and how far from the writer who records it: 'Non fu sì santo né benigno Augusto | come la tuba di Virgilio suona.'[33] The question is sustained in Ovid's farewell speech. In a complex demonstration of the relationship between the panegyrist/satirist and the political system he serves, Ovid departs for exile asserting his loyalty to the tyrant who is banishing him and dedicating both sword and pen to the battle against Augustus' enemies (II. i. 359–63). In *Alcibiades* Otway had dealt with the displaced, exiled hero. Lee here deals with the displaced, exiled poet, the servant of a system where others control language and wield the thunderbolt.

The place of the woman in the heroic world is also considered in Thomas Durfey's first play, the absurdly bombastic *The Siege of Memphis* (King's, c. July 1676). As in *The Empress of Morocco*, the main focus of interest is a flamboyant villainess (Zelmura), but here the villainess is allowed to challenge the masculine hierarchies of the heroic world, performing courageously in battle, killing a general who resents female competition, and inducing her husband to surrender power to her for three days, during which saturnalia she tries and executes him as a traitor. Moaron, the ranting, Almanzor-like hero, is her prisoner for most of the play, removed from the sphere of heroic action, and only able to fight against her in the final act because she has released him.

---

[33] 'Augustus was not as saintly or beneficent as the trumpet of Virgil proclaims' (Lodovico Ariosto, *Orlando Furioso* (4 vols., Milan, 1955), xxxv. 26 [vol. iii]). Ariosto observes that Augustus and Nero have different reputations because the former patronized writers and the latter persecuted them. Lee's Augustus and Nero are much the same, and both persecute writers (Nero condemning Seneca to death).

Zelmura remains a villainess, murdering her sister through sexual jealousy, but she is the tragic equivalent to those many women of spirit who, in Durfey's comedies, asserted themselves against a culture created in man's image.

The obvious primary inspiration for Durfey's play is *The Conquest of Granada*, and this remained the most influential of Dryden's heroic plays. But two new Duke's Company tragedies from this period—Settle's *Ibrahim The Illustrious Bassa* (by March 1676) and Otway's *Don Carlos Prince of Spain* (June 1676)—are clearly indebted to *Aureng-Zebe*, both portraying a monarch engaged in sexual rivalry with his son. In *Ibrahim* Solyman falls in love with the heroine Isabella and obstructs her marriage to Ibrahim, though both are his surrogate children. 'Is Justice in a King | So strange?' (II, p. 16), he asks when first agreeing to their marriage, only to be transformed by sudden infatuation into another of Settle's criminal monarchs, seeking to circumvent an earlier vow not to kill Ibrahim. For Ibrahim, Solyman is so godlike that life itself is a privilege depending on his discretion (IV, p. 49), but Solyman himself presents a different view of the relationship between kingship and divinity, seeing power as the arbiter of right in both (III, p. 37), and Ibrahim's viewpoint is counterbalanced by that of the captive Persian Prince Ulama, who is at one point prepared to head a rebellion against Solyman. The plan is not accomplished, but neither is it condemned, and *Ibrahim* joins the significant group of mid-1670s plays that give some countenance to rebellion against a criminal ruler. Solyman reforms, but—in contrast to King Edward in Orrery's *The Black Prince*—the reforming king is not a symbol or agent of social renewal, for his folly has destroyed his court. Ibrahim and Isabella depart for exile, Solyman's Queen has committed suicide, and the play's two Orrerian noble rivals also die, isolated martyrs who fail to find a society to which their virtues are appropriate.

In Otway's *Don Carlos* King Philip has actually married his son's fiancée before the beginning of the play, and Carlos consequently faces an extreme and insoluble conflict between the demands of desire and his social duties as son and subject, which drives him into the alienation characteristic of Otway's characters: 'a stranger' to his father (IV. 463), banished by him, becoming 'a naked wanderer' bound for 'some solitary shoar' (III. 442–47). Like Alcibiades, therefore, Carlos is a hero without a society, and indeed the gap between the hero and his milieu has widened, for libertine sentiments that in *Alcibiades* were confined to the villains now occur to the most noble and principled. In *Alcibiades*, only Tissaphernes or his like could have dismissed obedience as 'a false Notion made | By Priests' (I. 14–15), but here the speaker is Carlos, who indeed later decides to join a rebellion against his father, claiming that his participation will make the cause 'just' (IV. 25). The social unassimilability of the hero is due to the indomitability of sexual desire. As Carlos greedily smothers his stepmother's hand with kisses, she at first offers Platonic love, but quickly recognizes a deep moral disorientation that parallels Carlos's sense of displacement: 'Oh whither am I run astray!' (II. 299). Their passion remains unconsummated, but the tension between desire and social prescription is intolerable. The play opens with a ceremonial court scene in which Carlos's passion prevents him from enacting the expected gestures and roles of deference, and desire weakens the language of social category and obligation: '*Father!* and *King!* both names bear mighty sence: | Yet sure there's something too in *Son*, and *Prince*' (IV. 16–17), exclaims Carlos immediately before announcing his decision to join the rebels. Later, he actually curses 'the name of *Son*,' declaring the King to be 'not my Father' but a 'Tyrant' (IV. 160–3). Nevertheless, the 'Title' of father (though not of king) dissuades him from murder (IV. 488–90).

If Carlos echoes Tissaphernes, Queen Deidamia's sexual libertinism is echoed by the King's promiscuous bastard brother, Don John, nostalgic for the primeval state when 'Each of himself was Lord' (II. 5). Yet, even before his eventual renunciation of libertinism, Don John is a just and magnanimous prince, whose virtues stand in clear contrast to his brother's destructive jealousy, and who demonstrates with particular clarity Otway's growing interest in the universal persistence in human nature of elements alien to the disciplines of community. The incorporation of libertine elements into the heroic character leads to a corresponding decrease in the importance of the villainous libertines, here represented by the aged courtier Rui-Gomez and his young, lustful wife Eboli, who conspires the Queen's death because of her own unrequited love for Carlos. Though they arouse the King's jealousy and provoke his murder of the Queen, the King has much to be jealous about, and Rui-Gomez does not have to work very hard to achieve his goal:

R. GOM. Alas! 'tis only that I saw him here.——
KING. Where? with the Queen? Yes, yes, 'tis so I'm sure.

(IV. 295–6)

Whereas Iago imposes an entirely fictitious pattern of guilt upon innocence, Rui-Gomez and his wife marginally accentuate disruptive forces that are already raging in those they would manipulate. Rui-Gomez' manipulative menace is diminished by his ridiculous ignorance of his own cuckoldom, and a climactic scheme to expose Carlos and the Queen instead exposes his own wife *in flagrante* with Don John. Indeed, he cannot keep pace with the characters' own self-destructiveness: when he poisons Carlos's bath, Carlos promptly upstages him by climbing in and slitting his own veins. Iago, the disruptive outsider, is once again redundant, for there is a destructive alien within each individual.

The royal family is also fatally divided in *Abdelazer; or, The Moor's Revenge* (Duke's, by July 1676), Aphra Behn's adaptation of *Lust's Dominion*, by Dekker, Day, and Haughton. Both source and adaptation have much in common with *The Empress of Morocco*, for once again a lustful Queen

Mother commits adultery with an ambitious villain, has her husband poisoned, conspires against her offspring, and is betrayed when her lover falls for the heroine. Behn, however, avoids Settle's problems of authority, and indeed reduces those in her source, tactfully diminishing the young King's lechery, the strong anti-Catholic satire, and the personal acrimony between the two royal brothers, though the King is still duped into thinking his brother a traitor. Conversely, the divinity of kingship is accentuated. The play is further evidence of the gathering political crisis, reflecting (in Haley's words) 'the serious attitude which people had to the succession problem well before the hysteria of the Popish Plot'.³⁴ For the play concerns the unsuccessful attempt to exclude the King's brother from the succession, because of alleged bastardy and the religious scruples it provokes: 'The giddy Rout are guided by Religion, | More than by Justice, Reason, or Allegiance' (IV, p. 68). The brother is rash but brave, a warrior of Almanzor-like prowess who does without the foreign army with which his Dekker counterpart had fought for his right. In minimizing the problems of identifying just and legitimate authority, the play moves away from recent trends in tragedy and looks forward to the simplest forms of Tory drama of the Exclusion Crisis.

What is again noticeable, however, is the decay of the imagery that had formerly supported monarchic ideology. There is not even any explicit providential agency in the restoration of the true heir, and the generalized symbolic associations which cling to the original villain (Eleazar) are removed: Behn, for example, omits the comprehensive exclusion of the stranger, the expulsion of the Moors from Spain, with which *Lust's Dominion* concludes. At the beginning of *Lust's Dominion* the villain silences music claiming that he hates 'all unity' (I. i. 2) whereas Abdelazer silences the music because he 'hates all Softness' (I, p. 9). Enmity to the cosmic principles of harmony and unity dwindles into mere personal brutishness. Moreover, although Behn characteristically emphasizes the importance of vows, she diminishes the imagery which represents Eleazar as a foe of the celestial word, such as his comparison of his prisoners to books in an infernal library (V. iii. 65–6). *Abdelazer* was roughly contemporary with *The Man of Mode*, and, although its sense of possible crisis is signally absent from Etherege's play, both plays contemplate the standing of the vow in a world where language has lost its sanctity.

³⁴ Haley, *The First Earl of Shaftesbury*, 424. Shaftesbury had published his *Letter from a Person of Quality* in 1675.

CHAPTER FOUR

'The freedoms of the present': Comedy, 1668–1676

Until the mid-1670s, tragedy was the more radical genre than comedy. Although, with hindsight, *She Would If She Could* can be seen to herald a distinctive and dominant mode of Restoration comedy, it was not well received, and successors were slow to appear. *An Evening's Love* also exercised little specific influence, though it illustrates a continuing drift away from the hierarchical outlook of *The Committee* and from Tuke's didactic celebration of human rationality. By now, indeed, intrigue plays which preserve Tuke's outlook are few and mostly of very poor quality. One Tukean fossil is John Corye's *The Generous Enemies* (King's, June 1671), but even this complicates Tuke's simple faith in the woman's dependence on the protecting male. Alvarez rescues Alleria from a fire, but she swoons and initiates a chain of misunderstandings by mistaking another man for her benefactor. The male rescuer has, however, far less authority than in Tuke, for he was contracted to another woman, who follows him in male guise, selflessly assists his love for Alleria, but ultimately gains him for herself. In Thomas Duffett's *The Spanish Rogue* (King's, *c.* March 1673) two friends are each obliged to marry the sister of the other, and each discovers that the woman he really loves is the long-lost sister of the other. Desire and duty are fully reconcilable, and civic norms are clearly affirmed: a disloyal servant is implicitly judged against the kinds of ideals of service that Sir Robert Howard had embodied in Teague, and the play ends with the purging of the community, as a murderous guardian and his accomplice are expelled from the city. And in the anonymous *The Amorous Old-woman* (King's, March 1674)[1] the entangled affections of three couples are sorted out when men virtuously redirect their affections to their first loves, though moral seriousness is not consistently maintained (the old woman of the title is seen removing her false eye, wooden leg, etc.). Another departure from Tuke is that the author shows women intervening to moderate the male enthusiasm for duelling.[2]

Epigraph: Etherege, *The Man of Mode*, I. i. 120.

[1] The play was tentatively attributed to Duffett by Langbaine (*Account of the English Dramatick Poets*, 526) but, as Milhous and Hume observe, Duffett was hardly the 'Person of Honour' specified on the title-page (Judith Milhous and Robert D. Hume, 'Attribution Problems in English Drama, 1660–1700', *Harvard Library Bulletin*, 31 (1983), 5–39 (p. 9)).

[2] See Rothstein and Kavenik, *Designs of Carolean Comedy*, 168.

It is noticeable that all three of these plays were staged by the King's Company.

Perhaps the most striking departure from the outlook of *The Committee* came from Sir Robert Howard himself, now part of a group who, under the leadership of the Duke of Buckingham, 'made themselves' (in Clarendon's understandably hostile words) 'remarkable by opposing all Things which were proposed . . .for the King's Service'.3 They had contributed to the toppling of Clarendon (the target of Howard's *The Great Favourite*), and their other causes included a campaign for investigation of financial and naval mismanagement, opposition to the Duke of York, and toleration of Dissenters. The political alliance of Howard and Buckingham achieved literary expression when Buckingham contributed a scene to Howard's last completed play, *The Country Gentleman*. The play satirizes Sir William Coventry and his ally Sir John Duncombe under the names of Sir Cautious Trouble-all and Sir Gravity Empty, and Buckingham's scene mocks Sir William's pet contribution to office technology: a circular table with a hole in the middle.4 News of the scene provoked Coventry to send a challenge to Buckingham, and the play was consequently banned shortly before its scheduled performance by the King's Company in February 1669. It was assumed lost until a scribal copy was located in the 1970s by Robert D. Hume and Arthur H. Scouten.

The country gentleman of the title is Sir Richard Plainbred, a representative of the old gentlemanly values in a world where they are becoming obsolete: 'Your Countrymen scarce know theyr Landlords, and are grown too poor to care for 'em,' he complains. 'Fy upon't Trim, in former times we liv'd by one another, and now we live upon one another' (v. i. 405–8). Yet Trim himself, Sir Richard's former servant, has emerged from the paternalistic system which sustained Teague and has become an upwardly mobile barber, tricking Sir Cautious and Sir Gravity into marrying his daughters. Inverted order is everywhere to be seen. Whereas Sir Richard unfailingly desires a straightforward correspondence of word and thing, the language of London has been corrupted by 'new coin'd words',5 and is less a means of communication than a support for the pretensions of the false or degenerate gentry, whose very names suggest insubstantial sound and air: Slander, Vapor, Fart. In *The Committee*, the prime source of social dislocation had been the Days, servants who had usurped the rights of the gentry. Here, the genuine gentleman

---

3 *Life*, iii. 701.

4 Duncombe was an able Treasury Commissioner and future Chancellor of the Exchequer. Coventry, a fellow Treasury Commissioner, shared his tormentors' opposition to Clarendon (who writes about him with considerable hostility), but was on all other grounds objectionable to them: as former secretary to the Duke of York, as a naval administrator much identified with the Dutch War, and as an ally of Buckingham's great enemy, Arlington. Annabel Patterson perceptively analyses the politics of the play ('*The Country Gentleman*: Howard, Marvell, and Dryden in the Theater of Politics', *Studies in English Literature*, 25 (1985), 491–509).

5 I. i. 477–8; II. i. 8.

is an outsider in a milieu that has forgotten his values, and (in the scene provided by Buckingham) dislocation now comes not from the upstart bureaucrats of Mr Day's committee but by the two careerist servants of the Crown, spinning insanely in the middle of two circular tables, one representing England and the other the rest of the world.

London is the seat of law, and Sir Richard has (like Pinchwife in *The Country-Wife*) come to London on legal business, to see his attorney in the aftermath of his brother's death (I. i. 209–12). The attorney, however, is something of a Godot—the last reference to him is a complaint that this agent of Astraea has not turned up (V. i. 383–6)—and London is never a centre of order, the table scene providing the chief image of administrative activity. The characters therefore rely on private rituals of justice. Sir Richard's daughters are courted and won by two young country gentlemen who share his outlook, and their developing love is repeatedly represented in imagery of judicial process, as is the lovers' punishment of the fops Vapor and Slander.[6] It is these improvised games of justice that chiefly facilitate the final harmony, when Sir Richard and his newly enlarged family depart to their ancestral estates to honour the traditions of their class: 'we'l to the Countrey with our wifes; where we'l cheerfully spend what we have, and wast nothing that our Ancestors left us. . . . we'l love our King, and be true to our Countrey' (V. i. 538–43). Nine years after the Restoration, these traditional gentlemanly values of good lordship are as remote from the centre of power as they were in the Interregnum of *The Committee*.

Representations of traditional gentlemanly ideals are now very much confined to the margins. For example, the next celebration of the country estate occurs five years later in an exceedingly marginal play by another writer of noble origin: *The Triumphant Widow* (Duke's, by November 1674), which the Duke of Newcastle wrote in collaboration with Shadwell. This play gave Shadwell another opportunity to laud the social virtue of hospitality, a theme at this stage virtually confined to his work, though it later re-emerged in that of Southerne and Farquhar. Lady Haughty preserves herself from the fortune-hunting upstarts who invade her house in order to seek her hand and who (in a foreshadowing of *The Beaux Stratagem*) are paralleled with a footpad. She benevolently exercises her rank by rescuing the footpad from execution (gleefully awaited by her social inferiors) and receiving him into her household, and hierarchy is further vindicated when two gentlefolk ruined during the Rebellion recover their fortunes.

On the whole, however, the threatened traditions of gentlemanly existence are of less interest to Restoration dramatists than to their predecessors, and the once popular subject of the gentleman recovering his threatened estate or prosperity (preserved in *The Committee*) becomes peripheral until the

---

6 II. i. 509–12, 579–81; III. i. 741–2; IV. i. 237–40; V. i. 240–3, 253–78, 503–4.

1690s,7 when the morality of gentlemanly existence again starts to interest major dramatists. Plays which do deal with this subject are minor indeed: Orrery's *Guzman* (Duke's, April 1669), Elizabeth Polwhele's *The Frolicks; or, the Lawyer Cheated* (?1670–1), Edward Revet's *The Town-Shifts; or, The Suburb-Justice* (Duke's, March 1671), and *The Mock-Duellist; or, The French Vallet*, probably by Peter Bellon (King's, before May 1675). In *Guzman* three decayed Spanish gentlemen make rich marriages through a series of deceptions, including imposture as an astrologer (courtesy of Dryden) and rescue from apparent rape (courtesy of Tuke, though Tuke's celebration of benevolent machismo is again modified, since two of the brothers fake the rape attempt so that the third can appear as a heroic rescuer). In *The Town-Shifts* a further trio of impoverished gentlemen defraud a *nouveau riche* usurer's son of money and his intended bride, and in the more morally elevated *The Mock-Duellist* an errant lover is tricked into marrying the lady he has deserted, Lady Lovewealth eventually prefers poor, gentlemanly Peregrine Airy to a wealthy bumpkin, and a young heiress marries Peregrine's brother after escaping a fortune-hunter and a *senex amans*. In the two last plays the initial disruption of traditional order is emphasized by the presence of inadequate Justices, Justice Frump and Sir Amorous Frost (the *senex amans*), the latter of whom ends up as a prisoner awaiting trial by himself. There is yet another flawed Justice in *The Frolicks*, where Rightwit marries the daughter of the usurer-Justice of the Peace who threatens to foreclose on his estate, after a gay couple courtship manifestly modelled on that of Philidor and Mirida in *All Mistaken* (though the woman has a more sober sense of the dangers of surrender than Mirida does). The festive playfulness proclaimed in the title culminates in the obligatory inversion of judicial authority, when the Justice is tricked into approving the marriage of his daughter and intended victim. The other plots feature an indulgently viewed, but not explicitly consummated, wifely infidelity, and a more harshly portrayed seduction of an ingenuous virgin.8 The gentleman is also vindicated against the outsider in Orrery's second comedy, *Mr. Anthony* (Duke's, December 1669), which seems to take a hint from the banned *The Country Gentleman* of his kinsman Sir Robert Howard: two witty gentlemen win two witty ladies (Philadelphia and Isabella in both plays) at the expense of two fools, Mr Anthony and Cudden, son and nephew of the lecherous usurer Sir Timothy. Orrery, however, still gives his disrupted social order an Interregnum setting, and Sir Timothy's lechery and avarice are finally neutralized in a mock ritual of justice (the term is laboured)

---

7 The interpretation of mortgage laws was liberalized during the first quarter of the seventeenth century, 'assuring the defaulting debtor virtually automatic protection from sudden forfeiture' (Stone, *Crisis of the Aristocracy*, 527).

8 There is no evidence for a performance of this play, though it may well have been performed. See Polwhele, *The Frolicks*, ed. Milhous and Hume, 36. The play remained in manuscript until this edition.

which, remarkably, formalizes a gynocracy, Sir Timothy's neglected wife being granted 'the Soveraignty of the House' (V. 573). In this respect, like Edward Howard's two dramatizations of gynocracy in the following year, the play shows a fundamentally old-fashioned mind essaying some responsiveness to new ideas.

Plays such as these, however, are the fading reflections of older forms. If comic dramatists in the years immediately following 1668 were slow to imitate Etherege and Dryden, they were not content simply to adore the ancient glories of the gentry. What is most noticeable in the years from 1668 to 1672 is a sustained attempt at both theatres to absorb and Anglicize Molière. The series of close Molière adaptations is suddenly suspended in late 1672, when the movement towards a sex comedy of contemporary English life received new impetus from two Duke's Company plays: Henry Neville Payne's *The Morning Ramble; or, The Town-Humours* (November) and Shadwell's *Epsom-Wells* (December), the first clearly indebted to *The Comical Revenge* and the second to *She Would If She Could*. This first sequence of Molière adaptations is noticeably different from the later sequence initiated by *The Country-Wife* in 1675, for the later group radically transforms Molière into conformity with established English genres, whereas the earlier adapters use him as a medium for discovering a new form of native social comedy. One consequence of the interest in Molière was that it demanded some portrayal of bourgeois life, with sympathy at least for the younger generations of bourgeois families (which also appears in *The Town-Shifts* and Wycherley's *The Gentleman Dancing-Master*). But even the early Molière adaptations generally take a more complex and sceptical view of authority than their originals, as *Sir Martin Mar-all* and *The Sullen Lovers* had already done. For example, when Richard Flecknoe conflated *Les Précieuses ridicules* and the two *École* plays into his elephantine *The Damoiselles a la Mode* (King's, September 1668),[9] he rescued the false *précieuses* from humiliation by permitting them to marry their original lovers after playing a successful counter-trick on them, so that they display the same self-liberating initiative as the other heroines. Most importantly, their ruse gives them some linguistic autonomy: having alarmed their lovers with feigned longing for the stifling discipline of a nunnery and a passion for pious tracts (of which Arnolphe, the oppressive guardian of *L'École des femmes*, would have approved), they are allowed to pursue their fondness for romances in a more moderate form. A play which opens with Sganarelle (Arnolphe) praising 'the blessed state of ignorance' (I, p. 4) in which he has brought up his ward thus concludes with women determining their literary tastes and rights.

The female voice receives far more limited vindication in John Lacy's *The Dumb Lady* (King's, by 1670), which adapts *Le Médecin malgré lui*, with

9 The play was published, with details of Flecknoe's ideal cast, before it had been performed.

some borrowing from *L'Amour médecin*.[10] As in Molière, the heroine (here called Olinda) escapes an unwanted marriage by feigning dumbness, refusing to participate in imposed forms of language that will destroy her freedom: 'if she had said but *to have and to hold*,' says Squire Softhead, the suitor favoured by her father, 'we had had no further use of her tongue as I know of' (I, p. 3). There is, indeed, much satiric concern with verbal rituals of authority: Softhead fires servants who do not call him 'Squire' frequently enough (I, p. 1), Drench (the farrier) excites reverence by pretending knowledge of various learned tongues ('A Gentleman and not speak Arabick?', II, p. 22), and one of the doctors in the jargon-laden consultation scene insists on 'submission to *sic dixit Galenus*' (V, p. 70). But the chief contrast to such bogus forms of verbal authority is not so much the genteel love of hero and heroine as the far-cical plebeian promiscuity and violence that everywhere proceeds in defiance of them. Even an aged crone is energetically cuckolding her husband, and of the five children of Isabel, the farrier's wife, four were extramaritally con-ceived. Like Olinda, she resists the verbal prescriptions of established author-ity, never heeding the word '*duty*' or anything else that the parson says and claiming the liberty of the 'free born subject' to be as promiscuous as her so-cial superiors (I, p. 5). But there are more effective forms of control than the parson's preaching, and Drench restores the marital 'home' (V, p. 81)—and avenges an earlier beating which his wife had contrived for him—by having her caged as a bawd and sent to Bedlam. Authority belongs to the body, not the word. This point is repeated in the consultation scene, when Drench—the 'stranger' with 'strange' name and humours[11]—triumphantly discounten-ances established medical authority by using cow-itch (a plant which causes itching) to deceive 'a Doctor wedded to Rules and Method' (V, p. 80) into thinking himself ill; for his assistant in this pre-eminently corporeal assault on verbal authority is the parson (V, p. 74). His pulpit discourses unheeded, the preacher retains control by coarse action.

Problems of authority are more seriously examined in another conflation of the *École* plays, *Sir Salomon* (Duke's, April 1670) by the Catholic gentle-man John Caryll. Whereas the repressive guardian in Flecknoe's adaptation is as much a 'stranger' to the rules of 'humane Society' as 'the very *Savages* in America' (I, p. 2), Sir Salomon—as his lawgiver's forename suggests—is a more socially representative figure. Unlike Arnolphe, he is not a bourgeois so-cial climber but a gentleman, and his abuse of authority is more wide-ranging. As well as denying his young ward (Betty) knowledge and literacy, he threatens to disinherit his young son, claiming over him the absolute author-ity of a Hobbesian monarch, and he is yet more despotic to his servants than Arnolphe, treating them as 'Slaves', 'Traitors', and 'Vermine' (III, p. 44).

---

[10] Flecknoe's lost *The Physician Against his Will* is conjecturally dated by Pierre Danchin to 1669–70 (*The Prologues and Epilogues of the Restoration, 1660–1700* (4 parts in 7 vols., Nancy, 1981–8), i. 345).   [11] V, pp. 70 (twice), 75–6 (thrice).

Moreover whereas Molière isolates Arnolphe and Sganarelle by opposing them to men of sense, Chrysalde and Ariste, Caryll takes the opposite course of duplicating his central figure: the Justice of the Peace Wary Woodland, who takes Chrysalde's role in the opening discussion of Sir Salomon's plan for the perfect marriage, nevertheless quickly reveals himself as another despot, denouncing his daughter Julia's 'Crime of Rebellion' (II, p. 20) in preferring the penniless young Single over his own choice, Sir Arthur Addell. And Sir Arthur himself is no harmless buffoon but an arrogant abuser of his station, with a potential for nastiness that is thwarted only by his gross folly: 'I defie all the Justice of *England*: For, I have Fifteen Hundred a year, and owe never a Groat' (II, p. 32).

But justice will not be defied, and ultimately triumphs over despotic oppression. When Sir Salomon attempts to have his rival (Woodland's son Peregreen) beaten up, the plan unexpectedly results in the apparent murder of Sir Arthur, and Salomon finds himself in a role very different from that of the archetypal judge whose name he bears: 'Whither shall I fly——I hear the noise of Justice', he exclaims (V, p. 86). Justice, however, first claims Sir Arthur, who is arrested for his own murder and brought to be examined by Wary Woodland, so that Julia has the satisfaction of keeping her unwanted suitor in custody, gloating that he is 'now in the hands of the Law' (V, p. 90). As the various young lovers gain their partners, their happiness is associated with the establishment of legal right: Betty's lover, Peregreen Woodland, is pronounced by young Single to have a lawful right to her, since they are bound by a promise of marriage, whereupon Providence seals the triumph of justice by arranging the opportune return of Betty's long-lost father, the India merchant Barter, from foreign parts. Even young Single is subjected to a benevolently enquiring justice, undergoing trial (III, p. 55) by Julia, to ensure that he does not become a tyrant after marriage. Like Caryll's *The English Princess* (where, indeed, a tyrant also imprisons his desired bride) *Sir Salomon* portrays the providential ending of tyranny. The difference from the earlier play is that the tyranny here is not usurpation but the exercise of legitimate authority in arbitrary acts of exclusion: disinheritance, and denial of education. The long-delayed home-coming of Barter emphasizes a wider re-entry of the excluded into their due places, and his socially ambiguous role as merchant has more potential point than in Molière, for the excesses of the *gentilhomme* are corrected by the agency of the bourgeois.

Matthew Medbourne's *Tartuffe* (King's, May 1670, or earlier?) is the most obviously topical of the Molière adaptations, not only in its concern with a hypocritical zealot who threatens (like the Days) to dispossess an established family of its heritage but in its portrayal of a fundamentally decent man who has been compromised by association with treason. It is perhaps a sign of the changing political climate, however, that Medbourne does not follow Molière in making the King an active *deus ex machina*. The King remains a benevolent figure to whom intercession will be made, but Orgon is saved primarily by the contrivance of his social equals and inferiors: an intelligent friend and a pair of intelligent servants. A different sign of the times is provided in Thomas Betterton's, *The Amorous Widow* (Duke's, November 1670). The plot which gives the play its title is fairly trite, portraying the attempts of a mature woman (Lady Laycock) to gain the affections of young men. More interesting is the other plot, which follows *George Dandin* in portraying the humiliations of a rich bourgeois (Barnaby Brittle) married to the daughter of impoverished but haughty gentlefolk. As Aphra Behn was to do in adapting *Le Malade imaginaire* as *Sir Patient Fancy*, Betterton modifies Molière so as to concentrate upon the young wife's plight and viewpoint. Brittle is an aged boor, with none of the semi-tragic status that Dandin acquires, and Mrs Brittle is a young and lively beauty who has been sacrificed by her parents' greed. Whereas Dandin ends his play abjectly humiliated and on an inexorable course towards cuckoldom, Mrs Brittle learns the dangers of playing with fire and Brittle the dangers of jealous oppressiveness, and there is some hope that the bourgeois and the gentlewoman will live in tolerable peace. In *George Dandin*, rigidities of class attitude create a situation which progresses with mechanical inexorability, whereas here it is the specific dispositions of husband and wife that first mar and then mend the marriage. Adultery is not endorsed, but the temptation is treated with understanding, and this is a sign of the direction in which drama was moving.

In his lost *The Hypocrite* (probably another *Tartuffe*) and in *The Miser* (King's, January 1672) Shadwell added the run of French adaptations, as he to a lesser extent did in *The Humorists* (Duke's, December 1670), whose main plot seems indebted for its general outline to Quinault's *La Mère coquette*, and which (like *The Sullen Lovers*) imitates *Les Fâcheux* in its portrayal of intrusive bores. Both *The Humorists* and *The Miser* sustain Shadwell's preoccupation with the decay of gentility, both feature solemn, truly gentle, couples, and both weaken the association between gentility and birth. Goldingham (Harpagon) in *The Miser* is one of the few Restoration successors to Quomodo and Sir Giles Overreach, a monstrously subversive outsider; yet the son of this bourgeois menace is a paragon of gentility. In *The Humorists*, concern with birth and rank is reserved for the vacuous and fraudulent: if the foolish Drybob's statements are not true, he is the son of a fishmonger, baboon, or scavenger, and two strumpets of undistinguished birth engage in regular disputes about honour and precedence. In this play, indeed, the threat to gentlemanliness is posed not by a Goldingham but by the newly defined (rather than newly made) gentleman of the 1660s, the wit and the libertine declining into the vacantly facetious Drybob (presumably Dryden)[12] and the poxed Crazy, whose syphilis symbolizes the social decay

12 See Winn, *John Dryden and His World*, 222.

with which Shadwell was obsessed. It is a sign of Shadwell's distaste for currently dominant mores that the original version of the play had to be withdrawn because it had offended some unnamed but manifestly influential people.[13]

But more soundly established norms of gentility are also scrutinized, and in *The Humorists* Shadwell begins his process of detaching gentility from its origins in feudal chivalry, and the romances which perpetuated feudal attitudes. (The process was particularly explicit in *The Woman-Captain* (1679), where Heildebrand, a gentleman hooligan named after a hero of the Charlemagne cycle, enters after a night of drunken violence boasting with lofty arrogance that his sword 'is stain'd in gore of filthy Peasant' (III, p. 48).[14]) Repeatedly, Shadwell highlights ways in which the residual language of chivalry, that is, the language of honour and courtly love, can dignify conduct that is essentially oppressive or socially corrosive. Crazy's syphilis exceeds the sufferings of knights for their ladies (I, p. 194), and in *Epsom-Wells* the language of chivalric romance (and of the heroic play) becomes that of seduction, violence, and decadence: the heroes Bevil and Rains treat hangovers and claps as wounds of honour (I, p. 108), and represent themselves as knights errant when they rescue the heroines, Carolina and Lucia, from the two hectors Kick and Cuff (I, p. 115), though they clearly hope that knightly prowess will facilitate easy seduction. And, whereas Rains compares the duellist to a knight at 'Tilts and Turnaments' (I, p. 119), Lucia sees duelling as a 'Gentleman-like murder for . . . Honour' (V, p. 169). True gentlemen must do without such meretricious survivals of archaic codes; thus, in *The Virtuoso*, Bruce tries and quickly abandons heroic cant in his courtship of Clarinda.

Apart from Shadwell, the most important early adapter of Molière was Edward Ravenscroft, author of the highly successful *The Citizen Turn'd Gentleman* (Duke's, ?December–January 1671–2). Obviously, the main debt is to *Le Bourgeois Gentilhomme*, but (like Shadwell at about the same time) Ravenscroft also turns to *L'Avare*, adding Harpagon's rivalry with his son to the catalogue of Mr Jorden's follies, and paralleling *The Miser* in portraying the citizen's son as an ideal gentleman. More interesting than the way in which Jorden's follies are multiplied, however, is the way in which they are softened. As in the original, Jorden is tricked into believing that he has been awarded the Turkish dignity of Mamamouchi, and he receives the meaningless title amidst a Babel of gibberish and meaningless ceremony which symbolizes his alienation from the signs and forms of his native world. In Molière, M. Jourdain remains dislocated, locked in his Babel of illusion. Ravenscroft's Mr Jorden, however, returns to his world, changed and wiser, resolving no longer 'to play

[13] The original version has been edited by Richard Perkin (*The Humorists by Thomas Shadwell 1670*). Perkin conjectures that Lady Loveyouth and Oldpox (the original name of Crazy) may have been construed as satires on Lady Castlemaine and Henry Jermyn (pp. 2–4).

[14] Heildebrand is also mentioned in *The Humorists*, IV, p. 232. See Summers's notes (p. 310).

the Gentleman,' but instead (without irony) to 'shew my self a Gentleman' (V, p. 107), and throughout the play his folly lies less in his social affectation than in his belief that gentility is a matter of biological inheritance rather than conduct: he even distinguishes his two children by genetic punctilios, since his first wife was a citizen and his second a gentlewoman (I, p. 9). The biological folly of this belief is shown when he insists on his daughter's marriage to Sir Simon Softhead (M. de Porceaugnac), even though he believes him to be riddled with venereal disease (III, p. 52); and it is Sir Simon who is the 'stranger',[15] whereas Young Jorden really is a citizen made gentleman.

The two greatest Restoration Molière adaptations were to be produced by Wycherley—*The Country-Wife* and *The Plain-Dealer*—but they came later, and at this stage Wycherley stood apart from the main trend, busying himself with the Anglicization of Spanish drama,[16] though in ways which took it well away from the old intrigue pattern. *Love in a Wood; or, St James's Park* (King's, March 1671) resembles *The Country Gentleman* in portraying a world of universal dislocation, but differs by withholding any fixed original order of place against which the dislocations might be measured. Physical, social, economic, and perceptual disorientation abound, all of them combined in the complex nocturnal wanderings and misunderstandings in the park, where signs become ambiguous, and identity, social rank, and moral character are alike obscured and misconstrued. In the opening scene, the ageing husband-hunter Lady Flippant introduces the sense of chaotic flux that is to run through the play, complaining that her late husband's escutcheon has 'walk'd as much ground as the Citizens Signs since the Fire' (I. i. 17–18). Social mobility is translated into physical mobility, and into a literal instability of sign, and this image of physically shifting signs foreshadows the less tangible shifts and uncertainties of signification that are to cause so much jealousy and misunderstanding; the darkness in the park is paralleled by other deficiencies of sight and light, such as the short-sightedness arising from Lady Flippant's excessive use of mercury water, or the virtuous Christina's seclusion in her room, away from the sun, during her lover's exile. But Lady Flippant also describes a changing social landscape, in which the categories of town and city, so clearly designated in the Dramatis Personae, do not correspond to fixed geographic standards. Place is amorphous, incapable of intrinsic symbolic significance, but receiving transient meaning from human imposition, and throughout the play characters engage in the imaginative transformation of place, as when Dapperwit describes his mistress's tiny alley-house as 'the Cabinet, in which I hide my Jewel' (III. ii. 1) or Lady Flippant transforms the

---

[15] III, pp. 42, 61; IV, p. 64.

[16] *Love in a Wood* is indebted to Calderón's *Mañanas de abril y mayo*; *The Gentleman Dancing-Master* is indebted, to a lesser extent, to his *El maestro de danzar*. See John Loftis, *The Spanish Plays of Neoclassical England* (New Haven and London, 1973), 121–30; James Urvin Rundle, 'Wycherley and Calderón: A Source for *Love in a Wood*', *PMLA* 64 (1949), 701–7; P. F. Vernon, 'Wycherley's First Comedy and its Spanish Source', *Comparative Literature*, 18 (1966), 132–44.

park into an exotic pastoral landscape, complaining that it 'affords not so much as a Satyr for me' (V. i. 170).

Lady Flippant is a personification of social dislocation. She is vagabond, impoverished, and homeless, being forced to lodge with her socially incompatible brother, the Puritan usurer Gripe, and feeling 'most properly at home in her Coach' (I. i. 68). Sir Simon Addleplot is another drifter, having bought a knighthood and lost an estate, reduced to pursuing a rich marriage in the menial guise of Gripe's clerk. But less ridiculous and socially endangered characters are also uprooted. Valentine, the jealous lover of the virtuous Christina, has been exiled after a duel with an imagined rival; Ranger (obviously) ranges; and, though he seeks to keep his mistress, Lydia, at 'home' so that he can 'Ramble' (I. ii. 81–3) undetected in the park, she instead leaves home to pursue her own wandering. Even the virtuous Christina is unwillingly drawn into the confusions of the park, despite her resolve to remain fixed in the seclusion of her dwelling-place until her lover returns from exile; for Lydia invades her privacy, seeking to avoid the embarrassment of meeting Ranger in the park, and Ranger—a disruptive 'stranger', as he is later called (IV. iii. 203, 215)—follows close behind, believing he is pursuing a new conquest and mistaking Christina for the object of his pursuit. The consequent jealous misapprehensions of Valentine provide one of the chief demonstrations that signs can be epistemologically slippery as well as physically mobile: for example, when he hears from his friend Vincent of Christina's exemplary conduct during his exile, he suspiciously detects ambiguities and alternative meanings in the evidence (II. iv. 31–8).

Towards the end of the play, Ranger announces an end to the prevailing disorientation: 'when we are giddy, 'tis time to stand still' (IV. iii. 331). But what has hitherto been opposed to the wandering in the park has not been a shared and comprehensive order, such as Howard recalled in *The Country Gentleman*, but dispersed and fragmented confinement in separate, enclosed spaces. Christina, as we have seen, mourns Valentine in the seclusion of her lodgings. Gripe officiously tries to restrict his sister, and also wishes to fornicate with Lucy in the privacy of her lodging, resisting all appeals to decamp to the greater spaces (and expense) of the Mulberry Garden. Martha, Gripe's daughter, jealously pent up by her father, elopes with Dapperwit and thereby escapes into the disorder of the park, only to find that her ultimate destination is merely another small room: disappointed in his hopes of becoming Gripe's heir, Dapperwit is advised to 'hire a little room in *Covent-Garden*, and set up a *Coffee-house*' (V. ii. 91–2). The characters' separate confinements in separate enclosures reflect their diverse isolations within distinct social codes and viewpoints: 'Thou seest but the order and policie of this little little Cell wherein thou art placed. . . . This law thou aleagest is but a municipall law.' The little cells include the hypocritical Puritanism of Gripe and the bawd Joyner, the libertinism of Ranger, the romantic idealism of Christina, and the mistaken social self-conceptions of Dapperwit and Sir Simon Addleplot, and the fragmentation of code produces a Babel of competing dialects and idiolects:[17] Alderman Gripe's Puritan cant, Dapperwit's compulsive similes, Sir Simon's constant failures to make language ('the words in fashion', I. ii. 188) carry his intended meaning. Among the fools, language becomes a means to assimilate events to the favoured viewpoint, to impose signification rather than to express it, as when Gripe and the Puritan bawd Joyner praise each other, in an antiphony of absurd metaphor, as 'the Muffler of Secresy,' 'the Head-band of Justice,' and so on (I. i. 127–8). But the fools are pushing to extremes processes that underlie subtler forms of delusion, such as Valentine's jealousy of Christina; for there, too, signification is imposed by the observing consciousness.

Valentine's misinterpretations of Christina proceed from errors of social expectation: from confusions endemic in the Babel of codes. Sir Simon Addleplot's descent into clerkly clothes deceives only the short-sighted Lady Flippant, but Christina's impersonation of Lydia creates real perplexities; for, once she is drawn into complicity with Lydia, she inevitably deviates from the patterns dictated by the values which she and Valentine uniquely share. Christina's principles of self-denying loyalty are not a universal social ideal but one code in a multitude. Secluded in her lodgings during her lover's absence, she *ipso facto* cultivates isolation from the full span of her society, living in the isolated confinement of her own ideals, one of many inhabitants of closed, cramped spaces, and equally one of many characters cut off from the light. When Lady Flippant facetiously greets her as 'faithful Shepherdess' (II. ii. 51, 196) she is hailing not a Fletcherian expression of fixed, hierarchical ideals but a solitary devotee of an incomprehensible creed. Pastoral, a genre which pre-eminently attaches a fixed moral significance to place, is diametrically opposed to the kind of drama which Wycherley is creating, and the term 'faith' itself—the foundation of social existence—becomes not a unifying force but a protean expression of conflicting viewpoints: for example, in Sir Simon's addiction to the socially gauche phrase 'Faith and troth', which constantly undermines his imagined knightly dignity, the term paradoxically becomes a token of social incohesion and disarray.

Justice, that other mainstay of social cohesion, dissolves into similar diversity. The troubled relationships of Lydia and Ranger, and Valentine and Christina, are repeatedly portrayed in terms of trial and justice,[18] and Christina is finally shown to have been 'injur'd' (V. i. 425, 436, 449), a term literally suggesting denial of justice. But the first and last references to justice in the play come from the double-dealing bawd and match-maker Joyner, who hails Alderman Gripe as 'the Head-band of Justice' (I. i. 128), and marries off the impoverished Lady Flippant to the equally impoverished Sir Simon with

---

17 The diversity of dialect is also discussed in Markley, *Two-Edg'd Weapons*, 140–50.
18 III. iii. 115–21; IV. iii. 21–2; V. i. 279–80, 387–8, 521–2.

the aside, 'like the Lawyers, while my Clients endeavour to cheat one another; I in justice cheat 'em both' (V. ii. 16–17). The justice attained by Christina and Lydia expresses private ideals, not a comprehensive order, and the choric voice of justice is given to the bawd. Like faith, it loses its character as social absolute and becomes a term whose value shifts from dialect to dialect in the hubbub of codes. Wycherley here foreshadows his greatest representation of Babel: Westminster Hall in *The Plain-Dealer*.

Social and spatial dislocation also provide the unifying motif for Wycherley's *The Gentleman Dancing-Master* (Duke's, February 1672), a play concerned with the follies of two social upstarts, the merchant James Formal and his nephew Mr Parris, whose discontent with their social place is magnified into a total alienation from their birthplace. Renaming themselves Don Diego and Monsieur De Paris, the two citizens respectively cultivate the roles, language, and codes of honour of a Spanish and French gentleman. In short, Wycherley is again portraying Babel. He is not, however, portraying his ambitious and alienated cits as subversive violators of a fixed social order; after all, the chief focus of sympathy is Diego's vivacious daughter Hippolita, who far outshines her rather put-upon gentlemanly lover, Gerrard. Rather, the proliferation of national styles, customs, and speech habits draws attention to the arbitrary and purely customary nature of national codes and characters: of the systems of behaviour that contribute to the creation of social identity and status.

The instability of social role affects even Gerrard, the gentleman, who falsifies his status in order to court Hippolita in the guise of a dancing-master: a disguise which pre-eminently illustrates the arbitrary relationship of code to practitioner, for the dancing-master is a non-gentleman who teaches genteel accomplishments,[19] an authority on a code which signifies a status he does not himself possess. The image of the dancing-master thus parallels the cits' more farcical separations of code from character, suggesting that these accentuate incongruities that are present in the normal conduct of social existence. The connection is explicitly made in the most blatant of all separations of code from actor, when Monsieur De Paris is instructed in Spanish gravity not (as one might reasonably expect) by a Spaniard, but by a blackamoor; for the blackamoor is twice described as Monsieur's dancing-master (IV. i. 135; V. i. 1–2). Indeed, what is signally absent from this play is any portrayal of characters conforming to norms in which they have an innate proprietorial stake. The prostitutes Flounce and Flirt insist on being treated as ladies of quality, but nowhere in the play does a real lady of quality appear; the fiction is all that we are given. And Gerrard (unlike Horner and Manly) is never seen in his own home, but is always in some sense on foreign territory, displaced: in the French-House (a French restaurant) or Don Diego's Spanish household.

---

[19] See C. J. Rawson, *Henry Fielding and the Augustan Ideal under Stress: 'Nature's Dance of Death' and other Studies* (London, 1972), 3–34.

There is never a simple correspondence of person and place, or of person and social role.

The pretence of giving dancing-lessons enables Gerrard to court Hippolita in the presence of Diego and his sister, Mrs Caution, the main point and joke being that the gestures are equally appropriate to the dancing-master and the gentleman, but have different meanings according to the performer; the code is ambiguous. As in the more famous China scene in *The Country-Wife*, a single set of signs assumes alternative significance according to the framework in which it is viewed. The signs are not impenetrably ambiguous, since they become clear when the framework is known, but they are arbitrary, and Wycherley delights in confusing terms and signs which traditionally define a natural and univocal order. The term *Master*, in the context of courtship and marriage primarily associated with the husband's authority, becomes nicely detached from its customary usage when Hippolita uses it, with perfect appropriateness, to an apparent employee and social inferior. The holding of hands, so often a natural sign of fixed social order and interdependence, similarly becomes meaningless without a context to define it:

DON. Can he dance with her without holding her by the hand?
HIPP. Here take my hand, Master.
GER. I wish it were for good and all. . . .   [*aside to her.*
CAUT. Nay de' see how he squeezes her hand, Brother, O the lewd Villain!

(III. i. 370–87)

But, in the China scene, Horner and Lady Fidget at least know what the sign means to them. Hippolita, in particular, is for a long time unsure whether the linking of hands actually corresponds to a linking of hearts: 'you are a Stranger to me,' she has earlier said to Gerrard; 'to know your heart, would require a great deal of time' (II. i. 458, 475–6); but, eventually, she does fix the sign which the joke dancing-lessons have clothed with uncertainty, giving 'my hand now in earnest' (V. i. 181).

Throughout the four and a half years following *She Would If She Could*, the only essay in libertine comedy had been the comic plot of Dryden's tragicomedy *Marriage A-la-Mode*, which takes a sceptical and secular view of established sexual mores, but in the end redefines the imperative to fidelity instead of rejecting it; though it has no sacred authority, it is enforced by the inescapable human instinct for property. Dryden's next comedy, his unsuccessful *The Assignation* (King's, by November 1672), completes the line of his early comedies (he did not produce another until *The Kind Keeper* of 1678), and continues their combination of polemically secular outlook and relatively chaste action; and, once again, it examines the interaction between the libertine and the heroic, though without the separate line of elevated action that had characterized *Secret Love* and *Marriage A-la-Mode*. Other dramatists (notably Aphra Behn in her earliest plays) had also used tragicomedy as a vehicle for examining libertine principles, but the failure of *The Assignation* heralded a shift away from heroic comedy:[20] Dryden abandoned the genre until *The Spanish Fryar* (1680), Crowne did not follow up *Juliana*, and after *The Dutch Lover* (1673) Aphra Behn started to move in different directions. Appearing at the very time in which the movement towards sex comedy was starting to quicken, and in which the fairly straightforward recycling of Molière was starting to peter out, *The Assignation* appears at the point of a pronounced shift in the nature of comedy. If Dryden had alone sustained a sympathetically critical interest in libertinism in the years immediately following *She Would If She Could*, he only partially anticipated the genre which others were to make the distinctive vehicle for such interest.

The play retains some of the carnivalistic attitude of the first crop of innovative Restoration comedies, such as *The Comical Revenge* and Dryden's own *An Evening's Love*. Formality is relaxed, and widely differing degrees of gentility and nobility mingle on virtually equal terms. Servants, it is true, do not benefit: although Dryden revived from *Sir Martin Mar-all* the saturnalian role-exchange of servant and master, it is here the servant, Benito, who is the incorrigible blunderer. But Benito also participates in another, implicit, role-exchange which leaves hierarchy less comfortably vindicated, for his miscalculation of his capacities is paralleled by that of the most exalted member of the cast, a 50-year-old Duke who attempts to usurp his son's role as lover. Indeed the Duke steps into the role of fop for which Benito had at first apparently been prepared: the play opens with Benito (Jo Haynes) admiring his clothes in the mirror, not yet identified as a servant, but identified as a fool by the casting of his part. But, in the event, it is the Duke who is 'that Fop-gravity' (IV. iii. 34), and one of the tribe of 'antient Fops' (IV. iv. 41). The Duke appropriates the title which had apparently been reserved for his social antithesis, the most plebeian and stupid character in the cast. This is saturnalia of a subtler kind.

But the ancient fop is also a figure of violence and menace, and although the play repeatedly shows institutional authority inverted by the power of the flesh it is not a pure celebration of carnival, as *An Evening's Love* had been. A carnival does form a point of reference for the action, but now it is in the past (I. i. 149–50), and the relationship between desire and power is now more menacing. Nevertheless, the flesh is again prominent, and is here linked with two other terms with which it has an ancient and familiar association: the world and the Devil.[21] The Devil is almost always invoked jocularly, and is chiefly associated with Benito, whose ambition to prove himself a

---

[20] Hume, *Development*, 281.

[21] For the flesh, see I. i. 219; II. i. 170–1, 177; III. i. 11–20, 75–6; IV. i. 5–6, iv. 125–6. For the world, II. i. 146; III. i. 79–80; IV. i. 12–14, iii. 22, 69–70, 83, iv. 3–4, v. 33; V. i. 30, 90, iv. 235, 257, 263, 268. For the Devil, III. i. 75–6, 122–3, 359–61; IV. ii. 25, v. 18–20; V. ii. 80–1, iv. 118.

manipulative wit brings repeated embarrassment upon his master's circle: at one point, for instance, he is likened to a picture of 'the Devil . . . grinning behind the Witch upon the Gallows' (V. ii. 80–1). If the demonic shrinks from cosmic malevolence to buffoonish blundering, the world and the flesh lose their evil potency and become principles to be affirmed: at the end of the play Lucretia, a love-struck novice nun, is released to 'the World' (V. iv. 268), and the humane abbess who releases her is herself anxious that her conduct be justified 'to the world' (V. iv. 235). Appropriately, the worldly love that claims Lucretia and the other young characters is explicitly and defiantly carnal in character. Violetta, a temporary resident in the convent, has no 'Nuns flesh' (I. i. 219), and Platonic love is mocked: for example, Prince Frederick quickly discards Platonic pretensions and decides that he loves Lucretia 'all over, both Soul and Body' (IV. iv. 125–6).

The social and cosmic orders are also interpreted in materialistic terms. Events are governed by chance, and all relationships are of power and subjection. Family authority is repeatedly combined with institutional power—Prince Frederick's father is also his ruler, the guardian uncle of Violetta and her sister Laura is Governor of Rome, and their aunt is an abbess—and the opening scenes show power to be the basis of all human relationships: Aurelian kicks his foolish servant Benito to discourage his dreams of social advancement, complains of being 'commanded' (I. i. 83) by his father to employ the dolt, and unsuccessfully urges his friend Camillo to 'Be rul'd by me' (I. i. 75). Laura and Violetta also suffer from the whims of paternal power, being doomed 'by a Clause in their Fathers will' (I. i. 98) to forfeit their fortunes if they marry without their guardian's consent. And, when we first see Laura and Violetta, we find them engaged in an amicable power struggle, Violetta complaining that Laura's slight seniority encourages her to abuse her 'authority' and 'Soveraignty', Laura reproving her junior's rebellion and claiming the 'double right' of greater years and greater wit (I. i. 157–62).

The exercise of power is most naked and threatening when the Duke of Mantua becomes the rival of his son, Prince Frederick, for the love of the nun Lucretia, and eventually attempts to rape her. When Frederick and his companions intrude at the critical moment, the Duke is humiliated at his exposure before 'that Son, | O're whom the right of Nature gives me power' (V. iv. 129–30). And, although Frederick at this point has not only moral authority but the cruder power of armed supporters, the Duke still asserts that his power exempts him from the judgement of one who is 'doubly . . . my slave, | Both Son and Subject' (V. iv. 147–8). As at the culmination of *An Evening's Love*, formal justice collapses into a contest of naked power, but the possibilities of power are now more threatening; unlike the confrontation at the end of *An Evening's Love*, this cannot be resolved with a cry of 'it was only a Carnival merriment, which I mistook for a Rape' (V. i. 434–5); it is far closer to the grim enigmas created by Settle's criminal rulers. Here matters are settled by an appeal not to carnival but to death: Frederick moves his father by surrendering his military advantage and—unable to abandon his love—offering his life instead. Though incapable of rapid Orrery-style triumph over his 'violent' (v. iv. 202) love, the Duke nevertheless combats desire by putting its object out of reach, permitting Lucretia to marry Frederick. The power struggle cedes to an arduously and incompletely achieved glimpse of the rights and integrity of others, but there is none of Orrery's simple faith in the compatibility of individual desire and sociable reason; for the egotistic pursuit of power is a fundamental human instinct, the conquest of which is long, painful, and never complete.

The difficulty of giving social acknowledgement and expression to the demands of the flesh is everywhere evident. The nunnery—into which all the young female characters are drawn—becomes an embodiment of a tyrannical order at odds with the nature of human flesh, tolerable only because its abbess has a worldly understanding that is quite incongruous with her spiritual function. The frequent encounters in darkness, masks, or disguise, with the associated misapprehensions or conscious misrepresentations of identity, create circumstances in which individuals are constantly separated from fitting social attributes. This separation is most extreme when the masked Lucretia tantalizes the Duke (himself disguised as his own emissary) with a sequence of false self-identifications, each asserting her relationship to a different noble house, and each instantly inspiring the Duke to detect a family likeness. Further division of identity, and suspension of social character, occurs in a double reversal of roles between superiors and servants: Benito's aspirations to gentility are imaged in reverse when his master, Aurelian, assumes the role of Benito to accompany his friend Camillo on his assignation with Violetta, and in the darkness becomes attracted by the wit of Laura, who is accompanying Violetta in the guise of the maid Beatrix. Since Aurelian has already admired Laura's beauty in daylight, his apparently divided attraction to the seen beauty and unseen female wit creates another variant of the Invisible Mistress convention, so often used in this period to depict an incoordination between public role and personal desire.

As the confusions of identity indicate, knowledge, language, and visual representation of the self and others are elusive and uncertain: 'let us discourse [a recurrent term], and know each other better first,' says Violetta to Camillo (iv. v. 31–2). But knowledge can be hard to find: 'I know you for *Lucretia*', the Duke says to the masked Laura (v. ii. 67); 'Knowing my own merits, as I do,' says the bumptiously self-deceiving Benito (iv. vi. 1). It is noteworthy that Camillo's initial approaches to Violetta, imprisoned in her uncle's house, display the efforts of discrete individuals to make contact over a dividing barrier, and also noteworthy that there is no shared system of meaning, since each party uses a different species of sign: Camillo has shot messages with arrows, 'and by the signes she made me I find they were not ill receiv'd' (I. i. 111–12). Unmediated self-disclosure is impossible, desperately though Lucretia longs for it when the Duke persecutes her with his love:

> Yet, could you see my heart, 'tis a white Virgin-Tablet,
> On which no Characters of earthly love
> Were ever writ.
>
> (IV. iii. 107–9)

The Duke does believe her, but only because he cannot bear the thought that Frederick might have enjoyed her: the reasons for his trust are inside him, not inside her. When Lucretia and the nun Hippolita are locked out of the nunnery, the page Ascanio produces the lost key with the exclamation '*Ecce signum*' (III. iii. 52), and the fumbling for the key that will unlock the barrier typifies much of the play's action.

If the carnivalesque had become menacing in *The Assignation*, it remains cheerfully uncomplicated in Henry Neville Payne's *The Morning Ramble* (Duke's, by November 1672), one of two plays from this period which at last made constructive use of Etherege's example. The other, Shadwell's *Epsom-Wells*, owes much to *She Would If She Could*, but Payne's inspiration is clearly *The Comical Revenge*. Although it has no rhymed heroics (and indeed explicitly mocks them, I, p. 11), its nocturnal saturnalia re-creates the ethos of Etherege's first play: Merry's courtship of Honour Muchland recalls Sir Frederick's of the Widow Rich (Merry, like Sir Frederick, was played by Henry Harris), and the cowardly Ruffle relives several of Sir Nicholas Cully's experiences, finally retiring to the country to pass off a new but sexually well-practised wife as a virtuous lady. Payne follows both Etherege and Dryden in his cheerfully amoral view of the gentleman's responsibilities—only an oyster-crier would reprehend a gentleman for drunkenness (IV, p. 53)—and in his satiric scrutiny of male and female professions of honesty and honour, particularly the honour of the duellist and of the prostitute. But Payne—a friend of Aphra Behn—goes beyond Etherege and Dryden in the extent to which he allows women to inspect and test male codes. When two of the heroines disguise themselves as men about town in order to observe the mysteries of the stag-night, the female experimentation with masculine identity is far more complete and complex than in any earlier Restoration comedy by a man, and paves the way for later plays such as the anonymous *The Woman Turn'd Bully* and Shadwell's *The Woman-Captain*. Moreover, it is a woman who delivers the most extensive critique of honour (IV, p. 54), and a woman who actually bears the forename of Honour.

Although no fornication actually takes place (two long-established lovers are interrupted as they are on the point of going to bed), the play provides an exceptionally explicit and sustained critique of received sexual morality, its viewpoint being that of an open-minded and sceptical moral relativism. 'Since no Action, be it good or bad, but hath it's vouchers,' says the libertine

Townlove, 'I am for letting every one have his humour' (I, p. 10). It portrays the pre-dawn exploits of a group of gentlemanly revellers—Merry, a drinker, Townlove, and Muchland, a staid country *Justice* who comes along for the experience. The freedom and suspended order of night are contrasted with the sober business of day, and the suspended order results in a saturnalian inversion of judicial ritual, when Merry's shoemaker confronts him in his night-time authority of constable, only to have his authority removed when Merry himself takes over the administration of justice, trying and freeing four prostitutes. 'We'l know no other Justice hereafter but you, Sir' (II, p. 27), says the Constable. Merry's version of justice ratifies the intrinsic subversiveness of the prostitutes' existence, for they have been loud in their professions of honour and gentility, and one of them is in fact the Constable's wife, mocking her captor's cuckoldom from the safety of her disguise. In his two tragedies, Payne shows apparently fallen women fixed in their fallen roles by the arbiters of narrative; he here rescues real fallen women from the arbiters of justice. Increasingly, judicial ritual and narrative—generally historical narrative— were to be paralleled as areas in which women risked passive subjection to definition by men.

While Payne re-created the uncomplicated festivity of *The Comical Revenge*, Shadwell in *Epsom-Wells* (Duke's, December 1672) at length acted upon his avowed admiration for *She Would If She Could*, creating a quartet of witty lovers that is manifestly inspired by Etherege's, and dividing the characteristics of the Cockwoods among three married couples, the Woodlys, the Fribbles, and the Biskets. Characteristically, Shadwell is concerned to uphold the very traditions of sexual morality that Etherege was questioning, but he nevertheless outdoes Etherege in allowing his foolish husbands to be cuckolded. The heroes, however, turn out to have made their last cuckolds before the play starts, for their attempts at intercourse are constantly interrupted, and at the end they are on probation as the prospective husbands of the virtuous heroines: here, as in many later plays, Shadwell portrays the maturing of the gentleman.

From the outset, where Rains and Bevil boast of the 'Honourable' hangovers they have suffered (I, p. 108), their rakish outlook is associated with outrageous definitions of honour and gentility: in a parody of the love–honour debate of the heroic play, for example, Bevil decides that he is not a 'Villain' (I, p. 109) to cuckold his friend Woodly, because the cuckoldom commenced before the friendship. Their rakishness also links them to characters with whom they would not willingly acknowledge affinity: the foolish libertine Woodly (another man of honour, and by no means so gross a fool as his model, Sir Oliver Cockwood) and, still more, the hooligans Kick and Cuff, who outdo the heroes by accomplishing a pair of cuckoldings during the play. All these characters initially share a contemptuous view of women as mere sexual prey or property, most crudely expressed when Kick and Cuff treat the heroines, Lucia and Carolina, as prostitutes, attempting (upon their 'honour') to buy their favours (I, p. 114). Yet it is the heroines, not the men, who are the true repositories of honour. It is Lucia who describes a duel as 'a Gentleman-like murder for . . . Honour' (V, p. 169), and it is a sign of the heroes' growth that Rains comes to like Lucia 'too well to dishonour her' (III, p. 148). The redistribution of honour between man and woman benefits even that stereotyped figure of fun, the strumpet obsessed with her reputation. Woodly believes that 'it is a silly Honour that will hinder a man the satisfying of his love' (V, p. 165), but—a true devotee of the double standard—he will not allow the same latitude to his wife. On discovering her infidelity, he summons the heroes and heroines to a public ritual of divorce, promising to 'behave my self like a man of honour' (V, p. 175). But, unexpectedly, she gains more dignity from the ritual than he. Hitherto she has seemed a more sexually successful version of that paragon of honourable adultery, Lady Cockwood, but she now acquires the authority to discredit the equally spurious honour of her husband, blaming her infidelities on the 'lewd disorderly life' which made him a virtual stranger to her (V, p. 180).

The ceremony of divorce places events in a more solemn judicial setting than had become normal in genteel comedy, and it provides an appropriate counterbalance to the 'tryal' (V, p. 181) which the heroes must now undergo to prove themselves worthy of Lucia and Carolina. And this legal sifting and ordering of conduct is the point at which the foolish country Justice, Clodpate, gains his one moment of glory. Clodpate is a lover of English country life in whom the old Jonsonian virtues of care for estate and tenantry have declined into antiquated idiosyncrasy: he is, indeed, at one point forcibly and very appropriately dressed as a ghost. But here, uniquely, Justice Clodpate can vindicate his title rather than his name, gaoling Kick and Cuff for adultery and violence. Shadwell thus repudiates the carnivalistic dismissal of justice that had concluded *An Evening's Love*, showing libertinism contained by law.

In *The Careless Lovers* (Duke's, March 1673) Ravenscroft followed the drift from imitation of Molière to imitation of earlier Restoration models, although he took some hints from *Monsieur de Pourceaugnac* for his portrayal of the foolish Lord De Boastado (as he had already done for Sir Simon Softhead). Like Payne, however, he turned to a relatively early model: shamelessly (since the prologue mocks Dryden for plagiarism), he reworked the Celadon–Florimell plot of Dryden's *Secret Love* as the courtship of Careless, a libertine gentleman, and Hillaria, the niece of Alderman Muchworth, juxtaposing this with the more solemn courtship of the Alderman's daughter Jacinta (whom he designs for De Boastado) and the idealistic and easily jealous Lovell. Gay couple comedy has come to the City, and indeed Ravenscroft was one of the few dramatists before the 1690s to acknowledge the obvious enough fact that gentility both of conduct and ancestry could be found within its limits. The Alderman is of gentle stock, as is Beatrice, the servant whom De Boastado inadvertently marries and ennobles; and Muchworth is not an object of ridicule but a decent if rather old-fashioned man, wanting the best for Jacinta but initially having rather out-dated ideas about the importance of lords and inferiority of women. 'Have not we Rational Souls as well as Men,' Hillaria protests to him; 'what made Women Mopes in former Ages, but being rul'd by a company of old Men and Women[?]' (III, p. '33' [25]).

The real outsider in this play is not the prosperous citizen but the fatuous lord. De Boastado is a 'Traveller', and is associated with the kinds of cultural and linguistic dislocation that had characterized the Mamamouchi scene in *The Citizen Turn'd Gentleman*: 'He speaks some few words in most Languages, but Sence in none' (I, p. 3), and even his clothes are a sartorial Babel, designed by an international consortium of tailors so that onlookers may be able to '*read* all the Countries of my Travels' (II, p. 18; italics added). Yet this pre-eminent outsider, with his supreme unfixity of place and sign, is a nobleman of unimpeachable descent (though his pride in ancestry is pungently mocked, I, pp. 4–5). Despite his credentials of place and ancestry, he becomes a force for dissolution and estrangement, and indeed when the term *stranger* is used, it is generally De Boastado who has provoked its usage: desiring alliance with the nobleman, Muchworth tells Lovell to 'be a stranger to' Jacinta (I, p. 5), and Lovell does indeed become 'strange' (II, p. 13)—and threaten to 'turn Wanderer, and spend my dayes in Travel' (II, p. 14)—when he suspects Jacinta of coveting De Boastado's title. But there is one character towards whom De Boastado does not merely function as a ludicrously disruptive alien. On first greeting the libertine Careless, he insists that he 'must not be a Stranger' (I, p. 3), and the greeting prepares the way for some gently satiric parallels between the oafish lord and the fashionable gentleman: much of the comedy arises from deceptions practised on the two by disguised women (Hillaria as a man and Beatrice as an heiress), and Careless as much as De Boastado is an embodiment of unfixity, having 'wandring Thoughts' (I, p. 2) and praising the freedom of a bird or of a colt in the fens (I, p. 1).[22] Indeed, De Boastado ends up as the more stable of the two, for Careless and Hillaria enter into a very open marriage, whereas De Boastado retires to his country house with his unexpected wife, promising her that she will 'take place' over her former mistresses (V, p. 74). This is a nice climax to a play in which traditional roles of class (and gender) have been consistently revised, not to produce the Hobbesian free-for-all of wit and aggression that distinguishes *Sir Martin Mar-all*, but to suggest that gentility is not always to be found where one has been taught to look for it.

The Morning Ramble, *Epsom-Wells*, and *The Careless Lovers* all develop native models of comedy that had evolved since the Restoration, and in

[22] Cf. I, p. 9; II, p. 22; V, p. 62.

addition all portray the position of women with some sympathy. This sympathy re-emerges two years later in the anonymous *The Woman Turn'd Bully* (Duke's, March 1675). Here, as in *The Morning Ramble*, a woman not only assumes male guise but actually experiments with male characteristics and language: in order to avoid an unwelcome marriage in Derbyshire, Betty Goodfeild comes to London disguised as a gallant, and quickly acquires the knack of swearing and talking like a man (I, p. 7). This linguistic liberation contrasts with the oppression of Lucia, niece of the lawyer Docket, who is forced to read *The Whole Duty of Man* and subjected to a course in law French, but it is noteworthy that Betty often depends for her language on texts written by men, quoting from plays such as *Marriage A-la-Mode* and *The Assignation*. There is no genuine crossing of boundaries (Betty's male mentality and vocabulary vanish as soon as the clothes are abandoned, IV, p. 56), and it is principally the men who thwart Docket, the embodiment of injustice and linguistic obfuscation. Essentially, this is a socially conservative play: thus, a witty maidservant is rewarded not with the now customary upwardly mobile marriage but with a place—'service'—for life (V, p. 82).

Another play which points in two directions is Joseph Arrowsmith's *The Reformation* (Duke's, ?May 1673),[23] in which an attempt to import English sexual liberty into Venice fails because it is false to human nature. A similar attempt at sexual freedom in *Marriage A-la-Mode* (a clear target of Arrowsmith's) had failed because wife-swapping was incompatible with the male instinct for property, but here libertinism is defeated by sheer love. Reaction against recent drama is most obvious in the well-known caricature of Dryden as the Tutor who instructs the Venetians on English dramaturgy and sexual customs. Yet, at the same time, these customs prevail when an unhappily married couple agree to set up with separate lovers.[24] Another concession to recent trends is the satire of male tyranny over women, and in particular of the identification of the wife's chastity with the husband's honour (V, p. 62).

All five of these plays were Duke's Company plays. Following the burning of their theatre, and the failure of *The Assignation*, the King's Company produced a sequence of weak and generally old-fashioned comedies that was only broken by the appearance of *The Country-Wife* in January 1675. During these years, their most prolific writer of comedies was Thomas Duffett, who in addition to *The Spanish Rogue* produced three animated (if schoolboyish) burlesques of successful Duke's spectaculars: *The Empress of Morocco* (?summer 1673), *The Mock-Tempest* (?late spring 1674), and *Psyche Debauch'd* (August 1675). These are saturnalian and festive works, reducing life to sex, drinking, feasting, and (an interesting addition) infantile play, all

---

[23] This is conjectural, and 'any date up to a year earlier than May 1673 is quite possible' (Milhous and Hume, 'Dating Play Premières', 388).

[24] The unresolved diversity of sexual standards in the play is discussed in Rothstein and Kavenik, *Designs of Carolean Comedy*, 170–1.

stripped of any mendacious veneer of social refinement. Through the levelling force of appetite, the noble or divine characters of the Duke's Company plays become plebeian in outlook and generally in rank: in *Psyche Debauch'd*, for example, two princes and princesses end up in prison on charges of murder and theft, and are stripped and then formally tried and sentenced by the common prisoners. The obvious, if infinitely superior, forerunner is Rabelais, but Duffett is not only Rabelais in miniature but Rabelais in reverse, emphasizing not the heroic exaltation of appetite but the anti-heroic deflation of those who delude themselves that life holds anything else: when Rabelais himself is mentioned, in *Psyche Debauch'd*, it is not as the celebrant of giants but (in a nice inversion) as the author of a heroic poem about Tom Thumb (IV. iii. 69–71).

Authority, with its apparatus of religion and justice, wages a vain battle against desire, generally manifested in low-life criminals. When the character in *Psyche Debauch'd* who corresponds to Shadwell's Cupid is asked his name, he reveals himself as that embodiment of eros, the late highwayman Claude Duval. Often, the criminals invade and take over the ceremonies of authority. In *The Empress of Morocco* a country parson, his mystique already compromised by his fleshly passion for devouring sheeps' heads, is tied to a post by a drayman-pimp, who represents his feat as an act of 'justice' (I. ii. 220). In *The Mock-Tempest*, as in *Psyche Debauch'd*, the inmates of a prison (in this case, a bawd and some prostitutes) conduct an extended trial of one of their fellows, with much labouring of the term *justice*. And in *Psyche Debauch'd*, a confidence trick designed to inveigle women into sex is preceded by a veritable Feast of Fools: 'the Chief Priest in a Fools-coat, his Train supported by two in like habit, two Priests in Surplices follow them; then come two Judges playing on Jewes-trumps followed by a Cardinal, playing on a Childs Fiddle; two in grave habits follow him playing on Childrens Pipes' (II. ii. od–h).

At the end of *Psyche Debauch'd* Justice Crab invites Claude Duval and his mistress back to his hall for a festive mumming, which turns out to represent the union of Cupid and Bacchus, but in general figures of authority enforce the irrational suppression of desire. Prospero, whom Dryden and Davenant had turned into a Hobbesian autocrat, becomes in Duffett's hands the Governor of Bridewell, the prison for punishing prostitutes. He twice intervenes to prevent his daughters from pre-marital copulation, and Duffett's version of the magically interrupted banquet confirms his role as the foe of festivity (prisoners have previously dreaded the moment when the depletion of their own supplies would leave them only with the prison diet of bread and water, III. i. 96–103). Finally, however, Prospero does relent, foreshadowing the benignity of Justice Crab by releasing the prostitutes to resume the joys of the flesh, and it is at this juncture that Caliban makes his first appearance, as the foe of discipline, the champion of fun, and the herald of the union of Cupid and Bacchus: '*let Correction cease;*' '*be merry, be merry, be merry, | Be merry;*' '*Now your drink, and your Drabs you shall safely enjoy.*'[25]

The Duffett burlesques were by far the bawdiest plays to appear on the Restoration stage, outdoing even Lacy's farces, though in both cases the low-life buffoonery sharply distinguishes them from the threatening and disturbing plays that were shortly to come. Nevertheless, they seem to show that, along with its desperate reliance on the amateurish and the old-fashioned, the King's Company was also taking the lead in audacity. Both tendencies can be seen in Dryden's only contribution to comedy in this period: the bringing to the stage (with a prologue by Duffett) of an old city comedy, *The Mistaken Husband* (King's, March 1674), in which the unscrupulous Hazard permanently gains the wife of his friend Manley, who has been out of the country for many years, and robs his father-in-law. In its explicit portrayal of prosperous crime, it parallels the growing amoral and anti-providential trend in new drama. Far more innovative, however, was J. D.'s *The Mall* (King's, January 1674), which exceeds any previous Restoration comedy in its sympathetic portrayal of genteel adultery, and links its polemic on behalf of sexual freedom to a striking portrayal of man's tyrannical violence to woman: a violence which is held to be incompatible with the ideal of the gentleman.[26] Old Mr Easy beats and imprisons his young wife and tries to marry his niece, Grace, to the foolish Sir Ralph Spatter, at one point attempting to coerce her by the forcible letting of her blood. And Ralph himself (like Sir Arthur Addell) is no mere buffoon, but is a figure of ugly and menacing male violence and economic power: he has power over the rake Lovechange's estate, locks Grace's true love in a cellar (IV, p. 50), and attempts to have him beaten and Grace imprisoned.

Sympathy for the woman's lot is most striking in the portrayal of the rich, old, ugly widow Woodbee, whom the rakish Lovechange has married for her wealth, and who emerges as a victim of both monetary and sexual oppression, gaining little for the £10,000 she has settled on her husband (V, p. 62). She does, however, gain one significant triumph: seeking to trick her husband into sleeping with her in the darkness of St James's Park, she inadvertently cuckolds him with his friend, who gloats over the beauty he imagines he has enjoyed (III, p. 42). But, when she discovers the mistake, she reacts not with the simpering lasciviousness that one might expect from a crone but with horror and dignity, which contrast with Lovechange's coldly egocentric exposition of the double standard: 'when you offend, I bear the dishonour on't, when I, you but the little griefs' (V, p. 61). Her dignity reappears when—a true noble rival—she persuades Easy to resign his wife to her husband, who reciprocates by urging Easy to take over the Widow (V, p. 71). Like the sexual deception in the park, the final exchange of partners is part of a widespread

[25] V. ii. 299, 329–30, 349.   [26] I, p. 7; IV, pp. 51, 56.

switching of social and sexual roles: Mrs Easy swaps roles with her servant, and another servant, Jo, is mistaken for Grace's suitor, Amorous; Mrs Easy and Sir Ralph exchange clothes (the tyrannical Mr Easy being beaten by his apparent wife); in the end, Sir Ralph knowingly and voluntarily marries the servant Betty; and the Spanish lady Camilla pursues her beloved Courtwell in male disguise, under the appropriately alienating name of Perigreen. Amidst this protean fluidity of role, marriage can seem a strait-jacket, a tyranny sustained by masculinity and money, fittingly challenged by the concluding adulteries and by the release from known identity in the liberating darkness of the park.

In quality, Wycherley's *The Country-Wife* (January 1675) clearly stands quite apart from the other comedies that the King's Company had staged since *The Assignation*. Yet it also stands apart in outlook from Wycherley's own previous comedies, for in revealing the chaos of desire beneath the conventional decorums of social existence it goes far beyond his earlier fairly playful dismantling of accepted codes,[27] and parallels developments evident in *The Mall*, whose mechanical adulteries and role-swappings, however inexpertly, depict a profound instability of social and sexual character. Indeed, there can be few greater unsettlings of sexual stereotype than to show a Don Juan operating in the guise of a eunuch.

In the opening lines, Horner prepares us for a conflict between the arbiters of society and the ministers of nature, the latter lying beyond the margins of respectability and law: 'A Quack is as fit for a Pimp, as a Midwife for a Bawd; they are still but in their way, both helpers of Nature' (I. i. 1–3). Horner here sees himself as a free agent of untrammeled natural instinct, whose pose as a eunuch will be a kind of Ring of Gyges, conferring an invisibility that will carry him unnoticed through the barriers created by sexual convention and give him alone the 'freedom' that all desire. He aspires to be 'the *Pas par tout*' (I. i. 160) of the town: the master-key to open the doors that are so assiduously locked throughout the play, abolishing distinctness and security of property and covertly creating a private state of nature in which he alone recovers the primitive right of all to all. Yet, in the concluding scene of the play, this anarchic foe of property and society has himself become the property of a secret society of sexually voracious women:

LA. FID.   this is *my* false Rogue. . . .
                          this is *my* false Villain.
SQUEAM. And *mine* too.
DAYN. And *mine*.

                (V. iv. 149–59; italics added)

[27] In a stimulating essay, Helen M. Burke has argued that *The Country-Wife* 'seeks to disclose and denaturalize sexual categories, putting into question the very symbolic system that designates woman as "Other" ' ('Wycherley's "Tendentious Joke": The Discourse of Alterity in *The Country Wife*', *The Eighteenth Century: Theory and Interpretation*, 29 (1988), 227–41 (p. 228)).

Even sexual instinct must create social systems in which to express itself. More fully than in any previous Restoration comedy, humanity straddles the boundaries of the city and the wilderness, able neither to reconcile their claims nor to become simply savage or simply citizen; hence the conspicuous but temporary splittings of identity, when Margery becomes Alithea's *doppelgänger*, and both she and Harcourt pose as their own brothers.

The demands of social existence persistently exercise the characters' minds and shape their vocabulary: they are constantly defining their desired (and very exclusive) forms of *society* and *company*, revealing a natural gregariousness that is tempered with a determination to lay down personal and very selective conditions of community. Human sociability is both ineradicable and profoundly limited, and the sexual co-operative which is formalized in the banquet scene is the last and fullest expression of the general impulse to form small communities (Montaignesque little cells) with private rules and—as the China scene shows—private systems of signs. What never appears is the universal interdependence that is traditionally summed up in the image of the city. The term *civil* itself is, as is well known, subjected to constant ironic misuse, as are all the traditional rituals and terminologies of social existence. Honour, friendship, and obligation become façades for lust and cut-throat rivalry. So, likewise, do hospitality and service: both Harcourt and Horner insist on presenting their *service* to their rivals' women,[28] and one of Horner's first attempts to ensnare Pinchwife is through a dinner invitation. The feast at which Horner's mistresses ratify their social compact of time-share adultery finally destroys the value of hospitality as a traditional social microcosm.

If the vocabulary of a universal social morality is destroyed, so is the vocabulary of shared and verifiable knowledge. Belief, deception, certainty, plainness, riddles, knowledge, truth, and falsity are recurrent and increasingly problematic issues: problematic not because knowledge is simply and absolutely unattainable but because the criteria are of sporadic and partial availability. To Lady Fidget's 'certain knowledge', Horner has no China left (IV. iii. 187–8). But what does *China* mean? Certainty of knowledge is paradoxically affirmed in a riddling ambiguity of sign. Margery has 'certain knowledge' (V. iv. 370) of Horner's potency, but certainty is here accompanied by a far cruder imperfection of sign, for her mouth is stopped before she can share her certainty with the world. Harcourt's determination to 'believe' (V. iv. 252) in Alithea's innocence is just and admirable, but it is juxtaposed with Sir Jaspar's decision to 'believe . . . truly' (V. iv. 347) in his wife's innocence, and Pinchwife's more grudging agreement to 'believe' what he wishes to believe: that his wife, too, is chaste (V. iv. 410). Epistemologically, it is hard to distinguish Harcourt's noble faith from Sir Jaspar's foolish credulity, and

[28]   III. ii. 436–7; IV. i. 78, 106, iii. 330.

indeed it is the former whose faith is more at odds with the available evidence. Harcourt's moral and intellectual superiority is not in question, but it is troublingly difficult to give it an objective basis. As so often in this play (and many others) the ideal and its apparent contrary are riddlingly linked in character and origin.

Difficulties of acquiring and sharing knowledge are, of course, difficulties of signification, and the thematic prominence of the sign in *The Country-Wife* has long been recognized.[29] Characters repeatedly ponder the 'meaning' of each other's words and actions, and *sign* is itself a recurrent term. But the signs repeatedly demonstrate their own insufficiency, since (as Hobbes had observed) their agreed public range of meaning is contaminated and contradicted by private associations. Where, then, does the meaning of the sign actually reside? And what communication can the visible segment of its meaning effect between individuals whose private, invisible segments differ?[30] The doubleness of the sign, with its compound of private and socially disseminated meanings, corresponds to the doubleness of human nature, with its inextricable entanglement of the citizen and the solitary creature of inarticulate instinct, and indeed the covert meaning of signs is generally sexual: although the rules and rituals of social existence persistently deny or exorcize sexuality, it inevitably emerges as a latent meaning in signs which are ostensibly restricted to the chaste decorum of the social world: signs such as the word 'China', or that sexless 'sign of a Man' (I. i. 288–9) Horner. Signification is self-annihilatingly divided between the contradictory expression of public fictions and covert sexual motives, as is nicely illustrated in the final round of deceptions and non-explanations, when the illusion of universal chastity is being painstakingly reconstructed; for here the word 'communicate' is used in successive lines to indicate verbal and sexual communication (V. iv. 293–4).

But language itself remains a primarily social instrument, and the intrusion of private and unsanctioned meanings into the sphere of the sign is frequently accomplished by reversion to a more archaic mode of expression, for the social invention of language repeatedly cedes to that more individualistic, corporeal, and powerful means of signification, the hand. For the high-minded Alithea, the two go together: she has given Sparkish 'my word, and will my hand too' (IV. i. 39–40). But harmony between the hand and the word is rare. With reason, Pinchwife repeatedly fears the 'hands' of Horner,[31] and his inexorable progress towards cuckoldom is marked by constant triumphs of the desiring hand over the less tangible restraints of social and marital duty: Horner grabs Margery in the New Exchange, and on receiving her

---

[29] The best recent studies are Deborah C. Payne, 'Reading the Signs in *The Country Wife*', *Studies in English Literature*, 26 (1986), 403–19; Michael Neill, 'Horned Beasts and China Oranges: Reading the Signs in *The Country Wife*', *Eighteenth-Century Life*, 12 (1988), 3–17.

[30] 'And therefore in reasoning, a man must take heed of words; which besides the signification of what we imagine of their nature, have a signification also of the nature, disposition, and interest of the speaker' (*Leviathan*, ch. iv, 109). [31] III. ii. 382, 433; IV. ii. 119.

letter claims that she has 'stretch'd forth her hand' (IV. iii. 403–4); shortly afterwards, Margery tricks Pinchwife into leading her by the hand to her lover. At this point, the hand actually takes over from the word, for Margery dismisses Pinchwife with a gesture of the hand, lest her voice betray her true identity (V. ii. 71b). Elsewhere, the hand similarly intrudes into the domain of the word. When Harcourt is bemusing Sparkish by his ambiguous dialogues with Alithea—seeming to speak for his 'friend' while in fact speaking for himself—he sustains his ruse with frequent manual gestures. And, when the ladies finally admit to each other their true relationship with Horner, moving towards the construction of a mini-society based on shared sexual interest, the process is started when Lady Fidget identifies Horner as her lover by clapping him on the back. As is often the case in more socially conservative drama, the re-establishment of social cohesion is accompanied by a ritual of identification, but the ritual is here not one of naming: a community whose principle is the covert gratification of the body is appropriately initiated by a corporeal sign distinct from the verbal discourse of the public world.

Conversely, the approved and conventional forms of life tend to be represented as systems of words. Harcourt gives credibility to his pose as a parson by restricting his vocabulary to that of the Church, and Pinchwife's fears of cuckoldom focus upon the socially unacceptable 'name' of cuckold (I. i. 343; V. i. 78). Similarly, he reflects gloomily that Alithea and Margery lack the attributes customarily associated with the 'names' of sister and wife (V. i. 99–101). Alithea is also involved in the crudest reduction of moral judgement to the imposition of approved and conventional systems of names, when Sparkish resolves to confront her 'and call her as many Crocodiles, Syrens, Harpies, and other heathenish names, as a Poet would do a Mistress, who had refus'd to heare his suit, nay more his Verses on her' (V. iii. 19–20). Characters such as Pinchwife and Sparkish are mentally confined in systems of language, mistaking glossaries of moral terms for permanent and substantial criteria of conduct. As Pinchwife's fear of being entitled a cuckold shows, names have genuine power to become the objects of fear and desire.

One function of Wycherley's emphasis on the instability of the sign, on the ease with which it accumulates private meanings dictated by forbidden desires, is to show that language is essentially unsuited to be an unalterable instrument of an unalterable moral order. But its unsuitability for this purpose does not only invalidate the outlook of fools such as Pinchwife and Sparkish, for commitment to the binding power of the word pre-eminently distinguishes the socially principled Alithea. In this respect, she is truly Pinchwife's sister and Sparkish's partner. But they attempt to exercise power through the word whereas she, initially, is its slave. For one social function of language is to enable men to control women. In the New Exchange, Pinchwife censors Margery's reading, forbidding her to buy plays (III. ii. 145). Later (wishing that she had never learned to write at all, IV. ii. 64), he not only insists that Margery write a letter denying her desire for Horner but reinforces his insistence by threatening to carve 'Whore' on her face (IV. ii. 92–3): in this ugly literalization of Harcourt's earlier claim that 'Mistresses are like Books' (I. i. 197),[32] he is clearly trying to endow language with corporeal tangibility and power (to make it an agent of the hand), and also to make his wife a passive vehicle for the signs which he imposes; it is the most brutal example in all Restoration drama of the man's desire to write the character of the woman, a domestic equivalent to the dealings of history with Lee's Julia and Payne's Irene. But Margery, whose ineffectuality is initially indicated by her confinement to baby-talk, matures by gaining control of the art of signification (and, thereby, falsification), writing to Horner, learning the use of the hand, and becoming adept in visual display by disguising herself as Alithea.

When the ingenuous Margery assumes the guise of the apparently worldly-wise Alithea, she hints at some fundamental affinity between their conditions, and it is Alithea herself, with her determination to honour her 'word' to Sparkish, who most fully exemplifies the power of language to control and restrict female sexual conduct; for in her the power is supported not by the external tyranny of a husband but by internal principles and inhibitions. If Horner commences as a champion of antisocial freedom, Alithea commences as a champion of social bonds. She is obliged to Sparkish but not to Harcourt (II. i. 217; IV. i. 50), and consequently obliged also to tell Sparkish about Harcourt's advances to her (II. i. 250–1). Yet the manifest discrepancy between the dictates of obligation and those of the heart and even of common sense means that this pure embodiment of the social impulse is as problematic a figure as her antitype; for the life of pure sociability is as foreign to the intricacies of human nature as that of pure, unrestrained instinct, and Horner and Alithea consequently follow complementary and converging courses away from their original positions, the symmetry being emphasized by the sustained parallels between Harcourt's deception of Sparkish and Horner's of Pinchwife, which culminate when Margery disguises herself as Alithea in order to have sex with Horner. Horner gradually finds that his libertine designs do not create total exemption from social bonds, for his gang of mistresses quickly starts to exercise the kinds of claims and pressures from which he had sought escape, interrupting his privacy as remorsely as the public world interrupts that of Courtall and Freeman in *She Would If She Could*. He becomes a kind of sorcerer's apprentice, struggling to control the forces he has unleashed, and ultimately devoting more effort and ingenuity to keeping mistresses at bay than he did to acquiring them. And, in the banquet scene, he becomes the shared property of a consortium of women.

[32] The treatment of women as texts in this and other plays is well analysed in Jon Lance Bacon, 'Wives, Widows, and Writings in Restoration Comedy', *Studies in English Literature*, 31 (1991), 427–43.

From her opposite position of resolute social principle, Alithea too moves towards an accommodation of sociability and desire. Her name is derived from ἀλήθεια (truth), and she thus seems to symbolize the correspondence of word and deed, sign and substance, that is the foundation of perfect social existence. Yet her initial inflexible truth to her word threatens to stultify her personal life, and she takes her first, significant, step towards personal happiness when she violates the implications of her name by lying in order to prevent Sparkish from lunging at Harcourt with his sword (having been told that Harcourt disparaged his 'parts', II. i. 274). As her progress towards marital happiness proceeds, so her experiences become more and more linked and comparable to those of Horner's circle. Sparkish unwittingly co-operates in his own dispossession, as Sir Jaspar and Pinchwife do in their own cuckoldings, and both Sparkish and Sir Jaspar are bemused by extended conversations in which signs assume one meaning for them and another for the lovers. Whereas Lady Fidget is a willing conspirator in the China scene (and indeed takes the lead in it), Alithea is an unwilling and protesting conspirator when Harcourt declares love to her under the guise of praising Sparkish, and when he masquerades as his own twin brother. But the scenes work upon her passions despite her principles, and she is edged from her simple rigidity of word and value towards the ambiguities of conduct that receive their fullest manifestation in Horner's lifestyle.

Significantly, the Harcourt–Alithea and Horner–Margery plots are causally interdependent, for Harcourt's wooing of Alithea in the Exchange delays the departure of the Pinchwifes and makes possible the first meeting of Margery and Horner, and Alithea's ultimate union with Harcourt proceeds from Horner's seduction of Margery, who has by now become Alithea's double. The interdependence of the two plots continues to the end of the play, confirming the paradoxical blurring of distinctions between the marriage of the ideal couple and the stabilization of Horner's seraglio; for not only is Harcourt's trust in Alithea epistemologically similar to the cuckolds' renewed faith in their wives but, in the final moments, Alithea helps to persuade Pinchwife of Margery's innocence. Here, in the final intertwining of Horner's and Alithea's fortunes, the nominal representative of truth becomes unwittingly instrumental in the propagation of a lie. Just as the antisocial deceiver is bound to society, so the socially responsible symbol of truth becomes dependent upon Horner and his subversive masquerade. Alithea thus discredits the expectations that her name initially arouses, although her name is one which peculiarly insists on its own veracity, and she thereby demonstrates the difficulty of encompassing the totality of the self within the public world and the signs by which it coheres. The representative of truth fulfils herself through falsehood, and thereby becomes the prime example of the self-contradictory sign whose private meaning evolves in directions increasingly remote from its public origins.

If Alithea's name initially presents her as a symbol of truth, it finally suggests that truth and falsehood have merged in an enigmatic interdependence, as guilt and innocence had done in *Aureng-Zebe*. Such merging is in fact widespread, arising from an obsessive if misguided concern to discover whether the sexual partner is true or false, which in turn reflects a more general tendency to impose the structure of language upon the structure of life, this tendency being illustrated by the reduction of moral systems to glossaries of names. Truth is the goal and attribute of discourse, though it is problematic enough even in this area; but, as soon as one looks for it in the world which is the subject of discourse, it proves self-annihilating, as Alithea's career shows, and as the careers of Dryden's Cleopatra and Cressida will further demonstrate. As Hobbes wrote, '*True* and *False* are attributes of Speech, not of Things' (*Leviathan*, ch. iv, 105). Yet there can be no clearer attempt to impose the qualities of language upon the composition of life than to name a woman Truth.

If the entangling of truth and falsity parallels that of guilt and innocence in *Aureng-Zebe*, a still closer parallel is provided by the treatment of guilt and innocence themselves, for their stark and absolute antithesis provides another pattern demanded by the pure symmetries of syntax yet denied by the organic impurities of life. Here the problems of signification and social regulation become inseparably linked, for the administration of justice requires verifiable public signs of interior character, and valid, publicly agreed categories for classifying such character. London is from the outset identified as a judicial centre, since Pinchwife has been brought back to civic life by the demands of a lawsuit; yet London also becomes (as it was still more to do in *The Plain-Dealer*) an area in which the rituals and language of justice are progressively emptied of meaning. Alithea's sense of obligation to Sparkish derives from her sense of 'justice' (IV. i. 18), but she is freed from its influence through a series of misapprehensions about her moral character that is repeatedly imaged as a judicial ritual moving inexorably towards the wrong conclusion: 'in these cases', murmurs Horner, 'I am still on the criminal's side, against the innocent' (V. iv. 224–5).

The image of the trial continues after the exoneration of Alithea, encompassing the enquiry into Horner's and Margery's conduct: when the Quack arrives to testify to Horner's sexual incapacity, Horner thanks him for bringing 'a reprieve;' for, otherwise, 'I had died for a crime, I never committed' (V. iv. 341–2). This mock-trial of Horner, Alithea, and Margery forms the climax to a play in which sexual conduct is repeatedly discussed in terms of guilt, crime, and innocence: 'unlawful pleasures' and 'innocent diversion' (I. i. 118–19). The repeated description of Margery as a rustic 'innocent' acquires, in the overall context, the resonance of a judicial pronouncement. But the problem is not only that the signs of guilt and innocence are misleading: the very categories of guilt and innocence are themselves open to question, for there is nothing in this world of bored, neglected, or oppressed wives, deluded fiancées, and fatuous or tyrannical husbands to give any intelligible basis for the legal terms that define the duties of one partner to another. In the final mock-judicial ritual, where the inadequacy of public forms as guides and measures of private life receives its climactic demonstration (as it had in the trial by combat of Almahide), the socially responsible Alithea demonstrates their inadequacy as much as the subversive Horner, for even she can only gain private happiness by being tainted with the appearance of guilt.

The grand system of antitheses that supports the traditional order of civic life—guilty and innocent, true and false—has the simple and final symmetry to which linguistic structure easily tends, but to which the ambiguities and anomalies of human conduct can rarely conform. It belongs with linguistic artefacts such as Sparkish's list of crocodiles, harpies, and sirens. But there is another antithesis fundamental to the established social order: that between man and woman. Definition of sexual difference is a widely shared interest: Horner professes to find 'manly' pleasure both in 'good fellowship and friendship' (I. i. 192–3) and in 'being very drunk, and very slovenly' (I. i. 218–19), and Sir Jaspar and Pinchwife both base their marriages on simple, man-centred ideas of female nature, Sir Jaspar seeing women as 'gentle, tame' companions (II. i. 453), Pinchwife as natural but 'indocile' slaves moved to rebellion against 'their Politick Lords and Rulers' by their greater capacity for lust (IV. iv. 37–8). But, however powerful these fictions may be in determining the theoretical patterns of social existence, they remain fictions. Clearly, there is no uniform differentiation of intelligence and desire according to sex: though the word *fool* is liberally bandied around, there are three male fools (Sparkish, Sir Jaspar, Pinchwife) to one female (Margery), and the men remain imprisoned in their folly in a way that she does not. One of the significant features of Horner's banquet is that the women are able to dispense with feminine decorum, drinking and boasting of sexual conquests in a manner that is customarily the privilege of the male. And, if the women cast off the stereotypes of femininity in private, Horner, the pseudo-eunuch, has already publicly sacrificed the most cherished attribute of his sex. In the banquet we witness the collapse of the grand ordering polarities of social existence which are so blindly and complacently reasserted at the end of the play, where the deluded cuckolds' measured dance converts one of the archetypal images of universal order into one of desperate fantasy. At the end of the play, truth, innocence, and femininity are reasserted as pure absolutes, incapable of surviving contamination by their contraries, but in the banquet scene the immutable opposites of the public world coalesce. Illicit sexual desire paradoxically drives its devotees to social arrangements and contracts. Still more surprisingly, Horner's sexual vigour simultaneously proves him a 'true' and a 'false' man, providing another coalescence of ἀλήθεια and falsehood:

LA. FID. By this brimmer, for truth is no where else
  to be found, [Not in thy heart false man.　　　　　　　　*[Aside to* Hor.
HOR. You have found me a true man I'm sure.　　　　　　*[Aside to* Lady Fid.

　　　　　　　　　　(V. iv. 22–4)

Such advanced terminological collapse is a long way from the simple role-confusion of a play such as *The Mall*; but, at opposite extremes of quality, both are raising similar questions. To some extent, the saturnalian suspension of order in the banquet scene recalls the carnival licence of *An Evening's Love*; but it is a private, secret carnival, and one that inevitably mimics the order against which it rebels. And it is not a scene of joyous liberation: the disappointed division of shares in the male permits no such impression.

The next two King's plays, however, are far more traditional in outlook. Peter Bellon's *The Mock-Duellist* (before May 1675), already discussed, rewards virtue and gentility at the expense of a fortune-hunter, a bumpkin, and a *senex amans*, and tricks a faithless lover into marrying the woman he has deserted. More complex and adventurous is Sir Francis Fane's *Love in the Dark* (May 1675), which—like *An Evening's Love*, whose title it possibly echoes—portrays a conflict between the impulses to carnival and the regulating processes of social order. Like *The Country-Wife*, it opens with a rake-hero (Trivultio) dethroning custom and formal justice in favour of a liberated and festive nature:

> The Carnival's begun; the Feast of free-born Souls,
> Where Nature Reigns, and Custom is depos'd:
> That Magistrate of Fools.

　　　　　　　　　　(I, p. 1)

The liberty of carnival is then contrasted with the unfestive rigidity of the foolish Intrigo: while others appoint Lords of Misrule at their feasts, he appoints 'Clerks of the Uniformity' (I, p. 3), and abstains from flesh all day if a single dish appears out of its rank.

Expectations of another sexual romp are, however, disappointed, for the virtuous Aurana manages to end Trivultio's moral dislocation: to 'fix' her 'wandring dear *Trivultio*' (II, p. 26). Indeed, Fane portrays the unruly flesh from an explicitly Platonic viewpoint: an unexpected outlook in a play written by one of Rochester's friends, dedicated to Rochester, and bearing an epilogue by him. Trivultio's rambling lusts form a subordinate contrast to the divided loyalties of the virtuous Sforza, who is tested (like Wildblood) by means of the Invisible Mistress ruse, being courted by the masked Parhelia in the guise of three different women but remaining true to the first. Whereas Jacinta's triple disguise merely entangles Wildblood in the undiscriminating instability of the flesh, Sforza's loyalty to the masked unknown is associated with a transcendence of sense towards an apprehension of immaterial light. 'The Soul will show it self as clear/ Without the Face, her weak Interpreter,'

Parhelia instructs Sforza (I, p. 15), and she is repeatedly associated with the light of the sun. A *parhelios* is a false sun appearing by the side of the true, and Sforza describes Parhelia's disguises as 'Two Suns reflected streaming from the true one' (III, p. 49). Whereas *The Country-Wife* portrays truth disappearing amidst multiplicity of sign, Fane portrays a process of simplification and distinction which leads to the truth. Thus, although the play explicitly and repeatedly confronts its characters with problematic signs, it repudiates the scepticism of Wycherley and Dryden in favour of far older certainties: the world is a place of confused shadows, but the enlightened mind can ascend from the secondary sign to the primal form. Religion, Sforza says, is 'veil'd in Types from vulgar Eyes' (I, p. 8).

For Fane, as for Plato, the sun symbolizes the ultimate goal of the intellect.[33] Conversely, the darkness of the play's title, which is recalled throughout the play in imagery of night, cloud, and mist, denotes the blindness of fleshly lusts, as does the imprisonment that is inflicted upon Trivultio and Intrigo, and the apparent imprisonment that forms one of Parhelia's tests of Sforza. Intrigo, for example, is imprisoned after painting his face black in order to pursue a sexual intrigue in the guise of a negro, and one indication of Sforza's as yet imperfect enlightenment is that he mistakes the blackened face peering from a prison cell for that of his masked unknown: 'Oh, now my Heaven appears; but clouded still' (IV, p. 60). At Intrigo's level of life, signification is impossibly difficult. Whereas Parhelia's beauty is 'the Book of Fate' (II, p. 33), Intrigo's blackened face is a blotted book (II, p. 30), and he and another character gabble at each other in fake Moorish, each fearing that the other really knows the language (II, p. 29). Some illiterate officers imprison another fool, Cornanti, for treason simply because his name is as long as the name on the warrant. Intrigo's prolix servant Circumstantio constantly buries sense in a mass of distracting detail. And Intrigo misguidedly sees hieroglyphics and symbols in the most base and earthly of locations: in the scrawls on a lavatory wall (I, p. 11) and in lavatory paper itself, which, like all other torn paper, he reassembles and misdeciphers with the aid of a special frame, equalling the zeal of a country parson in perplexing an unambiguous text (I, p. 3). (Few other comedy writers of the period would use the clarity of Holy Writ as a model of perfect signification.)

The recurrent portrayal of imprisonment culminates in Act IV, when Trivultio and a number of other eloping lovers are imprisoned on the Doge's orders. Trivultio escapes by perverting the Myth of Er,[34] faking a suicide attempt and giving such glowing accounts of the other world that the guard tries to hang himself in order to share them—though he sees only 'a black Mist' (IV, p. 75) and 'a great Fog' (IV, p. 76). All then seems prepared for a

---

33 See Plato, *Republic* 507–20.

34 In book x of the *Republic* (613d–21d) Plato gives an account of the afterlife which ostensibly repeats that of Er, the son of Armenius, who is said to have revived twelve days after his death.

carnivalesque inversion of justice. Trivultio impersonates Cardinal Colonna and presides at the public trial of the lovers, sentencing them (and himself *in absentia*) merely to the prison of marriage, and conducting his inversion of judicial process to such good effect that the true judge is arrested as an impostor. But Fane once again departs from the example of *An Evening's Love*, for authority is restored when Trivultio throws off his disguise and begs the pardon of the Cardinal, who promptly ratifies all Trivultio's judgements. The civilizing of the rake is reflected in the reconciliation of carnival and justice.

Love in the Dark inspired no imitations, though the Invisible Mistress plot was reused in the following year in Edward Ravenscroft's intrigue play *The Wrangling Lovers; or, The Invisible Mistress* (Duke's, July 1676). Here mistaken identity and misconstrued circumstance produce jealous quarrels between one of the two pairs of lovers on whom the play concentrates. The other pair feature in the Invisible Mistress plot, in which a woman tests her lover's constancy by appearing to him in two different guises, veiled and unveiled. Remarkably, the woman's split identity arouses no mental conflict whatsoever in her lover, with the result that one of the favourite sources of tension in contemporary sex comedy is completely neutralized. The tested hero, Gusman, at first wrongly assumes that the veiled lady is the other of the two heroines; and, since the other woman is loved by his friend and host, he resolves to suppress his passion. When the veiled lady appears, unveiled, and apparently as a completely different person, love for the seen at once banishes any interest in the unknown woman. There is no perplexing conflict between the rational and the carnal: the unseen version of the heroine remains a complete cipher, and the hero is right to choose the seen, for she is the more fully known. If the play lacks Fane's insistence on the immaterial form beyond the visible sign, it shares his belief that signs may be implicit in nature as well as instituted by convention. 'These signs are the Language of Nature, by which she declares her wants,' says the servant Sanco as he awakes and rubs his eyes. 'Draw but the Teat from the mouth of a Babe, and still the lips retain a pretty sucking motion, which tells us with a silent sort of Oratory, that it is still a hungry' (I, p. 1). The impasses of *The Country-Wife* vanish: signs yield the meaning endowed by nature, and desire submits to the obligation imposed by society.

If it is unsurprising that *Love in the Dark* failed to start a fashion, it is perhaps more surprising that *The Country-Wife* contributed so little to the future course of Restoration comedy. Its influence is perceptible in Durfey's *A Fond Husband* and (especially) Ravenscroft's *The London Cuckolds*, cuckolding extravaganzas in which the rake is again portrayed with irony but without moral criticism, but these essentially farcical plays simplify and trivialize their model. The play which really set the agenda for sex comedy over the next few years was *The Man of Mode*, performed fourteen months after Wycherley's play, though the effect was almost wholly to produce reaction rather than imitation. Neither play is an archetypal pattern of Restoration comedy; each is exceptional, even unique. There are no other 'Horners and Dorimants' in Restoration comedy.[35]

Of the five new comedies performed between *The Country-Wife* and *The Man of Mode*, two were innocuously moral (*The Woman Turn'd Bully* and *The Mock-Duellist*), one a coarse burlesque (*Psyche Debauch'd*), and one (*Love in the Dark*) a philosophically elaborate rejection of sex comedy. Only Crowne's *The Countrey Wit* (Duke's, ?March 1675/January 1676)[36] actually contributes to the genre, and even here the emphasis is on the reform of the extravagantly outrageous Ramble, who eventually marries Christina, the virtuous daughter of Sir Thomas Rash, despite that tyrannic patriarch's determination to marry her to Sir Mannerly Shallow, who mistakenly marries the daughter of Sir Thomas's employee and namesake, the porter Tom Rash. In a parallel disturbance of the master–servant hierarchy, Ramble's servant Merry marries the man-hungry Lady Faddle by posing as a gentleman. Ramble has a last fling of libertinism by courting Betty, the kept mistress of Lord Drybone, and in the dark Sir Thomas mistakes Drybone's remarks about Betty for remarks by Ramble about Christina. Her anger at the apparent slander is the stimulus for Ramble's reform.

As the cross-purpose conversation indicates, this play resembles *The Country-Wife* in its concern with problems of signification. These appear at their most harmless in the lifestyle of Sir Mannerly, who is accused of writing anagrams and acrostics (I, p. 11)—Crowne repeatedly shows language declining into meaningless patterning and metaphor—and whose life is cluttered with inane signs. In the cultural isolation of Cumberland, he cultivates a taste for the non-realistic theatrical genres of pastoral and the heroic play, adoring the rants and far-fetched similes of the latter (IV, pp. 52–3). He has also staged an allegorical masque on the lines of Crowne's own *Calisto*, in which 'I was *London*, or *Augusta*, and I had a high crown'd Hat, to signify *Pauls Steeple*, and I had one acted the River *Thames*, I had a great Nose made on purpose to signify *London Bridge*' (IV, p. 52). Sir Mannerly's hat represents a landmark from before the Great Fire, and this enthusiastic signifier of a vanished city is hopelessly inept at reading the signs in the actual one, mistaking the propositions of coachmen and prostitutes for the civilities of gentlefolk and marrying the daughter of a porter because, in a confounding of both verbal and visual sign, the porter has the same name as Sir Thomas Rash and wears a badge displaying Sir Thomas's coat of arms (V, p. 74). Finally, the man who had so proudly signified the city in his allegorical masque resolves to

[35] The most recent use of this absurd phrase is in Julie Stone Peters, *Congreve, the Drama, and the Printed Word* (Stanford, Calif., 1990), 24. Robert D. Hume has already observed that Dorimant and Horner inspired very few imitations (' "The Change in Comedy": Cynical Versus Exemplary Comedy on the London Stage, 1678–1693', *Essays in Theatre*, 1 (1982–3), 101–18 (pp. 108–9)).

[36] The first known performance was on 10 Jan. 1676, but Nell Gwyn saw a play called *The Country Knight* on 19 Mar. 1675. See Danchin, *Prologues and Epilogues*, ii. 205.

return home and remove all its signs from his house: 'I will burn my Map of *London* that hangs in my Parlour' (v, p. 89).

Sir Mannerly's iconography of the city comically reflects Crowne's interest in the dependence of civilization on the sign that signifies without direct resemblance: the map is the perfect example of such a sign (recurring in a far more serious context in *The Destruction of Jerusalem*), but the allegorical tokens of London landmarks are others. So is the sign which bemuses Sir Mannerly on his arrival in the real city: the single name shared by two quite distinct people. But there are problems even in representational signs: in pictures, which form one of the commonest kinds of sign in the play. For pictures reduce dimension and complexity to pure surface. The central epistemological problem in Crowne's plays of this period is of how to interpret a many-dimensioned world on the basis of pure, flat, impenetrable surface; the kind of pure surface that is comically evoked in the name Sir Mannerly Shallow.

Far more serious problems of signification, both verbal and visual, occur when Sir Thomas is misled into thinking that Christina is unchaste:

CHRIS. I know not the sence of your discourse; your language has to me no meaning. . . .

SIR THO. Oh, you are for the substance, and not the *Picture* in words and phrases;— I'le tell you my meaning more plainly.

(III, p. 38; italics added)

Indeed, Christina's relationship with Ramble consistently creates problems of interpretation, since the isolation and verification of his true character are prerequisites of their marriage, and it is here that the problem of the picture is most fully treated: 'The scurvy Picture is too like the Life,' says Christina's maid, Isabella, after denouncing Ramble (I, p. 8).[37] Ramble the rake is the creator of spurious pictures. Seeking to sleep with Betty, he follows the ruse of the true lover in Molière's *Le Sicilien* by posing as a portrait painter. But Betty knows that both pictures and words can deceive: 'If your Pencil, Sir, flatters, as much as your Tongue, the Picture you will draw, will not at all resemble me' (IV, p. 60). Ironically, indeed, while the picture itself is a representational sign, the word 'picture' becomes arbitrary and ambiguous, exactly equivalent to 'China' in *The Country-Wife*: a random synonym for illicit intercourse (IV, pp. 65–6).

Confusion of sign breeds confusion of rank, manifested in the two marriages between gentle and servant classes. But the consequent implication is that rank is as arbitrary a sign as any other, and the blurring of social distinctions is treated with genial indulgence. At the end of the play Sir Thomas accepts Tom Rash (for the day) into 'our Society', though retaining a rather odd power to control the representation of his employee: 'I will have both

---

37 For other imagery of pictures, in addition to those discussed here, see I, p. 10 ('here's one glimpse of the Fool's picture I am to marry already') and II, p. 22 ('handsome Fools are her [Nature's] Pictures').

your Statues made in Ginger-bread, and set up in Costermongers-Hall' (v, p. 90). But such control is no more than the prostitute Betty exercises over her aristocratic lover. Scorning him as a mere sign without substance, a 'nothing with a Title' who is titular in lordship, manhood, and everything but money, she tyrannically censors his rights of expression: 'not a syllable he speaks to night, but shall cost him dearer than printing a Book in Folio' (II, pp. 24–5). At the end of the play, they are permanently and happily reconciled, their liaison accepted (like the elevated marriage of Tom Rash's daughter) into the 'Society' that Sir Thomas welcomes into his house. But it is a condition of their happiness that the prostitute controls the lord. Actual and titular authority are at variance. These liberal attitudes contrast remarkably with the servile support for Stuart absolutism in Crowne's serious drama. Monarchic authority is affirmed without any enthusiasm for the smaller, analogical systems of authority that traditionally support it.

Like Fane's Trivultio, Ramble is a genially festive extravagant in the line descending from James Howard's Philidor and Dryden's Celadon, though Crowne also shows the distressing impact of his extravagance on his virtuous mistress. Horner, too, develops and complicates the example of Celadon, for the limitations of his festive lifestyle are clear enough, though it is less clear that he is a reprehensible or destructive figure. Certainly, his actions raise more doubts than Celadon's: perhaps Margery's sexual awakening merely opens her eyes to the walls of her prison; and his refusal to clear Alithea is disturbing, even if it accidentally benefits her. A director may legitimately emphasize such questions as he will, but they are not explicitly foregrounded, and Horner's most visible victims are his eminently deserving (yet comfortably ignorant) cuckolds. Moreover, the initial casting of the play suggests a fairly light interpretation: Hart's previous record, predominantly in impressively heroic or charmingly outrageous characters, hardly suggests that he would have portrayed the nightmare sadist of some readings, and the cast lacked Rebecca Marshall (the first Olivia in *The Plain-Dealer*), who could have created a fearsomely voracious Lady Fidget. Instead, this part was played by the plump and sprightly Elizabeth Knepp. Nevertheless, once adultery and fornication are portrayed rather than merely talked about, the way is open for a more serious and complex treatment of human sexuality than had been called for by the insouciant reminiscences of a Philidor. *The Country-Wife* broke the taboos which restricted the earlier versions of libertine comedy; but, in breaking them, it created the conditions for an entirely different kind of play. By liberating festive drama, it destroyed it.

The change first appeared in Etherege's *The Man of Mode* (Duke's, March 1676), which creates a dramatic revolution out of surprisingly formulaic elements: the rakish Dorimant is tamed—perhaps—by the witty Harriet; in a more idealistic love plot, Young Bellair marries his beloved Emilia, despite his father's desire to pair him with Harriet and marry Emilia himself; and mirth is contributed by the subtle gaucheries of one of the best Restoration fools, the emptily ornate Sir Fopling Flutter. Etherege's innovation is to extend the scope of comedy to include the pain and bitterness of the rake's former conquests; and the inclusion of this alters everything else. When the hero's interesting past was a mere topic of conversation, ex-mistresses could be figures of uncomplicated fun: in *All Mistaken*, six of Philidor's conquests are trapped in a funeral vault, along with a man who has overdosed on laxatives. But Dorimant's victims, Loveit and Bellinda, are allowed to establish their own viewpoints, and to create circumstances which are not mere confirmations of Dorimant's outlook. As a result, Dorimant is disturbing in a way that Horner was not; for Horner preys only upon men. Nevertheless, the viewpoints of the victims are not allowed to predominate or to control the play: on the contrary, they are set against a social milieu where the acknowledgement or expression of such earnest concerns is a laughable *faux pas*; a milieu of perpetual festivity, where the fundamental hunger is for diversion and the fundamental metaphor for social life that of the game.

Entertaining Emilia and the fashionable hostess Lady Townley, Dorimant's friend Medley anatomizes a society committed to play: the obsessive gaming of Lady Dealer (II. i. 99–107), Dorimant's latest prank of serenading Loveit 'with kettledrums and trumpets' (II. i. 122), the tedious party games listed in 'The Diversions of Brussels' (II. i. 130), the postures catalogued in the fictitious 'The Art of Affectation' (II. i. 135), and gossip about new lovers recently 'brought into *play*' (II. i. 156; italics added). Medley himself is the arch-embodiment of his own theme, for his sole function is to supply diversion, to alchemize the base matter of life into pleasant and outrageous narrative. As early as *The Comical Revenge*, Etherege had been interested in the transforming power of narrative, but he had nevertheless allowed the festive actions of Sir Frederick Frollick to shape events; here, Medley (another Harris role) acts merely as a distorting lens, disengaged from the events that he turns into comedy. The festive outlook has been qualified, becoming a mode of interpretation rather than a mode of life, and permitting the contrasting mode of the tragically engaged Loveit to merit a hearing, if not to monopolize the play.

Medley attributes compulsive play both to the glamorous and the ridiculous, indicating that *homo ludens* is to be the subject of sceptical analysis rather than uncritical celebration, and he associates play with such a comprehensive range of social activity that it becomes nothing less than a generalized model of social existence. The game is Etherege's version of Montaigne's municipal law. For games involve not only amusement but arbitrary rules and conventions, and these are often explicitly equivalent to the rules and conventions of fashionable life: Sir Fopling Flutter, for example, cultivates the 'diversion' of studying 'his motions and his dress' in a mirror (IV. ii. 86–92). But play (in the sense of gambling) also symbolizes the characters' constant battle against the random and unforeseen contingencies which dominate life: Old Bellair chances to lodge in the same house as his son's secret love, Emilia, and falls in love with her himself; immediately after Bellinda has betrayed her friend Loveit by sleeping with Dorimant, the chairmen embarrass her by their 'unlucky' (IV. iii. 15) mistake in taking her to Loveit's house; after Dorimant has arranged that Fopling shall meet Loveit in the Mall (in the assumption that Fopling will be humiliatingly rebuffed by her), he finds that his own unforeseen meeting with Harriet there turns Fopling's carefully planned arrival into an unwelcome disruption; and events spin still further out of control when Loveit fails to act as predicted and wrong-foots Dorimant by feigning eager interest in Fopling. As in *She Would If She Could*, the Epicurean vision of a world ruled by chance indicates that there are no fixed natural principles of order which can be replicated in the laws and hierarchies of the community. Rather, the games of London society are localized and arbitrary systems of order constructed in the face of constantly encroaching chaos.

Language and other codes of expression are part of the social game, instituted by arbitrary and potentially mutable compact, their origins and sphere of operation lying in social interchange, not in the recesses of personal experience (words do not have the substratum of private significance that they possess in Wycherley). As a means of communicating the intimate, language is gravely defective, and when Dorimant wishes to convince Harriet of his genuine passion, he has to use signs of the same category that he has used in his trickery of Loveit: signs bearing no natural or verifiable relationship to thought or intention. Language is still more incapable of moving from expression of the social to expression of the transcendent, since the characters' many references to celestial or demonic agencies merely diminish these agencies to the scale of fashionable artefacts, as when Loveit's tearful destruction of her fan is mockingly described as a diabolically raised storm (II. ii. 153–61) or when, in the final invocation of the demonic, she calls on a horde of devils to carry off that walking artefact, Sir Fopling (V. ii. 361).

Private desires and cosmic terrors are alike denatured by translation into social discourse, the social artifice of language converting everything into its own substance. The diversions of the *beau monde* constantly appropriate private concerns as matters of general amusement, Medley announcing that new love-affairs have been 'brought into play', and urging Young Bellair to risk disinheritance by marrying against his father's wishes, in order that he might be publicly 'pointed at' (I. i. 448): all aspects of the personal life risk losing their quiddity by becoming figments in his repertoire of diversions. Consequently, Loveit's attempts to give tragic articulation to her suffering become self-negating, because their violation of linguistic decorum invites laughter, and because she perforce uses vehicles which cannot bear her intended weight of meaning: the vision of Fopling in the talons of a demonic horde shows how tragic rage may express itself in comic spectacle. Because it remains a system of game-like rules, moreover, and because it lacks sacred authority, language cannot actually bind or direct that which lies outside its compass. Loveit's impotent curses show that language is losing its sacred or magical efficacy, the curse showing only the powerlessness of the tortured and isolated mind to affect the world with the word. As with the curse, so with the oath: unsurprisingly, Dorimant argues that oaths are valid only for the duration of the desires that produced them, but even the virtuous Emilia recognizes that the fixity of the oath is incompatible with the flux of bodily existence, and forbids Bellair to swear constancy to her (II. i. 27–8).

Nevertheless, private desires cannot be pursued in perfect isolation from the signs and forms of the public world. Dorimant must speak to Harriet, and indeed she initiates a working relationship between the play of language and the earnest demands of personal desire; for Dorimant's interest in her is first excited by the linguistic descriptions of Medley, elsewhere the purveyor of playful fictions (I. i. 121–40), and when Dorimant first sees her he declares that Medley has, unprecedentedly, come near to speaking 'truth' (III. iii. 130). The play of language has become contaminated with seriousness, and henceforth Dorimant's gamesmanship, both in language and life, falters, since his desires now need the sanction of the public world. Dorimant thus experiences the characteristic problem of 1670s drama: that the social and private are as irreconcilable as they are interdependent. Exceptionally, Etherege does portray characters who confine themselves to only one: Loveit to passion, Fopling to social ritual. They are manifestly stultified, but what lies in between is not a balanced golden mean but a state of constant and shifting tension, whose rules vary from person to person. Emilia and Bellair gamble that the form of marriage will continue in harmony with the desires of the flesh, and their gamble seems safer than the one which Dorimant initiates with his first words to Harriet: 'You were talking of play, madam. Pray, what may be your stint?' (III. iii. 62–3).

Dorimant moves from dispassionate mastery of the game to experience of the risks and humiliations of pursuing earnest and intimate aims amidst a society whose customs he has hitherto been able to manipulate and reverse at will. He must, Harriet declares, learn to 'bear being laughed at' (IV. i. 166–7): to endure the embarrassment of seeing his passions become public property. Throughout the first half of the play, Dorimant is in virtual control of everything (though even here his planned rupture with Loveit is planned and dictated by Bellinda):[38] he encourages Bellair's marriage to Emilia in the hope that it will facilitate his own seduction of her, domineers jokingly over menials, announcing that the next servant to catch a clap 'shall rot for an

---

[38] See N. J. Rigaud, 'Les Faiblesses d'un héros: Dorimant dans *The Man of Mode*', *Études Anglaises*, 41 (1988), 24–36 (p. 26). Dorimant's failures to control events are also analysed in Professor Rigaud's earlier *George Etherege: dramaturge de la Restauration anglaise* (2 vols., Paris, 1980), i. 407–11.

example' (I. i. 20), enables a prostitute to sit in the most respectable region of the theatre, proclaims his right to ride an elephant through the streets of London (I. i. 487), insultingly triumphs over Loveit in her own lodgings, and easily outshines Sir Fopling. Once he meets Harriet, however, he loses his grip, and becomes subject to the random and unforeseen. Indeed, this meeting co-incides with the humiliatingly unexpected outcome of his attempt to stage-manage Fopling's courtship of Loveit in the Mall. Thereafter, mishaps multiply. Sir Fopling regularly (if unintentionally) embarrasses Dorimant by uttering his name in the presence of Harriet's mother, Lady Woodvill, who be-lieves him the Devil incarnate from his reputation alone. Dorimant's second visit to Loveit, immediately after his seduction of Bellinda, signally fails to re-create the easy triumph of the first, not least because he unexpectedly finds that Bellinda too is there, and he has to retreat in confusion before the telling accusations of his two mistresses. The discomfiture is the greater in that it arises from the actions of plebeians, since Bellinda has been brought to Loveit's through a mistake on the part of the chairmen who collected her from Dorimant's lodging: even the menial classes are no longer the easy victims of Dorimant's wit, as they were in Act I, but have the power to embarrass him. There is a similar shift in the balance of power between Dorimant and Emilia; for, in Act V, the designated sexual prey of Act I becomes his adviser in courtship strategy, preventing him just in time from the blunder of publi-cizing her marriage and thereby removing the emotional pressure on Harriet, who still believes that she herself is in danger of being married to Bellair (V. ii. 102–4).

Dorimant's embarrassments have been insufficiently noticed by critics, but they remain simple embarrassments, different in kind and scale from Loveit's humiliations, and lacking all character of moral retribution. If Etherege goes beyond earlier dramatists in displaying the emotional distress that the rake's life could inflict, he never supplies an obvious moral response to that distress. Few later dramatists reproduced this stance of detached, amoral observation, and *The Man of Mode* remained an exceptional play. Nevertheless, Loveit is not simply a ranting bore, for she scores enough points off Dorimant at the beginning of Act V to ensure that her viewpoint merits a hearing. Once again, the main point at issue is the conflict between justice and the flesh. Dorimant retains some of the carnival licence of Wildblood and Trivultio, indulging his 'flesh and blood' (IV. i. 324) with Bellinda before the 'Lent' imposed by Harriet (III. iii. 79), and delighting in images of decorum subverted by crude, fleshly presence: a prostitute in the best part of the theatre, an elephant in the fashionable streets. References to draconian or exemplary justice do run through the play, but they reduce the processes of justice to those of playful fantasy: the next clapped footman 'shall rot for an example' (I. i. 20), and the orangewoman will be prosecuted as a murderess (I. i. 83–6), her husband as a public nuisance (I. i. 247–8), and the shoemaker as an atheist and libeller (I. i.

244–6). A more serious invocation of exemplary justice occurs when Loveit interprets her unhappiness as retributive and exemplary suffering, advising Bellinda to 'Take example from my misfortunes' and 'give thyself wholly up to goodness' (V. ii. 348–50). But we already know that her example has had no deterrent influence on Bellinda. Indeed, judicial authority is suspended from the outset, when the orangewoman describes the judge who could not resist making himself ridiculous by kissing Harriet. Judges, Dorimant reflects, 'have not been wanting by their good examples to countenance the crying sin o' the nation' (I. i. 148–50): the flesh destroys the authority of the magistrate, and judicial example authorizes carnal licence. In Dorimant's own vocabulary, justice ceases to be an absolute and becomes synonymous with victory in his combative bachelor games: he will 'justify' his 'roguery' (I. i. 227) and 'justify' his 'love to the world' (V. i. 227–8). But Loveit still demands absolutes of justice: she is 'satisfied in the justice' (V. i. 190) of her flirtation with Fopling; and, when Dorimant mocks her 'growing infamy,' she protests that 'This from another had been justice; but from you, 'tis a hellish and inhuman outrage' (V. i. 172–5). In many plays of the mid-1670s, the woman is the victim of the judicial mentality. Here the female victim clings to it in a society where revelry and justice have changed places, with revelry now the ruling social principle and justice a challenge to prevailing order, but where the reversal of the pattern does not fundamentally alter the picture.

Dorimant's subversion of justice is thus harder to categorize than Wildblood's diversion of the approaching *corregidor*, or Merry's deposition of the cuckolded constable. It is not Justice in the Stocks, an assault on established social forms, for the marginal, transgressing woman has none of the attributes or customary authority of the judge. But she has the authority of the injured party, and throughout the second quarrel she consistently outpoints Dorimant with cogent and reasonable answers, forbidding him the easy triumphs of their first skirmish and ensuring that, when he does manipulate her into public repudiation of Fopling, his victory is one in which the viewpoint of the conquered is represented. If Loveit's tragic insistence on absolutes is embarrassingly eccentric in this relativistic world of comic play, her alien voice sometimes outreasons that of Dorimant, and the absolutes to which she appeals are ones commonly accepted. She creates one of the many unresolved elements in the play. She certainly represents the debit side of Dorimant's account, but debit and credit are given in different currencies, and we are not told the exchange rate. *The Man of Mode* is the first of several plays in which revelry, or festivity, or carnival lose the simplicity which they had before *The Country-Wife* broke the taboos.

Shadwell's *The Virtuoso* (Duke's, May 1676) followed too quickly upon *The Man of Mode* to show its influence, and indeed reveals that Shadwell was still mesmerized by *She Would If She Could*. In creating the part of Lady Gimcrack for his wife, Shadwell clearly drew on her earlier role of Lady

Cockwood, creating another mature lady who lustfully interferes in the affairs of two couples: her nieces, Clarinda and Miranda, and their lovers, Bruce and Longvil. It is a revealing sign of changing dramatic taste, however, that Lady Gimcrack is—unlike her predecessor—permitted to bed both heroes. A less localized affinity with Etherege is to be found in Shadwell's Epicureanism, ostentatiously signalled when, in the opening speech, Bruce approvingly recites (in Latin) Lucretius' famous description of the gods' care-free remoteness from human affairs (I. i. 7–12).[39] Shadwell is not, however, primarily interested in the rule of chance, and the Lucretius passage is chiefly introduced as a criterion of discourse: unlike bombastic heroic poets (i.e. Dryden),[40] Lucretius demonstrates 'that poetry and good sense may go together' (I. i. 5–6), and his ideal union of sense, eloquence, and practical wisdom stands in judgement upon the intellectual and linguistic decay of the present. Bruce and his friend Longvil go on to deplore the decline of the gentry into a class of illiterate, clap-ridden ignoramuses, and the play's trio of fools destroys the Lucretian balance of knowledge, language, and experience: Sir Samuel Hearty with meaningless verbal tags and physical pranks, Sir Nicholas Gimcrack with jargon-ridden investigation of the subhuman and microscopic, and Sir Formal Trifle with rhetorical inflation of the trivial. The greatest negation of Lucretian discourse occurs when Sir Formal tests Sir Nicholas's stentrophonical tube (megaphone) by reciting some lines of Homer through it, choosing Homer simply because his high proportion of vowels makes him peculiarly resonant. Contemplation of great poetry shrinks to contemplation of the physics of sound. But even the Lucretian passage polemically limits the range of human discourse, explicitly separating the human from the transcendent and divine. Human language does not echo a celestial archetype: as in Etherege, it is an earthbound and purely social instrument.

Despite his secular viewpoint, Shadwell propounds an unambiguous social morality, continuing to champion the traditions of gentility and citizenship that other major dramatists were finding outmoded and contradictory: the satire of diseased and ignorant gentlemen is satire of a class that has departed from the ideals of Henry Peacham's *The Compleat Gentleman*. Accordingly, whereas Wycherley exploits the ambiguities of the term *civil*—civilized, sexually compliant—to question established standards of social behaviour, Shadwell exploits it to reinforce them. For example, when Lady Gimcrack represents adultery as a 'civil' engagement in 'discourse' (III. i. 216–17), there is a simple contrast between the true and false versions of citizenship and

---

[39] See Lucretius, *De Rerum Natura*, ii. 646–51.

[40] David M. Vieth has persuasively argued that *The Virtuoso* was the immediate stimulus for Dryden's attack on Shadwell in *Mac Flecknoe* ('The Discovery of the Date of *Mac Flecknoe*', in *Evidence in Literary Scholarship: Essays in Memory of James Marshall Osborn*, ed. René Wellek and Alvaro Ribeiro (Oxford, 1979), 63–87).

language, parallel to that between the literacy of the old gentry and the debauchery of the new. Degeneration of citizenship is accompanied by that of human nature itself, for the title of the play signals a widespread corruption of *virtus* (literally manliness), not only in the activities of the virtuoso but also in the frequent and fraudulent claims to virtue by an assortment of prostitutes and whoremongers: the prostitute Figgup, for example, pronounces herself 'civil and virtuous' (IV. ii. 185).

Virtus, man-ness, cedes to animality and decay. Gimcrack learns the theory of swimming by imitating a frog, studies maggots and cheese mites, tours Italy to see not its civilization but its spiders, transfuses sheep's blood into human veins so as to produce a woolly man with—another corruption of discourse—a bleating voice, and (in a gross subordination of language to decaying flesh) reads a Geneva Bible by the light of a decomposing leg of pork. His philosophy of decay dissolves the fixed forms of social existence: man and sheep merge into a confused, equivocal existence, and he hopes to proceed from imitation of the frog to creation of an 'amphibious' humanity (II. ii. 28), *amphibious* very specifically suggesting the suspension of fixed limits and appropriate place. To the end, he pursues the dissolution of fixed form, finally hoping to recuperate his dissipated fortunes with the transmuting power of the philosopher's stone (V. vi. 130–3). When he does seek taxonomy and order, his systems belong to the alien realms of ants, spiders, and moon-men. In ants and spiders he detects 'government' and educability (III. iii. 29–30, 69–70): the principles of sociability that are disappearing from the human realm. He is 'no *stranger*' (III. iii. 45; italics added) to the tumbler spider, and amidst all the confusion and disintegration of human nomenclature he seals his intimacy with the spider world with an act of naming, endowing a spider with a version of his own name ('Nick', III. iii. 73) and training the creature to recognize it. The one human taxonomy to be attempted is a taxonomy of decay, when Sir Formal 'ranks the diseas'd people in their several classes, forms, or orders of diseases' (IV. iii. 235–6) so that they may receive prescriptions from Gimcrack, and even this pseudo-order collapses when the call 'Pox' (IV. v. 34) floods the stage with a chaotic mob. Traditional taxonomies of human rank, worth, and genealogy do not interest Gimcrack. What interests him are creatures believed to be spontaneously generated from decaying substances (III. iii. 5): maggots and the frog, to whose condition he himself aspires. He lives in a world from which ancestry has been erased, not only as a social but even as a biological principle, and he challenges the form of both human identity and civil society. According to Henry Peacham, travel abroad prepares the gentleman for exercising the native responsibilities attendant upon his degree, enabling him to 'haue rule ouer and instruct the ignorant'.[41] Gimcrack has learned only to instruct spiders.

41 Peacham, *The Compleat Gentleman*, 235.

Like many other dramatists, Shadwell repeatedly places his characters in situations of confinement: the dark vault into which Sir Formal and Sir Samuel plummet, the concealments in the woodhole (represented by the same trap as the vault) as couple after couple come to the same, seedy room for furtive sex, the box in which Sir Samuel has himself delivered to Miranda. Generally in this period, however, confinement—the little cell—represents the inescapable parochialness of any human code. Here, it represents a culpable deviation from the rational and the universal. In part, the confinement suggests deviation from the rational because it represents the constraint of what Sir Formal terms 'the clog of my sordid, human body' (I. ii. 229–30):[42] in the vault, deceived by the woman's clothes that Sir Samuel is wearing, Sir Formal tries to rape him, and this episode is paralleled and repeatedly replicated by the abortive sexual encounters in the small enclosure of the rented room, with its still smaller enclosure of the woodhole, which in turn foreshadow the converging crowd of pox cases at the end of the act. But elsewhere the confinement is of intellectual scope and enquiry, an insulation from contact with widely dispersed culture. The vault where Sir Formal assaults Sir Samuel is also the place where Sir Nicholas stores the bottled air of various regions, contracting many climes within a single prison prior to releasing and enjoying the air in the equally confined space of his chamber. Indeed, Sir Nicholas's schemes regularly have the effect of negating travel, of fixing the operator in one place: he learns to swim upon an immobile table, and the intended advantage of the stentrophonical tube is that it will facilitate oral communication without travel, to the point of rendering ambassadors obsolete. The contraction of intellectual horizons is pointedly illustrated when Gimcrack and Sir Formal describe a spider hunting a fly upon and underneath a table, and Sir Formal describes the spider coming 'to the antipodes of the fly' (III. iii. 56). The dimensions of their world have shrunk within the limits of a spider's existence. Gimcrack's confinement and immobility reflect his repudiation of rational social pursuits, and eventually he literally loses his place in the community when his estate is seized to cover the costs of experiments.

The plots that are woven around Gimcrack's scientific demonstrations transfer to the human level (where they properly belong) the kinds of problem and enquiry that he inappropriately pursues among the spiders. Epistemological concerns and language permeate all parts of the play—the non-scientists, for example, repeatedly strive to *understand* or determine the *meaning* of events—and the vocabulary of knowledge, discovery, and deciphering is equally prominent in both the scientific and non-scientific strands of plot: *knowledge* and *to know*; *to find* (most commonly *find out*), *discover*, and *invent* (Anglo-Saxon, Romance, and Latinate versions of the same idea);[43] *phenomenon* and *show* (Greek and Anglo-Saxon versions of the

---

42 The boast is recalled at IV. iii. 143–4 and V. i. 8–9.

43 *Invenire* literally means to find. *Invent* is restricted to the scientific plot, but its synonyms are not.

same idea); to *observe*, *watch*, or *see*. Preoccupation with acquiring or conveying knowledge is general, from Gimcrack's lofty if misguided conviction that 'Knowledge is my ultimate end' (II. ii. 86) to Sir Samuel's fondness for assuming a disguise and reiterating variants of the question 'don't you know me?' (II. i. 106).[44] Sir Nicholas's determination to 'find out' the scientifically recondite[45] is suddenly transferred to the human sphere when, catching each other in the same seedy room for the same illicit purpose, he and his wife seek to outface each other by claiming to be engaged in detection of the other's infidelity: 'Have I at length *found out* your base lascivious haunt?' (IV. ii. 97–8; italics added) demands Gimcrack, while Lady Gimcrack assures him that she came for 'discovery' (IV. ii. 93) of his own malpractice.

Similarly, Gimcrack's concern with observation of phenomena, and Sir Formal's complementary preoccupation with show,[46] misapply a decoding of appearances that is an essential skill in the sphere that Gimcrack explicitly rejects: that of human manners and conduct. Disguise and the misreading of outward signs are central elements in the plot: in the dark vault Sir Formal spectacularly misconstrues Sir Samuel's sex and attractiveness, and Sir Samuel himself farcically misinterprets all his humiliations at the heroines' hands as evidence of love. Sir Samuel, too, superintends the culminating proliferation of disguise and misinterpretation, the masquerade. Here, for example, Sir Formal elopes with the maid Betty instead of Clarinda; for, while he dutifully wears the costume whereby Clarinda is to 'know' him, Betty wears the costume whereby he is to 'know' Clarinda (V. i. 15–19). The heroines (exceptionally) are sensible enough to read signs correctly, giving tartly apposite answers when Sir Samuel and the whoremaster Hazard successively approach with the question 'Do you know me?' (V. iv. 10, 21). But Bruce and Longvil are less perceptive, for each is deceived into sleeping with the masked Lady Gimcrack, and each fails to recognize her, despite an insistent desire to 'know' who she is.[47] Instead, she forges notes in the heroines' names which lead each man, apparently, to 'discover' the 'discovery' (V. v. 14–16) that he has slept with the other's beloved. As a result, the friends begin to duel, and their mistresses temporarily repudiate them, outraged at the misconstruction of their characters. Lust has led the heroes to re-enact the moral and perceptual errors of Sir Formal in the dark vault, and, to emphasize the way in which lust pushes them towards the condition of the witless, their illicit dalliance is closely juxtaposed with an episode in which the hypocrite Snarl is publicly derided for his furtive whoring.

The ruse whereby Lady Gimcrack eventually enjoys the heroes, successively concealing her own identity in two different disguises, combines two popular

[44] See also II. i. 156, 164–5; III. iv. 162, 171; V. iv. 10.

[45] I. ii. 12; II. ii. 94, 96, 101, 102; III. iii. 6, 39, 81.

[46] For Gimcrack's interest in observation, see III. iii. 19, 86, 89; for his interpretation of phenomena, see III. iii. 6, 39, 92, 107–8; IV. iii. 213; for Formal's association with show, see I. i. 284; III. iv. 86; IV. iii. 159–60; V. ii. 124.

[47] V. iv. 72, 79, 99, 177.

devices for exploring the tension between man's social and instinctual character: the splitting of identity, freeing instinct from the constraints of social
role, and the bedroom trick, a special form of the divided self. There is, however, no implication here that the self is intrinsically and unalterably divided.
As in *The Libertine*, the bedroom trick corrupts potentially clear signs essential for social coherence, the corruption of signs culminating in the false
nomenclature of the forged letters, and the corruption of community in the
duel of the friends. In dividing her identity, Lady Gimcrack mimics her husband's dissolution of fixed forms and boundaries: a woman with two incarnations is, in a literal if exceptional sense, amphibious. But, if Lady Gimcrack's
carnality turns her into a personified ambiguity, the more rational lovers
easily clarify the false signs which had alienated them, and the men just as
easily transcend the life of pure, brute instinct. *Finding* (V. v. 80) that each
loves the woman who loves the other, they redirect their own affections with
the rational ease of an Orrery hero, regarding it as mere 'rape' to 'have the
body without the mind' (V. v. 77–9). In accommodating their desires to those
of the heroines, they endow women with rights of signification, departing
from the custom which, as Miranda complains, treats women as natural
'ciphers' (III. iv. 3). The lovers have, as Lady Gimcrack discontentedly remarks, 'come to a right understanding' (V. vi. 62). Gimcrack, by contrast,
who never cared 'for understanding mankind' (I. ii. 13) ends the play as an
entirely isolated figure, 'deserted by all' (V. vi. 130).[48] Shadwell's moral
schematism and earnest emphasis on the proper ends of knowledge are poles
apart from Etherege's open-minded relativism and Wycherley's labyrinthine
scepticism.

No such moral coherence distinguishes *Tom Essence* (Duke's, August
1676),[49] which even-handedly dispenses both sex and traditional morality. In
a plot closely derived from Molière's *Sganarelle*, Theodocia succeeds in
marrying Courtly rather than the debauched Loveall, whom her father
favours, though they are for a while estranged by the allegations of the per-
fumier Tom Essence and his wife, who suspect each other of infidelity with
one of the lovers. Loveall is in turn pursued and reclaimed by Luce, a widow
whom he has seduced on promise of marriage (and who therefore has a legal
claim to him), but this edifying plot is set off by one which portrays the
cuckolding of old Monylove, Theodocia's father. Even here, however, the rake
cuts a rather poor figure, being so submissive to his mistress that he is actually
willing to marry someone else at her command, and the stress on his submissiveness is consistent with the leading role given to women throughout the
play. Luce at one point uses the name Manly (III, p. 36), and Mrs Monylove's

---

[48] Shadwell's adaptation of *Timon of Athens* was first staged about Jan. 1678. The influence of
Shakespeare's play is evident here, and also in *The Woman-Captain*.

[49] Langbaine (*Account of the English Dramatick Poets*, 552) attributes the play to 'One Mr.
Rawlins'. See Milhous and Hume, 'Attribution Problems', 33.

adultery arises from her assumption of male disguise, when she enters her house disguised as her own brother; for, anxious to save money on linen, her husband accommodates the apparent youth in the same bed as her lover. *The Man of Mode* had been the first Restoration comedy to focus on the sensations of the discarded mistress (though Aphra Behn had already done so in her tragicomedy *The Amorous Prince*). *Tom Essence* is the first play to follow the lead of *The Man of Mode*, and (like a number of later responses) it rejects Etherege's morally non-committal stance, condemning the man and siding with the woman. Indeed, the play predominantly affirms the social and linguistic absolutes that *The Man of Mode* had rejected. Vows 'are in Heav'n Recorded' (II, p. 24), and the injured[50] characters seek and obtain justice: Luce, for example, vindicates her claim to be Loveall's 'Lawful Wife' (III, p. 36). Inconsistent and unoriginal as it is, this play provides the first sign of the impact created by *The Man of Mode*, and of a substantial modification of the direction taken by comedy.

[50] *Injury* is a recurrent idea: see II, pp. 19, 24; III, p. 30; IV, p. 39; V, pp. 51, 54, 55, 56, 57.

CHAPTER FIVE

'A Song expressing the Change of their Condition': Tragicomedy and Opera, 1668–1676

Tragicomedy, the dominant genre of the early Restoration, did not survive long into the 1670s, killed off by declining faith in the heroic and the hero-king. The decreasing convincingness of early Restoration forms is strikingly shown by Shadwell's recycling of John Fountain's unperformed *The Rewards of Vertue* (1661) as *The Royal Shepherdess* (Duke's, February 1669). The plot is one of restoration, the shepherdess Urania being saved at the last minute from decapitation by the revelation that she is the daughter of the deposed and martyred King of Thrace (she had been condemned for marrying and conceiving the child of a prince, but her exalted birth removes the scandal). Urania is also pursued by the married King of Arcadia, but he is reformed in a signally chaste bedroom trick (like that in Shirley's *The Gamester*), wherein his Queen impersonates Urania and talks him into chastity without the need for feigned adultery. When the King brazenly enforces the double standard by committing his wife to trial for infidelity, judicial ritual vindicates her without complication, and justice is thus universally triumphant. In the Urania plot Fountain seemingly tries to mitigate the early scandals of the reign, the King's philandering and the Duke of York's marriage to Anne Hyde, and reflects the early, vain, hopes that marriage would stabilize Charles II's wandering lusts. But, by 1669, his gauche but well-intentioned predictions about royal family life (if such they were) were almost satirically remote from the truth, and although Shadwell did not emphasize this remoteness he did present the play as a corrective to contemporary moral malaise: in his preface he again deplored his rivals' idealization of the debauched gentleman (p. 100), and the prologue amplified his concern with the abuse of class privilege:

> *In our times*
> *Small Faults are scorn'd, the Great are worthy Crimes,*
> *Onely for Noble Sparks, who think it fit*
> *That the base Vulgar should mean Crimes commit.*

(p. 101)

Epigraph: Dryden, *The State of Innocence*, I, p. 35.

There is another reform of royal infidelity, and perhaps another allusion to the Anne Hyde affair, in Frances Boothby's *Marcelia* (King's, ?August 1669),[1] the first original play by a woman to be staged professionally in Britain. Reprehension of royal philandering is clear enough when one of the heroes asks, topically, 'How strictly then are they to Virtue ty'd, | Who by Example, are a Nations Guide?' (IV, sig. K), but royalty is treated with great respect, and the King's infidelity lies simply in trying to abandon his fiancée for the heroine. Like Behn's slightly later *The Forc'd Marriage*, this play betrays the influence of *Othello*, yet, despite its place of honour in the history of women's writing, no other Carolean imitation of this much imitated play shows less interest in the mentality and mechanics of male power.

Melynet, an ambitious upstart who (like Iago) has 'miss'd the place | He thought himself so sure of' (I, sig. B), creates mistrust between his kinswoman Marcelia and her beloved Lotharicus, hoping to advance his interests by marrying Marcelia to the King, and plotting to cover up his scheming by arranging Lotharicus' murder. But the murder plot fails, the lovers are reconciled, and the placeless villain is banished from the court, the errant king rising to his proper role as fountainhead of justice. The play is less a feminist document[2] than a lament for the decay of feudal values, the corruption of honour, service, friendship, faith, and the oath being constantly stressed, with the King implicated in the general decline until his final enlightenment. The assault on the old order reaches an extreme, if innocuous, form in the rich fool Moriphanus, who pretends to have been ennobled by Cromwell and buys liveried servants (ex-beggar-boys) from an entrepreneur who plans to start a rent-a-livery service. Like Melynet, Moriphanus is eventually consigned to his proper placelessness, being finally seen departing for travel. In a yet more naked, but also more corrigible, conversion of bond, trust, and society into

---

[1] This is not the place for extended discussion of Frances Boothby's identity, but I must point out that the one identification so far proposed is clearly false: for Frances Milward, who married Sir William Boothby in 1653, died the following year (the identification is suggested in Maureen Bell, George Parfitt, and Simon Shepherd, *A Biographical Dictionary of English Women Writers 1580–1720* (New York, London, Toronto, Sydney, Tokyo, and Singapore, 1990), 31). The one suitable Frances in the Boothby pedigree is the daughter of Walter and Catherine Boothby of Tottenham, who was born *c*.1635 and was still alive (as Mrs Edw. Brewester) in 1690 (see L. Bazely, *The Family of Boothby* (London, 1915) repr. from *Miscellanea Genealogica et Heraldica*, 5th ser., i (1914), 7–56, 115–18, 179–94). Through the two marriages of her half-relative Elizabeth Basset, Frances was related both to the playwright Howard brothers and to the Duke of Newcastle. I have not, however, managed to link her to the two ladies whom our authoress names as relatives: Lady Yate, the dedicatee of *Marcelia*, and Anne Somerset, née Aston (*Tixall Poetry*, ed. Arthur Clifford (Edinburgh, 1813), 228–9). The Astons and the Yates were closely linked by marriages with the Gage family, and all three were Catholic families. I am most grateful to Sir Brooke Boothby for his prompt and very painstaking response to my enquiry about the history of his family, and to Mr Michael Hodgetts for generously sharing his knowledge about Lady Yate.

[2] Feminist readings are provided in Elaine Hobby, *Virtue of Necessity: English Women's Writing 1649–88* (London, 1988), 111–13, and Jacqueline Pearson, *The Prostituted Muse: Images of Women & Women Dramatists 1642–1737* (New York, London, Toronto, Sydney, and Tokyo, 1988), 133–5. Pearson does, however, write interestingly about Boothby's preoccupation with service.

rootless cash, the young blade Lucidore gets his friends to pay him for a look at his mistress, who turns out to be not a lady at all but a great heap of money, derived from the sale of all his lands. He does, however, reform and marry, and the play in general portrays the re-establishment of order and hierarchy: the curing of post-Restoration ills by a fulfilment of Restoration expectations.

By contrast, Aphra Behn's first performed play, *The Forc'd Marriage* (Duke's, September 1670),[3] portrays a serious conflict between social structure and personal desire, which can only be resolved when the the former is reconstructed in conformity with the latter. The play opens by portraying a culture dominated by masculine values: a celebration of a heroic warrior, Alcippus, in which all the male characters participate, but from which the women are absent, the acme of the ritual of masculinity being the victorious Alcippus' request to marry the heroine Erminia as reward for his valour. This replays the opening of *The Indian Queen*, with two differences: the king approves the match and the heroine does not want it (since she and Prince Philander are in love), but is forced into it by paternal authority. Behn thus disrupts the conventional plot pattern, in which the claims of love and heroic prowess coincide, and instead shows that the code of the warrior may blind men to the interests and rights of women: indeed, Alcippus' possessive jealousy leads him to attempt—successfully, he for a long time believes—to murder his wife. Once again, Restoration drama turns to the model of *Othello*, and once again we see that the cultural outsider has become redundant. As in Porter's *The Villain*, it is the culture itself that is at fault: the same impulse to possess by conquest that makes Alcippus its prime representative makes him also the 'strange wild thing' (IV, p. 344) who duels with his prince, attempts to murder his wife, and, even in his fits of penitence, consoles himself with the thought that no murder could approximate more to *justice*.

Such destructive aggressiveness is general. Even Philander treats Erminia with blinkered and possessive egocentricity, and the banter of the gay couple, Aminta and Alcander, is tinged with genuine fear and mistrust; hardly surprisingly, since Alcander nearly kills Aminta's brother. Nor does masculine disruptiveness arise solely from the vigour of young love. Like Urania in *The Royal Shepherdess*, Erminia was born in deceptively humble circumstances, but she is the daughter not of a king but of a rebel: her father, a general, was banished for using his military power to 'undermine the Government' (III, p. 337), and has only been pardoned because of Philander's love for her. The discovery of Urania's royal birth in *The Royal Shepherdess* reconciled the apparently subversive choices of personal desire with established order, but the prince's love for the displaced daughter of a suspected traitor implies that the operations of desire do not mimic an ideal pattern of social harmony, just as the father's ambition shows that male militarism may prove disruptive in

---

[3] By Behn's own account, her first play was *The Young King*, though this was not performed until 1679. See the dedication of *The Young King* (p. 105).

areas quite removed from sexual passion: the mentality that sustains the state also threatens it.

Nevertheless, Behn does not leave us with the sense of incurable inequity and unresolvedness that marks her mature plays. There is no strong hint that the passions provoked by the forced marriage will persist when partners are finally and properly redistributed, and the self-sacrificing noble rival Pisaro shows that bellicose possessiveness is not the inevitable attribute of the male, for he works to unite Alcippus with the Princess Galatea despite his own love for her. In moving towards the final concord, Behn abandons the model of *Othello* for that of *Much Ado About Nothing*, Erminia returning from apparent death to claim a happier form of existence, and the mode of her return clearly associates it with a new representation of the female role. Alcippus has a portrait of Erminia with a mirror on the reverse, their conjunction literally reducing the woman to a sign reflecting the male, and Erminia's return from death is first conveyed to Alcippus when she stands behind him, so that her reflection appears alongside his, announcing that women have a separate and equal significance. Whereas Hero's symbolic resurrection permits the completion of her original marriage ceremony, however, the precondition for Erminia's symbolic resurrection is a divorce which amounts to a wholesale dismantling of established order: for her marriage has been initiated as an expression of the royal will and celebrated amidst full court ceremonial. In Behn's mature plays, by contrast, the victims of forced marriage can only escape into unequal and unsatisfactory adulteries: the dreams of a new order have been abandoned.

New feminist orders are the subject of two characteristically eccentric plays by Edward Howard. Scythia in *The Womens Conquest* (Duke's, ?spring 1670) is a male supremacist culture in which, in obvious satire of the contemporary state of British marriage, husbands betray their wives with impunity and enjoy the right of arbitrary divorce. It is set against its mirror-image, the kingdom of the Amazons, and the Scythian males experience the role-reversal of capture by the Amazons. But the golden mean which emerges from this clash of extremes is merely a more benevolent and tempered exercise of male authority; for, as the Queen of Scythia concedes, 'nature and the worlds best Laws | Have dignify'd the man superiour' (I, p. 15). Howard clearly sees that Restoration sexual liberation is liberation only for the male, but his plan to improve the woman's lot is merely to remove abuses in the status quo. A similar design marks his *The Six Days Adventure; or, The New Utopia* (Duke's, March 1671). In Howard's Utopia power constitutionally alternates between the sexes, and during the play the women assume the government (cf. Aristophanes' *Ecclesiazusae*), endow themselves with the right to make the first move in courtship, and set up a court to regulate male misdeeds in love, with much stress on the creation of justice. But the experiment ends when men go on strike by withholding their love (*Lysistrata* in reverse), and

democratic experiments give way to the restoration of monarchy. In his preface, Howard concedes that women might, if equally educated, prove equal
to men in ability; nevertheless, he has sought 'to confirm the judgement
and practice of the world in rendring them more properly the weaker Sex'
(sig. A3ᵛ).

The attainment of justice for women was also the subject of Behn's second
play, *The Amorous Prince* (Duke's, February 1671), performed shortly before
The Six Days Adventure. Topically enough, Behn portrays a philandering
ruler: Prince Frederick has seduced Cloris, the sister of his friend Curtius, and
also uses his power and status in an attempt to deprive Curtius of his mistress
Laura. There is a new explicitness in the portrayal of sex, the opening scene
depicting the immediate aftermath of Cloris's seduction. Frederick's philandering is one of a number of parallel abuses of male power, all of which
push women into what is loosely called whoredom. For example, in an abuse
of husbandly authority which parallels Frederick's abuse of royal power,
Antonio tests his wife, Clarina, by persuading his friend Alberto to court her:
'For this uncertainty disturbs me more, | Than if I knew *Clarina* were a—
Whore' (I, p. 144). Alberto is tricked by Clarina's sister Ismena into courting
her instead, but nevertheless puts loyalty to his friend above growing attraction to the imagined Clarina, until the trick is exposed. The real Clarina is,
however, courted (unsuccessfully) by the whoremaster Lorenzo, whose
attempt to buy her favours by relaying lavish gifts via her woman, Isabella
(who in fact keeps them), is the fullest and most flagrant attempt to prostitute
the object of desire. Frederick's tyrannical domination of women is nevertheless conducted in the language of the courtly lover, courtly love being merely
a disguised exercise of male power.

The discrepancy between social and moral 'Quality' is repeatedly emphasized, as is the divorce of power from justice. Access to justice is once again a
key concern. Victims complain of 'injustice', 'injury', 'wrong', 'crime',[4] and
the central enigma of criminal authority creates a derangement of classifica-
tion in which the innocent are repeatedly classed as criminals: Curtius is proclaimed a traitor for opposing Frederick, and Alberto, believing that he loves
his friend's wife, considers himself a traitor, criminal, and much beside. The
collapse of authoritative justice leads to a proliferation of revenge schemes
and, in a climactic dislocation of roles, Frederick is lured into a supposed
brothel, where the various abused women of the cast confront him in the guise
of prostitutes (the first occurrence of a recurrent Behn image), and where
Curtius and (apparently) some hired ruffians menace him with pistols and
reproach him for his 'Injuries' and 'Crime' (V, pp. 204–5).

In Settle, the problems of the criminal ruler permit no easy solution. Here,
however, all is put right by the reform of Frederick and Antonio, and by a

4 II, pp. 149, 158; III, pp. 161, 167, 170; IV, pp. 183, 191; V, p. 205.

harmonious sequence of appropriate marriages in which the only jarring element is the unwilling marriage—on Frederick's command—of Lorenzo to Isabella, who has ensnared him by a bedroom trick in which she masqueraded as Antonio's wife. Frederick's abuse of monarchic authority thus leaves no lasting questions about the nature and validity of monarchy, and he always remains God's vicegerent: 'where lies this Power divine,' ponders Curtius, 'That can so easily make a Slave of mine?' (IV, p. 183). Though Curtius believes he is employing genuine ruffians in the brothel episode, they are in fact his friends in disguise, determined to avert any genuine threat to their ruler. The uncaging of the rabble is averted, and passion submits to social discipline. The order established, however, is not one of sexual equality. Throughout the play, men can act directly, whereas women can only pursue their ends by disguising themselves—temporarily escaping their prescribed roles—in order to elicit action from men. In the brothel scene, Antonio and Alberto appear as bravoes, figures of pure, brute action, whereas the women appear as prostitutes, objects of male purchase. For men exercise control not only through force but through money, and also through language. Frederick, for example, 'has a Tongue and a Purse that seldom fails' (III, p. 164).

Cloris does gain some linguistic authority, but only when disguised as a man. Unrecognized by Frederick, she tells him of her sufferings, reversing the sexual roles of oppressor and oppressed, both gaining the ability to narrate and making this ability the subject of her narration: '[I] told so oft the story of my Passion, | That she grew weary of the repeated Tale' (IV, p. 184).[5] The greatest female linguistic triumph is secured by Isabella, appearing (at great profit to herself) to assist Lorenzo's courtship of Clarina, yet leaving him in a condition in which he is 'confin'd to Signs and Grimaces only, | To declare his Mind in' (I, p. 132). But all linguistic ability is strikingly removed from women in the brothel episode, where they lose the capacity not only for action but for speech: Laura, the woman Curtius loves, '*shakes her Hand, as not understanding*' and '*answers in Grimaces*' (V, p. 203). In their masquerade as silent prostitutes, the heroines sum up the condition of women as the objects of men's desire, men's money, and men's language. The prostitute is what remains when a woman is not recognized as a sister, wife, or daughter (Laura is 'a Stranger', V, p. 203): when, instead of being classed by her relationship to a particular man, she is classed by her relationship to all men. The masquerade is the episode which restores justice; yet women (literally) have no voice in the restoration of justice, just as Almahide literally has no voice in the trial by combat towards the end of *The Conquest of Granada*.

A woman seeks her rights with more complete success in John Crowne's *Juliana; or, The Princess of Poland* (Duke's, June 1671), a late example of

---

[5] Women exercise greater authorship and authority in Behn's fiction, though their power is still viewed with considerable ambiguity. See Jacqueline Pearson's excellent 'Gender and Narrative in the Fiction of Aphra Behn', *Review of English Studies*, NS 42 (1991), 40–56, 179–90.

drama celebrating restoration, with the familiar cycle of restoration being transferred to a woman ruler, who is rescued from the prospective slavery of marriage to a Muscovite prince to assume the throne along with her chosen husband. The plot is ramshackle and implausible. In a ceremony conducted in complete darkness, Prince Demetrius of Muscovy has married the Czar's daughter Paulina by impersonating Duke Ladislaus, whom she loves. A number of misunderstandings inevitably proceed from this bold deception, Paulina being puzzled by the neglect of the real Ladislaus, and Juliana—who also loves Ladislaus—being enraged by his apparent infidelity, though the play ends with clarification and reconciliation. The play's coherence, in so far as it has any, derives from two linked and recurrent images. One is of displacement and estrangement. Despite her 'quality', the Princess Paulina has become a 'wandring Exile . . . in a strange Country' (III, pp. 23–4) in pursuit of her imagined husband, and characters are repeatedly introduced or identified as strangers,[6] so that the ludicrous improbability from which the Plot proceeds—marriage in the dark to an unrecognized man—at least has the merit of symbolizing Crowne's view of the human condition. The suspension of social coherence is illustrated when a supposedly comic Landlord steals a travelling bag containing Demetrius's princely garments, hoping thereby to set himself up as a landed gentleman. Social quality is, briefly, represented by possession not of place and estate but of mobile property (as it was also to be, a generation later, when Farquhar's Archer and Aimwell lugged from town to town the box of money that was the chief surviving token of their status). But the ultimate restoration of order is, for 1671, unusually uncomplicated.

Not so the restoration in Dryden's *Marriage A-la-Mode* (King's, ?November/December 1671). Dryden here pushes to extremes the popular avantgarde theme of identity divided and destabilized by the conflict between social regulation and private desire, his protagonist being a man whose information about his identity keeps changing with bewildering rapidity, until he is finally revealed as the true, hereditary monarch of Sicily. There is no progress of an innately royal character to his preordained royal place, as there is in Dryden's source.[7] Rather, the relationship between social role and the intrinsic self (if there is such a thing) becomes increasingly perplexed and paradoxical.

The Sicilian usurper Polydamas goes in search of his long-lost only child, of whose sex he is ignorant. He at first fixes on the young fisherman Leonidas and commands him to marry Amalthea, the daughter of his former partner in rebellion. Despite Amalthea's virtue and beauty, Leonidas remains loyal to his peasant sweetheart, Palmyra, whom Polydamas consequently resolves to execute. In the nick of time, however, *she* is identified as his true child, whereupon Leonidas returns to peasanthood and Palmyra is commanded to

---

[6] I, pp. 4–5, 7; II, pp. 17–18; III, p. 27; IV, p. 36.

[7] 'The History of Sesostris and Timareta', in *Artamenes; or, The Grand Cyrus*, vi/ii, pp. 76–125; vi/iii, pp. 126–8; vii/i, p. 13; vii/ii, p. 92.

marry Amalthea's wicked brother, Argaleon. Leonidas then turns out to be
the son of the deposed, rightful king, and is sentenced to death. Divided in
loyalty between her lover and her new-found father, Palmyra swoons helplessly as Leonidas is led to the scaffold, but Amalthea provokes a successful
rising in his favour. Leonidas and Palmyra marry, Polydamas is forgiven, but
Amalthea and Argaleon remain—despite their opposed moral characters—
fixed in parallel states of painful unfulfilment. This heroic plot of restoration is juxtaposed with a comic plot, also depicting an imbroglio of four
lovers: more obedient to paternal command than their heroic counterparts,
Palamede and the scatty social climber Melantha are about to enter an
arranged marriage, but nevertheless become entangled with Rhodophil and
Doralice, a bored husband and wife, each man and woman coveting the
other's partner. But the illicit pairs keep meeting and frustrating each other's
attempts at adultery, and the men's possessive jealousy finally convinces them
that fidelity is pragmatically advisable.

Both plots re-establish a legitimate status quo, and indeed Palamede and
Rhodophil assist decisively in the restoration of Leonidas. But both reveal
problems that survive the return to legitimacy: most notably, the problem of
discovering an interior principle of selfhood amidst the forms imposed by the
public world. Leonidas and Palmyra strive to maintain a consistency of self
amidst bewildering and rapid shifts of social identity, while the comic lovers
are trapped in fixed states which they wish to vary: whereas Leonidas struggles
to cope with his triple change of identity, Rhodophil resents Doralice's unending sameness, indulging in sexual fantasies in which—more protean even
than Leonidas—she is transformed into every beautiful woman in Sicily.[8]
Rebellion against social impositions on the self is expressed in both plots in
constant attempts to gain sexual privacy, which are thwarted by the equally
constant intrusion of the public world. The comic lovers' attempts at adultery
are invariably interrupted, the last interruption coming when the men are
summoned by the usurper to arrest Leonidas (IV. iii. 160–87): a clear triumph
of public concerns over private appetites. Similarly, crowding and interruption constantly inhibit the conversations of Leonidas and Palmyra, and
even interfere with Leonidas's discovery and declaration of his identity: when
the loyal Eubulus is about to make the revelation, approaching strangers force
a retreat to 'much more private' surroundings (IV. i. 117), though even these
are later invaded (IV. iv. 119), and the threat of public scenes to self-definition
culminates when Leonidas is prevented from naming himself on the way to
the scaffold. The comic lovers' desire for privacy is thus not merely a desire to

---

[8] 'La constance en amour est une inconstance perpétuelle, qui fait que notre cœur s'attache succes-
sivement à toutes les qualités de la personne que nous aimons, donnant tantôt la préférence à l'une,
tantôt a l'autre; de sorte que cette constance n'est qu'une inconstance arrêtée et renfermée dans une
même sujet' (François de La Rochefoucauld, *Maximes*, ed. Jacques Truchet (Paris, 1967), 325).
(Truchet's edition contains texts of all the substantive editions. I am quoting Maxime 184 in the first
edition (Paris, 1665).)

copulate, but part of a more widespread, and generally thwarted, aspiration to liberate the intrinsic self from the pressures of the outside world.

But liberty and the self are irreconcilable ideas, and privacy merely brings an alternative expression of bondage. On the one hand, the self has the bondage of the puppet, passively influenced by external forces; on the other, it has that of solitary confinement, for it cannot directly apprehend the agencies which work upon it, perceiving only the mental phantasms of objects, never the objects themselves. Once again, the mind is a sealed dungeon. One consequence is that sex is an even more private affair than is usually assumed, for desire is directed at the phantasm rather than the corporeal partner, who becomes a mere medium for the enjoyment of imagined forms (as when Doralice is transformed in Rhodophil's sexual fantasies). Repeatedly, the outward, corporeal partner is eclipsed by the partner inwardly created in the imagination. The attachment of Doralice and Palamede derives its intensity from its unfulfilment, retaining its charm because corporeal reality has not intruded on the anticipating imagination ('we might upon trial have lik'd each other less,' Doralice muses, V. i. 252–3), and when the comic lovers visit a court masquerade, Palamede praises the masks for obliterating the actual identity of the partner, creating unindividualized forms that the imagination can transmute as it will (IV. i. 136–44). So entirely is desire aroused by the imagined rather than the seen that Palamede begins to lust after Melantha only when he has had an erotic dream about her (V. i. 194–6).

When the characters seek to escape control by public pressures and forms, therefore, the alternative is not a life of unconstrained private companionships but the total isolation of Almanzor's 'Pris'ner of the Mind'. The same is true of the heroic lovers. Opposing Polydamas's insistence that he marry Amalthea, Leonidas tries to remain true to a fixed sense of inner identity untouched by his change in outward circumstances: 'something too | I owe my self' (II. i. 310–11), he urges. But, for him too, autonomy of self leads to entrapment within the imagination, as he reveals when he ponders how to express love during a life of constant public ceremony:

> Our souls sit close, and silently within;
> And their own Web from their own Intrals spin.
> And when eyes meet far off, our sense is such,
> That, Spider-like, we feel the tender'st touch.

> (II. i. 499–502)

Strikingly, love is here portrayed as the lonely imaginative creation of the lover, created, like a spider's web, from the solitary inward resources of a single being. In heroic love, as in comic, the corporeal partner is perceptually inaccessible.

The personal life which is so earnestly sought is thus not an ideal state of self-fulfilment but a problem-ridden isolation amidst the phantasms of the mind. Yet, within the deepest privacy of the imagination, the characters are nevertheless insidiously manipulated by extrinsic forces. Even Leonidas, who makes the most determined effort to retain a consistency of self, cannot suc-ceed completely. When first promoted from peasant to prince he acquires the mannerisms of power with surprising rapidity, brusquely ordering Argaleon about within seconds of his elevation and receiving the apt riposte, 'You . . . over-act your part, and are | Too soon a Prince' (I. i. 423–4). And, though abrasively wilful as the usurper's son, he becomes benign and forgiving when established as the legitimate king: the man inevitably changes to meet the potentialities of his role.

Susceptibility to external influence is far more flagrantly obvious in Melantha, who is a human chameleon. As Montaigne found that he spoke dif-ferently at Paris and at home,[9] so she changes in conduct and self-perception as she alternates between country and court: 'when I have been once or twice at Court,' she explains, 'I begin to value my self again, and to despise my Countrey-acquaintance' (III. i. 150–1). We might expect nothing else from such a mercurial social climber, but her experiences are strikingly paralleled in Palmyra's elevation from peasant to princess; for Palmyra too makes the journey from country to court, and she too changes with remarkable rapidity to fit her new circumstances. When her true identity is first disclosed, her relationship with Polydamas changes instantly from that of condemned crim-inal and hanging judge to that of daughter and father, and there is a equally abrupt change in inner inclination, for she immediately acquires the dutiful affection of a daughter, her instant closeness to her new-found father intro-ducing a corresponding distance in her relations with Leonidas:

> If I know the King, though you are not his son,
> Will still regard you as my Foster-brother,
> And so conduct you downward from a Throne,
> By slow degrees, so unperceiv'd and soft,
> That it may seem no fall: or, if it be,
> May Fortune lay a bed of down beneath you.

> (III. i. 445–50)

This adapts a speech which in Dryden's source is given to the usurper,[10] and by transferring it to the heroine Dryden introduces an unsettling sense of change and distance which is preserved in the lovers' later dealings. For example, when Leonidas requests 'One hours short audience' (IV. ii. 27) at their foster-father's house, she accepts with surprising reluctance and gracelessness ('Perhaps I should [refuse], did I consult strict vertue', IV. ii. 29), and through-out the meeting itself her disturbing reserve continues. 'Fear nothing; and hope, all' (IV. iv. 38), she reassures Leonidas, only to withdraw the reassur-ance at once: 'Think what a Prince, with honour, may receive, | Or I may give,

---

[9] *Essays,* iii. 103 (ch. v).   [10] *Artamenes; or, The Grand Cyrus,* vi/ii, p. 115.

without a Parents leave' (IV. iv. 39–40). Throughout the encounter, Leonidas doubts her love for him, and her divided loyalties do almost drive her to renounce him irrevocably, for Leonidas just manages to silence her as she begins an oath to repudiate him should he take arms against her father (IV. iv. 79–86). He then arrests and imprisons her to protect her from the claims of her new self, kneeling as he does so to express his continuing love. In their pastoral life, Leonidas had knelt to Palmyra when she was crowned as May Queen, the incident demonstrating a perfect harmony between public ceremony and private inclination, and the ironic recollection of the gesture at his point emphasizes that the actions demanded by the lovers' new roles can no longer signify the passions which arose in different and lost circumstances.

Later, Palmyra's new and old identities conflict so much that she can only escape from both into unconsciousness, swooning so that she need not choose whether to save her lover's life at the cost of her father's throne or her father's throne at the cost of her lover's life (V. i. 426–34). Yet, as the loved Palmyra proves increasingly reserved and helpless, the rejected Amalthea acts generously and decisively on Leonidas's behalf, securing his meeting with Palmyra at the masquerade (IV. i. 73–95) and eventually saving him from execution as Palmyra swoons (V. i. 438–47), though to do so is to endanger her own brother. Finally, the elaborate permutations of status and identity equal the lovers once more and make their union again compatible with the exactions of the outside world. But it is a new world, and the lovers (like Doralice and Rhodophil at the beginning of the play) are new people joined by the commitments of an old existence. Though the pairing of Leonidas and Palmyra had a natural symmetry in their lost pastoral paradise, the symmetry which emerges from more recent events is that of Leonidas and Amalthea (the problem does not arise in the source, where the lovers remain ideally matched, and where Amalthea's equivalent, Liserina, is unscrupulous and ambitious). Pastoral simplicity yields to tragic untidiness, and the claims of the vanished world frustrate the potentialities of the actual. The lovers have changed enough to prevent us from rejoicing in their union, but not enough for them to abandon it.

So vulnerable is interior life to external control that language serves less to express thought than to impose public values. In Leonidas and Palmyra's pastoral life, language had seemed a natural vehicle for personal affection: Leonidas had taught a starling to speak Palmyra's name, and had carved both their names on trees. But they now rarely converse, for language reflects the claims of their new selves: Palmyra 'cannot tell' (I. i. 441) her feelings for him, and he, equally, 'cannot | In publick' (I. i. 456–7) speak his thoughts to her. He has to silence her to prevent her from renouncing him, and she cannot save him from execution by proclaiming his true identity. The social tyranny of language also dominates the lives of the comic lovers. The men's quest for private, furtive copulation is also a desire to escape into pure, silent, inarticulate instinct: on the point (as he believes) of sleeping with Doralice, Palamede is 'past talking,' (III. ii. 33), and Melantha so compulsively socializes and talks that Rhodophil has never had sex with her; indeed, Palamede has to drown her voice in order to make her marry him, this incident closely paralleling Leonidas's silencing of Palmyra, whose language has become equally inimical to the prospect of marriage. It is Melantha, also, who provides the extreme illustration of language as an exterior, public convention, with no expressive relationship to the personal consciousness. In one of the play's funniest scenes, her maid reads from a paper the daily list of French words which she has chosen for her mistress's use. The words are mechanically learned and explicitly unconnected with Melantha's own experience, yet they are essential to preserve her sense of her social position. But, though Melantha's folly is extreme, it is an extreme form of a general condition: in the following scene, another subordinate produces another paper, which instantly transforms Palmyra from peasant to princess, and consequently determines and inhibits her future range of speech.

The private self is elusive and ultimately undiscoverable: the more intimately one penetrates into the human constitution, the more it retreats from view, even the imagination, that last sanctuary from public influence, turning out to be essentially a creation of outside forces. The characters are trapped in an endlessly circular paradox, unable to escape from the prison of the mind to unmediated apprehension of the world beyond its limits, yet at the same time constantly subject to that world. On the one hand, Palamede praises the masquerade for liberating the imagination from all debt to the objective, and indeed for suspending familiar social forms and investing the partner with the allure of the strange and savage: 'she's all *Terra incognita,* and the bold discoverer leaps ashoar, and takes his lot among the wild *Indians* and Salvages' (IV. i. 141–2). Yet he also describes the masqueraders as 'Puppets' (IV. i. 133), and thereby points to an important and recurrent truth: that, even when the imagination is most apparently unconfined, man still has his strings tugged by external forces. If Palamede starts to lust after Melantha because he has dreamed of her, representing lust as a mere response to an internal phantasm, he also lusts after her because his rival Rhodophil does, just as Rhodophil regains interest in Doralice because he respects Palamede's judgement in women. Lust is, equally, a response to the private, solitary imaginings of a dream and to the public pressures of social example; what it is not is a direct, unmediated response to the intended partner. Melantha's closest approximation to a sexual encounter with Rhodophil occurs when she acts out a complete seduction by him; but the enactment is imaginary and solitary (III. i. 248–58), and she is attracted to Rhodophil not by his charms as an individual male, which she never considers, but by his mastery of public fashions, his letters being 'so *French,* so *gallant,* and so *tendre*' (III. i. 244–5). Melantha's solo fantasy of seduction illustrates the almost solipsistic nature of the imagination, its subordination of the physical partner to the image-forming mind, yet her lonely imaginings are primarily shaped by the public world. Man is at once too lonely and too public to be capable of sexual partnership and understanding. The opening song about a dead marriage which Doralice seeks to practise in solitude may sound like a heart-felt call for sexual companionship (I. i. 3–18), but it is in fact being memorized by rote at the command of a public figure, 'the Princess *Amalthea*' (I. i. 2). And, with its description of the sexual uncoordination of premature ejaculation, the play's second song declares (for a decidedly public audience) the essential solitariness of sexual enjoyment, which persists even when the pleasure is less one-sided: '*Then often they di'd; but the more they did so,* | *The Nymph di'd more quick, and the Shepherd more slow*' (IV. ii. 66–7).

Despite the similarities of situation and psychology that unite the heroic and comic lovers, their attempted responses to their problems remain consistently opposed, the comic lovers pursuing change and the heroic lovers pursuing constancy. But, torn from its native, past, surroundings, rustic love can produce only gestures that cannot be substantiated in a world where the actual is shaped by present, public imperatives. 'Let me die before I see this done' (III. i. 316), exclaims Leonidas as Palmyra is sentenced to death, providing a startling echo of Melantha, for whom 'Let me die' is a favourite catch-phrase. And, in the event, Leonidas's words prove as meaninglessly divorced from corresponding action as Melantha's. At first, he vows to follow Palmyra to execution and to die with her, but Polydamas easily frustrates this vow by ordering his guards to part the lovers (III. i. 330–6). Then Leonidas vows to die in Palmyra's defence, but promptly changes his mind at her instigation (III. i. 336–40). Then, in a useless gesture, he presents his sword to Polydamas, asking that his heart be pierced on the spot (III. i. 341–3). His request ignored, he impracticably boasts that he will 'hold' his 'breath and die' (III. i. 348). Then, with Palmyra's plea that Leonidas should delay his death until after hers (III. i. 349–52), the scene seems to approach a genuinely moving tragic climax—which is promptly forestalled as the dramatist intervenes to switch the public roles in which his characters are cast. Heroic intention here produces only a repetitive sequence of empty, frustrated gestures.

The permutation of the characters' roles leads ultimately to a precise reversal of Palmyra's near-execution, in which Leonidas is the condemned criminal and Palmyra the royal intercessor. Here, once again, the public world hinders the translation of heroic intention into heroic action. Hounded and parodied by Melantha, with her renewed cries of 'let me die', Palmyra vows to join her disgraced and arrested lover in death: 'Death shall never part us; | My Destiny is yours' (V. i. 120–1), she exclaims. But, when Leonidas is shortly afterwards hustled towards the scaffold, Palmyra can only swoon (V. i. 426–34), her prayers for death (V. i. 433–4) now evasive of moral responsibility, her swoon effectively a choice of Polydamas's party. Even Leonidas's final show of resistance on the scaffold (V. i. 439–47) has all the characteristics of another futile gesture until the comic characters come to the rescue of the heroic; for Leonidas would have been 'lost for ever' (V. i. 444) had not Rhodophil and Palamede come to his aid. In the new milieu of the court, then, the surviving sentiments of the pastoral world have become powerless, incapable of translation into external act. Decisive, saving action comes not from the devotees of the love that is enshrined in the play's concluding moments but from the devotees of those loves which it opposes or rejects: from the lonely, unloved courtier, Amalthea, and, even more, from Rhodophil and Palamede, still sexual pragmatists for all their new-found marital and political loyalty.

The final dependence of the heroic lovers on the comic shows just how equivocally Dryden compares their opposed modes of life. Finally, the two plots create a teasing vicious circle, each side embodying qualities deficient and desirable in the other without itself benefiting from those qualities. The comic plot amply displays the psychological inconvenience of change, and there is no doubt that the marriage of Rhodophil and Doralice would be more satisfactorily saved by the constancy of a Leonidas than by the makeshift arrangements that in fact prevail. But, if the comic plot reveals the inconvenience of change, the heroic plot finds equal inconvenience in constancy. Polydamas, who adapts gladly and with relief to his new role (V. i. 477–81), is happy. Argaleon, who cannot outgrow his former self, becomes a prisoner of it (V. i. 510–19). Amalthea, immovably attached to Leonidas, withdraws to sterile retirement and speedy death (V. i. 523–8). Leonidas, faithful to a love belonging to a lost world, is unable to assuage or even to mention her grief (V. i. 529–30). And Palmyra, who engulfed Leonidas in danger and then failed to save him, gains the reward that seems Amalthea's proper due. How much more satisfactory things would be if the heroic characters could adopt the shifting affections of the comic.

As in Etherege and Wycherley, private desire and public compulsion exist in simultaneous tension and interdependence, though Etherege and Wycherley do not create the paradox that the self is at once irremediably solitary and utterly open to public control. Dryden does not create a simple theory of the self that is identically realized in each character, and the proportions of impressionability and constancy are widely varied. But the greater the constancy, the greater the imprisonment: the ultimately pliable Polydamas is happy, whereas Argaleon and Amalthea, constant and oddly parallel in their contrasting extremes of virtue and vice, end the play by literally choosing prison, true prisoners of the mind. What disappears among these complications of personal autonomy is any idea of the man born to be king, for it is never entirely clear how far Leonidas's kingliness precedes his kingship and how far the man is perfected by the role. But it is clear that the public impact of the man is entirely conditioned by his role. Melantha's very perception of Leonidas's physical form depends on whether he is peasant or prince at the moment of perception: 'when he was a private man he was a *figure;* but since he is a King, methinks he has assum'd another *figure:* he looks so grand, and so August' (v. i. 498–500). Remarkably, this is the closest account of any subject's motives for joy at the process of restoration. Hitherto Leonidas has been a cipher, entirely without presence in the public mind, his very existence unsuspected. But he is King, and the general response to him changes as quickly and convulsively as Palmyra's response to Polydamas on discovering that he was her father. With this deeply sceptical view of the nature of restoration, the drama of restored authority came to an end. Earlier in the year, Settle's *Cambyses* had already introduced the anxiety-ridden drama of succession.

In *The Dutch Lover* (Duke's, February 1673), Aphra Behn also turned to the typical tragicomic figure of the child ignorant of noble parentage, the confusions of the play arising because two of its heroes are unaware of their true origins. Like Dryden, too, she uses ignorance of origins to examine the tangled relationship between social expectations of identity and the actualities of personal desire. Behn, however, now concentrates entirely on the hierarchies and categories of domestic life, abandoning her earlier explicit analogies between political and sexual power. The suspension of social and familial relationships was to be a regular feature of Behn's plays and novels, long-lost spouses or relatives returning as strangers, and brothers failing to recognize sisters. When the nomenclature of kin disappears, what remains are indiscriminate patterns of male lust and oppression, often for unnamed and undifferentiated women. In *1 The Rover* Pedro heads a queue baying for gang rape of an unseen and unnamed woman, not realizing that she is his own sister. In *The Dumb Virgin* two sisters fall in love with the same 'Stranger',[11] whose strangeness and potential sexual oppressiveness are emphasized by the fact that he is first seen at a masquerade, in the guise of a Turk. He eventually turns out to be their long-lost brother, but not before he has seduced one of them (without ever discovering her name) and killed his father. The seduced sister exemplifies an extreme suspension of nomenclature, in that she is dumb, whereas her sister is highly articulate but sexually undesirable, the contrasting and complementary deficiencies emphasizing the anomalies of femininity, in that women are equally marginalized by ugliness, which renders them ciphers no matter what their control of language, or beauty, which makes them the passive objects of male desires and values. All women outside the forbidden categories of kin are fair game, and when those categories are temporarily obliterated the women within them are fair game too; but the terms brother and sister, or father and daughter, which prescribe relationships between man and woman from which predatory lust is absent, generally record an alternative form of oppression.

    [11] *The Works of Aphra Behn*, ed. Montague Summers (6 vols., London and Stratford-upon-Avon, 1915; repr. New York, 1967), v. 427–9, 434, 437, 439. All references to Behn's fiction are to the texts in this volume.

The category which defines the unindividualized female object of lust, outside the limits of kinship, is that of the prostitute. Behn repeatedly emphasizes that the prostitute is a creation of men, both in the simple sense that women are forced into prostitution by the actions of men and in the broader sense that the figure of the prostitute answers to and realizes a fundamental element in man's perception of woman: hence the appearance of women in the guise of prostitutes at the end of *The Amorous Prince*. But, again, the roles in which women are perceived when their identities are concealed clarify the implications of their customary roles, for Behn repeatedly and obviously stresses that the marriage-market is a particular and socially accepted manifestation of the universal male impulse to prostitute the female, and in another of her novels, *The Unfortunate Happy Lady*, we see the accepted forms of prostitution leading to their illicit counterpart when an extravagant brother attempts to force his sister into literal prostitution so as to avoid paying her marriage portion.

The Dutch Lover is the first play in which Behn·extensively examines the undiscriminating urge to seduce and prostitute that the terminology of kinship half proscribes and half validates. There is repeated stress, even in the play's title, on the lover as *stranger*, the term being particularly associated with the most ungoverned of the male lovers, the roving libertine Alonzo, who emphasizes his role as stranger by imitating the Dutchman of the title. The prominence of the stranger reflects a widespread suspension of familial and social role, which is pushed to comic extremes when the Dutchman sees his impersonator and wonders which is the real he. Generally, however, the suspension has a more serious purpose, in revealing how feebly social morality directs the blind operations of desire. Ignorant of his true parentage, Silvio and his apparent sister Cleonte fall in love, and Silvio rejects as incomprehensible the inhibiting terminology of kin: 'The empty Words of Nature and of Blood, | Are such as Lovers never understood' (III, p. 281). Equally ignorant of his true parentage, Alonzo allows his wide-ranging lusts to include his own sister as their object. In addition, in a prime instance of man's undiscriminating lust for anonymous and unseen women, he has an agreement to share his sexual booty with his friend Lovis; and, inevitably, the unseen conquest on which Lovis wishes to take up the option turns out to be Lovis's own sister. When she first appears to Alonzo, he takes her for a prostitute, and she then arranges to meet him at a brothel. And another heroine, Hippolyta, has been unwittingly lodged in the brothel by her seducer, advertised as 'a *Venice* Curtezan to hire, | Whilst you believ'd it was your nuptial Palace' (III, p. 276).

In isolation, the passion of Silvio and Cleonte might seem to reconcile natural desires and social taboos, for the bar to their love turns out to be illusory, but the pseudo-incest is complemented by Alonzo's attraction towards his genuine sister. There is no mysterious process directing desire in conformity with moral order, and the vindication of Silvio and Cleonte's love is little more than an arbitrary stroke of luck: desire is blind. It is also violent. Despite himself, Silvio is inhibited by the 'Name' of sister (III, p. 281; V, p. 316), but the inhibition produces its own chaos of passion, in that he is willing to kill Cleonte when he mistakenly believes that she is prepared to sleep with him: social imperatives are as wild and oppressive as the appetites they prohibit. The sense of oppressiveness is not carried over into the harmonious set of pairings that concludes the play, but the previous view of both sexual desire and its social containment has been pessimistic, and the endings of later plays were less harmonious.

At the same time as such disturbing and exploratory plays, audiences were being offered musical spectacle on an increased scale, made possible by the opening of the Dorset Garden theatre, where Betterton mounted a spectacular new production of the Davenant *Macbeth* and an operatic reworking of the Dryden–Davenant *Tempest* (April 1674). In March 1674 a French opera, *Ariane; ou, le Mariage de Bacchus*, with libretto by Pierre Perrin and music by Cambert and Grabu, was staged on a more modest scale at Drury Lane by the short-lived Royal Academy of Musick, in honour of the recent marriage of the Duke of York to Mary of Modena.[12] The inglorious Third Dutch War had recently been concluded by the Treaty of Westminster (9 February) and the dedication praises England as a paradise of peace in a world of war. In the prologue, the rivers of the world pay homage to the Thames and the King,[13] in a rather wishful display of mercantile and diplomatic supremacy, and the opera itself celebrates peaceful hedonism: the rejected Ariane gains a new love in Bacchus, and some satyrs resurrect a bottle from the tomb and enthrone it. Divine (and royal) amours had been more pessimistically portrayed in the masque of the rape of Eurydice in *The Empress of Morocco*, and the mini-genre of musical entertainments on this subject was continued in two further works, Crowne's court entertainment *Calisto* (February 1675), whose leading parts were acted by court ladies, including the Princesses Mary and Anne, and Shadwell's *Psyche*. The heroine of *Calisto* preserves her chastity from Jupiter, who initially behaves as a voluntaristic tyrant, equating right with his power and will (II, p. 15), but eventually grows into a sovereign and impartial 'Judge' (V, p. 74), vindicating Calisto's slandered chastity and sentencing 'my self the greatest Criminal' (V, p. 78) to eternal separation from her.

In the same month, the Duke's Company staged Shadwell's spectacular *Psyche*, based on the Molière–Corneille–Quinault collaboration of 1671, and similar in its fundamental subject to *Ariane*.[14] Here (as often) spectacle is

---

[12] See Robert D. Hume, 'The Nature of the Dorset Garden Theatre', *Theatre Notebook*, 36 (1982), 99–109 (p. 101); Price, 'Political Allegory', 6–7; Pierre Danchin, 'The Foundation of the Royal Academy of Music in 1674 and Pierre Perrin's *Ariane*', *Theatre Survey*, 25 (1984), 55–67. For the authorship of the music, see ibid. 62–3, and the articles on *Ariane* and Robert Cambert in *The New Grove Dictionary of Opera*.

[13] The English translation enhances the level of compliment. See Price, 'Political Allegory', 7.

[14] Price suggests another allusion to James's marriage, with James as the monster who turns out to be Cupid (ibid. 8–9). This seems forced.

achieved at the cost of intellectual coherence. The original had reflected the ethos of the court milieu in which it was first performed, opening with praise of Louis XIV as peace-maker, stressing the demands of *rang* (rank), and concluding by praising the therapeutic virtue of pleasure after '*les soins du jour*' (V. vi. 2051); for Louis XIV (unlike Charles II) was a diligent administrator. But Shadwell is uncomfortable both with the Olympian and with the court mythology of his original. His opening portrays royal courts as predatory jungles of ruthless place-seekers, and in the concluding masque the original's praise of pleasure as respite from toil is vulgarized into a paean to '*Loves great Debauch*': '*Nor would Kings rule the World, but for Love and good drinking*' (V, p. 338). In both versions Psyche's rival suitors, Nicander and Polynices, act as noble rivals, but Shadwell's are not the bloodless embodiments of princely *rang* that their predecessors had been. At their first encounter, indeed, they are virtually in a Hobbesian state of war with each other, and consequently derive their subsequent magnanimity not from their princely station but from Psyche's persuasion. Nicander, indeed, is a materialist, scornful in his denunciations of priests and seeing love as an irresistible mechanical process, and there is no indication of how the noble self-denial taken from the source coexists with the principles which Shadwell grafted on to his character. Indeed, the strong advocacy of rational, natural religion, devoid of mystery, miracles, and priestcraft, constantly subverts the spectacular emphasis on wonder-working Olympians. When Apollo is induced by Venus to issue an unjust oracle commanding that Psyche be exposed to a serpent, Nicander and his associates extensively mock the cruelty and folly of religion:

CH[IEF]. PR[IEST]. Heav'n does again to you in Thunder speak!
NICAN. 'Twas nothing but a petty cloud did break.

(II, p. 300)

The argument is indebted to Lucretius,[15] who would also be evoked at the beginning of *The Virtuoso*, again to confirm the disjunction of human and divine language. And the attack on the oracle here quickly leads to a restatement of Lucretius' most famous attack on superstition: 'Such horrid ills Religion can perswade' (II, p. 300).[16]

A more consistent combination of scepticism and the supernatural was, however, achieved by Dryden in an abortive attempt to imitate Betterton's Dorset Garden spectaculars. In 1674 he took the remarkable course of turning *Paradise Lost* into an opera libretto, *The State of Innocence, and Fall of Man*, but failed to secure a production, presumably because the effects he demanded were beyond the resources of King's Company. For the Platonist Milton, the unfallen Adam apprehends God by intellectual ascent from the secondary order of the material world to the primary, immaterial order of

---

[15] Lucretius, *De Rerum Natura*, vi. 96–422.
[16] 'Tantum religio potuit suadere malorum' (ibid. i. 101).

which it is a shadow, but in portraying Adam's first moments of consciousness Dryden ostentatiously employs a different philosophic tradition: 'For that I am', Adam reflects, 'I know, because I think' (II, p. 36). In Milton, of course, it is Satan who makes his own consciousness the touchstone of reality, and indeed Satan's solipsism directly recalls absurdities which Gassendi postulated as the necessary precondition of Cartesianism:

An te probasti creatum esse? An meministi te aliquando non fuisse? An meministi ejus momenti, quo transivisti ex non esse ad esse? . . . An fuisti quo tempore omnia fuere creata, ubi fuere creata; et percepisti quomodo creata?[17]

> Who saw
> When this creation was? Remember'st thou
> Thy making, while the Maker gave thee being?
> We know no time when we were not as now;
> Know none before us.[18]

The philosophy of Dryden's Adam belongs to the intellectual environment of Milton's Satan.

Descartes's opponents feared that his preliminary rejection of all received certainties had released a genie which could not be returned to the bottle, and that his arguments would support the very scepticism which he opposed. Dryden proved them right, using Descartes in *The Rival Ladies* to support a materialistic theory of consciousness and in *Aureng-Zebe* (the play which followed *The State of Innocence*) to support the portrayal of characters locked in the very prison of consciousness which Descartes had postulated but had endeavoured to open.[19] Indeed, Adam himself quickly moves from exultation in his mind to the belief that it is a prison, his decisions the inevitable product of a long sequence of cause and effect: 'But the long Chain makes not the Bondage less' (IV, p. 52). The visit of Raphael—who here has Gabriel to give him moral support—is entirely devoted to countering Adam's determinism, though brevity makes the angels' arguments unsatisfactory, and it is difficult to know how intentional the unsatisfactoriness is: the mechanical movement of the heavenly bodies is, for example, a poor analogy for the freedom of the will, and the argument that free will is necessary so that God may punish his creatures is unimpressive (IV, pp. 52–3). What is certain is that Adam remains

---

[17] 'Have you demonstrated your own creation? Do you remember when you did not exist? Do you remember the moment when you passed from non-being to being? . . . Did you exist when and where all things were created; and did you see how they were created?' (Pierre Gassendi, *Disquisitio Metaphysica*, ed. Bernard Rochot (Paris, 1962), 309). The French philosopher and mathematician Gassendi (1592–1655), who revived Epicurean atomic theory and sought to reconcile it with belief in Divine Providence, produced the most impressive and extensive of the early rebuttals of Descartes's *Meditations*.

[18] *Paradise Lost*, v. 856–60, in Milton, *Poetical Works*, ed. Douglas Bush (London, 1966).

[19] A more flippant misappropriation of Descartes occurs in Payne's *The Morning Ramble*, in a character's defence of free love: 'This is the prettiest sort of new Philosophy in Love; right *Descartes*, it depends all upon motion' (IV, p. 52).

unsatisfied, eventually convinced of his freedom, but not of its purpose or justification. Even in the unfallen state, linguistic contact between heaven and man is flawed and inconclusive. In general, commentators on this debate have assumed that Dryden is reproducing the debates between Hobbes and Bishop Bramhall on the freedom of the will, and that he is siding with Bramhall.[20] But even if we assume that the case for free will *has* been conclusively won, however grudging Adam's assent, there is no escape from the double-bind that Dryden has created: if Adam is right, the absence of free will makes the doctrine of the Fall morally meaningless; but, if he is wrong, it is equally meaningless, for what is ideal about a prelapsarian state in which man rushes headlong into intellectual error? Dryden's Adam, like that of his former school-fellow Robert South, 'came into the world a philosopher'.[21] But South went on to praise a titanic intellect that dwarfed into invisibility the total sum of postlapsarian genius. Dryden's Adam, by contrast, is a thoroughly modern man.

It is sometimes difficult to interpret Dryden's abbreviations of Milton, since abbreviation on the huge scale enforced by circumstances produces transformations that may not always be the result of calculating artistry. But, however necessary it was for Dryden to abbreviate his source, it was a startling decision to avoid even the most indirect reference to the Son: an alteration far more breathtaking than anything Tate later did to *King Lear*. Direct represcentation was, of course, impossible, but total silence was none the less extraordinary. When Raphael first appears to Adam, his exposition of man's religious duty would have satisfied any deist: reason will teach all men to give God 'Pray'r and Praise' (II, p. 37), and nothing more is necessary. After the Fall, all that is necessary to mitigate the doom is repentance. As Dryden put it in *Religio Laici* (1682), in his by then hostile summation of deism:

> This *general Worship* is to *praise*, and *pray*:
> One part to *borrow* Blessings, one to *pay*:
> And when frail Nature slides into *Offence*,
> The *Sacrifice* for *Crimes* is *Penitence*.

> (ll. 50–3)

The State of Innocence propounds a religion without mystery or sacrificial atonement: a religion which, like Shadwell's in *Psyche*, conflicts with the myth that expresses it.

When Milton's Raphael converses with Adam and Eve, he shows that they have their own special places in a universe consisting of an ascending hierarchy

---

[20] King, *Dryden's Major Plays*, 95–115. Noting Dryden's debt to the Bramhall–Hobbes controversy, Bredvold also notes that the angels are unsuccessful as instructors ('Dryden, Hobbes, and the Royal Society', 329). Their shortcomings are analysed at length in K. W. Gransden, 'Milton, Dryden, and the Comedy of the Fall', *Essays in Criticism*, 26 (1976), 116–33.

[21] Adam 'came into the world a philosopher, which sufficiently appeared by his writing the nature of things upon their names' (South, *Sermons Preached upon Several Occasions*, i. 37).

of forms, but Dryden's entirely new conversation about freedom and necessity leaves the relationship between the self and the cosmic order beset with problems, and when the angels have left Adam is still wondering 'Why am I trusted with my self?' (IV, p. 53). Because of the problems in understanding the self, there are no satisfactory scenes of naming: as Milton's prelapsarian clarity of communication between earth and heaven vanishes, so does his prelapsarian harmony of sign and signified. After the omission of the Son, Dryden's most remarkable omission is perhaps that of Adam's naming of the beasts, in which essence is perfectly rendered in linguistic sign. But Adam does not even name Eve, and their names are only pronounced when Eve mistakes Satan for 'some other *Adam*' (IV, p. 57) and when she deludedly fears the creation of 'Some other *Eve*' (V, p. 60). The name is used as a point of reference to define something else, but not to define the thing itself. Coherent identity is an elusive concept, easily obfuscated by the structures of thought and language.

In Eden, as in Aureng-Zebe's India and Horner's London, the structure of language insidiously and inevitably shapes the mind's ordering and interpretation of the world: there was no original correspondence of word and thing, and in any case the relationship of particular signs to particular objects is unimportant when the interrelationships of signs cannot reproduce the structure of the world which they describe. Dryden plays with circular paradoxes in which the self becomes the object of its own subject—'Why am I trusted with my self?' (IV, p. 53), 'I my self am proud of Me' (II, p. 41)—and with situations in which the self is actually apprehended via an external object. As in Milton, Satan devotes his first speech to reflection upon his companion's now uncertain and unstable identity, but unlike Milton's Satan he uses his companion as a means of apprehending himself: 'I see | My self too well, and my own Change, in thee' (I, p. 30). In this context, Eve's bemusement with her reflection externalized in the pool is no longer a remediable error but an illustration of the inevitable contradictions that attend the attempt to apprehend the self, which in the very act of apprehension turn it into the not-self. Adam and Eve's relations with each other are further expressions of this quest for the self in the not-self. Eve accepts Adam because he is 'like my self' (II, p. 42), and Adam's desire for Eve as his 'better Half' (II, p. 41) (not 'other half', as in Milton, iv. 488) becomes not an exercise in self-completion but self-inanition, in which he surrenders his inward and essential qualities to his double: 'I yield my boasted Sovereignty'; 'Made to command, thus freely I obey' (II, pp. 41–2). (Just after defining himself against Asmoday, Satan similarly calls him his 'better Half' (I, p. 31).) Indeed, Adam's desire for his 'better Half' expresses a moment not of triumphant union but of bewildered isolation, for he has as yet seen Eve only in his dream, and is suspended between a sense of reality and unreality, existence and non-existence: 'If this be Dreaming, let me never wake'; 'I seek my self, and find not, wanting thee' (II, p. 41). And, when union is accomplished in a highly disordering and passionate copulation, surrender to the double for a moment extinguishes both the sense and expression of self: 'And speechless Joys, in whose sweet Tumult tost, | I thought my Breath, and my new Being lost' (III, p. 44). In a negation of the Cartesian axiom, thought here seems to guarantee the absence of 'Being', and there is a total separation between the self as thinker and as object of thought. What Satan's temptation of Eve does is, apparently, to reconcile the habitual linguistic and conceptual ways of rendering the self with the order of things. Before Eve's eyes, a serpent enters, eats the forbidden fruit, and returns as Satan: 'I was he' (IV, p. 58), he explains, quite truthfully, bringing into being that division between self as subject and object that has been Adam and Eve's constant way of understanding themselves, and which has already been reified in Eve's tempting dream, in which her desires are enacted onstage by a *doppelgänger*, '*a Woman habited like* Eve' (III, p. 47).

Even the Cartesian *Cogito* assures the self of its existence by splitting it into subject and object. Adam's first words are 'What am I?', and the self divides as soon as he starts to elaborate the question with 'that I am | I know, because I think' (II, p. 36), as it also does when the newly created Eve proceeds from the same question to 'I my self am proud of Me' and to bemusement with her reflection (II, p. 41). Even thought, the pledge of existence, can disintegrate in an infinite regression of subject and object: 'why do I my Bliss delay | By thinking what I thought?', Adam exclaims, as sexual desire dethrones the priority of thought (II, p. 41). Gassendi had objected to Descartes that the self could no more contemplate itself than the eye can, and Culverwell had derived an absurd and unwarranted infinite regression from the *Cogito*, arguing that to think that I think that I am ('thinking what I thought', in Dryden's words) must provide greater certainty than merely thinking that I am, and so *ad infinitum*, the constant recession of certainty leaving the mind with nothing but 'Sceptisme'.[22] Dryden shares Gassendi's view that the self cannot contemplate itself, and in exposing the difficulties of self-contemplation he traps his characters in infinite regressions far more ingenious than the feeble reasoning of Culverwell could contrive.

There are other, cruder, suggestions that Adam and Eve are ripe for the Fall from the outset: Eve, for example, is a vain coquette throughout. But Dryden is suggesting not merely that egocentric appetite is an inevitable part of any imaginable human constitution, but also that the Fall reflects the way in which the structure of language governs the apprehension of the self. Both suggestions are apparent when Eve first accepts Adam, expressing an unexpected self-regard in the characteristic doubling of the self as subject and object: 'I next my self, admire and love thee best' (II, p. 42). Humanity is inevitably appetitive, and language inevitably creates structures that arise from its own

---

[22] Gassendi, *Disquisitio Metaphysica*, 279; Nathanael Culverwel [*for* Culverwell], *An Elegant and Learned Discourse Of the Light of Nature, With several other Treatises* (London, 1654), 129–30.

laws rather than from those of the world it ostensibly represents. As is implied by the omission of the naming of the beasts, and the bewilderment to which Adam is reduced by conversation with the angels, there is no perfect signification in Eden; no perfect antithesis to that undecipherable sign, the forbidden fruit. When Eve reaches the Tree of Knowledge, she knows by many 'Signs' that she is standing before the forbidden fruit (IV, p. 58): that is, she can correlate what she now sees with previous descriptions of it. But this is to interpret signs with reference to other signs, in a potentially infinite regression: how to comprehend the essence of the fruit? Satan argues that its appearance and position are signs of excellence, and so they would be if signs signified by resemblance. The Tree of Knowledge embodies the inescapable disjunction of sign and essence. If the model of signification in *Paradise Lost* is the naming of the beasts, that in *The State of Innocence* is Eve's attempt to converse with her reflection, where her own language becomes transformed into something external, alien, and incomprehensible (even more alien and incomprehensible than the French words which Melantha acquired from her maid): 'When I begin to speak, the Lips it moves; | Streams drown the Voice, or it would say, it loves' (II, p. 41). We have encountered many divisions of the self in sex comedy, where they generally reveal the tensions between appetite and social inclination. Dryden, characteristically, postulates a far more intricate problem: that the self can no more comprehend itself than the eye can, and that language can only represent the self to the mind by inverting it and turning it into something separate and other. Gazing at the mimic self beneath the surface of the pool, tantalized by illusory communication offered by the unreal simulacra of speech, Eve represents the I gazing at the Me.

CHAPTER SIX

'Senseless Riot, Neronian Gambols': Comedy, 1676–1682

By late 1676, the predominant character of comedy was clearly darkening, as dramatists reacted with various kinds of moral earnestness to Etherege's morally dispassionate portrayal of Dorimant's sexual Machiavellism. Sex comedy became largely critical of the faithless male, and often very pessimistic in its portrayal of human sexuality. In addition, some plays (on the whole poor in quality) directly reject sex comedy. Cheerful bedroom romps are rare, and when they occur are explicitly farcical in character, not claiming the status of high comic art. The transformation of drama was soon accentuated by the grave political crisis which began in September 1678, with Titus Oates's first allegations of a popish conspiracy to murder the King and initiate a general rebellion. These led to the Whig attempts, increasingly orchestrated by the Earl of Shaftesbury, to exclude the Duke of York from the succession, the eventual favoured substitute being the King's eldest illegitimate son, the Duke of Monmouth (who had first been mooted as a possible successor in the 1660s). The crisis produced a drama that was often heavily politicized, though not always in predictable ways, since several leading dramatists changed tack according to the fluctuating fortunes of the Exclusionist cause,[1] and even some of James's natural supporters were deeply uneasy about their man. The genre chiefly affected was tragedy, but in some of the comic work of Otway, Behn, and Dryden growing concern with painful and unresolvable sexual dilemmas became a means for glancing at more comprehensive dilemmas of order.

Painful sexual dilemmas dominate Aphra Behn's *The Town-Fop* (Duke's, September 1676), her first portrayal of London society. It is a sign of her

Epigraph: Lee, *The Rival Queens*, dedication, l. 35.

[1] Susan Jane Owen, 'Drama and Politics in the Exclusion Crisis: 1678–83', Ph.D. thesis (Leeds, 1992), and 'Interpreting the Politics of Restoration Drama', *The Seventeenth Century*, 8 (1993), 67–97. Dr Owen argues that there was a pronounced move towards the Whig outlook during the season of 1680–1. Her approach is more flexible and convincing than that in J. Douglas Canfield, 'Royalism's Last Dramatic Stand: English Political Tragedy, 1679–89', *Studies in Philology*, 82 (1985), 234–63. Matthew H. Wikander, 'The Spitted Infant: Scenic Emblem and Exclusionist Politics in Restoration Adaptations of Shakespeare', *Shakespeare Quarterly*, 37 (1986), 340–58, argues that the Shakespeare adaptations reveal anxiety about the policies of the Crown, but that their authors 'see as the only alternative to these policies not loyal opposition, but civil war' and present 'a Shakespeare that is more conservative, more patriarchal, and more hysterically terrified of civil disorder than the original' (p. 357).

seriousness that she should have based her comedy upon a domestic tragedy, George Wilkins's *The Miseries of Inforst Mariage* (1607), and it is a sign of her distance from Etherege that, a few months after his portrayal of Dorimant's triumphant perjury, she should emphasize the binding moral force of the vow: as in Wilkins, the hero (Bellmour) is forced by his guardian's threats of financial ruin into abandoning his betrothed and entering an unwanted marriage, and is consequently driven into a confused state of tormented dissipation. Characteristically seeing prostitution as the fundamental image of the relations between the sexes, Behn portrays Bellmour as joining Sir Timothy Tawdrey, the fop of the title, in a sordid brothel and courting the prostitutes, conscious that he has rendered himself their moral equal. Equally characteristically, she emphasizes the fragility and deceptiveness of nominal social relationships by showing intimates reverting to the condition of strangers. Bellmour's brother and sister are, for example, told by their guardian (and uncle) to 'expect no more Friendship at my Hands, than from those that are absolute Strangers to you' (v, p. 78).[2]

In Wilkins the rejected woman kills herself, but here she and the hero are united after a legally improbable divorce. In his confused torment, however, Bellmour has denied his sister her portion, and she therefore desperately enters a disastrous marriage with Sir Timothy, who is not a Fopling-like butterfly but an actively loathsome figure in the line of Sir Arthur Addell and Sir Ralph Spatter, who plans to spend his bride's portion on his prostitute. In Behn's world, women are the victims even of fools. The order to which the play moves is thus partial and inequitable, and even the central moral principle of the play, the binding vow, is a principle whose rationale is elusive. Wilkins validates the sanctity of the vow by repeated imagery endowing language with a tangible existence and power which extends from earth to heaven. 'God writes sin' upon the head of an adulterous bed (sig. D), and the hero is reconciled to his marriage when a Doctor of Divinity (omitted by Behn) argues that a marriage vow is a deed sealed by God (sig. K2). Behn, however, removes all reference to a transcendent language of authority to which human language is answerable, and attributes no authority at all to the vows of the hero's actual marriage, which easily cede to the power of true love. The desire to ground life upon the sanctity of the oath outlives the beliefs that explain that sanctity.

In later works, indeed, Behn quite explicitly refuses any sacred power to speech. When Isabella protests in *Sir Patient Fancy* against an unwanted marriage, she treats the dreaded ceremony as a ritual of magical mumbo-jumbo, and threatens to 'stand as silent in the inchanting Circle, as if the Priests were raising Devils there' (v, p. 91). In *The Widow Ranter*, as the tormented Indian Queen stands in state with her unloved husband, priests

---

[2] See also III, pp. 46, 48.

conduct a sacrificial ritual '*with ridiculous Postures*' and meaningless in-cantations (IV, p. 279). The Indians in Behn's novel *Oroonoko* regard the word as inviolable and almost omnipotent, concluding that the English governor must be dead when he fails to keep a promised appointment (for 'when a Man's Word was past, nothing but Death could or should prevent his keeping it', p. 132), and using as a magical charm the written name of a European they saw creating fire with a burning glass. The Indians' view of language is not terribly different from that in *The Miseries of Inforst Mariage*, where the hero returns to his family after a bombardment of titles—'Kinsman', 'Brother', 'Husband', 'Father' (sig. [K4])—which have such tangible potency as to be likened to bullets. With such a conception of language it is easy to attribute authority to oaths; but Behn does not have it, and a very secular view of the oath is provided in *Oroonoko* itself by the hero, who (with the author's evi-dent approval) is associated with a deistic rejection of Christian mysteries, constantly making 'a Jest' (p. 175) of the Trinity. Oroonoko, though a persis-tent victim of European faithlessness, scorns those who keep oaths from fear of damnation, arguing that honour and the judgement of one's fellows are more potent and admirable restraints. Behn, however, deals with groups where some species of perjury have become institutionalized and applauded, whether it be the perjury of the European to the Negro or that of the seducer to his mistress.

Just as Behn was finding her mature voice in *The Town-Fop*, the most prolific—if not the most consistent—male writer of feminist plays was appearing on the scene. Durfey's *The Siege of Memphis* had treated its dominant villainess with unusual sympathy, and his first two comedies, *Madam Fickle* (Duke's, November 1676) and *The Fool Turn'd Critick* (King's, November 1676), both provide strong criticism of the predatory male. In the former, a witty woman outsmarts her unscrupulous suitors, exploding their claims to be 'princes and lords of nature' (IV. i. 120–1), while the latter gives a sober portrayal of faithlessness in love and friendship, foreshadowing Otway's *Friendship in Fashion* in outlook if not quality. Both plays establish what were to be standard Durfey preoccupations. Women are championed, brainless and ruffianly would-be gentlemen ape and discredit the libertine machismo of their wittier counterparts (Old Winelove in *The Fool Turn'd Critick* actually engages a tutor to instruct his son to 'quarrel with Bullies, | And pick a Wench up with alacrity', I, p. 4),[3] and authority-figures are locked in outmoded social outlooks, marked by restrictive interpretation of social and sexual roles. The dinosaurs in *Madam Fickle* and *The Fool Turn'd Critick* are Sir Arthur Oldlove, an antiquary, and Sir Formal Ancient, nostalgic for the heyday of Puritan power. Examples in later plays include the Cavalier Sir Roger Petulant in *A Fond Husband* (remarkably, a greater fool than

---

[3] There is perhaps a reminiscence of Old Barnacle's attempt to secure a 'gentlemanly' education for his son in Shirley's *The Gamester*.

the Puritan Sir Formal) and Sir Wilding Frollick (in *Trick for Trick*), who successfully hopes that his son will continue the 300-year-old family tradition of senseless debauchery that he equates with ancient gentility.

The resourceful heroine of *Madam Fickle* avenges apparent betrayal by her one true love by toying with a series of suitors, most of whom veil a fundamentally despotic view of male–female relations in a conventional and patently artificial language of adoration and submissiveness. She thwarts them all, effortlessly shifting styles of speech as her suitors come and go, and gaining her greatest triumph when she persuades one of them (named *Manley*) to act the part of a madman and talk gibberish. (Incidents of total linguistic collapse in Durfey generally reveal the superior manipulative power of the female.) The main custodian of the traditions which this new woman challenges is the antiquarian Oldlove: a figure who once again implicitly raises the question of how far women can control the interpretation of history. And, since this is a play in which men do *not* control language, the antiquary's achievement is not the composition of historical narrative but the uncritical and disordered assembly of objects from the past. These objects nevertheless testify to a past that was overwhelmingly male-dominated: Sir Gawain's skull, Sir Lancelot's sword, Pompey the Great's breeches, the tears of that patron saint of anti-feminist writing, St Jerome, and a host of other male relics. The only female relic in the collection is appropriately insubstantial and decorative: the Queen of Sheba's shoe-horn. The continuing force of nostalgia for a man-centred past is indicated when another of Fickle's suitors, Harry, vents his bafflement and frustration by lapsing into his own brand of antiquarianism, longing for the time 'before the deluge, when love was like the storming of a castle, attain'd by violence, not as now, with fair words' (IV. ii. 70–2). As in *The Siege of Memphis*, the male prerogatives of strength and action are baffled by an upstart female.

Fickle thus has to cope with impulses to inarticulate domination that are, literally, antediluvian. Archaic traditions of male hooliganism are also honoured by the family of Captain Tilbury, an 'old fashion'd' country gentleman (according to the Dramatis Personae), obsessed with the antiquity and customs of his clan: with patriarchal lineage. His two foolish sons aspire to a life of brainless gentlemanly violence—wife-swapping, beating up the watch—and dignify their brute machismo by assuming burlesque names suggestive of the world of knightly romance which so excites Oldlove: Filloflorido and Rounsivell. They are, however, regularly humiliated by the repartee of women, even of prostitutes, and—no intractable problems of justice here—they eventually fall victim to the forces of law and order, the Constable and Watch.[4] One of the more intelligent men sees their lives as narratives without structure

4 K. E. Robinson plausibly suggests that the fools' fight with the constable alludes to the notorious episode at Epsom in which Rochester's folly caused his friend Downs to be killed by the watch ('A Glance at Rochester in Thomas Durfey's "Madam Fickle" ', *Notes and Queries*, 220 (1975), 264–5).

and interpretative criteria: 'A fool is a vacuum in nature, a prolix story without marginal notes' (II. i. 3–4).

Fickle deludes her suitors by feigning conformity to the traditions of a past shaped by male design. For each suitor she assumes a false name, each name evoking centuries of male writing, male invocation of the female, and polite male fictions about woman's importance. As Sir Arthur Oldlove approvingly exclaims, 'They are names of antiquity' (V. iii. 58–9). One is Celia (heavenly), glancing at her suitors' technique of enslavement through deification. Another, Corinna, is the name of a Greek poetess, stolen from her by Ovid to be the pseudonym of his poetic mistress. And the third is Cleio, the name of the Muse of *History*: fictitious patroness of a male preserve. Tragedies such as *The Siege of Constantinople* and *All for Love* show women as the victims of historical writing, but comedy tends to be more optimistic and, like later Durfey heroines (Cordelia, Penelope, Fulvia), Fickle reacts against a nomenclature whose connotations reflect a man-centred culture.

Like Lurewell in Farquhar's *The Constant Couple*, Fickle is finally reunited with her first love, who is still faithful despite earlier appearances to the contrary. As the humble and socially despised agents of justice contain the excesses of Tilbury's sons, so Fickle manages to claim a just and appropriate social existence in the face of male power and selfishness. Here, Durfey's view of the woman's prospects was simpler and rosier than that now held by Aphra Behn. But *The Fool Turn'd Critick* was far less optimistic, and is the first of several Durfey plays to suggest that the woman's only security from male tyranny lies in spinsterhood. It depicts the cynical betrayal and counter-betrayal of two gentleman friends, Frank and Bernard: Bernard is representing his mistress Lucia as an heiress in order to trick Frank into marrying her; meanwhile, the equally slippery Frank is courting Penelope on Bernard's behalf, but realizes that she is more attracted to him, and decides to enjoy her himself as an aperitif to Lucia. Penelope herself is being pressed by her father, Sir Formal Ancient, to marry the buffoonish would-be spark Tim Winelove, so that she faces the conventional choice between a fool of her father's choice and a wit of her own. What is not conventional is Durfey's emphasis on the meaninglessness of the choices before her: Frank and Bernard, between whom she hesitates, are equally callous and selfish, and Frank perfects the condition to which Tim Winelove aspires, even at one stage being appointed as his mentor on the grounds of his gentlemanly ability 'to accost a Wench, Strut and talk Bawdy' (III, p. 32). The wit and the fool are Tweedledum and Tweedledee. Equally unconventionally, Penelope is saved from unwise love by her hitherto ridiculous father: at last realizing Frank's infidelity, she deludes herself that Bernard is better and attempts to marry him, but in the usual contretemps inadvertently marries Frank instead. Fortunately, however, the ceremony was invalid, since the 'parson' was her father in disguise, and the buffoonish Sir Formal unexpectedly ends up as the hero of the play.

There is no concluding social harmony. All the young women seek marriage, but all remain single, even though one—Penelope—is named after a classical archetype of virtuous wifehood. The pregnant Lucia (whose name intermittently changes to that of another archetypal wife, Lucretia) seeks the respectability of a husband, but another false parson frustrates her attempt to cheat Bernard into marriage. And the maid Betty seeks social advancement through marriage to Tim, but is promptly disappointed when Tim's father announces that he will buy a divorce (on what legal basis remains unclear). While the women remain isolated and vulnerable, Frank and Bernard make the sole, empty, gesture of social reintegration, coolly renewing the friendship that has proved so consistently meaningless.

Such was the state of the theatre when Wycherley's last play, *The Plain-Dealer*, appeared (King's, December 1676). As in his earlier plays, Wycherley depicts betrayal and false friendship, but amused observation is now replaced by portrayal of the crushing personal experience of treachery. Another sign of change is that the play provides by far the most complex and disturbing comic role yet recorded for Hart.[5] Previously, the hero of sex comedy had descended either from Sir Frederick Frollick or—more typically—from the whimsical extravagants played by Hart during his early partnership with Nell Gwyn. With Dorimant, another prototype had been established, associated with another actor, and *The Plain-Dealer* is the first comedy to stretch Hart with a part equal in power and depth to that of Dorimant. No trace of the witty extravagant remains in this almost tragic figure, whose inflexible commitment to the ideals of manhood leads him to idealize the fickle, mercenary Olivia, who easily flatters his fantasies, and to ignore the loyal Fidelia, who follows him unrecognized in male disguise but cannot meet his ideals of valour. After Olivia, like her Shakespearian namesake, has fallen in love with the girl in boy's clothing, Manly copulates with her in the dark while Fidelia talks to her and deceives her into thinking that 'he' is her partner in bed. If this rape pushes Manly's code of virility to an extreme of moral insufficiency, it also reveals its practical incompleteness, for the supremely virile act is dependent on the agency of a woman.

Though very different in outlook from *Madam Fickle*, *The Plain-Dealer* parallels it in representing the male viewpoint in a character called Manly, and also in portraying an independent woman fighting for personal and linguistic autonomy, though instead of a spirited beauty Wycherley portrays a crazed and litigious harridan, the Widow Blackacre. The Widow is the least attractive of the many women on the Restoration stage who struggle against institutionalized systems of justice, and who try to control the writing of their own fate; she even attempts, unsuccessfully, to do so by commissioning acts of

---

5 We have no cast lists for *The Mall* and *The Fool Turn'd Critick*, which do have disturbing heroes; even so, neither equals Manly in stature or complexity.

forgery, after her *writings* are stolen by the fortune-hunter Freeman. Though her problems are those of many a more sympathetically viewed female character, however, it is doubtful whether she herself excites much sympathy.[6] Yet, if Wycherley seems not to side with her, he withholds the most obvious means of condemning her: of portraying a sexual insubordinate who transgresses the norms of her sex. For virtually everyone in this play violates gender stereotype, and a norm that is universally disregarded is no longer a norm. If this aggressively masculine woman fails to win sympathy, moreover, she nevertheless helps to rouse our suspicions about that other aggressively masculine character, Manly. In some ways, he seems a counterbalancing ideal to her folly. Most fundamentally, her addiction to obfuscating legal language is counterbalanced by his hatred of a society where speech has superseded archaic, inarticulate force (a hatred shared with Madam Fickle's suitor Harry). He despises 'talking Cowards' (IV. i. 106) and a London where the beaux 'are in all things so like Women' (II. i. 623–4), and longs for a state of primitive violence 'where honest, downright Barbarity is profest; where men devour one another like generous hungry Lyons and Tygers' (I. i. 595–7). Though he hates all disjunction of sign and intention and longs for a primeval purity of signification, he locates this purity not in Eden but the jungle; not in the naming of the beasts but the roaring of the lion, with its direct expression of the predatory hostility that is the fundamental principle of nature.

Manly is certainly right about London, for it is a place where language (or at any rate the production of words and noise) supplants sex and violence. At one point the compulsive poetaster Oldfox ties the Widow up in order to rape her 'through the ear ... onely' (V. ii. 426–7) with his poems: a clear confounding of the attributes of language and experience, recalling Aureng-Zebe's belief that the name 'Morat' gives Indamora an aural orgasm. Scenes of compulsive and uncommunicative talking and noise-making run throughout the play. The Widow has a bout of total non-communication with Oldfox (IV. i. 220–57), he talking about his poems and she (as always) about her litigation, each seizing the other's words and redefining them to suit his or her humour. Olivia compulsively finishes satiric portraits that the vacuous pseudo-wit Novel barely has time to start (II. i. 165–385). And even Westminster Hall, the home of justice, turns out to be a Babel, resounding to the senseless clamour of rival crooks; more flagrantly than in any other Restoration play, the rituals of justice fail. Here the Widow coaches her lawyers to produce rhetorical noise and nonsense; and here her grown-up son Jerry plays with toys mimicking animal noises. In all the above incidents—

---

[6] A good defence of the Widow is provided in Bacon, 'Wives, Widows, and Writings', 435–9. Bacon was the first to notice that the Widow only takes up forgery because Freeman has stolen her documents. In the 1988 Stratford production, the Widow emerged without forcing as a character with a case. But, to judge from her repertory, Katherine Corey does not seem to have presented the subtler shades of character.

most flagrantly that in which Oldfox and the Widow keep altering the meaning of each other's words—language ceases to be an agreed system of signs, declining either into sheer noise or into the rendering of private, unshared meanings: a decline also evident when Olivia expatiates with chaotic free association on the obscene connotations of the name 'Horner'; here, more than anywhere else, words 'have a signification also of the nature, disposition, and interest of the speaker' (*Leviathan*, ch. iv, 109). In another kind of assault on the representative character of language, Olivia claims that the China scene in *The Country-Wife* has so irrevocably sullied the word that all the corresponding objects must be destroyed: words cease to be the symbols of mental images and instead usurp the status of objects, yet again showing how easily the mind imposes the properties of language upon experience itself. The private, warring languages show that social existence does not so much replace the Hobbesian state of nature as translate it into another form and medium, language being not an alternative to brute and chaotic violence but a feeble surrogate for it, as when Jerry asserts his masculine vigour with toys imitating animal sounds, or Oldfox attempts his aural rape of the Widow.

Manly's contempt for what he deems an effeminate society is partly contempt for men who no longer imitate the action of a tiger, but instead conduct their battles in what are conventionally the woman's weapons: words.[7] But Manly is less distinct from his antagonists than he imagines, and he becomes increasingly dependent upon the very linguistic processes that he rejects. He, indeed, takes a leading role in one of the earliest instances of frantically loquacious non-communication when, in his first conversation with the Widow, she talks with blinkered monomania about her lawsuit while he talks with equal obsessiveness about his passion for Olivia (I. i. 413–50): a foreshadowing of the later incident in which Oldfox and the Widow each understand the other's words within the rival systems of meaning provided by their separate, isolating passions of poetry and law; by their 'nature, disposition, and interest'. Manly and the Widow, man of action and garrulous harridan, are here puzzlingly parallel in their indomitable garrulity. It is appropriate, therefore, it should be amidst the clamour of Westminster Hall (the Widow's spiritual home) that Manly starts to reveal his affinities with the society he rejects. He had loved in Olivia an ideal conjunction of sign and intention, but he continues to love her when she is exposed as a beautiful hypocrite, and his embarrassed dissimulation of his passion leads him into the very separation of sign and intention which she embodies, and to which Westminster Hall is consecrated: 'How hard it is to be an Hypocrite!' (III. i. 26), he muses. Then, immediately before the Widow instructs her lawyers in corrupt oratory, Manly

---

7 In Dryden's *Don Sebastian*, Dorax refers to 'this Womans War of tongues' (IV. iii. 402), and in Cibber's *Xerxes* Aranthes declares that 'the tongue's a woman's weapon' (I, p. 149). Cf. *Iliad*, xx. 251–8.

coaches Fidelia in the speaker's art, urging her to use all her 'Rhetorick' (III. i. 125) to win Olivia for him. Manly's sexual instincts cannot be pursued by direct, virile action, but depend for their fulfilment upon the language of another; indeed, though he does not yet realize this, upon the language of a woman.

In *The Plain-Dealer*, as in many Restoration plays, man hovers between rational sociability and appetitive savagery, each aspect of his divided nature hindering and frustrating the other. The impasse is especially evident in Manly's two bedroom tricks with Olivia: his purest attempts to free instinct from the complications of language and social judgement. Olivia herself wishes to escape from the web of language and sink into a state of wordless lust: ''tis not a time for idle words' (IV. ii. 179–80), and she did not expect to pass her time 'in talking' (IV. ii. 244–5). And, of course, the consummation of the deception provides the clearest disjunction between man's speaking and sexual self, with the antisocial Manly silently performing the deed after Fidelia—a man only in her public trappings—has done the talking. The literal division of the individual in Manly's bedroom trick symbolizes the constant tension between the warring yet interdependent social and instinctual aspects of the human character. Yet, because they are interdependent, the division is brief and unstable. Both encounters suffer interruption (a constant motif), the second being halted before consummation by the invasion of virtually the whole cast, when lust is hindered quite literally by society. But there is a yet more striking compromise of antisocial instinct, in Manly's decision that his copulation with Olivia will be insufficient revenge unless he can have 'Witnesses' to it (IV. ii. 291).

Just as the characters cannot entirely suppress their social natures, so they cannot entirely dispense with the forms and disciplines of law. The judicial regulation of the kingdom may be a chaotic sham, but the rituals of law express something that is intrinsic to man's nature, and throughout the play small groups of people spontaneously mimic the processes that in their larger forms are so empty of meaning. The verbal combat of Olivia and Manly in Act II becomes a formal altercation before the jury of Novel and Lord Plausible (II. i. 581–621), and when Oldfox and Freeman compete before the Widow for her hand, the contest naturally enough takes the form of a trial (II. i. 769–957). When Novel and Oldfox dispute about the nature of wit, Novel appoints Manly to 'be our Judge' (V. ii. 168). And, when Manly requires witnesses of his adultery with Olivia, his need for them shows that, even at his most appetitive and antisocial, he still wants the customary forms of communal existence. In attempting to give judicial solemnity to a rape, Manly (his name more than ever appropriate) pre-eminently illustrates the vulnerability of the woman to the improvised legal rituals of the male, though Wycherley seems to be far more interested in the social anomalies of the act than in the experiences of the victim.

Judicial rituals are exercises in the establishment and interpretation of signs. As Hobbes saw, social existence requires a stable and verifiable system of signs whereby the intentions (all too possibly hostile) of one's fellow citizens can be determined; but it is easier to desire such a system than to discover it, and Wycherley makes the instability of the sign a formal principle of the play, introducing abrupt and puzzling shifts of tone and genre, and also raising within the play the question of whether generic convention bears any relationship to the quality of what is being represented. In the prologue, Manly announces that Wycherley is no Lely but a *'course Dauber'*, who follows only *'Life, and Nature'* (ll. 32–3), implying (rather paradoxically) that excellence in art necessitates remoteness from life, and that the allure of the sign is in inverse proportion to its actual power to signify. Then, as Olivia pours out satirical descriptions of her acquaintances, her sensible cousin Eliza recurs to the example of Lely, drawing an analogy between his art and Olivia's satire; for, at Lely's studio, the pictures are 'much handsomer than they are, and like; here, much uglier, and like' (II. i. 213–14). Lely's and Olivia's portraits are opposite in character and equal in distortion, but they are nevertheless, paradoxically, 'like' their subjects, with the result that the relationship between sign and object is one of enigmatic incompleteness. The imperfect relationship of art and life reappears in Olivia's habit of defacing 'the nudities of Pictures, and little Statues' (V. i. 26), a campaign of artistic reform that seems to indicate revulsion at too gross an intrusion of man's appetitive character into the decorous, public world of art. But, as Eliza perceives, it is really a protest that art cannot re-create the most elemental, organic features of man's natural existence, for Olivia defaces the nudities 'only because they are not real' (V. i. 27). The defaced, sexually inanimate images epitomize the nature of public display and ceremony throughout the comedy.[8]

Wycherley constantly draws attention to the difficulty of finding stable and appropriate generic conventions for representing the events he is portraying. Fulfilling the roles of Heraclitus and Democritus, the weeping and laughing philosopher,[9] Manly and Freeman interpret the same patterns of life in opposed tragic and comic terms, neither adequate to the range and variety of events. Another generic complication is introduced by Fidelia, who appears at first to have strayed incongruously into Wycherley's London from an Arcadian romance, yet then compromises her standing as Arcadian heroine by assisting Manly to rape Olivia: an act of self-denial in view of her own love for Manly, but one that is far more morally complex than the noble rivalry of Orrery's heroes. She is not, of course, being crudely debunked; rather (like the comparable figure of Alithea) she displays anomalies that are alien to the uncomplicated values evoked by her name, for she is led by the very logic of those

---

[8] Eliza's jibe is vastly more subtle than Célimène's simple taunt to Arsinoé in *Le Misanthrope*: 'Elle fait des tableaux couvrir les nudités; | Mais elle a de l'amour pour les réalités' (III. iv. 943–4).

[9] See Birdsall, *Wild Civility*, 157–77.

values into an act which compromises her capacity to embody them. Alithea's name had signified truth, and Fidelia's signifies truth to word. But the possibility of such uncontaminated representation is the very thing that Wycherley questions. Manly was obviously wrong to believe Olivia to be 'all truth' (I. i. 557–8), but even Fidelia's career is one of consistent self-misrepresentation (she pretends to be a man), and the scene in which she most proves her loyalty to Manly (the rape) is not only the point at which she is most morally compromised but also that at which there is the greatest divorce of act from linguistic representation, the doer and the talker being apparently the same yet actually separate.

Fidelia is attractive, but she is not a paragon, and she lives up less to her given name than to her surname, Grey, which suggests the merging of one of the most fundamental of binary oppositions. For she exemplifies the imperfect, contradictory relationship between the confused composition of human nature and the simple stereotypes which we derive from it, and by which we seek to understand it. She remains a very different being from Olivia, her enforced career of dissimulation notwithstanding. But the signs available to differentiate them are simpler than the differences themselves, and the paradox of Fidelia—generically alien to a world of which she is increasingly part—again shows the discrepancy between conventional signs and the confused essence of human character. In the end, she does not prove that Manly's ideals exist but rather that his pet hates of cowardice and dissimulation can contribute to acceptable and in some ways admirable forms of life. When he at length recognizes her loyalty, Manly impulsively associates her with an exotic, distant realm remote from the drab banalities of Restoration England: 'you deserve the *Indian* World' (V. iii. 136–7). But her reply exorcizes all exoticism, revealing that she is the daughter of a well-extracted northern gentleman, left 'in the present possession of Two thousand pounds a Year' (V. iii. 143–4). After all the evocations of Arcadia, she turns out to be that most ordinary of beings, a provincial heiress.

But Fidelia also helps to question a yet more fundamental and comprehensive set of differences: that between male and female. After all, she spends the play dressed as a man, and thereby participates in a widespread disordering of expected sexual roles. The Widow is a virago, her son is a sexless dolt, and Novel and Plausible are, by Manly's standards, effeminate. Oldfox and Freeman each court the Widow in linguistic rituals empty of sexual desire, and Olivia falls for another woman. The only traditionally feminine woman, Olivia's sensible cousin Eliza (Éliante in *Le Misanthrope*), remains (unlike Éliante) entirely marginal, without influence or lovers, exercising no influence and entering into no social or sexual relationships. As in *The Country-Wife*, the stereotypes of male and female are imprecise and over-schematic classifications of the manifold and unpredictable patterns of human life. It is true that the biological signs of Fidelia's sex are among the few objective and reliable forms of proof to emerge in the play: when Vernish finds Fidelia in male disguise at his lodging, it is the discovery of her breasts which turns fears of cuckoldom into designs of rape, and it is the discovery of her long hair that reveals her true sex to Manly and puts all her previous conduct in a new light. But, if the breasts and hair are clear and simple signs, the condition which they signify is profoundly equivocal, for femininity has progressively been deprived of consistent and stable meaning. The same is true of the masculinity signified by Manly's name. Manly, who had championed a pure correspondence of sign and signified, ends up bearing a name which corresponds to very little, forming one-half of a verbal antithesis which is nowhere reproduced in the tangled composition of life.

The cheerful insouciance of early Restoration gay couple comedy was ceding to the seriousness and unresolved complexity displayed, at vastly different artistic levels, by *The Fool Turn'd Critick* and *The Plain-Dealer*. Cheerful sex is largely confined to farce, and even here there can be complications: Durfey's *A Fond Husband* and *Squire Oldsapp* are as farcical as one could wish, but they also highlight the serious inequity of the woman's position. There is also a growing reaction against sex comedy, both in new plays and adaptations. In *The Debauchee; or, The Credulous Cuckold* (Duke's, February 1677), for example, an anonymous adapter (possibly Aphra Behn)[10] reworked Brome's *A Mad Couple Well Match'd*, a play whose exuberant but deeply unattractive hero (Careless) is guilty of cynical ingratitude to his uncle and benefactor, to the point of trying to cuckold him. The adapter is still more critical of Careless (contemplating his raucously drunken lifestyle, the Butler expresses relief that he was not born a gentleman, and remarks on the gentry's taste for bawdy plays, III, p. 30), and there is more sympathy for female victims: Careless's mistress, Phebe, loses the shrill vulgarity of her original, and his brusque indifference to her is slightly intensified. Brome's Lord Lovely, another gentlemanly womanizer, is reproachfully renamed Lord Loveless. In both versions, the Lord is accompanied by a 'youth' who is actually a gentlewoman he has deflowered, but in Brome the injured woman is merely given money to secure herself a good husband, whereas here Loveless repents with an earnestness which looks forward to that of his Cibberian namesake: 'You melt my soul.——Pray let me make new vows to you, or well confirm the old. . . . Can you forgive what's past, and take a penitent man to your mercy?' (V, p. 62). Careless also shows a greater inclination to reform, and the adulteress, Mrs Saleware, another mistress of Lord Loveless, also displays an explicit reform that is not in Brome.

John Leanerd's *The Country Innocence* (King's, perhaps March 1677) is another rake-reformed adaptation, of T. B.'s (?Thomas Brewer's) *The Countrie Girle*, and its reaction against contemporary developments is quite explicit,

---

[10] 'This Play is by some ascrib'd to Mrs. *Behn*' (Langbaine, *Account of the English Dramatick Poets*, 529). See also Milhous and Hume, 'Attribution Problems', 13.

for its preface and epilogue protest against virtually every current trend in drama: scenery, dancing, French influence, '*bawdy Farce*', and the heroic play. Here, a lecherous landlord is induced to live up to the moral demands of his status, name, and reputation (II, p. 15) after being confronted with the social disorder implicit in his irresponsibility: turning up, as he believes, for an assignation with a tenant's daughter, he sees the victim and her family in noble dress (the father identified as a 'Justice', IV, p. 36), his wife being dressed as his victim's mother. For a moment, he becomes an outsider, as the inferior group on which he intended to prey becomes a socially established group which refuses to recognize him. Inverted social order also expresses moral inadequacy in the complementary plot, in which a number of worthless suitors of Lady Lovely are tricked into courting her disguised chambermaid, and duped into appropriately humiliating marriages. The sexual predator is also thwarted in *The Counterfeits* (Duke's, May 1678), an adaptation of Moreto's *La ocásion hace al ladrón* which has been ascribed to John Leanerd,[11] where a rake marries a woman whom he has deflowered after an insincere promise of marriage: as in *Tom Essence*, the deceived and rejected woman is treated with clear sympathy, and given a clear moral claim.

Two original plays, Edward Howard's *The Man of Newmarket* (King's, by ?February 1678)[12] and the anonymous *Tunbridge-Wells* (Duke's, ?March 1678),[13] also dispense earnest morality. In his Induction, Howard denounces the 'spurious Monopolizers of Wit' (sig. A2) and obliquely disparages Shadwell and Wycherley, and in the play itself he takes obvious issue with *The Plain-Dealer*, both in his sympathetic portrayal of a lawyer and in his critical portrayal of the malcontent Maldrin, who feels that his military service has not been adequately rewarded. Service, he is told (in a resurrection of a venerable ideal), is duty (I, pp. 4–5), and the wisest government cannot identify and recognize everyone's deserts (V, p. 62). There is heavy emphasis on the civic imperatives of obligation and law (to which, for example, Maldrin must subordinate his sense of individual grievance), and much insistence on the characters' 'worth': unlike many abler contemporaries, Howard has complete faith in the verifiability of intrinsic character. In a leaden transformation of gay couple courtship, Clevly tests the 'worth' of two suitors, including Maldrin. In another, the beautiful Quickthrift (surprisingly played by Katherine Corey) is courted by the lawyer Plodwell, who despite his name is

[11] 'This Comedy is ascribed by some to *Leanard;* but I believe it too good to be his Writing' (Langbaine, *Account of the English Dramatick Poets*, 528). Milhous and Hume consider the attribution to Leanerd suspect ('Attribution Problems', 12). For the Spanish source, see Loftis, *Spanish Plays of Neoclassical England*, 163–6.

[12] *The London Stage*, ed. Van Lennep, and Danchin (*Prologues and Epilogues*, iii. 103) conjecturally place the first performance in Mar. 1678. The play is, however, satirically mentioned in Leanerd's *The Rambling Justice*, IV, p. 49, and this play appears to have been premièred in Feb. 1678 (Danchin, *Prologues and Epilogues*, iii. 251).

[13] Langbaine (*Account of the English Dramatick Poets*, 554) attributes the play (like *Tom Essence*) to 'Mr. *Rawlins*'.

an exemplary gentleman of great moral authority: 'Can there be a more high inducement than to be legally good, or to submit to the divine perfection of Reason form'd into Law?' he asks. 'Believe me, Sir, it shall guide my civil being' (III, p. 32). This quite unconventional comic hero acts as a standard against which more conventional comic figures are measured: the genial extravagant Breakbond compromises his essential 'worth' (I, p. 8) by an underdeveloped sense of obligation, in that he refuses to pay debts to tradesmen; and the mercenary jilt Luce turns into an outright criminal when she robs her lover. Law and the *civil* are rescued from Wycherley's scepticism and re-established as guiding principles in society.

Tunbridge-Wells is similar in dullness and rectitude: the former womanizer Fairlove is converted to marital virtue by Alinda in a feeble gay couple courtship, and social degree is rigidly enforced. Alinda's brother, Sir Lofty Vainman, demonstrates by his folly the unworthiness of the baronetcy conferred on his family by James I, but his rank nevertheless induces the more sensible characters to rescue him from marriage to Brag, a prostitute masquerading as a rich widow: 'His very being a Gentleman obliges all Men of Honour to endeavour's rescue' (V, p. 43). The mercer Farendine, a social climber who wants to 'Purchase a Knight-hood' (II, p. 15), is released from a mock marriage to Brag's accomplice, but only on condition that he 'never more pretend to th' qualifications of a Gentleman' (V, p. 48). Brag and another prostitute are brutally returned to poverty and the streets, and Owmuch, the gentleman sharper who had sought to impose the fake widow on Sir Lofty, is dismissed as being unworthy of his rank.

Innocuous farce was, predictably enough, continued by Edward Ravenscroft and, more surprisingly, by Otway, whose first comedy was an adaptation of Molière's *Les Fourberies de Scapin*, performed as an afterpiece to his adaptation of Racine's *Bérénice*: the first example of the combination of tragedy and afterpiece that became popular in the eighteenth century. In *The Cheats of Scapin* (Duke's, ?November 1676), the two heroes pursue love in defiance of paternal authority, only to find that their fathers' choice coincides with their own, since each of the two young men loves the other's sister: love is nicely reconciled with duty, in a way that contrasts with the corrupting impasse of *Titus and Berenice*. It is in keeping with Otway's general outlook, however, that he should increase the tension between fathers and sons, intensifying Molière so as to express his habitual concern with dispossession and displacement: 'never think to come within my Doors, or see my Face more; but expect to be as miserable as thy folly and poverty can make thee' (II. i. 63–6).[14] He omits, however, the more romantic and unrealistic displacement of the long-lost daughter stolen in infancy by gypsies. Ravenscroft's *Scaramouch a Philosopher* (King's, May 1677), also based on *Les Fourberies de Scapin*, and

---

[14] Molière's version is 'je te renonce pour mon fils, et tu peux bien pour jamais te résoudre à fuir de ma présence' (II. ii, p. 611).

retaining the gypsy plot, reached the stage by May 1677 after some delay, probably caused by Otway's rival version. Whereas Otway fleetingly tinges farce with the darker vision of his tragedies, Ravenscroft expands the farcical element with overt debt to the *commedia dell'arte*, and turns the two fathers into unmenacing representatives of sham intellectual authority: a philosopher and a doctor. Here, however, only one of the courtships turns out to coincide with parental designs; in the other, the parentally favoured suitor is dissuaded from the match by a series of ruses which reveal Ravenscroft's continuing fascination with *Monsieur de Pourceaugnac*. He follows an identical pattern in his next comedy, *The English Lawyer* (King's, by December 1677), based on Ruggle's Latin *Ignoramus* of 1615, where the identification of a long-lost daughter again harmonizes young love with paternal designs, and where the eponymous lawyer provides more sham intellectual authority.

As well as ventures into innocuous farce, there were two ventures into pastoral, both at Dorset Garden: Elkanah Settle's *Pastor Fido* (December 1676), based on Fanshawe's translation of Guarini, and the anonymous *The Constant Nymph; or, The Rambling Shepheard* (July 1677). Settle turns Guarini's satyr into a Restoration rake, gives the faithless Corisca some of Lyndaraxa's qualities, and pairs them off in a marriage doomed to acrimony (the original Corisca is redeemed by penitence), whereas *The Constant Nymph* depicts the reform of an inconstant male, whose transformation coincides with a wider social stabilization, through the exorcism of old enmities.

The most backward-looking sex comedy of the late 1670s was Thomas Porter's *The French Conjurer* (Duke's, ?March or April 1677), in which the cuckolding of an elderly citizen and thwarting of an elderly father are conducted amidst intrigues reminiscent of *An Evening's Love* (including a mock-astrologer). Christianity is mocked by a scene of pseudo-incantations during which the citizen's wife descends to hell in order to consummate her adultery. The most up-to-date feature of the play is a disturbing emphasis on the ego-centric violence of the male: in an attempt to gain a woman's affections, Horatio knifes her and attempts to frame his favoured rival (and close friend) for the crime. Porter now mingles the ethos of festive comedy with that of his tragedy, *The Villain*.

In the early 1670s, Ravenscroft had used the prevailing forms of comedy—gay couple comedy, Anglicized Molière—as vehicles for his interest in farce, but he initially kept farce distinct from sex comedy, making his first, belated experiment with the genre in the very lightweight *The London Cuckolds* (Duke's, October 1681). It was Durfey rather than Ravenscroft who first experimented with sexual farce, in the extremely popular *A Fond Husband* (Duke's, May 1677), a favourite of Charles II, and *Squire Oldsapp* (Duke's, June 1678). But, unlike Ravenscroft, Durfey was not exclusively a *farceur*, sustaining his serious critique of male sexual conduct even in these predominantly light-hearted romps. Until the closing stages of *A Fond Husband*, a pair

of adulterers repeatedly evades apparently imminent detection by such ludicrous contrivances as disappearance through a trap-door, but even in this
almost slapstick context Durfey gives serious prominence to the feminine
viewpoint. Emilia, the adulterous wife, is a spirited and attractive girl trapped
in marriage to an impotent dotard, who alternates between abject uxorious-
ness and bouts of jealous tyranny in which he insists on his right of 'Government' (III, p. 24) to the point of wishing to mutilate her (III, p. 30). She is also
consistently superior in invention and resource to her lover, Rashley, being
alone responsible for postponing detection of their adultery until the closing
moments of the play. The forces set against her are those not of morality but
of sexual jealousy—the spoilsports Ranger and Maria combine to expose the
lovers because he lusts after Emilia and she after Rashley—and exposure,
when it happens, is not the triumph of inexorable moral process but the mere
product of 'Chance' (V, p. 61). The oppression of women is emphasized by the
condition of Emilia's stepdaughter Cordelia, pestered by the courtship of the
decaying Alderman Fumble and designed for marriage to the clap-ridden
Sneak, another rustic gentleman who affects the worst features of the town
gallant. Like many other Durfey heroines, Cordelia finds happiness not in
marriage to her true love (she does not have one) but in remaining single; in
doing so, she (like Durfey's Penelope) departs from the pattern of a literary
namesake whose excellence consists in service to the male.

   Whereas Emilia—'the mighty Sophistress' (V, p. 61)—is consistently distinguished by her wit, inventiveness, and articulacy,[15] the disagreeable suitors
and partners display various kinds of linguistic incapacity: Bubble, her husband, expresses love in baby-talk, Sneak, fresh from Oxford, cultivates absurd
rhetoric, and Fumble, unwilling to admit his deafness, makes consistently inappropriate contributions to conversation. The result is not simply a pointless medley of humours. Rather, authority of status is separated from that of
language, and there is consequently no clear vocabulary of moral authority.
Like Pinchwife in *The Country-Wife*, Bubble fears the *name* of cuckold (III,
pp. 25, 30). But, when the most important characteristic of cuckoldom is the
word itself, the value of wifely fidelity becomes questionable. Certainly, when
Bubble at last discovers Emilia's guilt the moral terminology is on his side, but
the arguments are on Emilia's:

EMIL. [to Rashley] Ah, who could have the heart to leave thy Blisses for such a Fool,
   such a Beast, such a dull, sordid, filthy, insipid Creature as my Husband? . . .
BUBB. Ah cursed Creature! is this thy Vertue? . . .   *[Goes to wound her.*

(V, p. 60)

---

   [15] Christopher J. Wheatley gives an interesting account of the association between adultery and
elevated language in this and other plays of the period: 'Thomas Durfey's *A Fond Husband*, Sex
Comedies of the Late 1670s and Early 1680s, and the Comic Sublime', *Studies in Philology*, 90 (1993),
371–90.

As Otway later did in *The Souldiers Fortune*, Durfey creates a situation in which the accepted vocabulary of sexual morality is deprived of its customary support. 'Vertue' simply becomes irrational loyalty to a partner so intolerable that he is prepared to enforce fidelity at knifepoint. At the end of the play, Emilia is finally denied language—'Shame ties my Tongue' (v, p. 60)—but those who are not denied language have throughout the play been denied authority.

Squire Oldsapp is even more farcical than *A Fond Husband*: at one point, for example, the eponymous dotard is kept out of his unfaithful mistress's way by being persuaded to take part in a magical ritual of rejuvenation. But, amidst the farce, the woman's viewpoint is again dominant, and the emphasis is not on the sexual conquests of the male but on those of Oldsapp's mistress, Tricklove. Even the formal operations of legal authority are diverted to the service of the female, and to the subversion of the double standard; for, when Oldsapp tries to have Tricklove arrested as a harlot, he is instead arrested himself (by contrast, in the more man-centred *The Adventures of Five Hours*, the virtuous Porcia had narrowly escaped arrest as a strumpet). But, if the female libertine Tricklove outsmarts the traditionally more predatory male, carefree libertinism appears less joyfully problem-free when we witness its impact on another female viewpoint: that of the faithful, betrayed wife. One of Tricklove's lovers, Henry, is married to the chaste Christina, whom he guards with the jealous suspicion that convention permits a faithless man; the other, Henry's friend Welford, actually attempts to rape Christina, not realizing that she is his friend's wife. At the climax, Durfey pits legitimate obligation against illicit desire by the common device of role-splitting, using a version of the Invisible Mistress ruse: Christina and Welford's betrothed, Sophia, don masks and, unrecognized, approach the two men, easily inducing them to betray their real characters in coarse sexual proposals. The dialogue between Henry and Christina implicitly exalts public values over private desires with none of Wycherley's or Dryden's ambivalence:

CHRIST. Sir, I desire a word in *private* with you?

HENR. In *private*? with all my Heart, Madam: this Room, I confess, is too *publick* for any business—if you please, Madam, I'll wait on you to your Lodging.

CHRIST. No, Sir, mine is a *publick* business——you will guess it so when you see my Face.

(v, p. 63; italics added)

And here matters are left, with Henry lamely promising an explanation when they get home, and the concluding moments of the play belong to Tricklove, who easily persuades Oldsapp of her love and fidelity. Christina and Sophia are likely to be less credulous, and the prospects of happy marriage seem uncertain.

Here, farce is tinged with seriousness. In *Trick for Trick; or, The Debauch'd*

Hypocrite (King's, March 1678), the play which comes between *A Fond Husband* and *Squire Oldsapp*, Durfey reversed the process, creating a protagonist for whom life is a sustained bedroom farce, but providing a dark and serious view of his impact on others. The play is a radical revision (and improvement) of Fletcher's *Monsieur Thomas*. Fletcher's Thomas is an engaging extravagant who returns from travel with the seeds of reform sown in him, but is reinforced in his old ways by his father, Sebastian, who complains that 'my name and quality | Has kept my land three hundred yeers in madnesse' (I. ii. 71–2),[16] and threatens to disinherit him should he break the tradition. The contrast between normative and corrupt versions of gentlemanly character is emphasized by the complementary plot, which portrays the magnanimity of an old man and his young friend (actually father and long-lost son), when both find themselves in love with the same woman. Durfey abandons Fletcher's emphasis on the exemplary. The noble rivalry plot is dropped, and Thomas becomes a genuinely noxious rake, who is feigning reform as part of a plan to horrify his father into parting with money. His nastiness is the more striking in that he clearly recalls one of the earliest and most successful examples of the cheerful Restoration roisterer, Sir Frederick Frollick: for Thomas's surname is also Frollick, and he resembles his namesake in having a comic French servant (one of the few simple outsiders in comedy of this period).[17] Equally strikingly, he was played by Charles Hart, here for the first time cast as an unequivocally contemptible character. Surnamed Frollick, played by Hart, Thomas provides comprehensive revaluation of the extravagant rake.

Thomas's full viciousness, however, only gradually becomes apparent, and at first he caters exuberantly to the hunger for the diverting, socially daring spectacle that is as dominant in this play as it is in *The Man of Mode* (as his surname might suggest, preoccupation with the *frolic* recurs throughout the play).[18] Early in the play, for example, his French servant Launce describes one of the pranks which, 'much like a Gentleman' in Thomas's own view (I, p. 6), he contrived during his recent stay in France: leading a prostitute through the streets of Paris on the back of a bear while acting as the orator to proclaim her virtues (I, pp. 7–8). By comparison, Dorimant's disturbances of civic norms—a prostitute in the most fashionable area of the theatre, a serenade with military instruments—seem rather tame, but Thomas's more straitlaced friend Franck approves: ''twas very extravagant, yet gave occasion for Mirth enough' (I, p. 8). Thomas, in short, is a one-man carnival; but, for the Restoration stage, the carnival season was over. The bear incident also

---

[16]   The complaint is retained by Durfey (II, p. 14).

[17]   Early in 1678, Charles had reluctantly been obliged to send troops to the Continent in order to defend the Netherlands against France. Danchin (*Prologues and Epilogues*, iii. 109) notes that the prologue and epilogue reflect 'readiness for a possible war against France'.

[18]   I, pp. 6, 7; IV, pp. 34, 35, 38, 44; V, pp. 50, 62.

introduces the linguistic idiosyncrasy which emphasizes Thomas's social ab-
errance (he is later rebuked for 'debauch'd Phrases' (I, p. 9) and 'vile Phrases',
II, p. 21): his ostentatious use of the civic instrument of oratory to provide
a panegyric upon a prostitute is complemented by the 'rhetorick, tropes,
figures, and such like' (I, p. 6) with which his only partially Anglophone
French servant recounts the incident.

Nevertheless, Thomas is generally regarded as a welcome contriver of diversion, and Franck's praise of him resembles Emilia's praise of Medley in
The Man of Mode. She had loved to hear Medley 'talk o' the intrigues. Let
'em be never so dull in themselves, he'll make 'em pleasant i' the relation' (II.
i. 88–9), and Thomas has a similar gift for pleasantly distorting narrative: 'a
graceful action gives an excellence to his Jest.—If he tells a Lye, he will be sure
it shall be a pleasant one: And he never tells a bawdy story for its own sake, but
the Companies, and the Mirth that followes after' (IV, pp. 41–2). Thomas's
courtship of the sprightly and virtuous Cellide at first follows the standard
pattern of the witty love duel. The duel is amiable enough in its early stages,
and is expressly regarded by others as a source of diversion: 'if he knew how
well she lov'd him, We shou'd have better sport', says Cellide's friend Sabina
(I, p. 9). Later, when Thomas is protesting love and Launce inopportunely announces that he has found two prostitutes, as requested, Sabina is again
amused ('a pleasant Jest', III, p. 31). The diversions become less innocent,
however, when Launce describes Thomas's boisterous hooliganism of the
previous night. In the inevitable conflict between festivity and the ministers of
justice, the Constable and other agents of 'the King's Peace' are routed, but
the destructiveness of the drunken gentleman is, with obvious satiric point,
assisted by that of some pigs whom he releases: one 'most villainously
tramples upon authority' and another demolishes the contents of a potter's
shop. 'Now Sir—you shall hear all—and laugh abundantly, he has such a
grace in telling it, Sir' (IV, p. 36), says Launce.

Thomas's Medley-like ability to transform anything into an object of diversion is starting to become a process of moral as well as aesthetic distortion,
and his fictions and spectacles soon become very ugly indeed. Caught hiding
in Cellide's room by her father, Thomas brazenly claims that she invited him
there for sex, and nearly leads her father to disinherit her. Her love turned to
vengefulness, she devises 'Rare sport' (V, p. 56), arranging an interview in the
hearing of both their fathers. Having elicited from Thomas an admission that
he slandered her chastity, she distracts his servant Launce by talking gibberish (turning the tables on the linguistically aberrant pair), has her servants
bind both of them, and proceeds to strike Thomas. But Thomas and Launce
struggle free, and the final, ugliest, diversion gets under way, as Thomas attempts to rape Cellide. Cellide's father, hitherto pompous though by no
means purely ridiculous, now becomes the authoritative voice of social and
moral judgement: 'Rascall, Villain, Debauch'd Villain'. Sabina, previously

entertained by the spectacle of the lovers' battles, echoes him: 'Savage, Barb'rous Villain'. But Thomas's father (Sir Wilding) cheers him on with delighted laughter, and Launce revels in the joke: ''Gads noones, this is sport' (V, p. 61).

Durfey has initially portrayed a world governed by the principles of Medley and Dorimant but has developed those principles to violent and repulsive conclusions. In *The Man of Mode* the detached aesthetic delight in the lusts, embarrassments, and extravagances of individuals—the pleasure of the Lucretian spectator—is the prime shared principle of community, and the prime social constraint upon the free indulgence of appetite. Here, the preoccupation with diversion attenuates the principles of community, diminishing compassion and prompting an amused tolerance of conduct which in its naked essence is destructive and antisocial. 'What Barbarity is this?' asks Valentine, Cellide's host and Sabina's brother, as he enters just in time to prevent the rape (V, p. 62), the iterated definition of Thomas as a villain and barbarian defining him as an outsider to his class and to society itself. In *The Man of Mode*, the repeated term *barbarous* emphasizes the multiplicity and mere conventionality of available social codes, in that it expresses a variety of individual condemnations of conduct acceptable by other available standards: Sir Fopling, for example, finds the names of English servants 'barbarous' (III. iii. 263) and Emilia, probably facetiously, condemns Dorimant's raucous serenade as 'barbarous' (II. i. 123), whereas Lady Townley gives it the prime accolade of the diversion-seeking society by finding it 'pleasant' (II. i. 121). Such usages diminish the objective significance of barbarity, with the result that when Loveit and Bellinda condemn Dorimant's 'barbarous' conduct (II. ii. 144; V. i. 266) they voice the isolated judgement of the individual rather than the unanimous judgement of the community. (As Charron wrote, 'Chascun appelle barbarie ce qui n'est de son goust et usage'.[19]) In *Trick for Trick*, however, the condemnation of the barbarous expresses the united voice of the community, and Thomas's idiosyncrasy of style and meaning now expresses his moral isolation: 'I was going to teach her a new Dance,' he says of his attempted rape (V, p. 62), with an insouciant trivialization and corruption of meaning. A popular etymology of the Greek word βάρβαρος was that it mimicked onomatopoeically the alien and incomprehensible chatter of a foreign tongue: that Sir Fopling should find his own mother tongue barbarous is a nice terminological inversion, but Thomas is barbarous in the literal and traditional sense, and it is appropriate that he should recently have returned from a foreign land with a foreign servant,[20] priding himself on pranks performed on foreign soil.

Durfey was still thinking about *The Comical Revenge* in *The Virtuous Wife*

[19] Charron, *De la sagesse*, bk. ii, ch. ii, p. 57.
[20] In *Monsieur Thomas* Launcelot is not foreign, though Fletcher (like Durfey) emphasizes his multiplicity of languages.

(Duke's, by October 1679), as we can see from several of the characters' names: Beauford, Jenny Wheedle, Sir Frollick Whimsey (a Sir Frederick who is well past his prime). Durfey shares Etherege's interest in the controlling power of chance, which is repeatedly invoked, but, still more explicitly than in *Trick for Trick*, he reassesses and rejects the comedy of carnival: 'Lying, Drunkenness', boasts the rakish Beverly, 'is the Souls Carnaval, where the noble Essence has liberty to range and divert it self, uncontroul'd by the severe Rules of Wisdom, Nature, Religion, or Honesty' (II, p. 22). Durfey in other plays also uses critical imagery of festivity (on three occasions he alludes to the Banquet of the Senses),[21] and Beverly's explicit rejection of wisdom and honesty emphasizes that his carnivalistic outlook is being censured. So do the numerous discomfitures (including a whipping, arranged by Beverly) which impede the attempted lechery of his fellow-rake, Beauford. Pointedly, his discomfitures keep bringing him into contact with representatives of the law: embodiments of structured social regulation. Once, when trying to cuckold a judge, he had got into the judge's bed rather than his wife's (I, pp. 6–7). Later, trying to evade recognition by another prospective judicial cuckold, the JP Sir Frollick Whimsey, he pretends to be an Irishman and talks gibberish, but finds himself sentenced to another whipping. He is only rescued from his plight by Sir Frollick's wife, to whom Beauford and his servant *make pitiful signs of discovery* (IV, p. 39); as in *Madam Fickle*, man is reduced to linguistic impotence and sexual subservience. Later still, Beauford actually becomes a criminal, attempting to sell a ring he had wrongfully acquired through a misunderstanding. But the goldsmith to whom he offers it is, unfortunately, the goldsmith who originally sold it; and, still more unfortunately, the goldsmith is a magistrate, so Beauford is again under arrest. In one of his characteristic revisions of sex comedy stereotypes, Durfey subjects the gentleman to the authority of a citizen, and (yet more revisionist) has him released by the magnanimous and good-humoured intercession of his intended cuckold, Sir Frollick, his 'good nature prompting [him] to forget and forgive' (V, p. 62). Finally, Beauford reforms, heeds the advice to 'live civilly and orderly' (V, p. 64), and arranges to marry Beverly's sister.

The legal form that is most extensively opposed to rakish carnival is marriage: like Otway's earlier *Friendship in Fashion* (April 1678), *The Virtuous Wife* depicts a miserable and disintegrating marriage, showing the effect of the rake's lifestyle—and double standards—on the neglected wife. Unlike Otway, however, Durfey resolves matters with facile reform. After Beauford fled abroad following a duel, his 'friend' Beverly assumed his name in order to marry Beauford's beloved Olivia, but he quickly loses interest in her and

---

[21] *Madam Fickle*, V. i. 76–7 (cf. v. i. 124); *The Fool Turn'd Critick*, V, p. 50; *The Royalist*, III, p. 31. Cf. *Squire Oldsapp*, II, p. 22. Harold M. Weber discusses the topos of the Banquet of Sense in his explication of *The Country-Wife*, but is unaware of its currency in Durfey (*The Restoration Rake-Hero: Transformations in Sexual Understanding in Seventeenth-Century England* (Madison, 1986), 56–68).

forms a liaison with Jenny Wheedle. Returning from exile, Beauford pursues both Olivia, virtuous despite her misery, and Isabella, the beautiful wife of Sir Frollick Whimsey, meeting with repeated frustration and ill luck. In another reworking of earlier, festive forms of comedy Olivia (as Dryden's Florimell and Ravenscroft's Hillaria had done) disguises herself as a man in order to win her rival's affections, promising Jenny marriage and thereby recovering the jewels which Beverly has lavished on her. The difference from earlier plays is that Jenny is no mere cipher, but is genuinely hurt by the deception and, for all her graspingness, voices her feelings and viewpoint sufficiently to claim some sympathy: dressing as a man in order to right her own wrongs, Olivia in the process inevitably creates another female victim, and to this extent Durfey does acknowledge that there is no simple end to adultery, despite the facile conversions of his rakes. Moral reform has its casualties as well as its beneficiaries. The most unsettling feature of Olivia's revenge is her attempt, with Beauford's aid, to subject Jenny to the kind of bedroom deception which another Olivia, in *The Plain-Dealer*, had herself suffered. In Wycherley, the significantly named Manly had planned the rape. Here the plotter is a woman, the namesake of Wycherley's victim, and the scheme only goes wrong because of Beauford's characteristic incompetence. For Durfey, no woman deserves to be raped; and it is disturbing that the assumption of masculine disguise should lead a virtuous woman to engineer a rape in order to sustain her appearance of masculinity.

The darkening of comedy also appears in two minor plays, both indebted to Middleton, and one showing some influence of *The Plain-Dealer*. *The Counterfeit Bridegroom* (Duke's, September 1677), an anonymous adaptation of Middleton's *No Wit, No Help Like a Woman's*, is speculatively attributed by Genest to Aphra Behn.[22] Both its plots concern the recovery of heritage. A young man goes abroad to ransom his mother and sister, squanders the money on good living, and returns with a bride whom he passes off as his sister. On her unexpected and embarrassing return, his mother declares that the bride really is his sister, but she is fortunately mistaken, and the true sister is finally identified. In the other plot, an impoverished gentlewoman who cannot gain redress by law recovers her fortunes by assuming male disguise and marrying the widow of the usurer who defrauded her father (husband in Middleton). During the illusory marriage the widow falls in love with someone else—actually her fake husband's brother—and finally marries him (the adapter adds an attempted bedroom trick, with the brother as substitute during the consummation of the marriage). Middleton repeatedly stresses the reversion of kinship to strangeness, and since this is also a favourite preoccupation of Behn, and since the anonymous adapter largely excises it, it seems likely that Genest's attribution is erroneous.

[22] John Genest, *Some Account of the English Stage from the Restoration in 1660 to 1830* (10 vols., Bath, 1832), i. 213.

Middleton also locates individual conduct in interlocking cosmic, religious, and social structures: wives should obey husbands, masters should look after tenants, and adultery is a damnable offence. After all their dislocations and estrangements, Middleton's characters have their 'right name and place' (V. i. 463), and their very names (Twilight, Sunset, Low-Water) link their social fortunes to an all-pervasive natural order. By contrast, the adapter shows the individual in revolt against oppressive constraints and arbitrary misfortunes. Learning of his possible incest, for example, the hero responds with typical 1670s libertinism: 'Pox on Kindred—like noble Savage, I wou'd range and choose my Mistress where I pleas'd—now must sacred Love be curb'd, and pleasures lost, and all long of dull fantastick Law' (IV, p. 38). Moreover, the allusions to cyclic process disappear, so that Mistress Low-Water (the destitute gentlewoman) becomes Mrs Hadland: a victim of mere economic collapse. In keeping with the reduced interest in natural systems, the adapter gives less emphasis to the dispersed family than to Mrs Hadland's contrivances for economic redress, which are portrayed as individualistic efforts to secure rights denied by the social mechanisms of justice: 'Wit now perform, what Justice could not do; | All ways are just, when we our Rights pursue' (I, p. 14). This insistence on rights which transcend established judicial forms is a new element in Restoration drama, and one which the Whig Shadwell later repeated in *The Woman-Captain*.

The other Middleton offshoot, Leanerd's *The Rambling Justice* (King's, February 1678), is far more sparing in its borrowing, transplanting a few episodes from *More Dissemblers Besides Women* into a new context.[23] Whereas individualism in *The Counterfeit Bridegroom* had produced an order acceptable to all, this play moves towards the unpleasantly unresolved tension that was becoming increasingly characteristic of comedy. In this respect, it is quite different from Leanerd's two reform comedies, though equally responsive to new trends. Sir Generall Amorous has in the past cuckolded Alderman Contentious Surly, and during the course of the play sleeps with Eudoria, the wife of another alderman, Sir Arthur Twilight. Rejected by her lover, Surly's wife (Petulant Easy) inveighs against the double imprisonment of marriage to a worthless husband and attachment to a perfidious rake (V, p. 57), and at the end of the play she remains a brooding and disruptive presence, plotting how to spoil the hero's eventual marriage to his new mistress's stepdaughter. Easy does manage to enjoy Amorous for one last time by means of a bedroom trick, the deception here highlighting the indiscriminate randomness of desire (as it did later in Otway's comedies): on two occasions Sir Arthur (a great follower of the double standard) propositions Eudoria when she has disguised herself to meet Amorous, and indiscriminacy of desire is reflected in the compulsive

[23] Langbaine (*Account of the English Dramatick Poets*, 320) damned the play as a wholesale plagiarism. Arthur Gewirtz correctly states that it cannot be counted as an adaptation (*Restoration Adaptations of Early 17th Century Comedies* (Washington, DC, 1982), 155).

attempts at womanizing by the foolish Sir Geoffry Jolthead, the rambling justice of the title, nominally an enforcer of social regulation, but actually a living exemplar of its fragility in the face of appetite. At the end of the play, Amorous comes close to killing Sir Arthur, who is only saved by the intercession of his faithless wife, and then has to rest content with Amorous's cynical justification of adultery: ''tis but a Veniall sin, and not so great as it is Common; for but few Women inviolably observe the Faith they owe their Husbands' (v, p. 67). The norms of human conduct are determined not by the absolutes of faith but by the empirical statistics of desire.

Rambling of a more literal kind—of gypsies (taken from Middleton)—is also featured: for her first assignation with Amorous, Eudoria disguises herself as a gypsy, but Easy gets there first in the same disguise and bags Amorous, leaving Eudoria to be pestered by her lustful and unrecognizing husband, the entanglements being further complicated by the arrival of a real company of gypsies. These alien nomads, outside the formal structures of society, symbolize the wandering lusts that drive the characters to mimic them. Although the play has many farcical elements—a fake ghost, a trap-door, an old man mistaken for a woman, etc.—it chiefly emphasizes the disagreeable inconclusiveness of a world where order is constantly compromised by appetite, and it concludes with a series of inversions of conventional familial authority. Sir Arthur's daughter Flora agrees to marry Jolthead because he will be easy to cuckold; Flora's sister decides to marry Amorous (the cuckolder and near-murderer of her father); and the vengeful Easy broods on how to disturb what is already a rather imperilled harmony.

The gypsy also symbolizes the suspension of fixed social order in Aphra Behn's *The Rover; or, The Banish'd Cavaliers* (Duke's, March 1677), here appearing in conjunction with that archetypal suspension of social order, the carnival; for the play portrays the search for love amidst the apparent freedom of the Naples carnival. But, once again, carnival has lost its innocence, expressing the darker side of male licence, its exuberance constantly spilling over into duels, and into attempted rape or battery. Willmore, a woman's-eye view of Dorimant, treats virtually every woman in the cast as a prostitute, and the soberly virtuous Florinda is twice threatened with rape, first by Willmore, secondly by most of the male cast, who clamour outside the room in which she is imprisoned incognita, none clamouring more loudly than her own brother. The danger, though also the attraction, of the carnival is that it creates a suspension of social identity. The gypsy disguise in which Hellena and her friends first go masquerading suggests a nomadic independence from local social structure, and Hellena thereafter pursues Willmore in an ever-shifting sequence of disguises. Men (especially Willmore) are repeatedly described as 'strangers', and sexual encounters are frequently anonymous: after the prostitute Lucetta has robbed Blunt, a fool from Essex, she boasts that he does not know her name; when Willmore molests Florinda, he reassures her—

as some sort of palliation for rape—that he cannot brag, because he does not know her name; and, most strikingly, Willmore and Hellena each discover the other's name only when the carnival courtship gives way to the socially approved institution of marriage.

Such suspension of usual forms is not, however, confined to the carnival: the courtesan Angelica Bianca takes little part in it, but nevertheless stands outside received norms and, unlike the revellers, cannot finally be assimilated into society. Willmore, the Rover, is geographically as well as sexually unfixed (he is a royalist privateer), and he and the other banished Cavaliers remind us that the saturnalia in Naples coexists with another, more durable and sinister, inversion of order in England. But one need not look back to Interregnum England to find disruptive Englishmen; for, with their compulsive violence and sexual molestation, the banished Cavaliers are themselves forces of disruption, despite their identification with a political cause to which Behn herself was entirely committed. Disorder, at least that of male tyranny, is inevitably implicit even in the most legitimate order (as is again shown by the Tory rake Tom Wilding in *The City Heiress*). The carnival is not so much an inversion of the typical as a special case of the typical, and its function, therefore, is less to suspend established order than to expose the elemental patterns of power which underlie it: patterns in which the woman is likely to become victim or commodity. Florinda, who twice narrowly escapes rape during the carnival, has already narrowly escaped it in that other free play of power, war. And, as carnival liberty turns into nightmare for Florinda, so the autonomy of the prostitute turns into slavery. Lucetta, who robs Blunt, is herself the prey of her husband's avarice and sexual fantasy, and Angelica's alluring power is inseparable from her status as commodity. Indeed the very sensation of prostration before the adored mistress is a luxury made practically and psychologically possible by the man's unbroken retention of actual power. Even Belvile, the most decent man in the cast, who repeatedly rescues women from male violence, reveals how deeply interlinked are the impulses to worship women and to assault them; for, when Willmore emerges from Angelica's house, Belvile crudely enquires how successful he has been by asking, 'Are we to break her Windows, or raise up Altars to her!' (III, p. 45). There is the thinnest of distinctions between adoration and violence, and indeed when Willmore attempts to rape Florinda he does so in the language of courtly self-abasement, asking to 'salute thy Shoe-string' (III, p. 56) and claiming that he is compelled to molest her by the power of her eyes. In Behn's early tragicomedies, oppression in the guise of worship is part of a phase that men outgrow; now it is a permanent part of male conduct.

The most serious (virtually tragic) element in the play is Angelica's discovery that the power of the courtesan is an illusion. In the first stages of their courtship, as Willmore is veering between denunciation of Angelica's 'Trade' and assurances that he is her 'Slave' (II, p. 41), she recognizes that he has 'a

Power too strong to be resisted' (II, p. 42), and, when she is finally rejected for Hellena, she laments the lost illusion of power:

> I was a Slave——
> Yet still had been content to've worn my Chains . . .
> Had I remain'd in innocent Security,
> I shou'd have thought all Men were born my Slaves;
> And worn my Pow'r like Lightning in my Eyes. . . .
> Why woud'st thou then destroy my fancy'd Power?

(V, pp. 95–6)

Willmore, however, has two more substantial forms of power: language and muscle. Like Dorimant, he combines ruthless perjury with the power of linguistic fascination: 'His words go thro me to the very Soul,' Angelica confesses (II, p. 39), expressing Behn's surprising yet consistent sense of the woman's linguistic vulnerability; she shares neither Durfey's confidence in the woman's linguistic manipulativeness, nor the hyperbolic enthusiasm of the unknown female admirer who credited her with rediscovering the language of Adam.[24] But Willmore also has power in the most primitive sense. When Pedro, the stock tyrannical brother, hears that his sister Florinda has taken the husband of her choice, he exclaims 'Does he not fear my Pow'r?' (V, p. 98), only to be subdued by Willmore's 'Sir, my Power's greater in this House than yours' (V, p. 99), and by the threat of kidnapping. Inescapably, power such as this shapes events and the social order. Briefly, Angelica possesses the means, but not the ability, to exercise it, when she threatens the unfaithful Willmore with a pistol, but—unlike the habitually duelling men—she lacks the killer instinct.

In her murder attempt, Angelica wears carnival guise. This is her only extensive experiment with the form of escapist disguise that the protean Hellena constantly exploits, and indeed Willmore here initially mistakes her for Hellena. The carnival inversion for Angelica is an attempt to escape from the constraints of femininity into the boundlessness of male violence, but she remains fixed in what she is: she cannot escape from womanhood into manhood, or from the forbidden transgression of the prostitute to the licensed transgression of carnival, and she cannot therefore take the final step from carnival licence to social assimilation. Finally, she remains an outsider incapable of finding a place in the order which is chosen in the concluding marriages (whereas the wandering Willmore, the male outsider, is easily accommodated, even though he has prostituted himself by receiving money from Angelica). When the marriage of Willmore and Hellena is mooted, the proposal is put to the votes of the cast and carried,[25] in an expression of the

---

[24] Behn, *Works*, ed. Summers, vi. 127.

[25] The democratic vote of the cast also overrides the wishes of the fallen woman at the end of Catherine Trotter's *Love at a Loss; or, Most Votes Carry It* (1700).

social consensus to which Angelica cannot belong, and the social consensus is ratified in a time-honoured way, by an act of naming, when Hellena and Willmore finally declare their names to each other. But, for Angelica, the saturnalia cannot end with an act of naming that draws her into a new social role in which her individuality and social position are reconciled: as she has previously recognized, her 'Name' and 'Infamy' (IV, p. 78) are already fixed, and already damn her.

Behn's interpretation of the linguistic status of the prostitute may be compared with that in a piece of conventional prostitution literature written in Charles I's reign: Cranley's *Amanda*, the story of a reformed prostitute. Before her reform, Amanda is a being outside the accepted system of nomenclature and place, having no fixed name and no fixed lodging (she is *'like a wandring vagabond'*).[26] Her reform is accomplished by language: by poems of exhortation sent by the narrator, and by the preaching of a pious divine. But the appropriate aftermath to reform is not marriage to the narrator (despite his initial strong attraction to her) but sorrowful penitence and early death. The same complex of values is retained in *The Rover*, but it is now examined critically, with emphasis upon its anomalies: Willmore, whose title of the Rover emphasizes his initial status as a placeless outsider, can be brought within the received system, but the errant female is subject to different rules.

Accordingly, one of the recurrent problems of *The Rover* is that of female self-definition. Angelica first appears—and first attracts Willmore—not in the flesh but in a multiplicity of signs, in three portraits hanging outside her house, and Willmore's first move towards the conquest of Angelica is to steal one of her signs, pleading the crude right of 'Possession' as he fights over it with her rich admirer, Antonio (II, p. 35).[27] Similarly, Hellena first attracts Willmore as a masked unknown. Florinda also has to make herself known via extrinsic signs: in another reminiscence of the Invisible Mistress, she talks unrecognized with her beloved Belvile, who believes her to be a gentlewoman of loose morals, and she leaves her picture with him, which Willmore first mistakes for another prostitute's advertisement (III, p. 51); and, when (mistaken for a prostitute) she is threatened by Blunt and Frederick, she offers a diamond ring as a sign of her gentility (IV, p. 85). In the intervening incident, when Willmore similarly mistakes her for a prostitute, there is again a suspension of usual signs, in that Willmore does not know her name (III, p. 57). In Florinda's case, suspension of the normal tokens of social identity pushes her towards the condition of the prostitute; for, as already observed, the category of prostitute is what—in men's eyes—remains when the categories of wife, daughter, or

[26] Thomas Cranley, *Amanda; or, The Reformed Whore* (London, 1635), 46. Behn's debt to the literature of prostitution is discussed in Eva Simmons, ' "Virtue Intire": Aphra Behn's Contribution, in her Comedies, to the Marriage Debates of the Seventeenth Century', Ph.D. thesis (London, 1990).

[27] The relationship of this incident to the play's systems of patriarchal power is discussed in Elin Diamond, '*Gestus* and Signature in Aphra Behn's *The Rover*', *ELH* 56 (1989), 519–41.

sister are absent (which is why Behn's heroines adopt the disguise of prostitutes when they wish to escape from the limits of those categories). What is distinctive about Angelica is that she ostentatiously signifies herself a prostitute. But she, too, loses control of her signs and becomes a victim. Willmore steals her picture, and in the speech recognizing and lamenting the illusoriness of her power she retreats from confident public self-representation:

> But when Love held the Mirror, the undeceiving Glass
> Reflected all the Weakness of my Soul . . .
> —Oh how I fell like a long worship'd Idol.

> (V, p. 96)

The power of the portraits is replaced by the impotence of the discredited idol.

The carnival thus amplifies an ambiguity that is always present in men's treatment of women. Still more than in her earlier plays, Behn shows how fundamental the category of prostitute is to man's perception of woman, and how precarious the boundary is, both in perception and actuality, between the prostitute and the gentlewoman: Blunt mistakes Lucetta for a gentlewoman and Florinda for a prostitute. As the carnival both suspends the official order and reveals its intrinsic, hidden character, so the prostitute is both the antithesis of the gentlewoman and the image of her fundamental condition: the marriage-market is, as Angelica points out, prostitution by another name (II, p. 40), but the external resemblance of prostitution and marriage as financial transactions is explored far less than the convolutions of the male mind in comprehending the categories of prostitute and gentlewoman: so separate and irreconcilable, so interchangeable and synonymous. These convolutions are best illustrated in Antonio's division of sexual interest between the courtesan Angelica, whom he loves, and the gentlewoman Florinda, to whom he is betrothed, and who therefore figures yet again in a complex intermingling of gentlewoman and prostitute. The misunderstandings caused by Antonio's deviousness culminate when the strait-laced Belvile is induced by his male code of honour to disguise himself as the cynically promiscuous Antonio, in order to fight a duel which he believes to concern Florinda, but which actually concerns Angelica: in this incident, opposing stereotypes of male and female conduct are simultaneously blurred and confounded; and the dissolving agent is the prostitute.

Men exercise control through money, force, and language, and women are consequently consigned to categories shaped by men, and to observance of their arbitrary differentiations of value between the sister sold in marriage and the stranger sold in prostitution. The order of society is founded upon natural principles, namely what Behn increasingly came to see as unalterable principles of power, but the principles of nature are not principles of justice. Florinda complains about her brother's 'unjust Commands' (I, p. 10), and

Angelica reproaches Willmore for his 'unjust' breach of vows (IV, p. 71). And, appropriately, it is Willmore himself who gives the most forceful image of a judicial order created in the likeness of male desire. Molesting Florinda, and arguing that her own attractiveness is to blame, he protests, 'a Judge, were he young and vigorous, and saw those Eyes of thine, would know 'twas they gave the first blow' (III, p. 57). Early in *The Man of Mode*, Etherege used an anecdote about an amorous judge to signal the defeat of justice by play. Behn's procedure is quite different, and different also from that in Dryden's *An Evening's Love*, where the approach of the killjoy magistrate is halted by the revellers (though there is some resemblance to Manly's attempt to invest the rape of Olivia with judicial formality); for here, as carnival merriment threatens to turn into rape, a judge is invoked to grace the excess with the character of a social norm. For women, the indignities of the saturnalia are normality.

Behn examines the linguistic vulnerability of women still further in *Sir Patient Fancy* (Duke's, by January 1678), whose preface and epilogue also polemically assert the woman's right to be heard: '*We once were fam'd in story, and could write | Equal to Men*'.[28] The play is largely derived from Molière's *Le Malade imaginaire*, though it also contains a learned lady, Lady Knowell, based on Bélise in *Les Femmes savantes*. Molière's learned lady is an ageing and foolish man-hunter, convinced that her niece's lover is really in love with her, but Behn changes the part radically, as is indicated by its casting: not Elinor Lee, the specialist in ageing man-hunters (who later acted in Thomas Wright's *The Female Vertuoso's*), but Ann Marshall Quin, a specialist in commanding beauties, who had played Angelica in *The Rover*. Moreover, Behn's learned lady has no real interest in the younger man (here wooing her daughter), merely pretending to pursue him in order to test his worthiness. Nevertheless, she is in large measure ludicrous, for she never discovers a proper linguistic decorum in which to display and communicate her learning. When she unites her daughter with her true love, for example, she pushes a dignified gesture towards farce by crowning it with a pedantic Latin cry of 'Thalessio, Thalessio,' the cry uttered at Roman weddings (V, p. 95).[29] The acquisition of linguistic learning in itself bestows no authority, because it makes the woman a linguistic outsider who violates accepted norms of discourse while lacking any power to create new ones. An earlier display of learning portrays her insecure position quite clearly. On her first appearance, she proclaims her delight in books, singling out for enthusiasm the embraces of Rinaldo and Armida, and the divine resonance of Homer: '*Ton d' apamibominous prosiphe podas ochus Achilleus! Ah how it sounds!*' (I, p. 14).[30]

---

[28] Epilogue, p. 115.

[29] Talasio (probably the name of a forgotten marriage god) was an exclamation uttered by immemorial custom at Roman weddings. See e.g. Catullus, *Carmina*, lxi. 127.

[30] 'τὸν δ' ἀπαμειβόμενος προσέφη πόδας ὠκὺς Ἀχιλλεύς' ('The swift-footed Achilles spoke in answer to him', e.g. *Iliad*, ed. D. B. Monro (2 vols., Oxford, 1888), i. 84).

There is comedy (of a rather poignant kind) in her purely vicarious experience of the realms of love and heroic action. But there is also something more. The Armida story portrays the ultimate failure of a woman to dominate a man through magical incantations—through language. And the formulaic Homeric line represents a man talking to a man.

Women do, however, gain linguistic victories early in the play. The university-educated Sir Credulous Easy, a specialist in rhetoric, is tricked into courting Lady Knowell's daughter through silent signs, which are wilfully misinterpreted as offers to surrender all his valuables. Later, when he does attempt speech, he uses rhetoric in the wrong context, and to the wrong person. The man from the university reduces signification to chaos, and this early satire on the male monopoly and perversion of linguistic education means that, when Behn takes over the satirical torrent of medical jargon with which Molière ends his play (with debts also to the consultation scene in *L'Amour médecin*), it becomes an extended display of the traditions of formalized gibberish with which men have cornered and sustained their wealth and power, and it is a display in which the linguistically fatuous Sir Credulous participates with aplomb. But it is also important to note that this fraudulent jargon represents one of the areas in which Lady Knowell admiringly seeks proficiency (III, p. 45). The privilege for which Lady Knowell combats is in part the privilege of talking like Sir Credulous Easy, and there is no sense that beyond the systems of jargon lies a stable and objective language of authority which it is possible to acquire by education. Unlike the heroine of Shadwell's *The Woman-Captain*, Lady Knowell cannot simply establish herself by learning some established public argot of authority, for the sources of linguistic power are more subtle, insidious, and internalized, and to see what Behn is doing we should look at another flawed image of female liberation that complements and interacts with the linguistic liberation of Lady Knowell.

Behn's mature plays are second to none in their explicit and polemic endorsement of adultery as a liberation from forced or loveless marriage. Yet, while adultery is always uncomplicated fun for the man, it increasingly creates its own kind of subjugation and indignity for the 'liberated' woman. In adapting *Le Malade imaginaire*, Behn turns the protagonist's wife from a scheming and selfish crook to a sympathetic young woman who has been denied her legitimate right to love and sex. And so, when she waits eagerly in the dark for her first sexual encounter with the man she really loves, she seems to be on the verge of an act of self-defining escape. And, at this point, she is raped by a passing third party. In the dark, she mistakes her stepdaughter's fiancé for her own lover and, although the young man is horrified when he thinks his own fiancée is inviting him to bed, he quickly recognizes Lady Fancy's voice and enjoys his future mother-in-law by the time-honoured device of the bedroom trick (which Behn reused in *The Lucky Chance*). The man rapes the woman because of his greater adroitness and experience in using language (it is he who recognizes her voice), and the silence of the bedroom trick signifies the exclusion of the woman from full participation in language, and completes the earlier linguistic imposture. Once again, the suspension of familiar social signs pushes the woman towards the condition of the un-differentiated sexual prey—the prostitute—and it is a symptom of the woman's vulnerability that Sir Patient actually addresses his wife as 'my little Harlot' (IV, p. 85).

Lady Fancy's linguistic vulnerability is apparent even in the adulterous relationship that promises to release her. As she waits for her unfortunate assignation, she feels that her vocabulary is contracting into a single, submis-sive utterance: 'I've no Ideas, no Thoughts but of *Wittmore*, and sure my Tongue can speak no other Language, but his Name' (III, p. 49). And, earlier, she had implored him not to use his 'softest Language' in front of her step-daughter, lest she become her rival (II, p. 33). Wittmore and Lady Fancy are at their most equal when they are outside language, reduced (like Sir Credulous) to silent signs. When her husband is overhearing, she successfully communic-ates with her lover by silent gestures: '*She endeavours to make Signs to* Wittmore. . . . As Wittmore *goes out, he bows and looks on her; she gives him a Sign*' (IV, p. 79). Later, when they are caught out by her husband's return, she orchestrates her lover's escape by means of silent signs, the concluding one being '*a little kick*' (IV, p. 88)—a slight gesture of command and superiority. But she never exercises or desires such control in free conversation. In allegor-izing the ideal condition of love in *Lycidus; or, The Lover in Fashion*, Behn described it as a state outside official languages, conducted in physical signs and private dialects, there being 'as many Languages as there are persons'.[31] But the ideal condition of love never prevails in *Sir Patient Fancy*. Lady Fancy's retreat from language is not a retreat to primitive freedom but a response to the threatening official presence of her husband, and she generally has to work, at a disadvantage, within the man-created conventions of language, and the man-created structures of power which they support. Even towards the end of the play (when she briefly and falsely believes Sir Patient dead), her sense of liberation is simply a sense that she is now free to bestow submission where she desires, for she creates Wittmore 'Lord' of her pleasures and for-tunes (V, p. 111), and hands over Sir Patient's property to him.

The Rover and *Sir Patient Fancy* are the first plays in which Behn found her mature style, and provided patterns which she went on to develop in her suc-ceeding work. *The Rover*, obviously, is imitated in *The Second Part of the Rover* (Duke's, *c.* January 1681) and also in *The Feign'd Curtezans* (Duke's, by March 1679), while *Sir Patient Fancy* was followed up by another Molière adaptation, *The False Count* (Duke's, ?October 1681), which also deals with a young wife's escape into adultery, and with the limitations of her apparent

---

[31] Behn, *Works*, ed. Summers, vi. 323.

liberation. Most elements of *The Rover* survive in *The Feign'd Curtezans* and 2 *The Rover*: again, prostitute and gentlewoman are as rigidly separated in theory as they are thoroughly confused in practice; again, sexual encounters are generally cases of mistaken, or unknown, identity, in which the partner becomes a characterless object of desire; and, again, lovers are repeatedly described as strangers. In *The Feign'd Curtezans* two sisters, Marcella and Cornelia, attempt to escape forced marriage and a nunnery by disguising themselves as prostitutes under the names of Euphemia and Silvianetta. Believing Silvianetta to be a real prostitute, another gentlewoman, Laura Lucretia, poses as her in order to gain exploratory freedom in the face of an impending forced marriage, thereby creating considerable sexual confusion. As usual, the sole alternative feminine role to those of wife, daughter, and sister is that of prostitute, the only other possible disguise being that of a man (a disguise all the heroines also assume). There is no actual prostitute in the cast, but the women have an imaginative fascination with their parts that is quite absent from Behn's earlier feigned courtesans, in *The Amorous Prince* and *The Dutch Lover*. In prostitution, Cornelia claims, 'there are a thousand Satisfactions to be found, more than in a dull virtuous Life' (II, p. 329). Laura wishes to use her prostitute disguise to sleep with her preferred partner, Galliard, before her marriage to the unwanted Julio, but inadvertently sleeps with Julio instead, only discovering her mistake after the event. An apparent night of prostitution thus turns out to be the premature consummation of a marriage. The sisters pursue the role of prostitute at a more speculative level, but Cornelia nevertheless parallels Laura in a number of ways: also calling herself Silvianetta, also in pursuit of Galliard. Indeed she assures him, after ensnaring him into marriage, that her training as prostitute will be a marital asset: she will 'be the most Mistress-like Wife. . . . I have learnt the trade, though I had not stock to practise' (V, p. 408). Both Laura and Cornelia show, with differing degrees of literalness, that the prostitute is precursor and precondition of the wife, and indeed the conjunction of the two is fundamental to Julio's experience, since he falls in love—and sleeps— with Silvianetta-Laura without realizing that she is his designated wife. When the chosen partner turns out to be the same as the designated partner, the normal result is a reconciliation of desire with authority (as in Ravenscroft's *Scaramouch a Philosopher* and *The English Lawyer*). Here, the result is to reveal the fundamental interdependence of the socially sanctioned and the socially forbidden.

This interdependence also appears in the courtship of the third couple, Marcella (posing as the prostitute Euphemia) and her lover Fillamour, a sober and principled man after the pattern of Belvile. As Florinda had adapted the Invisible Mistress trick to tempt Belvile in the guise of another and less chaste woman, so Marcella tempts Fillamour in the guise of a prostitute, presenting him with her own physical form transposed into an ostensibly alien moral dimension. Originally, the Invisible Mistress device emphasized the compatibility of desire and social codes, in that apparently divided and wandering passions turned out to be respectably concentrated upon a single object. But, apparently confronted with two physically identical women in radically different sexual contexts, Fillamour by contrast discovers the essential ambiguity of male desire (as Julio also does in that analogous situation of divided identity, the bedroom deception). Fillamour resists temptation, but his fascination is more protracted and painful than that of Belvile, and he does defer an assignation with Marcella for a final meeting with 'Euphemia', though at the meeting he attempts to convert her. To emphasize this unexpected side of Fillamour's character, Behn juxtaposes his vacillation with a parody of the virtuous man fascinated with the forbidden, wherein the hypocritical clergyman Tickletext tries to visit Marcella's sister, Cornelia-Silvianetta, pretending that he wishes to convert her. His combination of bogus virtue and enthusiastic frailty reverses Fillamour's character but at the same time emphasizes that it too is tinged by the universal fascination with the prostitute. The legitimate bonds between man and woman constantly mirror and contain their proscribed antitypes.

The constant confounding of nomenclature (*two* Silvianettas, multiplying the confusions of gentlewoman and prostitute), the mismatch of partners, and the frequent misapprehension or ignorance of the object of desire all reduce social existence to confused patterns of lust and power, and the reduction is furthered by the farcical plot involving Tickletext and his upstart pupil, Sir Signal Buffoon, both in hot pursuit of Cornelia-Silvianetta. Here an ostensible process of social, gentlemanly education keeps resolving itself into gross corporeal action: most gross when an elegant ritual of snuff-taking is in fact conducted with powdered excrement; most corporeal when both master and pupil forget their avowed aims in the universal pursuit of prostitutes, or when the same character, in different and unpenetrated guises, serves the fools both as '*Civility-Master*' (II, p. 336) and pimp.

In 2 *The Rover* Behn reverts to concentration on a real prostitute, La Nuche, though the prostitute and the lady are still repeatedly confused. La Nuche's entanglements conflate the main elements of the Florinda–Antonio–Belvile and Hellena–Angelica–Willmore triangles: Beaumond, who provides Behn's most searching study to date of the mentality behind the double standard, is to marry Ariadne, but loves La Nuche; Ariadne pursues Willmore (now a widower), who vacillates between her and La Nuche as he had earlier vacillated between Hellena and Angelica, while La Nuche alternates (like Fletcher's Scornful Lady) between desire and scorn for the impoverished Willmore. Here Willmore reverses the choice he had made in Part I, linking hands with La Nuche and agreeing on an extramarital union, while Ariadne and Beaumond tentatively agree to try to make the best of marriage. Previously, however, the distinction between the prostitute and the lady has been characteristically obscured. Mistaking La Nuche for Ariadne, Beaumond denounces his imagined fiancée as a whore, only to find himself speaking to the whore he loves: 'And is a Whore a thing so much despis'd?' La Nuche coldly asks, as she reveals herself (IV, p. 173). Later, Willmore sleeps with La Nuche in the belief that she is Ariadne, while Ariadne almost sleeps with Beaumond in the belief that he is the anonymous 'Stranger' (V, p. 205), Willmore. If such incidents reiterate Behn's interest in the deep ties between the psychology of marriage and of prostitution, the common element of barter is also once again stressed, most obviously in a widespread eagerness to marry a rich dwarf and a rich giantess. What seems, if not new, at least more fully developed, is the constant visual stress upon the handling of women. The hand is a repeated visual motif, emphasizing the liability of women to external control, and—in the conventional contrast—setting the ways of the hand against the desires of the heart. Here, the contrast is resolved: Willmore and La Nuche link hands, and Ariadne agrees 'With all my Heart' to a marriage with Beaumond conditional upon amendment of 'Hearts' (V, p. 211). But no later play was to reconcile heart and hand.

The increasing pessimism is evident in *The False Count*. Like *Sir Patient Fancy*, this portrays the ostensibly liberating adultery of a young wife, Julia, forced into marriage with an elderly ex-leather-seller, Francisco, who treats her as a 'Prisoner' and 'Slave' (I, pp. 107, 111). In the other plot, which gives the play its title, Behn adapts Molière's *Les Précieuses ridicules*, showing the courtship of Francisco's socially pretentious daughter, Isabella, by an aristocratic 'Stranger' (III, p. 137) who is actually a chimney-sweep, Guiliom. In the original, and the two other seventeenth-century adaptations (by Shadwell and Flecknoe), the joke stops short of marriage, and Flecknoe actually adds a triumphant female counter-ruse, but here the marriage is concluded and consummated, and Isabella's steady and wilful march towards humiliation acts as significant counterpoint to Julia's struggles for freedom. When Guiliom resumes his sweep's clothes and takes his astounded wife by the hand (V, p. 174), the enforced linkage of hands is anything but an expression of harmony (though it is important to note that Behn's attitude towards the non-gentle classes—'*Th' industrious noble Citizens*' (V, p. 175)—is here by no means contemptuous).

Throughout the depiction of Julia's marriage, Behn stresses that she is barely allowed a voice. Her husband baby-talks to her, and habitually tries to prevent her from speaking in company, at one point claiming that 'the Doctors have prescribed her Silence' (I, p. 113). When she does commit adultery, the healthy sensuality of the act is not in doubt, but Behn goes out of her way to avoid clothing it in imagery of liberation. The ruse by which it is accomplished is one in whose planning—still voiceless—she has no say. And it is one in which Julia and Francisco are apparently captured and enslaved by the Great Turk (actually her lover, Carlos, in disguise). The trick certainly turns the tables on Francisco, who experiences both the slavery and the enforced silence that he had inflicted on Julia, the silence being at one point enforced with a bowstring (IV, p. 159). But a cuckolding in which the mistress acts the part of a slave and the lover that of the Great Turk, the archetype of sexual despotism, is a profoundly limited act of female emancipation, and indeed Carlos habitually regards union with Julia as an act of possession: '`Tis certain, *Julia*, that thou must be mine' (II, p. 124). Even in the conclusion, where Carlos and Julia are permanently united, she is a piece of passive property to be negotiated over by her lover, her husband, and her father. 'I but seiz'd my own', says her lover, while her husband shrugs off her father's objections by saying he can surrender his 'Goods and Chattels' to whomever he pleases. She's 'my Lumber now,' he argues (V, p. 173). Even the union of true lovers turns out to be a union of male owner and female property. The play consistently indicates that all the language and titles of power are male: Carlos is a figure of power both with his false title as Great Turk and his real one as Governor of Cadiz (he is repeatedly referred to as 'the Governor'). Both in her marriage and in the ruse which releases her from it, Julia's role is that of slave. Yet, whereas a gentlewoman gains her man in the guise of a slave, a chimney-sweep gains his woman in the guise of a lord. There is no evident remedy for the fact that language *de facto* enshrines and validates a system of male supremacy.

Uncomplicated carnality survives only in Dryden's *The Kind Keeper; or, Mr. Limberham* (Duke's, March 1678). For reasons which are now probably beyond discovery, this play was quickly banned,[32] even though it was written at the King's suggestion, and the offensive parts were excluded from the printed text. As Dryden reveals in a letter,[33] his generic model was *A Fond Husband* (a favourite of the King's), though he omits the concern with female oppression which Durfey retained even amidst the slapstick chaos of farce, providing a more purely comic stress on female resourcefulness and the outwitting of the absurd male chauvinist Brainsick. Almost alone among dramatists of the late 1670s, Dryden continues to delight in the sheer triumph of the flesh over customary and theoretical patterns of order. The play is set within the confined space of a boarding/bawdy-house run by the lustful Puritan Mrs Saintly, the house becoming an enclosed and complete world in itself, like the island in *The Tempest*. 'We are a Company of our selves' (I, p. 292), says Mrs Saintly to her new lodger, the sexually voracious Woodall; 'He's a Fellow-lodger, incorporate in our Society' (I, pp. 298–9), says an established resident, Aldo (who does not recognize Woodall as his own son). The prime characteristic of this society is that sexual potency and allure become the sole principles of power and order. When dressed to kill, the cobbler's daughter Tricksy 'looks like any Princess of the Blood' (I, p. 299). Although he

[32] See Susan Staves, 'Why Was Dryden's *Mr. Limberham* Banned? A Problem in Restoration Theatre History', *Restoration and 18th Century Theatre Research*, 13/1 (1974), 1–11.
[33] *Letters of Dryden*, ed. Ward, 11–12 (letter 5).

fails to recognize his real son, Woodall (who is 'a Stranger' to him, I, p. 294), the elderly pimp and whoremaster Aldo acts as 'Father' (I, p. 296) and 'Patriarch' to a bevy of prostitutes (IV, p. 339), is addressed as 'Father' by the elderly keeper Limberham (I, p. 301), and readily welcomes Woodall as a 'Son' (I, p. 296) in his large family of sexual dependants. Paternity, which for Filmer and others was the foundation of political society, lacks intrinsic force and authority, and is universally redefined to signify seniority of experience in shared sexual interests.

The cohesion of the community receives the same sort of redefinition as that of the family. Shared language and a shared sense of national identity are diminished. Woodall, newly returned from France, is introduced by his father as 'A young *Monsieur*' (I, p. 298), imagines himself into the condition of a Turk in his seraglio,[34] and finds himself imitating an Italian essence-seller and conversing in sign language and pseudo-Italian with his prospective cuckold, Limberham. Brainsick, a ranting cuckold who prides himself on his domination of his wife, also inhabits an imaginary Turkey, and also pushes language towards dissolution. 'I am the *Sultan* of this Place: Mr. *Limberham* is the *Mogol* of the next Mansion' (IV, p. 346), he boasts, investing the cramped boarding-house and its little cells with the vastness and diversity of Asia. Later, tricked into guarding the door at his own cuckolding, he strips language of all significance: 'Clangor, *Taratantara*, Murmur' (V, p. 356). Dryden thus pushes to extremes of literalness the common image of humanity distributed into separate cells and separate dialects, and the dissolution affects not only the traditional forms of familial order, but those of community itself. The language of government persists, but it describes a world ordered only by sexual appetite: 'my People is dissatisfy'd, and my Government in danger' (III, p. 335), says Woodall of his harem. And, predictably, the administration of justice is converted into the management of sexual concerns. When one of his strumpets loses her keeper at Tyburn, Aldo promises to set her up with the judge who sentenced him while leering upon her (IV, p. 337)—another unsettling transformation of the amorous judge in *The Man of Mode*. And Aldo himself sits as judge when one prostitute complains that another 'has violated the Law of Nations' by stealing her aristocratic cully (IV, p. 338).

The play ends with a reconstruction of conventional forms of relationship, though without their conventional substance. Woodall acknowledges Aldo as his father and undergoes the traditional ritual of reassimilation, the resumption of his proper name (V, p. 370). But the father–son relationship is, explicitly, to be without order and hierarchy, banishing 'all Pomp and Ceremony' (V, p. 368). By Woodall's arrangement, his servant Gervase impersonates his master in a bedroom trick with Mrs Saintly and then goes on to marry

---

34 I, pp. 295, 300–1; III, p. 334.

her, becoming his master's landlord and—since his wife is his superior—taking her surname. Woodall agrees to marry Pleasance, Mrs Saintly's apparent daughter, whom he had fallen for at a play and traced to Saintly's house, but of whom he had initially been wary because of her apparent ancestry (as Careless had been with Ruth in *The Committee*). In uniting the couple, Dryden flippantly reworks two standard motifs for bringing desire into harmony with social authority: Pleasance turns out to be the match who had been all along designed for Woodall by his father and (like Ruth) she turns out to be the daughter of gentry. But paternal authority has been thoroughly discredited, Pleasance's respectable birth accounts not for an innate nobility of character but for her constant spitefulness and rudeness, and the actual identity of her parents is evidently of no import, since it is not revealed. Woodall agrees to marry her with the ostentatiously ambiguous words, 'All I can say is, I do not now begin to love you' (V, p. 369), and some still less promising bonds are tied: Limberham marries the faithless Tricksy, and Brainsick, deludedly convinced of his wife's fidelity, turns from a jealous into a doting husband. 'The Moral on't is pleasant, if well consider'd' (V, p. 371), says Woodall of Brainsick's transformation. The detection of an unspoken moral in an insignificant event is an appropriate accompaniment to the ritual reaffirmation of social patterns that have lost all justification and function.

Perhaps about the same time as Dryden's *The Kind Keeper*, Shadwell's *A True Widow* (Duke's, ?March 1678)[35] provided a quite contrary response to *A Fond Husband*, setting Act IV in the playhouse and engaging his characters in fornication, intrigue, and misunderstanding during the performance of a play which is obviously a malicious parody of Durfey's hit. (Neatly, Shadwell continues to portray sex, but transposes it into a dramatic culture from which his own play is dissociated.) For good measure, the obsessive poetaster Young Maggot is a caricature of Durfey, being similarly ugly, and having similarly deserted law for the pursuit of poetry. In *The Virtuoso* Shadwell had to some degree swum with the tide, criticizing sex comedy from within the genre, but now he reverts to a more direct attack. The sensible heroine Isabella prefers a humble marriage to the most prosperous mistresshood ('A Lord? a Beast', II, p. 303), while her foolish sister Gartrude sacrifices even prosperous mistresshood by succumbing to two seducers in quick succession.

Characteristically, Shadwell portrays a social order that has departed from its ancient functioning and order. Lords are fat and contemptible lechers who devote themselves to meaningless rituals of sexual pursuit (such as 'side-glassing', I, p. 290) in the park. Ladies have become bawds and confidence tricksters. Language is so debased that the racing and hunting fanatic Prig has stood godfather at the christening of the dog Ranter, a ritual of naming which (like Gimcrack's naming of the spider) has lost any social function, and the

---

[35] The date of the première is uncertain, and may have been as late as Jan. 1679. See Danchin, *Prologues and Epilogues*, iii. 116; Milhous and Hume, 'Dating Play Premières', 387.

linked decay of language and social structure is represented in the contracts written in disappearing ink with which Lady Cheatly defrauds her victims. Amidst the moral and linguistic chaos, gentlemen and gentlewomen of sense learn to surmount stultifying indulgence of self and prepare for the responsibility and community of marriage (one of the ineducable fools is in fact called Selfish). Etherege's Harriet wins Dorimant by her abrasive independence, and this is not responsible for his brief dalliance with Bellinda; when Shadwell's Carlos nearly seeks solace for Theodosia's coquettish evasiveness in the arms of the foolish Gartrude, however, it is Theodosia's conduct that is to blame, and the result is a critique of gay couple comedy that complements the critique of sex comedy. In the other courtship, the solemn Bellamour renounces fornication and marries the virtuous Isabella, despite the fact that she breaches comic convention by being penniless.

In *A True Widow* the moralistic concerns inhibit dramatic invention and interest. An altogether more subtle and inventive play is *The Woman-Captain* (Duke's, *c.* September 1679). This is yet another reassessment of festive comedy, for the duration of the play is coextensive with the duration of a feast: the twenty-fourth birthday party of Sir Humphrey Scattergood, celebrating the day on which he comes into his father's estate. Judicial norms are inverted ('Chastity shall be Felony, and Sobriety High-Treason', III, p. 52), and the regulating principle is the flesh: Humphrey takes a book, that familiar symbol of civilization, and reads from it a Rabelaisian profusion of different species of edible flesh (I, pp. 21–2).[36] Like the revellers in *Epicoene*, Humphrey brings his festivities into the house of a signally unfestive character, the usurer Gripe, whose wife he wishes to seduce, and who even before their arrival is complaining that 'my Family is turn'd Topsy-turvy' (II, p. 38). In defiance of expectation, the wife remains unseduced, but the intrusion does enable her to escape her husband's tyranny (a key word) and contrive her own saturnalia: she returns disguised as her brother, a recruiting officer, and then bullies her husband into, apparently, enlisting in the army, whereupon all his customary authority dissolves for he is not only, unwittingly, under his wife's thumb, but equal in rank with the servant he had also oppressed, who now offensively addresses him as 'Comrade' (V, p. 78). Mrs Gripe also, however, manages to discredit the pride in manhood and rank that informs the rakes' merry-making, stealing the affections of three prostitutes (as Florimell in *Secret Love* had stolen Celadon's mistresses), and enlisting and beating some hectoring libertines previously distinguished by mindless violence against their social inferiors.

But, in order to impersonate a man, Mrs Gripe has to learn to talk like one. How? An improbably feminist sergeant has the answer: 'Oh, use, use! 'tis nothing but use' (III, p. 54). Custom and practice alone differentiate man and

---

[36] Cf. the list of the Gastrolaters' sacrifices in *Pantagruel*, iv. 59–60.

woman, and Mrs Gripe quickly learns to swear and hector as to the manner born: like Durfey, and quite unlike Behn, Shadwell can envisage few obstacles to the linguistic liberation of women. As usual, the issue of access to language is closely bound up with that of access to the rituals and processes of justice, and Mrs Gripe's pose as commanding officer gives her, apparently, judicial authority over her husband: 'if you run from your Colours,' she threatens, 'I can hang you by Law' (IV, p. 59). The ambitions of the Widow Blackacre are here given a fairer and more sympathetic representation.

If Humphrey's feast assists in the liberation of Mrs Gripe, however, this is the only good thing about it. Extravagance, so often a term of approval in portrayals of the whimsical rake, here becomes a term of disapprobation,[37] and Humphrey's extravagance is the disordered excess of a society whose hierarchical forms have become discreditable fictions. Gentlemen whoremasters are exposed as the slaves of their mistresses, and as the moral inferiors of their social inferiors: an old family servant witheringly refuses the new heir's command to associate with whores by retorting that it is beneath his dignity (III, p. 51), and an honest citizen is manhandled by gentlemanly hooligans and then arrested for their crimes by a venal watch, who show (yet again) that the forms of justice and the priorities of social order have no relationship to the actual distribution of quality. (Here, exceptionally but not uniquely, a Carolean dramatist supports the bourgeois.) There is, indeed, much stress on the violence of gentry against non-gentry (the hector Heildebrand boasts that his sword is 'stain'd in gore of filthy Peasant', III, p. 48), and on the skewing of legal process to favour an unworthy upper class: 'Poor Bawds are carted, while great Mens Pimps are Company for Lords,' and magistrates 'commit Adultery themselves, and whip poor Wenches for simple Fornication' (I, pp. 24–5).

Like the Gimcrack plot in *The Virtuoso*, the Scattergood plot reflects Shadwell's intellectual engagement with *Timon of Athens*, his adaptation of which had been staged near the beginning of the previous year: Humphrey comes close to dissipating his estate on his own pleasures and those of a grasping mistress and two false friends, and is only saved from destitution by marrying the low-born prostitute on whom he has bestowed his ancestral dwelling. Humphrey's dissipation illustrates the decline of the gentleman's estate as a focus for responsible and interdependent society: the opening of the play witnesses the dissolution of a coherent community, as Humphrey dismisses his father's Fool and other servants and replaces them with Frenchmen. Like La Foole's feast in *Epicoene*, this feast is deprived of those who most properly belong to it, turning from a communal gathering into a gathering of strangers: 'let every Stranger and Servant in my House have his *Cher entirè*,'[38] Humphrey proclaims (III, p. 52). The ejection of the Fool inspires the inevitable taunt that fools are redundant now that gentlemen fulfil their roles for

[37] Dramatis Personae, p. 16; V, pp. 71, 82, 83.   [38] i.e. *Chère entière*—slang for 'whore'.

themselves, and the subtler jibe that Shakespeare's fools speak more sense than all the wits and critics of the present generation (I, p. 20). Festive subversion of order has no point when the order no longer exists, and the general allusion to the Shakespearian fool is complemented by one that is more specific and pointed, for Humphrey's final words to the Fool, 'take away the Fool!' (I, p. 20), are those which also conclude the dialogue between Olivia and the Fool in *Twelfth Night*, where the question is likewise whether the Fool or his employer is greater in folly (I. v. 69–70).[39] Feste has no place at Humphrey's feast. Similarly, when the Steward announces that Humphrey's estate has been seized, he laments, 'Many a good *Christmas* has my old Master kept there, and must it now be parted from his Family—' (V, p. 70). Christmas—with its culmination in Twelfth Night—represents the hospitable and sociable feast that is the mean between the opposed unsociabilities of Humphrey and Gripe (whose loans, appropriately, finance Humphrey's excesses). The estate is recovered, but the household has gone, and the relationships established at the end are founded upon money: Mrs Gripe tricks her husband into signing a deed that gives her financial independence, Humphrey recovers the remains of his estate by marrying a prostitute, and the friends who had refused to help him instead expend their money in making settlements on other prostitutes, who reject their previous and now impoverished keepers.

There is a political as well as purely moral point to the representations of decaying order and authority. Humphrey is replacing his father's servants with Frenchmen, bred in his view 'for Service' but in the Steward's 'for Slavery' (I, p. 19): the native traditions of England are being threatened not only by French fashions but—still more—by French absolutism. Similarly, Mrs Gripe's campaign against her husband's tyranny is a campaign for the rights and liberty of an Englishwoman.[40] Implicitly, the play addresses the threat to the native constitution posed by an authoritarian heir of alien outlook. But, if Shadwell laments the disappearance of the old England, he is no mere apologist for hierarchy, as his championship of women and (far more limited) championship of the non-gentle classes shows. His point seems to be rather that the language and privilege of the old order survive when the system justifying them is no longer observed, and when the estate—Humphrey's literal place in the social order—comes not from patrilineal descent but from union with a prostitute. The threat of absolutist tyranny comes at a point when the abandonment of old, if serviceable, forms is rather pointing the way to a more comprehensive order.

---

[39] There are few surviving records of Restoration performances of *Twelfth Night*, but there are several allusions to it in Restoration plays. Shadwell himself quotes the opening line, as a well-known text, in *The Squire of Alsatia* (II, p. 225), and Wycherley and Behn make extended allusion to the play in *The Plain-Dealer* and *The Younger Brother*, Behn at one point reworking Olivia's itemization of her beauty (II, pp. 341–2).   [40] I, pp. 27–8; II, p. 38; III, p. 54.

The prime exponent of the comedy of social disintegration was, however, Otway, whose first original comedy, *Friendship in Fashion* (Duke's, April 1678), has some similarities of design with Shadwell's later play. It too is a comedy of constant festivity; and, whereas *The Woman-Captain* opens with the expulsion of the traditional Fool, *Friendship in Fashion* concludes with the expulsion of two foolish gentlemen-parasites, who have been forcibly clad in the traditional Fool's costume. Like so many grand, symbolic gestures in Otway, this in fact achieves and signifies very little, but it ostensibly purges the transference of the Fool's role to the gentleman that Shadwell reaffirms at the beginning of his play. The festivity in *Friendship in Fashion* is an endless, desperate round of entertainment, party-going, and drunkenness (the protagonist, Goodvile, is drunk for much of the play), a desire for *company* (a recurrent word) that is unrelated to any genuine social instinct. As Mrs Goodvile says, copulation is 'almost the onely way Relations care to be kind to one another now a days' (II. 52–3), and, as the title indicates, friendship has declined into an empty form, a mask for mutual manipulation and deception. Truman cuckolds his friend Goodvile, while Goodvile, tired of his mistress Victoria, attempts to trick Truman into marrying her. Even lust loses any vestigial social element: Lady Squeamish and Goodvile mistakenly commit adultery, each thinking the other to be someone else, and so determined is Otway to remove this bedroom trick from any traces of social existence that he does not even locate it in a bedroom, but out of doors, in a metaphorically apt 'Wilderness'.

Goodvile (Betterton) is an uglier version of Dorimant, and his social round is a degradation of the smart social gatherings that Lady Townley had supervised. *Pleasant* is again a fashionable term of approval, though chiefly associated with the fatuous Lady Squeamish, and generally elicited by descriptions of foolish or sordid spectacles, such as a bawd with a 'a great deal of Paint, variety of old Cloaths, and nothing to eat' (III. 225–7). This Lady Squeamish finds 'extravagantly pleasant' (III. 228–9). It is, however, a sign of the emptiness of the social rituals that the other key term of approval, again distinctively associated with Lady Squeamish, should be one that traditionally denies the accomplishment of cohesive community: *strange*. The oafish Sir Noble Clumsey, for example, 'is a strange pleasant Creature' (III. 410). Another sign is that the parties become increasingly detached from any fixed sense of domestic dwelling: the ball of Act IV is situated in a garden leading to the 'Wilderness', and Mrs Goodvile's party in Act V depends upon the absence of her husband, who has allegedly, though not actually, gone to fulfil the duties of his place by visiting his estate and tenants in the country. When Goodvile disrupts the forced festivity, it is in an attempt to dissolve his marriage and household, and introduce a group of prostitutes in his wife's place; and, although Mrs Goodvile manages to outface him, there is no doubt that their relationship has lost all coherence and purpose. Perhaps the most striking dissociation of festivity from community occurs when Otway joins Durfey in redefining and darkening that favourite word of the merry-maker, *frollick*. For the fool Malagene, a 'Frollick' is that ultimate destruction of domesticity, the burning of a house (IV. 194–7).

The empty social rituals reflect the displacement and disorientation of a society where place (in the sense of degree) has become meaningless, and where lord and lady are synonymous with pimp and prostitute: when Goodvile attempts to hand his household over to prostitutes, he prescribes a hierarchy of precedence between them. Disorientation is visually represented in the frequent drunkenness of the characters, and the still more frequent requirement that they engage in awkward or inappropriate movement on stage (there are characters named Clumsey, Saunter, and Caper). Characters dance at inapposite junctures, and drunkenly overturn furniture and china; Caper hates 'to stand still' (III. 209), and Lady Squeamish is a 'Whirligig' (III. 656). But beyond the visual collapse of order and orientation is the portrayal of a society with no appropriate forms of representation, whether ceremonial or verbal. Chaotic ceremony is a recurrent motif. Clumsey, predictably, makes elaborate and unsuccessful attempts at ritualized bowing (II. 310–13), but meaningless ceremony is not confined to buffoonish louts: when Mrs Goodvile, chronologically accurate however insincere, wishes her husband 'Good morning', he responds with 'Good night', adding, 'Ceremony is the least thing I take care of' (V. 56–60).

The characters are as given to inappropriate bursts of song as to inappropriate excursions into dance. Malagene prides himself on his ability to imitate the rumbling of a wheelbarrow and the roasting of mutton, and attempts to argue his way out of a tight corner by playing a Jew's trump. Charged with indecorum against the ladies, Sir Noble responds—if that is the right word—with anecdotes about a barber skilled in music and poetry. In *A Midsummer Night's Dream* it was the untutored mechanicals who provided 'very tragical mirth', but ignorance has been upwardly mobile, and Sir Noble has composed three acts of a tragedy, full of laughter and waggery: the gentlemen have again made Shakespearian fools redundant. But yet more striking is the lack of any adequate customary language to describe serious moral situations. We know where we are when Lady Squeamish, scorned by Goodvile, lapses into self-dramatizing fustian: 'So *Theseus* left the Wretched *Ariadne* on the shoar, so fled the false *Æneas* from his *Dido*' (V. 153–4). But it is less easy to classify a similar rant from Mrs Goodvile to her husband: 'Let me be gone; send me to a Nunnery; confine me to a charnel House, Vile Ungrateful Wretch, any thing but thy presence I can endure' (IV. 313–16). These tones of heroic innocence have an obvious inappropriateness from an adulteress attempting to escape detection, even though her adultery is a reasonable response to extreme neglect and provocation; for there is no linguistic decorum whereby the adulteress can represent herself as an injured innocent. In portraying a woman without a socially prescribed language of self-defence, Otway (like

Durfey) comes closer than any other male dramatist of the 1670s to the viewpoint of Aphra Behn.

Victoria, the fallen woman, also falls victim to the inadequacies of social terminology: no male character questions the conventions that make her a pariah, but Victoria is in fact one of the most decent characters in the play, condemned by her past to marriage with Sir Noble Clumsey. Shadwell associates the decay of the old order with the emergence of an independent woman, who quickly acquires the language of authority and alike escapes the tyranny of her husband and the lusts of his would-be cuckolder. In Otway, there is no visible alternative to the old, corrupted structures (indeed, the class structure in itself is unquestioningly accepted). There is reiterated concern with justice, but a justice that is explicitly synonymous with revenge, and a male justice: to punish Goodvile's duplicity in attempting to impose Victoria on him, Truman administers justice by cuckolding him, but this is a justice in which women become the passive expressions of a male viewpoint. Mrs Goodvile does gain a triumph of sorts over her husband, luring him to catch her with his friend Truman and then proving that she knew of his coming. As he brandishes the letter making the assignation, she trumps it with a letter (from Victoria) warning her of his arrival. It would be tempting to see this climax of letter trumping letter as an emblematic linguistic triumph for the woman, but—like the expulsion of the fools—it in fact achieves and proves little, beyond shoring up another shaky and discredited system of society, the Goodviles' marriage.

Displacement is also a pervasive condition in Otway's next comedy, *The Souldiers Fortune* (Duke's, June 1680), in which he offers his most explicit criticism of the social order which, perhaps for fear of finding something worse, he continued to support throughout the Exclusion Crisis. Disbanded after the short-lived Flanders campaign, the loyal gentlemen soldiers Courtine and Beaugard are reduced to the status of impoverished vagabonds, while former vagabonds, regicides, committee-men, footmen, and pimps prosper in a society where degree and authority have lost any basis in birth or merit. The heroes' displacement is confirmed by their preoccupation with cultural archetypes of home-coming: their 'cold wet March' (V. 331) in the Flanders campaign is imaginatively transformed into a 'rowling in the Lands of Milk and Honey' (IV. 9–10), the pimp Sir Jolly Jumble (Anthony Leigh) is hailed as bringing 'news from Paradise' (IV. 128), and the prospect of wine and prostitutes is described by Beaugard as 'the land of *Canaan* . . . in little' (IV. 200–1). But, shortly after these anticipations of paradise regained, even paradise itself is transmuted into an image of farcical and humiliating placelessness: lured into a basket with the promise that he will be drawn up to the beloved Sylvia's bedroom, Courtine is left helplessly dangling, 'in *Erasmus* Paradise between Heav'n and Hell' (IV. 536–7). Dislocation here takes its most extreme and literal form. And here, remarkably, Courtine launches into a song praising the established social order, as administered by Charles II: '*God prosper long our*

Noble King, | *Our Lives and Safeties all'* (IV. 541–2). Otway certainly satirizes the Exclusionists in the person of Beaugard's elderly and evil cuckold, Sir Davy Dunce, but this spectacle of a dangling, dislocated man, bawling into the dark loyal sentiments learned by rote, hardly provides a reassuring alternative.

Human relationships constantly resolve themselves into relationships of naked power and violence, as when Sir Davy Dunce attempts to avoid cuckoldom by hiring a cut-throat to murder Beaugard, or when (in the familiar association of rape and judicial authority) he interprets his power as magistrate as power to rape Courtine: 'I'll Ravish you, you Buttuck, I am a Justice of the Peace' (IV. 452–3). Traditional hierarchy survives only in the entourage of the pimp Sir Jolly, 'the Flower of Knighthood' (I. 232–3), who regulates a society of genteel prostitutes—one of them allegedly, and not implausibly, the daughter of a knight—with exemplary 'discipline' and 'command' (II. 13–14). Even the attractive figures of Beaugard and Lady Dunce—lovers before Lady Dunce's enforced marriage to an aged husband—are reunited after she sends him money via Sir Jolly. Their union begins in pimping, develops amidst Sir Jolly's inarticulate gibberings of desire for Beaugard (and for a privileged location under the couple's bed), and is consummated when Beaugard's 'corpse' is left with Lady Dunce after Sir Davy has been duped into, apparently, hiring a thug to kill him. Young love blossoms amidst the trappings of prostitution and murder, and the solicitudes of a senile voyeur. Love is similarly darkened in the other romantic plot, in which Courtine and Sylvia act out an unpleasant transformation of gay couple courtship, replacing witty one-upmanship by a more earnest and ruthless struggle for supremacy; at one point, Courtine is even subjected to bondage and the threat of whipping.

As in *Friendship in Fashion,* the social disorientation is reflected in the decay of shared and fitting conventions for signifying value and place. Decorum and ceremony lose all expressive or regulatory force. The meetings between Sir Davy Dunce and Beaugard—potential cuckold and potential corpse—tend to begin with elaborately formal courtesy, so that the rituals of civility become essentially rituals of violence, and Beaugard is compelled by poverty 'To use respects and ceremonies' (IV. 69) to the stinking families of idiotic tradesmen (a piece of social prejudice that Shadwell would have deplored). Finally, Sir Davy reacts to his cuckoldom with laughter and ceremonial submissiveness, declaring himself 'thy Lady-ships most humble Servant and Cuckold' (V. 702–3). The uneasy combination of violent hostility and ritualized deference is emphasized by Otway's repeated comparison of man to the dog (a comparison which recurs throughout his mature plays); for the dog is a creature which pre-eminently combines fawning civility with predatory wildness.

Particularly in the sphere of sexual conduct, fixed and appropriate forms of language and justice are as lacking as those of ceremony. *Toad* is a regular term of endearment (as in *The Country-Wife*), the pseudo-assassin Bloody-

Bones rants in Pistol-like heroics, Sir Jolly lusts in inarticulate squeaks, and Courtine and Sylvia woo each other in a depressing perversion of gay couple banter which mixes sordid abuse with mock lyricism without ever finding a mid-point of engaging wit. Detected in an attempt at adultery, Lady Dunce lacks any received language with which to explain her situation, and consequently reacts with the tonally false (if essentially justifiable) protestations of injured innocence that had earlier been perfected by Mrs Goodvile ('Curse on my fatal beauty! blasted ever be these two baneful eyes', III. 551–2). Nor does she have any commonly agreed categories of justice on her side. Although the scene is permeated by the language of justice, it is Sir Davy, the JP, whom it favours: whereas Lady Dunce passively demands to 'be justifi'd' (III. 557), Sir Davy actively threatens to have Beaugard 'hang'd for Burglary' (III. 563). As in much contemporary tragedy, female vulnerability to the verdicts of justice is paired with vulnerability to those of history; for, feigning a determination to stab herself in order to erase the stigma of attempted rape, Lady Dunce implicitly mimics the culturally approved pattern for female response to sexual dishonour: Lucretia (one of the heroines of *The Atheist*, Otway's sequel to *The Souldiers Fortune*, was indeed named Lucrece, and the example of Lucretia figures as an oppressive cultural presence in several tragedies). As a counterpart to the woman's inability to determine the writing of history, she must work within the female stereotypes purveyed by historical writing. Sir Davy confirms his wife's customary role of linguistic subordination by baby-talking to her, and, although he himself falls into a bout of linguistic derangement, he does so in the course of imitating a historical stereotype of a distinctly manly and active kind, threatening to 'crack the frame of nature, sally out like *Tamberlain* upon the *Trojan* Horse' (III. 574–6). And he is sufficiently in the mould of Tamerlane to try to arrange Beaugard's murder. There is in this scene an absurd discrepancy between the actual worth and standing of the characters and the cultural flotsam which is used to signify their masculinity and femininity. But the cultural roles have some power: it is only when Sir Davy loses his authority as magistrate, becoming a criminal terrified of the gallows after his apparent murder of Beaugard, that he is successfully cuckolded. Amidst the constant derangement of signs and hierarchies, the only authoritative codification of desire—indeed, the only emblem of socio-linguistic order—is the book in which Sir Jolly categorizes his prostitutes.

A reminder of older and simpler ways is provided by Lewis Maidwell's *The Loving Enemies* (Duke's, January 1680), where two young men divided by ancestral enmity fall in love with each other's sisters, neither realizing the identity of his loved one, and both therefore misinterpreting sisterly concern for the enemy as amorous affection. A benevolent Providence, however, inevitably rectifies misunderstanding and brings reconciliation. Misunderstanding is disseminated in other areas of the plot by the inflated rhetoric of the valet Circumstantio, but his linguistic excesses are mere defects of understanding, revealing no defects in the medium of language itself: 'are not words to express thoughts by, and the plainest expression of our meanings best?' (I, p. 1), asks his employer. Such morally and socially unreflective plays were, however, increasingly rare, partly because of the serious and often pessimistic interest in human sexuality, and partly because of the increasing engagement of dramatists with the Exclusion Crisis.

The only other similarly unreflective play, Ravenscroft's highly successful *The London Cuckolds* (Duke's, October 1681), is very different in moral outlook. This is the only Restoration sex comedy to show no interest whatsoever in analysing or evaluating sexual conduct, simply sanctioning the romps with a token religious scepticism: chance rules, and adultery is an act of faith, hope, and charity (III, p. '27' [29]). The play depicts the cuckolding of three foolish Aldermen, each with a pet but doomed scheme for avoiding his predestined horns (viz., marriage to a pious, a witty, and a foolish wife). The epilogue mocks the cits and Whigs with a cheerful lack of realism ('*There's not one* Cuckold *amongst all the* Tory's'), though there is a darker element in Ravenscroft's complaints about the London Grand Jury's refusal to return politically acceptable verdicts.[41] The play itself, however, retains some of the pro-citizen sympathies of Ravenscroft's earlier plays, for the most engaging of the three cuckolders is himself a merchant. Conversely, the rakish gentleman Ramble is farcically discomfited by upended chamber-pots, flatulent chimney-sweeps, and the like before making the easiest conquest, of the foolish wife.

Other comedy writers, however, were starting to produce an overtly and polemically Tory drama: *The London Cuckolds* appears at roughly the same time as Durfey's *Sir Barnaby Whigg; or, No Wit Like a Womans* (King's, ?summer 1681) and *The Royalist* (Duke's, January 1682), the anonymous *Mr. Turbulent* (Duke's, ?October 1681), and Aphra Behn's *The Roundheads* (Duke's, by December 1681.) (Dryden's *Absalom and Achitophel* was published on or about 17 November 1681.) The lost *Sir Popular Wisdom* (1677) had caricatured Shaftesbury and his associates, and there is incidental satire of factious citizens in *Sir Patient Fancy* and *The Souldiers Fortune*, though the latter play is also critical of royal policy, but it is noticeable that this clutch of plays represents the first concerted emergence of comedy as Tory propaganda and that they appear fairly late in the Crisis, some months after the dissolution of the Oxford Parliament, when the final push against the Whigs was under way.[42] (By contrast, Shadwell had—though very indirectly—initiated

---

41 As Danchin points out (*Prologues and Epilogues*, iii. 328–9), '*he's piqu'd at by the* Ignoramus *Jury*' cannot chronologically refer to the jury which on 24 Nov. refused to commit Shaftesbury to trial for treason. But 'the new London Grand Jury declared a verdict of *ignoramus* in the case of a Whig named Rouse on 18 October, a likely sign of how Shaftesbury's case would be settled' (Winn, *John Dryden and His World*, 349). Rouse was the under-sheriff of London, who was subsequently executed in the aftermath of the Rye House Plot.

42 'Political comedies are largely a phenomenon of 1681–82 when the Tory triumph was practically certain, and playwrights set about rubbing it in' (Hume, ' "The Change in Comedy" ', 110). Hume

opposition comedy with *The Woman-Captain* in 1679.) This group of Tory comedies provides a mini-re-enactment of the earliest phase of Restoration comedy, *The Royalist* imitating *The Committee* at almost the same time that *Mr. Turbulent* in a single breath imitated *The Committee*, *Cutter of Coleman-Street*, and *The Cheats*, and that Aphra Behn revised *The Rump* as *The Roundheads*. The Whigs were marked with the stigma of forty-one and forty-nine, while the Tories sought to revive the triumphalism of 1660, though in the process they produced some very weak plays. In *Sir Barnaby Whigg* Durfey pillories the originator of Whig comedy, repaying Shadwell for Young Maggot by caricaturing him in the title part as an unprincipled turncoat who changes sides and betrays old associates, being eventually duped into espousing Islam and agreeing to revolt in favour of the Grand Signior. As Whigg moves towards championing this ultimate of male tyranny, Durfey shows women subverting the pettier tyrannies of doltish husbands and smug rakes. They out-talk and out-manœuvre both, and one rake is left dangling unaccompanied in a suspended bed. Women in Durfey frequently have the power to make men linguistically impotent, and here a suspicious husband is paralysed by the task of interpreting a nonsensical letter which his wife has handed him. And, once again, Durfey envisages a justice that can serve the interests of the woman: contemplating adultery, a neglected wife opines that 'If my Cause were to be tryed in a Court of Equity, I question whether the most Reverend Head could blame my proceedings' (III, p. 31).

The hero of Durfey's *The Royalist* is Sir Charles Kinglove, owner of the oak in which Charles II had hidden, who (like the heroes of *The Committee*) risks losing his estate to crooked sequestrators. But Durfey modifies Howard's championship of birth and class, writing a walk-on part for a loyal citizen, and marrying his hero to the virtuous daughter of a regicide. He also again takes the woman's side: the seduced Aurelia convincingly denounces the double standard before being married off to the corrupt Justice Eitherside, whom she promptly cuckolds. Political corruption is, indeed, confined to men: all the female relatives of the Puritans are well-intentioned, and there is no Mrs Day to combine social with sexual insubordination. Nevertheless, this is an archaic play, portraying a world turned upside-down of disloyal tenants and uppity inferiors. Justice is subverted (in a foreshadowing of *The Recruiting Officer*, Eitherside tries for rape a heroine in male disguise), but the imminent Restoration will reinstate paragons such as Sir Charles, whose 'Actions still in this Plebeian Age' are 'Grounded on Justice' (V, p. 63).

In *Mr. Turbulent* Fairlove rescues Lucia Well-bred, a gentleman's daughter, from the clutches of the sectarian fanatic who is her uncle and guardian. The play is fiercely hierarchical, condemning the fanatics as social upstarts,

also points out that, following the failure of four sex comedies in 1678 (*Sir Patient Fancy*, *The Kind Keeper*, *A True Widow*, *Friendship in Fashion*), only one new comedy (Behn's *The Feign'd Curtezans*) was staged in the 1678–9 season (pp. 108–9; cf. *Development*, 333).

enemies of universities (one character wishes to abolish reason and logic, IV, p. 66), and subverters of male supremacy (they include a learned lady). Appropriately, these foes of rational social order are consigned to Bedlam. In Behn's *The Roundheads; or, The Good Old Cause* partisanship again numbed creativity, resulting in the least interesting of her mature plays. In reworking Tatham's *The Rump*, she characteristically increases the centrality of the woman's viewpoint. Mrs Cromwell and Lady Fleetwood (a small part) remain much the same, but Behn deepens the character of the haughty Lady Lambert,[43] initially misled by 'the Lyes and Cheats of Conventicles' (V, p. 418) but reformed by love for a Cavalier, and she adds the entirely admirable Lady Desbro, a covert royalist who has married a Puritan grandee so as to retrieve her lover's estate. She also adds a royalist maid-servant. This play does not go as far as *The Royalist* in detaching women from male power structures, but it certainly moves in that direction.

Behn's other Exclusion Crisis play, *The City Heiress* (Duke's, April 1682) is, however, one of the finest works to emerge from the Crisis. The hero, Wilding (Betterton), is (like Dorimant) involved with three women: he has slept with the lowly-born Diana before the start of the play, seduces Lady Galliard during its course, and marries the virginal city-heiress Charlot at the end. He even responds to female tears (albeit of a Puritan bawd) with the same aesthetic insouciance as Dorimant ('So Tempests are allay'd by Showers of Rain', II, p. 222), and he provides the vehicle for one of Behn's most searching portrayals of the impact of the rake's lifestyle on the women he mesmerizes. Yet Wilding is also an ardent Tory (albeit an ex-Whig), and he reflects Behn's ambivalence towards a system of authority to which she gave unwavering support, but which nevertheless seemed inseparably bound up with the irrationalities of male supremacism. (Another Tory is a double-dealing fortune-hunting parasite called Foppington.) The Whig outlook is represented by Sir Timothy Treat-all (Shaftesbury), Wilding's tight-fisted and hypocritical uncle, from whom Wilding recovers his estate in a burglary modelled on Dick Follywit's first robbery of Sir Bounteous Progress in *A Mad World My Masters*. Whereas Follywit is tricked into marrying his uncle's mistress, however, Sir Timothy is here duped into marrying Wilding's, so that the rake emerges with total impunity. In a contrast reminiscent of that between the two father-figures in *Adelphi*, the oppressive, miserly Whig uncle is set against an indulgent Tory uncle, the exuberant Sir Anthony Meriwill (modelled on Durazzo in Massinger's *The Guardian*), who is constantly dismayed by the solemnity and timidity of his nephew, Sir Charles. Yet Sir Anthony is by no means uncritically portrayed. He represents yet another degradation of the festive character, a Sir Joslin Jolley on the way to becoming Sir Jolly Jumble (the part, like that of Sir Jolly, was written for Anthony Leigh, exploiting Leigh's talent for

---

[43] In Tatham's play the syllables of many of the historical characters' names are transposed, Lambert becoming Bertlam, Fleetwood Woodfleet, etc.

playing old men of excessive and misdirected sexual enthusiasm). If the ultimate corruption of festivity lies in the cold and venal political junketing supplied by Treat-all ('every Day mighty Feasting', II, p. 226), the manic roistering of Sir Anthony is hardly a counterbalancing ideal, engaging as it sometimes is.

This trio of Tories comes under most detailed scrutiny in the young men's rivalry for Lady Galliard, courted by Wilding with arrogant boisterousness and by Sir Charles with a timid deference which outrages his uncle, though the deference is merely to her social quality, for he can, as Sir Anthony reminds him, 'be leud enough upon occasion' (I, p. 218). In Lady Galliard, Behn again shows how slight is that seemingly immense boundary between the lady of quality and the 'common Hackney' (IV, p. 260). Though she loves Wilding, she initially has a firm sense of her virtue and social dignity, most clearly expressed when, desperate to believe that Wilding could not net a catch such as Charlot, she demands to hear a song which Wilding has written for his last mistress (Diana). This, she smugly asserts, is 'not like the Description of a rich Citizen's Daughter and Heir, but some common Hackney of the Suburbs;' and, even if the addressee is a gentlewoman, many gentlewomen live 'as rank Prostitutes' (IV, p. 260). In defining the gap between Diana and Charlot, she also defines that between Diana and herself, as she makes clear when (immediately afterwards) Wilding enters and treats her with some familiarity:

> [If] I ever suffer you to see me more,
> Then think me what your Carriage calls me,
> An impudent, an open Prostitute.
>
> (IV, p. 261)

But then, shockingly, her world falls apart, and all the hierarchical differences between her and the common mistress disappear. For, by the end of this very scene, Wilding has browbeaten her into sexual surrender, and her words specifically erase the distinctions she had so confidently drawn between Diana and herself:

> have I promis'd then to be
> A Whore? . . .
> The Slave, the *Hackney* of his lawless Lust!
>
> (IV, p. 266; italics added)

In the following scene, the hitherto deferential Sir Charles turns up in a mood of ugly macho aggressiveness, inspired by wine and the encouragement of Sir Anthony. He then blackmails her into marriage (and probably pre-marital consumption)[44] in a sequence that is essentially a rape, made none the more attractive by the enthusiastic commentary of the concealed Sir Anthony. Still

---

[44] There is some critical uncertainty on this point. Nancy Copeland, for example, believes that Sir Charles simply spends the night in her lodgings in order to incriminate her (' "Who Can . . . Her Own Wish Deny?": Female Conduct and Politics in Aphra Behn's *The City Heiress*', *Restoration and 18th Century Theatre Research*, 2nd ser., 8/1 (1993), 27–49 (p. 40)).

more than Belvile, Sir Charles shows that within every man of principle lurks an ape.

It is an odd manifesto which portrays the favoured party as burglars, rapists, Foppingtons, and voyeurs, yet such is *The City Heiress*. Sir Timothy's joyless and treacherous lifestyle has nothing to recommend it, whereas that of Wilding and Sir Anthony has an undeniable vitality. But that vitality has its unacceptable side, and Behn combines clear support for the establishment with gloomy recognition that women are excluded from its workings. When Sir Charles throws money to a group of musicians to drink the King's and the Duke's health (V, pp. 289–90), the gesture of loyalty is also a gesture of sexual triumph: he is, in full public view, *'undrest'* (p. 289) on Lady Galliard's balcony, and he is paying off serenaders sent by Sir Anthony to hymn his conquest. Like Courtine's Tory song in *The Souldiers Fortune*, this is a very unsettling expression of loyalty. Once again violence is the ultimate arbiter of order, and Lady Galliard's rank proves a frail protection. Its inhibiting influence on Sir Charles vanishes with drunkenness, and in the aftermath of her surrender to him, when he turns into a domineering household tyrant, she loses authority even over her own servants; it is not only Sir Robert Howard's Puritan subversives who dissolve the bond of service.

All the distinctions between Lady Galliard and the despised Diana have vanished in an instant, and they finally face similar futures, each saving respectability with an unwanted husband while continuing to long for Wilding. Both have been linguistically dominated by their seducer (Lady Galliard complains that Wilding's 'feign'd Vows debaucht my Heart' (I, p. 215), and Diana laments that he 'talkt away my Heart', III, p. 245), and as usual in Behn the vulnerability of the female heart to the male tongue is the inevitable consequence of physical vulnerability; for the female heart is also powerless before male physical control. Our final glimpse of Lady Galliard, *'Sighing and looking on* Wilding, *giving Sir* Charles *her Hand'* (V, p. 298), presents Behn's persistent image of female vulnerability, the inability to make the hand execute the desires of the heart. Earlier, Diana has given her hand to her elderly husband, falsely saying that her 'foolish Heart' has taken leave of Wilding (V, p. 288). But Sir Charles's conquest of Lady Galliard has been a triumph of manhandling. 'Did I not put her into your Hand?' asks Sir Anthony (IV, p. 268), and as Sir Charles's confidence rises he does indeed start to pull her around (IV, p. 275). In this depressing contrast between the conquering hand of the man and the helplessly outstretched hand of the seduced woman as she redeems her dishonour, Behn illustrates how literally the roles in which women live their lives may be the result of male manipulation. By some standards, Lady Galliard comes off well, for fallen women in Restoration drama rarely make good marriages unless they marry their initial seducer.[45] But

---

45 Other such marriages (i.e. when the fallen woman marries a gentleman who is neither the original seducer nor a fool) occur in Elizabeth Polwhele's *The Frolicks*, Crowne's *The English Frier*, and

these standards reflect a male viewpoint, and respectability is a poor compensation for the crushing of the personal life.

Some months before the surge in Tory comedy, Shadwell had followed the implicitly Whig *The Woman-Captain* with the far more overtly polemic *The Lancashire Witches, and Tegue O Divelly the Irish Priest* (Duke's, ?spring 1681), which had to be performed with heavy cuts because of its anti-Catholic satire. Factional dispute drew from Shadwell some of his weakest work, as it did from Durfey, and the price for this feeble piece was heavy, for Shadwell was silenced for the next eight years.[46] Shadwell again presents himself as the guardian of the traditional English political order, now threatened by an alien and superstitious tyranny. Sir Edward Hartfort lives like the gentry of 'the Golden Days of Queen *Elizabeth*', untouched by French fashions, residing on his estate, exercising hospitality, and treating his servants as part of his family (III, p. 136). He is sceptically open-minded, tolerating Dissenters and scorning the ignorant credulity which can condemn simple old women as witches. Contrasted with him is the superstitious, hypocritical, and intolerant Irish priest Tegue O Divelly, who is eventually arrested for complicity in the Popish Plot. If the tyrannic superstition of the alien priest is opposed by the benevolent scepticism of the native English gentleman, however, it finds no worthy opposition in the Anglican Church: Sir Edward's chaplain, Smerk, is a timeserving rogue, an adherent of Glanvill's view that belief in witches is necessary to religious belief (II, p. 131),[47] and a social upstart, who is finally degraded to the more fitting occupation of farming, 'an Office you were born to' (V, p. 187).

In rejecting belief in witches, Shadwell was—though perhaps not as a primary aim—rejecting one of the darkest representations of femininity (his prime aim seems to have been to create a parallel between the fraudulent rituals of the witches and of the Catholic and perhaps even the Anglican Church).[48] Unfortunately, however, stage spectacle called for real witches and so, though Shadwell's men of sense rationally deplore belief in magic, witches nevertheless perform it. But Shadwell also provides more mundane and consistent revisions of feminine stereotype. Though otherwise excellent, Sir Edward's Elizabethan principles do not include feminism, and he plans to marry his doltish son and witty daughter to a witty woman and doltish man. Applying Whig principles to the woman's lot, the daughter decides that she is 'a free English woman, and will stand up for my Liberty, and property of Choice' to

---

Craufurd's *Courtship A-la-Mode*. Mrs Fainall in *The Way of the World* makes a socially acceptable marriage, but it has even more inconveniences than that of Lady Galliard.

[46] See the dedication of *Bury-Fair* (1689), p. 294.

[47] Shadwell refers tartly to Glanvill's *Saducismus Triumphatus* in his preface (p. 101).

[48] See Judith B. Slagle, 'Thomas Shadwell's Censored Comedy, *The Lancashire-Witches:* An Attack on Religious Ritual or Divine Right?', *Restoration and 18th Century Theatre Research*, 2nd ser., 7/1 (1992), 54–63 (p. 60).

the point of being 'a Rebel' (I, pp. 111–12), and the two heroines eventually marry reformed and sensible gentlemen of pleasure.

A more thoughtful and sophisticated anti-Catholic drama was Dryden's split-plot play *The Spanish Fryar* (Duke's, November 1680). As one would expect, this has none of Shadwell's polemic Whiggism, but its sustained satire of popery does indicate that Dryden had not yet acquired the role of official Tory champion that he assumed a year later in *Absalom and Achitophel*.[49] Indeed, when it was published (in the run-up to the Oxford Parliament, when the success of Exclusion still seemed distinctly possible) it was dedicated to John, Lord Haughton, a member of the strongly Whig Holles family: 'a *Protestant* Play to a *Protestant* Patron' (sig. [F6]).[50] The comic plot reworks some elements of *The Kind Keeper*, now set in a clear Christian order, but still emphasizing the impasses that arise when desire clashes with authority. Like Woodall, the rakish Lorenzo pursues sexual intrigues under a false name that initially prevents his father from associating them with his son, coming as a handsome 'Stranger' (I, p. 144) into the life of Elvira, the young and sexually unfulfilled wife of the elderly Gomez, and attempting to satisfy her with the aid of Friar Dominick, her venal confessor (another of Anthony Leigh's senile voyeurs). So attenuated is family consciousness that the 'Stranger' does not until the denouement realize that his intended mistress is his sister. This pattern of forbidden desire and forgotten kinship is recapitulated in the heroic plot, where Lorenzo's seeming cousin Torrismond ('a Stranger almost', I, p. 143) discovers that he is the son of the deposed King only after marrying the King's apparent murderess (the current Queen, Leonora, whose father deposed his father). The two heroes are explicitly paralleled as addicts of ruinous love (I, pp. 143–4), and, like Lorenzo's inadvertent love for his sister, Torrismond's love for his father's apparent murderess creates an extreme conflict between the claims of appetite and of social role. Indeed, when Torrismond is first told by his nominal father that the true heir survives, his first instinct (before learning that he himself is the heir) is to fight for the usurper:

49 This play used to be taken as evidence of Dryden's dalliance with Whiggism, but modern scholarship has tended to see Dryden as a true-blue Tory throughout the Exclusion Crisis. A corrective has, however, been supplied in Phillip Harth, 'Dryden in 1678–1681: The Literary and Historical Perspectives', in *The Golden & The Brazen World: Papers in Literature and History, 1650–1800*, ed. John M. Wallace (Berkeley, Los Angeles, and London, 1985), 55–77; id., *Pen for a Party: Dryden's Tory Propaganda in its Contexts* (Princeton, 1993), 52–9. Harth persuasively rebuts the view of Dryden as an unwavering and committed court apologist from the beginning of the Exclusion Crisis, arguing that he emerged 'at the eleventh hour as a Tory spokesman' ('Dryden in 1678–1681', 67; *Pen for a Party*, 106) in mid-1681, after the dissolution of the Oxford Parliament, but was not producing politically committed literature in the earlier years of the Crisis. Harth underestimates the political content of Dryden's drama in the late 1670s (see Owen, 'Drama and Politics in the Exclusion Crisis', 197; id., 'The Politics of John Dryden's *The Spanish Fryar; or, The Double Discovery*', *English*, 43 (1994), 97–113). Some of this is Tory in tone—notably the attack on Shaftesbury and Buckingham in *Troilus and Cressida*. But Dryden (like Crowne) made marked concessions to the anti-Catholic cause in the middle of the Crisis, when the Whigs appeared strong.

50 See Harth, 'Dryden in 1678–1681', 68–72; id., *Pen for a Party*, 58–9.

I dare him to the Field with all the Odds
Of Justice on his Side, against my Tyrant:
Produce your lawful Prince, and you shall see
How brave a Rebel Love has made your Son.

(IV, p. 195)

As he had already done in *Oedipus*, Dryden dramatizes the moral complexities of power by unifying in one person the antitypes of lawful king and usurping rebel: at this moment, Torrismond is in intention what Oedipus is in fact.

Other characters, too, are placed in paradoxical and discordant relationships with legitimate authority. The loyal Raymond, who has brought up Torrismond as his son, is led by reverence for the old King into increasing opposition to his infatuated charge, eventually trying to suppress publicization of Torrismond's true identity. Conversely, the cynical Lorenzo readily supports Torrismond (and in the process fights against his own father), sustained merely by belief in the virtue of superior might: 'Now, Sir, who proves the Traytor?' he says to his father; 'My Conscience is true to me, it always whispers right when I have my Regiment to back it' (V, p. 205). The usurping Queen, who orders the true King's death and (apparently) countermands her order too late, wholly engages the audience's sympathies. And the play's villain spares the King, through intelligent assessment of his own interests. Dryden creates perplexing paradoxes in which loyalty proves rebellious, villainy and libertinism prove loyal, the true heir defends usurpation, and the passions of a would-be regicide compel our sympathy. The polarized antitheses of factional language are insufficient to convey the real moral texture of experience.

More fashionably, Dryden also lays the usual stress on the imprecision of judicial ritual and language. In the comic plot, Gomez prosecutes Elvira for adultery, but is reduced to incoherence and contradiction when Lorenzo menaces him from behind the seat of justice: the inflexible, insensitive justice which vindicates the impotent, grasping dotard is met by its equally unacceptable alternative of brute force. The romantic plot also portrays painful clashes between justice and an illicit but poignant love. In a more heroic version of Lorenzo's courtroom tactics, Torrismond dares to do battle against the true heir, 'with all the Odds | Of *Justice* on his Side' (IV, p. 195; italics added), and the lovers are repeatedly confronted with the hostility of justice, which Torrismond eventually regards as a 'Tyrant' (V, p. 206). Dryden's extraordinary decision to focus attention on the extenuating circumstances which can make a potential regicide an object of sympathetic concern strikingly confirms his determination to explore those areas where the most incontestable of social imperatives may seem imprecise in its regulation of particulars. The imprecision reappears when Raymond, that rigid adherent of justice, is led by his very rigidity into rebellion, refusing to allow the true King to rule until he learns 'Justice' (V, p. 204). At this point, justice dissolves into enigma. While the revelation that the old King survives removes the circumstances that created the problem, it cuts the Gordian knot without untying it. In the comic plot, similarly, the discovery that Lorenzo is Elvira's brother prevents their adultery but does not remove or alleviate the unfulfilled passions that Lorenzo as lover had promised to gratify. The tension between desire and order is contained but not resolved.

The Spanish Fryar affirms paternal and regal authority in the face of its manifold limitations and imprecisions, and the affirmation is accompanied by a stabilization of language and place which contrasts with the irremediable incoherence and dislocation portrayed in Otway's plays of this period (and which is never attained in that earlier study of love for a usurper's daughter, *Marriage A-la-Mode*). Place is most emphasized in the comic plot, where the invasion of Gomez' home is repeatedly stressed, where the young lovers long for an existence of vagabond wandering (III, p. 165), and where the final unfrocking and chasing out of Dominick shows a decisive expulsion of the moral alien that is new to Dryden's drama. Disordered language is still more pervasive. At the beginning of the play, the usurping Queen's name is used by soldiers as a password, a talisman of public order (I, p. 135); at the end, Torrismond is organizing public proclamations of the name of the true king (V, p. 214). In between, there is linguistic confusion and impotence, reflecting the bitter conflicts of desire and social imperatives: Lorenzo's false name, the sophistries with which the false father, Dominick, justifies breach of the marriage vow, the corresponding sophistries with which the Queen justifies the murder of the true father, the wordless signs with which the murder is ordered (IV, p. 188), the cessation of language between the Queen and the anguished Torrismond (V, pp. 198–200), Gomez' incoherence in the courtroom, and the outraged Raymond's denial of Torrismond's 'Title' (V, p. 204). At this point, nomenclature has become entirely unstable, and power remains the only arbitrator of meaning: 'Take your Rebel back again, Father mine,' says Lorenzo to Alphonso. 'The beaten Party are Rebels to the Conquerors' (V, p. 205). Such chaotic relativism of title is ended by the survival of the old King, but prior to that even Torrismond's legitimacy has lacked intrinsic linguistic authority, depending simply on the authority of force.

Appropriately, conflicts in the experience of authority, and difficulties in the articulation of those conflicts, converge on that prime sign and archetype of authority, the father. Lorenzo fights against his father, Alphonso, and later, when Gomez prosecutes Elvira for attempted adultery with Lorenzo, Alphonso is the judge. Torrismond is unable to subordinate love for his wife to duty to his newly found father, and in consequence quarrels with Raymond, his foster-father. The crooked Friar Dominick repeatedly boasts of his 'Authority' and exploits his title of 'Father', yet uses his quasi-paternal authority for the subversion of Gomez' house and family. The play concludes with the expulsion of this false father and the revelation that the true father, the old King, still survives. Yet the true father never appears, remaining a shadowy off-stage figure, like Caesar in *All for Love*. Perhaps the reason is just dramatic tact: what would the true father say to the daughter-in-law who had yesterday ordered his murder? But the very necessity for such tact testifies to the difficulties which paternal authority throughout the play creates for those subject to it. The patrilineal transmission of power is sacrosanct, but the relationship on which it is grounded is endlessly problematic.

CHAPTER SEVEN

'Not one mark of former Majesty':
Tragedy, 1676–1682

By 1676 the festive comedy of the early Restoration had given way to darker treatments of human desire. In serious drama, the heroic idealism of Orrery—the butt of such festive plays as *The Comical Revenge*—had all but disappeared, though Dryden, Otway, and Lee had continued to use the old genres and subjects to criticize the ideals formerly associated with them. But, by the end of 1676, all three had abandoned the heroic play, though minor writers protracted the genre into 1678, chiefly in the form of Siege, Conquest, and Destruction plays. One late exercise in the heroic mode which did not follow the Conquest pattern was Charles Davenant's rhymed opera *Circe* (Duke's, May 1677), the last operatic spectacular until Dryden's *Albion and Albanius* (1685). Davenant pads out the plot of *Iphigenia in Tauris* with Circe (married to King Thoas), Ithacus (her son by Ulysses), and Osmida (Thoas' daughter by an earlier marriage), the extra characters making possible complex patterns of love returned and unrequited after the fashion of *The Indian Queen*.[1] Unrequited love can inspire magnanimous acts of renunciation; but, still more than in Dryden, and in complete contrast to Euripides, ideals fail, and only Pylades and Iphigenia survive. (In 1699 John Dennis reworked Euripides' play in a contrasting fashion, allowing civilization to triumph over xenophobia and cultic barbarism.)

The least undistinguished of the late group of heroic plays was Crowne's two-part *The Destruction of Jerusalem by Titus Vespasian* (King's, January 1677), which portrays a Jerusalem torn by division between fanatical Pharisees ('Proud Separatists', Part I, I, p. 9) and the pious priests of the Sanhedrim (Anglicans), who are accused by their foes of importing Roman idolatry (Catholicism). The Sanhedrim have the assistance of a valiant, Almanzor-like and atheistic stranger, Phraartes, whose Epicurean atheism (while not endorsed) is intellectually attractive, and is opposed only by other species of

Epigraph: Lee, *The Rival Queens*, IV. i. 171.

[1] In *The Indian Queen* the villainous Queen Zempoalla and her lover Traxalla respectively love the hero and heroine Montezuma and Orazia, who of course love each other. Zempoalla's virtuous son Acacis also loves Orazia. Here, Thoas and Circe love Iphigenia and Orestes. Ithacus also loves Iphigenia, and Osmida loves Ithacus. Pylades and Iphigenia love each other. There is a good discussion of *Circe* in Paul D. Cannan, 'New Directions in Serious Drama on the London Stage, 1675–1678', *Philological Quarterly*, 73 (1994), 219–42 (pp. 230–2). Cannan's article provides an excellent account of the diversity of form and impulse in serious drama of the mid-1670s.

error. Crowne's level of religious commitment may be gauged from a song urging that fear of hell should not deter from sexual enjoyment, and that the vagina is the true gate to paradise (Part I, II, p. 17); and later, in the preface to *Caligula* (1698), he confessed that the character of Phraartes had made atheism appear *'too reasonable and lovely'*. On the Roman side, Titus (a just prince whose clemency has been abused by rebellious subjects, Part II, III, p. 23) struggles to relinquish his beloved but unpopular Berenice (presumably the Duchess of Portsmouth, the dedicatee), who resembles Phraartes in being a religious sceptic (e.g. Part I, II, pp. 15–17). Having renounced his loved one and conquered Jerusalem, the triumphant Titus (plausibly, in view of the available evidence) concludes that he is the king promised in ancient Jewish prophecies, so that the hero's triumph creates another erroneous system of interpretation.

Phraartes loves the High Priest's piously virginal daughter, Clarona, who tormentedly reciprocates his love, and lectures her unbelieving suitor on the epistemology of faith. Phraartes argues that we see only the surface of an infinitely deep ocean (Part II, III, p. 30), developing one of the chief ideas of *The Countrey Wit*: that human knowledge depends on two-dimensional signs of a three-dimensional reality. The portrait and the map are again important images. Clarona counters Phraartes' scepticism by arguing that prophecies are 'Maps' or 'Pictures' of things to come, verifiable by comparison with the things themselves, but for Phraartes the relationship of sign to event is less fixed: the prophecies are 'draughts', 'Which with some small addition may with ease | Be drawn to what resemblances you please' (Part II, III, p. 31). One of the ironies of this debate is that Clarona has herself misinterpreted the prophets, for the pious Jews who represent the Anglican Church are also (in their literal identity) a sect abandoned by God, bewildered by the hostility of an incomprehensible Providence and as baffled as the Epicurean Phraartes by the menacing omens and voices which disrupt the Passover (Part I, III, pp. 22–8). Once again, humanity is estranged from the celestial word, and the High Priest Matthias later concludes that God has stopped speaking to him (Part II, II, p. 11)

Though humanity seeks absolutes, it is fragmented into ideologies determined by culture and bodily composition: Berenice attributes her worldliness to her 'Complexion' (Part I, II, p. 17), and, more remarkably, Clarona admits that her religion springs from the 'frame' of her personality, and suggests that, in a pagan culture, her constitution would have expressed itself in devotion to Diana (Part I, II, pp. 21–2). The fragmentation is frequently expressed as estrangement: for example, Berenice and Phraartes, the two sceptics, are 'Strangers' to the cultures of their unattainable loved ones,[2] and the Jewish priests are baffled by the 'strange' prophecies of God (Part I, III, p. 28). For

---

[2] Part II, II, p. 13; IV, p. 37.

Crowne, the enduring literary image of mankind as a gathering of strangers expresses the incoherence of a world where creeds are determined by culture and even bodily composition, and where the transcendent may be unrecognizable even when directly seen.

The remaining heroic plays are feeble indeed. Two, John Banks's *The Rival Kings* (King's, June 1677) and Samuel Pordage's *The Siege of Babylon* (Duke's, September 1677), capitalize on the success of Lee's *The Rival Queens* (discussed below), all three being indebted to La Calprenède's *Cassandre*, though Banks and Pordage concentrate on the love of Lysimachus and Oroondates (Orontes in Pordage) for Parisatis and Statira, the daughters of the defeated King of Persia. The nobility of Banks's Alexander is greater than that of Lee's, and Banks (unlike Lee) defies history by punishing the regicide Cassander with immediate death; but Alexander is still marred by cruelty and excess, and heroic militarism is clearly denounced. In Pordage, however, there is no ambiguity, and indeed no Alexander. Instead, there is a reassertion of vanishing certainties: providential order (written in the book of Fate, I, p. 5), Orrerian noble rivalry, and sexual hierarchy (the Amazon Thalestris abolishes her tribe's way of life, V, p. 65). Banks returns to the bankruptcy of heroism in his unrhymed *The Destruction of Troy* (Duke's, by November 1678), where war is a process of treachery, theft, deceit, and dishonour. With this unambiguously hostile representation of the heroic life, the sequence of Conquest plays came to an end.

The changing fashion is acknowledged in the prologue to Ravenscroft's *King Edgar and Alfreda* (King's, ?September 1677): the play, Ravenscroft claims in the prologue, was written '*at least Ten Years ago*' but has only become stageable now that the fashion for rhyme and heroic supermen has passed. The story of an evil counsellor tricking a king into an ill-advised marriage would indeed have been topical at the time of Clarendon's fall, though no anti-Clarendon play kills off Catherine of Braganza, and the play's sympathetic treatment of unsanctioned royal love does correspond to a mini-trend of the late 1670s (witness *The Destruction of Jerusalem* and *All for Love*). Like Crowne, Ravenscroft repeatedly uses the portrait to exemplify the nature of human perception, but for him the portrait leads to truth, and one can always (as in *The Wrangling Lovers*) transcend the false or incomplete sign. In all three plots, love is excited by a picture, and eventually emerges from incomplete signification. One pair of lovers is tongue-tied, and another courtship features an illiterate, linguistically incompetent sailor who (like Congreve's Ben Legend) is trapped in the vocabulary of naval life. In the main plot, Ethelwold has been sent to court the beautiful Alfreda on behalf of King Edgar, but has married her himself after misinforming Edgar about her looks. By the time the King sees a true picture of Alfreda, he too is married to another. Edgar and Alfreda fall in love, but each virtuously tries to save the other's marriage, though an attempted bedroom trick in which Alfreda tries to reconcile Edgar with his Queen unexpectedly results in the deaths of both unwanted spouses. The lovers' attempts at magnanimous self-sacrifice are conventional enough, but it is not conventional for such efforts to result in the happy demise of the rivals. The balance between desire and social obligation has shifted in favour of desire, and desire is sanctioned by justice: when Ethelwold and the entirely virtuous Queen die, 'Justice | Seem'd to strike the blow' (v, p. 70).

A sterner view of life, however, appears in Thomas Rymer's version of the same story, *Edgar; or, the English Monarch* (unperformed?), a rhymed 'Heroick Tragedy' (according to the title-page).[3] All three of its heroes are given the dignity of kingship—no comic mariners—and there is much rebellion, usurpation, and restoration, so that love is always seen in relation to state responsibility and to the re-establishment of an invariably masculine authority, the greater frailty of the female being one of the fundamental assumptions of the play. The play overtly celebrates the British monarchy, but it does so with the kind of tactfully critical loyalty that had been current in the mid-1660s: after a masque which (astonishingly) celebrates British naval supremacy, Edgar exclaims that the show is less of a shadow than his power, and that he is 'dethron'd' by love (IV, p. 40).

Whether *King Edgar and Alfreda* had really lain unperformed for ten years is impossible to say. If it had, it was not the only tragicomedy to be optimistically unearthed at this time. William Chamberlayne's previously unacted *Loves Victory* (1658), a structureless romance about rebellion and reconciliation, was transformed into *Wits Led by the Nose* (King's, June 1677), its old-fashioned sub-plot about a trickster and a bumpkin being replaced by a marginally more up-to-date one involving two cowardly pseudo-wits. And when Aphra Behn claimed to be raiding the bottom drawer for *The Young King* (Duke's, ?September 1679),[4] her claim had every appearance of truth, for the play has much in common with *The Forc'd Marriage* and *The Amorous Prince*, and little with the plays that she had more recently produced. Part of the plot is a condensed version of Calderón's *La Vida es sueño*: Orsames, a Dacian prince imprisoned from birth because of oracles about his future tyranny, is given a day's reign, behaves tyrannically, and is consequently persuaded that the day of power was a mere dream. But the oracle is now fulfilled, and the prince is free to change and reign justly. One of Behn's modifications is to make the prince a prisoner of his mother rather than his father, so that the imprisonment involves a reversal of sexual roles and a suppression of masculine privilege and identity. Such reversal is further developed in the complementary plot, taken from La Calprenède, featuring the problems of sexual identity experienced by Orsames' sister, Cleomena, who has been

---

[3] There is no record of a performance. *The London Stage* suggests that it 'may have been acted in opposition to Ravenscroft's play' (i. 264).

[4] In the dedication she describes it as 'this first Essay of my Infant-Poetry' (p. 105).

brought up as an Amazon in order to take the place of the suppressed brother. Her problems of identity are paralleled by those of her lover, Prince Thersander (i.e. 'Bold Man') of the enemy kingdom of Scythia, whose love induces him to fight on the Dacian side as—it is repeatedly stressed—a 'Stranger', under the assumed name of Clemanthis. As so often, a conflict between social imperatives and personal desire enforces a splitting of identity, and so radical is the division in this case that a single combat is arranged between Thersander and his *alter ego* of Clemanthis. He chooses to fight as Thersander, privately appointing a friend to fight, and lose, in the guise of Clemanthis. But the friend is wounded before the fight, and Cleomena secretly takes his place, entering the battle disguised as her lover's other self, and being gravely wounded by his primary self. Thersander's allegiance to political authority triumphs over his personal desires, and the triumph of political authority is also a triumph of male violence, the two (as usual) being inevitably intertwined.

From this early study of the Amazon to the later, far subtler, study of the virile heroine of *The Widow Ranter*, Behn never envisages effective female challenges to male authority. The remarkable thing about this early play is her ready acquiescence in a situation which she later came to view with increasing gloom. Cleomena's Amazonian upbringing has not altered 'a Heart all soft . . . all Woman' (I, p. 115), and she experiences a conflict between her Amazonian role and feminine nature, begging the gruffly macho general Vallentio to 'tell me who I am' (IV, p. 171). She then gladly instructs Vallentio to restore her brother, complying with the popular desire for a male ruler. Conversely, Orsames retains his instinctive belligerence, although brought up in cultural and sexual isolation, exposed only to the platitudes of a moralistic tutor. He attempts to rape the first woman he sees (while professing religious adoration of his victim), and is sexually aroused by the first glimpse of his mother, again showing that lust is the primal male response to woman, ready to take over when consciousness of kinship lapses.

Behn repeatedly implies the insecurity of female command. If women exercise linguistic authority, it is self-negating: when lots are drawn for the duel with Thersander in which Cleomena is to be overcome, it is she who writes Thersander's name on the lot; and, when she assumes the authority of an 'Oracle' (IV, p. 172), it is to resign power to her brother. But the differentiation of sexual power is most extensively represented in the imagery of bondage, for the two sexes experience distinct kinds of subordination. Thersander wears the 'Fetters' (II, p. 132) of love for Cleomena, but nevertheless dominates her in single combat; and, when Cleomena later attempts to murder him, believing him to have murdered Clemanthis, she is captured and constrained by literal 'Fetters' (V, p. 177), until Thersander's father releases her, with the fetters replaced by—or rather transformed into—'Garments suitable to her Sex' (V, p. 179). The distinction between the illusory servitude of the adoring male and the actual bondage of the woman is particularly evident in the experiences of the captive Scythian heroine Urania. Upon finding her, the Dacian general Vallentio claims her with a *captor captus* cliché: 'you must be my Prisoner, unless your Eyes prevent me, and make me yours' (I, p. 113). But Urania herself is a captive of love as well as war, for she has deliberately sought captivity in order to join her beloved Amintas in bondage. Inadvertently, however, she enters the cell of Orsames, who mistakes her for a god, professes submission and devotion, and tries to rape her, but is prevented by the fettered Amintas. Urania's submissiveness internalizes the constraints imposed by social subjection and physical vulnerability, whereas Orsames' sense of emotional bondage expresses itself in violence and physical domination, and the fettered Amintas has a power that the unchained Urania cannot attain. In subjecting Orsames to lifelong imprisonment, his mother exercises a power of physical constraint not generally granted to women, but it is an unstable power. When Orsames leaves the prison for the throne, and Cleomena assumes first fetters and then the subtler bondage of female garb, the patterns of command and subjection are normalized. Orsames' ascent to the throne is, of course, a restoration, and the enthronement of one who is initially presented as a mere compound of lustful and destructive impulses shows that from the outset Behn imaginatively linked her cherished political cause with a distribution of sexual authority from which she was excluded. Here 'the God of War' is finally overcome by 'The God of Love' (V, p. 191), but in the new plays which Behn was producing at this time machismo was less easily civilized, and the stranger less easily made a partner.

The Young King emerges from the bottom drawer with a set of attitudes that had become strikingly dated since the time of Behn's first plays. Whereas desire is here finally reconcilable with the institutions of society, serious drama from the mid-1670s parallels contemporary comedy in emphasizing the unresolvable complexities of sexual passion: in Lee's *The Rival Queens*, for example, Alexander is torn between the competing claims of two wives. Although this development is obviously not a mere response to current affairs, it does intermittently draw upon a contemporary situation, in that there appears a small clutch of plays concerned (from various standpoints) with a ruler's liaison with an unpopular foreign mistress. *The Destruction of Jerusalem* is one of two plays on the Titus and Berenice theme; there were two Antony and Cleopatra plays; and in *Brutus of Alba* (Duke's, June 1678) Nahum Tate transferred the Dido and Aeneas story to the eponymous founder of Britain,[5] showing the royal exile renouncing love in order to gain and make great the British throne (there is topical prophecy of war against France, V, ii. 292). In part, Tate's approach is that of the tactful rebukes to royal amorousness in the mid-1660s, but he gives greater emphasis to the

5 In the preface Tate reveals that the play was originally about Dido and Aeneas, but was altered on the advice of friends so as to avoid comparison with Virgil (p. 75).

claims of the personal: the Queen (like his later Dido) is the innocent victim of sorcery (there is much *Macbeth*-style incantation), though here the sorcery drives the lovers together, whereas in *Dido and Æneas* (which emphasizes the personal still more) it separates them. Even here, however, the lovers part less like Virgil's Dido and Aeneas than like Titus and Berenice, each tormented by the parting, yet each aware of its necessity.

The claims of the personal had been still more emphasized in Otway's rhymed *Titus and Berenice* (Duke's, by November 1676), where, as Jessica Munns has shown, Racine is inverted in the portrayal of a ruler corrupted by the sacrifice of the personal to the public.[6] But a contrary view of a parallel dilemma is presented in Sir Charles Sedley's *Antony and Cleopatra* (Duke's, February 1677), where Antony is a critical portrayal of Charles II:[7] Actium stands for the Third Dutch War, and the besotted hero is blind to the cunning of his mistress and inept both in his clemency and severity. The voice of the people is treated with unusual sympathy, for, when the common soldiers rebel to prevent the whipping of Thyreus, Antony recognizes that they are right: 'just Heaven, what am I, | Whom the rude People, teach Humanity?' (III. ii. 331–2). There is nostalgia for the freedom of the Roman republic (III. i. 112–15) but no simple escape from the present: two reformist and ultimately rebellious Egyptian lords are fatally misled by the villainous Photinus. Sedley's first play had celebrated the Restoration; nine years later, he combines censure of Stuart absolutism with acknowledgement of the difficulties that beset right-thinking men in seeking an alternative.

The emotionally divided ruler also features in the work which first pointed the way beyond the heroic play, Lee's unrhymed *The Rival Queens* (King's, March 1677), but the emotional conflict is between love and love rather than, as is more customary, love and imperial duty. The opposition between love and empire, and East and West, is reduced to a very subordinate status, and Alexander is principally divided between the competing attractions of two wives: the haughty, lustful Roxana (his first wife) and the gentle Statira. Nor does Roxana have any claim through priority of nuptials, for the wife with the better claim is the wife with the better character; discrete individuals are the criteria of value, not universal principles. But the absence of more general criteria of order does not liberate the individual, for Lee again portrays a morally disordered world in which the innocent die and (exceptionally in Restoration drama), the guilty survive; for, like Augustus in *Gloriana* and the murderers in *The Massacre of Paris*, the villainous Cassander outlives the tragic chaos he has brought about.[8] For the first time, however, Lee suggests

[6] Jessica Munns, 'Thomas Otway's *Titus and Berenice* and Racine's *Berenice*', *Restoration*, 7 (1983), 58–67.

[7] See John Dryden, *All for Love*, ed. N. J. Andrew, New Mermaids (London and Tonbridge, 1975), p. xvi.

[8] Machiavelli also survives in *Caesar Borgia*, though he is handed over to the Inquisition. And Nemours in the unclassifiable *The Princess of Cleve* enjoys complete impunity.

that such disorder is inevitably implicit in the nature of political authority. Nero and Augustus had been tyrants, but such monstrous extremes of tyranny tend to seem special cases. By contrast, *The Rival Queens* lacks monsters, but also lacks the felt moral order that gives meaning to the idea of the monster; allowing the fixed political categories and antitheses of the earliest heroic plays to merge in indistinct confusion. Alexander simultaneously sustains the traditionally opposed roles of hero and tyrant, lover and faithless libertine, and his assassin, Cassander, is at once a typical scheming villain (like Rustan in *Mustapha*) and a victim of tyranny who provides the clearest analysis of the tyrant's pride and cruelty.[9]

The absence of fixed, palpable design is reflected in the impenetrable obscurity of divine language. Otherworldly language chiefly makes arbitrary announcements of destruction, and there are also chillingly silent omens. One verbal announcement of unexplained calamity occurs when a divine oracle proclaims, 'in abrupt Thunder' (II, i. 182), that Babylon is doomed. Another, more complex and dreadful, occurs when the gentle Statira is menaced with daggers by the ghosts of her parents, who affirm her innocence and yet declare that her death is decreed (v. i. 1–20). Mortals in Lee's earlier plays have complained about the indifference of the gods to suffering virtue, but here the gods explicitly and directly reveal their indifference, and the conversion of parental figures into forces threatening the innocent child reflects Lee's persistent suggestion that the family is naturally alien to the child which is born into it (another omen involves 'a monstrous Child' (II. i. 22) that utters a terrible, inarticulate shriek). The ghost of Alexander's father also appears, similarly as a figure of menace, though here the menace is wordless: like the ghost of Hamlet's father, that of King Philip walks in mysterious silence, but unlike his predecessor he does not even communicate with his son. The image of paternal silence is recalled and amplified when Statira lies dying, and Alexander desperately appeals to his imaginary father, Jupiter: 'Answer me, Father, wilt thou take her from me?' (v. i. 148). But Jupiter does not answer, and Statira herself lapses into the silence of death, in which 'the talking Soul is mute' (v. i. 171). But another episode of celestial silence is yet more terrible, and suggests a yet more comprehensive incoherence:

> A pale Crown'd head flew lately glaring by me,
> With two dead hands, which threw a Chrystal Globe
> From high, that shatter'd in a thousand pieces.

> (IV. i. 80–2)

The integrity of the bodily organism and of the world, of microcosm and macrocosm, is here dissolved.

---

[9] The ambiguous presentation of Alexander is emphasized in Laura Brown, *English Dramatic Form, 1660–1700* (New Haven and London, 1981), 71–6; Brown, however, claims that it is not 'deliberate and artful ambiguity . . . but rather the inchoate and involuntary ambiguity of formal transition' (p. 75).

The silent omens and supernatural voices of doom are supplemented by thunder. But its mysteries require translation, the translation is always ambiguous, and the translator on all but one occasion is the predominantly villainous Cassander or his associate Polyperchon. On the one occasion when Cassander is not involved—when Alexander's subordinates Perdicas and Meleager tell him of an omen of ghostly ravens in combat—the ambiguity extends to the question of whether thunder has actually been heard: 'Whilst dreadful sounds did our scar'd sense assail, | As of small Thunder, or hugh [*sic*] Scythian Hail' (II. i. 208–9). When the assassins hear thunder, its existence is not in doubt, but its meaning is, as when Cassander attaches two contrary meanings to the same thunderclap:

> The Lords above are angry, and talk big,
> Or rather . . .
> . . . seem to groan for Alexander's fall.
>
> (I. i. 139–42)

The gods are inarticulate, and, more persistently than Hannibal in *Sophonisba*, Alexander attempts to make his own language the arbiter of events. He repeatedly claims to control thunder, as when he addresses his associate Clytus as his 'Lightning' and 'Thunder' (II. i. 131–2), and when Clytus refuses to be Alexander's thunder—the mere voice of his will—and rebukes his degeneracy and tyranny, he is struck through with a javelin. Another insubordinate, Lysimachus (rival in love to Alexander's favourite, Hephestion), is thrown to a lion with the command that neither he nor his associates should speak (II. i. 402–3). Like many libertines of comedy, Alexander can conquer women through language ('Then he will talk, good Gods how he will talk!', I. i. 379) and through insouciant perjury: vows—submission of human language to divine sanction—cannot restrain the man who claims the power of thunder. Alexander's imagined divinity of speech fails when he cannot prevent the silencing of Statira's 'talking Soul', but there is no greater, transcendent language beyond the capricious words of the earthly ruler. When Roxana curses Alexander for his perjury to her, he is promptly seized by a mortal sickness, and attributes this to the workings of the curse (V. i. 225–39); but he is in fact dying because he has been poisoned by Cassander, before the curse was pronounced. The transcendent order here postulated is based on misinterpretation of a purely material process.

The omens of the shattered globe and deformed body dissolve the traditional correspondences between body, state, and cosmos: individuals now wander in a world of shadows, unable to pattern their lives according to a fixed cosmic order. Frequently, they rejoice in their liberation from the numinous: commanded by Alexander to resign Parisatis to Hephestion, Lysimachus says he would disobey such a command even from the gods (II. i. 241–2). The word *body* is insistently repeated, frequently in order to elevate the corporeal over the celestial: grasping her 'body', Roxana recalls, Alexander swore that her breasts outvalued 'the Globes of Heav'n and Earth' (III. i. 108–11); and Statira loves the 'Body of the Sun' less than 'the least part' of Alexander (I. i. 365–8). But the exaltation of the body alternates with its dismemberment. Partly, this is associated with Roxana's disordered passions: 'I cou'd tear my flesh' (IV. i. 117); 'I am lost, torn with imagination!' (IV. i. 223); 'hew me into smallest pieces' (V. i. 198). But it is also associated with Alexander's tyranny: in the torture of Philotas (I. i. 229–32), the sufferings of Lysimachus, and, finally, in the death of Alexander himself, who is torn by the poison (V. i. 302). The bodily disintegration associated with Roxana's wild lusts is also, more disturbingly, manifest in the ruler of the world, and indeed Alexander's militaristic destructiveness transfers the same processes of disintegration to a larger scale. If Roxana feels her body torn by sexual passion, Alexander has destroyed Persepolis at the whim of Thais (II. i. 343–4), and in agony at Statira's rejection of him he threatens to destroy Babylon in terms which clearly foreshadow his later cleaving of Clytus' body: 'I'le strike my Spear into the reeling Globe | To let it bloud; set Babylon in a blaze' (III. i. 381–2). After the deaths of Hephestion and Statira, he crucifies Hephestion's physician and plans, Tamburlaine-like, to destroy cities in order to commemorate Statira (V. i. 258–76). And yet this violation of the individual and civic organism is, at the same time, an apotheosis of the body—Statira's corpse—and a further elevation of the corporeal over the celestial: 'To build her Tomb, no Shrines nor Altars spare, | But strip the shining Gods to make it rare' (V. i. 275–6).

Here lies the tragic paradox of the play. The celestial has retreated into muttering incomprehensibility, not to liberate man but to render his oppression arbitrary and incomprehensible. Man is left with the individual body, stripped of the symbolism and correspondences that made it once both part and image of an integrated cosmic and political whole and reduced to a principle of anarchy, dismembering the rival bodies and communities that impede its claims and seized by passions that conspire its own disintegration. Alexander is not the earthly personification of a divine order but a supreme actualization of the body, with its destructive and contradictory impulses, re-enacting on earth the omen of the shattered globe, and leaving chaos to his successors with the famous bequest of the empire 'To him that is most worthy' (V. i. 371). Like so many tragedies of this period, *The Rival Queens* alludes to problems of succession, and it does so in the context of a monarchy that has been thoroughly secularized and rendered an agent of corporeal process.

In *All for Love* (King's, December 1677), Dryden followed Lee in abandoning rhyme and Sedley in dramatizing the deaths of Antony and Cleopatra, providing the greatest Restoration treatment of the hero torn between his nation and a personal life vested in an alien, unpopular mistress. In depicting the conflict between personal and public, he reinstated the choices which Lee had banished to the periphery, but at the same time he complicated their conventional moral associations. Sedley had contrasted a meek, self-sacrificing Octavia (Mary Betterton) with a powerful Cleopatra played by Mary Lee, a specialist in dominant, passionate women; but, as already noted, Dryden's Cleopatra and Octavia were played by the small, vulnerable Elizabeth Bowtell and the strapping, forceful Katherine Corey. A year earlier Corey had played the Widow Blackacre in *The Plain-Dealer*, and she returns to a spirit of aggressive legalism in stating her claim to Antony: 'he', Cleopatra taunts, 'whom Law calls yours, | But whom his love made mine' (III. 433–4). Octavia's destructive, unimaginative attachment to law receives one particularly striking expression. When she first claims her right to Antony's hand, the words with which she does so—''tis mine, and I will have it' (III. 266)—are the very words with which Shylock claims his pound of flesh.[10] Nor does the echo emphasize merely her blinkered legalism, for it signals a blurring of what distinguishes the city, and all that it stands for, from the amorphous wildness that it traditionally opposes. Shylock is an 'alien' seeking the life of a 'citizen' (IV. i. 345–7), whereas Octavia is an embodiment of civic virtue seeking to convert Antony to what she represents, and doing so with a conventional image of social harmony, the taking of the hand. Similarly, when Ventidius, the archetypal Roman citizen, attempts to confirm Antony's moral homecoming by persuading him of Cleopatra's infidelity, he does so by echoing the words with which another Shakespearian outsider, the bastard Don John in *Much Ado*, slanders Hero's chastity:

> Your *Cleopatra*;
> *Dollabella*'s *Cleopatra:*
> Every Man's *Cleopatra*.
>
> (IV. 296–8)[11]

The representatives of the city are transformed into and absorbed within their opposites, and the opposition between ordered Rome and the untamed, individualistic East becomes unstable and potentially reversible.

Indeed, although the play depicts a Roman's fascination with an alien queen, the word *stranger* is exclusively used of Roman citizens. Ventidius is introduced as a 'Stranger' (I. 89), and, when Dollabella is reunited with Antony, he likens himself to a man who has become 'a stranger' to his own home (III. 126); when Octavia arrives with the children, Antony's displeasure prompts Ventidius to ask (with reason) whether they are 'strangers' (III. 241), and Octavia complains that she has not even received the welcome due to 'a stranger' (III. 254). But the images of the stranger are used in isolation from what normally gives such images meaning: a counterbalancing sense of fixed place and culture. There is no global clash of national cultures, only the clash

---

[10] *The Merchant of Venice*, IV. i. 100. See H. Neville Davies, '*All for Love*: Texts and Contexts', *Cahiers Élisabéthains*, 36 (1989), 49–71 (pp. 63–4).

[11] Cf. *Much Ado About Nothing*, III. ii. 95–6 ('Leonato's Hero, your Hero, every man's Hero').

of broken intimacies within the featureless space of Alexandria, and Dryden never gives a sense of concrete, particularized place, setting his characters instead amidst impalpable, universal forces of change, such as the union of creation and death symbolized in the devastating yet fertilizing Nile floods which Serapion describes in his opening speech, and which reappears in various forms throughout the play.[12] The idea of place is associated not with fixed, objective localities but with private, subjective states: 'What place have I to go to?' asks Cleopatra in her second estrangement from Antony, envisaging herself as a global wanderer, 'banish'd from you' (IV. 552–6). Later, believing Cleopatra dead, Antony sees the world as 'a black Desart' (V. 287), blank, insignificant, and undifferentiated without her. Though the choice between Rome and Egypt, nation and self, is constantly made and remade, no order greater than the self is given imaginative substance or tangible manifestation; indeed, the representative of the triumphant nation, Octavius Caesar, never appears, entering immediately after the end of the play.

Accordingly, language becomes limited in its range of reference, incapable of signifying cultural norms or providential designs. In the opening speech, the priest Serapion proclaims that 'Portents, and Prodigies, are grown so frequent, | That they have lost their Name' (I. 1–2), indicating that the contrast of natural and unnatural which survives as a linguistic possibility no longer exists in the world itself; the patterns of language again falsify those of experience. Linguistic contact with the supernatural perhaps remains, but as in Lee the supernatural voice is inexplicable in its menace and ambiguous in its origin: Serapion has heard an otherworldly voice announcing the downfall of Egypt (I. 27–8), though his experience is promptly dismissed by the Hobbist Alexas as either a fabrication or a dream.[13] In Dryden's early heroic plays the supernatural voice had been directly heard; here it is reported at second hand, through human agency, and its reality immediately becomes a subject for debate between two characters of limited authority. Finally, when Egypt does fall, Serapion again invokes a superhuman source of language, the book of time, but only to suggest that the book is now closed, obsolete, and inaccessible: for 'Time has unrowl'd her Glories to the last, | And now clos'd up the Volume' (V. 74–5).

As in *The Man of Mode*, descriptions of the transcendent regularly turn out to be descriptions of the human: in Cleopatra's 'when he gave his answer, | Fate took the word, and then I liv'd, or dy'd' (II. 38–9), for example, fate is a superfluous element in the statement that she cannot live without her lover. A redundant linguistic term becomes promoted to the status of a cosmic agency. The language which enshrines social or political values is similarly presented as mere language, sanctified by convention yet remote from the true principles

---

[12] See Derek W. Hughes, 'The Significance of *All for Love*', *ELH* 37 (1970), 540–63.

[13] 'From this ignorance of how to distinguish Dreams, and other strong Fancies, from Vision and Sense, did arise the greatest part of the Religion of the Gentiles in time past' (*Leviathan*, ch. ii, 92).

of human action. In Act III, Ventidius, Dollabella, Octavia, and her children briefly recover Antony for Rome with a naked and formulaic barrage of titles, successively hailing him as emperor, friend, husband, father (III. 361–2). In George Wilkins's *The Miseries of Inforst Mariage*, a very similar bombardment of titles ('Kinsman', 'Brother', 'Husband', 'Father') had permanently restored the erring hero to a sense of social and familial responsibility, and the titles had emphatically been credited with solid and substantial force: 'Harke how their words like Bullets shoot me thorow', he had exclaimed (sig. [K4]). In Wilkins the ritual of naming produces lasting social reintegration, but here the titles are mere titles, falsely reducing Antony's nature to the mere sum of his external obligations, and producing an effect of notable transience. In the next act, Ventidius and Octavia attempt to fix the effect of the naming scene by confronting Antony with the apparent infidelity of Cleopatra (the woman whose claims do not figure in their glib list of publicly approved labels), but they succeed only in destroying the fragile fiction which their moral glossary has conjured up. (As in *The Country-Wife*, moral codes become word-lists.) When Cleopatra finally claims the 'Title' of Antony's wife (V. 414), it is a title justified purely by love, and the private act of self-entitlement recalls and cancels the Romans' oppressive incantation of Antony's public labels.

In other ways, too, language becomes oppressive and distorting, and Dryden once again shows characters confusing the nature of language with that of experience itself. As in *Aureng-Zebe*, they repeatedly mistake the signifier for the signified, regarding the linguistic representations of will as accomplished reality: 'in that word | *Octavius* fell' (I. 429–30).[14] They also create imaginary versions of what others have said or are about to say, so that language becomes an agent less of communication than of solipsism, a means of making independent beings passive puppets in a script of the speaker's devising. When Ventidius and Octavia see, without overhearing, Cleopatra's flirtation with Dollabella, Ventidius confidently creates his own words for Cleopatra, disastrously misconstruing the unheard spectacle:

> She look'd methought
> As she would say, *Take your old man*, Octavia;
> *Thank you, I'm better here.*
>
> (IV. 228–30)

Cleopatra is, indeed, the chief object of the recurrent compulsion to articulate the silence of others. She begins and ends her liaison with Antony as a passive, silent object of male contemplation: the inert spectacle on the Cydnos; the corpse, clad in the garments of the Cydnos, whose smile—in the

---

[14] The autonomy of language in *All for Love* is noted by Anne Davidson Ferry (*Milton and the Miltonic Dryden* (Cambridge, Mass., 1968), 189–205). Words, she writes, 'are the only instruments by which the world may penetrate to the inward self, and yet the self remains forever separate' (p. 205). See also my 'Art and Life in *All for Love*', *Studies in Philology*, 80 (1983), 84–107.

last of many speculative elucidations of silence—Serapion falsely interprets. In rendering Cleopatra's apparition as Aphrodite on the waters of the Cydnos, Shakespeare modifies the North–Plutarch account so as to make her the creative centre of a scene of fervent energy, but Dryden creates a contrary modification, making Cleopatra and her companions blank, passive ciphers: all the movement in the spectacle is associated with the artefacts, not the actors, and Cleopatra becomes an image possessed and interpreted by the minds of the spectators: 'The hearing gave new pleasure to the sight; | And both to thought' (III. 178–9).[15] And so she remains throughout the play, constantly perceived as either fascinating goddess or fascinating siren—as Aphrodite or Circe—and never as the vulnerable, Bowtell character, as cruelly miscast by history as she has been ingeniously miscast in the theatre: 'Nature', she complains to Alexas, 'meant me | A Wife, a silly harmless houshold Dove' (IV. 91–2).

Enraged and uncomprehending when Cleopatra's vulnerability and frailty in flirting with Dollabella disrupt the illusion he retains from the Cydnos, Antony veers from worship of a non-existent goddess to execration of a non-existent monster, never seeing the woman. He judges in terms of innocence and guilt, truth and falsity, faith and treason: terms which, as usual, are crudely inexact for the assessment of individual motives. Cleopatra laments that 'one minutes feigning has destroy'd | My whole life's truth' (IV. 521–2), and an absolute such as truth certainly cannot accommodate one minute's falsehood; all the more reason, therefore, not to use it as a measure of human quality. Truth may be the goal of narrative but, as Wycherley had already demonstrated in the portrayal of Alithea, it paradoxically annihilates itself when one looks for it in the experiences which are the subject of narrative. Once more, it is pertinent to recall Hobbes's observation that '*True* and *False* are attributes of Speech, not of Things' (*Leviathan*, ch. iv, 105).

Innocence is as zealously sought and as persistently self-erasing as truth. Still more than *Aureng-Zebe*, *All for Love* emphasizes the trial of the heroine. Even the Cydnos voyage was an exercise in judicial self-defence, in which Cleopatra attempted 'To clear her self' (III. 160) of responsibility for the death of Dollabella's brother, and during the play Antony conducts two mock-trials of Cleopatra, arraigning her at the end of Act II for her prior liaison with Julius Caesar and her flight at Actium, and at the end of Act IV for her enticement of Dollabella. On both occasions Cleopatra tries to make Antony understand the complex human frailty that governed her actions, and on both occasions she fails, emerging from the first trial revered as a goddess and from the second reviled as a betrayer worthy of Tartarus; for Antony can only judge in antithetical absolutes, and cannot comprehend the flaws and stains which, as Dryden's imagery constantly emphasizes, are intrinsic to the

---

[15] See Derek Hughes, '*Aphrodite katadyomene*: Dryden's Cleopatra on the Cydnos', *Comparative Drama*, 14 (1980), 35–45.

flesh. The contrast between Antony's idealizing vision and Cleopatra's acute sense of carnal flaw is particularly clear at the beginning of Act III, immediately after the trial scene. Here Cleopatra is restored to the role of a goddess, radiantly free from flaw, hailed by Antony as 'My Brighter *Venus!*' (III. 11). But Cleopatra has a different vision of Antony, imagining him covered with the marks of love-bites (III. 10): as a fleshly lover, covered with the marks and stains that are organic to the flesh. It is part of the tragedy that Antony can never perceive Cleopatra in this fashion.

As Cleopatra was silent during her trial on the Cydnos, so Antony attempts to deny her language during the two trial scenes within the play. In the first, he forbids her to speak unless he utters a falsehood (luckily, he does); at the end of the second, he repeatedly refuses to 'hear' her pleas of innocence. Cleopatra is thus compelled to enact ritual tests of innocence in which the ration of language allowed to her is doled out by her accusers. The exclusion continues even during Cleopatra's progress to apotheosis in death. Her mock-suicide sustains the image of the voiceless woman in the lawcourt, for the story is invented without her knowledge by Alexas, as a final attempt to 'clear' her 'innocence' (V. 105), and indeed it does persuade Antony of her 'Truth' and 'Innocence' (V. 242). But even in their final scene Antony still invents speech for her, and still needs the crudely reductive categories of truth and falsehood: 'Say but thou art not false' (V. 374), he urges, in yet another of the numerous attempts to control and dictate the words of others. But not the last. This is reserved for the very last speech, when Serapion enters and elucidates the meaning couched in the smile on Cleopatra's now eternally silent corpse, turning the body into a text decoded by a man. Unlike Serapion, we have witnessed Cleopatra's death, and have seen not a triumphant entry into immortality but the panic of a woman blinded by poison, seeking a last comforting contact with her lover's corpse; we have seen, that is, a farewell to the flesh, but not an entry into eternity. But for Serapion the smile is evidence that Cleopatra 'went to charm' Antony 'in another World' (V. 512), and he goes on to prescribe the future narrative of her life and death, falsifying both in the process: 'And Fame, to late Posterity, shall tell, | No Lovers liv'd so great, or dy'd so well' (V. 518–19). Cleopatra is here fixed in a role against which she has rebelled throughout the play: as the great embodiment of eroticism. And her smile, the last sign which she created, now passes out of her control into an alien and male scheme of interpretation.

Like Payne's heroines, Cleopatra cannot dictate her posthumous story, remaining as powerless over the verdicts of history as she is over those of justice. Her double powerlessness is foreshadowed in Alexas' unauthorized fiction about her suicide, which is couched as a court-room defence of the accused, but which is also, obviously, an unsanctioned narrative of her death, based for good measure on an earlier narrative about another female stereotype:

> and, with such looks
> As dying *Lucrece* cast,——...
>
> She snatch'd her Ponyard.
>
> (V. 226–8)

Cleopatra is an even more unlikely candidate for the role of Lucretia than Otway's Lady Dunce. But the potentially infinite regression of narrative based on narrative, of archetypal woman characterized with reference to an earlier archetypal woman, vividly illustrates the woman's inability to emerge as self-defining individual from the elaborate chains of male narration.

Dryden's treatment of Cleopatra is paralleled by the treatment of Tarpeia in the anonymous and generally old-fashioned *Romulus and Hersilia*. This was not performed until August 1682, when it appeared with a fiercely Tory prologue and epilogue, an attack upon Monmouth in the latter causing the imprisonment of its author and speaker, Aphra Behn and Lady Slingsby (Mary Lee). According to the prologue, however, the play itself was '*writ before the times of* Whig *and* Tory' (though a specific echo of *All for Love* gives a *terminus post quem*).[16] The play features an old-fashioned self-denying lover in the Orrery vein, his passion eventually diverted from Hersilia to her sister by a trick involving a chaste substitution of partners. More interestingly, it shows women shaping their own lives and adopting roles of their own choice. Hersilia has been willingly abducted during the rape of the Sabine women, investing a classic instance of female passivity with a dimension of female decisiveness, and she later aids Romulus with a troop of female warriors. The most provocative redefinition of femininity is provided by the treatment of Tarpeia, the archetypal Roman traitress, who here redeems her treachery by assuming male guise and acting bravely in battle, and whose name is offered to posterity not as the familiar eponym for the punishment of treachery but as a sign of feminine virtue:

> Queens when they'd Name a Maid of mighty Courage,
> And vindicate their Sex above the Male,
> Will say *Tarpeia*.
>
> (V, pp. 61–2)

An ancient stereotype fixed by centuries of male narrative (and male judicial ritual) is reclaimed—as Dryden's Cleopatra was not—by the narrative of women.

All for Love had not been an adaptation of *Antony and Cleopatra*, but its title-page proclaimed it 'Written in Imitation of *Shakespeare's* Stile', and it provided the first evidence of renewed interest in the use of Shakespeare,

---

[16] 'Thou brighter *Venus*' (I, p. 2) and 'My greater *Mars*' (III, p. 27) echo *All for Love*, III. 11 ('My Brighter *Venus*!', 'O my greater *Mars*!').

which was to result in a stream of adaptations—all politically partisan—over the next few years. The first was Shadwell's revision of *Timon of Athens* as *The History of Timon of Athens, The Man-Hater* (Duke's, January 1678), which displays its author's familiar concern with the decay of the gentleman and of gentlemanly hospitality, but for the first time gives an explicitly political dimension to social discontent. Alcibiades represents the Duke of Buckingham, to whom the play is dedicated, and who, along with Shaftesbury and two other opposition peers, had been committed to the Tower early in 1677 for attempting to secure the election of a new parliament.[17] Timon is a Restoration libertine who is appalled when his principles are turned against him by the infidelity of his friends, and Shadwell turns Shakespeare's sycophantic poet into a caricature of the chief celebrant of the libertine gentry, Dryden. Polemic morality is again allied to a polemically secular outlook: the virtuous fallen woman Evandra is emphatically preferred to the mercenary virgin Melissa (marriage being not 'a bond of Truth' but merely 'a few trifling Ceremonies', I, p. 212), and Alcibiades' mutilation of the Hermae is defended, in Shadwell's first contribution to the growing assault on Catholicism, by mockery of the very idea of a sacred object (IV, p. 248).

Timon denounces Athens as a 'Forest of two legg'd Beasts' (III, p. 242), but, characteristically, Shadwell does not leave us with an irreversible merging of the city and the wilderness. Unlike Wycherley's Manly, Timon does make the journey to the wilderness, but this is where he discovers the redemptive loyalty of the Fidelia-like Evandra.[18] Within the city, moreover, Alcibiades resolves to free public order from the contamination of individual appetite, decreeing that the 'base corrupted wills' of a few shall no longer be made 'the scope of Justice' (V, p. 272). Justice, so often wrapped in epistemological enigma, is here attained by a simple political reform. And the reform is democratic. Earlier in the play, Apemantus had savagely denounced aristocratic rank as corrupt when not merited and corrupting when it was (III, p. 231). Here Alcibiades, who had helped to establish the tyranny of the Four Hundred, now realizes that government should be 'in the Body of the People' (V, p. 272), and the play concludes with the people shouting '*Liberty*' (V, p. 273). For the first time, Shadwell articulates a radical opposition to the Stuart regime, heralding the overt and partisan politicization of drama that began in earnest later in the year, after Titus Oates's allegations in September initiated the Popish Plot scare.

In *Mithridates* (King's, February 1678), however, Lee continued more generally to contemplate the insoluble perplexities of political authority,

---

[17] See Gunnar Sorelius, 'Shadwell Deviating into Sense: *Timon of Athens* and the Duke of Buckingham', *Studia Neophilologica*, 36 (1964), 232–44; Alan S. Fisher, 'The Significance of Thomas Shadwell', *Studies in Philology*, 71 (1974), 225–46.

[18] John Edmunds rightly stresses Shadwell's debt to *Le Misanthrope*, but in my view understates the debt to *The Plain-Dealer* (' "Timon of Athens" blended with "Le Misanthrope": Shadwell's Recipe for Satirical Tragedy', *Modern Language Review*, 64 (1969), 500–7).

portraying not democratic activism but moral paralysis before the anomalies of paternal, royal, and providential power, though with a perhaps significant emphasis on a power struggle between a good and a bad heir. Once again, sexual rivalry between a king and his sons is used to test the limits and excesses of authority: the villainous Pharnaces lusts after Monima, the young wife of his father Mithridates, and eventually allies himself with his Roman enemies, while Mithridates is induced to fall in love with Semandra, who is betrothed to his virtuous son Ziphares. Mithridates is, like Alexander, a complex character, but Lee nevertheless takes father–son rivalry to new extremes by portraying Mithridates as forcibly marrying and then raping Semandra, and so provides a darker portrayal of paternal tyranny than even Otway had yet managed. In so doing, he repeatedly represents the family as a concatenation of hostile strangers: Ziphares, Mithridates reflects, is a 'Bosom-Wolf' (III. ii. 136). In a tableau at the beginning of Act IV, immediately after the rape, Mithridates is menaced with daggers by the ghosts of his sons (as Statira had been menaced by the ghosts of her parents), and in explicating the dream represented by the tableau, Mithridates describes how the form of Ziphares had (in a confounding of opposites typical of Lee) merged with that of his enemy Pompey and pierced his heart (IV. i. 60–1). The merging of opposites again illustrates the collapse of the moral systems that had informed the earliest heroic plays. When the father-king turns rapist, pat antitheses between love and filial duty become trite oversimplifications. The son's powerlessness to oppose paternal authority is no longer teeth-gritting loyalty but moral paralysis on a cosmic scale:

> Heav'n here is Bankrupt;
> The wondring Gods blush at their want of pow'r,
> And, quite abash'd, confess they cannot help me.
>
> (V. ii. 148–50)

And, for Semandra, the fundamental distinctions of religion itself lapse into amorphous uncertainty: 'Holy, Profane, | All things are now alike to my distraction' (III. ii. 604–5).

As political authority becomes problematic, so does linguistic authority, for the play depicts a constant struggle for control of language and the criteria of interpretation: characters, for example, are much concerned with the way in which their stories will be told, but are frequently unable to control the narratives of their lives. Mithridates, master of many languages (I. i. 433), regards his speech as an invincible expression of his power, his name as a word 'that comprehends all Honors, | All Titles, Riches, Power, all Majesty' (I. i. 226–7). By threatening to execute Ziphares, he forces Semandra to repudiate him, preventing her from expressing in language the love which she still feels, and deceiving Ziphares into seeing her as a stereotype of linguistic fallaciousness: 'What Story is not full of Womans falshood!' (IV. i. 293), he exclaims, imposing the wrong narrative pattern on her life and recalling her earlier fear that, should she betray Ziphares, men who 'read my Story' would 'Tear all the Rolls, or throw 'em to the Flames!' (II. i. 194–5). But Ziphares too feels that he has lost narrative control over his own life: Semandra, he laments, has 'told the story of my utter ruine' (IV. i. 498). Even Mithridates is linguistically vulnerable. Though 'Skilled in all Speeches of the babling World' (I. i. 434), he is readily suggestible, desiring Semandra and suspecting Ziphares as a result of linguistic manipulation by villainous subordinates. Finally, he dies wishing that his own story should never be told: 'No tongue relate the deeds this Hand has done' (V. ii. 404).

Nor can the 'babling'—Babel—of earthly discourse be elucidated by appeal to an ordering logos in the heavens. Semandra, for example, vainly asks the gods to heed her prayers, and on two occasions concludes that they are deaf.[19] As the play moves towards its bloody ending, Ziphares and Semandra's despairing sense that the gods are absent is only accentuated by transient mirages of order. As Mithridates faces defeat as a result of Pharnaces' rebellion, Semandra sees in his sufferings the providential justice she has so frequently demanded, and feels she can speak to the gods: she and Ziphares will tell them Mithridates' 'Story' (V. ii. 214). But Ziphares hears only the undistinguishable 'Voice of Fate' (V. ii. 245) in the din of the final carnage, and in its chaos he fails to recognize Semandra and fatally stabs her (V. ii. 280). In a characteristic confounding of moral categories, the virtuous man becomes the blindest destroyer in the cast. As she dies, Semandra at first envisages posthumous reunion with Ziphares, and even an assimilation of human nature into divine, but her actual experience of death (like that of Dryden's Cleopatra) is very different, being one of dislocation and the final extinction of speech:

> Methinks your Voice is faint
> As distant Ecchoes; and I am now far off:
> Alas, I know not where.
>
> (V. ii. 328–30)

Omens in Lee's earlier plays were supernatural, despite their impenetrability. But the events of *Mithridates* are initiated by a fraudulent omen, contrived by Pharnaces and a venal priest in order to halt Mithridates' marriage to Monima by playing on his 'mighty Faith | In holy Fables' (I. i. 77–8), the jibe asserting both his linguistic vulnerability and the unreality of celestial speech. The false omen moves the virtuous Ziphares to deride those who 'call the schreme of every hooting Owl, | Or croaking Raven, Fate's most dreadful Voice' (I. i. 328–9), and in the circumstances we can hardly disapprove. Yet this fraudulent omen of defeat is as perfectly fulfilled as any of Lee's genuinely

---

[19] II. i. 253; IV. i. 202–3.

celestial omens, though fulfilled by the very human agencies that created it. Fate and its signs originate not in the order of the heavens but in the chaos of human intentions. Despite his earlier scepticism about 'Fate's most dreadful Voice,' Ziphares claims to hear 'the Voice of Fate' (v. ii. 245) in the tumult of Pharnaces' rebellion; but even here the voice is man-made, uttered by drums and trumpets. When there is a genuine omen towards the end of the play, it is a curiously self-negating one, representing the extinction and reversion to formlessness of the cult objects with which men attempt contact with the gods:

> every shining Altar
> Dissolv'd to yellow puddle, which anon
> A flash of thirsty Lightning quite lick'd up.
>
> (v. ii. 46–8)

The licking lightning is imitating the tongue, though not a speaking or communicating tongue. Rather, it is reversing the most famous communication through tongues of flame: the miracle of Pentecost, which annulled the curse of Babel. Here the curse remains, and the tongues descend only to remove any apparent community of sign between the human and the divine.

A few months after the première of *Mithridates*, Titus Oates plunged the nation into chaos. As might be expected during a crisis of authority, the oppressive father remained a favourite dramatic figure, and its handling even by generally Tory writers implies a more divided and reserved interpretation of authority than that promoted by the exhumation in 1680 of Filmer's *Patriarcha* as a defence of patrilineal royal succession. Obviously, there were passionate and uncomplicated opponents of Exclusion, among playwrights as among the country at large (though the country at large persistently refused to provide a parliamentary majority of such people). But firm belief in James's divine right to the throne did not prevent grave worries about what he would do with it, and the predominant message from the pulpit was not that a popish successor presented no problems (though there certainly were defences of James's character), but that God commands obedience to any legitimate ruler, however tyrannical. In a sermon which stressed the iniquity of Rome and the sufferings of the Huguenots, the future non-juror George Hickes also emphasized the Christian's duty to accept martyrdom: 'when ever it shall please God to call them [the martyrs], or us, to such a degree of Persecution, that we shall be killed all the day long, and be counted as sheep for the slaughter; I question not but he will assist us in it'.[20] 'Although unrelenting in their attacks on the "senseless Superstitions of Rome," ' Margaret Jacob has written, 'churchmen like John Moore warned that "when we are so

---

[20] George Hickes, *The True Notion of Persecution Stated* (London, 1681), 32–3.

terrify'd about the events of things" we must resist under any circumstances recourse "to Cunning men for a Resolution." . . . . Moore and many of his colleagues were deeply troubled by the prospect of a Catholic monarch, yet they urged the passive acceptance of whatever might come.'[21] Several loyal dramatists were likewise 'terrify'd about the events of things'.

Precise correlation of plays and events is hazardous, since the dating of premières is so often imprecise or conjectural, and since the première date is manifestly not that of composition. Nevertheless, a fairly clear overall picture emerges. During the year or so after Oates's allegations, anxiety about government is the rule, though the anxiety is not necessarily subversive. By the second quarter of 1680, acquittals of Plot suspects became the norm, and although the conviction and execution of Lord Stafford at the end of the year gave some boost to the Plot's credibility, most onlookers at his execution believed him innocent. But Exclusion—first broached in Parliament in May 1679, with James's daughter Mary as the preferred successor—became an ever more obsessive question, especially after Charles's brief but serious illness in August 1679 gave the succession question new urgency. Nor were the King's own intentions clear: apart from the period of Charles's illness, James was in exile from March 1679 to February 1680, and he left for a further seventeen months of exile in October 1680. After the dissolution of the First Exclusion Parliament in July 1679, the newly elected Parliament was continually prorogued until October 1680, and during the winter of 1679–80 the Whigs kept up pressure on the King by mass petitions; by 'the fall of 1680, Whig strategy depended upon hovering close to the brink of civil war'.[22] From late 1679 until the Lords' rejection of the Exclusion Bill in November 1680, when expectations that Charles would cave in received a sharp setback, drama is extremely unsettled:[23] Otway's *The Souldiers Fortune*, with its memorable image of Courtine dangling in mid-air and singing loyal sentiments into the dark, dates from the middle of this period (June 1680). Crowne, who is normally considered a Tory writer, moved towards the opposition (or at least towards loyalty of particular complexity and gloom). In *The Loyal General* (*c.* December 1679) Nahum Tate, the future continuator of *Absalom and Achitophel*, produced a transparent pro-Monmouth and anti-Danby polemic. In *The Spanish Fryar* (November 1680) Dryden celebrated restoration of the true king, but catered to anti-Catholic sentiment. It is probably no accident that in the unsettled and uncertain year of 1680 there is also a move

[21] Margaret C. Jacob, *The Newtonians and the English Revolution 1689–1720* (Hassocks, 1976), 74. The reference is to John Moore, 'Sermon Preach'd before the Lord Mayor . . . Jan. 27, 1683/4', in *Sermons on Several Subjects*, ed. Samuel Clarke (London, 1715), 62.

[22] Ashcraft, *Revolutionary Politics*, 288.

[23] Susan J. Owen writes that 'The 1680/81 season sees an extraordinary . . . shift towards either moderation or outright Whiggery during a period of apparent Whig ascendancy' ('Interpreting the Politics of Restoration Drama', 71). My interpretation of the chronology is slightly different from hers, but her work on Exclusion Crisis drama is of the greatest importance.

towards a serious drama of domestic or at least private experience, avoiding a primary concern with politics: Otway's *The Orphan* (February 1680) is a key example. But, at the same time, there were new extremes of partisanship: William Whitaker's *The Conspiracy* (March) and Settle's *The Female Prelate* (May), dedicated to Shaftesbury, were the most virulent Tory and Whig plays yet to be staged. Settle followed up *The Female Prelate* by organizing the 1680 Pope-burning, and in the following year wrote *The Character of a Popish Successour*. After the Lords' rejection of the Exclusion Bill and, still more, after the dissolution of the Oxford Parliament, drama is predominantly, though not at first uncritically, Tory (both sides portray the King as weak and easily misled), and after the Oxford Parliament, during the final push against the Whigs, there emerges a comedy that is primarily rather than incidentally Tory in its message. From December 1680, with the banning of Lee's *Lucius Junius Brutus*, drama is also increasingly subject to political interference. Towards the end of the Crisis, even Lee was indulging in crude Tory triumphalism. The last Whig play is Settle's *The Heir of Morocco* (March 1682), but by 1683 Settle had become a Tory pamphleteer.

Appropriately, the onset of the crisis of authority was accompanied by a dramatization of the most archetypally problematic story of paternity and kingship, the Dryden–Lee *Oedipus* (Duke's, ?November/December 1678),[24] which resembles Lee's earlier plays in portraying the disintegration not only of specific social groups but of the very intellectual basis of order. For there is a persistent and bewildering collapse of normal social categories and polarities, Oedipus being both son and husband, citizen and 'stranger',[25] and—most disturbingly—regicide and rightful king: he is, as it were, both Cromwell and Charles II. Shocking syntheses of opposites are prominent: the same brands serve the same couples as nuptial and funeral torches (I. 44–6), the city is 'a crowded desart,' and there reigns 'A Midnight silence at the noon of day' (I. 419–20). And there is another, less absolute but nevertheless shocking, blurring of differentiation: between the unscrupulous would-be usurper Creon and the noble and just Oedipus, who incomprehensibly merges the roles of usurper and legitimate monarch. The deformed Creon is himself a synthesis of opposites, 'Half-minted with the Royal stamp of man; | And half o're-come with beast' (I. 140–1), so far outside known categories as to constitute a unique species in himself (I. 160–1). Though his uniqueness means that he cannot be contained in language, which describes the general and the customary, he of himself embodies no moral mystery and (most atypically for a figure in major Restoration drama) he is a character whose outward form is

---

[24] According to Dryden, 'I writ the First and Third Acts of *OEdipus*, and drew the *Scenary* of the whole Play' (*The Vindication of The Duke of Guise*, in *Works* (1735), v. 347). According to Alan Roper, 'the play was almost certainly completed before the Popish Plot became public knowledge in September 1678. But if, as seems likely, *Oedipus* was given its final form in the summer of 1678, then it would have been written at a time of growing suspicion' (California Dryden, xiii. 461–2). I follow Roper's tentative dating (pp. 443–4).

[25] I. 73, 226, 231, 298.

a direct sign of his instrinsic nature. But the chaotic visible form of the 'Monster' (III. 72) Creon becomes an unexpected counterpart to the chaotic moral essence of the '*Monster*' Oedipus (V. 145), whose nature embodies a riddle implicitly comparable to that of the Sphinx (III. 439–41).

Rituals of naming again cease to represent the reinstatement of the socially dislocated individual, and instead confirm his alienness. Throughout *Oedipus* there is a repeated and often unearthly naming of Oedipus and Jocasta, marking a gradual progress towards the final identification and disclosure of the guilty. Early in the play, for example, two human figures appear in the sky, crowned with the names of the couple. But the namings chart their progressive moral and social dislocation. Oedipus finds himself 'wandring in the maze of Fate' (III. 590), Jocasta longs to fly to 'some barren Island' (IV. 377) never before visited by man, and both are estranged not only from the community they have ruled but from all the received social patterns of human existence, to the point that the language which reflects those patterns cannot reflect the conditions of their union: 'What shall I call this Medley of Creation?' (V. 155), Oedipus asks, contemplating his sibling offspring.

Oedipus is not a unique monster, but an extreme example of a general condition: of the discrepancy between conventional visions of the family and its actual turmoil of hostility and desire. The menacing ghost of Laius (Oedipus' father), who appears to Tiresias in Act III, is yet another implacable Restoration father; Jocasta kills her children before her own suicide; she is plainly attracted to Oedipus because of his likeness to Laius, so that the marriage is essentially as well as accidentally incestuous (and indeed the attraction persists after the fatal disclosure); and, when Oedipus' Corinthian foster-father dies, his foster-mother promptly sends him a diamond ring along with a sexually inviting message (IV. 267–75). The special categories of parent and child have no special and particular passions belonging to them: only the general, universal passions of lust and hate. The accepted norms of civilization are not the true normality of human nature, and it is not merely Oedipus or Creon who is the monster, 'But Man, the very Monster of the World' (IV. 449). Nor is there a cosmic order beyond the chaos of human desire. Oedipus comes to feel that the most fitting image of his condition is a collapsing, lightless, and chaotic universe, where 'Gods meet Gods, and justle [joust] in the dark' (IV. 626). Tiresias advances the common argument that man, seeing only the bottom links of the chain, cannot comprehend the whole design (III. i. 239–48), but the ghost of Laius then portrays a malevolently deterministic universe in which the benign power that gave Oedipus 'every Kingly vertue' was overruled by an inexorable 'Fate, that sent him hood-winckt to the world' (III. 365–6) to be an agent of crime.

Sometime about the beginning of the Popish Plot crisis Ravenscroft turned to another archetypal dissolution of parent–child relationships, but his streamlined adaptation of *Titus Andronicus* presents a bald sequence of events, stripped of interpretative elaboration. The mutilated Lavinia communicates so quickly that she represents physical outrage far more than linguistic dispossession, and the book is no longer used as a criterion of civilization and a repository of knowledge and precedent: Lavinia has not instructed her nephew in Cicero, and does not use the text of Ovid in explaining what has happened to her. As the book, the icon of civilization, disappears (to be replaced by the rack which forces Aaron to narrate the truth in the final act), so do those opposites of civilization, the forest and the hunt, for Lavinia is now raped in the wild recesses of the imperial *garden*. (Similarly, Titus captures Chiron and Demetrius after luring them into his garden.) Rome remains a wilderness of tigers,[26] but there is no longer any implication that the wilderness and the city are normally distinct. Tamora's body is not cast into the wilderness, and Aaron is not captured near Shakespeare's 'wasted building' (V. i. 23) outside the city; both aliens remain within the city bounds at all times, and indeed the two gardens are the wildest settings that Ravenscroft creates. The play was not published until 1687, when it was dedicated to Lord Arundell of Wardour, who had been named by Titus Oates as one of the chief popish conspirators. In the prefatory material Ravenscroft states that the play had appeared very early in the crisis, and that it had condemned the rampant perjury of the time. Yet a play which sanctions tyrannicide, likens its heroes to Lucius Junius Brutus (IV, p. 37), declares that justice has fled from the earth, and shows disaster resulting from adherence to patrilineal succession does not at first glance seem tailor-made for the Tory cause, and Ravenscroft would have been exceptionally prescient to have seen through the Popish Plot in its earliest stages.

John Bancroft's *The Tragedy of Sertorius* (King's, by March 1679) portrays the destruction of an idealized defender of republican ideals, though there appears to be no detailed analogy to current politics, besides the portrayal of an assassination plot and a constant emphasis on mysteries and mazes. There is a more divided representation of authority in Crowne's *The Ambitious Statesman; or, The Loyal Favourite* (King's, March 1679), a play which parallels *Titus Andronicus* in incorporating allusion to the myth of the Thyestean banquet, which Crowne portrayed directly two years later. The plot is an intricate story of jealousy and political duplicity with some debts to *Othello*, though with the usual complication and blurring of roles: the Iago-figure is himself a dupe (as in *Don Carlos*), and the (loose) counterparts to Othello and Cassio each misinterpret the heroine's relations with the other. (The Constable of France has by deception alienated his son, the Duke of Vendosme, from his loved one, who then secretly marries the Dauphin; the Constable persuades Vendosme that she is the Dauphin's mistress, while the Dauphin becomes convinced that she is Vendosme's.) As usual, too, outsiders are omitted:

---

[26] Shakespeare, III. i. 54; Ravenscroft, IV, p. 29.

the jealous husband is, ominously, the heir to the throne, and the Iago chiefly works upon his own son. 'Were all mankind my Children,' he boasts in a chilling version of patriarchalism, 'I wou'd hang half, to rule the other half' (IV, p. 69). And, having duped the Constable into permitting Vendosme's torture and death, the Dauphin mockingly likens him to that archetypally destructive parent, Thyestes: 'Now thou maist eat thy Son' (V, p. 80).

In portraying characters destroyed by false appearances, Crowne reverts to his preoccupation with the sign as impenetrable, two-dimensional surface, as of the sea or a painting. 'Massy substances of things sink down,' muses Vendosme, 'And nothing stay's but Colours, Sounds, and Shadows. | What mighty things derive their power from Colours' (III, p. 32). When the King belatedly recognizes Vendosme's worth, Vendosme responds with a striking image of pure two-dimensionality, 'You guild a vanishing Shadow' (V, p. 86). And, as in *The Countrey Wit*, an actual portrait is the prime example of the incomplete sign, for the heroine's possession of Vendosme's portrait persuades the King of his guilt (IV, p. 67). The picture both symbolizes and furthers the incomplete representation of the self from which the tragedy arises. It has none of the barbaric exoticism of Othello's handkerchief, but rather denotes the everyday world of unpenetrated surfaces in which life is inescapably conducted. The pervasiveness of ambiguity necessitates royal authority, and exculpates it when it errs: tortured and dying through unmerited royal condemnation, Vendosme denies receiving 'Injuries,' because 'My present sufferings | Are what appearances gave warrant for' (V, p. 82). But to vindicate royal justice through the mouth of a dying and innocent victim of its fallibility is to do so only through a terrible paradox, far removed from the simple certitudes of 1660.

It is tempting to ask whether this play makes any reference to the current political situation. The play has no historical basis, and since Crowne freely chose to name his fictitious king Charles, and gave him a problematic but ultimately reformed heir, some parallels are probably being drawn. But who is the Constable? There is a temptation to identify every villainous statesman in late Carolean tragedy as Shaftesbury, and there are certainly telling resemblances to the Shaftesbury of Tory demonology and caricature: hypocritical championship of liberty, atheism masquerading as religious toleration (I, p. 8), physical infirmity (II, p. 23), record as a former rebel. But, overwhelmingly, the resemblances are to Danby, the recently fallen Lord Treasurer and chief minister, who had been impeached for high treason at the end of 1678 after the exposure of correspondence demanding money from France during the recent peace negotiations.[27] Danby's own inclinations, which he obviously had to subordinate to those of Charles, were pro-Anglican and anti-French, and he had at first been very keen to exploit the Plot, and indeed to use it to

---

[27] In his edition of *All for Love* (p. xvii), N. J. Andrew suggests that Photinus, the villain of Sedley's *Antony and Cleopatra*, might be a portrait of Danby (to whom *All for Love* was later dedicated).

oust James from politics.[28] At the time, he was suspected of wanting James out of the way 'so he might have the king the more absolutely in his own power',[29] and the Catholics blamed him even more than Shaftesbury for the prosecution of the Plot.[30] Danby did, however, decide by the end of 1678 that his interests were linked to those of James, and his initial zeal against the Plot did not prevent the absurd charges in his impeachment that he was popishly affected and had concealed the Plot. He was granted a royal pardon in mid-March, but the Commons nevertheless hoped to proceed with the impeachment.

All these details and more enter into the portrayal of the Constable. He has exercised power in the king's place, flattered tyranny (I, p. 3), amassed great wealth, and has a reputation for corruption (II, p. 24), as Danby very justly did; and, at the beginning of the play, he is secretly and treasonably corresponding with a foreign king (I, p. 2). He receives a royal pardon (II, p. 20) which does him no good (our uncertainty about the première date here becomes exasperating).[31] The portrayal of the fallen favourite's neglect by former flatterers is conventional enough, but also accurate, down to the detail of the sycophant who had bought a place but who was turned out without enjoying its profits.[32] His initial attempts to undermine the Dauphin may suggest Shaftesbury, but his subsequent hollow alliance with him certainly does not: the combination is more appropriate to Danby. And the sedition in which he is involved would, in early 1679, most compellingly evoke the Popish Plot (the word *plot* has some prominence). Vendosme's stoical acceptance of injustice certainly follows orthodox Anglican teaching on how to respond to tyranny. But Crowne does portray tyranny: the tyranny of a benevolent but misled king and a brutal, unscrupulous heir. Both reform, but not before their bad rule has exacted a terrible cost. The image of the parent eating the child, which occurs four times in Exclusion Crisis drama, is a signally pessimistic representation of authority.

The misinterpretation of innocence was a recurrent tragic theme during the Exclusion Crisis, being appropriated by the supporters both of Monmouth (*The Loyal General*) and James (*The Loyal Brother*). When Dryden revised— or rather reversed—Shakespeare in *Troilus and Cressida; or, Truth Found Too Late* (Duke's, by April 1679), however, he was still preoccupied with the misinterpreted innocence of the royal mistress (and, as the subtitle suggests, with the perils of seeking Truth in the treacherous texture of experience), though there is certainly topical stress on the dangers of faction, with some allusion to personalities: Patroclus, gifted in mimicry and nothing else,

[28] Keith Feiling, *A History of the Tory Party 1640–1714* (Oxford, 1924), 173.

[29] *Memoirs & Travels of Sir John Reresby Bart.* (London, 1904), 182. See also p. 189.

[30] Haley, *The First Earl of Shaftesbury*, 461.

[31] The play was entered in the *Term Catalogues* in June 1679 'and must have been performed two or three months earlier' (Danchin, *Prologues and Epilogues*, iii. 148).

[32] IV, p. 56; *Memoirs & Travels of Sir John Reresby Bart*, 190–2.

caricatures the Duke of Buckingham; Achilles and Ajax keep open house, like Shaftesbury; and Thersites becomes a satirist without guiding moral principle (Durfey later likened Shadwell to Thersites).[33] The play concludes by denouncing faction and exhorting 'obedience to . . . Kings' (V. ii. 326) and Ulysses' speech on degree is simplified into a homily on 'Supremacy of Kings' (I. i. 38). If the speech loses the problematic character that it has in Shakespeare, however, it also presents a greatly contracted rationale of authority. The vision of degree as a universal cosmic principle is dropped, the only natural analogy to the political order of men being that of the bees, and even here Agamemnon is the hive—the provider and refuge—rather than the ruler (I. i. 35–7).[34] On the Trojan side, Hector forthrightly denies that the degrees of nobility are unalterable cosmic principles. Reproving Troilus' aristocratic contempt for the rabble, he argues that the worshipper makes the god:

> And what are we, but for such men as these?
> 'Tis adoration, some say, makes a God . . .
> Ev'n those who serve have their expectances,
> Degrees of happiness, which they must share,
> Or they'll refuse to serve us.

> (III. ii. 313–19)

Moreover, although Dryden cuts some ugly elements from Shakespeare—Paris and Helen are not directly portrayed, and Achilles and Ajax are less overtly thuggish—he mitigates Shakespeare's ironic portrayal of power without entirely abandoning it: the re-establishment of Agamemnon's authority follows, and proceeds from, a terrible on-stage massacre in which the Trojans are unchivalrously surrounded and slaughtered by the superior force of Achilles' Myrmidons. As so often, authority is affirmed, but not glamorized.

The clearest departure from Shakespeare, however, comes in the transformation of Cressida into a slandered innocent, forced by Calchas (a more directly destructive father than in Shakespeare) to strengthen his position by dissembling love to Diomede. Yet more clearly than in *All for Love*, a woman becomes the victim of a posthumous reputation which obliterates her essential character. Dryden retains from Shakespeare the episode in which Troilus, Cressida, and Pandarus predict, with varying degrees of unconscious irony, the future significance of their names as synonyms for truth, falsity, and pimping (III. ii. 56–83),[35] but he adds the irony that the woman's name is to become a false sign. Regularly, indeed, Dryden associates control of language with men and male activities. Agamemnon opens the play meditating on 'every Action of Recorded Fame' (I. i. 3),[36] clearly thinking of military action, and

---

[33] *Sir Barnaby Whigg*, III, p. 28.

[34] In 'Dryden's *Albion and Albanius*: The Apotheosis of Charles II', Paul Hammond perceptively argues that the perception of monarchy which had shaped the iconography of the pre-Civil War masques was no longer available to Dryden when he wrote *Albion and Albanius*.

[35] Cf. Shakespeare, *Troilus and Cressida*, III. ii. 171–203.   [36] Cf. ibid. I. iii. 13–14.

Hector hails Nestor as a 'good old Chronicle' (IV. ii. 125).[37] But Cressida can never earn such a title. Urging Troilus to renounce her for the public good, Hector asks whether he can 'stand the shock of Annals, blotted thus, | *He sold his Country for a womans love!*' (III. ii. 298–9); and, when Troilus concludes that Cressida is unfaithful, he prays that 'blushing Virgins, when they read our Annals,' may 'Skip o're the guilty page that holds thy Legend' (IV. ii. 389–90).

During the scene in which Hector steels Troilus to renounce love for the sake of 'The publick' (III. ii. 302), the question is whether Troilus deserves the name of friend and 'the name of man,' or merely 'The name of Brother' (III. ii. 341, 372, 377). Traditionally enough, recovery of the social self is here associated with the recovery of social nomenclature, as when Antony yields to the barrage of his Roman titles. Hector's claims are more sympathetically presented than those of the Romans, though the surrender of Cressida in fact destroys the city whose claims Hector here urges. But Hector's nomenclature is not only social but, quite flagrantly, masculine ('man', 'Brother'). Earlier, when Andromache had wished to cast off womanhood so as to attain the 'nobler name' (than wife) of Hector's 'friend' (II. i. 145), Hector had granted it her: 'thou manlier Virtue come; | Thou better Name than wife!' (II. i. 156–7). But Cressida remains outside such terminology, and she starts at a disadvantage, for, when she and Troilus first swear fidelity to each other, he gives particularly ungracious expression to the male preoccupation with female truth: 'Oh that I thought truth cou'd be in a woman!' (III. ii. 56). Their love scenes are marked by hesitancy and inarticulacy, and she is unable to talk Troilus out of his suspicion: it 'Has struck me dumb!' (V. ii. 208), he will 'stop [his] ears' (V. ii. 223), and she can only persuade him by abandoning speech for self-annihilation. The other Trojan women (even, ultimately, Andromache) are also linguistically impotent: Polyxena writes a letter to Achilles, dissuading him from combat with Hector, and Andromache attempts to dissuade Hector from entering the fatal battle, but the two moves cancel each other out, since the discovery that Polyxena has written to Achilles induces Hector to disregard Andromache's advice.

Andromache's and Polyxena's voices are voices of peace, raised against the male specialism of war, and they reflect a consistently emphasized contrast between male and female outlooks: Hector sees his debate with Andromache as one between the 'manly' and the 'woman' (V. i. 80–2). Every Trojan male, regardless of age, participates in the final battle (V. i. 181–4), Troilus laments for the dead Cressida 'like a woman' (V. ii. 283), and Calchas has 'a womans longing' to return to the city he has betrayed (IV. ii. 251). The primary death of Dryden's tragedy is not that of Hector, which is almost casually narrated, but that of Cressida. But, although women become the source of compassion, citizenship, and peace, they lack the means to represent themselves within the

---

[37] Cf. ibid. IV. v. 201.

preordained polarities of innocence and guilt, truth and falsehood. Cressida is determined to 'be justify'd or dye' (V. ii. 182), but her 'innocence' can only 'appear like guilt' (V. ii. 213), and she dies. The question of Cressida's loyalty is, indeed, impossibly distorted by the terms in which Troilus poses it: namely, whether she is an incarnation of truth. For Cressida becomes caught in a version of the Cretan paradox: she can only symbolize truth because she was lying to Diomede; had her words been truthful, she would have symbolized falsehood. Alithea—'Truth'—becomes involved in a comparable aporia at the end of *The Country-Wife*. In both cases truth and falsity, the fundamental categories of interpretation, dissolve into oneness before the paradoxes of experience.

Troilus and Cressida had acknowledged a crisis without allowing it to become the *raison d'être* of the play. But, in most tragedies, it now was. Lee's *Caesar Borgia; Son of Pope Alexander the Sixth* (Duke's, May 1679), for example, vigorously lampoons Romish cruelty and corruption, and comes complete with a murdered corpse in a chair, obviously alluding to that of Sir Edmund Berry Godfrey (V. ii. 4b–c).[38] The dying Borgia quotes Milton's mockery of Catholicism in the description of the Paradise of Fools,[39] and then prophesies that his own spirit will inspire the assassinations of Henri III and IV of France and threaten the happy England of Charles II. Perhaps we should not overinterpret the suggestive synthesis of opposites achieved by putting Milton in the mouth of a deranged and regicidally minded pope's bastard,[40] but there are clearer signs that Lee is as uneasy about the opponents of Rome as he is about Rome itself; for Machiavelli, the principal villain, is an Epicurean and a republican.[41]

Lee once again stresses the general incoherence of the state and family. In the past, Borgia and his brother, the Duke of Gandia, have both slept with their sister (I. i. 269), Lucretia, and now both love Bellamira. Although Bellamira loves Gandia, her father forces her to marry Borgia, who eventually murders brother, wife, and father-in-law; briefly, he feigns willingness to surrender Bellamira to Gandia, but this hypocritical display of noble rivalry only serves to emphasize how distant the social hero of early Restoration tragedy now is. *Caesar Borgia* is yet another version of *Othello*, with Iago's role taken by a re-creation of Iago's literary prototype, Machiavelli, and once again the absence of literal aliens shows that the sources of chaos lie within

---

[38] Godfrey, the magistrate who had taken the first depositions of Titus Oates, was found murdered in a ditch on 17 Oct. 1678. It was later alleged that the body had been removed from Somerset House in a sedan chair. Here, the Duke of Gandia's body is taken to the Tiber in a chair and thrown in.

[39] V. iii. 326–32; *Paradise Lost*, iii. 490–6.

[40] I am not sure whether the Milton quotation is functionally allusive. In the previous act, Machiavelli freely reworks the exiled Suffolk's curse from 2 *Henry VI*, and this reworking appears to be simple theft (*Caesar Borgia*, IV. i. 263–91; 2 *Henry VI*, III. ii. 308–37).

[41] The republican Henry Neville had published a translation of Machiavelli's works in 1675, and his *Discourses* were of course an important source of republican theory, used by Lee in his critical portrayal of republican revolution, *Lucius Junius Brutus*.

family and society: Borgia, the jealous husband, is a bastard, but he is also head of state, and Machiavelli is not an unpromoted malcontent but an admiring associate who wishes to make his lovesick master as superior to passion as Cato Uticensis (III. i. 333). The opening visual image of the play is of an invasion of the strange, with 'American Boys' and Indian screens cluttering an Italian chamber of state, but the ultimate effect is of a confounding of cultural styles and norms rather than of a challenge from the barbarian to the civilized, and the newcomers pointedly fail to shape the plot in the way initially expected: they are intended as a bribe to turn Machiavelli against Borgia, but the temptation of the exotic never figures among his motives. Indeed, while clearly a figure of shocking cruelty, he idealizes the glories of ancient Rome and wishes to re-create them in Borgia; Iago is now the character with the most coherent attachment to political order. As Machiavelli moves into social centrality, so the virtuous victims move in the opposite direction: after all, Gandia not only loves his brother's wife, but has also slept with his sister.

Sometime in this period, Lee wrote a more exclusively anti-Catholic play, *The Massacre of Paris*, which was not staged until after the Revolution (see below, p. 358).[42] A weak but not evil king (named Charles) is pressured by a fanatical close relative—here his mother—into sanctioning the St Bartholomew Massacre: an act described as 'Royal Justice' (III. ii. 223), though it in fact denies 'Justice' (V. iv. 51) to thousands. The play is also remarkable for its favourable treatment of a former rebel, the Huguenot Admiral (?Monmouth), who champions 'Liberty of Conscience and Religion' (II. i. 107). If the rebel becomes morally central, royalty is correspondingly degraded, the Queen Mother becoming the stranger within the gates, threatening (as her own son admits) to 'turn a City to a Wild' (I. ii. 75). As in *The Rival Queens*, the deconsecration of the traditionally sacred is associated with reiterated imagery of the body and its dismemberment, culminating in the display of the Admiral's mutilated corpse.[43] Even the soul becomes deeply implicated in the body: the dying Admiral's soul, for example, is reluctant to leave it (V. iv. 44). As a result, Catholicism (possibly religion itself) resembles the self-apotheosis of Lee's Alexander: a pretended divinity, masking the self-fulfilment of the body in the destruction of other bodies.

[42] Hume argues that the banning is unlikely to have occurred before June 1680, since at that time Settle's *The Female Prelate* was holding the stage, whereas bannings and excisions became frequent after the banning of *Lucius Junius Brutus* ('The Satiric Design of Nat. Lee's *The Princess of Cleve*', *Journal of English and Germanic Philology*, 75 (1976), 117–38 (pp. 118–23), repr. in Robert D. Hume, *The Rakish Stage: Studies in English Drama, 1660–1800* (Carbondale and Edwardsville, Ill., 1983), 111–37 (pp. 114–18)). J. M. Armistead argues on internal grounds that the play 'was composed in late 1678 or 1679' (*Nathaniel Lee*, 96). Antony Hammond, 'The "Greatest Action": Lee's *Lucius Junius Brutus*', in *Poetry and Drama 1570–1770*, ed. Coleman and Hammond, 173–85 (p. 176), argues for 1679. One difference between *The Massacre of Paris* and *The Female Prelate* is that the former constitutes a direct attack on Charles.

[43] Candy B. K. Schille notices the imagery of physical dismemberment ('Reappraising "Pathetic" Tragedies: *Venice Preserved* and *The Massacre of Paris*', *Restoration*, 12 (1988), 33–45).

Factional massacre also figures in Otway's impressive revision of *Romeo and Juliet* as *The History and Fall of Caius Marius* (Duke's, October 1679),[44] in which the love story is relocated amidst the conflict between Marius and Sulla ('Sylla'),[45] Romeo becoming Marius Junior and Juliet Lavinia, the daughter of Metellus, who was once a benefactor of Marius but is now allied with Sylla, and wishes him to marry Lavinia. The conflict is ostensibly one of class, Sylla being a patrician and Marius a *novus homo* (I. 60–5), but this is one of many areas in which social terminology proves unstable, since Marius' side also denounces Sylla as a presumptuous upstart (I. 269), and the prevailing impression is that man, the political animal, is simply a predator who can shout slogans at his victims:

SYLLA. My Name thou hast heard,
   And fled from. I am the Friend of *Rome*,
   The Terrour and the Bane of thee her Foe.

(III. 361–3)

The litanies of each side are meaningless and interchangeable.

Sylla here treats his own name as a symbol of political power, though the actual effect is quite contrary: to draw the personal name into the relativism and insignificance of the political Babel. In Shakespeare, despite Juliet's 'What's in a name?' (II. ii. 43), the name records the inescapable claims of social origin, but here the heroine's question is supported by a widespread weakening of the power and stability of names: hailed as 'Father' by his son, Marius wishes to be called 'by some other Name' (III. 197) and commands him to 'Go where I never more may hear thee nam'd' (III. 220), rendering names and the social bonds which they signify equally mutable and vacant. At one point, successive and virtually identical speeches from the two opposing factions shift the crowd from cries of '*Marius! Marius! Marius!* No *Sylla!* no *Sylla!* no *Sylla!*' (II. 441) to those of '*No Marius!* no *Marius!*' (II. 490). But the mass chanting of names is as redundant as it is mindless, since Marius promptly conquers by force. Nomenclature is fixed by power. As the turncoat Cinna remarks after switching to Marius' side and gaining the semantic authority of an army,

How many Slaves,
Traitours, and Tyrants, Villains was I call'd
But yesterday? Yet now their Consul *Cinna*.

(V. 1–3)

---

[44] There is an excellent discussion of this play in Jessica Munns, ' "The Dark Disorders of a Divided State": Otway and Shakespeare's *Romeo and Juliet*', *Comparative Drama*, 19 (1985), 347–62.

[45] In the course of their political conflict Gaius Marius (*c.*157–86 BC) and his erstwhile protégé Lucius Cornelius Sulla (*c.*138–78 BC) both seized power in Rome by military force, revealing the vulnerability of the Republic to ambitious generals.

Even the lovers' marriage is a 'blessed *deed*' (III. 129; italics added), performed by a bribed and anonymous friar. There are no 'holy words',[46] and a
ceremony of sacred language is consequently transformed into one of mere
materialistic action.

Marius and Sylla alike use the rhetoric of the liberator in an attempt to enslave Rome. *Slave* is a standard term of political abuse, and the indiscriminate
massacre of senators, matrons, and children which constitutes Marius' final
triumph is represented as a slaughter of slaves. Beneath the sham political
creeds, the essential distinction is simply between those who seek to enslave
and those who accept bondage. The Roman mob alternate in their acclama-
tions of two indistinguishable despots, and the craving for bondage colours
even the relationship of Marius Junior and Lavinia, Marius Junior describing
himself as 'the Slave of strong Desires' and a 'Slave that lies | Chain'd to the
Floor' (I. 339–43). There is not yet a sense, as there is in *Venice Preserv'd*, that
the craving for bondage is universal, but it is clearly implied that politics are
rooted in man's propensity to enslave and be enslaved, and that the language
of political principle is a façade behind which the primitive processes of
subjugation are enacted. The lovers' passion is no longer a redemptive persistence of harmony, but is rather the noblest variation of the instinct for subjection, their participation in the general condition being indicated when, in the
end, they become two casualties in a mass carnage.

Names define not fixed and immutable identities and relationships but
transient roles and alliances arising from the fluctuations of political circumstance. Such fluctations threaten even the continuity of personal identity.
Marius Junior protests that his father must 'Create me o're agen' if he wishes
him to renounce Lavinia (I. 337), but later does (briefly) allow himself to be
new created, agreeing not to consummate his marriage without Marius' approval (III. 227–39). And Marius Senior finds that his political decline challenges his felt continuity of self:

> If I am *Caius Marius*, if I'm he
> That brought *Jugurtha* chain'd in triumph hither;
> If I am he that led *Rome*'s Armies out . . .
> Why does she [Rome] use me thus?
>
> (I. 171–8)

And the felt continuity *is* deceptive. At the nadir of his political fortunes, he is
a hunted and exiled outcast in the countryside, betrayed by former clients and
dependants, who disregard the obligations that are fundamental to social
existence. At this stage he appears a noble and Lear-like victim of injustice,
and the resemblance to *King Lear* becomes overt when Lavinia takes on the
role of Cordelia, aiding the destitute Marius in a moving scene of reconciliation. Yet the suffering and reconciliation in the wilderness yield no enduring

---

[46] *Romeo and Juliet*, II. vi. 6.

knowledge, constituting a closed, separate phase of Marius' identity that lapses when another return to power re-creates his old arrogance and cruelty. In this final version of his self he forgetfully kills Lavinia's father, perpetrating the very violation of obligation that he had lamented in his destitution, and only remembering her benefactions when the deed is done. Obligation, which is so repeatedly dishonoured in this play, is the foundation of society; yet, to be honoured, obligation must be recorded and remembered, and signification and memory are too unstable and transient to permit this.

The illusory pastoral idyll does, indeed, seem to promise a stabilization and reordering of language. When Lavinia enters after wandering through the woods, she describes finding her name carved in the bark of a 'well-grown Oak' (IV. 313), incorporated in the processes of nature and enshrined in a stereotype of permanence. The discovery impels her to call for her beloved Marius, but—a hint of the continuing imperfection of nomenclature—the wrong Marius answers (IV. 315–16). Nevertheless, Marius Senior addresses her in speech that rejects the nomenclature of faction: 'let me bless thee, though thy Name's my Foe' (IV. 335). But his change of language is as transient as his change of nature, and shortly before his murder of Lavinia's father he is calling,

> Let every Tongue proclaim aloud *Metellus;*
> Till I have dasht him on the Rock of Fate.
> Then be his Name forgot, and heard no more.
>
> (V. 246–8)

As the killing of Metellus shows, Otway's version of *Romeo and Juliet* brings no concluding reconciliation of faction, no final affirmation of community. Even as Marius' bloody victory runs its course, news comes of yet another re-distribution of power, with Sylla once again marching on Rome to subject it to his will.

Social incoherence is, predictably, reflected in Otway's habitual stress on disorientation and isolation: characters are repeatedly imaged as wanderers in the wilderness, and the image is literalized when Lavinia and the Marii meet in just such circumstances, Lavinia banished as a 'Vagrant' by her father (II. 143), the Marii exiled from their native city. Exile and slavery sum up the warring but inseparable aspects of man's biform nature, for man imaginatively veers between nostalgia for the solitude of the primal wilderness and a cringing acceptance of bondage. This unusually grim representation of man's twin character as savage and citizen was to generate the calamities in Otway's two mature tragedies, but a social vision such as this forms a poor basis for partisan panegyric. Marius is one of the many stage versions of Shaftesbury to appear during this period,[47] but Otway does not respond to the great

---

[47] John Wallace ('Otway's *Caius Marius* and the Exclusion Crisis', *Modern Philology*, 85 (1987–8), 363–72) argues against the traditional identification of Marius and Shaftesbury. But see Barbara A.

subversive by affirming any contrary scheme of order: when Marius plans 'inverted Order' (II. 506), he is planning to liberate slaves, and slavery can hardly constitute a social norm. Rather, Otway simply contemplates man's infinite capacity for chaos. In portraying a Rome divided in its support for rival yet equally worthless masters, Otway reached his mature view of the human condition: as a state of agonized suspension between meaningless choices.

Far less complex, though just as pessimistic, is Tate's pro-Monmouth play *The Loyal General* (*c.* December 1679), whose unjustly misrepresented hero, Theocrin, defeats a rebellion, is suspected of courting popular favour, and loses his general's commission, all of which provides a fair résumé of Monmouth's fortunes over the previous year.[48] Another familiar figure is the villainous favourite Escalus, undone by the discovery of his treasonable correspondence with a foreign ruler: Danby once more. There does not appear to be a direct representation of James, but the haughty Thracian King Abardanes, who offers his troops to quell native unrest, clearly reflects fears about the royal brothers' relationship with Louis XIV (the initial Plot hysteria had brought fears of a French invasion). There is criticism of the court, and the King eventually abdicates, after a reign marked by spectacularly bad judgement in the choice of favourites, and culminating in a general death of the innocent. It is left to the Senate (Parliament) to choose his successor.

Serious drama in 1679 is thus predominantly anti-court, even when (as in *The Ambitious Statesman*) the exhortation is to loyalty. The prologue to *Caius Marius* expresses hearty relief at Charles's recovery from illness, but the only tragedy which is positively supportive of court interests is Dryden's *Troilus and Cressida*, and even that is hardly a paean to divine right monarchy: ''Tis adoration, some say, makes a God' (III. ii. 314). Dryden supportively portrays the quarrel and reconciliation of two royal brothers (Hector and Troilus), but otherwise there is not an iota of specific support for James in the drama of 1679. This is hardly surprising, since James's cause seemed hopeless once he had been exiled in March. But, by the end of the year, the situation had become more complex. On the one hand, Charles's illness concentrated the minds of those who feared a popish successor. On the other, James's brief return from exile at this time provoked far less hostility than had been feared, and Charles felt able to recall him early in 1680. 'By 1680

Murray, 'The Butt of Otway's Political Moral in *The History and Fall of Caius Marius* (1680)', *Notes and Queries*, 234 (1989), 48–50.

[48] Monmouth started to 'affect popularity' (John Miller, *Charles II*, 300) in 1678, and in May and June 1679 he defeated a Covenanters' rebellion in Scotland. During Charles's serious illness in Aug. 1679, the King's ministers recalled James from exile in Flanders, fearing that Monmouth might stage a coup. And, when James left for a second, brief, exile in Edinburgh, Monmouth was deprived of his generalship and sent to Holland. After his unbidden return in Nov., he was stripped of all remaining offices.

the nascent Tory reaction against the Whigs' radicalism was apparent, but Charles hesitated to throw all his weight behind the Tories, despite James's urging.'[49] But, as the seventeen months without a parliamentary sitting drew to a close, James became vulnerable again. By September 1680 he was fearing impeachment; and, on 20 October, the day before the opening of the Second Exclusion Parliament, he again went into exile, lest Parliament commit him to the Tower. It should be no surprise, therefore, to find dramatists during this period variously partisan, uncertain, and ducking for cover.

Crowne is a useful barometer. Like Otway, he raided Shakespeare in order to portray the horrors of faction, adapting the third and subsequently the second parts of *Henry VI* as *The Misery of Civil-War* (Duke's, December 1679 or January 1680) and *Henry the Sixth, The First Part* (Duke's, ?January–March 1681). But the two plays, separated by at least a year, are very different in outlook. *The Misery of Civil-War* is the most polemic Tory play yet written, its theme being the prolonged horror which results from the disturbance of patrilineal succession. The fundamental postulate of the play is that the Yorkist claim to the throne is unquestionable, and that Henry's is vitiated by the ancestral crime of usurpation: shortly before his murder, Henry is visited by the ghost of Richard II, who promises him salvation but asserts the inalienable right of the blood-line to the throne. To emphasize the point, Edward IV becomes a clear representation of Charles II, absolved of the complicity in murder that tarnishes his Shakespearian original and given a correspondingly greater amorousness and negligence. These are largely extenuated, though his Dorimant-like faithlessness, supported by the belief that the Pope can nullify his oaths, drives Lady Elianor Butler to suicide. This is the most favourable dramatization of Stuart kingship yet to appear in the Crisis, but there is nevertheless ample stress on the brutality of each faction, and it is unnerving to hear the conventional Tory rhetoric against rebellion being uprooted and put in the mouths of the wrong (that is Henry's) side. The fundamental message (even if delivered by the wrong king) is that gloomy axiom of loyalism, 'the greatest Tyrant | Is to be chose before the least Rebellion' (IV, p. 44). This axiom is all the gloomier because Edward IV resembles Charles II not only in amorousness but in the possession of a terrifying younger brother. Crowne's gloom, however, is not so obviously loyal in his adaptation about a year later of 2 *Henry VI*, probably produced in the interval between the second Exclusion Bill and the Oxford Parliament, and dedicated to the Whig Sedley. Indeed, the play was suppressed because of its fiercely hostile portrayal of Catholicism.[50] (It was about the time of the Second Exclusion Bill that Dryden's anti-Catholic *The Spanish Fryar* appeared, and this was likewise to be dedicated to a Whig.) The murder of Duke

---

49 John Miller, *James II: A Study in Kingship*, rev. edn. (London, 1989), 94–5.

50 In the dedication of *The English Frier* (1690), Crowne says the play 'was stifled by command' (sig. [A3ᵛ]).

Humphrey provides another allusion to that of Godfrey,[51] and the Yorkist pursuit of power is now associated more with cynical ambition than hereditary right.

In between these adaptations Crowne produced his *Thyestes* (Duke's, March 1680), which is also pessimistic about royal and patriarchal authority. It is dominated by images of estrangement and exile ('Man is a vagabond', Atreus proclaims in the final speech, V, p. 55), the insecurity of relationship and place proceeding from insecurity of knowledge. Certainty is unattainable, and the political consequences of uncertainty are disastrous. Himself misled by jealous delusions, King Atreus vengefully ensnares his victims in cruel and fatal deceptions, to the point that the philosopher Peneus, who has spent eighty years cultivating innocence, is tricked into being an accessory to murder. In the past, Thyestes has raped the wife of his younger brother Atreus, and has subsequently lived a life of penitent exile in a cave. Believing his wife a willing adulteress, Atreus has cruelly imprisoned her, and wrongly doubts the legitimacy of his heirs; and doubt has transformed him from a benevolent man into a monstrous tyrant. He lures Thyestes back from exile by sending him the golden ram which signifies the transmission of royal power, and then accomplishes his famous vengeance, feeding the father on the flesh of his son at what is apparently a feast of reconciliation. In the process he drives to suicide his own daughter, who loves Thyestes' son and is used as the bait to draw him to destruction. This is a play of intense political anxiety, with its portrayal of hollow amity between royal brothers, and of a tyrant who deceives his victims with promises of reconciliation and then performs abominable murder with the aid of a priesthood plainly modelled on that of Rome. 'Shall I trust my Brother and a Crown, | Two of the *uncertain'st* things?' (IV, p. 36; italics added), ponders Thyestes, rightly, for neither family nor kingship offers any sources of certainty: the father unknowingly devours his son, satisfying his oppressor's deranged sense of 'Justice' (V, p. 50); the King is unsure of his heirs; the sacred token by which kingship is transmitted becomes an instrument of homicidal fraud; and intrinsic character is unstable, providing no assurance of kingly quality, for the good man has become a tyrant and the rapist a good man. Elsewhere, Crowne uses the elusiveness of knowledge to portray kingship as a necessary guarantee of stability, but here kingship is itself irremediably contaminated by uncertainty.

At about the same time, however, was staged the most fervently Tory play so far to appear: William Whitaker's *The Conspiracy* (Duke's, March 1680), in which a Sultan is murdered, despite quieting popular discontent about his 'lustful Scepter' (III, p. 27), and there is an unsuccessful attempt to replace his rightful heir (the first favourable stage representation of James) with another of his sons. Even here, all around the King is not well, since he is deceived by

---

[51] Wikander, 'The Spitted Infant', 348.

corrupt relatives, mistrusts his loyal Queen, and (without being personally culpable) presides over a court where merit is neglected:

> The Royalist in vain to Court does go;
> The Rogue that made him needy, keeps him so. . . .
>   we blame the Emperour
> Sometimes for things that are not in his pow'r.

(IV, pp. 41–2)

The prologue and Ravenscroft's epilogue reveal a significant new mood, the former urging loyalty to the King and suspension of judgement about the Plot, the latter condemning the lust for executions. When Ravenscroft eventually published his *Titus Andronicus*, reinterpreting it as an attack upon the Plot hysteria, he used this prologue and epilogue, stating that the original ones were lost.

But *The Conspiracy* was an early swallow, and concerted opposition to Exclusion perhaps does not start to appear until after the Lords' rejection of the second Exclusion Bill (some première dates are too conjectural to state this with confidence). Shortly after Whitaker's play there appeared the most violently anti-Catholic drama yet to reach the stage, Settle's *The Female Prelate* (Duke's, May 1680), which lampoons popish lust, cruelty, and hypocrisy, and claims to authority over princes, and was later published with a dedication to the Earl of Shaftesbury. Whereas Lee's banned *The Massacre of Paris* directly attacks Charles, Settle's professed and perhaps sincere stance is the standard one of reverence for the King combined with fear of the dangerous influences around him: in *The Character of a Popish Successour* (1681) he singles Charles out as 'the best of Kings',[52] and in the dedication of *Fatal Love* (?summer/ September 1680) he praises him as '*the Glorious Son of the Unhappy Charles*' (sig. [A3]). The hero of *The Female Prelate* is, indeed, the son of a murdered ruler.

Joanna Anglica, one of the few Tamora-like outsiders in Carolean drama, is a rejected mistress of the old Duke of Saxony, and has poisoned him after returning to his court in the guise of a priest. She retains her priestly disguise and during the course of the play is elected Pope. In one of Settle's many intricately flawed judicial rituals, the criminal acts as judge and the innocent 'King' is labelled 'a Criminal' (I, p. 17); for Joanna uses forged evidence of the old Duke's heresy to ensure that the Consistory Court blesses the murder and condemns his son and successor to imprisonment. The absence of justice is repeatedly stressed and, with the human criterion of justice neutralized, there is the familiar descent into competing schemes of vengeance. As usual, however, Settle establishes no standards to distinguish between permissible and impermissible schemes of vengeance: the young Duke is obviously right to

---

[52] [Elkanah Settle], *The Character of a Popish Successour, and what England May Expect from Such a One*, 3rd edn. (London, 1681), 10. Loyalty to Charles is also Shadwell's constant position.

wish to avenge his father, Joanna was obviously wrong to avenge her sexual betrayal, and that (apparently) is that. Other dramatists deliberately show the difficulty of defining civilized absolutes amidst the Hobbesian clash of competing wills, but there is always the suspicion that Settle is doing so by accident, as the by-product of a more simple attempt to show just individuals trapped in an unjust order. The image of the just person in the unjust order is clearly conveyed in the co-ordinated bedroom tricks in which Joanna and her former lover Lorenzo gratify their lusts for Saxony and his wife, Angeline, Joanna impersonating Angeline in the Duke's bed while Lorenzo impersonates the Duke in Angeline's (to her considerable, though subsequently regretted, satisfaction). The suppression of identity for the sake of lust does not highlight (as it does in Otway and Wycherley) any fundamental tension between man's instinctual and social natures. Settle's dual bedroom trick simply puts the wrong individuals in the wrong places. *The Female Prelate* is a tragedy of leaders in the wrong religion, and lovers in the wrong beds.

By the end of the year, however, support for James was growing. If Crowne and Dryden grew more concerned about him, Tate moved in the opposite direction. In choosing to rewrite *King Lear* as *The History of King Lear* (Duke's, *c*. New Year 1680/1), he chose as his source a play triply concerned with traduced, dispossessed, and exiled loyalty, and altered Shakespeare so as to ensure that loyalty was recognized and restored.[53] In addition to the notorious happy ending, he equally notoriously supplied a romance for Edgar and Cordelia, which reworks the doomed romance of Theocrin and the Princess Arviola in *The Loyal General*.[54] But Theocrin had been Monmouth; Edgar, the legitimate heir of Gloucester and, through his attachment to Cordelia, of Lear as well, can only evoke James. Tate cannot, indeed, wait to signal his sympathies, for the very first speech of the play is a rewriting of Edmund's speech on bastardy, with 'Now, gods, stand up for bastards!' (I. ii. 22) replaced by the more topically precise 'And base-born Edmund spite of law inherits' (I. i. 21). To portray unregarded loyalty, however, the dramatist must also portray an unregarding king. *The History of King Lear* does not offer the *Angst*-ridden loyalty of *The Ambitious Statesman*, but (like much Tory drama) it does offer a critical loyalty.

But Tate's modifications of Shakespeare are not only political, for he also abolishes the problems of signification which dominate the original. 'I cannot heave | My heart into my mouth' (I. i. 91–2), for example, is inverted into 'I can't dissemble' (I. i. 103), and indeed Cordelia never has any difficulty in controlling language, for her coldness to her father *is* in fact dissembled, in order to avert an unwanted marriage to Burgundy. The play concludes not

[53] For a detailed study of the play's politics, see Nancy Klein Maguire, 'Nahum Tate's *King Lear*: "the king's blest restoration" ', in *The Appropriation of Shakespeare: Post-Renaissance Reconstructions of the Works and the Myth*, ed. Jean I. Marsden (London, 1991), 29–42.

[54] See Nahum Tate, *The History of King Lear*, ed. Black, pp. xvi–xvii.

with language dissolving before the incomprehensible but with Lear looking forward to a tidily ordered narrative, 'Cheered with relation of the prosperous reign | Of this celestial pair' (V. vi. 150–1), and with the triumph of 'truth' (V. vi. 160), free of the difficulties which had shrouded it in Dryden's *Troilus*. Yet, at the same time, language is now a vehicle more of private than of social values. When Edgar reclaims his name it is not after his public combat with Edmund—there is no concealment of identity here—but in a private *éclaircissement* with Cordelia, conducted in a field (III. iv. 57–9).[55]

The flaws of monarchs in Tate's *King Lear* and *The Loyal General* are extravagance and unwise promotions. These reappear in his *The History of King Richard the Second* ('yet still the Court dances after the *French* Pipe . . . Knaves in Office, all's wrong', II, p. 12),[56] but they are Richard's only faults, for he has not murdered his uncle, and he merely borrows Bolingbroke's inheritance. Bolingbroke correspondingly becomes a mere cynical villain, a combination of Cromwell and Shaftesbury. Nevertheless, usurpation was a sensitive topic, and the play was banned (King's, December 1680), a disguised staging as *The Sicilian Usurper* (January 1681)—perhaps in a desperate attempt to compete with Part II of *The Rover* at Dorset Garden—resulting in the silencing of the company for ten days.[57] Ultimately, it was more important to try to make a living than to try to please the monarch. There were, however, no offensive complications in Charles Saunders's *Tamerlane the Great* (King's, by March 1681), a straightforward account of an attempt to divert lineal succession to an outsider, which was performed before Charles at Oxford, two days before the meeting of Parliament. The young author received some help in polishing the play from Dryden, who supplied a jocular epilogue for the London première and a politically inscrutable epilogue for the Oxford performance.[58] In a parallel to *King Lear*, an evil prince for a while supplants his good brother, but the villain is exposed as a changeling, his true father being the unscrupulous Odmar (Shaftesbury). Such simple triumph of inherited nature over nurture is by now exceptional in drama.

A more problematic account of misunderstood virtue is John Banks's *The Unhappy Favourite; or, The Earl of Essex* (King's, *c.* May 1681), for which Dryden provided a vehemently Tory prologue and epilogue when it was performed before the King and Queen. Here Essex is portrayed as a virtual innocent, destroyed by the jealousy of the Countess of Nottingham and the malice

---

55 Tate's emphasis on the private is discussed in Michael Dobson, *The Making of the National Poet: Shakespeare, Adaptation and Authorship, 1660–1769* (Oxford, 1992), 84–5.

56 It is clear from the dedication of this play that *The History of King Lear* came first.

57 See Timothy J. Viator, 'Nahum Tate's *Richard II*', *Theatre Notebook*, 42 (1988), 109–17; Hume, *Development*, 345 (correcting *The London Stage*).

58 Saunders acknowledges Dryden's help in the preface, where he also denies any assistance from Marlowe's *Tamburlaine*, of which he loftily claims total ignorance: '*how good it is, any one may Judge by its obscurity.*' For the politics of the Oxford epilogue, see Harth, 'Dryden in 1678–1681', 73–4; id., *Pen for a Party*, 102–3.

of Rawleigh and Burleigh (Banks having confused Robert Cecil with his father). If any contemporary parallel is being implied, the aim would seem to be a defence of Monmouth, though in extenuation of his flaws rather than vindication of his claims. More provocative, however, is the handling of Queen Elizabeth. Banks emphasizes her role as the opponent of Catholic Spain (a role which made her a favourite Whig icon), but he also portrays a monarch who is linguistically manipulable and cut off from the perception of real events. Elizabeth herself sees her linguistic vulnerability, recognizing that if she had the 'spirit' of her father she would silence her manipulators 'With one short syllable' (I. i. 412–13). But she has not and does not. Although Burleigh derides Spain as 'the place | Where Babel first was built' (I. i. 230–1), the Queen's constant vulnerability to misrepresentation and flattery shows that Babel is nearer at hand. Indeed, the words which influence her are often distortions of other words rather than direct representations of action. Even the reporting of Essex's rebellion is the reporting of an act of signification rather than of a mere act:

> To those that stood
> Far off he bended and made taking signs;
> To those about him raised his voice aloud.

(IV. i. 111–13)

The corruption of communication leads inexorably to the flawed judicial ritual of Essex's condemnation, and justice declines into revenge, the Queen authorizing Essex's execution 'to be revenged' (V. i. 228) for an imaginary slight concocted by the vengeful Countess of Nottingham, and repenting only when it is too late. The famous, apocryphal, ring which Essex sends to request mercy, but which fails to reach the Queen, epitomizes the non-exchange of signs between ruler and ruled.

Increasingly, however, the role of misrepresented hero was being fulfilled by James. A year after *The History of King Lear*, Tate returned to the maligned servant of the state in *The Ingratitude of a Common-Wealth* (King's, December 1681), an adaptation of *Coriolanus* whose hero becomes simply a brave nobleman (James) with too overt a contempt for the mob. Accordingly, Coriolanus is destroyed not by internal flaws but by extrinsic rivalries: the resentment of the Iago-like Nigridius, and Aufidius' lust after Virgilia. As in *The History of King Lear*, however, Tate places increased emphasis on private experience, turning the play into a family tragedy; for, in Act V, Virgilia commits suicide to avoid rape by Aufidius, Young Martius is tortured to death, and Volumnia goes mad with grandmaternal grief. Finally, Coriolanus sets out for eternity carrying his dead child, like 'th' Inhabitant of some sack't Town' fleeing with 'his most precious Store' (V, p. 64). Though this last speech is dominated by the image of the burning city, the calamity of the city has shrunk into a metaphor defining that of the nuclear family. Obsessively lost in grief for his dead son, Tate's Coriolanus reverses the image of Aeneas bearing Anchises from Troy.

There is another James-like paragon of misrepresented virtue in Thomas Southerne's first play, *The Loyal Brother* (King's, February 1682). Seliman, the Sophy of Persia, covets Semanthe, the lover of his brother Tachmas, and is easily induced by the villainous, Shaftesbury-like Ismael to believe Tachmas guilty of treason; but the brothers are reconciled, Seliman magnanimously renounces Semanthe (in an archaic gesture of Orrerian self-sacrifice), and Ismael is executed. There is much imagery of dislocation and wandering, but, in contrast with the displacement in Otway's plays (or in Southerne's own works after the Revolution), the dislocation is remediable, and Seliman finally comes to his brother's breast as to 'the haven, where | My beaten mind rides safe' (V. iii. 251–2).

At about the same time there appeared Durfey's revision of *Cymbeline* as *The Injured Princess* (King's, February/March 1682): another Shakespearian adaptation concerned with misrepresented loyalty and imperilled blood-line (though one which, according to the epilogue, was written nine years before). One of Durfey's many alterations is to omit Jupiter's conveyance of the inscribed tablet to the sleeping Posthumus: as so often, humanity loses access to a transcendent or natural system of signs[59] (Durfey also omits the 'natural stamp' (V. v. 367) of the mole on Guiderius' neck).[60] Similarly, Durfey dilutes or contradicts Shakespeare's grounding of social order upon a benignly ordered nature. In Shakespeare, for example, Posthumus is a poor but worthy gentleman, moulded by ancestry and 'Great nature' (V. iv. 48); D'Urfey's hero (renamed Ursaces, after a character in *L'Astrée*) is a 'plebeian' (I, p. 2). Conversely, Cloten is not, as he is in Shakespeare, an upstart outsider despised by other noblemen, but a representative of a degenerate aristocratic culture, who helps another lord attempt to rape Pisanio's daughter and then (in an echo of *King Lear*) blinds Pisanio. The correlation between social origin and intrinsic quality has here disappeared, and, although Durfey retains some of Shakespeare's emphasis on the innate nobility of Cymbeline's long-lost sons, he omits 'Cowards father cowards, and base things sire base' (IV. ii. 26), with its recollection of the most influential affirmation of hereditary character, Horace's 'fortes creantur fortibus et bonis' (*Odes*, IV. iv. 29). Indeed, Durfey's own images of nature are predominantly menacing, evoking grim or desert landscapes and savage beasts: as in the blinding of Pisanio, he is imposing the vision of *King Lear* upon *Cymbeline*. He does not, however, achieve a consistent and total transformation, but rather leaves an unresolved clash of outlooks—even though the outlook of the original offers a sounder philosophic basis for patrilineal succession.

---

[59] In one of the musical interludes in Part I of *The Famous History of the Rise and Fall of Massaniello*, however, the protagonist has a vision of Fate and Saint Genaro, who interprets the 'Book of Dooms' (II, p. 11).   [60] Guiderius is renamed Palladour.

The opposition reclaimed the figure of traduced integrity for one last time in Settle's *The Heir of Morocco* (King's, March 1682), written a year before he abandoned the apparently doomed Whig cause, and published with a dedication to Monmouth's mistress, Lady Henrietta Wentworth. Albuzeiden, King of Algiers, is determined to marry his daughter to Gayland, the blustering tyrant of Morocco, despite her love for his virtuous admiral, Altomar. Though Altomar continues to express fervent loyalty to Albuzeiden, he eventually kills Gayland and is tortured to death on Albuzeiden's orders, only to be revealed when on the point of death as the true king of Morocco, whereupon the penitent Albuzeiden and his distraught daughter commit suicide. The usual elements of Settle's work reappear here, for there is an oppressive parent, a failure of justice whereby a ruler is placed in the role of criminal, and a succession wrapped in enigma even more impenetrable than that in *Cambyses*, both true and false heir sharing the status of stranger: Gayland is 'an Imperial Stranger' (I, p. 5), and Altomar—constantly despised on account of his birth—a 'Stranger to his own great Quality' (V, p. 47). This is the story of an essentially just and merciful king (IV, p. 42) whose error about the succession leads him into tyranny and disaster: 'See here the dire Effects of unkind Parents' (V, p. 51).

Loyalty is also maligned, and justice perverted, in Banks's tear-jerking *Vertue Betray'd; or, Anna Bullen* (Duke's, March 1682), which even-handedly condemns Catholicism and supports absolutism. Anne and her brother Rochford are compromised and destroyed by the jealous Lady Elizabeth Blunt and the popish villain Woolsey, who fears 'A *Lutheran* Queen' (I, p. 3), and Banks again extensively stresses the role of flawed signs in denying justice and isolating the monarch. Anne and Piercy are, for example, accused of communication by 'Signs and Tokens' (II, p. 22). Truth is again belatedly signified: after the execution, Anne's head confounds Lady Elizabeth by 'Making a motion with its Lips to speak, | As if they meant t'upbraid her Cursed Treason' (V, p. 78) and thereby driving her to lunacy and confession. Finally, the King dispenses with his advisers ('Slaves') and resolves on personal rule, with the astounding announcement that 'Heav'n n'ere made a King, but made him just' (V, p. 79). The pattern of restored royal authority and restored justice is a familiar one: witness David's second Restoration in *Absalom and Achitophel*, with its infrastructure of bribed witnesses and hanging judges. But the particular formulation is here exceptionally chilling.

Still more depressing is Banks's *The Innocent Usurper; or, The Death of the Lady Jane Grey*, a play of uncertain date whose sympathy for its usurping heroine rendered it as unperformable before the Revolution as its insistence on loyalty to a popish successor did afterwards.[61] The Protestant Jane has

---

[61] The play was published in 1694. In the dedication, dated 5 Oct. 1693, Banks claims that it '*was written Ten Years since*' (sig. A2). Its sentiments do seem to link it to the period of Tory triumph. Banks's *The Island Queens; or, The Death of Mary, Queen of Scotland* was also banned for political

sacred language on her side—one syllable of *'Luther, Cranmer, Latimer'* is preferable to all the saints of Rome (V, p. 59)—but she has it on her side only as she heads for the block; during her period of usurpation, she is (like Shakespeare's Claudius) unable to pray (III, p. 26). No other play so nakedly follows the host of sermons which commend martyrdom before resistance. In doing so, it shows how deeply anxious a state of mind loyalty could be.

If such anxieties inspired a profusion of deeply political plays, they also, especially in the confused year of 1680, inspired a drama of flight from polit-ics. In Otway's *The Orphan* (Duke's, February 1680) Acasto has retired from public life to his country estate, torn between loyalty to his King and con-tempt for his entourage. On the whole, dramatists could not retire to country estates, but amidst all the partisan drama of this period there is also a tend-ency to retreat from political to private subjects, which receives its first and best manifestation in *The Orphan* itself, or to portray characters tragically divided between domestic existence or aspiration and the destructive, im-personal claims of political life, as in the two best tragedies of the Exclusion Crisis, *Lucius Junius Brutus* and *Venice Preserv'd*.

Otway appears never to have wavered from the cause of James. He dedic-ated *Don Carlos* to him, and *The Poet's Complaint of his Muse* (1680), writ-ten before James's return from exile in February, denounces the Whigs, idealizes James, and concludes with an affecting description of his departure from the kingdom. The prologue to *The Orphan* celebrates James's very recent return from exile, and the play on publication was dedicated to the Duchess of York. There are further espousals of James's cause in the three epilogues to *Venice Preserv'd* and the dedication of *The Atheist*. It would be wrong to doubt the genuineness of Otway's principles, but also wrong to as-sume that the rhetoric of panegyric permitted him to express every nuance of his political thought; and, for whatever reason, he did not extensively use drama itself as a vehicle for partisan panegyric or satire. The two plays from 1680, *The Orphan* and *The Souldiers Fortune*, are only incidentally polit-ical. There are no plays from 1681. And, despite some incidental (and often over-emphasized) satire of Shaftesbury in *Venice Preserv'd*,[62] considerable intellectual contortions are required to see it as a triumphalist Tory parallel

---

reasons, an altered version finally being performed in 1704. (Danchin raises the possibility of a per-formance *c.*1684 (*Prologues and Epilogues*, iv. 505–6), but this seems ruled out by the statement in the dedication of *Cyrus the Great* (1696) that the play was 'Cast and ne'er Try'd, Condemn'd and never Heard', sig. [A3ᵛ].) This is *The Unhappy Favourite* in reverse: amidst rumours of a Catholic plot, Queen Elizabeth executes an innocent Catholic monarch.

62 There are some occasional hits at Shaftesbury in the portrayal of Antonio, but I do not see that he can be interpreted as a sustained caricature of the Earl. Antonio, after all, is an Establishment fig-ure who survives a failed revolution of which he is an intended victim: in all these respects, he is the very reverse of Shaftesbury. There are many caricatures of Shaftesbury in late Carolean drama, from Payne's Chancellor to Lee's Arius. These figures have a shared and easily recognizable iconography, in which Antonio does not participate.

play.[63] In 1682–3 Dryden, Lee, Southerne, and Crowne all produced such plays, but Otway did not. *The Atheist* (1683), produced when the Tory Reaction was well under way, is strikingly apolitical. Otway's attitude was the common one of loyal gloom, though (exceptionally) there is no sign that James was the focus and inspiration of that gloom: unlike Dryden, Crowne, and Banks (but like Behn) he never expressed any hostility to Catholicism. His gloom appears to have been a more metaphysical one, of pessimism about man's political nature, and about the political structures he is capable of creating.

The Orphan is one of the finest renderings of that characteristic preoccupation of avant-garde Carolean drama, man's inability either to reconcile or to separate his twin natures as social, communicative being and solitary, signless savage: Acasto's two sons, Castalio and Polydore, make parallel attempts to isolate and cultivate the citizen and the savage, and these attempts are the complementary causes of the tragedy. The brothers are rival suitors of Acasto's orphaned ward, Monimia, and, although Castalio and Monimia are secretly betrothed, Castalio adopts the pose of an Orrerian noble rival—the perfect citizen—in allowing Polydore to court Monimia (much to her distress and bewilderment). His motives are nostalgia for the perfect childhood friendship with his brother, before the disruptive onset of sexual desire, and also resentment at the bondage of desire itself: a resentment which goes far to explain the secrecy with which he surrounds his betrothal and marriage. For fear of sexual desire recurs throughout the play: in their dialogues, Monimia and Castalio both see themselves as enslaved to the other's tyranny (e.g. II. 305–412), and, when Polydore reveals his impatience with social existence by longing for the carefree sex-life of the bull, he envies not its promiscuity (as an ordinary libertine would) but its freedom from the prolonged agony of unfulfilment imposed by custom and the inhibiting rituals of language, the point being less that the bull can freely enjoy his desires than that he can quickly escape from them (I. 362–77). Monimia too is troubled by sexuality, to the extent that, when Polydore courts her, she is disturbed not by the (considerable) coarseness of his approach but by the inner turmoil which he arouses in her, and which makes her long for the innocence of Eden, where Adam and Eve did not suffer the distraction of alternative sexual possibilities (I. 351–61).

Overhearing Castalio make an assignation with Monimia, and not realizing that the couple have just married, Polydore takes Castalio's place on the wedding night by means of a bedroom trick. In the darkness of the bedroom, temporarily released (like Wycherley's Manly) from language and social

---

[63] Recent attempts to read *Venice Preserv'd* as a detailed allegory of Whig iniquities are David Bywaters, 'Venice, Its Senate, and Its Plot in Otway's *Venice Preserv'd*', *Modern Philology*, 80 (1982–3), 256–63, and Harry M. Solomon, 'The Rhetoric of "Redressing Grievances": Court Propaganda as the Hermeneutical Key to *Venice Preserv'd*', *ELH* 53 (1986), 289–310. A decisive corrective is provided by Phillip Harth, 'Political Interpretations of *Venice Preserv'd*', *Modern Philology*, 85 (1987–8), 345–62.

identity, Polydore for a moment attains the pure, inarticulate and asocial, sensuality of the bull. But Manly had emerged from his bout of sensuality demanding witnesses, craving the forms of law, and Polydore also undergoes a necessary return to social consciousness. Morning, and the restoration of language, bring the knowledge that the seeming fornication was in fact incest, and the knowledge destroys all three parties: Polydore provokes Castalio to kill him, and Castalio and Monimia commit suicide. Once again, man belongs to both society and the wilderness, able neither to reconcile the warring elements of his nature nor follow one to the exclusion of the other: Castalio briefly attempts to mimic a Platonic paragon of reason, and Polydore briefly attempts to mimic a bull, but the attempts are alike in their tragic consequences. Man is, as Castalio says, 'the Beast of Reason' (v. 27), each aspect of his biform nature mocking him with aspirations whose fulfilment the other prevents.

The outward Eden of Acasto's pastoral retreat forms an ironic setting for the turbulent and tortured desires of its inhabitants, and these repeatedly express themselves in fantasies of decidedly unpastoral landscapes, for—in another instance of Otway's preoccupation with dislocation—the characters often imagine themselves as solitary wanderers in desolate wildernesses, amplifying the emphasis on dispossession initiated by the play's title. Monimia envisages herself 'Thrust out a naked Wanderer to the World' (IV. 343), Castalio imagines himself 'alone', standing 'upon a naked beach' (V. 287–8), and, learning of his unintentional incest, Polydore proposes that he and Monimia should leave Acasto's retreat and 'roam, | Like the first Wretched Pair expell'd their Paradise,' seeking a dwelling of elaborate and inhuman grimness, where 'Adders nest in Winter' (IV. 448–50). The imagined scenes of savage desolation are projections of those parts of man's soul that have no part in his civilized and civilizing self, and it is significant that language never figures in these fantasies: they express the regions of the self in which language has no part.

In addition to the fantasies, there are two prophetic dreams (Chamont, Monimia's brother, has dreamt of her defilement (II. 222–37), and Acasto dreams of his sons' deaths, IV. 5–13), and, like the fantasies, the dreams exist outside language: Acasto 'strove to speak, | But could not' (IV. 11–12). Both dreams come true, but the fulfilment of the prophetic dream is here no tired and empty cliché; for, in one of the most ingenious and striking effects in all Restoration tragedy, Otway portrays the physical and the imaginary landscapes as gradually changing places, until nightmare is material actuality and the pastoral landscape an intangible dream. The process starts immediately after Chamont's narration of his dream, when he describes meeting a destitute, vagabond hag and asking directions of her (II. 244–65). The hag corresponds closely to Monimia's numerous self-projections in the role of desolate wanderer, and this meeting between a lost man and a mysterious vagabond is the point at which the worlds of dream and of solid physical reality start to change places, and at which the mental images expressing the dark regions of the soul start to become palpable and real. Thereafter, dream and reality become ever harder to distinguish. Excluded from Monimia's bedroom (because Polydore is already impersonating him inside), Castalio spends a solitary night amidst hostile nature (III. 556; V. 252–3), his real condition approximating to that of the dislocated destitutes in the fantasies. Yet those whose experiences intersect with his actualized nightmare have to assure themselves that he is not a figment of dream: hearing Castalio's complaints, the servant Ernesto wonders whether his 'sense has been deluded' (III. 560); Acasto, similarly, has to persuade himself that his son's voice was not part of his ominous dream (IV. 21–7); and, more accurately, Monimia asks whether she has not 'most strangely dreamt' (IV. 116) of making love with Castalio.

Facing the still ignorant Castalio after her terrible discovery, Monimia actually attempts to treat herself as a figment in a dream, exclaiming, 'No nearer, lest I vanish!' (V. 207), and provoking Castalio to respond, 'Have I been in a Dream then all this while! | And art thou but the shadow of *Monimia!*' (V. 208–9). At the beginning of her death scene, immediately after Polydore has induced Castalio to kill him, Monimia for the last time revives the imagery of ideal, pastoral beauty, likening Castalio's voice to 'the Shepherds Pipe upon the Mountains, | When all his little Flock's at feed before him' (V. 416–17). But, immediately, the pastoral vision is destroyed: 'But what means this? here's Blood' (V. 418). The original relationship between dream and reality has now been decisively reversed, for the world of rural beauty is now the insubstantial mirage, and the malignant creatures of nightmare have irrevocably been translated into solid form. Near the end, Castalio tries once more to restore the surrounding horror to the regions of mere nightmare, charging Chamont to 'Vanish' (V. 486) as though he were a figure in a dream. But nightmare continues to have fleshly solidity.

In showing the community of a country estate—the traditional microcosm of English society—being taken over by nightmares of the wilderness, Otway gives peculiarly compelling expression to the Restoration preoccupation with the interdependence of human civilization and human savagery. As usual, this results in a mingling of intimate and stranger. Ignorance of intimates is at the heart of the play: Polydore has been kept 'a stranger' to Castalio's passion (V. 347); bewildered by his exclusion from the marriage chamber, Castalio uses his wife Monimia 'strangely' (IV. 233); and, when Polydore's deception is discovered, Monimia vows to be a 'stranger' (V. 280) to her husband. The conflicts of the play are underlined by the intrusion into the pastoral world of a disruptive outsider, Monimia's brother, Chamont, who introduces himself to the Chaplain as 'a Stranger' (III. 159) and in quarrelling with Castalio over his treatment of Monimia expresses the baseless hope that he is 'no Stranger | To great *Castalio*' (V. 88–9). But even this turbulent outsider nominally belongs to the society he invades—he is the son of a close family friend—and it is he who provides one of the clearest glimpses of the mental processes of estrangement: in an astonishing episode, he rants abusively at Acasto, who is his father's old friend and the foster-father of his sister, loudly regretting that Acasto's advanced age renders it impermissible to strangle him. Then, suddenly, he cuts himself short: 'Hah, is not that good old *Acasto?* | What have I done?' (IV. 282–3). For a moment, the blind savagery of rage—the heritage of the state of nature—has obliterated all awareness of Acasto's identity, and all consciousness of social relationship, revealing the intrinsic tendency of such relationship to revert to alienness. Yet, as is often observed, Chamont has no causal effect on the unfolding of the tragedy: he is neither agent nor catalyst, but simply a projection of the internal processes which reduce the community to a chance cluster of wandering solitaries. The decline in the disruptiveness of the outsider reflects the increasing precariousness of community itself. If the play lacks the explicit political allusiveness of most drama of the period, its portrayal of a society literally overtaken by nightmare provides the most profound image of the Popish Plot years.

Monimia dies relying on men to tell her story (V. 466–9), the written narrative of events being left not by the victim but by the rapist (V. 493–4). In *The Revenge* (Duke's, January–April 1680), however, Aphra Behn[64] subjected a man's text (Marston's *The Dutch Courtezan*) to systematic feminist revision. In the main plot of each play a gentleman (Freevill, Wellman) tires of a prostitute (Franceschina, Corina), with whom his friend (Malheureux, Friendly) falls in love. The prostitute offers to gratify her new admirer if he kills her faithless lover (an incident Behn had already faintly recalled in *The Town-Fop*),[65] secretly planning to betray the friend and have him hanged. The two friends stage a mock-murder, but the 'victim' then teaches the 'murderer' a salutary lesson by disappearing and leaving him, apparently, in real danger of execution. Behn also retains Marston's secondary gulling plot, adding some satire of cit fears of popery but dropping the thematic links between the two plots: the pervasive reduction of human relationships to ones of exploitation and cannibalism. Instead, characteristically, she concentrates on anomalies in the perception and self-representation of women. Though in some respects a victim, Franceschina has slept with many men and becomes a figure of criminal malice, eventually punished with imprisonment and whipping. Corina has slept only with Wellman, and is far more a passive creation of circumstances. Like Angelica, she meditates upon the anomalies of the prostitute's position—of seeming power and actual servitude—and sees herself as belied by a false system of language:

---

[64] The attribution to Behn of this anonymous play seems overwhelmingly supported by internal evidence. For the external evidence, see Milhous and Hume, 'Attribution Problems', 28–9.

[65] Rejected by Bellmour immediately after their forced marriage, Diana offers herself to Friendlove on condition that he kill her husband.

A Whore! what tho to her that bears it 'tis a shame, an infamie that cannot be sup-ported? to all the world besides it bears a mightie sound, petition'd, su'd to, worship-p'd as a God, presented, flatter'd, follow'd, sacrific'd to, Monarch of Monarchs, Tyrant of the world, what does that charming word not signifie! (IV, pp. 39–40)

The sign is associated with the male mentality that creates the alluring image of the prostitute; it cannot evoke the self-disgust of the woman who fulfils the fantasy.

Whereas Behn's prostitute is a victim of false signs, Marston's is portrayed as a force of linguistic disruption: a foreigner—stranger—who speaks in broken English and whose bed becomes a Babel, her 'virginity' being suc-cessively sold to lovers of different nations. Conversely, it is Corina's linguistic vulnerability that drives her to a murderous plot that is 'strange' (I, p. 8) to her nature. Repudiating her, Wellman cruelly fixes her in another antifeminist stereotype, 'Do not turn Witch before thy time,' provoking Corina to a despairing admission of verbal impotence: 'I wou'd I were, that I might be an age in damning thee: But words are Air' (II, p. 19). Corina's first reaction to her admission of verbal impotence is attempted suicide; her next, to plan Wellman's murder. Her linguistic powerlessness reappears at the end of the play, when Wellman is marrying her off to a gull, and she signifies consent in an admission of linguistic subservience : 'What pow'rful Charms dwell in thy tender language! . . . I am still all thine, dispose me as thou pleasest' (V, pp. 61–2).

Behn uses the generic ambivalence of the play to stress her heroine's limited control of signs, for the play never turns into the tragedy she desires. Recognizing that she lacks the witch's power of words, she attempts suicide and murder, but fails. Then, at the beginning of the fifth act, she attempts to seize generic control: "tis I | Must end the last Act of the Tragedy' (V, p. 50). But, relentlessly, the play becomes a comedy. When Friendly escapes hanging, his prospective bride, Diana, recalls the passage from Ravenscroft's *The Careless Lovers* in which Careless jocularly prefers hanging to marriage: 'wou'd you not rather cry, Drive away Carman?' she asks (V, p. 61).[66] Appar-ently imminent tragedy modulates into an old comic joke. Then, marrying Corina off to Sir John Empty on the pretence that she is his sister, Wellman re-produces the ending of Etherege's first play: with ingenious aptness, *The Revenge* modulates into *The Comical Revenge*. But, as Corina's painful sur-render to Wellman's language indicates, the comedy is darker, arising from the woman's inability to dictate the terminology which defines her. Hence-forth she will live her life under an assumed identity, exchanging the mis-understood title of whore for the false title of gentlewoman. Whore and gentlewoman, so often linked in Behn, are here linked as forms of false sign,

---

[66] 'If I was going to *Tyburne*, I wou'd cry *Drive on Carman*; and choose to Sing my *Penitential Psalme* at the Gallows, rather than return to say, *For Better for Worse*' (*Careless Lovers*, I, p. 2).

obstructing expression of the essential character. But identical problems beset the reverse of the whore/gentlewoman, the faithful plebeian wife. In the Act V prison scene, Behn adds the character of a highwayman's wife, who has framed herself for robbery in order to be hanged with her husband. She, too, envisages her life as a tragedy, seeking a form of self-representation normally denied to women of her category: 'my Statue and History', she says, 'ought to be added to the Gallery of Heroick Women' (V, p. 63). But she is reprieved, and her husband attains the heroism of Tyburn without her. At about the time when Otway and Banks were establishing the genre of she-tragedy, Behn portrays the woman's unsuccessful attempts to gain tragic status. Although she takes over a man's text, she does so in order to portray a continuing male tyranny over language.

Shortly afterwards, Settle experimented with semi-domestic tragedy in *Fatal Love* (King's, ?summer/September 1680). But his view of language is aggressively man-centred: 'I had a Virtuous *Father*' (italics added), rants one of the heroines,

> Who taught me still, that *Whore* was such a word,
> As Conjur'd *Devils* up, Eclips't the *Sun*,
> Made Earthquakes, Blazing-Stars, and Blew *Hell*-Fire.
>
> (IV, p. 37)

As usual in Settle, authority is a problem, but—as this patriarchal view of language indicates—it is a male problem, and indeed Settle's recipe for domestic drama is simply to abandon conundrums about who is the true king for conundrums about who is the true husband (one of the candidates being, indeed, a prince): Philander and Olizia marry in the mistaken belief that their former partners are dead and then discover their error. But, as usual, there is no clear divine criterion for resolving the dilemma. On realizing the mistake, Philander deterministically blames the gods for permitting it to occur (I, p. 8) and, as the sexual entanglements move inexorably towards a bloodbath, his determinism leads him to postulate a divinely ordained chaos where ethical categories lose distinction and meaning: 'if your Dooms our Ruines have Decreed, | The noblest Cause can Act the blackest Deed' (V, p. 49). This is a striking vision of a world with no principles of moral cause and effect, and it illustrates one of the most exasperating paradoxes of Settle's work: that no Restoration dramatist had a more authentic tragic vision than he, though none was less equipped to realize it.

The diminished possibility of defining human affairs in relation to fixed, transcendent categories is also evident in Settle's treatment of Philander and Olizia's conflicting marital obligations. There is not—as there was to be, say, in Southerne's *The Fatal Marriage*—an unequivocal stress on the priority of the first vow. Rather, there is a confounding of titles which does not easily yield to simple resolution: Olizia, whose first husband was a jealous and ranting despot, seems clearly entitled to her decent and upright second choice, but Philander's first wife was no less admirable than his second, and here the problem is acute, though in the event the *second* marriage is preferred. There is a clash not of absolutes but of specific human characteristics and desires, the claims of the world resisting translation into values of a higher order. Vows are not irrevocable imperatives recorded in the Book of Heaven, and when Settle uses the image of the sacred book he presents it in a significantly diminished form. When Philander asks 'Must this fair Book of Life, writ by the Hand of Heav'n, | The Legend of a *God*, be all defaced?' (IV, p. 31) (the only passage in Settle, as far as I know, to be accorded the dignity of plagiarism),[67] he is referring chiefly to Olizia's beauty. The Book of Life, a traditional representation of God's redemptive scheme for the human race, becomes an image of a pretty face, and even the 'Hand' of God becomes an instrument of material action and design. We note, however, that the woman again becomes the passive recipient of meaning inscribed by a fatherly authority.

A subtler portrayal of the woman's relationship to male linguistic authority occurs in Lee's *Theodosius* (Duke's, by September 1680)—not a domestic tragedy, but one which depicts the unattainability of anonymous domesticity. The philosopher's daughter Athenais has by her father been 'bred up to Books | In Closets like a Sybill' (I. i. 70–1); but, if she is like a sibyl—a mistress of sacred language—in her book-lined closet, her subsequent experience of love and politics renders her a victim, and a victim of situations that generally involve some formalized act or ritual of language. Her lover, the Persian prince Varanes, prays that he may be 'Swept from the Book of Fame' if he breaks his solemn oath to prefer her to 'Persian greatness' (II. i. 357–9), but he is in fact unwilling, until too late, to seat a philosopher's daughter on the throne of Cyrus, and desires only to make her his mistress: though he fantasizes that they shall mate like birds, 'Without remembring who our Fathers were' (II. i. 388), paternally determined roles prove inescapable. After her anguished discovery of Varanes' slipperiness, Athenais participates in another linguistic ritual: that of baptism, where she receives the new name of Eudosia and is explicitly represented as a sacrificial 'Victim' (III. ii. 3), dedicated to that paragon of Christian rhetoric, Chrysostom (III. ii. 1), the golden-mouthed.[68] In the aftermath of this ritual, she performs more linguistic solemnities: a renunciation of Varanes and, under paternal pressure, a promise to marry the emperor Theodosius, Varanes' friend and unwitting rival.

When Theodosius learns of Varanes' love, he makes the Orrerian gesture of permitting his friend to court his fiancée, explicitly giving him total linguistic freedom and making Eudosia (as she now is) the object on which that freedom is to be exercised: 'say all you can to gain her' (III. ii. 361). But the noble

---

[67] Predictably, the culprit was that king of plagiarists, George Powell (*Alphonso King of Naples*, IV, p. 34).

[68] Atticus, the Bishop of Constantinople, is Chrystostom's successor (I. i. ok, 318).

gesture cannot—as it can in Orrery's plays—genuinely harmonize passion with social obligation and social identity: even before Varanes sees Eudosia, Theodosius has changed his mind, informing Eudosia that he cannot surrender her, and merely permitting their meeting to go ahead so as not to break his word. Moreover, whereas Orrery exalts the male friendship bond without considering the psychological effect of its rituals upon the woman, Lee is primarily interested in this effect—witness his emphasis that Eudosia is to be made the object of Varanes' linguistic pressure, and the concomitant emphasis that Varanes' courtship is to be an irresistible intrusion upon her privacy: 'you shall see her, | With all advantage in her own Apartment' (III. ii. 359–60), Theodosius assures him. In between this undertaking and its fulfilment, Eudosia is subjected to the ultimate ritual of linguistic victimization, in that Theodosius, distracted by his unexpected rivalry with Varanes, absentmindedly signs her death-warrant. The warrant is not implemented, but the interview with Varanes does the trick just as effectively.

Varanes initiates this last interview, like the first, by professing subjection to a transcendent book, claiming that he approaches Eudosia like a penitent approaching a shrine, conscious that his sins are recorded in the book of heaven. But such identification of the feminine with a linguistic absolute proves more futile than ever, and Eudosia/Athenais becomes an incarnate ambiguity, Varanes being compulsively drawn to call her by a name which she has now renounced, but under which she was free to be his wife. The division of names reflects a continuing and irreconcilable division between her original desires and the patterns of language to which she has subjected herself through baptism: to Varanes' face, she swears a formal oath renouncing him, and then proceeds to a contrary linguistic formality, of farewell accompanied by a confession of love. This scene of painful and oppressive speech, sanctioned by Theodosius, constitutes her real death-warrant, for the tensions it creates prove insupportable. Commanded by her father (V. i. 3), Eudosia—looking like 'the Ghost of Athenais' (V. i. 63)— proceeds to her last linguistic solemnity, of marriage to Theodosius. But first she takes poison, so that death is working within her even as she speaks the ceremonial words, and in her final moments she is insistently called once more by her original name.

The cycle of destructive speech ceremonies receives two strangely contrasting prefigurations in the opening moments of the play. Surrounded by inspiring portraits of Christian martyrs, Theodosius and two of his sisters prepare to take monastic vows in a 'Solemn last farewell' (I. i. 230). The doors close for ever on the sisters, but the arrival of Varanes deflects Theodosius from his renunciation (until it is completed for tragically changed reasons at the end of the play), and Theodosius and Varanes then reminisce about their innocent and harmonious youth. Whereas Athenais, as we have recently learned, was 'bred up to Books' (I. i. 70) the two men have spent their youth hunting in the forest, but their sojourn in the forest is associated not only with virile action but with virile power of speech. They too are beings of dual names but, unlike that of Eudosia, their second names are freely chosen expressions of strength, in that they hunted under the names of Alcides (Hercules) and Theseus: parallel archetypes of manly action, both associated with the destruction or conquest of women. In addition, they have acted in a court performance of Seneca's *Hercules Furens* (a play in which Hercules kills his children and his *wife*), representing the hero's fury

> In all that raging heat, and pomp of madness,
> With which the stately Seneca adorn'd him;
> So lively drawn, and painted with such horror,
> That we were forc'd to give it o're, so lowd
> The Virgins shriek'd, so fast they dy'd away.
>
> (I. i. 259–63)

The deeds of the superman are mediated through the pen of the master stylist, and the hero's destruction of his wife is complemented by the mass death-like swoon of women provoked by its poetic representation, the representation becoming more dangerous than the deed.

This complex enactment of death, theatrical imitation on the stage producing physiological imitation in the audience, foreshadows the later oppressive rituals of language. For the sorts of oppression which the play depicts are not primarily dependent on Herculean strength. Although Theodosius follows Hercules' example in consigning his partner to death in a fit of distraction, he does so by an act of writing; and, despite his youthful role-playing as Theseus, he is generally viewed as womanish. Conversely, the gruffly virile general Marcian is at first out of his depth in the city because of his linguistic inexpertise. Representation produces only ridicule, as when he is tricked into repeatedly narrating his 'Story' (II. i. 34) to mocking courtiers, and he becomes destructive only when he learns the art of representation: pretending that the death sentence on Eudosia has been carried out, and giving a feigned account of Eudosia's execution, he attempts to shock Theodosius from being a 'Player' hero (IV. ii. 99) to being a hero in truth. But his account actualizes not the fictitious hero but the fictitious death, for it inspires Theodosius to abandon his willingness to surrender Eudosia and (with Marcian's delighted approval) to proceed, disastrously, with the ritual of marriage. Marcian does, however, undergo another, more constructive, conversion from his original blunt machismo. He is originally opposed to Theodosius' subservience to his sister Pulcheria, deploring the rule of women and praising the Salic law of the Franks, but he gradually falls in love with her and at the end of the play is set to become her consort, deriving his authority from hers. Power has passed to a woman, though at the cost of Athenais' tragedy.

If language is the foundation of social existence, its essential and primary power is not to communicate but to enslave the mind with solemnity, ritual, and incantation. Even law, the codification of social existence, originates in ritual. The Salic law of the Franks, for instance, is yet another ritual oppression of the female,

> Blest by their Priests, the Salij, and pronounc'd
> To stand for ever; which excludes all Women
> From the Imperial Crown.
>
> (II. i. 136–8)

Moreover, though all-encompassing for their participants, the rituals are (like Salic law) manifestly local and arbitrary in character, further examples of Montaigne's municipal laws. They are, indeed, repeatedly associated with the distinction of one space from another: with farewell, banishment, exclusion ('excludes all Women'), or inclusion. Meeting after meeting turns into a ritual farewell, Pulcheria and Athenais both attempt to banish the men they love, women are excluded from the French throne, and 'Religion's Door' is eternally locked when Theodosius' other sisters take their vows (I. i. 362). Confined in her closet of books, the young Athenais prefigures the binding systems of language which enclose and separate throughout the play, to the point that the three principal characters have to change names in passing from one to another. The name, and the ritual of naming, no longer express a fixed and comprehensive system of moral and linguistic order. Only in the frequent pastoral fantasies (where, for example, 'Phillis *unlocks* her Charms')[69] is there escape from enclosure.

Theodosius is a Christian, Varanes a Zoroastrian, and Marcian a pagan, while Athenais/Eudosia is tragically divided, both in name and life, between Christianity and paganism. The diversity of creed corresponds to the diversity of ordering linguistic ceremony. Yet the play opens by asserting a unified process of providential history, ratified by legible divine signature, for the opening scene is of a temple adorned with representations of the early martyrs, converging on an altar bearing a portrait of Constantine's celebrated vision: a cross, surrounded by angels, inscribed with the legend 'In hoc signo vinces'. Here is the celestial writing that is so often absent from Restoration drama—except that the celestial writing is mediated through human representation, dwindling into yet another impressive ceremonial artefact. Never do we move from the secondary representation to a direct apprehension of celestial sign; for, unlike the majority of Lee's earlier plays, *Theodosius* is without omens or revelations of any kind. Leontine (Athenais' father) declares that the Emperor's retreat into monastic life will cause the angels to descend 'With Charming Voices, and with lulling strings' (I. i. 37), but the monastic vows are not uttered, and the angelic voices are not heard. When Theodosius does undertake religious vows—of marriage—these are counteracted by the secret processes of carnal destruction within the poisoned bride,

---

[69] Song at the end of Act III, l. 7 (italics added).

though the vain desire for angelic voices is repeated in the doomed Athenais' baseless hope that some angel may 'Whisper' to her loved Varanes what she is doing (V. i. 14).

A song near the beginning of the fifth act questions the beneficence of Providence, even in the afterlife:

> Why should the Heavenly Powers perswade
> Poor Mortals to believe,
> That they guard us here,
> And reward us there,
> Yet all our Joys deceive.

(V. i. 35–9)

And, shortly afterwards, when deceived joys drive Athenais to resolve on the mortal sin of suicide, she sees in her death an eternal condition of unguided dislocation:

> Through the dark Caves of Death to wander on,
> Like wilded Travellers without a Guide,
> Eternal Rovers in the gloomy Maze.

(V. i. 69–71)

The initial convergence of the scenery upon Constantine's revelation suggests the divinely guided movement of history towards the Christian Empire. Yet the rituals enacted within the temple increasingly contradict its iconography, and it is finally the scene of Athenais' suicide. As she dies, her baptismal name slips away from her, and she is known once again by the name of her pagan-hood. And the play concludes with the accession of the virtuous pagan Marcian, an admirer of Lucius Junius Brutus who is determined to restore the vigour of old Rome. Manifest providential design cedes to a more indeterminate sequence of pattern and counter-pattern.

There is obvious political relevance in the spectacle of an amorous, indolent, and priest-ridden regime being cleansed by a vigorous admirer of Roman republicanism,[70] but political analogy is peripheral, and the play primarily belongs with *The Orphan* as a tragedy of private experience. Nevertheless, Lee returned to political drama in his greatest play, *Lucius Junius Brutus* (Duke's, December 1680), which reconstitutes many of the elements of *Theodosius*; Marcian, after all, had admired Brutus. Here, his role-model expels a degenerate and lustful dynasty which is supported by a cruel and corrupt priesthood, and executes his sons when they conspire a Restoration. *Lucius Junius Brutus* is also, however, a play about the flight from politics, Brutus' nobler son, Titus, being destroyed by his vain attempt to escape from the demands of his father's vision. One striking specific continuity is Lee's

---

[70] Armistead argues that Theodosius' conduct implies criticism of Charles II's withdrawal 'into an unreal, pastoral world' (*Nathaniel Lee*, 129).

persisting interest in *Hercules Furens* as a source of allusive commentary on his own material: for when, after the execution of his sons, Brutus concludes the play by setting forth his ideal political agenda, in a speech envisaging a perfect world, free even from storms and comets (V. ii. 197–210), he is repeating the speech delivered by Hercules when he is seized by the madness that leads him to slaughter his family.[71] For all Lee's clear criticism of the Stuarts, this allusion makes it difficult to see Brutus as an ideal alternative, and it emphasizes—if emphasis were needed—that he is yet another example of Lee's favourite problematic figure, the destructive father. Indeed, destructiveness is associated not just with the character of a particular father, but with paternity itself: as Athenais and Varanes had been separated by their inherited rank, so Teraminta and Titus, the hero and heroine of *Lucius Junius Brutus*, are separated by their inherited historical roles, she being the bastard daughter of the tyrant, he the son of the revolutionary liberator.

In contrast to his father's unyielding determination to shape the course of history, Titus wishes only to seize the present moment. He represents yet another version of the impulse to flee the constraints of civilization into a life of untrammelled personal happiness; and, like other incarnations of that impulse, from Horner to Otway's Polydore, he finds it impossible to fulfil. 'Not all the expectation of hereafter' (I. i. 15), he boasts, could purchase one minute of his wedding night; but, in the event, his agonized crisis of loyalty renders him impotent. In Titus, as in many Lee characters, rebellion against the tormenting impositions of social existence leads to dreams of escape into a simple, pastoral life. Here, the insurmountable difficulties of his loved one's parentage and social origin might vanish:

> A God thy Father was, a Goddess was his Wife;
> The Wood-Nymphs found thee on a bed of Roses,
> Lapt in the sweets and beauties of the Spring.
>
> (I. i. 44–6)

At the end of the play, after Titus has been flogged, Teraminta undertakes a parallel flight from history into ideal mythology, fantasizing that Titus was sired not by the barbarous Brutus but by a god, who 'Slipt to thy mothers bed and gave thee to the World' (V. i. 72).

As so often, flight from the tyranny of social precept becomes flight from language itself; for, as well as providing imaginary, unattainable release from the constrictions of paternity and social identity, the fantasies also reveal longing for a world without language (though, as always, the need for language proves inescapable). Teraminta is first described as 'Melting' her 'sorrows in the murmuring Stream' (I. i. 7), desiring dissolution into the

---

[71] *Hercules Furens*, ll. 926–37, in *Seneca's Tragedies*, tr. Frank Justus Miller, Loeb Classical Library (2 vols., London and New York, 1917), i. See Derek Hughes, 'Lee's *Lucius Junius Brutus* and Seneca's *Hercules Furens*', *American Notes and Queries*, 19 (1981), 103–4.

mindless condition of natural process, and as 'poring, like a Sibyl, on the Leaves' of an aged tree (I. i. 10), seeking for a mysterious, hidden language in a source quite outside the province of ordinary discourse. When she tries to bind Titus with an oath of fidelity, he resists her dependence on language: 'When words are at a loss' on their wedding night, she will 'confess all language then is vile' (I. i. 65–8). But later the roles are reversed: he demands that she reaffirm a covenant that neither should survive the other, but she has 'no language left' (II. i. 519). Both are torn between a persisting and ineradicable need for the order which language imposes and an impulse to sink into the inarticulate individualism of instinct. Later, when Titus again wishes to retreat from language and absorb himself in the pre-linguistic sounds of nature ('With broken murmers and redoubled groans, | To help the gurgling of the waters fall', III. iii. 29–30), his escapism expands into longing for the alternative, mirror-world 'ten fathom down' (III. iii. 36) beneath the surface of the stream. But the mirror-world cannot be reached, and his only escape from articulate speech is amidst all the regulatory terror of the public world. Arrested for conspiring against Brutus, he demands to be bound and whipped, envisaging an agony that will force him away from verbal expression, 'till I shall howl | My Soul away' (IV. i. 196–7), and in the event his boast is that he remained silent during the flogging (V. i. 43–6). Titus can only relinquish speech by resigning his desires and becoming a mute instrument of his father's historical vision.

Lucius Junius Brutus was quickly banned for 'very Scandalous Expressions & Reflections upon yᵉ Government',[72] and few subjects could have been more politically sensitive than that of republican rebellion against a tyrannical and lecherous ruling house. But there is no enthusiasm for the victorious cause, and Brutus is suspect well before his final speech.[73] In the earliest stages of the revolution, he claims that his political calling is authenticated by celestial writing, describing a vision of a dragon 'with a Head that's mark'd | With Tarquin's name' (I. i. 325–6). But the vision is a fabrication—Lee once again reduces divine utterance to human fiction—and an innocently sceptical bystander is beaten up until he agrees that he has seen it.[74] Authentication by divine word turns out to be authentication by cynical thuggery, and the fraudulent boast of divine blessing is the more suspect for being supported by the brutal and cowardly Vinditius, a caricature of Titus Oates whose presence

[72] L. C. 5/144, p. 28, cited in *London Stage*, ed. Van Lennep, i. 293.

[73] A number of studies have emphasized Lee's ambivalence towards Brutus: David M. Vieth, 'Psychological Myth as Tragedy: Nathaniel Lee's *Lucius Junius Brutus*', *Huntington Library Quarterly*, 39 (1975–6), 57–76; Armistead, *Nathaniel Lee*, 130–43; Antony Hammond, 'The "Greatest Action": Lee's *Lucius Junius Brutus*'; Parker, ' "History as Nightmare" '. The best statement of the contrary case is Sue Owen, ' "Partial tyrants" and "Freeborn People" in *Lucius Junius Brutus*', *Studies in English Literature*, 31 (1991), 463–82.

[74] Cf. L'Estrange's charge that the Whig agitators invent '*strange Stories*; as that of the *Dragon* in *Essex*; *Earth-quakes*, *Sights in the Air*, *Prodigies*, and the like' (R[oger] L['Estrange], *Citt and Bumpkin, in a Dialogue Over a Pot of Ale*, 4th edn. (London, 1680), 2).

in Brutus' faction does much to diminish its dignity: 'the Gods are very angry: | I know they are; they told me so themselves' (I. i. 309–10), he boasts, in a parody of Brutus' sense of divine calling.

Brutus returns to the fabrication of omens when, after the suicide of Lucrece, he invents a vision of her hovering spirit, again showing how a dead woman may become a figment in a male vision of history and even attributing his own invented signs to the apparition ('She bows her Airy head to bless you', I. i. 454). The Lucrece legend is a favourite illustration of woman's passivity in the formulation of history, being also used in *All for Love*, *The Atheist*, and, implicitly, *The Souldiers Fortune*. Here, however, woman and man alike become creatures of the history-maker; for Brutus is not a divine agent but a creator of myths, fictions, and archetypes to ratify his vision of history and civilization, and his ultimate creation is the execution of his sons. Shocked by their treachery, he at first doubts the presence of a comprehensible providential pattern in history, but quickly takes it upon himself to generate one, deciding on the execution but representing the outcome of his own mind and will as submission to divine decree. In the process, he is quite explicitly designing for himself the role of political archetype:

> Yet after all I justifie the Gods. . . .
> Since then, for Man's Instruction, and the Glory
> Of the Immortal Gods, it is Decreed
> There must be patterns drawn of fiercest Virtue;
> Brutus submits to the eternal Doom.
>
> (IV. i. 293–302)

And yet, in his final farewell to his son, he reveals uncertainty about the very existence of the gods: '*If there be Gods*, they will reserve a room, | A Throne for thee in Heav'n' (IV. i. 574–5; italics added). Brutus apprehends the divine with confidence only when it serves to articulate or enforce his political will.

Brutus' will is his only criterion, and he becomes as increasingly intolerant of dissent. Having been carried to power with Lucrece's widower, Collatinus, by the public outrage following the rape, he quickly drops his associate on the grounds of his kinship with the Tarquins. Only he knows 'what is right' for the people (III. ii. 27), and indeed the liberator quickly turns against freedom, resolving to curtail 'the loose Liberty of Rome' (IV. i. 514). His insistence on Titus' execution ignores the wishes of Senatus Populusque Romanus (V. ii. 124–8), and, when a friend stabs Titus to save him from the ignominy of execution, Brutus' reaction shows that he can no longer distinguish the state from his own will: 'Why, *my* Valerius, did'st thou rob *my* Justice?' (V. ii. 150; italics added).[75] Tellingly, one of his last instructions to his dying son is to

---

75 In Madeleine de Scudéry's *Clélie*, one of Lee's chief sources, Collatine is deposed because he is opposed to the commonwealth and ambitious to be king, and Brutus assents to the execution of his sons in deference to the cruel anger of the people ([Georges (i.e. Madeleine)] de Scudéry, *Clelia, An Excellent New Romance* (London, 1678), iii/i, p. 227, iii/ii, pp. 284–'281' [irregular pagination]).

bear greetings to Romulus and Numa: two former *kings* (V. ii. 176). Brutus equates the state with his will because the will is the fundamental principle of human life, and the individual is not an innately social being, even towards his own family. As Tiberius, Brutus' other son, boasts,

> Like a grown Savage on the Common wild,
> That runs at all, and cares not who begot him,
> I'll meet my Lion Sire, and roar defiance.

(III. i. 169–71)

Indeed, the two archetypal incidents which sum up the old and new regimes both evince the fragility of the family. The worst crime of the Tarquins is that Queen Tullia has arranged the murder of her own father and driven her chariot over his body; the greatest justice of the new order is that Brutus impartially executes his sons. In the political mythology of the play, these represent opposing extremes of ambition and public spirit. Yet each entails the destruction of the family: of the fundamental social unit.

All the ostensibly providential signs of the new order—from the celestially inscribed dragon to the celestially ordained execution—are figments of Brutus' will. But in more mundane matters, too, Brutus prevails with signs that cannot be tested, for crucial events and persons are not directly shown: not only is the rape of Lucrece communicated only in the decency of retrospective narration; no member of the Tarquin dynasty appears in the play. Consequently, characters respond not to the direct influence of events but to rhetorical representation or transformation of them. The specific fictions, such as the visionary dragon, emerge from a persistent stream of transforming, intoxicating rhetoric reminiscent of the incantatory linguistic ceremonies in *Theodosius*. Indeed, incantatory repetition is a fundamental rhetorical principle throughout the play—'Still closing every Sentence, He's a Tarquin' (III. i. 99)—and it is clearly portrayed as a transference to the political sphere of a linguistic device that is ritual in origin. For this play, too, has an oppressive and destructive ritual, when Tarquin's priests administer an oath sealed with the drinking of human blood (IV. i. 103–19), and the solemn repetitions of 'Swear' in their incantation lay bare one of the play's most fundamental patterns of language. In Brutus' incantatory meditation on Lucrece's death, he too tastes blood (putting her dagger to his lips, I. i. 437), and he too exacts a conspiratorial oath with repeated intonation of 'Swear'.

Language becomes a closed and self-contained system, uniting the community not by signifying verities beyond itself but through intoxicating and essentially insignificant structures that are peculiar and exclusive to language itself. When Brutus delivers his oration over Lucrece's corpse, he verbally depicts a non-existent vision of her spirit—a non-existent vision making a non-existent sign ('She bows her Airy head to bless you', I. i. 454). His repetition of 'Swear' is a linguistic formula designed to produce another linguistic formula:

the massed 'We Swear' (I. i. 451). And the character of liberated Rome is defined by its ritual perpetuation of Brutus' linguistic solemnities: in an annual ceremony, the Tarquins will be cursed, as Brutus has just cursed them (I. i. 448, 459–65), while Lucrece will be famed, praised, mourned, and blessed. Brutus' linguistic ritual creates the future, and the linguistic rituals of the future will endlessly re-create their moment of origin. In a closed and perpetual circle, each ritual of language begets the other.

A similar circle appears in the following act, when Brutus again orates over Lucrece's corpse. Here, he wishes that the statues of Romulus and Numa were pointing at the corpse and then verbally evokes the impact of their imaginary, dumb presence, eloquently conjuring up a silence that renders eloquence impotent: 'what use would be of Tongues! | What Orator need speak while they were by?' (II. i. 153–4). His verbal signs evoke other signs which nullify the signs by which they are created: an elegant vicious circle which again forbids any straightforward progression from signifier to signified. There is no escape from the tyranny of signs. When Titus rejects his father and joins the conspiracy, the fatal evidence of his commitment is that he signs his name (III. iii. 163). Despite their moments of longing for a world without language, Titus and Teraminta constantly need to translate their love into oaths and other ceremonies of speech. Teraminta too reiterates the word 'Swear' (I. i. 51–7), and Titus derives an iterative ritual from her name, promising to groan it 'Till the tir'd Eccho faint with repetition' (III. iii. 45). (Revealingly, he lays less emphasis on the utterance than on the echo: not the sign but the replica of the sign.) When Titus rejects the call of history for the personal life, he is rejecting one set of oaths for another, and even when he speaks longingly of the other world reflected in the stream he is describing a world of pure sign, from which solid and primary reality has been excluded. Finally, when he resolves his tragic conflict, he attains not a perfection but an attenuation of identity, shrinking into a passive signification of Brutus' will. Then, in describing the world made possible by Titus' death, Brutus produces a series of completely unreferenced signs, for this is where he repeats the utopian visions of Seneca's mad Hercules, reciting by rote a pre-existent dramatic description of a world which cannot exist outside the beauties of poetic fiction.

The springs of motivation in *Lucius Junius Brutus* lie not in events but in the forms of expression by which the events are transmitted and coloured. In his first attempt to win Titus from Teraminta (marked by formulaic repetition of the words 'I' and 'I'll', II. i. 302–9, 341–7), Brutus is strikingly open in his search for the right signs: 'Perhaps it stood in a wrong light before; | I'll try all ways to place it to advantage' (II. i. 377–8). Single words—even key political words—are unstable and reversible in their application. Immediately after the rape of Lucrece, Brutus uses Collatinus' kinship with the Tarquins to increase the horror of the crime and make Collatinus an object of sympathy. But later, 'Still closing every Sentence, He's a Tarquin' (III. i. 99), he uses the name to sully Collatinus and depose him from the consulship. Conversely, characters compete in conflicting definitions of single objects: is Teraminta to be termed Tarquin's 'Daughter' or his 'Bastard' (I. i. 218), Titus' flogging his 'shame' or 'honor' (V. i. 38–40), or Brutus the 'Father' or 'murd'rer' of his son (V. i. 75–6)? Clashes of political principle become clashes of verbal definition, and the greatest problem of definition concerns the central event of the play: is Brutus' execution of his sons to be termed justice or tyranny? 'Perfect thy Justice, as thou, Tyrant, call'st it . . .' taunts the condemned Tiberius, 'And let thy Flatt'ring Orators adore thee' (V. i. 125–8).

Once again, the clash of individual desire and political authority places the nature of justice in doubt, and once again a play drives towards a judicial ritual in which the complexities of personal motivation are effaced by the rigid imperatives of state. Tiberius' chief reason for preferring the old regime of the Tarquins had been its flexible administration of justice, no longer possible under 'Laws that are cruel, deaf, inexorable' (II. i. 17). As in Lee's sources,[76] this is a defence of the corrupt impunity of court favourites, but (in contrast to the sources) the speech indicates ways in which corruption and equity may be interdependent:

> What, to depend on Innocence alone,
> Among so many Accidents and Errors
> That wait on human life?
>
> (II. i. 22–4)

The inefficiency of corruption may preserve innocents, and the unbending zeal of reform may destroy them with its own brand of unscrupulousness and ruthlessness: Titus is a traitor by the merest technicality, since he was forced into the conspiracy by a threat to Teraminta's life and left it almost immediately, yet he is doomed by Brutus' pitiless insistence on an exemplary execution. *Justice* is one of Brutus' watchwords, yet even here it is seen as a personal creation and possession: for Titus and Tiberius it is 'your' or 'thy' justice (IV. i. 481; V. i. 125), and for Brutus 'my' justice (IV. i. 533; V. ii. 150). Immediately after Tiberius' speech, we have a foretaste of the new justice, when a court hanger-on (Fabritius) is sentenced to death after a summary kangaroo court. He fatuously attempts to control the mob with forensic rhetoric, reworking the opening of *In Catilinam* I (II. i. 62–9), but power gives the mob both judicial and linguistic mastery, and the would-be Cicero shrinks into a schoolboy learning the language of his captors: 'Hitherto I have helpt you to spell,' says Vinditius; 'now pray put together for your self: and confess the whole matter in three words' (II. i. 114–15). Hereupon, Fabritius is dragged off to the gallows, as Vinditius celebrates democratic justice: 'this is Law, Right, and Justice: this is the Peoples Law; and I think that's better than the Arbitrary

---

[76] Livy, *Ab urbe condita*, ii. 2; *Clelia*, iii/i, p. 229.

power of Kings' (II. i. 123–5). The deadly language lesson is another ritual of verbal repetition, Fabritius repeating and accepting Vinditius' charges, and the incident epitomizes Lee's vision of a society divided between those who dictate and those who subordinately mumble the formulas of power. The oppressiveness and fallibility of language is a common enough theme, but Lee is quite unique in counterbalancing its indefiniteness as an instrument of meaning with its potency as an instrument of ritual.

Like Lee, Otway was inclined to see flaws in all factions, and in *Venice Preserv'd* (Duke's, February 1682) he clearly profited from the example of *Lucius Junius Brutus*, portraying a weak, uxorious hero torn between politics and domesticity, though here domesticity is not an impulse to conspiracy but an alternative to it—an extension of established authority. But, if Otway profited from Lee's example, he also profited from his mistakes: when he dramatized the inevitable ugliness of authority, he ensured that the authority was not monarchic, and that it survived the challenge of attempted revolution. Yet again we see paternal tyranny, familial disintegration, and physical and moral dislocation. In the opening moments, the elderly senator Priuli disowns his daughter, Belvidera, condemning her and her bankrupt husband, Jaffeir, to eviction from their home, and the literal dislocation of eviction forms the prelude to an incessant imaginative preoccupation with exile, wandering, and the wilderness, as when Jaffeir fantasizes about escape to 'some far Climate where our Names are strangers' (I. i. 365). At first Jaffeir and Belvidera dream (like Titus and Teraminta) of retreat from an oppressive social milieu to a solitude where they can indulge the personal and the domestic: on 'the bare Earth' Belvidera will 'pour the balm of Love' into Jaffeir's soul (I. i. 375–80). But the affinity with the wilderness reflects an antagonism to social ties that threatens even marriage, and by the middle of the play, after Jaffeir has been drawn into a conspiracy against the state by his friend Pierre, he and Belvidera are no longer intimates in a strange clime but strangers to each other within their native city: 'Why am I made a stranger?' (III. ii. 84), Belvidera asks after Jaffeir has surrendered her to the conspirators as a pledge of his loyalty. Finally, in Belvidera's madness, the wilderness possesses and utterly isolates her mind even in the midst of Venice: 'The Winds! hark how they whistle! | And the Rain beats: oh how the weather shrinks me!' (V. i. 483–4).

When Belvidera imagines comforting Jaffeir in the alien wilderness, she treats the self as a point of stability in an outwardly unstable world (characters frequently long for 'rest'). But the self offers no stability, for its essence is incoherence and dislocation, and the characters are subject to uncontrollable shifts of intention and outlook in which reason is revealed as the slave and creation of material desires. To his own considerable surprise, the chief conspirator, Renault, jeopardizes the plot by attempting to rape Belvidera, thus confirming his earlier complaint that man lacks the mechanical consistency of a clock (II. i. 206–7), and Jaffeir's vacillations of attitude towards the planned coup are associated not with articulated principle but with the vivid mental apprehension of some sexual image.[77] For example, he leaves the conspiracy not because he has discovered its bloodthirsty aims (for the discovery initially leaves him unmoved), but because he learns of Renault's attempt on Belvidera. When he wavers in his willingness to betray his friends, he remains unimpressed by Belvidera's evocations of the general massacre which they plan, but is easily moved by allusion to the failed rape and by the suggestion that she may suffer rape in earnest during the confusion of insurrection. 'It shews a beastly Image to my fancy, | Will wake me into madness' (IV. i. 33–4), he protests when she reminds him of Renault. Fearing lest his mind dissolve into madness before the 'beastly Image', Jaffeir reveals the fundamental causes of his incoherence of character, for consciousness throughout the play is an uncontrolled sequence of discrete sensory images. There is little capacity for abstraction, generalization, or codification: only specific response to the experience or imagination of specific sensation. 'Oh how the old Fox stunk I warrant thee' (III. ii. 245), Jaffeir exclaims when telling Pierre of Renault's attempted rape. When Jaffeir hears that Pierre has been condemned to death, his mind becomes dominated by the imagined sights and sounds of the execution (IV. i. 459–60), and he again fears 'madness' (IV. i. 461). And, when Belvidera begs Priuli to secure a pardon for the conspirators, she impresses upon his senses the spectacle of Jaffeir's murderous rage against her: 'Think you beheld him like a raging lion' (V. i. 95).

Because mental activity is essentially consciousness of sensation, vacillation between opposed states of mind is generally represented as vacillation between alternative sets of memories, Jaffeir almost becoming a precursor of the case later postulated by Locke, of one body containing 'two distinct incommunicable consciousnesses'.[78] From the opening dispute between Priuli and Jaffeir, memory is seen as the key to character, each man trying to excite in the other an appropriate and selected set of memories: 'remember,' says Priuli to Jaffeir (I. i. 13); 'remember,' replies Jaffeir to Priuli (I. i. 30). Belvidera, Priuli complains, 'forgot her Duty' (I. i. 69) to him, and he in turn will 'forget her' (I. i. 72): 'you're but my curs'd Remembrancers | I once was happy' (I. i. 74–5). At the end of the play, however, Belvidera reverses Priuli's character by soothing his dominant memories into oblivion and reviving those which are latent: 'do not call to memory | My disobedience,' she urges (V. i. 51–2). Jaffeir fluctuates far more rapidly, but vacillation of character is still consistently expressed as vacillation of memory. 'Remember | Thy *Belvidera* suffers' (I. i. 290–1), says Pierre, drawing him into the conspiracy. 'Remember' our appointment, says Belvidera, drawing him out of it, and

---

[77] See Derek W. Hughes, 'A New Look at *Venice Preserv'd*', *Studies in English Literature*, 11 (1971), 437–57 (pp. 440–3).

[78] John Locke, *An Essay Concerning Human Understanding*, ed. Peter H. Nidditch (Oxford, 1975), 344.

eliciting a promise that he will 'remember' her truth (III. ii. 211–12). A little later, Jaffeir represents his entire involvement with the conspiracy as a whole-sale act of forgetting: 'What a Devil's man, | When he forgets his nature' (III. ii. 303–4). But, when he is on the way to betray the conspiracy, he fears that the alternative set of memories may be revived: 'Secure me well before that thought's renew'd' (IV. i. 77). After the betrayal, however, Jaffeir's own mem-ories revert to his friends, and he longs to forget his very identity: 'Forget my self and this days guilt and falsehood. | Cruel remembrance how shall I ap-pease thee!' (IV. i. 215–16). Similarly, when he is struggling with the tempta-tion to stab Belvidera, he again vacillates between the claims of alternating memories:

> This dagger, well remembred, with this dagger
> I gave a solemn vow of dire importance. . . .
> Have a care, Mem'ry, drive that thought no farther . . .
> Oh for a long sound sleep, and so forget it!
>
> (IV. i. 378–88)

The shifts between the irreconcilable claims of competing memories reveal human character to be an unstable, fluctuating complex of discrete, extern-ally derived sensations. At times, Belvidera becomes Jaffeir's identity—'my Soul it self' (IV. i. 80)—but when he commits himself to the conspiracy he physically excludes her from his sphere of sensation by surrendering her as a pledge to his new allies. In the conspirators, the discontinuous self (or 'divided Soul,' as Jaffeir terms it, IV. i. 406) is most obvious in their alternat-ing stances as heroic liberators and anarchic destroyers, which they permutate with no sense of inconsistency or irony. But a more fundamental, and virtu-ally universal, discrepancy is that between longing for liberty and addiction to bondage.

Essentially, the conspirators aspire to recover the freedom of the wilder-ness. Pierre, for example, urges them to recover their 'natural Inheritance' of liberty, distinguishing such liberty from the social fictions of morality: 'There's no Religion, no Hypocrisie' in their cause (II. i. 155–6). But, as al-ready indicated, their imaginative erasure of social curbs is in no sense excep-tional. Similar erasure occurs when characters inhabiting the same physical space imaginatively project themselves into distant, separate, alien, and often solitary scenes, from Belvidera's joyful cry of love, 'Oh lead me to some Desart wide and wild' (I. i. 348) to the infinitely alien private landscape of 'Seas of Milk, and ships of Amber' (V. i. 369) that she sees in her final mad-ness. Such repeated retreat into private space is part of the general reversion of intimacy to strangeness, and it emphasizes that the conspirators' fascina-tion with the presocial state is not an anomalous violation of a prevailing order, but an expression of a virtually universal unassimilability into com-munity. At first glance *Venice Preserv'd* might appear to display a conventional portrayal of a society threatened by the destructive outsider, for the plotters include, besides native Venetians, a Spaniard, a Frenchman, and an Englishman, who all meet at the house of a Greek courtesan. But this multiplication of foreigners gives a special significance to foreignness: instead of a world challenged by the outsider, we have a world consisting of outsiders, in which even fathers and daughters are strangers to each other (V. i. 33), and in which rulers and conspirators reciprocally participate in each other's characteristics. There is no external distinction between citizen and stranger: only the unending warfare of opposites within the 'divided Soul'.

If a longing for primeval freedom is widespread, however, so is that for servitude. The Senator Antonio, a figure of power, craves humiliation, paying the prostitute Aquilina (Pierre's mistress) to abuse him, treat him as an animal, and trample upon him, subjection before the feet being his prime enthusiasm. As is now widely recognized, Antonio's comic case of power negated by masochism is tragically paralleled by many of the principals, including the conspirators, it being no accident that they play out their deluded and self-negating fantasies of heroic liberty in the very brothel in which he plays out his explicit fantasies of servitude. Frank and generally erotic longing for pain is frequent: for example, when Belvidera leads Jaffeir to betray his friends, he mimics both Antonio's masochism and his impersonation of the abject animal, imagining himself as a sacrificial lamb who, bound by a beautiful priestess, '*too hardly bleats, such pleasure's in the pain*' (IV. i. 94).[79] Still more frequent is foot-fetishism. 'Take our Swords and crush 'em with your feet' (III. ii. 467), begs one of the conspirators, after Pierre has calmed the hostility to Jaffeir roused by the guilty Renault. Had they known Jaffeir, Pierre responds, they would have 'Humbled' themselves 'before him, kiss'd his feet' (III. ii. 486). Later, repenting the betrayal of his friends, Jaffeir still more closely reproduces Antonio's desires, urging Pierre to 'Tread on me,' and longing to 'Ly at thy feet and kiss 'em though they spurn me' (IV. i. 339–42).

The dreams of regaining primal liberty thus alternate and conflict with a masochistic pleasure in servitude. Many dramatists of the period portray man as belonging simultaneously yet irreconcilably to the city and the wilderness, yet most see the city as expressing an inextinguishable, if imperfect, need for social co-operation. For Otway, man is naturally a citizen because he is naturally a slave. Alternating between impersonation of a rampant bull and a tame dog, with even his impersonation of the bull being conditional upon his ecstasy of sexual humiliation, Antonio demonstrates how the impulse to rebellion contains within itself the impulse to subjection. His fantasies of being a howling or roaring animal are clear rejections of the social and linguistic life of the city, and they are widely shared, for another sign of imaginative retreat into the wilderness is that the characters repeatedly visualize

---

[79] For fuller discussion, see Hughes, 'A New Look at *Venice Preserv'd*', *passim*.

themselves and their fellows as animals: Jaffeir, for example, perceives himself as a howling dog (II. i. 79) and bleating lamb (IV. i. 94), Renault as a fox (III. ii. 245), and the officers who arrest him as predators with 'paws' (IV. i. 104). These are not animal images in the usual sense, for they are not metaphoric, but rather show the mind of the wilderness persisting amidst the life of the city. As in Antonio's fantasies, however, the images shift between those of aggression and tameness, suggesting that the ambiguities of human nature are already present in the wilderness: man exists on the boundaries not of the savage and the civilized, but of the wild and the tame. For this reason, Antonio's—and Otway's—favourite animal representation of humanity is the dog: a creature that peculiarly combines servility and wildness. Antonio's comic scamperings before Aquilina's whip are shockingly transformed when the insane Belvidera dies scratching at the earth with her hands and muttering 'I'll dig, dig the Den up' (V. i. 503). The tenuous fiction of reason banished, she has entirely sunk into the mentality of the dog.

The most distinctive human capacity is not reason or articulacy but a propensity to systems of economic exchange: a system of equivalences in which object is related to object either directly or by a purely material sign[80] without the intervening abstraction of signification. The paradigm of economic exchange is the sexual act: from the petty rituals of Aquilina's brothel to the grand annual ceremonial of the trading nation's marriage with the sea, sexual and monetary exchange serve as equivalents to each other. Her life saved by Jaffeir at the marriage of Venice and the sea, Belvidera 'paid' the debt 'with her self' (I. i. 48). Jaffeir then bankrupts himself by maintaining Belvidera according to her ancestral rank, wishing to prove that he 'lov'd her for her self' (I. i. 94): an odd explanation, implicitly representing the self as a product of economic circumstances. Later, he surrenders her to the conspirators, causing her to complain (with justice) that she has been 'sold' (II. i. 400; III. ii. 1). Even Pierre draws Jaffeir into the conspiracy with pin-money, as though he were negotiating marriage with a prospective wife (II. i. 98). According to Lucretius, the invention of money created systems of subjection which superseded the mere rule of physical strength,[81] and this is the prime refinement of the city upon the wilderness.

Trade—the direct correlation of object with object—is an appropriate system for characters whose minds remain a clutter of separate sensory impressions. But higher forms of signification are treacherous. Antonio has, unaccountably, some reputation as an orator, yet he consistently exemplifies the decay of speech, with his lustful gibbering, his mimicry of animal noise, and his infantile distortions of Aquilina's name during his sexual routines—

---

80 Money was thought in the sixteenth century to possess an intrinsic value, but in the seventeenth it 'receives its value from its pure function as sign' (Michel Foucault, *The Order of Things: An Archaeology of the Human Sciences* (London, 1970), 176).

81 Lucretius, *De Rerum Natura*, v. 1113–16.

parodic rituals of naming. When he rehearses a political speech in the brothel, he provides the clearest demonstration of a mind limited to the retention of sense impressions, producing a chaotic sequence of free association that wanders from the image of the noonday sun to that of a ripe pumpkin, and thence to a pickled cucumber, sauce, a gander, and so on (V. i. 135–49). He manages a one-to-one correspondence of word to idea, but the signification of order and relationship exceeds his capacities.

In likening himself to a howling dog and a bleating lamb, Jaffeir shows that he shares Antonio's fascination with animal noise, and he and others fall into the primal chaos of inarticulacy represented by Antonio's babbling. Belvidera proclaims herself 'dumb with the big thought' of sexual passion (I. i. 346), and her final madness dissolves her sense not only of place and species, but also of linguistic coherence, as her thoughts ramble in a disorder like that of Antonio's speech:

> oh how the weather shrinks me!
> You are angry now, who cares? pish, no indeed.
> Choose then, I say you shall not go.

> (V. i. 484–6)

Such extremes of personal linguistic disintegration underline the more persistent failure of language as a socially ordering force. It was observed many years ago that the play is full of broken oaths, and that the only pledge ever to be honoured is the dagger which Jaffeir hands to the conspirators along with Belvidera, and with which (before stabbing himself) he finally renews the bond of friendship by saving Pierre from the shame of execution.[82] The emotive power of the dagger confirms the character of the mind as a repository of specific sense-impressions: signs are ineffectual in comparison with the apprehension and exercise of the pure object, and indeed the dagger brings an explicitly indicated extinction of language, Jaffeir dying with the words 'I'm quiet' (V. i. 478) and Pierre dying in a burst of inarticulate laughs and groans: 'Ha ha ha——oh oh' (V. i. 469).

But, if characters habitually break oaths, they must first habitually swear them. As humanity exists on the boundaries of society and the wilderness, so it exists on those of language and the inarticulate, needing the benefits of speech but unable to realize them. Jaffeir concedes the power of language when he fearfully imagines the future 'History' (IV. i. 209) of his actions, but desire for linguistic power is chiefly expressed in the many curses and rather fewer blessings. These share with the oaths the character of casting language in formal ritual (indeed, an oath can be a conditional curse or blessing, IV. i. 164–74), but their chief property is that they seemingly endow language with

---

[82] David R. Hauser, 'Otway Preserved: Theme and Form in *Venice Preserv'd*', *Studies in Philology*, 55 (1958), 481–93; William H. McBurney, 'Otway's Tragic Muse Debauched: Sensuality in *Venice Preserv'd*', *Journal of English and Germanic Philology*, 58 (1959), 380–99 (pp. 388–9).

a solid, material force: 'Oh for a Curse | To kill with!' cries Jaffeir; 'Daggers, Daggers, are much better!' replies Pierre (II. i. 122–3). When characters most desire language, they most equate it with the tangible, sensory bodies that are the only objects of their consciousness. But the curses and blessings, as ineffectual as the oaths, do not link earthly language to the workings of transcendent power. Like Loveit's curses in *The Man of Mode*, they are the impotent outpourings of raging minds eager to reconstitute the world as a sign of their own inner agony, as when Belvidera wishes to transfer her widowed sterility to the entire world (v. i. 348–353). The curses mirror the isolation of the individual mind, the absence of a larger order to contain and harmonize the atomistic conflict of individual wills. Human signs have no eternal prototypes: when Jaffeir says that 'Angels are Painted fair, to look like' woman (I. i. 339), he explicitly and specifically turns a sign of an eternal form into a fiction derived from a corporeal source.

Denied absolutes, humanity is left (as in *The Rival Queens*) only with the conflicting impulses of the body, which toss man between servility and impotent dreams of freedom, and between competing sets of conflicting and alternative memories. It is in this corporeal turmoil, and not in the timeless order of the heavens, that the roots of political society lie. The concluding images of the play are of individuals disintegrating under the tyranny of social existence, the dissolution of Belvidera's mind—the ultimate incoherence of memory—complementing the breaking of the conspirators' bodies upon the wheel (an image of physical laceration which particularly recalls *The Rival Queens*). Then Priuli, the most prominent figure of state authority in the play, concludes it by choosing permanent seclusion from society. There is no second Restoration here: only a chaos of crushed individuals.

CHAPTER EIGHT

'Dire is the Dearth and Famine on the Stage': Drama, 1682–1688

In November 1682 the ailing King's Company merged with the more adventurously and expertly managed Duke's, and for the next thirteen years the London stage became a monopoly. The absence of commercial rivalry induced an unenterprising reliance upon stock plays, and new plays for a while became scarce and unadventurous. Most comedies, for example, are farcical or lightweight, and in the period up to the end of the 1688 season only four plays (Lee's *The Princess of Cleve*, Otway's *The Atheist*, Behn's *The Lucky Chance*, and Sedley's *Bellamira*) provide a serious and exploratory treatment of human sexuality. The Tory triumph turned hitherto ambivalent dramatists into partisans and thereby assisted the decline of tragedy. With *The Duke of Guise* (November 1682) and *Constantine the Great* (November 1683) Dryden and Lee make their last, and least distinguished, contributions to Exclusion Crisis drama; Rochester's adaptation of Fletcher's *Valentinian* received a posthumous première by February 1684; but thereafter there is nothing until Mountfort's *The Injur'd Lovers* (February 1688) and Crowne's *Darius King of Persia* (April 1688).

The Dryden–Lee *Duke of Guise* had been prepared for performance the previous July, but had been banned, probably because its attack on Monmouth offended his much tried but still protective father. Despite Dryden's disingenuous assertions to the contrary in his defence of the play,[1] the play develops a clear (and intellectually barren) parallel between the sedition of the Catholic League against Henri III and that of the Whigs against Charles: Blois, where the sedition is crushed, corresponds to Oxford; Guise, who is murdered, to Monmouth; and Henri of Navarre (Henri IV) to James, though Navarre never actually appears.[2] Whereas Navarre is associated with

Epigraph: Behn, *The Lucky Chance*, prologue.

[1] [John] Dryden, *The Vindication; or, the Parallel of the French Holy-League, and the English League and Covenant, Turn'd into a Seditious Libell against the King and his Royal Highness, By Thomas Hunt and the Authors of the Reflections upon the Pretended Parallel in the Play called The Duke of Guise* (London, 1683). In the *Vindication*, Dryden claims only I. i, Act IV, and the first half of Act V (*Dramatick Works* (1735), v. 313).

[2] It is probably unwise to seek any close parallels between the ineffectual Henri III and Charles. He has been interpreted as a further expression of Tory exasperation with the King's apparent inaction, though, if so, the exasperation is surely retrospective (Anne Barbeau Gardiner, 'A Conflict of Laws: Consequences of the King's Inaction in *The Duke of Guise*', *English Language Notes*, 19 (1981–2),

plain, honest speech, the conspirator Malicorne (?Shaftesbury) is ensnared by the equivocation of the fiend, for his pact with the Devil turns out, through an optical illusion, to have been for twelve years instead of the apparent twenty-one (V, p. 295).[3] Such is the insecurity when institutions are grounded not on the immutable clarity of the divine word but on the ambiguities and deceptions of secular compact.

Lee's *Constantine the Great* develops parallels to both the Exclusion Crisis and the Rye House plot (a conspiracy to assassinate the royal brothers in the spring of 1683), providing the familiar figures of a ruler, his severe but upright brother, and a manipulative subversive, this time represented by the heresiarch Arius. But Lee's main, and well-worn, subject is sexual rivalry between father and son (Constantine and Crispus), whereby he displaces into the sphere of romance the political rivalry between Charles and Monmouth and leads it to reconciliation; for, exceptionally in Lee's work, the oppressive father relents.[4] Historically, Constantine (like Lucius Junius Brutus) executed his son, but Lee portrays an ultimately benevolent father-king,[5] though Constantine is initially a paler version of earlier egomaniacs such as Mithridates and Augustus. Exceptionally, too, Lee brings humanity into linguistic contact with a benevolent heavenly power. At the opening of *Theodosius*, the vision of Constantine had been represented through human artifice, but *Constantine* opens with the vision itself, accompanied by an angelic song—heard also by St Sylvester—which predicts the coming cycle of agony and resignation. The action of the play thus follows a celestially planned and enunciated narrative—a quite exceptional dramatic design for a major writer of this period—though for much of the play the point is that Constantine is not obeying the signs, but is sacrificing his kingly calling to passion.[6]

The last comedy to deal with the Exclusion Crisis, Crowne's *City Politiques* (January 1683, banned in June 1682), similarly dispenses with doubt and

109–15). George Hickes emphasizes the remarkable parallel between the Guise conspiracy and the Exclusion Crisis, but describes Charles as 'incomparably wiser and juster then was *Henry* III. of *France*' ([George Hickes], *The Judgment of an Anonymous Writer Concerning These following Particulars*, 2nd edn. (London, 1684), 10). There is a full discussion of the scope and limitations of the play's personal parallels in California Dryden, xiv. 493–512.

[3] The identification of Malicorne with Shaftesbury is proposed in Rachel A. Miller, 'Political Satire in the Malicorne–Melanax Scenes of *The Duke of Guise*', *English Language Notes*, 16 (1978–9), 212–18.

[4] The political allusions in the play are discussed in A. L. Cooke and Thomas B. Stroup, 'The Political Implications in Lee's *Constantine the Great*', *Journal of English and Germanic Philology*, 49 (1950), 506–15, and Richard E. Brown, 'Nathaniel Lee's Political Dramas, 1679–1683', *Restoration*, 10 (1986), 41–52.

[5] *An Antidote against the Present Fears and Jealousies of the Nation* (London, 1679), lauding Charles's unexampled clemency, compares and contrasts him with Constantine, who 'forgave his Enemies, advanced Religion, incouraged Piety, yet he imbrued his Fatherly hands in the blood of his own Son and Heir *Crispus*, upon the suspition of a Rebellion' (pp. 5–6).

[6] Richard E. Brown notes Lee's criticism of Charles ('Nathaniel Lee's Political Dramas', 48).

ambivalence. The play is set in Naples, but transparently satirizes the Whigs' recent use of the City of London as a power-base, portraying it as a no-go area in which the law of the land is finally re-established, but where social cohesion is initially suspended amidst the proliferation of mini-societies: clubs, cabals, associations, and various kinds of company (a recurrent word, yet again). Before the final reassertion of authority, two intruders establish themselves in this separate world: Florio, who cuckolds the Podesta (Mayor) by pretending to be a Whig convert dying of diseases contracted while a Tory rake; and Artall, another Tory, who cuckolds the old lawyer Bartoline by pretending to be Florio. Florio emphasizes the social fragmentation by representing his life in the city as life in an alien world of alien language: 'I am in a world very different from that I used to live in. I talk godly, a strange language to me' (I. i. 32–4). The city is indeed a place of 'strange language': the distorted, lisping speech of the toothless Bartoline symbolizes his debasement of law into perplexed ambiguity; doggerel, libel, and false news proliferate; and the Doctor (Titus Oates) equates his vulgar slanders with the primal Adamic language (V. ii. 60–1). The characters' habit of describing each other in imagery of texts—the Podesta's son Craffy describes his beautiful stepmother as 'a curious appendix . . . bound up with' his father's 'volume of nonsense' (II. i. 56–8)—indicates the extent to which the libels and nonsense have become a primary reality, governing the perception of quotidian experience.

The most ingeniously developed symptom of the general disorder is that space and place become elusive, confusing concepts, as in the following absurd exchange between Florio and Craffy:

CRAFFY. Oh, friend Florio, are you here?
FLORIO. Ay, sir, thanks to my distemper that keeps me prisoner.
CRAFFY. Whoo! But aren't you wi' my father yonder?
FLORIO. No, I profess I am here, sir.
CRAFFY. How are you able to be here?
FLORIO. I am not able to be anywhere else, I'm so ill.

(I. i. 168–73)

There proves as unmanageable a term for Craffy as *here*. He lusts after his father's young wife Rosaura, whom he has seen copulating with Florio in the garden house, and he wishes to expose Florio without alienating her: will she, he privately asks, meet him 'there'—he uses the word five times—as well (V. ii. 99–107)? Accordingly, he accuses Florio of solo adultery: 'I did not see her *there*, but that damned rascal I did see *there*' (V. ii. 109–10; italics added). The contradictions of this charge are then teased out, with *there* remaining a central term.

Such confusion in the basic terminology of space reveals lives no longer regulated by fixed categories of place: dislocated lives, in which conditions of aimless movement are anomalously superimposed upon conditions of aimless imprisonment. Florio's pretended sickness repeatedly leads him to claim, as in his dialogue with Craffy, that he is imprisoned within a confined space, yet he is equally repeatedly rushing on a spurious journey to the next world. The Podesta is given to pointless meanderings, which bring him back none the wiser to his own house, which itself becomes a proliferating set of separate prisons (little cells): Florio a 'prisoner' because of his pretended sickness (I. i. 169) and later 'locked up' (III. i. 358–9) in adultery with Rosaura (who is lodged there to prevent her from 'going abroad', II. i. 401), Craffy locked up because of apparent madness, and the whole eventually hemmed in by guards. To be alone with Rosaura, Florio fabricates news of a French fleet, its commanders appropriately enough disguised as 'pilgrims' (III. i. 215), and the Podesta promptly sets out with 'no guide' (III. i. 285) on his journey of investigation: 'Now he is gone he knows not whither, to catch he knows not whom,' says Florio (III. i. 325–6). Later, deceived into thinking that the Viceroy intends to make him Lord Treasurer, he is led on an ostensible journey to the viceregal court which is in fact a circular journey back to his own house, which has been disguised in the mean time. 'Do you not know where you are? Do you not know your own home?' (V. iii. 112–13) asks the Governor when he arrives to inflict the literal confinement of arrest.

It is a question which applies to all the dislocations and all the fragmentations of community in the play: the illusory metamorphosis of the home, its investment with a grandeur beyond its nature, represents the decay of community as a unifying ideal and also the disruptive aspiration beyond due social place, most extreme in the Bricklayer (a caricature of Stephen College, the Protestant Joiner). At the end of the play, the Governor restores social and linguistic order, depriving the Doctor of his power to nullify the titles of lords and dukes and bidding the citizens return to the callings they were bred to, just as, nearly ninety years before, Augustus had sent the cit social climbers home in *Poetaster*. Man in *Thyestes* had been 'a vagabond' (V, p. 55), but dislocation is here no longer an essential characteristic of human life—simply a remediable perversion of a coherent social hierarchy. In Crowne's other plays, monarchic authority is necessitated by the limitations of knowledge in a world of enigmatic, impenetrable surfaces. Here, hierarchy is based on knowledge—knowledge of place—and the Whigs are satirized for their failure to grasp knowledge that is perfectly verifiable and obvious. The old men do not *see* (a key word) the adultery that is taking place under their noses, and they do not *know* their places: the Podesta goes 'he knows not whither, to catch he knows not whom' and does not 'know' his own home. Like Lee and Dryden, Crowne here departs radically from the philosophic principles that had informed his earlier work.

Loyalist triumphalism received support even from the Duke of Buckingham, who had quarrelled with Shaftesbury and drifted away from the Exclusionists: an adaptation of *Philaster* (?February 1683), possibly by him, is loyally titled *The Restauration; or, Right Will Take Place*,[7] and he undoubtedly wrote the tasteless epilogue, which mocks '*Achitophell*' for, among other things, being dead. The play is more an abbreviation than an adaptation, though one significant addition is a speech urging kings to administer justice instead of battening off their people (V, p. 67). But, with the defeat of the Whigs, political drama largely ceases until the death-throes of James II's reign, and in the years between 1683 and 1688 the only new play to deal directly with Restoration politics is Dryden's opera *Albion and Albanius*. It is tempting to see some hostile commentary upon Charles II in Rochester's *The Tragedy of Valentinian*,[8] in which, for example, Valentinian's catalogue of flaws is extended to include imprudent clemency. As Hume observes, 'The satire—if any—cannot have been too disturbing, since Charles had the piece played at court,'[9] but the play is none the less strikingly prophetic of the anti-Stuart drama of the post-Revolution years, focusing on what was to become the popular figure of the rapist tyrant and treating the intricate paradox of the guilty ruler as a Gordian knot which is easily loosened by the sword. In both the original and the adaptation, Valentinian rapes Lucina, the wife of the great soldier Maximus, and is consequently assassinated, whereupon Maximus gains the throne. In Fletcher, Maximus is corrupted by ambition, arranges the murder of his steadfast friend Æcius, and is fittingly killed by a poisoned laurel wreath at the moment of his inauguration. Rochester, by contrast, portrays a world without fixed absolutes, and puts in Maximus' mouth one of the most extreme denials of divine Providence in Restoration drama: 'Evil . . . has Coeternity' with the gods (IV, p. 215). Whereas Fletcher implicitly likens Lucina's resistance of temptation to that of Christ, the new Lucina's response to Valentinian is an internal and ambiguous process, no longer evaluated by fixed, external standards: she acknowledges Valentinian's attractiveness, and her prophetic dream of the rape is one in which she is torn between the influence of angels and devils, and in which she finds herself in a clammy swamp, inwardly incapable of controlling her voice or limbs (III, pp. 192–3). The dream represents a conflict not between good and evil but between Lucina's own sexuality and her sense of the forbidden, the absence of transcendent marital laws being indicated by the fact that even the angels do not pronounce her husband's name.

As she sleeps, her virtuous attendant Claudia meditates upon the paradoxes of virtue, for those who possess it are perpetually fearful and tormented, while the unvirtuous live in 'Tranquility and Peace':

---

[7] It is not certain whether the play was acted. Danchin conjecturally dates the première, if any, to Feb. 1683 (*Prologues and Epilogues*, iv. 452).

[8] Rochester died in 1680. The manuscript (BM Add. MSS 28692, fos. 3a–59a) gives an intended cast for a projected King's Company performance *c.*1675–6. See *London Stage*, ed. Van Lennep, i. 238.

[9] Hume, *Development*, 364.

> Each man I meet I fancy will devour me;
> And sway'd by Rules not natural but affected
> I hate Mankind for fear of being lov'd.

> (III, p. 191)

With monarchy, as with chastity, inflexible metaphysical principles yield to principles determined by human regulation. Maximus views Valentinian (persuasively) as a 'Worm', 'More than my self in nothing but in name' (IV, p. 215), and he asserts to Valentinian's face that kings are subject to law, and that they originally shared the toiling lives of their subjects (V, p. 236). Moreover, whereas Fletcher cites the example of the two Bruti merely in order to reject it (I. iii. 81–6), Rochester makes Lucius Junius Brutus a worthy object of imitation (the rape of Lucina is, for example, synchronized with the rehearsal of a masque representing the rape of Lucretia). Rochester's Maximus is not corrupted by disloyalty (having no part in Æcius' death), and Rochester does not show usurpation punished in the moment of consummation. Instead of an ending figuring forth eternal principles of justice, Rochester leaves us with the unresolved ambiguities of human deliberation, in Maximus' 'Lead me to Death or Empire, which you please' (V, p. 238).

By contrast, Dryden's *Albion and Albanius* (June 1685) revives the uncritical loyalist fervour of the early Restoration. The return of Charles is, indeed, the subject of the first act, which culminates with explicit revival of early Restoration iconography, in '*the 4 Triumphal Arches erected at his Majesties Coronation*' (I. i. 246b–c).[10] In the remaining two acts, Democracy returns from Hell in a further attempt to subvert 'Degree' (II. i. 26) and engineers the crises of Charles's later years, though she is powerless to thwart his destiny to 'be restor'd agen' (III. i. 145). From beginning to end, Dryden affirms the simple absolutes that he had so quickly abandoned in the 1660s. In the Virgilian motto on the title-page, '*Discite justitiam, moniti & non temnere Divos*,' Justice is released from inadequacy and epistemological ambiguity as Astraea returns once again; for the same lines had supported the Astraea Redux theme on the first coronation arch.[11] Language is similarly redeemed from ambiguity, and the obsessive Carolean association of judicial enigma and linguistic enigma is for a while suspended:

> *He Plights his Faith; and we believe him just;*
> *His Honour is to Promise, ours to Trust.*
> *Thus* Britain's *Basis on a Word is laid,*
> *As by a Word the World it self was made.*

> (Epilogue, ll. 31–4)

---

[10] For the iconography of Charles II's coronation, see John Ogilby, *The Entertainment of His Most Excellent Majestie Charles II . . . A Facsimile*, introd. Ronald Knowles (Binghamton, NY, 1988).

[11] *Aeneid*, vi. 620, where the line is addressed to the souls in Tartarus, all of whom had offended against social or religious obligations. See Ogilby, *Entertainment*, 40. The return of Astraea is celebrated at I. i. 232.

In the event, however, the world and the word went their separate ways. Charles died before this celebration of his second Restoration could be mounted, and Dryden had to tack on an apotheosis and transference of power. Then the opening run was curtailed by the panic caused by Monmouth's invasion: Dryden had portrayed the forces of disruption as emerging from and returning to '*a Poeticall Hell*' (II. i. oa), but in fact they were uncontainable.

As dramatists on the whole eschewed the complexities of politics, so they eschewed those of sexual conduct. After the success of *The London Cuckolds*, for example, Ravenscroft produced the inoffensive *Dame Dobson; or, The Cunning Woman* (May 1683), in an attempt (according to the prologue) to cater for respectable ladies, some '*Females of renown*' having formed a hostile claque at the former play. *Dame Dobson* concerns a fraudulent sorceress who gets off scot-free because her frauds are on the whole beneficent, her pseudo-sorcery giving opportunity for the increasingly popular mixture of spectacle and farce, but the attempt to give chaste pleasure failed.

The most original experiment with sex comedy in this period appears in Lee's *The Princess of Cleve* (?December 1682),[12] where Lee follows Otway in creating a comedy of social disintegration, and in the process dissolves fixed categories of dramatic genre, creating a 'Farce, Comedy, Tragedy or meer Play' (dedication, p. 153). Lee debases Madame de La Fayette's tragic account of the unrealizable love between the virtuous Princess, married to an unloved but adoring husband, and the noble Nemours, turning Nemours into a faithless, cynical rake, who overtly parodies the recently dead Rochester. In addition to his involvement with the Princess, Nemours participates in a sex comedy sub-plot where seduction and courtship are regularly associated with disguise and impersonation, achieved through the two standard devices of bedroom trick and Invisible Mistress deception, each used on three occasions: the misused wives of two would-be libertines confront their husbands as alluringly masked strangers before marching off with other men, and later enjoy a night of bliss in a complex double bedroom trick (in which, among other complications, a woman who thinks she is sleeping with Nemours is in fact sleeping with his male lover); and a long-established mistress of Nemours recaptures his attention, and enjoys his favours, by passing herself off as a new conquest.

In the sexual encounters of the comic plot, then, public tokens of character are frequently effaced, leaving only blind carnal contact. But this farcical instability of perceived identity is more subtly reproduced within the serious plot, or in the characters' transitions from one to the other. For, although Lee's Nemours is alien to the noble decorum of the Princess's world, he also

---

[12] The date is conjectural. See Hume, 'The Satiric Design of Nat. Lee's *The Princess of Cleve*', 118–23, repr. in *The Rakish Stage*, 113–18. Hume argues that 'we may feel reasonably sure that *The Princess of Cleve* was conceived and written in late 1681 or early 1682' (*JEGP* 122; *Rakish Stage*, 118).

participates in it, having in the past saved the life of the Prince whom he now destroys. Conversely, the Princess's love for the worthless Nemours reveals that her character is less simple than her code (which is itself a municipal law, for the two comic wives are perfectly justified in cuckolding their husbands). The impression of biform characters within uniform roles is assisted by emphasis on the alternative existence of the dream: the opening song prefers erotic dreams to carnal sex, and during the comic double bedroom trick a husband is cuckolded as he sleepwalks, performing in his dream a complete act of adultery, with running commentary, at the same time as an interloper satisfies his wife. But, if a ridiculous cuckold dreams of sensual liberation, so does the noble Princess, who first reveals her guilty passion to another by narrating a dream of entry into an alternative, subaqueous world in which she caresses Nemours ten fathoms beneath the surface of a stream (II. iii. 83–99).

The division and incoherence of self persists even at the end of the play. After her husband's death the Princess reluctantly rejects Nemours, whom she still loves, but her repudiation has no consistency of purpose, for she wavers between moral principle and the fear that surrender would quickly lead to betrayal. Her confused, unstable emotions give some credibility to Nemours's cynical intimations of future seduction, and they confirm the suspension of human character between social imperatives and other, less rational imperatives which mock prescribed forms: the desires of that other world, deep within the stream. Of the noble characters, only the Prince is free from such divided impulses, and he is destroyed by their operations in others. Nemours remains unstoppable, concluding the play with a sudden repentance whose genuineness we are clearly invited to suspect, but which—whether genuine or not—again illustrates the capricious mutability of human character; for it prompts him to marry the old flame who, by appearing to him in a new identity, has reinvented her novelty. There is no continuity either in the perception or inner constitution of character, and the play's discontinuities of genre and social standards reflect the fundamental incoherence of human nature itself. In its outlook, quality, and neglect, *The Princess of Cleve* stands with the comedies of Otway.

Otway himself made one last contribution to the comedy of social disintegration. Whereas Ravenscroft had followed *The London Cuckolds* with something completely different, Otway in *The Atheist* (July 1683 or earlier) returned to the formula of his previous comedy, providing a sequel to *The Souldiers Fortune* in which the marriage of Courtine and Sylvia has declined into incurable emptiness, recrimination, and infidelity. As usual in Otway, physical, social, and personal dislocation are pervasive. Early in the play, Beaugard denounces his father for his negligent upbringing, complaining that he was never permitted to remain at home, and that he had finally been turned out of doors (I. 9–41). Throughout the play, characters see themselves as travellers in quest of (illusory) freedom, and the images of travel and dislocation reach extremes when Beaugard and Daredevil (the atheist) are captured on the orders of the heroine, Porcia, and persuaded that they have been transposed to a different time zone (IV. 273–5), after 'a long unmeasurable Journey' (III. 616) to 'A Chrystal Castle built by Enchantment in a Land unknown to any but the fair one that Commands it' (III. 640–1). In the final act, still set in Porcia's domain, characters blunder around confusedly in the dark, the confusion about who is where culminating in a bedroom trick of multiple misapprehension: Sylvia has fallen for a 'Stranger' (V. 58) who is actually another heroine, Lucrece, in male disguise, and sleeps with Beaugard in the belief that she is sleeping with the beautiful stranger; Beaugard believes that he is sleeping with Porcia; and Courtine, sharing his belief, guards the door during his own cuckolding.

The literal dislocation of place and role reflects a suspension of social order and authority, most strikingly manifested in the comic role-reversal whereby Beaugard has to support a spendthrift, debauched, and disrespectful father, whose comic inadequacies support a more serious questioning of patriarchal and male authority. Porcia has been bequeathed by her dead husband to his friend Gratian, a former rival for her hand, and Gratian's claims are violently supported by Theodoret, who is both Porcia's brother-in-law and Gratian's friend. Such male bonds of noble rivalry and idealized friendship had often been uncritically celebrated in the 1660s, but (as in *The Orphan* and in Lee's *Theodosius*) the emphasis is here on the viewpoint of the reluctant woman who is bandied about in the men's punctilious rituals of mutual regard. Theodoret is a crudely anti-feminist tyrant ('Their Sex is one gross Cheat', III. 370), his encroachment upon Porcia's autonomy being confirmed by his invasion of her house with armed bravoes. In her deception of Beaugard and Daredevil, Porcia had briefly turned her house into an expression of feminist fantasy: 'A Chrystal Castle' ruled by a woman, situated in a land known only to its mistress, and administered by a dwarf: a shrunken man. But male oppressors discover the route to the secret land, and the dream of freedom becomes a material prison, Theodoret bursting in and commanding the doors and windows to be barred (V. 228).

As he does so, he threatens a still more despotic pattern of control, over her access to language: he will make her curse her father and mother for allowing her to learn to write (V. 234–6), and he fixes the limits of permissible literacy by ordering her to her prayer book (V. 297). Indeed, the very name that seems to individuate Porcia expresses a dominant masculine culture, for she is named after a Roman wife (of the younger Brutus) who committed suicide for the sake of her husband. So, of course, is Lucrece. Conversely, Theodoret and Gratian represent an enduring male monopoly in language and authority, being named after a famous church historian and a still more famous canon lawyer, so that the parallel vulnerability of women in the spheres of law and history is indicated with peculiar clarity. When Lucrece assumes male guise at the beginning of Act V, in an attempt permanently to seize the power and privilege of the male, she emphasizes that skill in male argot is essential for 'Interest at Court' and 'Preferment' (V. 43–4), but (as in Behn) control of language is not the cause but the consequence of power, and the defeat of Theodoret and Gratian is a feat of male militarism in which the women have little part. As Beaugard storms towards victory, authority is no longer that of the romance heroine in her crystal castle: 'I am sure I reign Lord Peramount of this Castle now,' he boasts (V. 750–1). Durfey's Madam Fickle had successfully challenged the nomenclature determined by a man-dominated history; Porcia and Lucrece are less fortunate.

Alluding to a ruse whereby his father had impersonated a chaplain in order to expose Daredevil's latent fear of hell, Beaugard affirms that he is going to 'make' Porcia 'another sort of Domestick' (i. e. than the chaplain) (V. 1043–4); '*Thus still, with Power in hand, we treat of Peace,*' he continues (V. 1053). After all the fantasies of power in a crystal castle, Porcia ends up with a husband who has the power to 'make' what she is. Feminism is a nobler and more legitimate rebellion against entrenched authority than atheism—like Shadwell's Mrs Gripe, Porcia insists that liberty is 'an English Woman's natural Right' (V. 430–1)—but the two rebellions prove equally ineffective. Lucrece fares even worse than Porcia, for the grand schemes of seizing male power through male disguise come to nothing. All she achieves is to organize the bedroom trick in which Beaugard and Sylvia sleep with each other, remaining manifestly disengaged from the proceedings, although the male participant is the man whose love she was originally seeking, and the female participant thinks that Lucrece, in her male manifestation, is her lover. Lucrece is not returned to her feminine identity at the end of the play, but she has no part at all in the ending, remaining entirely unaccounted for once the bedroom trick is over. Through her role-change, she does not discover identity for herself but merely confuses it in others, as is emphasized by her function in a variant of the familiar Invisible Mistress plot (the pseudo-enchanted palace and the dwarf both feature in the original version of the Invisible Mistress story, in Scarron's *Le Roman comique*, where the heroine is indeed named Porcia). Porcia enacts a straightforward version of the plot, courting Beaugard in a mask and then appearing unmasked, apparently as another woman, to test his loyalty to her own masked self. But Lucrece complicates this pattern by also courting Beaugard in a mask, spoiling Porcia's nice pattern of unity within division by providing a genuine masked alternative. Then, in the bedroom trick, she divides her rival yet more fully, presenting Sylvia to Beaugard in the guise of Porcia. 'How's this?' cries Beaugard as he emerges from the bedroom to find Porcia outside: 'My Widow split in twain! My *Porcia* there, and *Porcia* here too?' (V. 910–11). Lucrece works against Porcia's attempt to maintain a unity of self within a controlled manipulation of social appearances, producing a division of appearance that Porcia cannot predict or manage: a total and ominous separation between the lady of the castle and the object of Beaugard's lust. But, in doing so, Lucrece achieves nothing for herself: all that her dreams of liberty accomplish is to interfere with the parallel dreams of a parallel heroine. Otway's *œuvre* began, in *Alcibiades*, with a rootless ancient hero; it ends with a rootless modern woman, cursed with an ancient, heroic name.

After *The Atheist*, no new sex comedy was staged until Behn's *The Lucky Chance* (probably April 1686), though a critical retrospect on the ethos of sex comedy is provided in Southerne's generically indeterminate *The Disappointment* (April 1684), which explores the tragic potential of libertine comedy, and in the process displays marked sympathy for the fallen woman. Juliana, seduced and abandoned by the rakish Alberto, employs bedroom tricks to impersonate two other intended victims, eventually inducing him to recognize her 'most amazing Goodness' (V. ii. 156) and marry her. The first bedroom trick, however, leads the hitherto uxorious Alphonso to suspect his virtuous wife of adultery with the Duke, and the confusion is remedied just in time to prevent him from assassinating his ruler. Libertinism is politically disruptive, and the actions of *The Man of Mode* have the potential to produce those of *Othello*. Like *The Loyal Brother*, this play asserts clear social and moral absolutes, and it provides no hint that, within a few years, Southerne was to be Otway's closest follower in the comedy of disorientation, though he certainly does portray states of moral and emotional dislocation: Alberto and his victims wander, imagine themselves in deserts, require a guide, and feel that they have become strangers to their normal patterns of existence.[13] But, whereas Otway's dislocations (and those of the mature Southerne) were unalterable features of the natural order, the dislocations here are curable deviations from moral normality. Accordingly, Southerne gives the bedroom trick its most conservative function, of tricking an aberrant character into conformity with the norms that he violates, and the violation of norms is explicitly associated with that of 'Justice'.[14] At the end, 'Innocence is prov'd' (V. ii. 330).

Amidst all its characteristically farcical horseplay (which in part involves a foolish Justice), John Lacy's posthumously produced *Sir Hercules Buffoon* (June 1684)[15] also steers comedy in the direction of potentially tragic violence, portraying the impoverished Sir Marmaduke Seldin's attempt to repair his fortunes by murdering his two rich wards and substituting his two daughters for them: an attempt frustrated by the virtue of the daughters. The play appeared with a prologue by Durfey, whose *Love for Money* (1691) perhaps betrays its influence, and the names of its two heiress-hunters, Bowman and Aimwell, seem to have impressed Farquhar. Elsewhere, there is an increasing tendency towards pure farce (often featuring magical transformation).

---

[13] I. i. 185–6; III. i. 11–12, 43, 91, 225–7, 244–5, ii. 8–17, 51–2.
[14] III. ii. 27–8, 43–4, 189; IV. i. 251; V. ii. 113, 302.   [15] Lacy had died in 1681.

Nahum Tate's *A Duke and No Duke* (August 1684), an adaptation of Aston Cokain's *Trappolin Creduto Principe*, and Thomas Jevon's *The Devil of a Wife* (March 1686) both portray a regenerative inversion of a repressive order achieved through a magical exchange of identities. In the latter (very attractive) play, the gentle wife of a violent and tyrannical cobbler changes place with the shrewish wife of the kindly lord of the manor, the result being a reform of both cobbler and lady. In her unreformed state the lady had been a foe of festivity, attempting to cancel the celebration of Christmas. In *A Duke and No Duke*, a clownish pimp changes place with a Duke and to some extent creates chaos: as in the original, there is a scene of farcically logical justice (for example, the killer of a widow's child is sentenced to impregnate her with another). But the pimp also reverses the Duke's unwise distribution of punishment and favour. The challenging carnival of early Restoration comedy is replaced by harmless and unrealistic saturnalia. Behn, who had unsuccessfully returned to sex comedy in *The Lucky Chance*, also turned to farce in *The Emperor of the Moon* (March 1687), in which two young noblemen marry the niece and daughter of a foolish astronomer by masquerading as the Emperor of the Moon and the Prince of Thunderland, with appropriate stage spectacle (showy farce was the limit of affordable spectacle in the couple of years after the expensive fiasco of *Albion and Albanius*).[16] Even Marlowe was called upon to serve the taste for farce, in William Mountfort's adaptation, *The Life and Death of Doctor Faustus* (spring 1688), in which the tragic elements are truncated to make room for the sorcery of Scaramouche and Harlequin.

Another farcical simplification of a pre-Restoration play was Tate's revision of *Eastward Ho* as *Cuckolds-Haven* (July 1685). The original title refers to an unaccomplished westward voyage to Virginia, which reflects a persistent concern with disrupted place: a concern which Tate largely excises (while taking a patronizingly satirical view of the citizen characters). Jonson's voyaging gulls and impostors are, for example, no longer morally relocated by being washed up in appropriate places along the Thames; nor does the goldsmith Touchstone's good daughter, Mildred, any longer deplore marriage between partners of different social *'place'* (I. ii. 34). Another weakening of moral structure appears in the reconciliation of Touchstone and his extravagant apprentice Quicksilver: in Jonson, Quicksilver repents, but in Tate he endears himself by a failed but witty deception. In his other adaptation of the mid-1680s, a reworking of the 1668 reworking of *The Island Princess*, Tate cultivated the other extreme of inoffensiveness, romantic tragicomedy: a Portuguese hero restores an Indian king to his throne, gains the love of his sister, and converts her to Christianity, both lovers clinging to their faith in the face of threatened torture. In 1668, such topicality as the play possessed had simply

16 Milhous, 'The Multimedia Spectacular', 56.

lain in its portrayal of restoration; now it lies in the spectacle of a restored monarch forcing idolatry upon the agent of his reinstatement. But Tate's overt aim is simply the portrayal of triumphant virtue.

The only other dramatist in these years to equal Tate's score of three 'new' plays was Thomas Durfey, who also tried to play safe: two were yet more adaptations of Fletcher, with none of the bold transformations that had marked his earlier revision of *Monsieur Thomas*. A *Common-Wealth of Women* (August 1685), an adaptation of *The Sea Voyage* (itself heavily influenced by *The Tempest*), deals with a pair of men and a group of women stranded on separate desert islands, whose eventual meeting brings the reunion of a long-separated husband and wife. Fletcher retains from *The Tempest* a consistently emphasized concern with the value of service and community. He also treats the isolation of the men from the women as a condition of sterile unfulfilment, in which the men become signs lacking the principle that will raise them to full actuality. Neither are of interest to Durfey: for him, the basis of restored community is the sexual appetite of the women, and he adds to the play a feminist speech asserting the perfection and self-sufficiency of the female.

This play at least retains Durfey's interest in the capabilities of woman, but his next two plays reveal a thorough social conservatism. *The Banditti* (January 1686), written at the suggestion of Charles II, affirms the impotence of nurture to alter inherited nature, for a bandit's son brought up by a gentleman remains a villain, and a gentleman's son brought up by a bandit remains a gentleman. Audience disapproval of the play was so great that the actors at times became inaudible: like Ravenscroft, Durfey miscalculated in his attempt to cater for a new set of tastes. He was more sexually daring in a further Fletcher adaptation, *A Fool's Preferment* (March/April 1688), based on *The Noble Gentleman*, which deals with a foolish country gentleman's attempt to get preferment at court, his wife's extravagance and infidelity during their stay there, and her attempt to prevent his return home by deluding him that he has been made a Duke (though Durfey modifies his source by curing the dupe of his delusion, as Ravenscroft had done when adapting *Le Bourgeois Gentilhomme*). Durfey again excises Fletcher's analysis of the nature of community, omitting his commendation of the gentleman's home and estate, with its attendant responsibilities to tenants; like Tate, he is uninterested in the ideology of place. With opportunistic flexibility of principle, however, he deserts his normal feminist stance, portraying the errant wife as an ultimately reformed transgressor against sexual hierarchy, who finally promises the 'Duty of a most Penitent, Obedient Wife' (v, p. '85' [77]) (whereas her Fletcherian counterpart is still duping her husband at the end). But the wife's reform did not preserve the play from complaints of obscenity, which Durfey vigorously rebuts in the dedication. Once again, he had sensed a change of mood, but could not cater to it.

Crowne's *Sir Courtly Nice* (May 1685) was more successful in giving chaste pleasure, though its epilogue notes nervously that new plays were generally failing. Like St Serfe's *Tarugo's Wiles* (1667), the play adapts Moreto's *No puede ser*, which had been proposed to Crowne as a model by Charles II.[17] The adaptation, however, is far more ambitious than St Serfe's, following the pattern of *City Politiques* by providing a detailed examination of authority within the family. Lord Bellguard, jealous of his sister's honour and anxious to thwart her true love, promotes her marriage to the fop of the title, and his tyranny both as brother and potential husband is repeatedly described as a form and theory of 'Government' (e.g. I, pp. 6–7), whether directly exercised by him or by the 'Governess' Aunt (Dramatis Personae) to whom he entrusts his sister. Other agents of his system of government are two moral watchdogs, Testimony and Hothead, an equally ridiculous and bigoted Puritan and Anglican. The play depicts the ending of tyranny and misrule. The bigots are expelled, and the long desired goal of 'liberty' at last awaits the two heroines: Leonora, the sister whom Bellguard subjects to 'Eternal Slavery' (I, p. 2), and Violante, the woman who loves him but fears to submit to his tyranny.

Bellguard's despotic habits are linked to a fierce concern with social rank, Leonora's offence being to love Farewel, whose family has since the Conquest been engaged with her own in a quarrel for precedence, which Bellguard's father sought decisively to win by acquiring his peerage. It is, Farewel stresses, a quarrel less over 'Land' than mere 'place' (II, p. 9), the severance of these two traditionally linked (and partially synonymous) tokens of rank indicating that social place has become largely titular, no longer expressing the holder's actual stake in the country. Appropriately, Sir Courtly, Bellguard's preferred brother-in-law, is ludicrously obsessed with the mere external forms of gentility, standing 'bare to his own Perewig' (II, p. 11). Sir Courtly's chief humour is a detestation of stench and contamination, which leads him to refuse wine because the grapes are trodden by the 'filthy naked Feet' of peasants (III, p. 22), but his humour is a special form of a more general folly, for most of the comically defective characters are isolated by a sense of unique rectitude in a diseased world: Hothead regards Testimony as 'a canker'd Rogue' (I, p. 3), and Bellguard is obsessed with the carnal frailty of woman. Indeed, to keep Leonora from sexual temptation he employs only physically deformed servants, pushing to absurdly literal extremes his aristocratic conception of himself as a solitary paragon in a world of degenerate inferiors. Yet his aristocratic disdain is itself a form of disease, the gentle blood on which he prides himself becoming an agent of contamination whereby the 'Scurvy' of pride is transmitted from generation to generation (I, p. 2). And Leonora can only gain happiness by opting for physical and social exclusion from the community

[17] See 'Some Passages of the Life of Mr. John Crown, Author of Sir Courtly Nice', in *the Critical Works of John Dennis*, ed. Edward Niles Hooker (2 vols., Baltimore, 1939–43), ii. 404–6.

governed by Bellguard's pride of place, arranging to be ejected from the house in the guise of a prostitute (V, p. 54).

Each possessed by a different illusion of special rectitude, the various cranks see themselves as the sole repositories of health in a world of disease. Their follies are satirically reproduced in the contrivances of Crack, an amiable and socially excluded trickster (he has been sent down from Oxford), who is employed by Farewel to bring about his marriage to Leonora. Crack introduces himself into the household by pretending to be the mentally diseased Sir Thomas Calico, a rich heir who has been entrusted to Bellguard's care. One of the pretended defects of 'Sir Thomas' is that he breaks into uncontrollable frenzy at the sight of a woman (a parody of Bellguard's despotic antifeminism). Another is a virtually non-existent memory for words and their meanings, so that his conversation produces bouts of sheer nonsense and, more interestingly, moments when the familiar language of social value suddenly becomes unfamiliar and unstable. For example, 'Sir Thomas' has been to Westminster Abbey to see the tombs of the glorious dead: the chief of the nation's blood. But the name Westminster eludes him, and the solid repository of tradition undergoes a dreamlike transformation: 'Is there no Monster in the West called *Westmonster*?' (III, p. 30). Later, during the contrived mêlée in which Leonora and Farewel escape from the house, 'Sir Thomas' cannot even remember the noises appropriate to his class: 'I ha' forgot every thing belongs to a Gentleman' (IV, p. 42), he exclaims as he tries unsuccessfully to imitate a hunting horn.

Crack's inventive malapropisms parody the spurious systems of language which support established forms of authority. Bellguard considers the words of the marriage service to be polite fictions veiling the absolute power of the husband: 'When I offer'd, Madam, to take you for better and for worse; those are Heroical Complements. The form of Matrimony out-does *Ovid* for passionate expressions' (IV, p. 33). But sometimes the attenuation of meaning is unintentional, as when the Puritan Testimony, an enemy of university education, gets trapped in a verbal circle of inarticulate zeal: the ministers of his sect 'would shew you the great——great sinfulness of sin, that sin is one of the sinfullest things in the whole World' (I, p. 4). Here, even more than in *The Country-Wife*, a moral system becomes a system of words. Rotating for ever in his closed and self-referential circle of meaning, Testimony illustrates that the rival codes of life approximate to the condition of competing idiolects, as Bellguard at one point virtually recognizes. When Leonora and Violante urge him that women of honour deserve liberty, he responds by claiming the right to a private code of meaning and value: 'This I confess is the English Dialect; and when I talk of Governing Women, I talk of a thing not understood by our Nation' (IV, p. 32).

Such private codes are pushed to absurd extremes by 'Sir Thomas', whose malapropisms constantly transform accepted verbal meaning, and whose

fake oriental retainers introduce into Lord Bellguard's house an entirely fictitious language. In his haughty treatment of his Bantam and Siamite 'Slaves'
(III, p. 27), 'Sir Thomas' provides an image of exotic, colonial tyranny that
comments satirically on Bellguard's domestic despotism (which is, indeed,
compared by Violante to that of a Virginian slave-owner, IV, p. 33), and in the
process reduces the language of hierarchy to total emptiness: 'How? the High
and glorious Emperour o' *Siam* with all his guards? Thou most invincible
Paducco, Farucco,—melmocadin—bobbekin' (V, p. 47). Still more pointedly,
a fourth-act song about seduction weakens the traditional analogy between
monarchic authority and male supremacy by making it depend upon a nonsensical term:

> The great Jaw-waw *that Rules our Land,*
>   *And pearly* Indian *Sea,*
> *Has not so absolute Command*
> *As thou hast over me.*

(IV, p. [60])

Crowne was no doubt delighted to discover that the play recommended by
Charles II made prominent use of a picture, his favourite device for locating
characters in a world of impenetrable and depthless surfaces. Crack first con-
veys a picture of Farewel to Leonora ('a Map of his Face' he later calls it, in another favourite Crowne image, III, p. 29), and he finally unites Leonora with
the man as well as the sign. Crowne's fops are generally epistemological casualties, devotees of the two-dimensional, and none more so than Sir Courtly, a
creature of pure exterior form (like a *picture* in a tapestry, IV, p. 40), who is so
absorbed in contemplation of the two-dimensional image of his reflection in
a mirror that he declares love to the wrong woman (and later marries her by
mistake). The heroine's progress from picture to person forms an obvious
contrast. Yet this is a private achievement, rather like Edgar's private naming
of himself to Cordelia in Tate's revision of *King Lear*. A picture is not a gen-
eralizable sign, and there is no final reconstruction; no new order and terminology to replace the old. The oppressive social microcosm disintegrates
with a centrifugal flight of fools, and we are left not with a miniature society
but with two sane couples (Leonora and Farewel, Violante and the converted
Bellguard) ready to live their own lives on their own terms.

In the mid-1680s, only Aphra Behn and Sir Charles Sedley experimented
with sex comedy, in *The Lucky Chance* (probably April 1686) and *Bellamira*.
Both were published with prefatory material combating charges of obscenity,
and Behn's preface and prologue gloomily note the dwindling number of
dramatists and the scarcity of new plays. Her play emphasizes the evils of
forced or mercenary marriage. Bellmour returns from reputed death to rescue
his beloved Leticia from her as yet unconsummated marriage to Sir Feeble
Fainwou'd, and Sir Feeble's daughter Diana manages to avoid the unwelcome

match he has arranged for her. But the principal heroine, Julia, is already ir-revocably married to Sir Cautious Fulbank, and the cuckolding plot in which she figures provides the complex and pessimistic study of male sexual atti-tudes that is characteristic of mature Behn. Like *The Princess of Cleve* and *The Atheist*, the play uses both of the conventional ways of representing divi-sion between the social and sexual selves: the bedroom trick and the Invisible Mistress plot (Julia's lover, Gayman, actually refers to his 'invisible Mistress', IV, p. 248). With much pseudo-demonic paraphernalia, Julia tempts Gayman in the guise of a rich woman of undisclosed age and face. A prearranged inter-ruption prevents adultery, but the trial nevertheless demonstrates that Gayman is willing to sleep with virtually anyone, '*be she young or old, Woman or Devil*' (III, p. 234) for money: as in *1 The Rover*, when Willmore accepts money from Angelica after denouncing her trade, the hero becomes the prostitute.

In its early stages, the love of Gayman and Julia displays a quite touching combination of sentiment and finance: he has ruined himself to supply her with presents; she steals from her husband to supply him; and he gives her the ring gained from the Invisible Mistress. Yet the prostitution latent in such transactions eventually surfaces. Although Julia evaded adultery in the Invisible Mistress episode, Gayman does eventually enjoy her by means of a bedroom trick, and here the tables are turned, for Julia is now, unwittingly, the bought sexual partner: indeed, she is a piece of bartered property whose will and consciousness are not considered. Gayman wins the adultery from Sir Cautious at cards, and sleeps with Julia by impersonating her husband, so that the pleasure is entirely on the male's side. Julia reacts with quite under-standable outrage when the trick is discovered, and, although Sir Cautious magnanimously makes Gayman heir to his property and his wife (a signific-ant conjunction), it is not completely clear that she wants him.

As in *Sir Patient Fancy*, where Lady Fancy is raped by her stepdaughter's fiancé, the bedroom trick emphasizes the physical and linguistic vulnerability of the woman. As in *Sir Patient Fancy* also, it is preceded by a scene emphas-izing her linguistic exclusion, when Julia hovers around the card game in which she is the stake, sympathetically questioning her husband and receiving answers that are as impenetrable to her as Horner's conversation about china is to Sir Jaspar Fidget, though far more personally loaded than the china remarks:

L. FUL. What are you playing for?
SIR FEEB. Nothing, nothing. . . .
L. FUL.   what have you lost?
SIR CAU. A Bauble——a Bauble. . . .
LADY FUL. What has my Husband lost?——
SIR CAU. Only a small parcel of Ware that lay dead upon my hands, Sweet-heart.

(IV, pp. 257–8)

When Julia discovers the imposture, she angrily commands Gayman to 'Un*hand*' her (V, p. 271; italics added): she has become another of Behn's victims of the male tongue and the male hand.

Sedley's *Bellamira* (May 1687) also features a rape, though Sedley's view of the deed was predictably more indulgent than Behn's. As in *The Mulberry Garden*, which had owed something to *Adelphi*, Sedley takes Terence as his starting-point, this time turning to the *Eunuchus*. In both comedies, Sedley was out of step with fashion: if *The Mulberry Garden* had failed to reflect the increasing daringness of comedy in the late 1660s, Sedley here dared too late, and was irked to discover how far things had changed: 'I am very unhappy', he wrote after condemnation of the play's obscenity, 'that the Ice that has borne so many Coaches and Carts, shou'd break with my Wheel barrow' (preface, p. 5). The protest was disingenuous, for Sedley portrays a world in a constant state of nature, perpetuated by the universal pursuit of sexual gratification: 'in matter of Women,' says the elderly lecher Merryman, 'we are all in the State of Nature, every man's hand against every man. Whatever we pretend' (III. iv. 115–17), and indeed his characters are engaged in a constant exercise of wit, money, and violence for the purpose of betrayal, rivalry, and aggression. One of the heroines, the gentlewoman Isabella, has from childhood repeatedly been the object of kidnap, purchase, and enforced possession. During the course of the play her current 'owner', Dangerfield, besieges Bellamira's house in an attempt to recover her, and, although Bellamira succeeds in rescuing Isabella from her life of slavery, she does so in the hope of making money from her family. And, although Isabella achieves the closest approximation to a romantically satisfying marriage in the play, her bridegroom is making amends in marriage for having raped her. The effective prevalence of power, wealth, and ingenuity replaces fixed standards of social, linguistic, or religious control. 'Of Children Mistresses, and Religions our own are still the best', Merryman says, with cheerful relativism (II. i. 276–7). At the end of the play, Bellamira and her keeper look forward to cohabitation undefined by the traditional terminology of sexual rectitude: 'a marri'd Life, | Bating the odious Names of Man and Wife' (V. i. 618–19).

Typically, the unfixing of traditional codes is linked to that of social place, for the play centres upon characters who are both socially and geographically displaced. Bellamira, daughter of a bankrupt merchant, has prospered as the leading prostitute in Jamaica before heading for a new life and reputation in London, and Isabella's degradation from gentlewoman to slave has involved her in a rootless and vagabond existence, shifting from Jamaica, to Spain, to London. The parasitic flatterer Smoothly is a decayed gentleman who has lost his estate (II. i. 53–6) and now survives by exploiting the network of manipulation and deception which is the true essence of social existence. Even the relationship of the prosperous gentry to their estates is a purely monetary one, divested of the moral and symbolic dimensions that were so important to Jonson: the lifestyles of the prostitute and gentleman are interchangeable for, as a friend says to Bellamira, 'Like the Gentlemen that live in Town, you have your pleasure in one place, and receive your Rent from an other' (I. iii. 90–2). The prostitute is, indeed, mistaken for a lady of 'Quality' (I. ii. 9); conversely, when a man about town takes his leave of Bellamira 'like a Gentleman' (I. ii. 94–5), he means that he fornicates with her before departing.

As in Aphra Behn, the confounding of prostitution and gentility subverts traditional categories of degree and authority, and the prostitute emerges as the figure of true power: power without the contradictions and illusions that Behn's more subtle insight detected in her dominion. Whereas the gentlewoman is enslaved and raped, the prostitute is a skilled exploiter of the monetary and sexual interests that are the ruling principles in life. Bellamira is repeatedly described as exercising monarchic power over her keeper and, at the end of the play, she and Keepwell agree to support Smoothly. In a more indulgently presented version of the irony that had concluded *The Woman-Captain*, the gentleman is no longer supported in his place by his estate, but by the benevolence of a successful prostitute.

An adaptation of Terence that was more in keeping with the time (and a far better play into the bargain) was Shadwell's enormously successful *The Squire of Alsatia* (May 1688). Like Sedley's own *The Mulberry Garden*, it reworks the situation familiar from *Adelphi*, in which a father brings up one of his two sons severely, while the other is brought up indulgently by the father's brother, indulgence proving (with qualifications) to be the better influence on character. This was Shadwell's first play since *The Lancashire Witches*, and in the dedication of the next, *Bury-Fair*, written after the Revolution, Shadwell complains that he had been silenced for his political views. These views are still evident, if tactfully implicit, in *The Squire of Alsatia*, for the incompetence of the biological father discredits inherited patriarchal authority, while the wise foster-father earns his charge's love in a kind of social compact: 'You are his Father by Nature, I by Choice,' he tells his brother (I, p. 220). When the father protests that 'he is mine by Nature,' he is told that ''Tis all but Custom' (I, p. 221). After the Revolution, Shadwell still more clearly associated inadequate or oppressive parents with the principles of Stuart absolutism.

The strict father, Sir William Belfond, is a former town debauchee turned country recluse, who has brought up the elder Belfond within the bounds of his country estate, educating him in nothing but farm management. His brother, Sir Edward, is a merchant 'possessed with all Gentlemanlike qualities' (Dramatis Personae, p. 206), who has given Belfond Junior the education of a 'a Compleat Gentleman' (a venerable formula that Shadwell repeats with some emphasis),[18] including foreign travel and education in classical authors. As in Peacham, the purpose of the education is to mould a gentleman 'fit to

---

[18] It occurs three times in II, pp. 232–3.

serve his Country' (II, p. 232). The boorish and uneducated Belfond Senior comes secretly to town to escape his father's strict tutelage and falls into the clutches of rogues and sharpers from Alsatia, whom he mistakes for 'Compleat Gentlemen' (II, p. 233), and who attempt to defraud him. When the misdeeds of 'Belfond' come to the ears of his father (also, unexpectedly, in town), Sir William for a long time assumes the culprit to be Belfond Junior, and congratulates himself on his superior skill in bringing up his own charge. Alsatia is an area in Whitefriars populated by thieves and debtors, where the forces of law did not dare to venture. The very name suggests the presence of an alien settlement in the heart of the nation's capital,[19] and Shadwell's extensive use of thieves' cant emphasizes that it is an alien settlement with an alien language. When Belfond Senior finally appears before his horrified and disillusioned father, jingling money and proudly babbling in the Alsatian jargon, his initiation into the uncivilized wilderness (he is 'very *Rhinocerical*', IV, p. 263)[20] appears as an inverted image of the classical education whereby Belfond Junior has been prepared for the life and duties of a gentleman: 'had I been Rul'd by you . . . all this fine Language had been Heathen Greek to me' (IV, pp. 263–4).

Many Restoration dramatists had dwelt on the lurking persistence of the uncivilized within the confines of the civic community, but for many the principle of anarchy had been ineradicably present in human nature. By externalizing it, Shadwell also suggests that it is subject to control and cure, and the method of control is law. When Belfond Senior, in his first night as a town gallant, breaks windows and abducts a wench, he renders himself liable to a legal process which brings him before the Lord Chief Justice: the supreme embodiment of legal authority (IV, p. 254). At the end of the play, Sir Edward resolves to prosecute the Alsatian rogues, thinking it '*strange*, that places so near the Kings Palace should be no part of his Dominions' when Scotland, Wales, and Ireland have been reduced to order (V, p. 280; italics added). But Alsatia is an external manifestation of an intrinsic tendency of human nature towards predatory anarchy: a tendency which education must eradicate in the individual, as the law must eradicate it in society. The traditional degrees of society have no intrinsic power to reflect or preserve order: the untutored squire finds Alsatia his spiritual home, and one of his seducers is a decayed gentleman from his own family. Other shady characters, such as the brother of young Belfond's cast mistress Termagant, also make claims to exalted and ancient ancestry, and Shadwell does not bother to question or deny them: they are, in equal measure, plausible and irrelevant. More surprising, however, is the treatment of Belfond Junior, the humanely educated man of principle. Shadwell amply demonstrates his sense and good nature, and these are indeed his predominant qualities. But, as he himself remarks, 'a young Fellow carries

---

[19] Etymologically, indeed, Alsatia means 'foreign settlement' (*OED*).

[20] *Rhino* is slang for money, but it is tempting to think also of its literal sense.

that about him that will make him a Knave now and then in spite of his Teeth' (II, p. 226), and, if he regularly discredits Sir William's dark suspicions of his corruption and degeneracy, he also falls short of Sir Edward's high estimate.[21] The persecution which he suffers from Mrs Termagant, the destructively vengeful mother of his illegitimate child, shows him that wenching has its dangers as well as its pleasures, and his insulting treatment of her shocks his friend Truman (II, pp. 227–8). But more troublesome is his seduction of Lucia (Bracegirdle), 'a young, beautiful Girl, of a mild and tender disposition' (Dramatis Personae, p. 207).

Defending Belfond Junior against Sir William's suspicious denunciations, Sir Edward is confident that 'you'll find him perusing some good Author' (I, p. 221). In fact, as we immediately learn, Belfond Junior has been deflowering Lucia, and the accomplishments of the mind are placed in an incongruous and ironic relationship to the actions of the flesh. Belfond Junior's language to the anguished and regretful Lucia is consistently evasive, dishonest, and condescending, and Lucia rightly reproves his 'Flattering Tongue' (II, p. 223). Indeed, he appears most comfortable when pushing language towards total insignificance: 'in Billing, Cooing, and in gentle Murmurs, we exprest our kindess; and Coo'd and Murmur'd and Lov'd on' (II. p. 222). Then Lucia is bundled into a closet as the singing-master and then Truman enter, and at Belfond's request Truman sings—of all things—a setting of 'Integer vitae scelerisque purus'.[22] Belfond's taste in poetic sentiment reflects ironically upon his taste in conduct, not only because of the opening line but because the poem goes on to celebrate a constancy of affection which is both expressed in and excited by speech. 'Speaking' is its last word, and the closing lines—'dulce ridentem Lalagen amabo, | dulce loquentem'[23]—create a picture of uncomplicated amorous discourse that is markedly different from the uneasy evasions we have just witnessed. Lucia's situation becomes still worse when, while she is still secreted within earshot, Belfond and Truman discuss their plans to marry a pair of beautiful heiresses, and when Mrs Termagant intrudes, rants, and finally discovers and manhandles her concealed rival. The gulf between the poetic image and the lived reality becomes wider and wider.

During Lucia's concealment, Belfond Junior is also visited by his father and uncle, and, when Sir William intemperately denounces him for excesses in fact committed by his elder brother, Belfond responds with an uncompromising assertion of his linguistic integrity: 'I scorn a Lye, 'tis the basest thing a Gentleman can be guilty of' (II, p. 229). But his need to protect Lucia drives him into the mendacity which he so abhors (II, p. 230; V, p. 275), and one

---

[21] Hume sees Belfond Junior's failings as unskilful contradictions on Shadwell's part (*Development*, 78–86). John T. Harwood convincingly argues that the failings are intentional and well managed (*Critics, Values, and Restoration Comedy* (Carbondale and Edwardsville, 1982), 124–38).

[22] 'Perfect of life and innocent of crime' (Horace, *Odes*, I. xxii. 1).

[23] 'I shall love the sweetly smiling, sweetly talking Lalage' (ibid., ll. 23–4).

consequence of the affair is that the antithesis between Belfond Junior and his errant brother becomes less complete than it had once seemed to be. For much of the play, the elder Belfond has acted as a malign *doppelgänger* to his brother, performing in the Belfond name misdeeds which Sir William unquestioningly lays to the charge of Belfond Junior and which Sir Edward correctly concludes to be the work of some unknown namesake. And so, when Lucia's father approaches the old men to complain of his daughter's treatment, they act true to form, Sir William blaming Belfond Junior and Sir Edward blaming the 'Rascal that has taken my Sons Name' (IV, p. 255). But this time Sir William is right, and the momentary confounding of the two brothers gives particularly striking expression to what is everywhere implicit: that all men are potential residents of Alsatia, and that it is the process of education and experience rather than the immutable gift of gentle birth that fits them for the civilized community. The benefit of Belfond Junior's education is not that it turns him into a finished paragon but that it provides him with the resources to learn from his foolish and injurious actions and renounce them for the future. But there can be no real redress for Lucia. Sir Edward does what can be done, providing generous financial compensation and ensuring that her dishonour remains a secret, but, as her father recognizes, 'there can be no Salve for this Sore' (IV, p. 255). Lucia's father speaks with the authority not only of a father but of a lawyer (he is an attorney), so that young Belfond, like his wilder brother, has his failings judged by an agent of the law.

A largely decent and well-intentioned young man has thoughtlessly inflicted irremediable pain on an innocent and vulnerable woman, and nevertheless goes on to forge a happy existence for himself. Shadwell far outdoes Durfey's *The Virtuous Wife* in his attention to the casualties of the hero's moral development, and the result is something very different from Cibber's reform comedies, with their effusive celebration of innate benevolence. For Shadwell, as for Etherege and Wycherley, the predator lurks within the citizen. The difference is that here the predator may be tamed and expelled by the civilizing process. But the civilizing process is something that each individual must recapitulate in his own life: it does not deliver born citizens or gentlemen.

The Squire of Alsatia covertly indicates that authority must be earned rather than merely inherited. But the two new tragedies that appeared in the months before the Revolution (the first since *Constantine the Great* in November 1683)[24] both more directly register the tensions of 1688, presenting contrasting responses to absolute authority. William Mountfort's *The Injur'd Lovers* (February 1688) is, as its title suggests, much concerned with the suffering and experience of injustice, the terms *injustice, justice,* and *wrong* recurring insistently, and like many post-Revolution tragedies it uses rape as a prime manifestation of tyranny. The King of Sicily rapes Antelina

---

[24] Or since Rochester's *Valentinian* in Feb. 1684, if that counts as a new play.

(Bracegirdle), whose true love, Rheusanes, is deceived into marrying and bedding the King's sister, Oryala, in the belief that she is Antelina. Unwittingly and innocently, he thereby heaps injustice, injury, and wrong upon both Antelina and his friend Dorelanus, who loves Oryala; and his manifest disappointment with his unexpected bride also inspires Oryala to a voluble sense of injustice. Apart from the rapist King, the agents of injustice are as helpless as the victims, and the bedroom trick whereby Rheusanes consummates his marriage with the wrong bride shows not a conflict between public order and the disordering impulses of private desire but a brutal suppression of legitimate desire by a public power indifferent to individual interests. For the sufferers, justice becomes difficult not only to attain but even to define, for the monarch's status as vicegerent of God means that he is not subject to human retribution. Though Rheusanes rebels and Antelina poisons her ravisher, their resistance is a crime which is expiated in their own deaths, and the land is left to face a barren and hopeless future.

Nevertheless, the characters throughout the play define the self with reference to its private circumstances rather than to a single, all-embracing public order with a single nomenclature of authority. Though Rheusanes is initially deflected from rebellion by his awe for the 'Name of King' (IV, p. 45), names generally possess potency as expressions not of hierarchical relationships but of special and individual circumstances: Oryala's name, for example, has a talismanic quality for the love-sick Dorelanus,[25] but her 'Name' of Princess loses its force for Rheusanes once he has, inadvertently, become her lord (III, p. 32), and she herself finds that Antelina's 'Name, | Withers my Hopes' (V, p. 61); and Rheusanes, who has revered the name of King, finds his own 'Name cry'd up by all for King' (V, p. 68). Monarchic authority is, by divine edict, unchallengeable, but it does not provide a naturally fitting framework for individual existence; and, whereas Orrery's characters use nomenclature as a reflection of a single, monolithic social hierarchy, the language of Mountfort's characters shows that the individual is the primary standard of definition: when the raped Antelina describes herself as 'A Ravish'd Virgin in a stranger World' (IV, p. 45), the idea of the stranger is used to judge the world in relation to the self rather than, as is more usual, the self in relation to the world. One of the major changes in post-Revolution drama is that conflicts between the claims of authority and of individual life are no longer so perplexedly insoluble.

Crowne's *Darius King of Persia* (April 1688) gives a sharply contrasting view of monarchic authority. In *Sir Courtly Nice* 'Sir Thomas' had satirized Bellguard's authoritarianism by translating it into images of oriental despotism, but here Crowne uses the absolute monarchy of ancient Persia to justify the monarchy of James II. Darius is betrayed and murdered by noblemen—

---

[25] II, p. 12; III, p. 31.

'Slaves' (e.g. V, p. 63)—whose opposition to arbitrary monarchy, the prerogatives of birth, and the absence of law is deeply entangled with fierce personal ambition, though it is an indication of the complexity of Crowne's attitude that he already opposed all these abuses himself when they were not attached to monarchic rule, and that the sentiments of his villains were after the Revolution to be put in the mouths of his heroes. Nevertheless, monarchy is here part of the order of nature, and the murder of Darius (like Macbeth's murder of Duncan) is reflected in disturbances of natural order: 'Lyons came roaring from their Caves, then dy'd. | The Cedars groan'd, then fell' (V, p. 69). Principally, however, Crowne stresses that the regicides violate obligations specifically conferred by their king (*oblige* and related terms being key words), and that in doing so they dishonour social principles that transcend the constitution of any particular society.

'In the midst of his great Monarchy,' Darius is 'all alone, as in a Wilderness' (II, p. 17), 'To my own Nation a Forreigner' (IV, p. 45). Yet this king whom his own subjects have isolated as a stranger ('you seem so strange to me' (III, p. 33), he says to the dissimulating conspirators) is sustained and honoured by strangers whom he has obliged: chiefly Patron and his Greek mercenaries (initially described as 'strangers, loose from any bonds', (I, p. 3);[26] as so often, the physical outsider is not the true stranger. The point is repeated in the domestic tragedy which complements the political tragedy. As in *The Ambitious Statesman*, Crowne here imitates *Othello*, once again removing the external stranger: in addition to killing his king, the chief conspirator, Bessus, is also driven by jealousy to kill his second wife and his son, who have been in love since before her forced marriage to him. Although Bessus' first marriage had been to an Amazon queen, it is not this obvious experience of the alien that fills him with a sense of the monstrous but the sight of his own son: 'thou frightful Monster——dye', he exclaims (V, p. 60). Nevertheless, we are not left with Otway's sense of the irremediable alienness of one individual to another, but with a simpler sense of inverted normality. Bessus destroys the principles of community in both family and state, the unnaturalness of his regicide being emphasized by his murder of his son, and his defiance of principles sacred even to strangers. Carolean tragedy thus ends in nervous contemplation of what its earliest specimens had confidently exorcized: usurpation and regicide.

[26] For other imagery of the stranger, see II, pp. 24, 27; IV, p. 45.

CHAPTER NINE

'The surprising success of the Baudy Batchelour': Comedy, 1688–1695

After the Revolution, there is an appreciable revival in the demand for new plays: between November 1688 and the opening of the actors' breakaway company in April 1695 there are forty-six known premières (a few of pre-Revolution plays). There is also a boost in quality, associated with the arrival of Congreve, the maturing of Southerne, and the brief returns of Shadwell and of Dryden, stripped of his laureateship and short of money. Dryden's four last plays contain two of his finest (and one of his worst), and respond to the deposition of James II with detailed studies of displacement and exile. Southerne, a Jacobite gradually and tentatively reconciling himself to the new order,[1] also becomes preoccupied with dislocation (whereas his first two plays had been plays of homecoming), but displacement was also later a major concern in the works of the Whig Vanbrugh, who retains his predecessors' sense of the incomplete assimilability of individual character into social institution. Nevertheless, there were clear and quite rapid breaks with earlier drama. The drama of displacement is no longer the norm, many dramatists celebrating the new political order by emphasizing the recovery of the home (or preservation of the homeland); and, as a concomitant to the renewed sense of stable and morally significant place (and to the long war with France), the figure of the simple outsider regains prominence. Tyranny continues to be a favourite tragic theme, and is often expressed in rape, both for its intrinsic symbolic appropriateness and for the opportunities it afforded of showing Anne Bracegirdle in titillatingly mauled states. But tyranny is now more easily subject to justice, and in both tragedy and comedy justice is frequently freed from the epistemological and linguistic problems that had bedevilled it in the 1670s. Preoccupation with the reconciliation of law and desire swamps sex comedy, which now forms a tiny proportion of the total comic output (though reform comedies show considerable variety in their treatment of promiscuity prior to the inevitable moment of renunciation).[2] As usual, Durfey forms a

---

Epigraph: Henry Higden, *The Wary Widdow; or, Sir Noisy Parrat*, preface, sig. [A3].

[1] For the course of Southerne's political affiliations, see *Works*, ed. Jordan and Love, i, pp. xiii–xix, xxiii–xxix.

[2] John Harrington Smith detects a marked shift from cynical to exemplary comedy in the years 1688–9, citing *The Fortune-Hunters, The Squire of Alsatia, Bury-Fair*, and *The English Frier* ('Shadwell, the Ladies, and the Change in Comedy', *Modern Philology*, 46 (1948–9), 22–33 (pp. 30–1)).

useful barometer of fashion: of the eight plays (including six comedies) which he produced between 1691 and 1695, none were sex comedies (there is a subordinate and critically portrayed cuckolding action in *The Richmond Heiress*, but even this was omitted when he revised the play after its initial failure).[3] Only in 1697, in the wake of *The Relapse*, does he briefly return to the genre. At the same time, however, there was a temporary lull in the sorts of farce that had been prominent in the mid-1680s (and which returned after the renewal of competition): the only successor to *The Devil of a Wife* and *A Duke and No Duke* was John Wilson's Machiavelli adaptation *Belphegor* (June 1690, but performed in Dublin *c.*1677–8 or 1682–3), about a devil who (like Pug in *The Devil is an Ass*) finds human iniquity too much for him.

On the stage, as elsewhere, the Revolution was justified and interpreted in various ways: abdication of the incumbent, succession of the lineal heir (Mary), breach of the king's contract with the people, or (rarely) conquest. There is some dip in overt support for William between the end of 1692 and mid-1696; that is, between the French defeat at La Hogue in May 1692, which ended the immediate threat of French invasion, and the disclosure early in 1696 of a Jacobite plot to assassinate the King as prelude to a French invasion. This boosted William's popularity, as did hopes of a successful end to the war against France, which were initially dashed, but eventually gratified by the treaty of Ryswick in the autumn of 1697. The result was a succession of pro-Revolution plays celebrating the overthrow of amorous, unwarlike tyrants. But, if support for William fluctuates in frequency and effusiveness, there are only occasional hints (in, for example, Dryden's plays, and Charles Hopkins's critical portrayals of militarism) of the fears and discontents of his reign. In this respect, post-Revolution drama is quite different from that of the Exclusion Crisis. There are digs at court corruption, but these are very formulaic, and it is hard among the paeans to national salvation to glimpse an unpopular King, still more unpopular Dutch favourites, military and political venality, defeat at sea and on land, collapse of trade, heavy taxes, bad harvests, and (at the end of the century) fears of a dangerously large army. Crowne's *Regulus* (June 1692) and the possibly unperformed *Timoleon* (1697), a direct response to the assassination plot, are Williamite plays which pronounce the nation to be unworthy of its saviour, and *Timoleon* does deal directly with the scandal of corruption, but the only play to deal seriously with a populace groaning under financial imposition (and foreign rule) was Durfey's *Massaniello*; and even here no direct parallel may be intended. Elsewhere, the unprecedented burden of taxation is reflected only in comic Whig satire of non-payers, such as Sir Polidorus Hogstye in Vanbrugh's *Æsop* or Sir Wealthy

As Robert D. Hume points out in ' "The Change in Comedy" ', however, Smith greatly exaggerates the currency and success of libertine comedy over the preceding fifteen years.

3 See Peter Holland, 'Durfey's Revisions of *The Richmond Heiress* (1693)', *Archiv für das Studium der neueren Sprachen und Literaturen*, 216 (1979), 116–20.

Plainder in Dilke's *The Pretenders*. And the trauma of the recoinage passes unnoticed.

There is possibly a glimpse of social tensions in the increased satire of the aristocracy, though what tensions are being reflected is less certain. In the work of William Burnaby (and perhaps in that of another brewer's son, Thomas Southerne) there is bourgeois contempt for an idle and unproductive class, but late seventeenth-century drama is not on the whole marked by bourgeois self-assertiveness, and at this time the interests of the aristocracy also clashed with those of the minor gentry, the former extending their estates while the latter struggled, sometimes unsuccessfully, to preserve theirs from disintegration. But the true explanation for Lords Brainless, Stately, Froth, Malepert, Whiffle, and Foppington[4] may lie simply in the growing confidence of the intelligent professional in his own worth and standing.

The continuing trend away from sex comedy is partially evident in James Carlile's sprightly rake-reformed play *The Fortune-Hunters* (March 1689), where a rich and vivacious beauty tames Frank Wealthy after 'tryal' of his faith (V, pp. 60, 61). Unlike *The Squire of Alsatia*, however, the play shows little interest in the pain which the seducer may have caused his former conquests. In the other plot, the sensible Sophia, fearful of making a false step in marriage (I, p. 8), cures the jealousy of Frank's elder brother Tom, who at one point is dressed in the alien guise of a Spaniard to signify the un-Englishness of his tyranny. The trial of the prospective husband and the abolition of familial tyranny were to be important comic themes throughout the 1690s (most notably in Congreve's *Love for Love*). Though they probably do not do so here, both can reflect in miniature the defeat of Stuart absolutism, and the successful trials indicate that judicial process is now conceived as an appropriate model for the regulation and examination of individual life.

The contrast between Spanish oppressiveness and English tolerance recurs, now clearly as the basis of a political analogy, in William Mountfort's *The Successful Straingers* (January 1690), a poor intrigue play in which true love triumphs over parental covetousness and unwanted, tyrannical suitors, the liberating males (the strangers of the title) being Spaniards who return to their country with their outlook formed by the England of William III.[5] Oppressive European regimes (France and, again, Spain) also figure in Shadwell's first two post-Revolution comedies. In *Bury-Fair* (April 1689) Oldwit's daughter Philadelphia has been driven from her home by the threat of a forced marriage, and the household is dominated by her affected, Francophile stepmother and -sister, Lady and Mrs Fantast; but the play ends with the reunion

---

4 In Durfey's *The Marriage-Hater Match'd*, Crowne's *The English Frier*, Congreve's *The Double-Dealer*, Southerne's *The Maid's Last Prayer*, W. M.'s *The Female Wits*, and Vanbrugh's *The Relapse*.

5 Mountfort had dedicated *The Injur'd Lovers* to the Earl of Arran, who was a Jacobite after the Revolution. This play, however, was dedicated to the radical Whig Thomas Wharton, and Mountfort dedicated two other plays to relatives of the Whig martyrs Algernon Sidney and the Earl of Essex.

of the true family and the flight of the intruders, much to the delight of Oldwit, an absurd but essentially kindly lover of Shakespeare and Jonson. The flight of the Francophile stepparent parallels that of the Francophile king and modifies the pattern of *The Squire of Alsatia*, where the stepparent had excelled the true parent: there, earned authority was preferred to the seemingly natural authority of the biological parent; now Shadwell implicitly stresses the natural basis of the new order, and reduces James to the status of an interloping stranger. So pleased was he with the image of the tyrannical stepparent that he repeated it in *The Scowrers* (in portraying an overt Jacobite) and *The Volunteers*.

There is no longer an Alsatia at the heart of the metropolis: the threats to English tradition now come from outlandish and easily exorcizable elements, and the dynamic relationship between Belfond Junior and the rogues whom he both opposes and inadvertently imitates is abandoned as Shadwell returns to static contrasts between the sensible and foolish. Cities remain full of 'Wild Beasts upon two Legs,' but the city has been left behind; and, unlike Belfond Junior, Lord Bellamy knows from the outset that 'He that Debauches private Women, is a Knave, and injures others: And he that uses publick ones, is a Fool, and hurts himself' (I, p. 309). The tension between the nature of the individual and of the state has disappeared. Philadelphia's sister, the sprightly and independent Gertrude, argues that the new order invests her by analogy with the right to choose her own husband ('I am a free Heiress of *England*, where Arbitrary Power is at an end, and I am resolv'd to choose for my self', III, p. 339), though there are limits to the extent of the analogy: '*Non resistance*', she admits, is 'a Doctrine fit for all Wives, tho for nobody else' (V, p. 368).

The determination to judge private conduct according to the ideals of the new political order is at its clearest in the portions of the play in which Shadwell reworks the plot of Molière's *Les Précieuses ridicules*, depicting the enthusiasm of the Fantasts for a French barber, La Roch, masquerading as a Count. Inexpert and excessive Francophiles such as Sir Fopling had been judged against those more knowledgeable and moderate in the absorption of the foreign mode. But Mrs Fantast's Francophilia is enthusiasm for a tyrannical hierarchy that oppresses and misrepresents human rights and potential. La Roch praises the militarism of Louis XIV and describes peasants as slaves, and Mrs Fantast herself despises 'the *Canaille*,' but Gertrude, an arch-liberal, has 'no such contempt for the common People: they come near Nature' (II, p. 318). The fraudulence of La Roch's nobility reflects the moral emptiness of the social order that he champions, and he initiates a line of Frenchmen in post-Revolution comedy who are seen as intruders from an alien, threatening, and oppressive political order. Against this alien order Shadwell sets his old ideal, revivified by new political circumstances: the country gentleman at home on his estate, attentive to the rights and needs of those for whom he is responsible. At the end of the play, La Roch is exposed, the Fantasts flee, and

Oldwit recovers his lost Philadelphia. Purged of intruders, the home welcomes its native and original member once more.

Shadwell's next play, *The Amorous Bigotte* (spring 1690), is actually set in an alien papist tyranny (Spain, as in Mountfort's *The Successful Straingers*), and again treats the family as a political microcosm: Belliza, the eponymous bigot, is fanatical as a papist and tyrannical as both a natural and an acquired parent (of her daughter Elvira and niece Rosania). By favouring the Irish priest Tegue O Divelly (revived from *The Lancashire Witches*) she forces a malevolent and alien surrogate 'Father' (*passim*) on her charges, and her auntly tyranny is replicated in that of the pious bawd Gremia, who has forced her niece Levia into prostitution after taking her from her 'Mothers hands' (I, p. 24). (Belliza, just as reprehensibly, wants to gain Rosania's estate by consigning her to a convent.) There is also a tyrannical father, Bernardo, and, although he and Belliza initially wish to marry each other's offspring, they eventually marry each other, thereby becoming fully-fledged stepparents— roles which they have long symbolically fulfilled. Rosania and Elvira make happy marriages, but Levia is treated with chilling callousness: when her reformed lover rejects her for the virtuous joys of marriage, she displays all the rage and some of the tactics of Angelica Bianca in Behn's *The Rover*, but is allowed none of Angelica's moral stature, and is expelled with contempt, despite the clear parallel between her circumstances and those of Rosania. She is not an ironic image of the society that excludes her, as Behn in almost identical circumstances made Angelica; she is, simply, a stranger to its values.

Shadwell portrays the most detailed domestic re-enactment of the Revolution in *The Scowrers* (December 1690), a post-1688 version of *The Squire of Alsatia*, in which he returns to the civilizing of the gentleman, and again portrays siblings with contrasting qualities as parents, though there is a more complex interplay between parent and stepparent than in the earlier play. Sir William Rant, whom education and parental fondness have hitherto failed to dissuade from a life of drunkenness, fornication, and vandalism, is finally won to the cause of virtue by the love of a good woman, and by the wise lectures of Mr Rant, his natural father, who is represented as a guide leading him home. Finally, Sir William and a fellow-rake are brought 'home to our selves', the 'stray' returning 'From all the crooked Paths, to the right way' (V, p. 148). As in *Bury-Fair*, Shadwell abandons the unresolved tension of *The Squire of Alsatia*, for although Sir William's dissipation is far greater than Belfond Junior's thoughtless sexual self-indulgence, it inflicts no lasting injury on anyone. The contrasting unwise parent is Mr Rant's sister, Lady Maggot, a tyrant whose daughters reject her and put themselves under Mr Rant's guardianship in a plot that is full of explicit parallels with the Revolution. Here Shadwell has it both ways: Lady Maggot's motherhood gives her no perpetual right to authority, yet the elected surrogate parent has earned his election by his virtues as a natural father.

The daughters have already had one inadequate stepfather, the Jacobite Sir Humphry Maggot, who is no homeward guide like Mr Rant but rather an ingenuous believer in the benevolence of exotic tyrants: Louis XIV, the Pope, and the Great Turk (III, pp. 112–13). Symbolically, he is bullied by his wife into abandoning his home for a new one, and towards the end of the play sits in his new house as magistrate in the trial of his own nephew (and adopted son), who has deserted the study of *law* to imitate Sir William's life of alcoholic hooliganism. But he has lost his judicial and domestic authority, since his nephew knows of his treasonable talk and can blackmail him. Jacobitism violates the integrity of the home and the integrity of justice. Shadwell recycles these elements for one last time in *The Volunteers* (November 1692), in which Mrs Hackwell, an adulterous wife and tyrannical stepmother, leaves the home she has betrayed, as does her spiteful and affected daughter. Realizing that he has been 'led away' (V, p. 223), her husband then readmits his true son and daughter into the household, and the reunion is sealed by a traditional image of social harmony that had lost much of its potency during the Carolean period: the joining of hands. Domestic reconciliation is paralleled by the decay of old ideological differences: the ancient antagonism of Hackwell (a Roundhead and Anabaptist) and the Cavalier Blunt has declined into bantering reminiscence, and the reconciliation is completed by marriage between their children.[6]

The paralleling of political and personal reform that is implicit in *The Scowrers* had already appeared in a more direct form in Crowne's *The English Frier* (March 1690), in which Crowne unblushingly abandons the Tory elements of his earlier drama, while retaining and developing the anti-Catholic sentiments which he had voiced in the midst of the Exclusion Crisis.[7] The play is set during the reign of James II, and parallels the personal reform of the coquettish Laura and the rakish Young Ranter with two linked processes of discovery: of the fraudulence of Catholicism, and the insignificance of rank and precedence. The empty social forms and hierarchies beloved of the foolish Lord Stately are consistently paralleled to the forms and hierarchies of the Catholic Church, the equation becoming explicit when the Tartuffe-like Father Finical, newly dignified with a meaningless bishopric *in partibus infidelium*, promptly claims to be Stately's social equal (IV, p. 35). Rank is repeatedly misused. Confident in her 'quality', the papist Lady Pinchgut virtually starves her servants (V, p. 49), and Father Finical attempts to seduce the serving maid Pansy, believing that her social insignificance will prevent her

---

6 Christopher J. Wheatley rather elaborately links this reconciliation of old enemies to post-Revolution changes in the understanding of honour and patriotism ('Thomas Shadwell's *The Volunteers* and the Rhetoric of Honor and Patriotism', *ELH* 60 (1993), 397–418).

7 In dedicating the play to the Earl (later Duke) of Devonshire, Crowne emphasizes the anti-court elements in his earlier plays, pointing to the anti-Catholic sentiment in *Henry the Sixth* (sig. [A3ᵛ]). (Devonshire had been a prominent Exclusionist, and one of the seven signatories of the invitation requesting William's invasion.)

from exposing him. The abuse of social place is also evident in Crowne's radical transformation of the gay couple courtship. The coquetry of Laura, Lord Stately's elder daughter, clearly derives from the heartless and mindless arrogance of rank, and is ultimately abandoned for marriage to the exemplary Lord Wiseman. The crisis which prompts her reform is near-rape by her conventional counterpart, the libertine Young Ranter, in whom agreeable gentlemanly irresponsibility is transformed into a criminal violence which he believes to be sanctioned by custom and status. (On being told that he 'has good blood in his body,' Laura's sensible sister, Julia, scornfully retorts, 'So has a Pig, wou'd he had some good manners, and good sence' (IV, p. 33).) The rape attempt clearly parallels Father Finical's attempt on Pansy, so that the gentleman-rake and the popish priest become interchangeable embodiments of the unshackled domination of power and privilege. (Similarly, Young Ranter's arrogance towards subordinates such as chairmen parallels Lady Pinchgut's mistreatment of her servants.)

Like many post-Revolution comedies, *The English Frier* portrays exclusion of the alien and readmission of the native: in his folly (when 'empty o' the *English-man*', III, p. 22), Lord Stately excludes the two men of sense from his house (III, p. 23), but invites them 'home' (V, p. 52) at the end to marry his daughters. Interestingly, the final social inclusion embraces a fallen woman. Lord Wiseman's wisdom has not prevented him from seducing Airy (an action he defends on the grounds that he is not a statue, III, p. 25), and, although he compensates her with £200 p.a., he is also willing to let her starve should she expose him to Laura (III, p. 25). On the other hand, he does force Young Ranter to marry her, although Ranter is fully aware of her past. Rarely does a fallen woman make such a good match, and to this extent Crowne's critique of irrational privilege embraces a critique of the double standard.

The English Frier failed—Crowne complains of a tumultuously hostile faction in the first night audience—but, along with *The Fortune-Hunters* and *The Amorous Bigotte*, it was a shaping influence upon Mountfort's best and most successful play, *Greenwich-Park* (April 1691). Like Lord Wiseman, Lord Worthy makes a happy marriage despite his previous seduction of a vulnerable young woman (for which he is forgiven by his new wife); and, like Carlile's Frank Wealthy, Young Reveller copulates with two women during the play and is then reformed by marriage to a third. Female reform is represented by the penitent reconciliation of the adulterous citizen's wife Mrs Raison with her husband, an indulgently portrayed bourgeois roisterer. Still more vigorously than Crowne, Mountfort denies any intrinsic value to social quality: for example, the mother of the two witty, wealthy heroines started life as a laundress.[8] He also gives a more harrowing account of the lot of the fallen woman. Dorinda was sold by her aunt to Lord Worthy for £500 and, after a

[8] See Martin W. Walsh, 'The Significance of William Mountfort's *Greenwich-Park*', *Restoration and 18th Century Theatre Research*, 12/1 (1973), 35–40.

long period of chastity, falls for and yields to Young Reveller. When she is exposed and the virtuous characters round on her, the villainous aunt transfers
all blame to her victim, claiming that Dorinda had forced her into acting as
go-between by threatening her with starvation. This we know to be false, but
the slander is never rebutted, and Young Reveller is disposed to believe it. Like
Dryden's Cleopatra and Payne's tragic heroines, Dorinda remains invisible to
the world that interprets her, unable to represent herself in categories which it
understands.

A far poorer reform play which has some common features with *Greenwich-
Park* and *The English Frier* is John Smyth's *Win Her and Take Her* (1690–1),[9]
where a rake is tamed into marriage by a pure woman, and a jealous man and
coquettish woman outgrow their follies and likewise marry. Here, however,
there is much reliance on buffoonish humours characters, and none of
Crowne's and Mountfort's moral and social vision. By contrast, Durfey's
Love for Money (January 1691) resembles Shadwell's last plays in using the
sexual and monetary intrigues of comedy as vehicles for praising the new
political order. The author of *The Royalist* now swiftly turned his coat. *Love
for Money* affirms the power of law and the triumph of justice, with explicit
reference to the struggle against James II and Louis XIV. Like Shadwell in
Bury-Fair, Durfey reinstates the old conflict between the laws of the city and
the disruptive stranger, portraying a foolish Frenchman, Le Prate, who intrudes from an alien tyranny that lacks the safeguards of law (to Le Prate's
rage, indeed, Louis is slandered by an English *lawyer*, I, p. 4). But true social
principles triumph: mercenary relationships (a recurrent motif, as the title
suggests) prove less stable than those based on natural regard and affection,
and contrasting versions of familial authority replicate the international conflict between absolutism and the rule of law. Lady Addleplot, a Jacobite conspirator who is finally subjected to legal process,[10] is an exponent of familial
and class tyranny, terrorizing and imprisoning her submissive second husband (a citizen), and drawing unwarranted distinctions between the blue-
blooded daughter of her first marriage and her bourgeois stepdaughter, two
amiably unthinking and appetitive boarding-school girls who are identical in
character because identical in education.

Justice also awaits another exemplification of corrupted authority, the villainous guardian Sir Rowland Rakehell (a counterpart to Shadwell's villainous stepparents), who applies the libertine's philosophic contempt for moral

---

9 The play shares two names, Florella and Dorinda, with *Greenwich-Park*. If one play did influence the other, Smyth seems more likely to be the debtor.

10 Lady Addleplot was played by Anthony Leigh as a caricature of Lady Fenwick (*London Stage*,
ed. Van Lennep, i. 393, quoting Earl of Ailesbury, *Memoirs* (London, 1890), ii. 390–1). Sir John
Fenwick, a consistent and foolishly unguarded opponent of William III, was executed in 1697 for complicity in the plot to assassinate him. His wife, Mary (d. 1708), was the daughter of Charles Howard,
Earl of Carlisle. Her sister, Anne, married Viscount Preston, who was active in an earlier Jacobite conspiracy.

inhibition not to the seduction of women but to the fraudulent acquisition of estates, having gained his nephew's 'by means unjust' (V, p. 54) and his ward's by having her abducted (as he believes) to the Indies. At the end of the play, Sir Rowland faces certain hanging, and this unusually dark element emphasizes Durfey's determination to subject the philosophy of the rake to a system of evaluation and judgement as removed as possible from that of libertine comedy. Dorimant's abolition of fixed judicial absolutes has been reversed, and the stabilization of moral order is ratified in that most traditional image of renewed stability, a homecoming and exclusion of the interloper: at the climax of the play, the heiress Mirtilla takes possession of her house and excludes Sir Rowland and Betty Jiltall, the prostitute who has impersonated her and married Sir Rowland in an attempt to gain her property.

Libertinism is also condemned in Durfey's *The Marriage-Hater Match'd* (January 1692), and dishonesty in sexual matters is again equated with financial fraud: Sir Philip Freewit attempts to defraud Lady Subtle of her estate, but eventually allows her 'Justice' (V, p. 54), and he also inadvertently bestows the 'Justice'[11] of marriage upon the innocent parson's daughter (Bracegirdle) who has borne his child (he arranges for his Irish valet to perform a fake marriage, but the valet cannot master the words and gets his clergyman brother to stand in for him). In *The Committee*, the incompetence of the Irish servant had vindicated the moral authority of the gentleman; here, it restrains his amoral privilege. In a separate critique of entrenched and irrational authority, Lord Brainless marries a retired minor actress, having mistaken descriptions of her former roles for descriptions of her actual rank. The obvious point is that his real lordship is worth no more than her stage fictions.

Durfey also pairs amatory and financial plotting in his excessively intricate *The Richmond Heiress* (April 1693), where heiress-hunting is paralleled with the mania for speculation in stocks (also satirized in Shadwell's *The Volunteers*),[12] though this structurally central element was cut in the revisions which Durfey made after the play's initial failure.[13] As in some of his earlier plays, the heroines (Sophronia and the heiress Fulvia) remain unmarried, and in using the name Fulvia he again takes a name associated with a classical female stereotype (Mark Antony's virago wife) and redefines it by freeing it from the control of the male viewpoint. As 'The Female Plain Dealer' (II, p. 11), conversely, Sophronia appropriates the manifestly and explicitly male

---

[11] I, p. 2; III, p. 32; IV, p. 38; V, p. 43.

[12] The need for national loans to finance the war 'emphasized the importance of the stockbroker' (David Ogg, *England in the Reigns of James II and William III*, corrected edn. (Oxford, 1957), 85). Lawrence and Jeanne Stone point out that, by the 1690s, dramatists' contempt for the moneyed class had shifted from the great merchants and 'was beginning to focus more exclusively upon the new parasitical monied men, the usurious scrivener-bankers, the speculative stock-jobbers and the like' (*An Open Elite?*, 287–8)

[13] See Holland, 'Durfey's Revisions of *The Richmond Heiress*', 118.

role of Wycherley's Manly (himself named after a character in Durfey's *Madam Fickle*). At the end of the play Fulvia dispenses 'Justice' (V, pp. 62–3) to her unworthy suitors, but the struggle for self-determination has been hard, and for some time her only means of resisting a society that denied her control over her own life and person was to feign madness. For Frederick, the leading male character, the fitting state for a woman is impotence of both language and action: 'a Lady', he says to Sophronia, 'should no more pretend to a Book, than a Sword' (III, p. '29' [33]).

In the three-part *Comical History of Don Quixote*[14] Durfey simply relied on the attractions of farce and song, and he abandoned the thoughtful treatment of birth and education in *Love for Money*, returning to the unquestioning equation of status and merit that had marked *The Banditti*. The vulgarity and pretentiousness of Sancho and his daughter Mary are constantly mocked, and Sancho (unlike his original) acts as a boorish clown when dispensing justice during his governorship. Don Quixote himself repeatedly fails in his self-appointed role of 'Protector of Justice' (Part I, I, p. 2) (for example, when he releases the galley-slaves), but the reformed seducer Fernando has justice in his soul by virtue of possessing 'Noble Blood' (Part I, III, p. 26). The trilogy features bawdy talk and song, but takes no risks in its action (though even the bawdy talk in the third part was too much for the ladies). *Love for Money* and *The Marriage-Hater Match'd* had made important contributions to moralistic comedy, but the bawdry of *Don Quixote* suggests that Durfey was hankering for other things, yet nervous about providing them. A few sex comedies (*Sir Anthony Love, The Old Batchelour*, and, though it barely counts as comedy, *Amphitryon*) were still being premièred with great success, but there was a widespread disinclination to take risks, and new dramatists (Congreve excepted) were ingenuously confident in the allure of morality: Henry Higden, for example, was taken aback to find that *The Wary Widdow* (March 1693) had been completely overshadowed by 'the surprising success of the Baudy Batchelour' (preface, sig. [A3]). Like so many aspirant playwrights in the 1690s, Higden was an amateur out of his depth, but his subjects were fashionable enough: a fallen women is treated with compassion, and a prudent woman carefully tests a prospective husband. The test uses the familiar ruse of the 'invisible Mistress' (II, p. 21), Lady Wary attracting Frank Fox both in her own person, when she assumes a pose of demure gravity, and in the guise of a masked, bejewelled extrovert. Her split identity, however, merely gives her the opportunity to observe, and we do not find the divided appeal to the hero's appetitive and social selves that the ruse generally produces in Carolean comedy; there is no wild man within. The fallen woman, Leonora, is another victim of a scheming aunt, and has slept with both Frank and his father, but finally marries Sir Noisy Parrat. Her husband is an odious fool, but her

---

14 Parts I and II were first performed, with success, in May 1694. Part III, a failure, was produced by Rich's company in Nov. 1695.

dignification as Lady Parrat nevertheless implies the social assimilation of 'a perfect stranger to the World' (II, p. 19).

The plight of the transgressing female is more subtly studied in Crowne's last surviving comedy, *The Married Beau* (April 1694),[15] where it is linked to his characteristic fascination with characters lost amidst surfaces and inadequate signs, and his concomitant interest in the epistemologically challenged fop. The closest descendant of Crowne's earlier men of surface is Sir John Shittlecock, a man of conspicuous ancestry and invisible identity, who is so mesmerized by life's endless sequence of surfaces that he loves whichever beauty he happens to be looking at, and at one point courts an inanimate post—a blank form without interior character—under the names of all the women he desires (IV, pp. 39–40). Here, the fool is humanized (to the extent that, unprecedentedly, he makes a very good marriage), but a corollary of the humanization of the fool is that a fool is now also a potential agent of tragedy.[16] The husband of the transgressing woman, Mr Lovely, resembles Sir John in being a fop of pure surface, but he lacks Sir John's childish contentment with surface in others, and wishes to penetrate to his wife's essence, to invent a telescope to search her thoughts and breast (I, p. 3), in order to discover whether she sufficiently esteems his own beauty of surface. He therefore (in a reworking of Cervantes' story of the Curious Impertinent) persuades his friend Polidor to attempt to seduce her. Polidor initiates his seduction attempt with a conversation about Crowne's favourite image of the enigmatic surfaces of fleshly existence, portraits, and, although Mrs Lovely attempts to treat these flat, impenetrable images as expressions of aesthetic or moral value (one claims her admiration because it represents her husband), she is later conquered by Polidor's carnality. The lovers repent, and Polidor transcends his preoccupation with carnal surface, marrying a virtuous woman whom he had earlier mocked as 'A Picture of Virginity in Marble' (IV, p. '48' [46]). But there is no general reconstitution of society on the basis of sound signification, and indeed the final harmony is only possible because Lovely attains the blindness of a Sir Jaspar Fidget.

The increasing interest in marriage is also reflected in two very minor plays, Powell's *A Very Good Wife* (April 1693) and Thomas Wright's *The Female Vertuoso's* (May 1693), an adaptation of Molière's *Les Femmes savantes* in which the literary follies of Molière's ladies are extended to include scientific schemes worthy of Sir Nicholas Gimcrack. *A Very Good Wife* reworks Brome's *The City Wit*, with added contributions from (at least) *The Counterfeit Bridegroom* and *Hyde Park*, to create a play in which a virtuous wife restores her impoverished husband's fortune, providing a redress which cannot be obtained from the corrupt and slow-moving law (I, p. 6). In the process of

---

[15] His *Justice Busy* (1698–9) was not published and is lost.

[16] Susan Staves points out the new weight given to the fop in this play ('A Few Kind Words for the Fop', *Studies in English Literature*, 22 (1982), 413–28 (pp. 422–3)).

conflation, the pro-city emphasis of Brome's play is entirely reversed. A more sympathetic treatment of the city appears in *The Female Vertuoso's*, where Molière's 'bon bourgeois' Chrysale becomes Sir Maurice Meanwell, 'An honest rich Citizen' (Dramatis Personae). In Molière Wright found the popular theme of the testing of a suitor (the hero's love for the heroine is undiminished by her apparent impoverishment), and also potential for the increasingly fashionable subject of marital discord: he altered Molière to show Sir Maurice leaving his domineering second wife. There is, however, no modification of Molière's ridicule of female intellectual aspiration, which is supported by heavy-handed emphasis on male supremacy: '*Man first was destin'd for the Sov'reign Sway*' (V, p. 51).

Despite the moralistic nature of much new comedy, however, some of the best and most successful plays (*Sir Anthony Love, Amphitryon, The Old Batchelour*) continue the traditions of sex comedy. They are, in addition, all plays of dislocation, contrasting with Shadwell's celebrations of reconstructed homes. If the expulsion of James II moved Shadwell to celebrate the reintegration of community, it moved Dryden to repeated meditations on usurpation, exile, and displacement. In *Amphitryon* (October 1690) Jupiter and Mercury usurp the household and even the physical forms of Amphitryon and his servant Sosia, Amphitryon being at the climax of the play denied entrance to his own house while Jupiter sleeps with Amphitryon's wife in yet another version of the bedroom trick (as in Mountfort's *The Injur'd Lovers*, the trick enables public power to override personal right).[17] Jupiter is a libertine absolutist who treats law as an expression of his monarchic will, but the nominal guardian of law, the venal judge Gripus, is just as adept at corrupting and perverting it. Unsurprisingly, Dryden did not join Shadwell and Durfey in portraying the Revolution as a re-establishment of law. Law does not restrain power: it serves it.

In taking over the names and forms of Amphitryon and Sosia, Jupiter and Mercury deprive them of all external signs and tokens of distinct identity: when Amphitryon brings home a gift for Alcmena, it is in a package sealed with his own sign, but there is nothing beneath the sign, for Jupiter has already spirited away the gift and given it to Alcmena. (The theft of identity inevitably transforms the familiar into the alien, Sosia approaching his own residence 'as a stranger', II. i. 284). The climax of the play is a trial before Gripus to compare and evaluate the rival tokens of identity and decide which is the real Amphitryon. Here judicial ritual emerges with particular clarity as epistemologically flawed, and as incapable of assessing personal essence; for the true and false Amphitryons produce the same external signs of identity, but Alcmena is so startled by the angry jealousy of her true husband that she makes the wrong choice. When she attempts to isolate essential character

[17] David Bywaters extensively interprets Jupiter as a hostile representation of William III (*Dryden in Revolutionary England* (Berkeley, Los Angeles, and Oxford, 1991), 56–74).

from the outward accidents of physical form, she fails utterly, and intimates once again become strangers. Amphitryon's threats of visiting 'Justice' on his rival are inevitably impotent, and the enigma is only solved when Jupiter appears with the grandeur and impunity of divine power, explains what has happened, and imposes his own signification and moral character upon events: 'What he enjoys, he sanctifies from Vice; | And by partaking, stamps into a price' (V. i. 399–400). This concluding subordination of justice to power repeats and confirms what has already happened in the secondary plot, portraying the courtship of Mercury and Alcmena's lively maid, Phædra. The courtship culminates in a proviso scene, where the metaphor of legal contract intrinsic to such scenes is literalized, in that the provisos are sworn in the presence of Gripus. But Phædra quickly realizes that contracts with gods are unenforceable (V. i. 379–84). Law is once again an illusory protection against power; Whig principles do not work.

Amphitryon reverses the situation of *Marriage A-la-Mode*, where Leonidas and Palmyra are subject to bewildering shifts of identity and status that shape their minds and characters and call in question the autonomy and consistency of their essential selves. Amphitryon and Sosia suffer a contrary division of the self: not a disorientating proliferation and splitting of their own roles, but conflict with external replicas of themselves. Their essential identity remains immutable; but it is also unverifiable and inexpressible. The self remains mysterious and isolated, and the rituals of judicial proof, imperfect and corrupt as they inevitably are, cannot alter or restrain a fundamental condition of life: that it naturally resolves itself into networks of power, that power is primarily an agent of appetite, and that the networks of power are the true determinants of what pass for signs of individual character.

Southerne's first two plays, *The Loyal Brother* (1682) and *The Disappointment* (1684), had portrayed the recovery of fitting social or moral place, but his plays in the last decade of the century depict loss or corruption of the home, and of natural social impulse, the emphasis on dislocation presumably reflecting the anxieties of the erstwhile Jacobite. *Sir Anthony Love; or, The Rambling Lady* (?September 1690) is (as its subtitle partially implies) a play about uprooted, expatriate, and wandering characters,[18] the most fully dislocated character being a disreputable Pilgrim, whom the other characters at once despise and recognize as an image of themselves. His next two comedies, *The Wives' Excuse* (December 1691) and *The Maid's Last Prayer* (February 1693), are both London comedies, but they explore another species of dislocation in their preoccupation with decaying homes, introducing a concern with marital unhappiness that became a new and distinctive feature of comedy in this decade.[19] Exile and the collapsing home also became the primary subjects

[18] Jordan and Love plausibly suggest that it may be evidence that Southerne himself retired abroad for a time in the aftermath of the Revolution (*Works*, i, p. xix).

[19] See Robert D. Hume, 'Marital Discord in English Comedy from Dryden to Fielding', *Modern*

of Southerne's mature tragedies, and in both comedy and tragedy the dissolution of the home is complemented by the decay of those traditional bonds of social existence, hospitality and service. Sir Anthony Love invites the Pilgrim back for a drink and drugs him, Oroonoko is captured through a fraudulent act of hospitality, and, in the parties which consume life in the two London comedies, enmity and rivalry are pursued beneath the thinnest guises of conviviality: when Granger in *The Maid's Last Prayer* omits his hostess from an otherwise comprehensive disparagement of the female company, he is reproved for being 'Inhospitable' (I. i. 15), and promptly remedies his omission. And service, which had bound Howard's Teague to his masters in a harmony of reciprocal obligation, is repeatedly replaced by crude economic oppression, whether in the slavery of *Oroonoko* (where *service* is a recurrent word) or in the exploitation of vulnerable women: in *The Wives' Excuse*, for example, the rakish and cynical Lovemore tries to seduce the unhappily married Mrs Friendall by pretending to 'serve' and provide 'Service',[20] and in *The Fatal Marriage* Isabella's unloved second husband gains the impoverished and desperate woman by 'Services' which she explicitly equates with purchase (II. iii. 42, 105).

Indeed, sale is the primary model of human relationships. In *Oroonoko* the literal trade in slaves is paralleled with the subtler barter of the marriage-market,[21] and *The Maid's Last Prayer* portrays with contempt an aristocracy whose rapacious acquisitiveness is expressed not only in card-sharping and shop-lifting (III. iii. 50–3) but even in literal prostitution. The class structure is a mere pecking order in theft and the sale of flesh; indeed, in *Oroonoko* it is asserted that great estates owe their beginnings to acts of treacherous plunder such as that with which the hero is captured (I. ii. 262–4). In the opening scene of *The Wives' Excuse*, servants mimic the conversation and mannerisms of their superiors, revealing a personal lifestyle that is virtually indistinguishable from that of their employers. The 'Service' (I. i. 40) which these subordinates provide is not a natural expression of social degree but a grudging response to adventitious differences of circumstance. But, although Southerne empties social procedures of significance, he does not inherit Wycherley's and Etherege's interest in the ineradicable presence of antisocial impulses within the citizen. On the contrary, social rituals in his comedies increasingly become the entire sum of human existence, for society is a precondition for the kinds of betrayal

Philology, 74 (1976–7), 248–72, repr. in his *The Rakish Stage*, 176–213; Michael Cordner, 'Marriage Comedy after the 1688 Revolution: Southerne to Vanbrugh', *Modern Language Review*, 85 (1990), 273–89.

[20] II. ii. 98–9; IV. i. 186–90.

[21] Thomas Southerne, *Oroonoko*, ed. Maximillian E. Novak and David Stuart Rodes, Regents Restoration Drama Series (London, 1977), pp. xxii–xxiv; Robert L. Root, Jr., *Thomas Southerne*, Twayne's English Authors Series, 315 (Boston, 1981), 95–8. An unconvincing denial of the parallel is advanced in Julia A. Rich, 'Heroic Tragedy in Southerne's *Oroonoko* (1695): An Approach to a Split-plot Tragicomedy', *Philological Quarterly*, 62 (1983), 187–200.

in which he specializes. His characters are not imaginatively fixed in the Hobbesian wilderness, but are rather lost in empty rituals of pre-eminence, such as the bout of uncommunicative one-upmanship in *The Wives' Excuse* in which Friendall recites hierarchies of wines, snuffs, and teas (IV. i. 1–66). For Lord Malepert in *The Maid's Last Prayer*, retreat from the city is as unthinkable as an hour spent at home, for in the country 'There's no *Levees*, no *Mall*, no *Plays*, no *Operas*, no Tea at *Siam*'s' (IV. i. 96–7). Even copulation becomes a mere social ritual, a confirmation of status rather than a gratification of lust.

The separation of sexual triumph from sexual desire is central to *Sir Anthony Love*, whose rakish 'hero' is in fact a woman (Lucia) in disguise. (Charlot Welldon in *Oroonoko* was a similar travesty role, written for the same actress, Susanna Mountfort/Verbruggen.[22]) In the 1690s, the woman turned bully generally assumes her disguise in order to test or tame a suitor, but Anthony has no such aim, for she enters entirely into the mentality of the rake and enjoys the excitement of conquest; after all, many men prefer the chase to the kill (I. i. 34–8). 'We make a Carnival; all the year a Carnival' (II. i. 573), she claims, boasting of a new woman in every town. But, for her, it is a carnival without flesh, and indeed throughout his three major comedies Southerne habitually disjoins sexual conquest from lust: even when copulation occurs, it is never a shared completion of specifically directed desire. Anthony, for example, tricks her friend Valentine into sleeping with her, but he does so without knowing the identity or seeing the face of his partner until the deed is done. The most extensive scene of lust in the trio of comedies occurs when a worldly Abbè makes homosexual advances to Anthony, only to lapse into total indifference when he discovers her true sex. In an earlier and parallel scene—the only other portrayal of lust in the trio—the Pilgrim suspects (without definite knowledge) that Sir Anthony may be a woman, and makes ambiguously defined advances: 'I'm resolv'd to like you in any Sex' (III. i. 113). Promptly, however, he falls into a drugged sleep. Similarly, though *The Wives' Excuse* and *The Maid's Last Prayer* portray a monotonous round of seduction and pandarism, the characters' sexual activities are only minimally tinged with sexual desire, and there is usually an explicit lack of interest in the sexual partner. For example, Courtall in *The Wives' Excuse*, like Vainlove in Congreve's *The Old Bachelour*, is interested in conquest rather than possession, thinking 'enjoyment the dull part of an Intrigue' (III. ii. 133), and Sir Ruff Rancounter in *The Maid's Last Prayer* is pursuing Lady Malepert purely for 'the Reputation of a Quality-Entriegue' (II. ii. 12).

The general dissociation of copulation from any specifically desired object is reflected in a remarkable proliferation of unconventional bedroom tricks. (In *Sir Anthony Love*, the heroine not only sleeps incognita with Valentine but

---

[22] Susanna Mountfort, née Percival, was initially married to the actor and playwright William Mountfort. He was murdered in 1692, and Susanna then married another leading actor, John Verbruggen (the first Mirabell).

enters a mock-marriage with a woman and attempts to get a male friend to substitute for her in bed—a ruse repeated with greater success by Charlot Welldon in *Oroonoko*.) In most of its various manifestations, the bedroom trick defines the tension between desire and the social values that regulate it: it may permit the enforcement of corrupt and oppressive values, as in *The Injur'd Lovers* and *Amphitryon*; it may trick a would-be transgressor into inadvertent conformity with an authoritative social code, producing an act that is less immoral in performance than in intention, as in Southerne's own *The Disappointment*; or the error may work in the opposite way, towards an unsuspected degree of transgression, as in Otway's *The Orphan*. In Southerne's mature comedies, however, the distinction between intention and act is morally meaningless. When Friendall in *The Wives' Excuse* commits adultery with the wrong woman, the moral difference between the intended and the accomplished adultery is nil, and the impression is simply that stability of liaison is impossible, and that uncoordinated sexual designs produce an uncontrollable randomness of association. Another morally neutral substitution of partners occurs in *The Maid's Last Prayer*, where Gayman diverts Sir Ruff Rancounter from an assignation with Lady Malepert and covertly takes Sir Ruff's place in her bed. Ignorant of the substitution, Lady Malepert spends the imagined night with Sir Ruff in sexual fantasies of copulation with the man she is actually, but unknowingly, sleeping with, but is then dismayed to discover that she has acted as prostitute to a man she truly loves. Again, the bedroom trick does not create a collision between the imperatives of desire and of social existence; it simply exposes the randomness of the processes which link desire and partner.

Sexual encounters in Southerne, then, are marked by indifference, mistaken identity, and even misconstruction of the partner's sex, the mismatch between desire and object of desire here arising because the physical signs have been deciphered according to the wrong code. Sexual desire is not an elemental impulse that predates and abrogates the forms of society, but is deeply dependent upon the procedures of social existence, and is excited by the sometimes fictitious roles and appearances that constitute social identity: most obviously, the mistaken sex of Sir Anthony and Charlot, but also the 'Quality' that is one of Lady Malepert's chief attractions, and the slick playacting that persuades the virtuous Mrs Friendall that Lovemore, as contemptible in every way as her husband, is the ideal partner she missed in the lottery of marriage. Consistently, Southerne abolishes the tension between desire and social existence that had dominated the best sex comedy in the 1670s, portraying instead a world in which desire is attenuated into a byproduct of social ritual.

So, perhaps, is identity itself. Sir Anthony's female disguise raises the question of how far the person (actual and perceived) is separable from the external fabrications of social role; for, as Harold Weber has persuasively argued, her assumption of a male role actually produces an assumption of male psychology.[23] Equally, every social and personal evaluation of Sir Anthony is conditioned by mistaken assumptions about 'his' sex and status. The dependence of interior character upon public role is less comprehensive than in the later comedies, for *Sir Anthony Love* is not littered by hollow figures who have no existence outside their public pursuits; there is, for example, a clear incongruity between the Abbè's rank and his character. Nevertheless, Sir Anthony's identity remains a problem. Unlike Shadwell's Mrs Gripe, she does not display an essential equality with men that has hitherto been obscured by externally imposed stereotype, for she achieves little self-expression or self-vindication, merely devising public rituals of jest, sport, and diversion. Still less, however, is she temporarily suppressing an essential and natural femininity, for she is never given a specific female identity. She does resume female dress at the end of the play but, as Weber observes,[24] the dress is not her own. She does marry a man but (in yet another mismatch of partners) does so disguised as someone else (hence the borrowed clothes), and does so only in order to extort a settlement of separation from him. We know nothing of her family or (beyond the fact that she is English) her origins, for the manor of Love-dale, the *home* to which she refers during the play (I. i. 316), is a fiction; all we see are the transient guises and appearances which become her medium of social intercourse.

Sir Anthony, indeed, denies that familial origin can transmit anything other than the pox ('Example, and Custom' (I. i. 108) are what count), and her claim is confirmed by the name and conduct of the foolish and unprincipled Count Verole (*syphilis* in French), whose blinkered concern with social degree provides a peculiarly clear identification of accidents with essence. Such folly is easy to reject, but the alternative is not appreciation of essence but (as Sir Anthony's career shows) subtler versions of the same error, which remains inescapable even when it is recognized: 'How Ceremony disguises any thing!' exclaims Sir Anthony's former keeper, Sir Gentle Golding; 'I can't take this civil Gentleman for a Pimp, tho' I have Occasion for him' (IV. i. 12–13). But the figure who most fully develops and duplicates the absorption of person into perceived role is the fraudulent Pilgrim, who resembles Sir Anthony in being a wanderer and a robber: he is 'a shifter of Shapes and Names' who has 'travell'd through every Profession, and cheated in all' (III. i. 99–100). As soon as the Pilgrim enters, Sir Anthony mocks the external 'Frippery' that bestows apparent sanctity upon him (I. i. 150), but the false authority of his religious garments is quickly seen to typify the nature of social authority, for fools in the state and atheists in the church—Count Verole and the Abbè—survive through 'the Authority and Countenance of their Cloathing' (I. i. 168–9). Later, the Pilgrim's dissimulation and villainy are recognized as universal human characteristics:

[23] Weber, *The Restoration Rake-Hero*, 166.   [24] Ibid. 171.

> Thus every Man to his own Interest tends,
> The Pilgrim makes his Converts, We make Friends,
> With the same Conscience all, for our own Ends.
>
> (II. i. 672–4)

Nevertheless, universal human characteristics derive their particular colouring from the clothes of the individual who embodies them, and it is never possible to judge nature apart from role. The Abbè is a priest, a pederast, and a humane and enlightened man, but his enlightenment impresses no one, and he is either respected as a priest or mocked as a priestly pederast. Similarly, although the Pilgrim's career as a thieving wanderer obviously parallels that of Sir Anthony, his falsification of his spiritual character provokes quite different judgements from her falsification of her sex and rank; and, despite the overt contempt for popish trumpery, his robbery of the shrine at Loretto appears far graver than her robbery of her stereotyped cully, Golding. The Pilgrim is recognized as an incarnation of universal characteristics, yet his particular garb causes him to be rejected with contempt as an outsider. He is a striking reversal of the stranger within, presenting not the alien disguised as the familiar but the familiar disguised as the alien. Yet again, the disruptiveness which earlier dramatists had attributed to the persistence of presocial instincts within social forms is by Southerne attributed to the social forms themselves.

In *The Wives' Excuse* and *The Maid's Last Prayer* Southerne dispenses with exotic wanderers, instead portraying the dislocation of collapsing domesticity. Wittwoud, the unprincipled sexual manipulator of the former play, 'lives, as she us'd to do, least at home' (I. i. 113), is banned from the houses of most of her relatives, and tries to arrange the seduction of the one kinswoman who will still acknowledge her. So tenuous is domesticity that to go 'home' with someone becomes a synonym for illicit copulation.[25] The play portrays the empty marriage of the virtuous, intelligent Mrs Friendall and her vacuous, philandering husband, the emptiness of their marriage being emphasized by the persistent dissociation of their home from any idea of domestic society. Friendall will 'go home' with his wife, but shuns her in public (III. ii. 28–9), and even his home is—as Mrs Friendall complains—'one of the publick Places of the Town' (III. ii. 12–13), for it is a perpetual venue for pointless and joyless parties, ostensible rituals of community which are in fact rituals of backbiting and rivalry, and which entirely obliterate the privacy and integrity of familial life. When Friendall is caught *in flagrante* with Wittwoud at one of his parties, he is outraged at the violation of the home-owner's privilege to commit adultery on his own premises: 'What a pox! disturb a Gentleman's pleasures! and in his own House too!' (V. iii. 267–8). Appropriately, the play concludes with the separation of the couple. In *The Maid's Last Prayer* the decay of domesticity reaches still greater heights when the foolish Lord

[25] I. ii. 71–3, iii. 32; II. i. 88; V. iii. 218.

Malepert is forcibly expelled from his own house by the man who (though she does not yet realize it) has just slept with his wife.

The constant mismatch of partners means that there is no companionship or community even in the most primitive union of sexual pairing, and other forms of companionship are also correspondingly empty. When, in *The Maid's Last Prayer*, Lord Malepert comes home to find Gayman with his wife, Gayman talks his way out of the embarrassment by persuading Lord Malepert that he spent the night in his company, that he was sent ahead to arrange for refreshments, and that Malepert is simply too drunk to remember being with him: companionship is here literally an illusion. But, if man is isolated amidst a web of illusory or non-existent partnerships, society is a necessary expression of his isolation, for, as already indicated, human competitiveness in Southerne is the competitiveness not of the Hobbesian wilderness but of the drawing-room: the crooked gambling, and the ostentatious catalogues of tea, are not expressions of some deeper and more atavistic urge to dominate; they are the thing itself. There is no weasel under the cocktail cabinet. When Lord Malepert's very memory is overridden and revised by his companions, the attenuation of self into socially created forms reaches an absurd extreme, but it is an absurd extreme of the typical. There is endless social activity without society itself, yet also without any prevailing sense of socially unassimilable individuality. The really anomalous characters are not the Lord Maleperts but the few characters, such as the almost tragic Mrs Friendall, who desire society in its usual sense.

The old carnivalistic attitude towards sex makes one last uncomplicated appearance in Ravenscroft's *The Canterbury Guests* (September 1694), probably inspired by the success of *The Old Batchelour* ('nothing's more ridiculous than an old Batchelor in Love,' says one of the characters, I, p. 5). The play is largely constructed out of the gay couple plots from *The Careless Lovers* and *King Edgar and Alfreda*, though De Boastado, the foolish suitor of *The Careless Lovers*, is replaced by a new fool, Sir Barnaby Buffler (the old bachelor), whose conversation consists almost wholly of proverbs. One of his proverbs is '*Maids must be seen, not heard*' (II, p. 19), and there is obvious irony at the expense of the male supremacist who denies women language while being unable to coin an original sentence of his own. Ravenscroft also creates another figure of sham authority, Justice Greedy, in whom the majesty and ceremony of justice constantly yield to unruly appetite: his trial (at the dinner table) of two prostitutes is frustrated when they bribe him with a profusion of food, and he later ends up in bed with both at once. (A later Justice, Vanbrugh's Sir Tunbelly Clumsey, also displays carnal disorder in both name and conduct, but Vanbrugh's attitude towards the flesh was more ambivalent than Ravenscroft's.)

No other sex comedies of the 1690s are as insouciant as *The Canterbury Guests*, and most share something of Southerne's outlook. For, although many dramatists responded to the Revolution by celebrating the remaking of the home, concern with intractable social and domestic dislocation is not confined to dramatists with a Jacobite present or past. The Whig Vanbrugh, for example, imitates Southerne's portrayal of collapsing homes, and, although his most obviously displaced character (Young Fashion in *The Relapse*) is a Jacobite, the point about his Jacobitism is that it does not mark him out as a special outsider but is merely one version of a universal condition. Dislocation, though of a rather different kind, also interests Congreve. Indeed the first line of his first play, *The Old Batchelour* (March 1693), shows its hero expressing surprise at finding his friend out of his customary place: '*Vainlove*, and abroad so early!' (I. i. 1). Vainlove is, however, out of place only because habit, and the hour of day, exclude his present surroundings from his set pattern of life, and he is obviously not an uprooted and disorientated figure such as Sir Anthony Love, Amphitryon, or Young Fashion. Nor do Congreve's comedies ever offer a counterpart to these figures: for all his concern with insecurity and threatened penury (and for all his avowed admiration for *The Plain-Dealer* and its rootless protagonist), he never portrays a condition of actual dispossession and dislocation. Except for *The Old Batchelour*, his comedies are centred within homes, and within intricate webs of kinship. When outsiders (such as Ben and Sir Wilfull Witwoud) intrude, they are paralysed within unfamiliar rituals of domesticity and lack the physical mobility of their more urbanized coevals: Sir Wilfull is seen only in Lady Wishfort's house, and among the principal characters is equalled in immobility only by Lady Wishfort herself. Yet he and Lady Wishfort are the two characters who talk most about travelling, albeit to vague and undefined destinations. A figure such as Sir Wilfull—a would-be traveller confined and baffled within the walls of a city house—is the very reverse of ramblers such as Sir Anthony or Young Fashion. Even Osmyn, the noble exile of *The Mourning Bride*, first reveals his true identity from the enclosure of his father's tomb: a tragic counterpart to the kind of enclosure experienced by Ben and Sir Wilfull in their return to ancestral territory.

Nevertheless, Congreve resembles Vanbrugh and Southerne in denying absolute symbolic or moral value to place. But, whereas they empty place of significance by portraying characters whose norms of dwelling and domesticity have disappeared, Congreve takes the opposite approach, already developed in Wycherley's first two comedies, of inspecting the apparently fixed and stable systems of place that govern his characters' existence: systems summed up in the title of his last play. Repeatedly, place turns out to have the same kind of purely accidental and customary significance that makes the streets of London foreign territory to Vainlove in the morning. Bellmour and Vainlove have a customary 'old place' (I. i. 130) for dining, and the accidental significance of place is still more clearly illustrated when Sir Joseph Wittoll enters, finds himself in the very place where he was beaten up on the previous night, and announces that he 'shall never be reconciled to this place heartily' (II. i. 14–15).

Unfixity characterizes both the heroes of *The Old Batchelour*. Bellmour is 'not contented with the slavery of honourable Love in one place' (I. i. 137–9), and Vainlove is portrayed as a restlessly moving object pursuing an unfixed and unlocalized goal, for his desired Araminta 'is a kind of floating Island; sometimes seems in reach, then vanishes and keeps him busied in the search' (I. i. 205–7).[26] Even the final marriages provide not stabilization but simply co-operative motion: Bellmour and Vainlove set 'forward on a Journey for Life' while Heartwell continues to 'plod on alone' (V. ii. 181–3). To the end, Congreve withholds fixed norms of social stability, portraying marriage as the conversion of independent motion into shared motion. After all, there is little in these unions to suggest stabilization, for the courtships consist simply of an interplay of shifting and mercurial surface, with singularly little impression of wandering souls finding their goal in the discovery of a natural mate. Their dialogues consist not of communication but of criticism of the signs by which communication is attempted, as when Belinda mocks the imagery with which Bellmour declares love and then finds still more fault with the 'dumb Rhetorick' (II. ii. 212) with which he replaces it. The lovers do not gaze intimately into each other's essence, but rather spar with sign systems that are as ironically assumed as they are received. When Vainlove and Araminta are eventually brought together, it is by means of a totally spurious set of signs: a counterfeit letter from Araminta concocted by a jealous rival. Love in this play consists of random collisions by which independently moving objects are sent in a common direction, and Congreve's persistent portrayal of characters fencing with signifiers denuded of signification reveals one of the most important and consistent aspects of his characters' unfixity: the public signs and categories through which individuals are perceived and classified have no natural or representative connection with the personal essence they seemingly represent. In a very fundamental sense, characters do not belong to the system in which they are placed.

In later plays, Congreve's characters continue to spar with arbitrary and deceptive systems of signs: hence his fondness for the image of life as a game of cards, the card-game being another system of rules restricted to place and context, and an activity which centres upon the competitive concealment of signs. The most obvious example is the card-game which opens *The Way of the World*, but even Angelica in *Love for Love* achieves her success by applying to life the principles of the expert cardswoman: 'I have plaid you a Trick' (V. i. 570), she says to the defeated Sir Sampson. But the outward sign which interests Congreve most of all is the face, perhaps because it has the appearance of being a sign constituted by nature itself. In the later comedies, the face is the supreme mask: in *Love for Love* Mrs Foresight and Mrs Frail parry each

[26] Cf. I. i. 385–8; V. i. 2–6.

other's accusations of promiscuity with inconsequential comparisons of their faces (II. i. 458–64), management and scrutiny of the face pervade *The Way of the World*, and in *The Double-Dealer* Maskwell's face displays 'Ten thousand meanings' (V. i. 394–5). But in *The Old Batchelour* the face does not so much conceal character as create the hallucination of its existence, imposing an illusory distinctness and identity upon the amorphous and inapprehensible mass of human nature. 'Nothing's new besides our Faces, | Every Woman is the same' (II. ii. 201–2), proclaims one of the songs, and the bedroom tricks whereby Bellmour enjoys Vainlove's sexual conquests suggest a similar interchangeability on the male side: expecting an assignation with Vainlove, Lætitia is at first dismayed to see another 'Face' (IV. ii. 18), but then decides that she likes it anyway. Indeed, sexual intercourse is twice described as a joining of faces (III. ii. 4; IV. iv. 156): the apparent tokens of character and individuation make contact, not to communicate, but to engage in an act which renders every partner 'the same'.

In *The Old Batchelour* the restless mobility of the main characters forbids any climactic attainment of harmonious union. But even when, in later comedies, such unions occur, they are still associated with the arbitrary imposition of meaning upon a place that is in itself blank and meaningless. In *The Way of the World*, in one of the most famous and enchanting moments in all the comedies, Mirabell finds Millamant alone and newly escaped from the awkward gallantries of Sir Wilfull, and enquires why the other door to the room had been locked:

MIRABELL. Do you lock your self up from me, to make my search more Curious? Or is this pretty Artifice Contriv'd, to Signifie that here the Chase must end, and my pursuit be Crown'd, for you can fly no further.—

MILLAMANT. Vanity! No——I'll fly and be follow'd to the—last moment, tho' I am upon the very Verge of Matrimony, I expect you shou'd solicite me as much as if I were wavering at the grate of a Monastery, with one foot over the threshold. I'll be solicited to the very last, nay and afterwards.

(IV. i. 155–65)

In its metaphorical elaboration, the locked door symbolizes the constant renewal of novelty that preserves marriage from stasis and satiety. But, of itself, the locked door is not an 'Artifice Contriv'd, to Signifie' anything, for it had been locked not on Millamant's initiative but on Mrs Fainall's. It has no intrinsic or premeditated significance, and is consequently ready to receive whatever meaning the couple care to impress upon it. Like words, places are blank tokens which gain significance by usage or compact, and just such a compact takes place in the proviso scene, which maps out the places appropriate to each partner and prescribes particular rules for each place.[27] The artificial imposition of value upon place is then, independently, taken up

[27] At the beginning of *The Double-Dealer*, it is clear that the men and women have retired to the separate places prescribed by convention.

by the drunken Sir Wilfull, who rants about exotic lands and proclaims, 'My Map says that your *Turk* is not so honest a Man as your Christian—I cannot find by the Map that your *Mufti* is Orthodox' (IV. i. 444–7). Principles more comprehensive than the private regulations of particular marriages are here reduced to the level of local by-laws, for if, as Sir Wilfull goes on to chant, '*Mahometan* Fools | Live by Heathenish Rules' (IV. i. 452–3), their folly lies solely in their unchristian abstention from alcohol, and a clash between absolute verity and absolute error is reduced to a clash between localized conventions: 'rules' (unlike laws) are exclusively the product of human compact and decree. Even time itself varies according to local interpretation: the London morning, as Sir Wilfull remarks, overlaps with the Shropshire afternoon.

Conversely, systems which derive social hierarchies from natural order are derided. The family is not a natural microcosm of social existence, for biological affinity creates neither fellowship of mind (Ben Legend forgets about the death of his brother Dick) nor parity of social standing: in attempting to apprentice his half-brother to a felt-maker Sir Wilfull Witwoud follows a course that earlier in the century had been portrayed as a culpable degradation of gentle birth.[28] Belief in the organic and naturally validated community is reserved for fools. It is Brisk in *The Double-Dealer* who describes Lord Touchwood's household in imagery of the body politic, complaining of Mellefont's 'Amputation from the body of our Society' (I. i. 36–7). In *The Old Batchelour* the still more foolish Sir Joseph Wittoll is positively addicted to describing human relationships in metaphors of bodily organism, habitually referring to the *miles gloriosus* Captain Bluffe as his 'Back' (and also, on one occasion, his 'Breast and Head-piece', II. i. 120–1). Indeed, in his very first speech in the play, Wittoll revealingly characterizes disturbance of the civic peace in imagery of dismemberment, for he speculates that the 'Cannibals' who attacked him the previous night 'would have flead me alive, have sold my Skin, and devour'd my Members' (II. i. 3–6). And it is yet another fool, Foresight, who most persistently sees human life as a microcosmic analogy to the organic and harmonious processes of nature, studying the celestial writing in the stars for the secrets of human life, and retiring to bed with a wonderful affirmation of his oneness with a constant natural order: 'just upon the turning of the Tide, bring me the Urinal' (III. i. 646–7).

[28] One of the villainies of Sir Perfidious Old-craft in *Wit at Severall Weapons* is that he apprentices gentle orphans to be felt-makers (I. i. 68, in *The Dramatic Works in the Beaumont and Fletcher Canon*, ed. Bowers, vii (though the authors are probably Middleton and Rowley)). This crime is retained in Cibber's adaptation of the play as *The Rival Fools* (I, pp. 102–3). A felt-maker is used as a type of social baseness in Behn, *The Roundheads*, I, pp. 344–7. It is also used by Clarendon, in a similar context of contempt for insubordinate sectarian mechanics (Edward [Hyde], Earl of Clarendon, *The History of the Rebellion and Civil Wars in England, Begun in the Year 1641*, ed. W. Dunn Macray (6 vols., Oxford, 1888), ii. 278 (book v)). See also Falkland, *The Mariage Night*, V, p. 44. One of the plebeians in Middleton's *The Mayor of Queenborough* is a felt-monger, and in Wycherley's *The Gentleman Dancing-Master* Diego's social pretensions are punctured by the revelation that he is descended from a felt-maker (V. i. 385).

An equally foolish conviction that life shadows forth a fixed celestial order occurs in *The Double-Dealer*, in Sir Paul Plyant's reiterated faith in Providence, which exemplifies Congreve's tendency to remove all colour of universality from Christian values by expressing them in the idiolects of fools, so that the Word dwindles into a dialect and the Truth into a municipal law. 'As I hope to be sav'd' is the catch-phrase of Tattle in *Love for Love*, and drawling invocations of the deity ('Gad', 'Lard', '*Jesus*') are the speciality of Belinda in *The Old Batchelour*; in the same play, the Christian condemnation of adultery is uttered only in the fanatic dialect of Fondlewife, and Bellmour, cuckolding Fondlewife in the guise of the Nonconformist preacher Spintext, is detected by his victim only because he oversteps the approved limits of that dialect by carrying a copy of Scarron instead of a prayer book. Even in naming his clerics—Spintext, Saygrace (in *The Double-Dealer*)—Congreve identifies them as rehearsers of insignificant verbal formulas, and he labours the point by portraying Saygrace, on his first appearance, as being preoccupied with the composition of an acrostic. Indeed, it is only the fascination of the acrostic (the ultimate trivialization of the text shaped by the Word) which prevents this custodian of Holy Writ from leaping at once to aid Maskwell in his villainy; and even here the lure of the word proves less powerful than Maskwell's offer of tithes.

Saygrace's venality is complemented by another satiric misemployment of celestial influence: for, while Maskwell is engaged in villainous collusion with the man of God, Brisk and Lady Froth are committing adultery under the pretext of star-gazing, Lady Froth subsequently attributing the exposure of Maskwell to the influence of Saturn. With the authority of the church in disarray, man has to seize control for himself: hence both Mellefont and Lord Touchwood pass judgement upon their betrayers in the guise of parsons, at once appropriating and secularizing the role which Saygrace has discredited. But the division of priestly power between the two mock-parsons itself indicates a movement away from the monolithic and universal system of value to the separate, personal, and local. In *Love for Love*, similarly, the constant secularization of the term *providence* (by association with its entirely worldly cognates, *prudence* and *foresight*) stresses that man must direct life by his own providence instead of relying on the celestial agencies in which Foresight trusts. Finally secure in the possession of Angelica, Valentine turns to Tattle and celebrates the triumph of providential justice: 'you would have interposed between me and Heav'n; but Providence laid Purgatory in your way— You have but Justice' (v. i. 595–7). But it is the justice of human providence, for the imagery has no consistency or comprehensibility as an eschatological allegory: it makes no moral or causal sense for Providence to defeat the enemies of the soul by dumping them, unwitting and unwilling, into purgatory, which is a state for willing penitents. The terms *heaven*, *Providence*, and *purgatory* are linked in an intelligible causal relationship only by the worldly

events to which they are applied. The statement does not invest human courtship with a transcendent or spiritual symbolism: on the contrary, it places religious terminology in a context where it can only bear a secular meaning.
Heaven is Angelica, purgatory Mrs Frail, and providence the foresight that
tricked her and Tattle into marriage. The individuals are the things themselves;
they are not, and cannot be, signs and shadows of immaterial universals.

Nevertheless, Congreve persistently concentrates on characters committed
to imagined absolutes of place and order, and bewildered by threats to their
stability; hence his recurrent concern with households facing the prospect
of collapse. Nowhere is the nominal unity, and essential incoherence, of the
social group more apparent than in Lord Touchwood's house in *The Double-
Dealer* (October 1693), which provides the setting for the most spatially confined of Congreve's comedies. *Company* is a recurrent term, though it never
describes more than a ritualized social gathering, and its chief devotees are
fools such as Brisk, who laments the 'Amputation' of Mellefont from the body
politic of the house party, and Lord Froth, who goes to join the ladies with the
words 'we are a Solitude without 'em' (I. i. 284–5). As Brisk voices an attenuated and meaningless survival of the organic definition of society, so Lord
Froth voices an equally worn-out version of the principle of degree (place),
claiming to sit straight-faced through comedies 'To distinguish my self from
the Commonalty, and mortify the Poets' (I. i. 227–8). It is noteworthy that
Brisk, with his expansively hierarchical 'you shall Command me from the
Zenith to the *Nadir*' (I. i. 49–50), also retains a comparably trivialized notion
of universality: of a total cosmic space undifferentiated by locally inscribed
customs and rules. For Lady Froth, too, local systems require the descriptive
apparatus of cosmography (Lord Froth 'wants nothing, but a Blue Ribbon
and a Star, to make him Shine, the very Phosphorus of our Hemisphere', II. i.
30–2), and even adultery becomes invested with language of the social and
cosmic, when she misrepresents her dealings with Brisk as *commun*ication
and star-gazing. The hen-pecked Sir Paul Plyant is another exponent of
enduring natural order, attempting to claim that a collapse in his husbandly
authority would be as unthinkable a disturbance of natural order as copulation between a tiger and a lamb. By mixing up the traditional rhetorical formulas, however, and listing normalities where he means to list impossibilities,
he inadvertently turns unvarying principles of nature into poetic stereotypes
of the inconceivable: 'I cannot incorporate with Patience and Reason,' he exclaims, thereby establishing himself as yet another Congrevian fool who
thinks in metaphors of bodily organism; 'as soon may Tygers Match with
Tygers, Lambs with Lambs, and every Creature couple with its Foe, as the
Poet says' (II. i. 223–6). Fittingly, this inexpert celebrant of natural order is the
most restrictively subject to arbitrary local decrees, tied up nightly in bed at
his wife's command so as to hinder the natural indulgences of copulation and
even urination.

The chaplain's absorption in an acrostic, and Sir Paul's appeal to 'the Poet', associate the collapse of the apparently universal into the actually local with the contraction of seemingly authoritative systems of language into private and artificial systems (as in the substitution of Scarron for the prayer book in *The Old Batchelour*); thus, when Lady Touchwood manœuvres Mellefont into the appearance of attempting to rape her, she is able to dismiss his moral expostulations as 'very Poetry' (IV. ii. 127). The contraction of linguistic authority is most vividly illustrated in Lady Froth's experiments with that grandest and most authoritative of literary forms, the epic, on that most slight and evanescent of topics, *The Sillibub*. Poetry is, she reminds us, a matter of generic conventions (that is, local rules): she prides herself on her knowledge of Le Bossu and garrulously lists the genres in which she is proficient (II. i. 16–17). Indeed, the absurdity of the poem lies in its confusion of locality: literally, by locating her dairy in her town-house, and linguistically by yoking together different dialects (and levels of generic decorum) in her naming of her husband and herself, as Spumoso and Biddy. This remarkable hybrid of place and language nevertheless aspires towards the universal, giving the family coachman a biblical name (Jehu) and a cosmic appearance, his red face resembling the sun.

But obvious fools such as Brisk, the Froths, and Sir Paul are not the only ones to see cosmic principles in local accidents, for a similarly, if less fatuously, misconceived devotion to the natural principles of community characterizes Mellefont himself, whose trust in Maskwell is based on a sequence of deductions whose premiss is the natural sociability of man: 'He has Obligations of Gratitude, to bind him to me; his Dependance upon my Uncle is through my means' (I. i. 149–50). Maskwell, he believes, intends to do him 'Service' (I. i. 156), and indeed the idea of service is Maskwell's exclusive, though constantly misused, property, whether in his adulterous 'Service' of Lady Touchwood (I. i. 302, 337) or his claim, in the mock-soliloquy delivered for Lord Touchwood's benefit, to have 'served a worthy Lord to whom I owe my self' (V. i. 25–6). And, when Maskwell expresses his libertine amorality, he does so by denying the universal currency of obligation. Social ties are local, specific, and therefore dispensable: 'Duty to Kings, Piety to Parents, Gratitude to Benefactors, and Fidelity to Friends, are *different* and *particular* Ties. But the Name of Rival cuts 'em all asunder' (II. i. 446–8; italics added). For Maskwell, the world is ordered not by stable and natural values but by competing names that can alter each other's importance and significance, and his reduction of social relationships to ones of clashing nomenclature seems to triumph when Lord Touchwood promises to disinherit Mellefont in his favour, representing the substitution of stranger for nephew simply as a choice between two virtually equivalent strings of letters. Here, more than anywhere else, the family becomes a formulaic abstraction, a verbal contrivance on a par with the chaplain's acrostic: 'The Writings are ready drawn, and wanted nothing but to be sign'd, and have his name inserted——yours will fill the Blank as well' (V. i. 61–4).

The problem is that Maskwell's nominalism and relativism are nearer the mark than Mellefont's almost suicidally ingenuous belief in the power of obligation to bind character. Maskwell is thwarted because his deceptions become too elaborate, whereas the less ambitious betrayals of Brisk and Lady Froth, and Careless and Lady Plyant, remain safely glossed over. In a cast in which, as Collier protested, three out of the four fine ladies are adulteresses,[29] the spectacle of humanity provides no argument for deriving moral principles from universal consent. If Mellefont and Cynthia form the most decent and attractive couple in the play, the play offers few grounds for translating our affection and sympathetic interest into admiration of them as moral absolutes. We do not readily admire characters as ludicrously gullible as Mellefont, and in any case Cynthia explicitly poses a difficult conundrum as to what wisdom is in a world whose standard is folly: 'If Happiness in Self-content is plac'd, | The Wise are Wretched, and Fools only Bless'd' (III. i. 633–4). The wedding of Mellefont and Cynthia brings no larger social reunification, for around the happy couple Maskwell and Lady Touchwood are being expelled and the Froths and Plyants continue in their routine of male folly and female infidelity. The virtuous couple remain outsiders, unassimilated into the still dominant milieu, whose fragmentation and universal mendacity discredit the formal unity of the domestic setting.

The villains are brought to justice in an overtly theatrical coup, when Lord Touchwood contrives a 'Plot' to outwit them and summons the company into the gallery to watch their exposure: 'let me hasten to do Justice, in rewarding Virtue and wrong'd Innocence' (V. i. 582–3), he says, discharging the function of the comic poet. The element of theatre within theatre again contracts the absolute—Justice—into the compass of a closed and local linguistic artefact, and the theatre of justice is enacted amidst the trivial chatter of an audience who display no moral reaction whatsoever, concerned as they are with concealing the infidelities which link them to the excluded rather than to the vindicated. Lord Touchwood's moral acts and sentiments are not universalized, but remain confined within the area on which they immediately impinge. Though *The Double-Dealer*, like Congreve's two subsequent comedies, moves towards a formal establishment of justice, and to this extent differs from the great comedies of the previous generation, it also differs from the simpler Whig drama of Shadwell and Durfey, for justice is not an articulation of fixed social principles but an artifice imposed on the largely alien, tangled, and deceptive workings of human nature.

[29] Jeremy Collier, *A Short View of the Immorality, and Profaneness of the English Stage* (London, 1698), 12; id., *A Defence of the Short View of the Profaneness and Immorality of the English Stage* (London, 1699), 22.

CHAPTER TEN

'A Cause like yours would summon the Just Gods:' Tragedy, 1688–1695

The first tragedy known to have been premièred after the Revolution is Nathaniel Lee's anti-Catholic pot-boiler *The Massacre of Paris* (November 1689), written during the Exclusion Crisis and banned (see above, p. 269). Here 'A hundred thousand Souls for Justice call' (V. iv. 51), but they cry in vain, for, as so often in Lee, the innocent die and the wicked remain unpunished. But in post-Revolution Whig tragedy monarchy and justice are no longer irreconcilable. The change first appears in George Powell's unimpressive *Othello* clone *The Treacherous Brothers* (January 1690), in which the chastity of a virtuous queen is slandered by two villainous brothers of low social place, but is providentially vindicated in time to prevent her execution. What is chiefly notable is the simple definition of the Iago-figures. In the many previous Restoration imitations of *Othello*, the villain had always been an essential part of the order which he subverted; now (as in *Bury-Fair*) renewed confidence in the social order means that the outsider regains meaning as a source of evil. In Joseph Harris's feeble tragicomedy *The Mistakes* (December 1690), rather similarly, the Viceroy's villainous favourite promotes jealousy and injustice, but is finally expelled from the city to a desert.

A more complex transformation of outlook is evident in Powell's second play, *Alphonso King of Naples* (December 1690), which resembles Mountfort's *The Injur'd Lovers* in its plot and outlook, yet dispenses with Mountfort's insoluble conundrums about the relationship between power and justice. Like the earlier play, it portrays the oppression of individual desire by cruel monarchic power, and treats the rights of the individual as the prime criterion of value. In a plot which recalls the unhappy love of Theocrin and Arviola in Tate's early Whig play *The Loyal General*, King Alphonso opposes his daughter Urania's love for the General Cesario on the grounds of Cesario's humble birth, favouring instead the suit of the arrogant Prince Ferdinand of Cyprus (an 'Inglorious titled Wretch', V, p. 41). The lovers' attempt to flee from the stultifying demands of public life into a private, humble, and pastoral existence is thwarted, and during the course of their flight Urania (Bracegirdle) narrowly escapes being raped by bandits. But pastoral dreams are no longer (as they were in Lee) the intrinsically impossible fantasies of

Epigraph: [?John Bancroft], *King Edward the Third; with the Fall of Mortimer Earl of March* II, p. 13.

characters who are irrevocably trapped in a tormenting public world. What is portrayed is rather a callous and unnecessary frustration of personal life. There is an explicit parallel with the suppression of '*Justice*' and '*Law*' under the arbitrary rule of James II (IV, p. 29), and when Cesario is imprisoned by Alphonso, to Ferdinand's great delight, the vocabulary of justice is clearly being indefensibly misapplied to the service of amoral power:

FERD. Thou darst impeach the Justice of thy punishment.
CESA. Justice, my bold Tormenter!
FERD. Justice, Miscreant.
    The just reward of thy too bold Ambition.

(V, p. 41)

The difficulties of defining a system of justice centred upon the monarch, so insuperable in *The Injur'd Lovers*, have simply disappeared. At the same time, however, there is no simple assertion that subjects are entitled to depose unjust kings, for the king is to be revered as a god (V, p. 37). Before the subjects' rebellion becomes decisively invincible, however, the god-king conveniently abdicates (as James was officially supposed to have done), anguished at the calamities his 'Guilt' has caused (V, p. 47).[1] The problem of the criminal monarch loses its complexity, and kingship and justice are reconciled. But kingship is still validated by divine right rather than contract or *de facto* power.[2]

If Powell was bolder than the pre-Revolution Mountfort, Mountfort himself was now bolder still. He brought to the stage two anonymous political tragedies, *King Edward the Third* (November 1690) and *Henry the Second* (November 1692), which are generally attributed to John Bancroft, the author of the republican Exclusion Crisis play *The Tragedy of Sertorius* (1679). Mountfort, a former member of George Jeffreys' household, dedicated the former play to Henry Sidney, Viscount Sheppey (subsequently Earl of Romney), a prominent figure in the negotiations inviting William of Orange to England, and a younger brother of the republican Algernon Sidney (whom Jeffreys had sentenced to death). Here, Mountfort quite uncompromisingly defines the king as the servant and choice of the people, though the play itself is more circumspect. Justice is again the main issue, and rape is used (as so

---

[1] Negotiations between the Lords and Commons on the legal justification of the Revolution led to abandonment of the Commons' argument that James had broken the social contract, but their claim that he had abdicated was retained (Ogg, *England in the Reigns of James II and William III*, 226–7).

[2] 'Most Whigs evaded any description of 1688 as an act of rebellion and deposition, justified by violations of the Original Contract by James II and justifying the making of a new contract with William; equally unwilling to describe 1688 as a conquest, they laboured instead, though uneasily, to give credibility to the implausible idea of James II's abdication and to the notion of the "divine right of providence", to disguise *de facto* power' (J. C. D. Clark, *English Society 1688–1832: Ideology, Social Structure and Political Practice during the Ancien Regime* (Cambridge, 1985), 46). Historians have in general abandoned the idea that the Revolution saw the establishment of a contractual theory of monarchy. See Gerald M. Straka, *Anglican Reaction to the Revolution of 1688* (Madison, 1962); John Kenyon, *Revolution Principles: The Politics of Party 1689–1720* (Cambridge, 1977); Ashcraft, *Revolutionary Politics*.

often throughout this decade) to image the arbitrary oppression of private rights and desires: the villainous Chancellor Tarleton (Jeffreys, transformed into another of Anthony Leigh's hypocritical lechers) perverts judicial process into an instrument of tyranny, and attempts to use his judicial influence to rape the virtuous Maria (Bracegirdle). Saved from dishonour, Maria goes on to receive the 'Justice' of love and marriage from the Earl of Mountacute, and the defeat of the three-year tyranny of Mortimer/James is a providential 'Act of Justice' reinstating the 'Rights and Priviledges' of a free people (IV, p. 36). But justice is achieved by the accession of the lineal heir: the Glorious Revolution is a Restoration (though restoration of kingly right is here associated with restoration of the people's traditional customs and liberties). In *Henry the Second*, similarly, the rule of James is implicitly associated with the disruption of legitimacy: while the evils of popery are topically displayed, its effect is not to inspire a rightful king to tyranny but to undermine the rightful power of an amorous king who patently recalls Charles II. In both plays, the approach is not to justify a new order but to present William's reign as a resumption of normality after the constitutional aberration of the previous reign. (Similarly, Shadwell after the Revolution portrays James not as the unjust father but as the unjust stepfather.)

A more sober, though still thoroughly Williamite, account of the early post-Revolution years was Crowne's *Regulus* (June 1692). The prologue celebrates the naval victory over the French at La Hogue on 19 May (the first military success since the victories in Ireland, and the last for several years), but the play itself addresses the dissension, conspiracy, and military insecurity that marked the early years of William's reign. The Punic war setting evokes the current war between England and France, with Carthage representing England: an England corrupt, faction-ridden, and in danger of embracing a tyranny validated by blood descent (Asdrubal, the pretender to the throne, is a lineal descendant of Dido).[3] The Senate is factious and erratic, profiteering merchants trade with the enemy, non-juring clergy look to Rome to protect their religion, and the gentry look to absolute monarchy to validate their own social privileges: 'a Prince is to have his will, for he's the Image of the Gods; a Gentleman is to have his pleasure, for he is the Image of his Prince; a common fellow is to drudge, for he is the Image of an Ass' (I, p. 2).

In his earlier works Crowne had simultaneously supported absolutism and criticized all other forms of inherited and entrenched hierarchy; now absolutism itself comes within the sphere of his criticism. Asdrubal is opposed by the exemplary Spartan general Xantippus, who praises the constitution of his native country (a limited monarchy) as one where every citizen 'owns

---

[3] 'It cannot be emphasized too strongly that the immediate aftermath of the Revolution was a period of weakness, confusion and something like demoralization. Had James been restored by the French in 1690 historians would have had no difficulty in explaining the inevitability of this happening' (J. R. Jones, *The Revolution of 1688 in England* (London, 1972), 326).

the whole Commonwealth' and where 'Titles and Distinctions' derive from 'Merit . . . not Blood:' 'Your high-sprung Blood in *Sparta* will be lost: | I mean all your Precedencies of Birth' (I, p. 8). Xantippus, the foreign saviour opposed to the tyranny of the blood-line, obviously evokes William III, and the play ends with the nation rejecting its saviour, and his transformation into an enemy. Regulus, released on parole to carry peace terms to Rome, successfully urges rejection of the terms, and voluntarily returns to certain torture and death, exemplifying Crowne's constant interest in the virtues of stoic endurance, already shown in Vendosme and Darius; here, Crowne gloomily acknowledges that high principle survives more among the opponents of the new order, and that the liberated nation cannot recognize or rise to the patterns of heroism required of a just society.4

For all his intellectual confusion, the most intricate analyst of authority during the previous regime had been Elkanah Settle, who returned to the stage after a long interval with *Distress'd Innocence* (October 1690). (In dedicating the play to the distinguished soldier and zealous Williamite Lord Cutts of Gowran, Settle regrets his 'long Ten Years silence' and his digression 'into *Politicks*' (sig. [A3]).) There are some topical touches—the haughty King of Persia is misled by priests into a policy of religious persecution—but the outlook is essentially that of Settle's earlier plays, and he again reveals his fascination with the ambiguities attaching to inherited authority. As in Saunders's *Tamerlane the Great*, a villainous schemer has intruded his own daughter into the royal succession, and the King here blindly authorizes the rape of his true daughter and heir (Bracegirdle), too late discovering her true identity, so that the ruler becomes a criminal against his own successor. As always in Settle, the identification of authority and of justice becomes hopelessly problematic, and there follows the usual widespread coalescence of justice and vengeance, and the usual reduction of human affairs to a sequence of discrete, unpatterned, manual acts. In the most vehement of the many hand images, the King regrets the acts of his 'butchering Hand' (V, p. 56), confirming the villain's earlier identification of the symbols of power with the instruments of violence—'One Hand a Dagger and a Scepter hold[s]' (V, p. 50)—and his own rejection of the divinity of kings: only a few lines after the villain's confounding of dagger and sceptre, he had deplored the 'mistaken popular Adoration' which terms 'Monarchs Heav'n's Vicegerents' (V, p. 50). In *Tamerlane the Great*, hereditary monarchy had perpetuated principles of command and subordination that were providentially incorporated in the patterns of nature. Here the providential blessing is absent, and heredity itself

---

4 J. Douglas Canfield points out that Regulus keeps faith, whereas the Carthaginians/English repeatedly break it ('*Regulus* and *Cleomenes* and 1688: From Royalism to Self-Reliance', *Eighteenth-Century Life*, 12 (1988), 67–75 (p. 69)). Obviously, however, I do not follow Canfield in reading *Regulus* as a crypto-Jacobite play. Internal evidence apart, such an interpretation conflicts with Crowne's position in both the dedications and texts of *The English Frier* and *Caligula*.

is not only hard to verify but morally indeterminate: whereas Saunders's spurious heir genetically reproduces the true father's villainy, Settle's is flawed but fundamentally noble, and is tragically driven to unnecessary suicide by the discovery of her origins, although the heir to the Byzantine empire is willing to make her his queen, her birth notwithstanding. The play contrasts sharply with 'Bancroft's' attempt to reconcile the new order with traditional patterns of patrilineal descent, and it reveals Settle's characteristic combination of Whiggery and confusion: 'One Hand a Dagger and a Scepter hold' is both radical and ungrammatical.

Settle's fascination with the criminal ruler is also evident in *The Ambitious Slave; or, A Generous Revenge* (March 1694, but dating from 1682). Orontes, King of Scythia, has executed his rival for the hand of a Persian princess, but ends his days, a penitent and powerless 'Criminal',[5] in the alien kingdom of Persia, willing to be hanged for his crime and eventually expiating it by suicide (this presumably being the generous *revenge* of the play's subtitle). But the displacement of the criminal king is complemented by that of characters whose authority is moral as well as titular. The low-born 'stranger'[6] Celestina fascinates the King of Persia and succeeds in reducing the true Queen to the condition of a displaced wanderer (a substitution structurally similar to that of the false and true princess in the Persia of *Distress'd Innocence*), and eventually the King executes his Queen and loyal brother (and heir presumptive) on suspicion of adultery: there is thus a total confounding of justice and authority, the genuinely criminal ruler being balanced by two figures of royal status wrongly reduced to criminal rank. In this confusion, social principles become impotent. The loyal brother is a noble rival, loving the Queen yet virtuously trying to reconcile her with her brother; but, unlike his predecessors in Orrery, he fails to gain social fulfilment through suppression of self. In Settle the fate of the noble rival, that supremely social being, is to be an exile or martyr.

Oddly, Dryden's first post-Revolution play, *Don Sebastian* (December 1689), also pairs opposing forms of criminal ruler. Sebastian, King of Portugal, and his beloved Almeyda, a Moorish princess converted to Christianity, have been captured in the battle of Alcazar by Muley-Moluch, a blackened version of William III: a tyrant who seized the throne of Morocco in conjunction with Almeyda's father and subsequently murdered him. Like all the Moors, Muley-Moluch sees his appetites as the sole criteria of value, believing that both religious truth and worldly reality are controlled by his desires: in short, he is an archetypal example of Fallen Man. By contrast Sebastian, in evident allusion to James II, carries the dignity of true faith and true kingship. But it becomes increasingly clear that the apparently exemplary Christian hero and his bride-to-be are also inevitably tainted by hereditary guilt, and

---

[5] II, p. 9; IV, p. 33; V, p. 49.   [6] II, p. 17; III, p. 18.

that they in subtler and less destructive ways elevate their desires to the status of moral criteria. Although Almeyda constantly assumes the moral dignity of the rightful heir of a murdered king—a female Charles II—it is clear that her father's kingship was just as much founded upon violence and conquest as that of his murderer; that hereditary right is contaminated by hereditary guilt. Sebastian's campaign to restore her to the Moorish throne is thus less an idealistic crusade to extend the boundaries of Christendom than a morally dubious piece of imperialism. Still more tainted is the heroic love of Sebastian and Almeyda, for after their marriage night Almeyda is revealed to be Sebastian's half-sister, the product of an adulterous union between his father and her mother. The ideal is again contaminated by hereditary guilt, and the contamination further devalues Sebastian's campaign of conquest, for the love which chiefly inspires it is impure and (a Settle-like touch) Almeyda is not, after all, the genetic heir to the throne to which Sebastian is attempting to restore her.[7] In rushing to marriage and consummation despite a series of mysterious warnings, the lovers show that they, like Muley-Moluch, make their desires the measure of moral truth, and the unwitting act of incest provokes emphatic iteration of a word that had been only intermittently associated with the clearly evil Muley-Moluch: *crime*. Indeed, the play's final couplet stresses not the lineal transmission of authority from king to heir but the lineal transmission of crime: 'That unrepented Crimes of Parents dead, | Are justly punish'd on their Childrens head' (v. i. 726–7).

At the end of Act IV, Sebastian had appeared to be the fountainhead of justice, rebutting the grievances of his vengeful renegade subject Dorax and forcing him to confess that Sebastian had acted 'justly' in spurning him (IV. iii. 587). But throughout the final act the links between Sebastian and justice are broken: clear evidence of his father's adultery nullifies his confidence that his 'Father shall be justify'd' (v. i. 242); his confidence that he can 'justify' his war (v. i. 289) is discredited when the crusade against the Infidel turns out to be inspired by forbidden love; and, despite Almeyda's contemptuous scepticism, the elderly counsellor Alvarez does manage to 'justify' (v. i. 325) his charge against Almeyda's mother. Finally, the embodiment of royal justice becomes subject to the inexorable scheme of crime and divine punishment asserted in the play's last couplet, and he and Almeyda abandon royalty for the life of the anchorite.

The discrepancy between individual desire and justice is a familiar enough topic, though most commonly the discrepancy has been between the crude generalities of judicial assessment and the ungeneralizable particularities of individual conduct. Here, by contrast, desire and social authority are on the

---

7 Bywaters plausibly sees Muley-Moluch as a portrait of William III (*Dryden in Revolutionary England*, 45–6), but he seems to me to be very offhand with the parts of the play that do not fit his reading of it as a Jacobite allegory: for example, in order to make Almeyda an ideal antithesis to Queen Mary (p. 47), he has to treat the incest element as essentially dispensable (p. 41).

same side of the scale, the former contaminating the latter, and both being set against a transcendent, mysterious justice which can expose the highest public and heroic ideals as the creations of fallen appetite. Equally, both are set against a transcendent, mysterious language which overwrites the fictions and ambiguities sanctioned by human desire. The villainous Muley-Moluch had seen the language even of sacred texts as receiving meaning from his desires, wishing to rewrite the Koran to make it permit his marriage to the Christian Almeyda (III. i. 72–4, 83–4) and forbidding the Mufti to preach against his lusts, whereas Sebastian had seemed to represent an ideal linguistic expression of just authority. During his reconciliation with Dorax, for example, he accomplishes both justice and Dorax's linguistic rehabilitation. Each disputant accuses the other of violating language, Sebastian recalling Dorax's 'noisy brawls, and windy boasts' (IV. iii. 410) and Dorax accusing Sebastian of cultivating flatterers and speaking nonsense, but it is Sebastian who gains linguistic mastery when he restores the now penitent Dorax to his baptismal name of Alonzo—a highly traditional association between recovery of social identity and recovery of personal name, comparable to Edgar's recovery of his name towards the end of *King Lear*. The recovery of the baptismal name is recovery of a name transcendentally recorded in the language of heaven (Dorax 'lost like *Lucifer*, my name above', IV. iii. 621), and at this point we appear to have the perfect concinnity between the heavenly word and the human institution that Dryden had celebrated in the epilogue to *Albion and Albanius*: '*Thus* Britain's *Basis on a Word is laid*, | *As by a Word the World it self was made*' (ll. 33–4). Indeed, Sebastian's renaming of Dorax has something of the force of Adam's naming of the beasts, since the order that is established at the end of the fourth act is compared at the opening of the fifth to 'the Scene of opening Paradice' (V. i. 2).

But the harmony between the word and the world has gone, and throughout Act V Sebastian and Almeyda are crushed by linguistic revelations that destroy all their public and personal ideals. In forcing them to recognize their incest, Alvarez is forced to 'speak,' despite his desire to remain 'silent' (V. i. 186, 207), but the lovers resist his words, and when he produces documentary evidence Almeyda tears it, as hostile to unwelcome writing as Muley-Moluch in his desire to rewrite the Koran. But Alvarez then produces writing that cannot be ignored, showing that the rings of Almeyda's dead mother and Sebastian's dead father, each bearing the name of its original owner, interlock to form a love token. This is a ritual of naming very different from the restoration of Dorax's name, for naming now sanctions not assimilation of the subject into a monarchy that replicates the order of paradise, but exclusion of the king himself as an outsider, a monster (V. i. 551). Adamic naming is no longer the model, for Adam did not name monsters. In a Christian transformation of the commonplace libertine contrast between the anomalies of desire and the trite formulas of the moralists, Sebastian does not know 'by what name to call' (V. i. 608) his sister-wife, for both these names are mingled 'into a common Curse' (V. i. 612). Almeyda, however, cannot at first comprehend that her state defies signification; for, like Indamora in *Aureng-Zebe*, she finds herself kissing her lover's name, still treating words as simple tokens to actualize desire (V. i. 625).

The lovers retreat from the perplexed language of the fallen world to a secret and quiet penance, but—like *All for Love*—the play ends with an image of public narrative:

> And let *Sebastian* and *Almeyda*'s Fate,
> This dreadfull Sentence to the World relate,
> That unrepented Crimes of Parents dead,
> Are justly punish'd on their Childrens head.
>
> (V. i. 724–7)

In *All for Love*, Serapion's prediction of the verdict of 'late Posterity' (V. 518) illustrates that public narrative cannot comprehend the hidden essence of thought and conduct; here, however, the narrative enshrines an infallible and inescapable judgement governing human essence, prescribing the intrinsic transmission of corruption from one generation to another. Man no longer inhabits the ordered Eden which had symbolized the just kingdom as recently as *Albion and Albanius,* and the loss of Eden is re-enacted when the lovers retreat to the austere landscapes of their hermitages, the first of several exiled figures in Dryden's last plays. Clearly, the exile of Sebastian suggests that of James II, and Sebastian's sexual contamination recalls (perhaps fortuitously) James's own conviction that he had been punished for sexual sin. But the play is no mere disguised lament for a lost leader. Rather, like the defeated Milton, Dryden remained true to his principles while attempting to understand the ways of a God who had willed their defeat; and, like Milton, he chose to do so by reinterpreting the loss of Paradise.

Dryden fell ill during the composition of his next and last tragedy, *Cleomenes* (April 1692), and brought in Southerne to help him complete the final act. Again, the theme is the exiled ruler, and indeed a Spartan king languishing in sensual Egypt seemed too close for comfort to James II in France, with the result that the play was briefly banned.[8] The ban was quickly lifted, but as Anne Barbeau Gardiner has shown, Dryden did insinuate into the play some of the major themes of Jacobite verse, such as that of starving loyalty.[9] Nevertheless, whether through necessity or choice, Dryden avoids simple idealization of his exiled hero, as he had already done in *Don Sebastian*. For example, when Cleomenes demands news of how the conqueror Antigonus is conducting himself, eagerly expecting and even desiring

---

[8] See Winn, *John Dryden and His World*, 453.
[9] Anne Barbeau Gardiner, 'Dryden's *Cleomenes* (1692) and Contemporary Jacobite Verse', *Restoration*, 12 (1988), 87–95.

stories of pillage and rape, he instead hears of the 'peaceful Progress' of a king 'Who lov'd his People' (I, p. 300),[10] and in these circumstances there is something deeply unattractive about his exultation on learning that Antigonus died in the moment of victory. Rather like Southerne's Oroonoko, for whom he was obviously a model, Cleomenes is restricted in his capacity for social impulse and imagination, deeply attached to the immediate ties of family and friendship, but deficient in imaginative identification with his people; and, as his wife chides, he is flawed by 'Ambition' (I, p. 297). His militarism is, indeed, consistently associated with male sexuality, as when he demands the narratives of rape ('let me hear their Howlings, | And dreadful Shrieks, as in the Act of Rape', I, p. 299), or when he recalls begetting his son in an erotic 'Fury' after his 'first Maiden battle' (I, p. 296). It is a virtuously controlled sexuality (he rebuffs the *femme fatale* Cassandra), the contrasting effeminacy of Ptolemy is clearly repulsive, and we must not expect much anti-machismo from an author who complained that a politically cautious management had gelded away *the very Manhood* of his play (preface, sig. [L6ᵛ]). But Cleomenes is perhaps humanly incomplete, and there is some emphasis on the fatal denial of the feminine: when the hero and his family are starved, his wife's breasts dry up, and she can no longer suckle their son (V, p. 343).

At the beginning of the play Cleomenes claims that which Amphitryon had been denied: the inviolable autonomy of the self. 'My Mind on its own Centre stands unmov'd,' he boasts; 'still I am *Cleomenes*' (I, p. 293). Southerne later introduced his own exiled warrior-king, Oroonoko, with a similar boast. But, like Oroonoko, Cleomenes becomes enmeshed in circumstances that confound the pure simplicity of his initial boast, and at the climax of the play, half-dead from starvation, he revives to ask 'am I in the Regions of the Dead? | And hear the Fables there; *my self a Fable*?' (V, p. 348; italics added). In the period between the initial confidence and the final bewilderment, Cleomenes has (like Amphitryon) been consistently denied the power of self-signification, though not because he is plagued by the activities of a malevolent double but because he is in a world whose codes he cannot use or grasp. Like Spartans generally, he is 'scarce of Words;' for 'We have but just enough to speak our Meaning' (II, p. 309), laconic even when leaving his loved ones as hostages: 'Mother! and Wife! and Son! the Names that Nature | Most loves to speak, are banish'd from my Mouth' (III, p. 325). And, throughout, he fails to impose his desired scheme of signs. When hearing of Antigonus' reception in Sparta, he desires not only representation but virtual re-creation of the imagined outrages, demanding to 'hear' the victims' 'Howlings' (I, p. 299). But there were no howlings, and the desired mimesis cannot therefore be given. At the end of

10 Bywaters has argued that Dryden was at this stage seeking an accommodation with the new regime that did not involve the sacrifice of his principles, and that the play shows 'how respect and admiration for James may be reconciled with obedience to William and patriotic devotion to English interests and institutions' (*Dryden in Revolutionary England*, 94).

the play, Cleomenes and his friend Cleanthes attempt to rouse the town with incantation of the words '*Liberty*' and '*Magas*' (King Ptolemy's just brother) (V, p. 351). But the populace remains inert, and Cleomenes ends the play as he had begun it, defeated by a world whose signs do not answer to his own. In the end, signification becomes death, the two friends opening their bosoms to each other in a suicide pact (V, p. 358).

Cleomenes is frustrated not by a fixed system of meanings that is contrary to his own, but by one whose signs are slippery and amorphous, for in Egypt there is no authority able to endow signs with clarity and stability. Egypt is a land of shadows, where Cleomenes has become 'the Shadow of a King' (II, p. 307) and the royal favourite Sosibius is a 'Shadow' following the sun of royal caprice (II, p. 310). The absence of authority to impose signs is clearly indicated by the conduct of the feeble King Ptolemy: whereas the impotent and marginal figure of Cleomenes proudly asserts his name, Ptolemy resents having to sign his on a document, complaining that it takes 'an Hour to write it' (II, p. 305), and his signet is handed over to his mistress Cassandra (IV, p. 330), who loves Cleomenes and uses the signet to try to establish power over him. In gaining the power of the signet, Cassandra is pursuing a temptation of the hero which has been characterized from the outset by the disputed interpretation of signs, in that her lasciviousness and Cleomenes' virtue are both measured by their contrasting reactions to Apelles' painting of the rape of Helen. Ingenuously desiring a virtual identity between sign and object, Cleomenes finds the masterpiece objectionable because it depicts a dishonest act, whereas Cassandra treats the picture as Wycherley's Olivia had *The Country-Wife*, as a free vehicle of private meanings, so that the representation of an oriental prince cuckolding a Spartan king becomes a sign capable of actualizing its own opposite: a Spartan king cuckolding an oriental prince. 'It speaks; the *Helen* speaks,' she urges. But Cleomenes' young son, who answers her, shares his father's belief that the sign shares the moral character of its subject: 'It speaks *Ægyptian* then; a base dishonest Tongue' (II, p. 315).[11]

Cleomenes' inability to co-operate in Cassandra's system of signs furthers his downfall. His failure to show 'signs of Pity' (IV, p. 334) enrages her, and she orders that he and his family be imprisoned and starved; and later, after he has failed to rouse the mob with his watchwords, she visits him with the signet and diverts his attention so that his family can be destroyed (V, pp. 354–5). Cleomenes and his circle can only achieve private acts of self-representation in which the transformation of self into sign is an act of self-destruction: the suicide pact in which Cleomenes and Cleanthes open each other's breasts, and the process of starvation whereby Cleora becomes, in some terribly half-literalized way, a 'Shadow' to the 'Substance' of her husband (IV, p. 339). 'The Bodies tell the Story as they lie' (V, p. 357), and Cleomenes wonders whether

---

[11] Gardiner suggests that the abduction of the willing Helen may symbolize England's faithlessness ('Dryden's *Cleomenes*', 91).

he is himself 'a Fable'. As in *Don Sebastian*, there is no mirroring of the just state in an uncorrupt system of language, and no way in which perspicuous signs can integrate the just individual in a corresponding social order. As in *Amphitryon*, self-realization and self-representation prove impossible in a world where order and meaning derive from the exercise and craven acceptance of power.

There is a more harmonious resolution in Dryden's last play, the tragicomedy *Love Triumphant* (January 1694), which again deals with displaced royalty. The play portrays the aftermath of the defeat of Ramirez, King of Castile (James II), by his former friend Veramond, King of Aragon (William III).[12] Ramirez' son Alphonso has been brought up as Veramond's son, and develops an apparently incestuous but actually innocent love for his nominal sister, Victoria. In addition, he is naturally drawn to his true rather than his ostensible father, to whom he increasingly becomes a stranger, and who wishes to visit on him the ritual alienation of expulsion into the desert as a scapegoat (III, p. 475). The most sacred and primal bonds of father-king and subject-son are transformed into a terrible and archetypal alienness, and it is a consequence of the overwriting and suppression of natural patterns of allegiance that the blameless affection of Alphonso and Victoria becomes culturally represented as unnatural. When the blood-line is interrupted, all dependent forms of order are thrown into confusion. Dryden almost reverses the outlook of his other play of royal changelings, *Marriage A-la-Mode*. There, in an ironic retrospect upon the Restoration cult, Dryden had stressed how the royal characters' rapid and arbitrary shifts of perceived identity inevitably coloured their interior selves, their emotional ties, and their standing in the eyes of others. But now he unambiguously asserts the power of heredity, quoting the most famous affirmation of its influence, Horace's 'Fierce Eagles never procreate fearful Doves' (III, p. 474).[13]

To some extent, the problems of Alphonso recall those of Amphitryon and Cleomenes, but they are now the consequences of a readily soluble clash between social forms and hereditary principles. For example, Alphonso is permitted the self-representation which they were denied. In an incident similar to that of the Apelles painting in *Cleomenes*, he and his supposed sister Victoria study Ovid's account of Canace's love for her brother, Alphonso for the first time realizing that Victoria returns his love. 'May we not represent the Kiss we read?' he asks (II, p. 455), attempting to actualize desires so far safely locked within the limits of the text. But the clarification of ancestry ends the incompatibility between what can be signified and what done, just as it ends the tension between the forms authorized by society and the aspirations of individual desire (a tension represented in the disrupted ceremonies that mark

[12] The Jacobite implications of the play, and the background to its emphasis on aliens and outsiders, are well analysed in Anne Barbeau Gardiner, 'John Dryden's *Love Triumphant* and English Hostility to Foreigners 1688–1693', *Clio*, 18 (1989), 153–70.   [13] Horace, *Odes* IV. iv. 31–2.

crucial points of the action). Finally, there is total social reconciliation: Alphonso refuses to conquer his erstwhile father (and prospective father-in-law), instead resigning his sword and inspiring him to penitent reform. How different from the family life of William III.

And how different from the comic sub-plot, which depicts a milieu in which a classless commercialism has overridden ancestral and marital values. Sancho, the rich illegitimate son of a Jewish usurer (an outsider in every way), successfully courts the beautiful Dalinda, defeating his wittier but penniless rival Carlos, discovers after his marriage that Dalinda has two illegitimate children by a nobleman, but quickly accepts the situation with good humour and gives the children his blessing. If Sancho's cheerfulness contrasts agreeably with Veramond's Leontes-like brooding over Alphonso's paternity, the price of his cheerfulness is a world reduced to unstructured farce by the absence of patrilineal principles. The amorphousness is particularly apparent in an inconsequential recycling of the central situation of *Amphitryon* (and of the contest between James and William), when both Sancho and Carlos approach Dalinda in the guise of her noble lover, and compete to prove their alleged identity as Jupiter and Amphitryon had done. In *Amphitryon*, however, one of the claimants had been genuine, and the oppressive divorce between identity and its social expression had been linked to theft of the fundamentals of his social existence: his home, his marriage, his paternity of his wife's child. Here the contest is about nothing: both claimants are impostors, the disputed identity has lapsed (since its real owner turns out to be dead), and there is no system of nuclear social existence at stake; there is simply the rival blustering of rival usurpers. As Dr Johnson observed, Dryden's theatrical career began and ended with a failure,[14] but there the resemblance between his first and last play ends, for *Love Triumphant* affirms everything denied in *The Wild Gallant*, with its sustained satire of patrilineal principles. In the face of a world to which he was now alien, Dryden concluded his career with his most backward-looking play: a play with very few parallels in the preceding forty years.

In between Dryden's last two tragedies came his opera *King Arthur* (May/June 1691), with music by Purcell, a revision of a piece to which *Albion and Albanius* had originally been designed as a prologue. Arthur in the original version would doubtless have been treated as an overt prototype for the Stuart monarchy, but Dryden made extensive alterations to avoid offence to the government (dedication, sig. Q5), the net results of which were to turn Arthur into a thinly disguised prototype of the Stuart monarchy, engaged in conflict with a Teutonic invader, and to praise for maritime security and commercial vitality a Williamite England reeling from naval defeat and crippled trade.[15] The opera depicts the struggle between Arthur and the Saxon Oswald

---

[14] Johnson, *Lives of the English Poets*, i. 365.
[15] Bywaters, *Dryden in Revolutionary England*, 91.

(superficially, William versus James, actually vice versa), Oswald attempting forcible conquest both of Britain and of Arthur's loved one, the blind Emmeline, a personification of Britain, who finally sees clearly, as Dryden hoped Britain would. The contrast of sight and blindness is one version of a diversely expressed conflict between heaven/truth/light and darkness/illusion/earth (characters may, for example, be magically or symbolically rooted in the earth), the conflict presenting a choice between a nation ordered by carnal desire or one ordered by heavenly guidance. When he is tempted by illusions in a magic forest, Arthur himself has to choose what kind of king he wishes to be.

Dryden perhaps grimly enjoyed his ironic praise of British prosperity, but it is melancholy to see a great poet reduced to sarcastic falsification of the balance of payments. What raises the libretto above a sterile exercise in self-subversion is Dryden's continuing interest in the difficult relationship between political power and self-representation (a relationship which proves equally difficult in the plays of the Whig Congreve). When Emmeline recovers sight and stares around in bewilderment, 'A Stranger yet, an Infant of the World!', the sight which is most alien to her is that of her own visible form, captured in a mirror: 'What am I two? Is this another Me?' (III, p. 398), she exclaims (like another Amphitryon), wonders whether the other self is her child, and settles on the explanation that it is her name. Dryden here reverts to the paradox that had dominated *The State of Innocence*, that the self can only apprehend the self by treating it as the not-self. But the paradox is no longer universal and inescapable, but is merely a special limitation of physical sight. One cannot see one's own face (a recurrent image, as in Congreve), but there are other forms of knowledge and self-knowledge, which Arthur acquires when he defeats the illusions of the enchanted, earth-rooted forest. Significantly, the chief illusion is a double of Emmeline, earthbound through confinement in a tree, who discourages Arthur from his quest: Emmeline's 'What am I two?' is briefly answered in the affirmative, with reminiscence of the doubling of identity in *Amphitryon*. Here, however, the bifurcation of the self is ended not by arbitrary power but by superior knowledge, when the aerial spirit Philidel uses Merlin's wand to provide 'Proof' that the impostor is the 'earthiest, ugliest Fiend in Hell' by destroying the illusory *face* (IV, p. 410).

Demonic temptation through doubling of the heroine's body had also featured in *The State of Innocence*, as had the heroine's bemusement on first seeing her reflection. Indeed, when Philidel rescues Arthur from the deceptions of Emmeline's *doppelgänger*, he explicitly prevents him from re-enacting the error of Adam (IV, p. 410). In *The State of Innocence* Eve's bemusement with her reflection had typified the nature of perception, for attempts to apprehend the self or decipher signs had never grasped the thing itself, and the elusiveness of certainty had left humanity with few resources to resist the Fall. Here, however, ambiguities are subjected to criteria of certainty: Merlin's wand exposes the false Emmeline, and the mirror becomes a symbol not of ambiguity but of clarity, since one instrument of Merlin's superhuman vision is a magic glass (II, p. 384). Dryden's Arthur thus escapes the errors of Dryden's Adam, and *King Arthur* becomes an anachronistic restatement of Dryden's vision of England as Eden: a kingdom whose principles are not earthbound or crudely based in material power, and where the transcendence of mere material process permits the integrity of individual life that had been unattainable in *Amphitryon*.

By contrast, Purcell's other extended essays in musical theatre for the public stage, masterpieces as they are, have little extra-musical interest, the texts being perfunctorily revamped versions of older plays. The first in the series was *The Prophetess; or The History of Dioclesian* (May/June 1690), the first new operatic entertainment at a public theatre since Dryden's *Albion and Albanius* of 1685 (*Dido and Æneas* (before December 1689), which may have provided the impetus for *The Prophetess*, had been performed at a girls' boarding-school, and probably before that at court). Curtis Price sees the original play as a ready-made satire on the final years of Charles II's reign,[16] but the applicability is not really close, and the added musical numbers refer rather to the immediate present: Dioclesian is praised as a liberator from tyranny but, especially in the final masque, the joys of peace are preferred to the glories of war (King William's war was one of the most contentious issues of the reign). The primary topicality of the original text is in its insistence that kingship is earned rather than inherited, and it is probably unnecessary to dig any deeper, though the play does show how a noble liberator may nevertheless be guilty of broken promises and unwise appointments.

The Fairy-Queen (May 1692) revises its source, *A Midsummer Night's Dream*, more extensively, cutting it to skeletal form in order to make way for ninety minutes of musical masques tracing the movement from night to day and from amorous mistrust to marriage; a Chinese episode in the finale provides both lavishly exotic display and affirmation of the global influence of love, revealing a comprehensiveness of shared experience which contrasts with the clashing voices and competing visions of the original. The comprehensiveness is also apparent in the fact that Titania and Oberon disclose themselves to the mortals; the harmony of voices in the fact that the mechanicals do not perform at court (although they receive permission to do so, the adapter uses Shakespeare's Act V performance for the rehearsal in the forest). Even the spectacular scenery portrays order emerging from disorder, imposing the symmetry of the garden upon the wildness of the forest. (There is little interest in this decade in the pure wildness of uncivilized or infernal landscapes such as are provided in *Psyche* and *The Tempest*.)

---

[16] Price, *Henry Purcell and the London Stage*, 270–1.

If Dryden had twelve years in which to produce dramatic and poetic responses to the Revolution, another stranded Jacobite, Aphra Behn, did not long survive it, and was dead by the time her fine tragicomedy *The Widow Ranter* (November 1689) was unsuccessfully staged, the victim of savage cuts and eccentric casting.[17] In its adoption of the tragicomic genre, it harks back to Behn's earliest plays, and indeed its preoccupation with the Amazonian figure provides a link with what was probably her first play, *The Young King*. In other respects, however, it is of a piece with her later work, and continues (though without any immediate topicality) her increasingly pessimistic examination of the male lust for power in sex and politics. In contrast to the early tragicomedies, *The Widow Ranter* withholds a progression towards pure justice, and indeed places its characters in situations of considerable and insoluble moral ambiguity. Bacon, an honourable heroic individualist, fights the Virginian Indians in an attempt to recover his inherited estate and to pursue his love for the Indian queen, Semernia, who returns his love but remains loyal to her virtuous husband. Bacon's campaign defies the laws of Virginia, and, although the Virginian council consists largely of venal upstarts who produce gross travesties of judicial process (one of the justices is illiterate), Bacon's opponents also include men of rectitude and principle. The Indians too have a case, for their king protests cogently against European treachery and imperialism, and Bacon's pursuit of Semernia provides Behn's greatest critique of the adulterer as liberator, for Bacon not only kills Semernia's decent husband but, in the chaos of battle, kills Semernia herself, who had entered the fighting in male disguise. Lady Fancy and the two Julias (in *The False Count* and *The Lucky Chance*) had experienced terribly flawed sexual liberations involving servitude or rape; now, the lover outdoes the character of rapist and slave-master by becoming a murderer.

The fatal consequences of Semernia's disguise correspondingly outdo earlier failures of Behn's heroines to enter the male sphere, though her fundamental weaknesses are the same: her inability to identify herself to Bacon in time completes her constant linguistic subordination, and her repeatedly emphasized submission to Bacon's hand, which wounds her heart (V, p. 300), confirms her lifelong inability to make her own hand the executant of her own heart and desires. Another favourite Behn image to reach extreme formulation in this play is that of the lover as stranger. Man and woman here face each other as beings from different cultures and language systems (witness the gibberish of the Indian religious rites, IV, p. 279), and the final fatal error of identity is a final confirmation of alienness. But this extreme alienness directs attention to the subtler forms of alienness that persist within cultures. In the civil war which develops between Bacon and the Virginian authorities, all the women become prisoners of war, and another of the play's wooers, the

---

[17] See the dedication by G[eorge] J[enkins] (pp. 221–2). The elderly and misshapen Samuel Sandford was incongruously cast as the youthful and vigorous Daring.

mercenary if amiable Hazard, is constantly described as a stranger. Semernia is a more tragic and impotent version of Cleomena in *The Young King*, possessing all the public forms of authority while being a born victim. She lacks, as she herself laments, '*Amazonian* Fire' (V, p. 299). To some extent she is counterbalanced by the drinking, pipe-smoking Widow Ranter, the comic heroine, who gains the love of Daring after defeating him at swordplay, and who also enters the battle in male disguise. But even she is vulnerable in battle and is easily captured: 'thy *Hands* are yet too tender for a Sword' (V, p. 303; italics added), Hazard remarks as he leads her in (clearly holding her with his hand). When she and Daring agree to marry, they express their agreement by linking hands (IV, p. 292), but the Widow nevertheless faces a public world in which the male hand dominates.

After this humane and intelligent play, it is depressing to turn to the traditionalist sexual attitudes of Nicholas Brady's *The Rape* (February 1692), in which a man brought up as a woman and a woman brought up as a man unflinchingly display the submissiveness and authority proper to their sexes, eventually resuming them and marrying. The rape victim, Eurione (Bracegirdle), is so irremediably contaminated by her experience that she can only die, and a test used to establish the innocence of a suspect is an offer of marriage to the victim; if he is willing, he must be guilty, for no man would wish to marry a woman defiled by someone else. Another rather tasteless exploitation of the raped Bracegirdle is the short masque *The Rape of Europa by Jupiter*, with music by Eccles, which was probably written by Peter Motteux for inclusion in Rochester's *Valentinian* at the point at which Lucina is raped offstage.[18] Europa appears, '*her Hair loose about her, as just Ravish'd,*' to demand 'Is then *Astrea* fled from Heaven?', only to be consoled by the promise of transformation into a star (pp. 7–8). Presumably, the point lies in the contrast with Lucina's incurable tragedy, and Eccles's music could well have transformed what on the page looks like pure titillation: the music for Europa's lament is lost, but she has a fine G minor aria earlier. This, however, is offset by a jolly G major interlude in which a shepherd tries out on a shepherdess the experience he gained from a London prostitute. All in all, the concoction seems an early example of Motteux's policy of pleasing as many tastes as possible, with rape here as part of the menu.

Closer approximation to Behn's outlook is (as one might expect) shown in Durfey's adaptation of *Bussy D'Ambois* (March 1691), streamlined into a sympathetic study of adultery (Tamira and Bussy were bound by prior contract). But the legacy of Behn is most overt in Southerne's study of inadvertent adultery, *The Fatal Marriage; or, the Innocent Adultery* (February 1694), whose serious plot liberally transforms that of Behn's novel *The History of the Nun*. (Southerne had already adapted a Behn novel in *Sir Anthony Love*,

---

[18] In her introduction to the Augustan Reprint Society edition, Lucyle Hook convincingly argues for Motteux's authorship, and for the inclusion of the masque in *Valentinian*.

and of course did so again in *Oroonoko*.) Behn's novel opens by asserting God's special concern to punish violated vows and tells of a nun, Isabella, who at the age of 15, after two years of exemplary piety, falls in love, unsuccessfully attempts to conquer her passion with harsh penances, marries, and lives a life of piety and goodness. Her husband presumed dead, she after a decent interval marries a childhood admirer, and lives a life distinguished by charitable works. But, when her first husband returns (as 'a Stranger', p. 321), she unhesitatingly murders him, gets her husband to dispose of the body, and covertly sews the sack containing it to his coat, so that he follows it into the river and is drowned. After her arrest, she devotes herself to prayers, charity, and pious exhortation, and on the scaffold delivers a half-hour speech against vow-breaking. The discontinuities in Isabella's character highlight gaps in the apparent moral logic of the tale, for Isabella's sudden and semi-comic bout of murder is neither a symbolically nor a realistically appropriate effect of her failure at 15 to honour the vows she made at 13. As so often, Behn desires the security of the vow yet cannot find a way of intellectually validating its claims, which are here wrecked by the simple incoherence of human nature.

Southerne rejects Behn's cynicism and purifies Isabella's character, turning her into a pathetic victim destroyed by the consciousness of her unwitting and venial adultery. As a figure who dies to expiate guiltless sexual contamination, she to some extent resembles the heroine of Brady's *The Rape*, but Southerne extensively questions the patriarchal authority and values which Brady simply accepts. As usual, he portrays dislocated characters in a world whose governing principles are arbitrary and irrational. The play opens with the ejection of a son from his father's house, and shortly afterwards the impoverished and apparently widowed Isabella approaches her father-in-law, Count Baldwin, for aid, is denied both assistance and admission to his house, and is consequently forced by indigence to remarry. The consummation of Isabella's second marriage is quickly followed by what is repeatedly characterized as the *home*-coming[19] of her first husband, Biron, from his 'weary Pilgrimage' (IV. iii. 97). But he has returned too late, and home-coming, so often an image of renewed moral stability, can here only complete the social disintegration, which is reflected in Isabella's descent into madness. As later in *Oroonoko*, there is emphatic imagery of wandering and misguidance,[20] and, at the climax of the tragedy, Isabella reverses the imagery of secure haven which had expressed the harmonious concluding reconciliation of *The Loyal Brother*: 'The Waves and Winds will dash, and Tempests roar; | But Wrecks are toss'd at last upon the Shore' (V. iv. 300–1). Isabella's dislocation generates other familiar symptoms of social disintegration: her exclusion from her father-in-law's house exemplifies the decay of hospitality (I. iii. 70–2), her second husband's courtship represents the corruption of service (II. iii. 42), as does the

[19] IV. ii. 1, 18–21, iii. 59, 225; V. iv. 100.   [20] e.g. I. iii. 161–2; IV. iii. 185–7.

slavery in Turkey which prevented Biron from returning, and everywhere the hand is excluded from any role in social bonding, becoming a mere instrument of individualistic violence.[21] In her final agony, Isabella vividly recognizes the failure of the bonding hand: 'Cut off my Hands,' she cries, throwing herself beside Biron's body; 'let me leave something with him, | They'll clasp him fast' (v. iv. 75–6).

The Fatal Marriage, like *Oroonoko*, portrays a protagonist self-destructively driven to honour primal social impulses in a world from which they have almost vanished: Isabella enters her second, fatal, marriage because it seems the only way to retain and feed her beloved child; and she commits suicide out of an anguished and inextinguishable sense of the bond that unites her to her rediscovered first husband. Southerne's emphasis on Isabella's unswerving interior fidelity to her familial bonds is a central element in his transformation of Behn's black comedy into pathetic tragedy, and he removes any quasi-supernatural connection between her breach of vow and subsequent misfortune, which is the product of sheer oppression and injustice. The broken vow certainly does destroy her, but solely because it excites her father-in-law's wrath (for even the Church has forgiven her). Like the nunnery, but still more rigidly, Count Baldwin enforces a systematic dissolution of natural patterns of community, for he not only repudiates his daughter-in-law and grandchild but draws arbitrary and calamitous distinctions between his elder and younger sons, allowing social and economic categories to replace those of kin and thereby setting in motion the tragedy: for the embittered younger brother has intercepted the letters in which Biron reveals that he is still alive, but in slavery, and begs to be redeemed. By making Count Baldwin a spokesman for the values of the nunnery, Southerne emphasizes that it is an instrument and expression of the patriarchal tyranny that he represents. Although the Church has forgiven Isabella, the nunnery still negates natural ties and appropriates the bequests and donations due to kin, Isabella being unable to feed her son because she has made over her property to the convent.

The authority of the nunnery is further diminished by the comic treatment of religious vows in the subsidiary plot. Here a disowned son acquires the property of his father, Fernando, by pretending (with the connivance of some indulgent friars) that he has taken religious vows, drugging his father and persuading him on his revival that he died and was restored from purgatory to earth by the prayers of his family, and claiming that during his father's period of death he was released from his vows so as to inherit the family property. The result of this improbable scheme is the restoration of harmony not only between father and son but between the father and his hitherto jealously oppressed second wife. In this secondary plot, all the elements of the main plot recombine in new relationships: a return from apparent death, a remarriage,

---

[21] v. i. 34, ii. 80, iv. 2, 15, 37.

an unwanted son, a renunciation of the religious life. Here, however, the result is the reconstitution of the natural family, of which the departure from the artificial brotherhood of the cloister is a precondition: Fernando revives from his apparent death in the burial place of the monastery, and the reconciled family then departs for life at *home*, immediately before Biron's very different home-coming. In the main plot, by contrast, the familial microcosm of social existence dissolves into moral and terminological anarchy. Fathers are not fathers, brothers brothers, or husbands husbands: 'Is he without a name? *Biron*, my Husband' (IV. iii. 136), exclaims Isabella; and, when Biron's villainous younger brother Carlos comes to murder him, he comes without a 'Name' (V. ii. 84), isolating himself from the language of kin. Carlos, of course, has assisted the linguistic disorientation by intercepting his brother's letters, and when all is exposed Count Baldwin finds that he cannot name his own son, transferring the power of definition to the courts: 'I leave the Judge to tell thee what thou art; | A Father cannot find a Name for thee' (V. iv. 241–2). But, once again, judicial authority cannot define individual character: the subtitle of *The Innocent Adultery* ostentatiously combines notions of personal integrity and judicial transgression, and the irreduceable incoherence of the paradox is manifested in Isabella's insanity. Indeed, her ravings promptly deny the authority which Baldwin has given the courts:

> 'tis a babling World,
> I'le hear no more on't. When does the Court sit?
> I'll not be bought, what! To sell innocent Blood!
> You look like one of the pale Judges here,
> *Minos*, or *Radamanth*, or *Æacus*. . . .
>   I did not hope to find
> Justice on Earth; 'tis not in Heaven neither.
>
>   (V. iv. 254–77)

Behn's Isabella concludes by proclaiming the sanctity of the vow; Southerne's, by envisaging a universal Babel in which language has no power to signify or prescribe the nature of justice, and in which the only regulating principle is the sale of human flesh. Justice is absent both from earth and heaven: Astraea has fled the universe.

CHAPTER ELEVEN

'Madam, You have done Exemplary Justice': Comedy, 1695–1700

On 30 April 1695, for the first time in over twelve years, London found itself with two rival theatrical companies, for the oppressive tactics of the new manager of the United Company, Christopher Rich,[1] had driven a group of senior actors under the leadership of Thomas Betterton to set up a breakaway company at the old Lincoln's Inn Fields theatre (LIF) (Rich retaining control of both Drury Lane and Dorset Garden). The renewal of competition hugely increased the demand for new plays, and between the secession and the end of 1700 over ninety premières are recorded.[2] In any circumstances, such a glut of new plays would have contained much that was mediocre or incompetent, but matters were made worse by the slump of the mid-1680s, during which many established dramatists fell silent without being replaced by new talent. The only significant new dramatist to appear in the 1680s was Thomas Southerne, and when the demand for plays increased there was not the trained corps of prolific theatrical professionals that there had been by the mid-1670s. Dryden, Shadwell, Behn, Otway, Lee, Crowne, and Durfey all knew their craft, whatever their disparities of talent, and their output had been augmented by the more sporadic productions of Wycherley and Etherege. By the end of 1692 only Dryden, Crowne, and Durfey were active, and the only new professionals were Southerne and Congreve (the latter hardly prolific). Vanbrugh did not appear until late 1696, and produced only two original plays. Not until the appearance of Cibber, Farquhar, Centlivre, and Rowe (the two last in 1700) does a substantial body of professionals start once more to take shape.

In consequence, the theatres lived dangerously: the Patent Company (PC) was, for example, saved from the brink by the success of *The Relapse*, and after a promising start the Lincoln's Inn Fields company had by 1698 hit considerable difficulties, both of income and morale. In the final years of the

---

Epigraph: Congreve, *Love for Love*, v. i. 619.

[1] Alexander Davenant had covertly sold virtual ownership of the United Company to Rich and his associate Thomas Skipwith, while retaining titular control. Davenant was a compulsive swindler, who fled to the Canary Islands in Oct. 1693 shortly before the discovery of his frauds. The company was thereafter run by Rich, a lawyer for whom the theatre was simply a source of profit, whether gained from receipts or saved from reduced emoluments to personnel.

[2] For analysis of the competition between the two companies, see Judith Milhous, *Thomas Betterton and the Management of Lincoln's Inn Fields 1695–1708* (Carbondale, Edwardsville, London, and Amsterdam, 1979).

century, new plays of all kinds were failing at an alarming, if merited, rate. As a result, there was a reliance on extraneous attractions (which came to include animal acts and circus performers), and a tendency to aim at as many targets as possible: a tendency epitomized in Peter Motteux's *The Novelty: Every Act a Play* and in Gildon's splicing of *Measure for Measure* and *Dido and Æneas* into a single show. The exploitation of variety produced an increasing reliance on song and dance (with, by the end of the century, imported foreign artists), and Rich's continuing possession of the two main theatres encouraged him to use Betterton's old speciality of the operatic spectacular against him. This was an often successful policy, although there were expensive fiascos (such as Settle's *The World in the Moon*, 1697), and although the premature death of Henry Purcell in November 1695 struck English music-theatre a long-lasting blow.[3] Lincoln's Inn Fields could rarely stage full semi-operas, and they instead combined short plays with musical masques, as in the coupling of Ravenscroft's farce *The Anatomist* with Motteux's *The Loves of Mars and Venus*, with music by Eccles and Finger. Often, the same masque could be incorporated in a variety of plays. More than ever, the scholar attending to texts is describing a fraction of what the management actually offered.

The new company made an unsurpassable start with the première of one of the greatest of all Restoration plays, Congreve's *Love for Love*. This provides the finest version of a commonplace 1690s plot: the lady's testing of her lover, couched in imagery of judicial trial and linked to a general harmonization of social justice and personal impulse. But it is a familiar subject in an anomalous setting, for the point of the testing plot is normally to affirm certainties of knowledge and value, whereas it here exposes their elusiveness and insecurity. For, more elaborately than ever before, Congreve sees the wide expanse of human life as a map written over with small and clashing systems of localized rules: Montaignesque municipal laws. Belief in a natural social and domestic order sustained by a natural system of signs is the exclusive property of fools, as is the fiction that the family is a pattern of social cohesion embodying natural principles of authority, subordination, and co-operation. For example, the two tyrannical fathers, Foresight and Sir Sampson Legend, both foolishly claim pre-eminence in a naturally ordained hierarchy, Sir Sampson actually projecting himself back to a time where political authority was purely paternal: 'I ɹ m', he boasts, 'of your Patriarchs, I, a Branch of one of your *Antideluvian* Families' (v. i. 39–40).

But Sir Sampson is antediluvian in both senses, and the household again proves to be an illusory centre in a community whose instincts are centrifugal. As Angelica points out to Sir Sampson, one of the original Samson's achieve-

---

[3] The other leading theatre composers were John Eccles and Daniel Purcell, house composers respectively at Lincoln's Inn Fields and with the Patent Company, Jeremiah Clarke, Gottfried Finger, and Richard Leveridge.

ments had been to pull 'an old House over his Head' (V. i. 159), and in his very first line Foresight—the foolish upholder of so many archaic patterns of order—sees his household as threatened by a sinister and incomprehensible diaspora: 'What are all the Women of my Family abroad?' (II. i. 1–2). His world is turned upside down by a simultaneous subversion of domestic and sexual hierarchy; but, although Foresight's hierarchical vision is thoroughly traditional, Congreve defamiliarizes his traditional lore by representing it as the teachings of a medieval Jew—someone from a different place, with different municipal laws—and by couching it in archaic dialect:

> When Housewifes all the House forsake,
> And leave good Man to Brew and Bake,
> Withouten Guile, then be it said,
> That House doth stond upon its Head.

> (II. i. 51–4)

It is not, of course, unnatural for healthy young women to seek pleasure, company, and sex away from the society of an impotent and garrulous dotard. The ideology of home misrepresents a nature whose actual governing principle is the discrete pursuit of individual appetite, and both here and in *The Way of the World* Congreve contrasts the spatially and ideologically restrictive setting of the household with the expansive private mental geographies of its inhabitants: Sir Sampson boasts of cuckolding the King of Bantam, while in the same conversation Foresight boasts of travelling in the stars; the illicit excursions of Mrs Foresight and Mrs Frail transcend their narrow urban setting by having as their goal the World's End tavern; Sir Wilfull Witwoud turns Lady Wishfort's household upside-down by roaring drunkenly about the Antipodes; Lady Wishfort herself wishes to 'leave the World' (V. i. 134) for an imaginary Arcadia; and Fainall (still more indefinitely) longs to 'retire somewhere, any where to another World' (II. i. 245–6).

Trapped in restricted spatial settings with private, localized rules, such as the absurd restrictions which govern Sir Paul Plyant's conduct in bed, or the regulations of Lady Wishfort's cabal-nights, or the rules which permit unlicensed marriages at '*Duke's Place*' (I. i. 118), Congreve's characters hanker for alternative and unrealizable mental landscapes, rewriting in fantasy the map of artificially defined and regulated localities which represents the actual shape and limits of their existence. They long, in fact, to escape from the Way of the World, 'Way' (with its twin connotations of 'path' and 'habit') being a term that perfectly encapsulates Congreve's persistent implication that ethics and topography are inseparably linked. Similarly, the recurrent use of *world* to describe the minute coteries of high society indicates the ease with which the local and accidental can be perceived as the universal and inevitable.

In the last two comedies, the tendency to universalize the local means that those who breach the municipal laws are regularly seen as transgressing a fixed, natural, and (in Sir Wilfull's term) 'orthodox' code; as being 'inhuman', 'monstrous', 'barbarous' (a term suggesting the geographically and linguistically alien), and 'strange'. Most of all, they are accused of being 'mad'. The frequent accusations of madness in *Love for Love* have led one critic solemnly to conclude that Congreve is portraying an insane world,[4] but madness in this play generally means non-conformity with the speaker's private system of interpretation, and accusations of insanity are regularly prompted by thoroughly commonplace conduct, as when female disregard for his imagined authority impels Foresight to claim that 'all Females are mad to day' (II. i. 46–7). When Sir Sampson discovers that the servant Jeremy has the same physical constitution—and therefore the same sensations and appetites— as a gentleman, he recoils in incomprehension from the 'unreasonable' (II. i. 389) failure of nature to mimic the social hierarchy that has formed his own habits of thought. And his ultimate (and widely shared) goal is a total imposition and realization of his own preferred rules of existence, in which natural subordinates (for so he classes children) become unthinking and mechanical agents of their superiors' will:

> thou shall set thy Watch, and the Bridegroom shall observe it's Motions; they shall be married to a Minute, go to Bed to a Minute, and when the Alarm strikes, they shall keep time like the Figures of St. *Dunstan*'s Clock, and *Consummatum est* shall ring all over the Parish. (III. i. 473–8)

The principles governing the mechanical figures on St Dunstan's clock provide an ingeniously pure and extreme form of rules peculiar to localized time and place, and the startling reinterpretation of Christ's dying words implies once again that the texts and tenets of religious orthodoxy are part of the mosaic of local rules and dialects.

It is well known that Congreve's last two comedies recapitulate the Revolution by showing the containment of parental or marital tyranny by law and contract. Many Whig comedy-writers, such as Shadwell and Durfey, re-enact the Revolution in the reconstruction of a microcosmic household that demonstrates the natural sociability of humanity, but Congreve is one of a number of Whig dramatists (Vanbrugh is another) who continue to emphasize the separateness of the individual from society. For Vanbrugh, the consequence is an unresolvable and painful conflict between precept and desire, but Congreve comes closer to suggesting the priority of the individual. Society is a necessary and beneficial artifice, but it is not a natural organism of which the individual is a subordinate part, one in nature with the greater whole. Social structure and individual consciousness have no community of nature or pattern, and the most that can be achieved is an artificial equilibrium between the two: the kind of consensual mapping of territory that Mirabell and Millamant achieve in the proviso scene. After all, even this

---

4 Weber, *The Restoration Rake-Hero*, 110–12.

careful negotiation of contractual harmony includes the stipulation that the married pair 'be very *strange* and well bred . . . as *strange* as if we had been married a great while' (IV. i. 207–8; italics added). Intimates must remain strangers because the individual is not fully integrated with his or her institutional role (as, say, Kate claims to be at the end of *The Taming of the Shrew*), just as Jeremy is not naturally shaped for the servile role prescribed by social accident. A more formal species of contract than the lovers' provisos (the conveyance of her estate to Mirabell) enables Mrs Fainall to live in some peace and security with a rapacious and contemptible husband, but it cannot transform the marriage into a human as well as a legal union. Both marital arrangements recognize that the individual cannot simply be absorbed into the institution: again, there is a marked difference from *The Committee*, where the characters are essentially part of a social and hierarchical order.

The difficulty of representing essence in external, socially familiar forms is particularly pronounced in *Love for Love*. In his opening banter with Valentine Legend, Sir Sampson's son, Jeremy claims to have seen the Spirit of Famine walking abroad, but when he describes this universal and symbolic constant it promptly dissolves into a mass of distinct particulars: a decayed porter, thin chairman, bilked bookseller, and worn-out punk (I. i. 94–102). Foresight, with his faith in the celestial 'signs' and his trust in physiognomy, believes that the individual is governed and disclosed by linked and complementary sign-systems that extend throughout the whole universe. But the gap between visible form and personal essence appears when Scandal describes a gallery of 'Hieroglyphicks' which give pictorial representation to moral character: 'I have a Lawyer with a hundred Hands, two Heads, and but one Face; a Divine with two Faces, and one Head; and I have a Soldier with his Brains in his Belly, and his Heart where his Head shou'd be' (I. i. 642–6). Corporeal form here becomes a sign of moral character, but the corporeal forms are biologically impossible: character and physical being cannot be accommodated in a single visible representation. Yet these disjunctions of outward form and personal nature represent the figures who uphold the order of the kingdom: the lawyer, the divine, the soldier. By contrast, the critics, regulators of the alternative worlds of the playhouse, are barely granted even a pseudo-biological existence, their essence (and even their language) lying almost entirely in artificial trappings: 'there are huge Proportion'd Criticks, with long Wigs, Lac'd Coats, *Steinkirk* Cravats, and terrible Faces; with Catcalls in their Hands, and Horn-Books about their Necks' (I. i. 653–6).

All the hieroglyphics distort or isolate the face, emphasizing its quality as pseudo-sign. The lawyer and divine have, respectively, a single face accommodated by two heads and two faces accommodated by a single head. The soldier has no face at all. And the critic is a disembodied face uncoupled both from the body and from language, which is transferred from the mouth to the cat-call and hornbook. Though the face is the apparent point of contact between the essence of the individual and the public world, it must be divided or erased if essence is to be truly represented. In *The Double-Dealer* Careless had suspected Maskwell on the grounds of 'Physiognomy' (I. i. 148), but now trust in physiognomy has dwindled into one of Foresight's follies: another illusory correspondence between the outer and inner worlds. But, for all its inconveniences, the remoteness of the private self from visible representation is essential to the integrity and pleasure of life. At the end of Act IV of *Love for Love* (ll. 795–816), Valentine and Jeremy volubly deplore Angelica's undecipherability: she is 'a Riddle', more incomprehensible than hieroglyphics, Hebrew, or 'an *Irish* Manuscript' (that is, than writing that follows the rules of alien localities). 'She is a Medal without a Reverse or Inscription' (that is, without a *legend*): a sign detached from any system of meaning. But Angelica has already urged the joys of 'Uncertainty and Expectation' (IV. i. 786) and—as Millamant was to do—has seen estrangement as the basis of the happy marriage: 'Never let us know one another better; for the Pleasure of a Masquerade is done, when we come to shew Faces' (IV. i. 789–90).

Defining the self is as problematic as disclosing it. When Valentine attempts definition, he creates an infinite regression in which all the aspects of character for which agreed terminology exists are stripped away as being not the thing itself:

My Cloaths are soon put off:—But you must also deprive me of Reason, Thought, Passions, Inclinations, Affections, Appetites, Senses, and the huge Train of Attendants that you begot along with me. . . . I am of my self, a plain, easie simple Creature; and to be kept at small expence; but the Retinue that you gave me are craving and invincible; they are so many Devils that you have rais'd and will have employment. (II. i. 339–48)

The self is linguistically intangible, approachable only through negatives. But the remoteness and incommunicability of the self are in many ways desirable; for the alternative is not a harmonious body politic in which individuals actualize their social potential in social forms, but a loss of autonomy that leaves characters as helplessly manipulated as the figures on St Dunstan's clock: the fop Tattle celebrates his sexual conquests by acquiring the picture of his partner, completing possession of the person with possession of the sign; Foresight, that great believer in the correspondence between the outer and inner worlds, is easily persuaded by Scandal to feel ill, and to see the signs of illness when studying his face in a mirror; and Tattle is manipulated with equal ease into betraying the secrets—those defences of the private self—on whose preservation he implausibly prides himself. Such characters become the passive recipients of signs originating in outside agencies: sheets, as Valentine wrongly says of Angelica, of 'spotless Paper . . . to be scrawl'd and blotted by every Goose's Quill' (IV. i. 637–9). The legible character is the one that is written by another hand, and it is to guard against such overwriting of the self that Angelica maintains her private, hieroglyphic, inscrutability. By contrast, the most triumphant overwriting of the self occurs when Tattle and Mrs Frail are tricked into assuming the guise of friar and nun and marrying each other, Tattle believing that his bride is Angelica and Mrs Frail that her husband is Valentine. Both dupes clothe themselves in signs of whose true function (contrived as it is by others) they are ignorant. Both disguises suggest the surrender of the self to localized systems of—in Sir Wilfull's words—'rules'. And both muffle the face: that unfathomable but necessary sign that enables the individual both to confront and to remain remote from the public world.

The most intricate attempt to protect the self by separating it from the terms of public communication is Valentine's feigned madness, in desperate response to his father's refusal to allow him any independence of identity. The incommunicability of essence is nicely summed up in the spectacle of a man posing as Truth in all its immaterial universality and yet becoming, through his apparent madness, legally incompetent to sign his own name. In a very literal sense, he is no longer *legendus* (to be read). Valentine thus protects himself by seeming to abjure the rules with which his father, and the nation's legislators, have circumscribed his life, and indeed the principal technique of his pretended madness is to describe the map of local rules that determines the lives of the allegedly sane: 'Oh things will go methodically in the City, the Clocks will strike Twelve at Noon, and the Horn'd Herd Buz in the Exchange at Two. . . . Coffee-Houses will be full of Smoak and Stratagem. . . . Is your wife of *Covent-Garden* Parish?' (IV. i. 503–17). Truth itself describes only the local and conventional: the parochial rituals that masquerade as universal precepts.

Language too is a parochial ritual, and is consequently neither a window into the heart nor a natural index of social health and order. In *The Way of the World* Sir Wilfull Witwoud, a Shropshire gentleman, is baffled by the language of London. Valentine's brother Ben Legend, another gentleman, has spent most of his life at sea, and consequently translates everything into the language of shipping, much as Dryden's Guyomar had described ships in the language of the land. By contrast Jeremy, Valentine's servant, has been employed at Cambridge, and consequently has 'the Seeds of Rhetorick and Oratory' (V. i. 184) in his head. Ben and Jeremy are oral equivalents to the scrawled-over sheet of white paper, again showing how the ostensible signs of the self may be imposed from outside.

The elusiveness of the essential self produces a widespread concern to *know*, *understand*, and *distinguish* the characters of associates and rivals (*know* is a particularly prominent word). Those who have no reason to reject the systems of authority also seek to be known in their terms: 'Not know thy own Father' (IV. i. 157), exclaims Sir Sampson to the apparently insane

Valentine. Conversely, a prominent part of Valentine's pose as Truth is—paradoxically enough—a failure to 'know' people. He can only describe the processes of social ritual that are so often mistaken for essential character, and in doing so follows a principle stated before the assumption of his pose: 'I *know* no effectual *Difference* between continued Affectation and Reality' (III. i. 40–1; italics added). Valentine does not say that there *is* no difference: he is concerned with the possibility of knowing and distinguishing, for without such possibility questions of fact become redundant.

The problems and paradoxes of knowledge appear with particular clarity in the courtship of Angelica and Valentine. Like many other comic heroines of the decade, Angelica feels compelled judicially to test the character of her prospective husband. Yet the difficulties and perils of self-disclosure are as great as those of continuing disguise, as she recognizes when she commends to Valentine the pleasures of uncertainty. At the climax of the play, Valentine divests himself of all external property, performing a unique, unrepeatable act of self-revelation by renouncing all security and social position. Thus satisfied of his unmercenary character, Angelica announces an end to her 'dissembling' (V. i. 605). Yet Angelica's knowledge of Valentine has required as its precondition his ignorance of her, so what does he love if this is the first time that he sees her without misconstruction? Unlike *The Man of Mode*, *Love for Love* does not invite us to speculate with misgiving upon the future conduct and happiness of the central couple. This is the best love that the world permits, but it is one that rests upon an incomplete attainment and unequal sharing of knowledge, and the lovers' concluding words to each other provide not simple affirmations about the future but rules for interpreting it. It is a miniature proviso scene, in which they agree the prospective meaning of signs:[5]

ANGELICA. I have done dissembling now, *Valentine*; and if that Coldness which I have always worn before you, should turn to an extream Fondness, you must not suspect it.

VALENTINE. I'll prevent that suspicion——For I intend to doat on at that immoderate rate, that your Fondness shall never *distinguish* it self enough, to be taken notice of. If ever you seem to love too much, it must be only when I can't love enough.

(V. i. 605–12; italics added)

The ultimate assurance that Valentine gives Angelica is that of invisibility: her love will not be publicly distinguished, and they will have a private compact of knowledge that prevents exposure of the naked self to the gaze of society.

While no other dramatist of the time had Congreve's intellectual stature, and while concern with spatially localized values is by now exceptional, he in many ways provides the finest statement of commonplace concerns (such as

---

5 Richard W. F. Kroll discusses 'The difficulty of discriminating among levels of discourse, and of discovering and interpreting natural and social signs' in *The Way of the World* ('Discourse and Power in *The Way of the World*', *ELH* 53 (1986), 727–58 (p. 732)).

the testing of the lover and the biological meaninglessness of social distinction), and perhaps the impetus to their further exploration by lesser talents. In addition, his use of the kinsman-outsider (Ben, Sir Wilfull) as both comic victim and man of sense reflects a new ambivalence towards metropolitan values. Yet Congreve was largely isolated in his scepticism and his belief in the benign alienation of the self from the social order, and most dramatists now saw no problems in self-representation, social existence, and justice. When Edward Ravenscroft portrayed a father and son battling over the hand of a beautiful Angelica (in his farcical *The Anatomist*, LIF, November 1696), he portrayed a straightforward reconciliation of authority and love, the father eventually accepting defeat magnanimously. There is more spice in Motteux's accompanying masque, *The Loves of Mars and Venus* (the closest competition which Betterton's company could offer to Rich's operatic spectaculars),[6] but even here adultery is frustrated, and January and May are reconciled by Cupid.[7]

Congrevian elements without Congrevian complications, indeed, feature in the second new comedy mounted at Lincoln's Inn Fields, the undistinguished *She Ventures, and He Wins* by 'a Young Lady' (September 1695), whose failure caused the temporary closure of the theatre.[8] As in *Love for Love*, a woman tests her lover (though, imprudently, she does so after marriage): having married the penniless Lovewell, the heiress Charlot pretends to be an impostor, getting a beautiful friend to pretend to be the real Charlot, and to feign love for him. Lovewell remains immovably faithful to his wife, loving the woman even when she has (apparently) been stripped of the name and station by which he initially knew her, becoming a nameless and placeless enigma. As with the Valentine plot in *Love for Love*, the self is bared—an outcome unimaginable in *The Country-Wife* or *The Man of Mode*—but the exposure has none of Congreve's unresolved contradictions.

A better, though still unsuccessful, play is George Granville's *The She-Gallants* (LIF, December/January 1695/6, but written in the mid-1680s),[9] whose two heroines disguise themselves as men, one to test the character of a prospective husband, the other to reclaim an inconstant lover, who is eventually moved to effusive reform. But female emancipation is not championed, for the heroines' pursuit of marriage is contrasted approvingly with the intellectual presumption (and sexual laxity) of a *femme savante*, Lady Dorimen. Writing, says Lady Dorimen's more conventional niece, is 'not a Talent for a

---

[6] See Robert D. Hume, 'Opera in London, 1695–1706', in *British Theatre and the Other Arts, 1660–1800*, ed. Kenny, 67–91.

[7] I do not know why Curtis Price describes Venus as 'a vain, ageing beauty, almost a pantomime dame' ('Political Allegory', 20).

[8] Maximillian E. Novak, 'The Closing of Lincoln's Inn Fields Theatre in 1695', *Restoration and 18th Century Theatre Research*, 14/1 (1975), 51–2.

[9] 'Offending the Ears of some Ladies who set up for Chastity, it made its Éxit' (Downes, *Roscius Anglicanus*, 94).

Woman' (III, p. 38), though women are not confined to alien and weakened forms of language: the play features, and ridicules, an absurd proposal for a feminine dictionary, expurgating words of all potentially obscene syllables. Women again test and reform lovers in the anonymous *Feign'd Friendship* (LIF, ?May 1699). In male disguise, Eugenia parodies the conduct of the wild Lord Frolicksome and shames him out of it (the day of Sir Frederick Frollick was long past). Lady Generous satisfies herself of Truelove's true love, since the pre-marital servant easily turns into the lifelong tyrant (II, p. 15). And, in a perfunctory version of the Invisible Mistress plot, Sabina tests Townely by courting him in two different guises. Like the bedroom trick, the Invisible Mistress device remained popular throughout the 1690s, but the division of the mistress's identity became pointless as the perceived tension between desire and social existence waned. Except in Congreve's hands, then, the trial of the lover leads to an uncomplicated discovery of real character, and the implied metaphor of successful judicial process constrasts with the widespread pre-Revolution view that judicial enquiry could not grasp the essence of the individual. (At the end of Elkanah Settle's semi-opera *The World in the Moon* (PC, June 1697), a piece of self-reflexive theatre partially set on the Dorset Garden stage, the hero dons the theatrical robes of the Lord Chief Justice in order to secure both his bride and his property.)

The exposure of essential character is the chief subject of Thomas Dilke's three comedies, *The Lover's Luck* (LIF, December 1695), *The City Lady* (LIF, December 1696), and *The Pretenders* (LIF, March 1698), which satirize a milieu of deceivers: the pseudo-rich, pseudo-gentle, and pseudo-poor (who evade war taxes), and also lords and knights too proud of the trappings of status. Amidst the pervasive deception, a few people of sense strive, with difficulty but ultimate success, to assess each other's 'reality' (a confident term).[10] The fraudulence of the town necessitates the cultivation of private virtue, and the hero of each play is someone who (like Ben Legend) challenges the town by entering it from outside: a Colonel who has been fighting abroad and has already renounced his rakish past (*The Lover's Luck*), a plain-speaking country gentleman (*The Pretenders*), a young and sensible merchant's son returning from educative travel on the Continent (*The City Lady*). The most interesting of the three plays is *The City Lady* (which failed because the actor Cave Underhill was incapacitated by a nose-bleed). This depicts the reform of the grasping and dishonest merchant Sir George Grumble, of his proud, extravagant, socially pretentious wife, and of Sir George's elderly rake of a brother. Lady Grumble is a different kind of stranger in the town, who claims equality with the nobility after two weeks' residence, but, as with Ravenscroft's *The Citizen Turn'd Gentleman* of a quarter of a century before, the emphasis is not on the exclusion but on the assimilation of the upstarts:

---

[10] For concern to establish the real, see *The Lover's Luck*, III, p. 26; V, p. 42; *The City Lady*, II, p. 21; IV, p. 40; *The Pretenders* II, p. 15.

Bellardin, Sir George's son by his first marriage, has already travelled and acquired the culture of a gentleman, and at the end Lady Grumble's son Pedanty is sent abroad, to 'see the World, and read Men' (V, p. 48). Massinger's similarly titled *The City Madam* had affirmed an immutably fixed social order in imagery of immutably fixed geographic relationships, asserting 'A distance 'twixt the City, and the Court' (V. iii. 155). Dilke provides a linked image of social and geographic mobility.

One way in which Congreve might have seemed isolated in 1695 was in his persistence with sex comedy. After *Love for Love*, the next great comic success was Cibber's celebrated rake-reformed play, *Love's Last Shift*, staged by the Patent Company in January 1696, and in the interval neither company had staged another new sex comedy (though the comic sub-plot of Southerne's *Oroonoko* is *risqué* enough). Betterton followed *Love for Love* with *She Ventures, and He Wins*, *The Lover's Luck*, and *The She-Gallants*, while the Patentees' first new comedy after the rupture was Thomas Scott's *The Mock-Marriage* (PC, September 1695), in which the rake Willmot is contrasted with a gentleman of sense, and ultimately heeds his advice to 'live as becomes a Christian' (IV, p. 40). Their next offering, the third part of Durfey's *Don Quixote*, was damned for bawdiness, but its sins are of the word rather than the flesh. Then came *Love's Last Shift*, a play which has a reputation for many-faced opportunism, in that it gratifies both the recidivist taste for sex comedy and the growing demand for theatrical morality.[11] Cibber's own epilogue boasts that the hero, Loveless, is *'lew'd for above four Acts'* (l. 16), and the gleeful rape of the serving-woman at the end of Act IV is one of the nastiest episodes in Restoration comedy. The rapist is forced to marry his victim, but there were dramatists who had the moral sensitivity to realize that predatory aggression was poorly redressed by lifelong attachment to the aggressor. Nevertheless, for all its cynical diversity of appeal, the play does have a visible ideology, which was to have a significant shaping force in many of Cibber's principal plays. Whereas sex comedy of the early 1690s portrays irremediable dislocation, Cibber follows Shadwell in celebrating the homecoming of the morally, socially, and physically displaced. And, whereas sex comedy stresses the slipperiness of the signs that nominally sustain social intercourse, Cibber associates the process of moral and social rebirth with one of linguistic purification: for him, as for Ben Jonson, linguistic health is a precise index of moral and social health.

Loveless returns, impoverished, from a period of peripatetic debauchery on the Continent. He is literally a wanderer, and he has fallen both materially and morally beneath his hereditary rank as gentleman, becoming the economic and moral equal of his servant, Snap. (One consequence of Loveless's

---

[11] See Helga Drougge, 'Colley Cibber's "Genteel Comedy": *Love's Last Shift* and *The Careless Husband*', *Studia Neophilologica*, 54 (1982), 61–79; Paul E. Parnell, 'Equivocation in Cibber's *Love's Last Shift*', *Studies in Philology*, 57 (1960), 519–34.

eventual moral and social recovery is that he regains authority over Snap, commanding him to marry the woman he had raped: whereas Southerne and Congreve portray the relationship between master and servant as arising from mere economic contingency, Cibber retains the hierarchical outlook of *The Committee*.) Loveless is redeemed by his abandoned wife, Amanda, whom he believes to be dead, and who presents herself to him as a new, voluptuous mistress, revealing her true identity only after treating him incognita to a night of ecstatic sensuality. Since she has inherited an estate in his absence, she redeems him economically as well as morally. Loveless is certainly reformed by the crude discovery that even wives can be fun in bed, but Cibber also purveys loftier morals, emphasizing the home-coming and renewed fixity of the erstwhile wanderer and the moral agency of language in his conversion. 'Good Heav'n inspire my Heart,' Amanda prays, 'and hang upon my Tongue the force of Truth and Eloquence, that I may lure this wandring Falcon back to Love and Virtue' (V. ii. 8–10). Later, feeling that 'Heav'n bids me speak undaunted' (V. ii. 159–60), she names herself, and shows Loveless his own name, indelibly inscribed (presumably on a bracelet) on her arm, and the hero's confrontation with his own name is the decisive moment in his moral regeneration: there is an intimate and necessary synthesis between the recovery of identity, of social rank, and of the nomenclature by which the self is socially registered (even if, awkwardly, that name happens to be Loveless). The fundamental harmony between sign and character is shown in Amanda's ability to 'read' the characters of men[12] (whereas Congreve's Angelica cultivates illegibility to insulate personal essence from the visible processes of social life). And the harmony of individual character and social existence is further displayed in Amanda's ruse, a division of identity that combines the bedroom trick and the Invisible Mistress device, here serving not to divide but to reconcile the appetitive and the social: to redirect illicit lusts into socially sanctioned forms. In an inverted version of this plot, the irredeemably false gentleman Sir Novelty Fashion (played by Cibber) is also tricked into meeting an old partner in a new guise, though here a strumpet (Flareit) masquerades as a gentlewoman rather than vice versa, and the upshot is not home-coming but a collapse of their *ménage*, with Flareit resolving to 'change my Lodging' (IV. i. 59).

Love's Last Shift is not a major turning-point in the development of Restoration comedy, for it reflects an already well-established trend without visibly modifying it. Indeed, it was followed by a minor resurgence of sex comedy, to which it indirectly contributed by inspiring *The Relapse*, which in turn fed the resurgence. There were more significant developments in the 1695–6 season than the arrival of Colley Cibber. One is the appearance of three plays (*The Country-Wake*, *Love's a Jest*, and *The Cornish Comedy*) which reject a metropolitan setting for one in rural England (continuing the

---

[12] I. i. 338–9; III. ii. 73.

migration of comedy already evident in *Bury-Fair, The Canterbury Guests*, and—marginally—*The Richmond Heiress*). The other is the appearance of a new generation of women playwrights (accompanied by the première, and undeserved failure, of Aphra Behn's last comedy). The new women writers contributed significantly to the development of reform comedy, but their viewpoint deserves to be considered separately.

There are, however, a few plays which, sometimes independently, do reproduce aspects of Cibber's outlook. One is John Dryden junior's *The Husband his Own Cuckold* (LIF, ?June 1696), written in Italy some considerable time before its production, and staged against his father's better judgement.[13] A bedroom trick is again used to reconcile desire and social responsibility, and there is a stark endorsement of male authority (and even violence), a husband diverting his wife from adultery by impersonating his rival in bed and lacerating her face, causing her to regard it as an image of her disfigured soul. With the author's full approval, he does what Pinchwife had been unable to do: he writes his wife's character upon her face. In the other two plots a 15-year-old wife is prevented from cuckolding her 50-year-old husband, and the daughter of a grasping father refuses to marry her true love until paternal consent is assured.

Cibber's own *Womans Wit* (PC, January 1697) has none of the thematic interest of his first comedy. Two gentlemen of sense eventually marry suitably steady and sensible women, after having been confused by the deceptions of a jealous coquette. Libertinism is confined to Major Rakish and his son, close copies of Crowne's Old and Young Ranter, whose schemes for marriage to Lady Manlove and control of her foolish son owe much to *The Plain-Dealer*. Even less accomplished is his *Love Makes a Man* (PC, December 1700), an inexpert stitching together of *The Elder Brother* and *The Custom of the Country* (minus the racy bits, which even in the early Restoration had caused audience outrage). Cibber merges characters from the two plays with cheerful disregard for consistency, his main innovations being to turn one of the spliced characters into a foppish part for himself, and to accentuate the reform of Louisa (Hippolyta in *The Custom of the Country*). The prologue boasts that the play has something for everyone (though no one seems to have liked it), and in this respect the play typifies a more widespread tendency to aim at every available target rather than to create a unified work of art. The acme of this tendency is Peter Motteux's *The Novelty: Every Act a Play* (LIF, June 1697).[14] Another Fletcher hybrid is James Drake's *The Sham-Lawyer*, '𝕯amnably ACTED' (according to the title-page) by the Patent Company (May 1697), which plunders *Wit Without Money* and *The Spanish Curate* to

---

[13] Dryden senior's preface comments that the play 'was sent me from *Italy* some years since' (sig. [A3ᵛ]). Winn suggests that he received it 'probably before the contract with Tonson of 15 June 1694, which mentions "my son's play" ' (*John Dryden and His World*, 481).

[14] The playlets are a cut-down version of Edward Filmer's *The Unnatural Brother*; a pastoral by Oldmixon; a comedy showing the reform of a financially imprudent hero, after desperate attempts to

provide two virtuous heroines and three reformed men: an extravagant, a libertine, and a tyrannical husband (reconciliation within a January–May marriage is a new trend, also evident in *The Loves of Mars and Venus*, *The Husband his Own Cuckold*, and in John Corye's later *A Cure for Jealousie*, LIF, ?December 1699). Cibber's interest in the symbolic value of the home is paralleled in John Dennis's *A Plot and No Plot* (PC, May 1697), where Bull Senior, a Jacobite merchant whose fondness for political tyranny is reflected in his worship of rank and his oppression of his own family, is gradually brought to himself by a series of ruses involving the misrepresentation of the home, first as a prison and then as a madhouse.

The anonymous *Love Without Interest* (PC, April 1699) treats love with overblown emotiveness and juxtaposes the courtship of a sober couple with the taming of the rakish Wildman by a broad-minded woman ready to forgive his 'old Trespasses done in Strangers Inclosures' (I, p. 8). David Craufurd's *Courtship A-la-Mode* (PC, July 1700)[15] is chiefly interesting for allowing a fallen woman to make a good marriage to a man who is neither a fool nor her original seducer. More conventionally, it portrays reform as an ending of dislocation (the libertine is like a nomadic savage, III, p. 23) and as a response to the moral power of signs (beauty is a sign of virtue, I, p. 3). The problems of fallen women are, however, less easily solved in Francis Manning's feeble Spanish intrigue play *The Generous Choice* (LIF, February 1700). Here a compulsive seducer marries one of his victims, but another is left to retire to a nunnery. The interest in the purification of love is also evident in Oldmixon's *Amintas* (PC, ?1697–8), a version of Tasso's *Aminta* which self-righteously (and unsuccessfully) attempted to force culture on an audience addicted, as the epilogue complained, to farce. Its lofty aim was, however, compromised by an added chorus demanding a greater supply of willing virgins (III, p. 38).

The three rural comedies that appear in 1696 have little in common besides their rural setting, which displays the tentative movement away from metropolitan norms that is also evident in Dilke's choice of heroes, and they differ particularly in sexual attitude. In Doggett's *The Country-Wake* (LIF, April 1696) the rakish Woodvill avenges the loss of his father's estate to Sir Thomas Testie by sleeping with Sir Thomas's young, unhappy wife (providing the last example in the century of a hero who proceeds from in-play adultery to marrying a rich virgin).[16] The emotional and financial justification of the adultery is powerful, but Woodvill is nevertheless clearly condemned. After painfully discovering his faithlessness, Lady Testie decides to make the best of her marriage (May again being reconciled with January, though here with much residual misery), and Doggett provides a virginal gentleman of sense

---

put off guests to a dinner party he cannot afford to give; an allegorical masque of Hercules and Omphale; and a farce.

[15] Craufurd withdrew it from Lincoln's Inn Fields after abortive rehearsals at which Bowman refused to learn his part.   [16] Smith, *The Gay Couple*, 167.

(Friendly) to rebuke and contrast with Woodvill. Again, the relationship between desire and responsibility is defined through a reworking of the venerable Invisible Mistress motif; for, having once slept with Woodvill as a masked unknown, Lady Testie proves his faithlessness by sleeping with him again as herself. But here the dual form of the divided mistress neither expresses nor resolves the tension between socially sanctioned and socially forbidden desires: in both her forms, she is outside the limits of the acceptable. Division of affection is now in itself a transgression of limits, and the primary consequence of the ruse is social disruption, when Woodvill concludes that he may have slept with Friendly's prospective bride, Flora.

Coincidentally, *The Cornish Comedy* (PC, June/July 1696), an anonymous play brought to the stage by Powell, reworked that other expression of split sexual identity, the bedroom trick, though in the context of a disrespectful attitude towards legal, paternal, and marital authority that was becoming increasingly rare. When a cuckolded inn-keeper seeks solace in the arms of his maid, his spoilsport wife tries to take her place in the dark, only to be serviced by a passing and opportunistic third party, the consequence of the mishap being that the marriage is rescued. In the courtship plot, young lovers demonstrate that 'By Nature all things covet liberty' (I, p. 2), tricking a grasping parent into choosing the worthy rather than the wealthy suitor, and in the process perpetrating the only fraudulent misrepresentation of tin-mining rights in Restoration comedy. Perhaps the most purposeful use of the rural locale is in Peter Motteux's good-natured (and successful) *Love's a Jest* (LIF, June 1696), set in Hertfordshire. Here the withdrawal from the metropolis permits human conduct to be viewed in isolation from the local and superficial standards of fashionable life (unlike Congreve, Motteux does not believe that local rules are the only rules available). London is extensively satirized, and that prime transgressor of urban ideals, the fop, figures only as a remote wonder to be mimicked at second-hand (the closest approximation in the cast to either a rake or a fop is the carefree and benevolent bachelor Sam Gaymood). Here, offences are against more substantial codes: against courtesy and considerateness. And here there is a gradual weakening of artifice, as true feelings emerge from mistrust, disguise, and inhibition.

A continuing robustness of sexual outlook is apparent in Joseph Harris's *The City Bride; or, The Merry Cuckold* (LIF, March 1696), an adaptation of *A Cure for a Cuckold* in whose comic plot a merchant returns from apparent death and, finding that his wife has produced a child with another's help, evades the stigma of cuckoldom by divorcing and remarrying her. But the treatment of infidelity is not searching, and in his next and last play, *Love's a Lottery* (LIF, April 1699), Harris turned to innocuous farce, portraying the triumph of true love despite a father's attempt to dispose of his daughter's hand by lottery. In 1696, however, there were still two authoritative voices calling for the serious and sympathetic examination of refractory sexuality. One was Aphra Behn's, speaking from beyond the grave; the other was Vanbrugh's, speaking for the first time. Behn's *The Younger Brother* (PC, February 1696), brought to the stage with some alterations by Charles Gildon, resembles *The Revenge* in being a woman's engagement with a man's text, conducting an implicit dialogue with *The Plain-Dealer*, and elaborating the dialogue which Wycherley in turn had conducted with *Twelfth Night*. In addition to recasting the characters of Wycherley's Fidelia and Olivia, who are themselves recastings of Shakespeare's Viola and Olivia, Behn combines elements of both Shakespeare heroines in a third character, Teresia, who parallels Viola in her (brief) assumption of male disguise, but who also takes over and transforms Olivia's itemization of her beauty (which has no counterpart in Wycherley). Here the catalogue no longer satirizes the reduction of woman to a passive list of attributes but polemically states her active power: the vigour of her 'Machine, call'd a Body' (II, p. 341), and the ability of her mind to take on men in any area. The Petrarchan icon has become a Cartesian mechanism. Yet there is still Behn's characteristic diffidence about the woman's chances of encroaching on male linguistic domination, and, after her other boasts, Teresia's claim to linguistic power is oddly muted and anticlimactic: '*Item*, One Tongue, that will prattle Love' (II, p. 342). The linguistic vulnerability of woman is a central concern in the treatment of the play's ostensible villainess, the inconstant Mirtilla, who is patently modelled on Wycherley's Olivia and, like her predecessor, falls in love with an exemplary heroine in male disguise. Mirtilla is constantly portrayed as a linguistic transgressor, being repeatedly accused of perjury, yet it is clear that all she does is appropriate the lifestyle of the male rake: how different that conduct looks, at least to men, when it is displayed by the wrong sex. Loveit's charges of perjury never began to seem a fixed norm by which to judge Dorimant, for she was plainly out of her depth with the social conventions of language; but Mirtilla is judged by the sex that creates those conventions, and their charges therefore carry more plausibility, though not more real weight. Her rash intrusion into male territory is emphasized by a small, subtle detail. Although plainly modelled on Wycherley's Olivia, Mirtilla is—obviously—not called Olivia. That name is reserved for the Fidelia-like heroine, the woman who spends the play in male disguise and excites Mirtilla's love. That Behn should give the name of Wycherley's villainess to her own heroine clearly implies a challenge to Wycherley's categories, and it also implies a parallel between Mirtilla and the pseudo-man who has stolen her name: the woman with the name of Wycherley's villainess assumes male clothes; the woman with her character assumes male mores. Indeed, when Olivia resumes female dress, the clothes she puts on are Mirtilla's.

Behn's transformation of *The Plain-Dealer* is constantly evident. George Marteen, an extravagant but good-natured younger brother who has been forced by parental tyranny into the indignity of apprenticeship to a tradesman, returns to England to find that his beloved Mirtilla, whom he rescued from poverty, has married Sir Morgan Blunder for his money. George's friend Prince Frederick then falls for Mirtilla—not knowing of George's passion—and cuckolds Sir Morgan. Mirtilla values Frederick's rank, but quickly falls for the disguised Olivia (George's sister), and the latter part of the play depicts George's attempts to use Olivia to open Frederick's eyes to Mirtilla's baseness. The debts to *The Plain-Dealer* are clear, but Behn's villainess is more ambiguous than Wycherley's, for Mirtilla has caused George neither financial nor emotional ruin (he quickly falls for Teresia), and the moral claims of Frederick upon Mirtilla are weak. Whereas Wycherley's Olivia is quickly exposed to Manly, Mirtilla repeatedly thwarts George's attempts to unmask her, until he himself is lost in admiration for her skill: 'thou hast jilted him so handsomly, thou'st vanquish'd all my Rage' (v, p. 391). The pattern of persistently thwarted detection recalls Durfey's *A Fond Husband* and, as George acknowledges, it inevitably creates sympathy for the deceiver.

Frederick does eventually see Mirtilla's nature, but the scornful rejection for which *The Plain-Dealer* prepares us never happens. On the contrary, when the various united couples enter at the beginning of the final scene, the first in line is '*Prince* Frederick, *leading* Mirtilla' (v, p. 395). He then proceeds to agree with Sir Morgan an arrangement whereby he can periodically cuckold him. If this is not the expected rejection, it is still humiliation on a grand scale. The lover who had earlier proclaimed himself Mirtilla's 'Slave' (III, p. 354) is now in total control, his *hand* leading her, negotiating over her favours with her husband—her other male owner—as the proprietor males had negotiated over the two Julias in *The False Count* and *The Lucky Chance*. The virago's reign is over and, as so often, the language of courtly love cedes to that of ownership.

Behn was speaking not only from beyond the grave but from a vanished age. Although Vanbrugh's *The Relapse* (PC, November 1696) debunks the smug and implausible sexual psychology of *Love's Last Shift*, he does not share Behn's willingness to see sexual ethics as ratifications of power, and he does not question the social validity of traditional sexual morality; rather, he observes the tenuousness with which it is internalized in the frail composition of humanity (and consequently rejects Cibber's belief in the natural harmony between character and social forms and signs). Equally, he enfeebles the religious texts and dialects in which sexual morality is customarily expressed. There have been several fine studies of the play's blasphemous wit, in which a language consecrated to fixed and eternal absolutes is diverted into ambiguity, flux, and self-subversion:[17] the most favourable moment for seduction, according to Loveless, is when the woman has just finished praying (IV. iii.

[17] Alan Roper, 'Language and Action in *The Way of the World*, *Love's Last Shift*, and *The Relapse*', *ELH* 40 (1973), 44–69; Michael Cordner, 'Time, the Churches, and Vanbrugh's Lord Foppington', *Durham University Journal*, 77 (1984–5), 11–17; James E. Gill, 'Character, Plot, and the Language of Love in *The Relapse*: A Reappraisal', *Restoration*, 16 (1992), 110–25.

8–10). Yet the need for the morality survives the texts which traditionally created it, even if some can dispense with text and moral principles alike. Foppington dislikes sermons, immediately before her seduction Berinthia rejects a book of sermons in order to read Durfey's *A Fond Husband* (IV. iii. 23–6), and Hoyden is so much a creature of deaf appetite that she undergoes two marriage ceremonies in quick succession. Nevertheless, for rational beings, adultery has a power to corrupt and injure which is quite absent from the great Carolean sex comedies. Moral values are deeply associated with written or internally inscribed absolutes, and it is hard to know where to find them when the texts have so far lost authority and respect that Worthy's expression of desire for Amanda can be likened to a preacher's exposition of a text (IV. ii. 52–62), and when language itself is so dethroned that the greatest verbal virtuoso in the play is its fool, Lord Foppington. But the values survive somewhere: Worthy's conversion of the text that forbids into the flesh that is desired effects no comparable conversion in our assessment of the man and his motives, which remain cynical and manipulative.

Cibber's belief in a clear and single morality is revealed in his association between moral reform and home-coming: life has a fixed and publicly recognized goal. By contrast Vanbrugh (like Otway and Southerne) specializes in a drama of dislocation: *The Relapse* opens with the rural domestic bliss of Loveless and Amanda, Loveless claiming that he has now rejected 'roving pleasures' and that his love 'stands . . . fixed' (I. i. 3, 54); yet he immediately decides to leave home for London, and his journey from the country to the metropolis (once again, no longer the hero's natural home) is the first dislocation of many. The couple apparently find another fixed home in London, Loveless introducing Amanda to their new lodgings with the promise that 'I shall hardly remove whilst we stay in town' (II. i. 2–3); but he does not need to, for Amanda unwisely introduces into the household her beautiful friend Berinthia, to whom Loveless has already been attracted at the theatre, and the home is therefore violated from within. Loveless first propositions Berinthia after learning that Amanda is away from home (III. ii. 1–2), though adultery is here forestalled by Amanda's unexpected return 'home' (III. ii. 115). And, when Loveless finally accomplishes his adultery with Berinthia, he gains the opportunity by pretending—significantly—that he is away from home: a pretence whose literal falsity is outweighed by its symbolic accuracy. 'My wife don't expect me home till four o'clock,' he murmurs as he prepares to betray her (IV. iii. 2–3).

Dislocation is, literally, universal: not for Vanbrugh do 'The heavens themselves, the planets, and this centre | Observe degree, priority, and place';[18] on the contrary, as the song at Lord Foppington's abortive wedding feast proclaims, 'Heaven and earth and all go round' (V. v. 117). Immediately after

---

[18] *Troilus and Cressida*, I. iii. 85–6.

Loveless's abandonment of his home, Young Fashion returns from abroad, indigent and homeless, and committed to the cause of that expert in self-dislocation, James II (I. ii. 55). Denied any assistance by his brother, Lord Foppington, he attempts a comprehensive invasion of his brother's place, impersonating his identity and rank in an attempt to steal his bride-to-be and the estate that goes with her ('Get but the house, let the devil take the heiress' (III. iii. 8), he says in another separation of dwelling from home). When the true Lord Foppington turns up at the estate after his brother, his displacement is literalized, in that he is mistaken for a vagabond. And his marriage feast, a ritual of hospitality and home-making, dissolves in the final assault on domesticity, when Young Fashion gatecrashes his brother's home and claims his bride.

If spaces and institutions lose their power to signify and enforce a moral order, so does language, which frequently falters as social principles yield to the disorder of desire, as in the episode in which Berinthia and her former lover Worthy discuss their designs on Loveless and Amanda:

BERINTHIA. What do you mean by that?
WORTHY. Nothing. . . .
BERINTHIA. Pray tell me what you mean?

(III. ii. 148–55)

The tension between language and desire, social impulse and antisocial appetite, is a commonplace of Restoration sex comedy, but Vanbrugh's version of it is distinctive; for, if he lacks Cibber's easy belief in the capacity of human language to echo the transcendent, he equally lacks Etherege's cheerful acceptance that it can only refer to the social sphere in which it originates. Rather, Vanbrugh examines the inappropriateness of seeing in language the ratification of values which it cannot ratify, but which are no less necessary for that. It is unsurprising that Foppington and Berinthia should be deaf to pious exhortation, but it has limited power even over Amanda, although she explicitly enjoys sermons and is so unfrivolous that she dislikes deriving diversion from Lord Foppington's affectations (II. i. 148–63). Yet even she can desert the *utile* for the *dulce*. Despite her reluctance to gain diversion from Lord Foppington's antics, she does question him about his 'intrigues' (II. i. 247), provoking him to an embarrassingly public misinterpretation of her interest in him. She is also fascinated by Berinthia's morally alien lifestyle (in part because of her own painfully curbed responsiveness to Worthy's advances), and her interest prompts her disastrous decision to admit her to the household: inevitably, her fascination with the mores of the female libertine makes her the victim of them. Even in Amanda's life, there is a clash between the discourse sanctioned by religion and that desired by instinct.

The division between Amanda's principles and inclinations—between a love of sermons and a taste for less edifying discourse, between a commitment to chastity and an increasingly painful attraction to its opposite—clearly reveals the limitations which attach to the sermon as a regulating norm of human discourse. It is not a direct fusion of the human word and the divine, as Cibber represents Amanda's rhetoric to be, and it has imperfect power to direct the mental and linguistic habits of even the most virtuously inclined. In the name and person of the country Justice Sir Tunbelly Clumsey the authority of law and the unruly exuberance of the flesh—the antagonistic forces of early Restoration carnival comedy—are yoked with a conventionally comic incongruity. But *The Relapse* is not a carnival play (it ends, after all, with a disrupted feast), and the opposites so ludicrously combined in Sir Tunbelly are repeatedly combined to more serious effect in other areas of the play, as in Loveless's failed resolutions, and Amanda's combined reverence for the text and fascination with the proscribed. They are even present in Worthy's renunciation of his designs on Amanda: the climactic moral conversion in which, unexpectedly, *The Relapse* parallels *Love's Last Shift*. For, whereas the conversion of Cibber's Loveless brings total assimilation into the ways of society, Worthy's new virtue is a state of painful tension, of equilibrium that might be easily lost. To emphasize the divisions within his characters, Vanbrugh (like Wycherley and Etherege) contrives external doublings of identity: two Lord Foppingtons, leading to two husbands for Hoyden; Loveless visiting the theatre and seeing himself upon the stage; Berinthia narrating her affair with Loveless to Amanda as though she were describing the actions of a third party (as Etherege's Bellinda had, in parallel circumstances, done to Loveit). Such divisions emphasize a disparity between the self and its social representations: for Vanbrugh, as for Congreve, humanity cannot totally absorb itself in the processes of social existence; but, whereas Congreve optimistically sees the way of the world as providing a protective carapace of arbitrary yet useful convention, Vanbrugh shows a humanity mocked by commandments that are printed on the page but not in the heart.

The insubordination and indignity of the flesh are also prominent concerns throughout Vanbrugh's other original comedy, *The Provoked Wife* (LIF, April 1697), where they once again reduce a home to worthlessness. The play opens, indeed, with an image of flesh (Sir John Brute's 'What cloying meat is love', I. i. 1), and thereafter it traces proliferating and unresolvable conflicts between the flesh and morality: trapped in a dead marriage, Lady Brute is 'spurred on' to infidelity 'by desire, and . . . reined in with fear' (I. i. 120–1); her lover, Constant, has 'more flesh and blood than grace and self-denial' (II. i. 125–6); when her husband seeks escape and oblivion in a carnivalistic night on the town, this most extreme liberation of the flesh receives fitting expression in his ranting cry of 'Blood and blood—and blood' (IV. i. 56); and when he encounters his wife and her niece Bellinda on a parallel flight from repressive decorum in the guise of whores, he crudely emphasizes their dalliance with carnality by describing the apparent punks as 'mutton' (IV. iv. 96).

'What a pleasure there is in doing what we should not do!' exclaims Lady Brute (III. i. 333–4). As usual, the conflict between the flesh and the prescriptions of social decorum leads to conflicts between individual desire and the demands and rituals of justice, and Vanbrugh denies justice the uncomplicated force that it has in the Williamite plays of Shadwell and Durfey: like the sacred texts in *The Relapse*, it has far more authority than influence, but (unlike justice in Etherege and Wycherley) it cannot be simply despised, and it does stand in the way of sexual freedom, being removable only by sophistry or outright fantasy. Denied legal means of dissolving her terrible marriage, Lady Brute speculates that 'a Court of Chancery in heaven' (I. i. 90–1) might release her, and Constant argues that, since 'no woman upon earth has so just a cause as you', she is permitted in equity to betray her husband: for 'where laws dispense with equity, equity should dispense with laws' (IV. iv. 174–80). Attempts to appropriate the language and rituals of justice are common: claiming the mere privilege of power, Heartfree proceeds to 'examine' Lady Fancyfull (II. i. 23), and a still more naked display of power permits Sir John to 'examine' the journeyman tailor from whom he steals the parson's gown (IV. i. 13). But, of course, the night of carnival that begins with Sir John's assumption of the role of Justice culminates in his own arraignment before judicial authority. In *An Evening's Love*, thirty years earlier, the confrontation between revellers and judiciary had been aborted, and carnival had reigned triumphant. Here, the confrontation takes place, and the equivocal comparison of judge and criminal reflects Vanbrugh's general recognition that the contest between authority and impulse is not one that permits a single- and simple-minded championship of either party. The Justice is sensible, humane, fatuous, and ineffectual, while Sir John alternates between exuberant wit and offensive buffoonery. The flesh retains much subversive attractiveness, but the authority of the judge cannot be lightly dismissed, as it is in an *Evening's Love*; for Sir John's carnival has (unlike Wildblood's) extended beyond venial sensuality to theft, grievous bodily harm, and the arrogant abuse of social privilege. Indeed, his carnival has overtones of quite serious subversion. Sir John turns 'Liberty and property', the slogan of the Revolution,[19] into a cry of carnival freedom (III. ii. 67–8); but perhaps we should listen more closely to his envy, expressed in the same speech, for the absolute power of Louis XIV (l. 65). This is the true image of desire without the regulating inhibition of justice. Indeed the Blue Posts, where the night on the town starts, was a favourite Jacobite tavern, and had been 'the nerve centre' of the recent plot to assassinate William III.[20]

The unresolved conflict between order and carnality recurs throughout the play, and Vanbrugh draws obvious analogies between the mutiny of Sir John's flesh and that of his wife's. At the end of his revels, his path crosses that of

---

[19] *Sir John Vanbrugh: Four Comedies*, ed. Cordner, 19–20.

[20] Jane Garrett, *The Triumphs of Providence: The Assassination Plot, 1696* (Cambridge, 1980), 121. See also pp. 41, 124.

Lady Brute, who is pursuing her own forbidden course in the guise of a prostitute; and, when he returns home, he smears his filth and (significantly) blood over her, identifying her carnal mutiny with his, and indicating that her attempts to free herself from a debauched and intolerable husband ironically lessen the distance between them and destroy her authority to condemn him. The distance is lessened still further in the revised version of Sir John's revelry, where he confronts the Justice in the guise not of a parson but of his own wife.[21]

Predictably, prohibited desires resist translation into language: secrecy is an urgent preoccupation,[22] and when Lady Brute admits to Bellinda that she is on the brink of adultery, she cannot utter the word, contenting herself with the evasive obliquity of 'you know what' (III. iii. 133). But the relationship between desire and language is as perplexed and unstable as that between desire and justice, for language is never permitted to convey a clear, objective morality. When Lady Brute shrugs aside the biblical injunction to return good for evil by saying that there 'may be a mistake in the translation' (I. i. 96), biblical authority certainly contradicts and condemns the sophistries with which she is edging towards acceptance of adultery, but her argument reminds us that even the sacred text is transmitted to us by the mediation of fallible and disagreeing humans, and its capacity to control and transform human action is thereby diminished. As in *The Relapse*, the language of religion is the language of men. We are a long way from the direct transmission of divine utterance to human capacities displayed when Jupiter places the inscribed tablet in the breast of the sleeping Posthumus, and indeed Vanbrugh repeatedly emphasizes the deafness of the flesh to the restraining word: 'women will do more for revenge than they'll do for the gospel' (II. i. 301–2). As Rasor recognizes, the texts that govern this milieu are of a less sacred nature: 'cuckoldom in folio is newly printed, and matrimony in quarto is just going into the press. Will you buy any books, Madamoiselle?' (V. iii. 47–9). Nor is an unambiguous language of morality to be expected in a play whose dialogue so repeatedly alternates between English and French, withholding even the most elementary of linguistic norms.

Attempts to impose formal linguistic order on the ambiguities of experience constantly fail. *Argument* and *reason* are prominent words,[23] and episodes of disputation and reasoning are frequent. But reason is invariably weaker than desire, and persuasive sophistry is defeated not by stronger argument but simply by inarticulate rejection or panic-stricken flight. Constant's seductive 'sophistry . . . puzzles, but don't convince' Lady Brute (III. i. 381–2), and when he goes on to urge that secrecy is sufficient to prevent the 'injury'

---

[21] For the circumstances of the revision, see *Four Comedies*, ed. Cordner, 247–8.

[22] II. i. 273–8; III. i. 344–50, 437–8; IV. iv. 152–3.

[23] For *reason*, see I. ii. 163–71; III. i. 376, 381–2, iii. 109; IV. iv. 184; V. ii. 109, iii. 128, iv. 28, v. 93. For *argument*, see I. i. 60–1, 65–6; III. i. 348, 392, 440; IV. iv. 182.

and 'wrong' of adultery, she can only run away, claiming that 'A surer way to prevent it is to hear no more *arguments* in its behalf' (III. i. 437–40; italics added). For Constant is satisfying her own earlier demand that the dictates of reason be reconciled with the cravings of nature: 'Perhaps a good part of what I suffer from my husband may be a judgement upon me for my cruelty to my lover. Lord, with what pleasure could I indulge that thought, were there but a possibility of finding *arguments* to make it good' (I. i. 57–61; italics added).

As this speech indicates, Vanbrugh is not following the libertines in equating the demands of reason with those of instinct. Even Madamoiselle, Lady Fancyfull's maidservant, sees their conflict: 'my nature make me merry, my reason make me mad' (I. ii. 170–1). But the interdependence of mind and flesh means that the prohibitions of reason are obscurely formulated and imperfectly grasped. Its authority is as precarious as that of the Justice who examines Sir John, and indeed the unresolved clash of competing voices in the episode with the Justice provides a pattern which is constantly reproduced in the many episodes of disputation, which are always unresolved, and where the points scored by the opposing disputants can sometimes be surprisingly distributed: the more Sir John is outsmarted by Constant and Lady Brute in the closing stages of the play, for example, the more he acquires the wit to mock and deflate his tormentors. When Constant uses the threat of a challenge to cow him into acceptance of apparent cuckoldom, Sir John's complaisance is undignified, but he also pungently exposes the irrationality of a code which permits Constant to palliate the gross injury of cuckoldom with the further gross injury of a threat to the aggrieved husband's life. In the process, he gives the most explicit statement of the impotence and inconsequentiality of disputation: ' "I wear a sword." It may be a good answer at cross-purposes; but 'tis a damned one to a man in my whimsical circumstance' (V. ii. 97–9). As Cordner notes, cross-purposes is 'a game in which a ludicrous effect is produced by connecting questions and answers which have nothing to do with one another':[24] argument is reduced to the random exchange of *non sequiturs*.

In exposing the limits of authority and inconclusiveness of argument, Sir John also exposes the ambiguous moral status of experience, for his subversive power to turn earnest into jest reflects a widespread fascination with the contiguity and even interchangeability of these apparently incompatible categories of interpretation. Characters repeatedly see their actions as being on the boundaries of jest and earnest: when Lady Brute decides on her assignation in the Spring Garden, for example, the appointment is ''twixt jest and earnest' (III. iii. 138).[25] In isolation, an example such as this could be taken as an evasive palliation of clearly reprehensible conduct, but the unfolding of the play as a whole suggests that there is a genuine confusion between the two

---

[24] *Four Comedies*, ed. Cordner, 406.
[25] See also I. i. 100–1; II. i. 66–7, 177–9; IV. ii. 51–2; V. ii. 80–1, 110–16.

modes of judgement. For example, at the end of the play Lady Fancyfull attempts to estrange Heartfree and Bellinda by persuading each that the other
has a murky sexual past. Her deception is exposed by her penitent accomplice
Rasor, who in his denunciation claims that he fell to the blandishments of
Lady Fancyfull and Madamoiselle as Adam did to those of Eve and the serpent (V. v. 191–206). This image of the Fall forms a climax to all the previous
imagery of triumphant and rebellious flesh, deriving it from the event that
first contaminated human nature with the principle of carnality, so that all the
manifold and petty transgressions of the body are traced back to the single
grand archetype from which they flow. Yet the universal response to the exposure of Lady Fancyfull as the tempting serpent is laughter: if this image
provides the climax to the persistent emphasis on unruly flesh, it also provides
the climax to the persistent association between the flesh and play, sport, and
jest, and there can be no greater blending of jest and earnest than to make the
Fall itself an object of comic merriment.

A far less provocative and iconoclastic passage, however, provides an
equally complex interplay of playful and serious. If Bellinda and Lady Brute
are insensitive to the claims of sacred texts, they are acutely aware of the problems of responding to plays, and devote some time to discussing a vexing
dilemma: should a lady of good character retain a serious expression during
dirty jokes in sex comedies? As Bellinda complains, 'laugh we must not,
though our stays burst for't, because that's telling truth, and owning we understand the jest. And to look serious is so dull, when the whole house is a-
laughing' (III. iii. 80–3). The differentiation of jest and earnest could scarcely
be more arbitrary, for the very bawdiness that creates the humour also pro-
hibits the laughter. Here, the claims of the serious become capricious and
irrational, and it is fitting that the claims of social decorum upon the flesh
should in this passage receive complementary and parallel treatment: in the
image of the body swelling with suppressed laughter to the point of bursting
the stays, Vanbrugh comically literalizes the ever-present conflict between the
flesh and regulating decorum, and creates a situation in which the restraints of
the serious and the decorous have no more authority than that of local
convention. The conflict between desire and prohibition is, indeed, the more
troublesome and perplexed because prohibition can at times have no greater
authority than that of convention: of, in Constant's phrase, 'the humour of
the country' (III. i. 371–2). As Constant points out, Dutch women are permitted a freedom and informality of conduct that is foreign to English norms
(III. i. 374–6). But he uses this disparity of convention to propound a total
moral relativism, in which chastity itself becomes a mere prescription of custom, and it is here clear that he is elaborating a disingenuous sophistry that
pushes the evidence beyond its permissible limits. But it is not clear where
those limits are, for the boundaries between local convention and absolute
morality are troublingly obscure.

The need for some degree of social organization is illustrated by the conduct of Lady Fancyfull, whose extreme of egocentric desire leads to a stultifying lack of assimilation into community (she finds the conduct and impact of others 'strange'),[26] and to impossible fantasies of release from social constraint, such as her dream of being queen of the moon. But she also demonstrates that social consciousness is a dim and flickering faculty. For, although she represents an absurd extreme of antisocial self-indulgence, she is an extreme to which others move: for example, Lady Brute's increasing vulnerability to temptation creates an increasing vulnerability to Lady Fancyfull's prying malice, as she increasingly approximates to Lady Fancyfull's example. And, as Lady Fancyfull's influence spreads, so does the use of what had initially been her pet word, *strange*, its dissemination emphasizing the increasing tension between the characters' desires and the regulating norms of society: the Justice finds Sir John 'a strange man' (IV. iii. 45), and Bellinda finds in the prospect of sexual experience an unsettling disturbance of the known, speculating that 'it must feel very strange to go to bed to a man' (V. v. 7–8).[27] Appropriately, Lady Fancyfull's concluding achievement is to create estrangement between Bellinda and Heartfree, persuading Bellinda that Heartfree already has a wife, and Heartfree that Bellinda already has a child. Appropriately, too, the play concludes with the expulsion of the agent of alienation and her alien servant. But it is quite clear that the formal expulsion of the stranger has not exorcized all the disruptive and socially intractable elements of human nature. Lady Fancyfull's lies found a depressingly rapid answering chord in the minds of Bellinda and Heartfree, and their easy mistrust of each other emphasizes the uncertain future that stretches beyond any marriage.

Regrettably, all Vanbrugh's other completed comedies were adaptations, and only one, *The Confederacy* (1705), is a substantially creative adaptation. Between the first performances of *The Relapse* and *The Provoked Wife* came that of *Æsop* (PC, December 1696), based on a play by Boursault. It has a sketchy romantic plot (Learchus tries to marry his daughter to the ugly Æsop, but Æsop finally unites her with her true love), but this is merely a frame for a series of self-contained episodes in which Æsop meets foolish characters and tells them appropriately instructive fables. One consistent modification is that Vanbrugh regularly expands or invents images of the disordered home. In transforming the extravagant bourgeoise Albione into Mrs Forge-Will, for example, he emphasizes her destruction of the marital home: there is nothing in Boursault equivalent to 'from the Moment I set foot in his House, bless me,

---

[26] Bellinda is the first (and last) person to use the word (I. i. 167; V. v. 213), but it is then prominently associated with Lady Fancyfull (I. i. 52, 103; II. i. 1, 28, ii. 105; IV. iv. 229); in the last usage, Lady Fancyfull and Madamoiselle appear as 'strangers' to disturb the illicit trust of Lady Brute and Constant.

[27] The related word *barbarous* is shared between Lady Brute, who twice applies it to Sir John (I. i. 84, 152), and Lady Fancyfull, who applies it to her cold (II. ii. 68).

what a Change was there' (IV, p. 43), and the curt 'j'ai presque vendu tout' (IV, p. 81) becomes a detailed portrayal of the dismantling of the home: 'his Creditors plunder'd my House. But what pity it was to see Fellows with dirty Shooes, come into my best Rooms, and touch my Hangings with their filthy Fingers' (IV, p. 44). Vanbrugh's main addition to Boursault is an explicit negation of all civilized habitation, 'Sir *Polidorus Hogstye*, of *Beast-Hall*, in *Swine County*' (IV, p. 47), and the encounters with domestic delinquents conclude with a usually pointless injunction, or resolution, to go home.[28]

Part II of *Æsop* (PC, March 1697) is a disconnected series of satirical portraits, one butt being Betterton's company, but Vanbrugh returned to the disintegrating home in adapting Dancourt's *La Maison de Campagne* as *The Country House* (PC, by January 1698). The plays deal with a husband (M. Bernard/Mr Barnard) browbeaten into buying a country house, the upkeep of which is ruining him. He first gets rid of his wife's parasitic guests by pretending that the house is a mere inn, of which he is the keeper, and at the end he unites his daughter with the hero only on condition that the hero take the house off his hands. Characteristically, Vanbrugh amplifies the concluding sense of domestic disintegration. There is no promise that Mr Barnard will be reconciled with the gentlemen who rejected him on discovering his apparent tradesmanly status, and at the end Barnard hopes that, having disburdened himself of his son, daughter, and house, he can get rid of his wife into the bargain. Vanbrugh's adaptation of Fletcher's *The Pilgrim* (PC, April 1700), incorporating Dryden's Secular Masque, is, however, a straightforward drama of dislocation and relocation, of flight from the city to the forest and back. The wandering gentleman Pedro, the Pilgrim, has lost his sense of social identity ('I want myself. . . . *I seek myself and am but my self's shadow*', I, p. 101),[29] and at the end of the play the gentleman-outlaw Roderigo seeks reintegration into the community. This is the social morality of *Love's Last Shift*, and indeed Vanbrugh's chief addition is to emotionalize the outlaw's final penitence, under the clear influence of Cibber's Loveless.

One consequence of the mini-resurgence of sex comedy was that Durfey returned to the genre in two of his most complex plays, which at once enforce and implicitly criticize traditional sexual codes. He had already provided a fairly straightforward critique of sex comedy in *A New Opera, call'd Cinthia and Endimion* (PC, December 1696), a pale imitation of *Amphitryon*, in which the Olympians live as mortals for a month, creating whimsical conflations of mythic and everyday figures: satyrs, for example, become libertine gentlemen who seize the women of their social inferiors, prompting the shepherds to rebellious republicanism. A concluding apotheosis elevates the gods above imperfection, Jupiter and Juno descend in matrimonial glory, and the opera concludes with praise of William III. Stuart libertinism is linked to

[28] II, p. 31; III, p. 37; IV, pp. 45, 49.   [29] Cf. Fletcher, *The Pilgrim*, I. ii. 159–64.

Stuart bad government, and both are swept away by the new order. The relationship between authority and morality is, however, far less tidy in Durfey's next two straight comedies. As its title suggests, *The Intrigues at Versailles* (LIF, May 1697) portrays the infidelities and adulteries of the French nobility, tactfully transferring to an alien culture and political system conduct that had until recently been portrayed as the essence of London life. The most original aspect of the play, however, is its emphasis on role-reversal, both within the plot and in the casting. When Durfey's *The Marriage-Hater Match'd* had been published, it had carried a commendatory letter from Charles Gildon debunking Southerne's *The Wives' Excuse*, but here Durfey nevertheless borrows one of Southerne's tricks, in that he portrays characters discussing how to write the play in which they are in fact appearing. In *The Wives' Excuse*, the author-within-the-play, trying (among other things) to make it move towards his union with Anne Bracegirdle, is a plausible projection of Southerne himself. In Durfey's play, two women and a man in female guise try to take intellectual possession of a man's play: a far more ingenious idea. One of the women, the 'Poetical' Duchess de Sanserre (Dramatis Personae), is indeed played by Bracegirdle. The ladies' attempts at authorship are, appropriately, halted by an intruding husband, just as the scenario reaches his cuckolding, and, although the infidelities are in fact accomplished, the play has an ending that the ladies do not foresee. The Duchess is exposed by the promiscuous, volatile, and irascible Madam de Vandosme (Barry) as an adulteress, and exposed—significantly—by her *writing*, for Vandosme has acquired one of her love-letters, and gives it to the Duke. Announcing herself 'struck . . . dumb' and unable to 'speak a word' (v, p. 56), the Duchess leaves the stage for the last time to endure without remission the tyranny of a vengeful husband. In the preliminaries to the exposure, Vandosme had attempted to give herself an appearance of respectability by ostentatiously reading from a penitential book, but the role which the public act of reading supports is destroyed by the ruthless revelations of a former lover.

Through the tension between male and female authorship (and authority), Durfey once again highlights the anomalous discrepancies in the standards by which the sexual conduct of the two sexes is judged. Although the episode in which the women try to establish imaginative control over the play is in itself brief, it grows out of and emphasizes a more pervasive disordering in the dramatic expression of sexual roles and sexual standards. There is a great deal of cross-dressing. The Count de Tonnerre spends the play dressed as a woman in order to evade the consequences of that pre-eminently virile act, the killing of an opponent in a duel. The Duke de Sanserre disguises himself in his wife's night-clothes in an attempt to catch her lover, and the Duchess and Lady Brissac disguise themselves as men. Seeing his wife (Mrs Bowman dressed as a man) with Count Tonnerre (Bowman dressed as a woman), the Count de Brissac is jealous, not because he recognizes his wife but because he does not:

he lusts after the false woman and envies the false man who is with her (II, pp. 21–2). Had the pair been dressed according to their sex, the Count's moral reaction would have been very different, and the convolutions of this incident nicely expose the intricate anomalies implicit in the double standard.

If the characters' cross-dressing deranges customary standards of sexual judgement, the derangement is amplified by the extraordinary casting of the female roles. In the epilogue, Elizabeth Barry emphasizes that she has deserted her stock-in-trade of passionate heroines and civil wantons to play a she-devil, and it is indeed without precedent that Barry should develop a violently eccentric attraction towards Cave Underhill, who specialized in ungainly and sometimes menacing comic figures, such as Sir Sampson Legend. Still more extraordinary is the treatment of Anne Bracegirdle. Although she had played non-virginal roles in some previous comedies,[30] there is no precedent for the climactic humiliation, in which she is morally exposed by Elizabeth Barry. This reverses the normal contrast between the chaste Bracegirdle and lustful Barry, as does the Duke de Sanserre's reaction to the exposure of his wife's infidelity: briefly posing the question of whether the married or unmarried whore (Bracegirdle or Barry) is the greater strumpet, he unhesitatingly nominates the former (V, p. 56).[31] The morality of the comparison is murky enough, but theatrically it is quite wrong: by now, Barry is the greater strumpet virtually by birthright. As with Brissac's response to his cross-dressed wife and cuckolder, perception of the act cannot be isolated from perception of the role, and judgements which we should wish to be absolute are insidiously contaminated and conditioned by the theatrical circumstances in which they are made. In the end, the 'Poetical' Duchess is convicted of moral transgression because she has failed to write the play herself; to write her life and the terms on which it is judged. She is one of the many heroines of the period who cannot control the narratives of their existence, and whose linguistic vulnerability makes them vulnerable also to alien and oppressive rituals of justice.

Durfey's *The Campaigners* (PC, June 1698) appeared after Collier's *A Short View of the Immorality, and Profaneness of the English Stage*, and accordingly contained a song lampooning Collier's Jacobitism, and was subsequently published with a preface asserting the moral purity of the Durfey

---

[30] Lucia in *The Squire of Alsatia* and Phoebe in *The Marriage-Hater Match'd* are vulnerable victims of seduction. Lady Trickitt in *The Maid's Last Prayer* is a whore of quality, a witty libertine who survives with her control and self-possession intact.

[31] For a discussion of the Barry–Bracegirdle partnership see Howe, *The First English Actresses*, 156–62. Lustful women were by no means Barry's only line, but they were certainly, by this stage of her career, a speciality: e.g. Dorinda in *Greenwich-Park*, Cassandra in *Cleomenes*, Lady Malepert, Lady Touchwood, and Mrs Frail. But several of her other parts have some strong dimension of temptation or contamination: Almeyda in *Don Sebastian*, Alcmena in *Amphitryon*, Mrs Friendall in *The Wives' Excuse*, Isabella in *The Fatal Marriage*, Lady Brute. Helga Drougge discusses Southerne's exploitation of Barry's tragic talents in his comedies ('Love, Death, and Mrs. Barry in Thomas Southerne's Plays', *Comparative Drama*, 27 (1993), 408–25).

canon. But, as in his previous play, Durfey was concerned both to enforce traditional morality and to criticize its underlying conventions. He portrays a good-natured hero, Colonel Dorange, who is nevertheless guilty of two deplorably immoral actions: seducing (indeed virtually raping) an innocent virgin, and purchasing the favours of his friend's wife. With some verve, Durfey sets about rescuing and dignifying the character of a hero whose actions at first glance seem more appropriate to a criminal than a gentleman. The conclusion is a genuine and wholly admirable conversion to marital virtue, but *en route* Durfey critically examines not only the moral conventions that permit a decent gentleman to act like a felon but also—more interestingly—those that underlie the gentleman's repudiation of his misdeeds. As usual, one of the main objects of attack is the double standard.

As in *The Intrigues at Versailles*, Durfey uses cross-dressing to suspend the customary distinctions of category and judgement which apply to the sexes. In the comic sub-plot, in which a fat and mercenary husband and wife struggle to assert authority over each other, the wife at one point dons armour so as to look 'like the figure of St. *George* in the Sign' (III, p. 29) and terrorizes her husband, earning the title '*Tamerlana*' in the process (III, p. 30). (Sir Davy Dunce, we recall, had used the image of Tamerlane in attempting to assert authority over his wife.) More remarkably, Dorange deflowers the virtuous Angellica while disguised as a woman: as with the duellist Count Tonnerre, Durfey startlingly transposes peculiarly masculine actions and attributes into feminine trappings, dissociating them from easy and automatic justification by male prerogative. Nevertheless, cross-dressing between sexes is less insistently common than in Durfey's previous comedy, for he now adds another, complementary, species of cross-dressing: that between social classes. The former species raises questions about the prerogatives of the man; the latter, about those of the gentleman. Like many better known comedies, *The Campaigners* opens by displaying two genteelly clad characters discussing their sexual affairs. Here, however, the characters are footmen (another debt to *The Wives' Excuse*). The confusion between servant and gentleman is then enhanced when Dorange is mistaken for one of the footmen, and thereafter he encourages the impression that he is not a gentleman, jokingly allowing those who believe him a footman to continue in their mistake, and—since Angellica's uncle hates soldiers—pretending to him that he is a merchant. It does not occur to him that his two acts of sexual betrayal compromise his gentility far more thoroughly than his two saturnalian masquerades.

The merchant and the footman share a naked interest in profit (the footman being as eager for tips as the merchant is for trade), and Dorange's twin disguises emphasize a pervasive uniformity of mercenary motives beneath the distinctions of class. For example, the Marquise with whom Dorange commits adultery is a usurer's daughter, and she charges Dorange 100 pistoles for his pleasure, regarding him as 'a Chapman' (III, p. 27) engaged in an exchange of necessities. As in *The Richmond Heiress*, Durfey suggests that the mentality of institutionalized finance is fundamental to all human relationships, and he comes closer than any other male dramatist to Aphra Behn in portraying prostitution as the essential model of dealings between the sexes. The period in which Dorange is taken for a footman and a merchant is one in which his mercenary motives are frequently in keeping with his profiteering guise (so that there is a satiric aptness in the spectacle of the gentleman-footman receiving tips), and his final reform coincides with the full resumption of his gentlemanly character. The difference from Behn is that Durfey does permit full, unambiguous reform, but previously Dorange has displayed a mercantile manipulativeness in his sexual attitudes that is all the uglier for its unconsciousness, and for his consequent readiness to condemn in others flaws that are deeply present in his own character.

In particular, his self-reproach after betraying Angellica with the Marquise is a fine combination of moral feeling and financial calculation: 'I have left now the fair *Angellica*, half dead with doubts; nay, and two thousand pound a year in *Posse*, to give a hundred Pistoles to a Jilt for one nights Lodging' (V, p. 52). He then becomes obsessed with recovering his money from the Marquise, even considering force, though he is nevertheless quite ready to censure her as 'mercenary' (V, p. 52). When the Marquise's husband unexpectedly returns, Dorange at first has no thought of gentlemanly discretion, wishing instead to stay and force his money out of his cuckold, and although he does take the customary course of hiding in the closet, he quickly declares himself from behind the door to his as yet unrecognized cuckold: 'First then, as I am a Gentleman, which let him assure himself I am, I am utterly ignorant of his Name or Quality, nor had I ever been familiar with the Lady, but by her consent and invitation. . . . I had the pleasure of her Company, and she the benefit of my Money' (V, p. 55). On discovering that he has cuckolded his friend, he is overcome with shame, and the two men engage in a self-congratulatory bout of mutual understanding that gives an unusually detailed analysis of the workings of the double standard, for the cuckold and cuckolder are united by a shared set of masculine axioms and values in which the woman cannot participate. The Marquis is perfectly satisfied by Dorange's argument that 'the temptation [was] too strong to be refused by human frailty,' conceding that 'I should have done de same my self' (V, p. 56). And, in proof of his 'honour and amity,' he returns 99 of the 100 pistoles, reserving only one for his wife: 'I never give my wench more,' he says (V, p. 57). As Dorange smilingly takes the purse, the Marquise states her case with some force and dignity: 'niggardly Sir, that think you can give too much for a Lady's favour, and for a petty summ can blast her honour, take this hearty Curse' (V, p. 57). But her case is neither answered nor noticed, and the adulteress is packed off to a convent by a husband who regards male adultery as venial and physiologically inevitable.

Immediately after his encounter with the Marquise's wronged husband, Dorange is confronted with Angellica's wronged brother, Don Leon, who duels with him in an attempt to secure 'Justice' (v, p. 57) for his sister. But, when Dorange disarms him and restores his sword, Leon decides that honour is satisfied: ' "No, were she dear as my Soul, as she's my Sister, I wou'd not fight again, thou brave young man; this honour has regain'd her honour lost, and fix'd me for thy Brother." *They embrace*' (v, p. 58). One wonders whether Angellica, with her illegitimate infant son, would regard the restoration of a sword to her brother as having any bearing or impact on her plight. Again, shared male values—manifested in the embrace—exclude the sensations and interests of the woman. Completion of the duel does, however, leave Dorange both able and willing to redress Angellica's wrongs, and he now surmounts his earlier avarice, being content to leave Angellica in control of her estate (v, p. 59). Apart from the Marquise there are no nagging loose ends, as there are in many of Durfey's other plays. But, prior to the happy ending, there is a skilful exposure of the insensitivity and greed with which even fundamentally decent men habitually treat women, and which underlie a male code of honour that takes no account of women's sensibilities. And, although the duel culminates in Dorange's genuine reform, there remains a remarkable disconnection between the masculine ritual and the feminine problem which occasions it. (Perhaps the most absurd ritual of male bonding occurs in the first meeting of the Marquis and Dorange. Though they had been on opposing sides in the recent war, each politely insists that his own side had lost (i, pp. 6–8).)

The problems of sexual authority are more farcically portrayed in the marriage of Angellica's fat and mercenary uncle and aunt, Min Heer Tomas (a merchant) and Anniky. Both see Angellica as a source of profit, Tomas scheming to gain £3,000 by selling her in marriage to the President of the Council of Trade. The competitive greed of the couple results in the second of the two instances of cross-dressing, in which Anniky counterbalances Dorange's act of sexual banditry by one of armed robbery, dressing in armour and browbeating her husband into surrendering the £3,000 bond. Tomas's brooding schemes to recover the money from his wife provide a telling parallel to Dorange's later schemes to recover his money from the Marquise, and his eventual triumph produces one of the most ingeniously satirical critiques of male authority in all Restoration drama. Recalling that Anniky has a phobia of monkeys, Tomas borrows one and terrorizes her with it, with the result that male prerogative literally rests upon simian aggression. In a scene of mock judicial ritual, Tomas acts as prosecuting counsel, with the defecating monkey sitting in his lap as judge: 'Now lookee, tho my Friend Pug here asks ye no questions, 'tis not egh for want of copious capacity, but to egh ease himself, and therefore leaves ye wholly to my examination, upon which he will chatter his judgment,——come, what have you to say for your self,—what

You are a Heteroclite I suppose now?' (IV, p. 48). Earlier, Tomas and Anniky had vigorously disputed whether or not she was a 'Heteroclite' (irregularly declined noun) (II, pp. 14–15), though neither understood the term. Now, still uncomprehending, the husband fixes his wife in the condition of a linguistic anomaly. But the basis of his verbal and judicial authority is the 'chatter' and 'judgment' of a monkey. Aphra Behn would have been envious.

The next new comedy after *The Campaigners* was the first work of an author who did not disdain minor plagiarisms from Durfey, and who shared his distaste for the social and linguistic deprivations of women: George Farquhar, whose *Love and a Bottle* was staged by the Patent Company in December 1698.[32] But, whereas Durfey was the last practitioner of Carolean sex comedy, Farquhar (born, probably, in 1677) was the first major dramatist for whom the premières of *The Country-Wife* and *The Man of Mode* belonged to another age. He was ready enough to portray male sexuality with rough humour, but any conquests belong to the characters' pasts, and his plays emphasize the frustration and (generally) the reform of the lustful male: like Cibber, he depicts the making of the gentleman, portraying this as the stabilization of the physically and morally dislocated. At the beginning of *Love and a Bottle*, for example, the libertine Roebuck arrives in London from Ireland, 'a stranger' (I. i. 58), penniless and dislocated. He soon realizes that he has been followed by the mother of his bastard, whom he has been trying to escape, but only much later does he realize that he has been shadowed by another 'poor Wanderer' (III. i. 21), the lovesick Leanthe, who eventually stabilizes his morally and socially uprooted existence.

With this trio of wanderers, Farquhar began as he was to continue; for, from Roebuck to the vagabond gentlemen of *The Beaux Stratagem*, his heroes are initially unfixed in place (and often in principles). His plays, however, depict a movement towards stability, an acquisition of estate and security that is often both reward and symbol of moral fixity, and they consequently differ from Southerne's and Vanbrugh's comedies of irremediable displacement. But they also differ from the reform comedies of Cibber, whose penitent protagonists justify their right to a pre-existent home and rank by conforming to the traditional definitions of the gentleman. Only in *The Twin-Rivals* does a displaced Farquhar hero recover an existing ancestral heritage (though the play nevertheless attacks the rationale of inherited rank). By contrast, many of his heroes gain new estates as the consequence of moral maturity, creating a new conjunction of rank and merit rather than vindicating the moral basis of an existing hierarchy. Frequently (as in Roebuck's case) the estate comes from the woman who induces the moral change, and Farquhar's chief contribution to the championship of women is to make them the sources of property and moral influence in a nominally patriarchal society (the real name of

---

[32] Lurewell in *The Constant Couple* is based on Madam Fickle, and Sylvia's trial for rape in *The Recruiting Officer* recalls that of Philippa in *The Royalist*.

Lurewell, one of the heroines of *The Constant Couple*, turns out to be Manly). In *The Beaux Stratagem* it is Lady Bountiful who discharges the gentry's responsibilities to tenants, while her son drinks and hunts. In *The Twin-Rivals* Hermes Wou'dbe, heir to his father's estate and virtues, reaches a point of destitution where the only prospect of security is the estate which his beloved Constance offers to share with him, and she indeed materially assists the recovery of his ancestral fortunes. As her name suggests, she is a principle of stability in a treacherous world: a principle whose value is declared in the titles of two of Farquhar's other plays, *The Constant Couple* and *The Inconstant*.

Farquhar is thus acutely concerned with the anomalies and inequities of the woman's position as an unacknowledged moral centre in a world whose systems of authority are controlled by the less stable and principled male. Consequently, like many other dramatists, he emphasizes women's exclusion from linguistic and judicial power. They may become dupes of the romantic or heroic fantasies of literature, as did Lurewell in *The Constant Couple*, seduced while her head was full of *Cassandra*.[33] In *Love and a Bottle*, the wandering libertine Roebuck quotes from Dryden's heroic plays, allusively identifying his sexual exploits with the military conquests of Maximin but also inadvertently likening himself to the absurd poetaster Lyrick, who bolsters his courage by reciting Almanzor's '*I alone am King of Me*' (III. ii. 204).[34] Through the character of Lyrick, Farquhar follows the lead of Southerne and Durfey in pitting the designs of the poet within the play against the outcome of the play itself, for Lyrick represents a contriving agency less compassionate to the female lot than Farquhar himself. At one point, he discourses condescendingly on the appropriateness of poetry for giving 'Instructions' to women, who require something easier than the complex and severe discourse of a sermon (IV. ii. 105–13), and he heartlessly uses the fallen woman Trudge as a tool for his own enrichment, gaining £100 by apparently securing her as a bride for the foolish Mockmode, who believes her to be the heiress Lucinda, and then extorting a further £500 in order to release him from the fraudulent match. In Lyrick's proposed drama, the fallen woman is a contemptible cipher to be used for male advantage, but Farquhar is more humane, and the £500 goes to Trudge herself.

Early in the play, the virtuous Lucinda stands bewildered on the stage, surprised at the absence of her beloved Lovewell, who must have 'miss'd us for want of the Sign' (I. i. 124). Her isolation exposes her to the attentions of Roebuck, who sees her not only as a passive object of his lust but as a passive sign for his decoding: 'You are a sort of Dream I wou'd fain be reading: I'm a very good interpreter' (I. i. 142–3). Later, when a forged letter causes Lovewell to mistrust Lucinda, she loses control even of her name: as he reads

---

[33] Cf. *Love and a Bottle*, III. i. 83–6.   [34] *The Conquest of Granada*, Part I, I. i. 206.

her apparent signature, her name ceases to individuate her, becoming a sign controlled by him, expressing his atavistic male contempt for womankind: '*L, U, C, I, N, D, A*; that spells Woman. 'Twas never written so plain before' (IV. iii. 90–1). Then, believing he has decisive proof of her infidelity, he assumes that inevitable concomitant of male linguistic power, male judicial authority, describing himself as both 'Accuser' and 'Judge' (IV. iv. 38).

At this stage, the only challenge to the judicial authority of the male comes from the judge's wife with whom Roebuck makes an assignation, who describes her husband's sexual inadequacy in imagery of handwriting and proposes as password for the assignation the name of that pre-eminent text of legal authority, '*Cook upon Littleton*' (IV. iii. 43). But Lovewell does eventually renounce the role of judge for that of guilty criminal (V. iii. 92–3), and the judicial downgrading of the male culminates when Mockmode announces his apparent marriage to Lucinda with the question 'Bring in the Jury there.——Guilty or not Guilty?' (V. iii. 139), only to have the question thrown back at him by a triumphant Lovewell when the true identity of the bride is exposed (V. iii. 150). The improvised ritual of law, granting just acknowledgement to the rights and dignity of woman, recurred at the end of *The Beaux Stratagem*; but there the improvised ritual is more patently and polemically incompatible with the actual condition of law. Nevertheless, Farquhar portrays the fair judicial representation and regulation of individual life as an attainable possibility. For Vanbrugh, such regulation is biologically impossible; for Dryden, Wycherley, and Etherege, it is epistemologically impossible.

As its title and subtitle indicate, Farquhar's *The Constant Couple; or, A Trip to the Jubilee* (PC, November 1699) opposes normative domestic stability to directionless pursuit of the alien and the insignificant. Four of the central male figures are actually or potentially in transit, for the disbanded soldier Standard and the travelling gentleman Sir Harry Wildair have recently returned from Europe, and the bumpkinly Clincher brothers are lost in ignorant dreams of exotic voyages. Of the other male characters, Alderman Smuggler complements the Clinchers' hunger for the exotic with his illicit importation of enemy produce, and the hypocritical Vizard cultivates a moral vagrancy, emulating the 'ranging' of an escaped lion (IV. ii. 101). To emphasize the contrast between aimlessness and fixity, the impoverished, uprooted hero who finds love and stability is called Colonel *Stand*ard;[35] and, to emphasize the woman's unhonoured role in ordering an ostensibly male world, the *femme fatale* Lurewell is finally identified as Standard's long-lost love, who has been punishing all mankind for his apparent seduction and rejection of her. The other hero, Sir Harry Wildair, resembles Standard in being a recently returned traveller, though (as he offensively stresses) he has the security of £8,000 per annum. But Sir Harry's income is the only solid token of his social

---

[35] A false but popular etymology associated *standard* with *stand* (OED).

status: we learn nothing about his estate or ancestry, and he spends the play in constant motion, sauntering between two houses that do not belong to him and misinterpreting the nature of each: Vizard arranges a misunderstanding whereby Sir Harry mistakes Lady Darling and her daughter Angelica for bawd and whore, while they take him for a suitor of Angelica, and he is one of the many sexual predators clustering around Lurewell, ignorant that they themselves are the true dupes. Both houses are thus mistaken for territories of male mastery. Again, however, women are given the established ancestral status that Farquhar ignores in his presentation of the hero, and Lady Darling can reproach Sir Harry for insulting blood that has run pure for many generations (V. i. 222–3).

In the male world, however, ancestry is no guarantee of status and character, for the blood that runs with 'unsully'd Honour' (V. i. 223) in Lady Darling's veins also runs in the veins of Vizard, Smuggler, and the Clinchers— all her relatives. Among men, money rather than birth is the guarantee of status and control, and only Standard resists the prevailing outlook, refusing to prostitute himself by accepting Lurewell's fortune (I. ii. 67–9). Sir Harry attempts to buy Angelica, and diverts her footmen by throwing money when they attempt to prevent him assaulting her; and Smuggler, having defrauded Lurewell of her money, attempts to buy her with it, significantly attempting to stick a coin in his mouth and thereby associating the power of money with the other male power: that of the word. Control (including financial control) is regularly exerted through books and writing, for the book is Vizard's characteristic prop, Smuggler's villainy is neutralized only when he loses his pocket-book, and Sir Harry conducts his courtships with inappropriately heroic quotations from play-texts (whereas Smuggler has financed the production of an alternative printed authority, Collier's *Short View*, V. ii. 40–2).

One way in which Lurewell lives up to her real name of 'Manly' is by rivalling the men in verbal manipulativeness (which she shares with her prototype, Durfey's Madam Fickle): like Smuggler, for example, she has a pocket-book, in which she records her depredations from her suitors. But even Lurewell was seduced while under the influence of a man's book (La Calprenède's *Cassandra*), her seduction completed by Standard's 'Rhetorick' (III. iii. 222), and Angelica is initially more vulnerable, deploring 'The strict confinement on our Words' which women suffer (III. ii. 3), and half prepared to believe that the hackneyed hyperboles with which Sir Harry courts her are 'real' (III. ii. 53). It is, however, a measure of her moral stature that she repeatedly places him in a condition of linguistic embarrassment in which he 'dare not ask the Question,' 'cannot speak to her' (II. ii. 45, 49), resorts to evasion, and eventually takes refuge in the decent remoteness of French (V. i. 179–80).

The conclusion of the play brings a redistribution of authority. Clincher Senior, the extreme manifestation of gentle ancestry unaccompanied by gentle character, appropriately changes clothes with the plebeian Tom Errand, and subsequently turns up as Errand's equal in the classless 'Commonwealth' of Newgate prison (V. ii. 65). Smuggler is also consigned to Newgate (having been framed on a charge of stealing Lurewell's spoons), and at the end of the play is promised 'Justice' (V. iii. 256) for his genuine crimes. But it is noteworthy that he initially renders himself vulnerable when he is tricked into relinquishing his male control by disguising himself as a woman. There is also a general movement from dislocation to stability. The Clinchers are dissuaded from shaming their native land by foreign travel, and Sir Harry and Standard opt (with varying motives and feelings) for the settled condition of marriage. Standard's marriage to some extent formalizes the linguistic authority of the woman, for he and Lurewell recognize each other by means of a ring which Lurewell had given him twelve years before, which bears the inscription '*Love and Honour*' (III. iii. 236). As Mary Astell had already complained, the terminology of the heroic texts is frequently perverted by men to the dishonour and deception of women;[36] but here it is controlled by a woman, and brings Standard the social position that his exploits on the battlefield have failed to provide.

On a number of occasions, I have used the backward-looking social vision of Sir Robert Howard's *The Committee* as a standard against which to measure the more innovative attitudes of younger dramatists. Farquhar in particular invited such comparison, for in a slightly later comedy, *The Twin-Rivals* (1702), he actually introduces a loyal, dim-witted Irish servant called Teague, and treats him as a moral standard in a world which rings with disingenuous professions of service.[37] But there is a fundamental difference between the two Teagues; for, whereas Howard's exposed the vice and pretension of basely born upstarts, Farquhar's exposes those of the gentry themselves, calling into question the very system that his predecessor had vindicated. The play reduces the principle of hereditary rank and wealth to absurdity, for its action depends on the question of whether a good or evil twin emerged from the womb first, and the honest citizen Fairbank displays the traditional virtues of the gentry while lacking their heraldic recognition (III. ii. 219–21). *The Committee* is also recalled, perhaps more fortuitously, in *The Beaux Stratagem*, which resembles Howard's play in depicting the plight of two impoverished gentlemen (Aimwell and Archer). But the honest retainer has now disappeared, and Aimwell and Archer alternately act the equally false roles of lord and servant, swapping parts with each successive town that they visit. Fixed dispositions of social role can no longer be imaged in fixed

---

36 Astell complains that the 'venerable Names' of love and honour are 'wretchedly abus'd, and affixt to their direct contraries. . . . And how can she possibly detect the fallacy, who has no better Notion of either, but what she derives from Plays and Romances?' ([Mary Astell], *A Serious Proposal to the Ladies, for the Advancement of their True and Greatest Interest* (London, 1694), 37).

37 I. i. 155–6; II. iii. 20–2; III. i. 19, 34, 40, 48, 61, 80, 84, 92, 96, 124; IV. i. 112–13, 245.

relationships of geographic place, and even the real servant, Scrub, has a different household role ('Place', III. iii. 89) on every day of the week. The unstable roles of the two wandering, displaced strangers indicate that social place has become a shifting index of the shifting conditions of material fortune, symbolized by the eminently unfixed and portable chest containing £200, which they lug with them as the last surviving token of their rank; a token which, however, is duplicated and compromised by the £200 which the highwayman Gibbet likewise deposits in the inn where they are staying, just as their role as strangers is duplicated by the more obviously alien and predatory figures of the French Count Bellair, a prisoner of war, and the Irish-French priest Foigard.[38]

Farquhar's critique of social and sexual hierarchy is closely paralleled in the small, neglected *œuvre* of William Burnaby, the son (like Southerne) of a gentleman brewer, whose brief life was increasingly entangled in litigation and penury. Like Burnaby's two later London comedies, *The Reform'd Wife* (PC, March 1700) portrays a woman who, trapped in an unsatisfactory marriage, plays with fire, discovers the dangers, and decides to make the best of what she has. The heroines of the three plays are all in varying degrees flawed, but they are sympathetically portrayed, and are all married to tyrannical and incorrigible dolts. Preoccupation with marital inequity continued even in Burnaby's adaptation of *Twelfth Night*, *Love Betray'd* (LIF, January 1703), where Villaretta's (Olivia's) reluctance to marry the Duke springs not from attachment to a dead brother but hatred of a dead husband, which makes her fear a second term of slavery.

In view of Burnaby's mercantile background, it is not surprising that he should constantly mock the vacuous pride of the gentry and nobility, and their ignorant contempt for the tradesman. Aristocratic identity suffers a particularly notable disintegration in *The Modish Husband* (PC, *c.* January 1702), where Lord Promise changes clothes with a pimp, who struts foppishly in his borrowed finery (III, p. 310), whereas Promise is mistaken for a thief and soundly beaten. Burnaby's embroilment in litigation makes his repeated satire of the judicial system equally unsurprising: 'Justice only waits upon the poor, and a 1000 *l*. a year is Gallows proof,' says Sir Testy Dolt in *The Ladies Visiting-Day* (LIF, *c.* January 1701) (IV, p. 248). But the attack on arbitrary rank and oppressive justice transcends mere personal pique, and contributes to a serious critique of customary distributions of authority, particularly in the prescription of female roles. Burnaby's repeated imagery of politics and warfare—his doltish husbands tend to be keen amateur politicians—implies that male interests and activities dictate the terms in which life is described and analysed, and his women clearly believe this. As Villaretta and her confidante Emilia argue in *Love Betray'd*,

---

[38] For Foigard as stranger, see III. ii. 174; IV. i. 221–3. For Archer and Aimwell, see II. ii. 24; III. i. 51, 95, iii. 123; IV. i. 141, 151; V. iv. 36, 117.

VILL. Those that make Laws will always favour themselves. They have made their own Honour consist in Bravery, which is for their advantage; but ours to consist in Chastity, which is not for ours.

EM. If we had order'd things, it had been the Mens part to be Modest, Faithful, Reserved, and hating everything they desired, and ours to ha' done what we please.

(I, p. 352)

In *The Modish Husband* Lady Promise, rebelling against the double standard exploited by her philandering husband, similarly wishes to centre justice upon the woman's viewpoint: women must be 'Judges' of whether they have received 'just provocation,' and be empowered 'to do our selves justice' (III, pp. 308–9). Finally, indeed, the play does reject the double standard in favour of a more equal distribution of justice: '*The Husband's Folly justifies the Wives*' (V, p. 340); and it is interesting that the first of Burnaby's female rebels should be named Astrea.

The typical situation of women in Burnaby's plays is imprisonment: Astrea in *The Reform'd Wife* and Lady Dolt in *The Ladies Visiting-Day* both have husbands who oppress and confine them, and at the end of *The Modish Husband* Sir Lively Cringe, no longer believing that cuckolds are as fictitious as fairies, also resolves to imprison his wife (V, p. 336). Conversely, Freeman in *The Reform'd Wife* vindicates his name by being, as is repeatedly stressed, a traveller. But women who desire such mobility (necessary if they are to seek and gain desirable husbands) can normally only gain it by assuming male guise.[39] Cæsario in *Love Betray'd* is a particularly interesting case, for she is not Shakespeare's helplessly displaced victim but a determined, active woman who has voluntarily left home to seek a man she has already seen and fallen in love with. The place which befits her is not one prescribed by ancestry or role but one that she has freely elected and defined: 'The little Spot that holds him, *Laura*, is all the Liberty I ask; the World without it is a Prison' (I, p. 356). There is still obvious emotional passivity in this attitude (Burnaby's redefinition of femininity was limited) but place is nevertheless determined by subjective and relativistic choice rather than by fixed and natural social norms: it is the fatuous Sir Lively Cringe who regards his wife as the pliant creation of her surroundings, removing her from court because ''twas the place that corrupted her' (*Modish Husband*, V, p. 336). Burnaby emphasizes that ideals of female conduct vary from place to place (Italy is the worst place for a wife, England the best, *Love Betray'd*, I, p. 350), and in *The Modish Husband* Lady Promise has been betrayed into marital misery by marrying a lord for the sake of 'place' (I, p. 279); for the sake of a role prescribed by external convention.

Burnaby's conception of place as individually elected rather than socially prescribed is reflected in his constant contempt for an idle, irresponsible, and

---

[39] As do Fulvia in *The Ladies Visiting Day*, Camilla in *The Modish Husband*, Viola in *Love Betray'd*. Fulvia and Camilla are both names of classical viragos: Mark Antony's bellicose wife, and the Amazonian warrior of the *Aeneid*.

blindly class-conscious gentry. The insouciant definitions of gentlemanly conduct that in Etherege had debunked Christian systems of social morality are here turned against the gentry themselves: 'to keep ones word looks like a Tradesman. . . . And is as much below a Gentleman as paying ones Debts' (*Ladies Visiting-Day*, III, p. 236). In *The Ladies Visiting-Day* the foolish Saunter claims a genealogy that goes back before the conqueror; but the imagery with which he justifies his rank inadvertently suggests a world of dynamic motion, where the idle stasis of the gentleman is really inert dependence on the control and movement of others:

the World is like a Ship where the inferiour Wretches guide the Vessel, order the Sails, and handle the dirty Ropes, while Gentlemen are the Passengers that have no business but only to look on.

> For we have Wit enough we ne're imploy it,
> Let others rule the World while we enjoy it.

(I, p. 208)

The various elements Burnaby's critique of received ideas of place—social and sexual—combine most fully in the female fops of *The Reform'd Wife* and *The Ladies Visiting-Day*, the hypochondriac Lady Dainty and the foolish enthusiast for exotic fashions, Lady Lovetoy. (Their affinity was recognized by Cibber, who merged them when cobbling together *The Double Gallant* from the labours of Burnaby and Centlivre.) Both characters display an extreme pride of place and contempt for inferiors, both are stultifyingly static, and both are trapped by a limited and crippling notion of female identity. Lady Dainty boasts of diseases too genteel for the lower classes: health is a distressingly boisterous characteristic of the vulgar, as is *mobility*, for walking is the activity of peasants, and she admires 'the *Chinese* Nobility; who . . . contract the Feet of their Infant-Quality'. 'That, indeed,' says the more sensible Clarinda, 'is one step to take away the Trouble of moving at all, and make 'em live the Life of a Plant' (*The Reformed Wife*, III, p. 165). As in Saunter's ship image, the fixed role of the gentry becomes a passive dependence on the mobility of others: indeed, as Lady Dainty says to the doctor who fraudulently exploits her hypochondria, 'to live without you, is Sailing without a Compass' (II, p. 137). Even the xenophile Lady Lovetoy is a static character, relying on tradespeople to stuff her home with the frippery of countries she will never see. When Fulvia asks why she does not actually visit the countries she so much admires, she responds that travel is inappropriate for women: 'Alas! the Men have usurp'd all the Pleasures of Life, and made it not so decent for our Sex to Travel' (*The Ladies Visiting-Day*, II, p. 215). But Fulvia has no such scruples about trespassing on male territory, for she assumes male guise in order to challenge her prospective husband to a duel, and so contrives matters that she alone has a sword with a blade: a clear, not to say crudely symbolic, theft of male attributes (V, p. 257), all the clearer because her lover only gains access to her, and permission to marry her, because her guardian mistakenly believes him to be a eunuch.

But, despite her fascination with distant places, Lady Lovetoy crosses no boundaries. When her lover, Courtine, tricks her into marriage by posing as Prince Alexander of Muscovy, the point is not only that he plays on her love of the alien, but that he identifies himself with a place where husbands were notoriously tyrannical to their wives, and indeed Lady Lovetoy admires the 'Manly Grace' of the bewhiskered bogus barbarian, contrasting it with the 'Effeminacy' (II, p. 213) of English suitors. Lady Dainty's cultivation of sickness similarly combines stultifying ideals of gentility and femininity: ''tis betraying our Sex, not to be Sickly and Tender!' (*The Reform'd Wife*, II, p. 136), she exclaims. When Cibber combined the two female fops in *The Double Gallant*, his Lady Dainty offends against the stable social values that he habitually associates with the idea of home, even her hypochondria becoming a rejection of English mores, in that her squeamish horror of hearty meals is associated—in a detail not in Burnaby—with rejection of the 'home-bred' (IV, p. 60).[40] In taking over two of Burnaby's plays—half his slender output—Cibber constrained his characters within the very fixed values of place that Burnaby himself had so consistently and subtly destabilized.

The election and creation of private space is also a prime aim in *The Way of the World* (LIF, March 1700), where Congreve again portrays a heroine seeking to protect and control her identity in a world where the self risks being overwritten by demanding yet various and localized rules of place, such as Lady Wishfort's attempts to mould her daughter's sexual morals by denying her all sight and likeness of man until she reached womanhood (a psychological equivalent to Lady Plyant's regime of binding Sir Paul in bed). Even the family ceases to be an expression of fixed natural principles, for the genealogical complexities of the Wishfort clan turn it into an elaborate theoretical abstraction whose relationships are dimly grasped and never felt. Moreover, social status is itself insecure and contingent in a way that is unique in drama of the period. Lady Wishfort has total and arbitrary power to displace Foible from a location of genteel security into a landscape of poverty and squalor ('Out of my house, out of my house', V. i. 1), yet her own comfort and respectability exist perilously on the brink of ruin and scandal, and Fainall's threat to the order of her world once again dissolves the seeming certainties of established status into Congreve's favourite exemplification of formlessness, directionless voyaging: 'This, my Lady *Wishfort*, must be subscrib'd, or your Darling Daughter's turn'd a drift, like a Leaky hulk to Sink or Swim, as she and the Current of this Lewd Town can agree' (V. i. 441–4). This is the final, darkest, transformation of an image that had first appeared in the comparison of Araminta to a floating island, and had recurred in the restless

---

[40] The speaker is not Lady Dainty herself but a friend—who is, however, obviously supporting Lady Dainty's viewpoint. Cf. *The Reform'd Wife*, III, pp. 163–4.

voyaging of Ben Legend; an image that exposes the indeterminate flux beneath the seeming fixities of social value. To change place is to change everything.

Even the self is threatened by flux. Its discontinuity is comically caricatured in Petulant's ruse of dressing as a woman to call on himself, and retire in ostentatious disappointment on finding himself not at home (not in the right place), but it can also take more serious and troublesome forms. Lady Wishfort and the younger ladies brood on the changes wrought by time, Lady Wishfort painting herself to become a sign of the picture that signifies her younger self, but continuity of self is more insidiously threatened by discontinuity of memory. Witwoud's newly acquired character as a public purveyor of similitudes is sustained by a memory that can fail him and leave him floundering, and Waitwell holds forth with some intricacy on the shifts of identity and memory caused by his changes of role, both pretended (to Sir Rowland) and actual (to married man): 'it will be impossible I shou'd remember my self. . . . 'Tis enough to make any Man forget himself. . . . For now I remember me, I am married, and can't be my own Man again' (II. i. 554–61).

The Cibberian social vision, of a fixed social order that expresses and accommodates individual social instinct, has no validity here: all that can be created are local regulations that do not constrict or derange the individual's sense of self. As usual, the existing official regulations are useless, and the threat of investigating Mrs Fainall's sexual conduct 'in a publick Court' (V. i. 209) manifests yet again the persisting fascination with the moral and epistemological imprecision of judicial process, for the noisy and prurient public interest that Mrs Marwood so terrifyingly predicts has no proportion or relationship to the private griefs and frailties at the centre of the enquiry. Even scandal, however, has its own rules of place. At the trial, Mrs Fainall may become a Latinate jest 'against a *Rule* of Court, where there is no precedent for a Jest in any record; not even in *Dooms-day-Book*' (V. i. 215–17; first italics added), and Mrs Marwood then describes the migration of the news through different localities, classes, and accents 'into the Throats and Lungs of Hawkers, with Voices more Licentious than the loud *Flounder-man's*' (V. i. 232–4).

But, if scandal has many dialects, Mrs Fainall (like Otway's Lady Dunce) has no acceptable language of self-justification. She can only use the publicly sanctioned language in order to lie: 'I know my own Innocence, and dare stand a tryall' (V. i. 177–8). Those whom she is seeking to convince are never conclusively assured of her guilt, and Mirabell's concluding coup manipulates the law to conceal that which it cannot appropriately assess, when the deed in his black box protects her false façade with legal sanctions. Like many tragic heroines of the 1670s, Mrs Fainall concludes the play with her essence remote from public disclosure, but what was tragic isolation in them is welcome protection for her. Our sympathies are obviously with the deception, for the false plea of innocence has more merit than the intolerant truths of public censure, and indeed the value of truth has been consistently slippery, for, whenever it is invoked, the invocations tend to be self-cancelling. 'If I have not fretted my self till I am pale again,' Lady Wishfort cries as her carefully falsified features disintegrate, 'there's no Veracity in me' (III. i. 3–4); when Sir Wilfull proclaims his attachment to truth, it is with the drunkenly incoherent bawling of '*In vino veritas*' (IV. i. 409); and, after engaging Mirabell in a baffling guessing-game as to the nature of Petulant's greatest and least tolerable fault, Witwoud—a sham from head to toe—triumphantly reveals the answer: 'he never speaks Truth at all' (I. i. 340). Concern for truth is reduced to the habitual yet meaningless rehearsal of a verbal formula: a mere quirk of dialect.

Like the final protection of Mrs Fainall, the playful devaluation of truth suggests that human essence has no presence or importance in the visible fabric of social order: Millamant follows Angelica in seeking to avoid external control and possession of the self by hiding in evasion and inscrutability, to the point of refusing to disclose any continuity of self. As Mrs Marwood says, she is reluctant to 'appear bare fac'd' (III. i. 314) by admitting to a liking for Mirabell, and for her bewildered suitor her mercurial shifts of pose imply complete instability of place: 'A Fellow that lives in a Windmill, has not a more whimsical Dwelling than the Heart of a Man that is lodg'd in a Woman. There is no Point of the Compass to which they cannot turn, and by which they are not turn'd' (II. i. 493–7). One of the main points of the proviso scene is to establish agreed rules attaching to agreed places, such as the schedule of beverages permitted at Millamant's tea table. It also prescribes the local dialect of marriage, outlawing the 'Nauseous Cant' (IV. i. 198) of over-affectionate spouses. Millamant, formerly reluctant to 'appear bare fac'd' now has in the most literal sense to do so, renouncing all masks and washes. But the face in Congreve is never a sign of the inner self, and the provisos constitute protective shells of convention within which the lovers may, in Millamant's words, remain 'strange' (IV. i. 207) to each other. Their arbitrariness is emphasized when Mirabell's proscription of virtually all alcohol from Millamant's table is closely followed by Sir Wilfull's attack on the Mahometan 'Rules' (IV. i. 453) that proscribe alcohol altogether—an attack which suddenly transposes Mirabell's domestic and familiar regime into one that is exotic, alien, and unaccountable. For rules are by nature exotic and alien: in the proviso scene, as throughout Congreve's works, the regulations that define the legal or contractual limits of individual life provide no more analogy to the inner order of human character than do the walls and doors that define its physical limits. In both cases, all that can be desired is an adequate, uncompetitive, artificially defined living space. This is what Mirabell and Millamant achieve, and this is what Mrs Fainall gains by the contractual conveyance of her estate to Mirabell, which gives her some protection against her husband's greed and unscrupulousness. But in neither case can the individual be harmoniously assimilated into the social institution, in the traditional comic ending; for there can be no assimilation where there is no community of form.

Congreve was the least feminist of the great Restoration dramatists, though in one respect *The Way of the World* does provide a woman's-eye view of comic convention, in that the plight of Mrs Fainall presents the human aftermath of the standard comic ending whereby the fallen woman is married off to the dupe: her story begins where most comedies end. Surprisingly, however, although a productive trio of female dramatists did emerge in the last years of the century they achieved little rethinking of comedy on their own account, and indeed Mary Pix distinguished herself as a slavish upholder of male authority. She also, in sharp contrast to Congreve, stressed the essential compatibility of desire and legally prescribed order. In both *The Spanish Wives* (PC, August 1696) and *The Innocent Mistress* (LIF, June 1697), for example, she ultimately reveals that apparently forbidden private desires in fact have the sanction of law. In the former play, the wife of a tyrannically jealous Spanish nobleman is liberated for marriage to her true love, since the nobleman is ultimately judged to have abducted her illegally, but this legitimization of desire is counterbalanced in the other plot by a redirection of desire according to the demands of law, and the overall view of women's position is strikingly quiescent. The jealous nobleman, Moncada, is contrasted with a good-humoured and elderly Governor (referred to only by his title of authority), who trusts and allows freedom to his young and attractive wife. The debt to Terence's *Adelphi* is obvious but does not prepare us for the consequence, which is that the wife is exposed while about to commit adultery with a visiting English Colonel: a 'wondrous Stranger' (I, p. '13' [10]) appropriately named Peregrine. By the end of the play, the Governor has decided that his wife, having learned her lesson, can safely be trusted again, but the trust which he bestows is inevitably more sober and watchful. A number of striking and unexpected features stand out in this plot. In *The False Count*, Behn had portrayed with sorrow a society in which the language of authority had reflected and perpetuated the tyranny of the male; the title of Pix's nameless Governor testifies to his natural authority, which he enforces by conversing with his wife in baby-talk (something Behn would have abhorred). Moreover, the portrayal of the libertine Englishman as a disruptive stranger in the more regulated world of Spain remarkably reverses the prevailing evaluation of English sexual mores.

The Innocent Mistress similarly reconciles desire and social regulation. The law frees Sir Charles Beauclair from his forced marriage to a raucous and ugly philistine (since her first husband turns out to be still living) and enables him to marry the virtuous and sensitive Bellinda. In another plot, the city-heiress Arabella surmounts a tangle of legal malpractice in order to marry the man of her choice. And, in a very formulaic rake-reformed plot, Sir Francis Wildlove discovers that matrimony is what suits his nature best. Perhaps the most noteworthy feature of this play is its treatment of gentility, which Pix (a merchant tailor's wife) sees as derived from character and education rather than birth; thus the two servants who help Arabella are, polemically, given names denoting noble ancestry (Eugenia and Gentil). But, characteristically, Pix combines her modest levelling impulse with enthusiastic acceptance of female subordination: though one heroine assumes male guise in order to tame Sir Francis, she is quickly 'tir'd with wearing the Breeches' (IV, p. 30).

When considering Pix's *The Deceiver Deceived* for performance by the Patent Company, George Powell had decided to steal rather than to produce the play: *Imposture Defeated* (PC, September 1697) thus marks the zenith of his career as a plagiarist, and the aggrieved Pix's play was subsequently produced by Betterton's company in November–December 1697. In both, a rich man feigns blindness to avoid the expense of public office, only to find that his wife takes advantage of his supposed sightlessness by entertaining her lover. Whereas Pix's wife is the attractive, decent victim of a forced marriage, and still attached to her first and true love, Powell's is merely cuckolding her husband with a criminal. Powell adds a plot in which a gentleman who has gambled away his estate sells his soul to the Devil in order to recover his fortune, uses his magic power to marry the Duke's daughter, and manages to keep his soul into the bargain. Pacts with the Devil are an extreme form of trangression, though they are here allowed to uphold the right of both the man and the gentleman. But female transgression of a far more ordinary kind is less indulgently treated, for Powell's adulteress is consigned, unrepentant, to a nunnery, where she plans to spend the rest of her life cursing. Female sexuality and language can be contained only by externally imposed confinement. In Pix, by contrast, the wife accepts her lot, discovering the pain of guilt and the beauty of virtue: women are still subordinates, but at least they are intrinsically moral beings.

Pix's most assertive characteristic, her championship of the non-gentle classes, appears most fully in *The Beau Defeated* (LIF, March 1700) which concludes with a polemic defence of the citizen, '*less in Name*' than the nobility, but

> *of greater Power by far,*
> *Honours alone, but empty Scutcheons are;*
> *Mixt with their Coin, the Title sweetly sounds,*
> *No such Allay as Twenty Thousand Pounds.*

(V, p. 47)[41]

[41] For a good discussion of this play, see J. Douglas Canfield, 'Dramatic Shifts: Writing an Ideological History of Late Stuart Drama', *Restoration and 18th Century Theatre Research*, 2nd ser., 6/1 (1991), 1–9.

The speaker of this eulogy is the sensible citizen Mr Rich. His viewpoint is opposed by his foolish sister-in-law, Mrs Rich, who values titles and escutcheons above all else, preferring to 'be the beggarliest Countess in the Town, than the Widow of the richest Banker in *Europe*' (I, p. 2). First, she is taken in by pseudo-aristocrats; then, wrongly thinking his boorishness to be a witty pose, she marries a bumpkin of noble ancestry who has not bothered to take up his title. But the thing without the word is no better than the word without the thing, since the thing is itself without value. In a reversal of this plot, Lady Landsworth sheds her name and rank (gained through a forced and unhappy marriage) and makes 'trial' (IV, p. 34) of Younger Clerimont by posing as a prostitute; but he is sensible enough to see the personal through the role, and to read that 'sweet Innocence is writ in that dear face' (V, p. 43). Finally, Mrs Rich and her equally foolish niece, Lucinda, are also offered the chance of essential rather than nominal gentility, to be gained from advice, example, and education.

Mrs Pix may redefine the social expression of moral order, but the new expression is perfectly achieved, and women return from their forays into the unsanctioned—the false prostitute, the false gentlewoman—to assimilation into a comprehensive order. There is less possibility of assimilation, however, in two other women's comedies of this period. In Mary Manley's *The Lost Lover* (PC, March 1696), Olivia, a merchant's wife, virtuously rebuffs Wildman, the man she really loves, and a fallen woman (Belira) fails to prevent her seducer's marriage to the virtuous Marina. But, if morality is enforced, the mentality of the male enforcers is clearly deplored. The iniquity of the double standard which condemns Belira is extensively exposed, and even a woman's virtue can be turned against her, for Wildman at first crassly and coarsely misinterprets Olivia's rejection of him.[42]

Catherine Trotter's *Love at a Loss* (PC, November 1700) deals still more wide-rangingly with the social vulnerability of women. In the past, Lesbia has groundlessly suspected her true love, Grandfoy, and engaged herself to Beaumine, the suitor preferred by her mother, sealing the engagement with a contract written in blood. Although she never loved Beaumine much, he seduced her in a 'yielding Minute' (I, p. 4), and now evades her demands for marriage with a cheerful insouciance reminiscent of Sir Harry Wildair.[43] Although Lesbia and Grandfoy still love each other, Grandfoy being eager to marry her despite her lost virginity, Lesbia feels compelled to repair her dishonour with marriage to Beaumine, and entitled to marry Grandfoy only if Beaumine proves faithless. Accordingly, Grandfoy sets out to unite his loved

---

[42] Jacqueline Pearson gives an excellent account of the reversals of sexual stereotype in Belira's altercations with her seducer (*The Prostituted Muse*, 199).

[43] Beaumine, like Wildair, was acted by Robert Wilks. For the influence of Wilks's talents on the development of a new kind of comic hero, see Shirley Strum Kenny, 'Farquhar, Wilks, and Wildair; or, the Metamorphosis of the "Fine Gentleman" ', *Philological Quarterly*, 57 (1978), 46–65.

one with his rival, his conformity with social precept being emphasized by his recourse to judicial imagery: he will bring the lawless libertine within the confines of law (Beaumine disdains laws as 'Chains to our Wills', I, p. 6), subject his character to 'Tryal', and secure 'Justice' for Lesbia.[44] Yet again, we encounter the familiar figure of the noble rival, and yet again he fails to exemplify the ideal subordination of the personal to the social demonstrated by his forebears of the 1660s; for Grandfoy's self-sacrificing nobility consists of submission to a set of oppressive social conventions that conflict with his and Lesbia's true needs and characters. The tyranny of social convention, and the inadequacy of the judicial forms which encode it, are tellingly dramatized in the mock judicial ritual that concludes the play, in which the other characters act as a jury, casting votes to decide whom Lesbia should marry. One by one, the cast alternately side with true love or public morality, until the airy coquette Miranda gives the casting vote: 'for him that she loves least' (V, p. 55). And so Beaumine is chosen, and Lesbia proposes that her true love be in future 'a Stranger to us' (V, p. 55). The sentence is, apparently, rescinded— Grandfoy will remain a friend—and Beaumine promises, quite sincerely, to be a good husband. But there is no doubt that an externally sufficient redress, marriage of the wronged woman to a thoroughly reformed seducer, is one that fails to assuage the real wound, and when the pressure of public morality pushes the more appropriate partner towards the role of 'Stranger' it is the norms themselves that are under question, not the man whom they exclude.

The two complementary plots explore related problems. In one, the virtuous Lucilia has believed the clichéd rhetoric of the foppish Cleon, who claimed to be dying of love, and has consequently sent him letters expressing a regard she did not feel. Phillabell, her fiancé, discovers the letters, but she persuades him that the letters were forged by her governess, Lysetta. The Lesbia and Lucilia plots both portray a woman trapped by writing—the letters, the contract in blood—and the male manipulation of language. The other plot, featuring the coquettish Miranda and the solemn Constant, apparently shifts linguistic power to the woman (Miranda, for example, torments her admirer with parodic love poetry); but her equality of control is transient and illusory, and she ultimately has to regain her alienated lover with the feminine passivity of tears.

As usual, then, limitations of public justice are linked to limitations of language. And, as so often, these limitations are linked to those of knowledge itself, manifested in the general and largely vain desire to isolate Truth. Lesbia recovers too late from her 'unjust' suspicions of Grandfoy to discover that he is 'all Truth and Goodness' (I, pp. 3–4), and is now determined 'to try *Beaumine*'s Truth' (IV, p. 39); Phillabell and Beaumine are both led to doubt the 'Truth' of their mistresses (III, pp. 28–9), and Miranda's tears persuade

44 For the trial of Beaumine, see I, p. 4. For the desire to compel him to justice see I, p. 4; IV, pp. 41–2; V, pp. 43, 48–9.

Constant that she is 'Truth it self' (IV, p. 40). But truth is an elusive goal. Miranda is not, after all, 'Truth it self' but an amiably deceptive flirt who finally realizes where her heart really lies. Though faithful to Phillabell, Lucilia can only regain his trust by 'innocent' deception, resolving 'to cheat a Man to a belief of truth' (V, p. 46). 'This is a new way to deceive by speaking Truth' (III, p. 21), says Lesbia, after Beaumine has concealed his intention of visiting Miranda by jokingly confessing it. Lesbia's marriage to Beaumine necessitates the concealment of her feelings for Grandfoy: 'the proofs of your innocence confirm my Love' (V, p. 55), says Beaumine, with a complacent missing of the point. And Grandfoy himself, the only pure embodiment of truth in the play, declines into a marginal figure, excluded from the community of whose professed values he is the only pure expression. It would be idle to claim that *Love at a Loss* is anything other than a minor play, but it does at least stand out from most minor drama of its period in capturing some of the moral and epistemological complexity of Wycherley and Congreve, and in rejecting the tidy harmonizations of social convention and individual need that were increasingly taking over the stage.

CHAPTER TWELVE

'Scarce a good One Play'd':
Tragedy, 1695–1700

The comic revival of the late 1690s had no counterpart in tragedy, which continued its general decline into clichéd political complacency and aimless sensationalism. As in the earlier part of the decade, the greatest artist in the sphere of serious drama was not a playwright at all but Henry Purcell, whose last opera, an adaptation of the Dryden–Howard *The Indian Queen*, was performed by the Patent Company, probably late in 1695. This is the first tragic semi-opera, though the tragedy is simplified by the idealization of Montezuma, purged of the affinities with his villainous antagonists that had been a primary feature of the original.[1] The only spoken tragedy which could possibly merit modern revival, however, is Southerne's long-popular *Oroonoko* (PC, November 1695), his most ambitious and complex study of moral and cultural dislocation. As in *Sir Anthony Love*, he portrays expatriate rambling ladies, but here he juxtaposes their comedy with the tragedy of an African prince and princess, torn from their native land and forced into slavery in the West Indies. The dislocation is explicitly given a moral and symbolic quality, for Oroonoko's ancestral sun-worship is interpreted as hunger for a guiding light (whereas his Christian oppressors ignore the guidance of 'the Heavenly Ray', V. v. 311), and his perplexing sufferings bring a diminishing sense of guidance and direction.

The general dislocation reflects the usual comprehensive failure of socially binding mechanisms: the fraudulence of the signs and bonds which traditionally declare the natural character of feudal society. The hand, that biological sign of human disposition to co-operation and subordination, is offered in sign of oppression rather than community, from the point at which the planters pull at Oroonoko on his first entrance to the lovers' ironic linking of hands in Imoinda's suicide, when she lays her hand on Oroonoko's to give greater force to the dagger (V. v. 274b–c). The word is treacherous, whether as oath or sign: during his revolt, Oroonoko is betrayed by Hottman, a 'Man of mighty words' (III. iv. 79), and he is twice the victim of broken oaths. His capture and enslavement by his ostensible host manifests Southerne's habitual preoccupation with the fraudulence of hospitality, and this fraudulence is

---

Epigraph: Henry Smith, *The Princess of Parma*, epilogue (by Peter Motteux).

[1] See Price's excellent discussion (*Henry Purcell and the London Stage*, 125–43).

once again paralleled by that of service. Slavery (*servitium*) encapsulates the social and linguistic ancestry of the condition which had been a fundamental ordering value in *The Committee*, and there are specific underminings of the term: for example, Oroonoko's 'noble services' (II. iv. 82) in saving the colonists from Indian attack are cruelly disregarded, whereas the 'honest Service' (IV. ii. 11) of Hottman in betraying Oroonoko after his rebellion is more highly regarded.

Service also recurs throughout the comic plot, where Charlot Welldon, fleeing a tattered reputation in London, comes to Surinam in male guise, defrauds the Widow Lackitt of money by marrying her, arranges a bedroom trick wherein her matrimonial duties are performed by Jack Stanmore, a mercenary younger brother, and eventually reveals her true sex, pockets the Widow's money, and marries Stanmore's brother, leaving Jack to the Widow. She has, she tells the elder Stanmore, tried to be 'serviceable' (IV. i. 204) to his family. Her amiable swindling cannot be equated with the inhuman duplicity of Oroonoko's captors, which she deplores, but it does help to emphasize that the universal principle of human intercourse is the sale of the body, whether in the marriage-market or the slave-market (or, as in *A Maid's Last Prayer*, prostitution). Reproaching the Captain for his breach of word, Oroonoko argues that faith is the foundation of human society and commerce, but for the Captain money is more powerful than language: 'I have the Money. Let the world speak and be damn'd' (I. ii. 210). Yet there is no need for the Captain to defy the world, for the world is of his mind. As Stanmore says, 'Enquire into the great Estates, and you will find most of 'em depend upon the same Title of Honesty: The men who raise 'em first are much of the Captain's Principles' (I. ii. 262–4). The aristocratic ideals of hospitality and service glamorize a world whose true principles are exploitation and plunder, and the imagined regulatory power of the word and the ideal thinly conceals the actual dominance of matter and force. There can, indeed, be no greater dissolution of feudal authority than for a king to be reduced to exile and slavery by commercial forces.

There are overtones of specific topicality, though overtones only: Oroonoko is not James II, and James II did not fall to a bourgeois revolution; but an exiled king was inevitably a figure of some resonance, and the presence of a king dethroned by mercantilism heightens the less precise but at the same time more far-reaching implication that the traditionally revered bonding principles of civilization are façades for commercial forces. In *The Fatal Marriage*, even the son's view of his father is psychologically shaped by their economic relationship, and Isabella's role as wife is remade by economic pressure. If Oroonoko is not James II, still less is Isabella's division between two husbands, one with the power of the oath, the other with the power of the purse, a direct figuration of Britain's transition between two kings, or two systems. Yet in both cases the collapse of a seemingly natural into a nakedly monetary order throws up suggestive if subliminal political parallels.

In the network of power and commerce, judgement of persons tends to be conditioned not by essential character but by the accidents of economically or forcibly imposed role. The two plots of *Oroonoko* juxtapose two characters confronting a new world in new roles, which expose them to new and hitherto unexperienced categories of judgement. Charlot Welldon, like Sir Anthony Love, is a woman in male guise, her apparent masculinity determining the character of all the relationships into which she enters, from friendship to marriage, and Oroonoko is a heathen prince facing a Christian world in the condition of slave, his status both as heathen and slave dictating the judgements to which he is subject: the Captain of the slave ship justifies his treachery to Oroonoko by saying that he is 'a better Christian' than to keep his word 'with a Heathen' (I. ii. 177–8). Throughout the play, Oroonoko continues to act as a prince, but he is increasingly judged as a slave, forfeiting the awed ambiguity of response that had greeted his first entrance, when the clash between his royal garments and servile condition created uncertainty and fascination, '*The Planters pulling and staring at*' him (I. ii. 217b).

Oroonoko's reaction to the Planters' inquisitiveness is to 'Tear off this Pomp' and accept the 'slavish Habit' (I. ii. 230–1), while asserting an integrity of identity that cannot be diminished by his change of quality: 'there's another, Nobler Part of Me, | Out of your reach, which you can never tame' (I. ii. 234–5). Later, he again asserts his invincible self-sufficiency: 'I am a Slave no longer than I please. | 'Tis something nobler:—Being just my self' (II. ii. 8–9). Oroonoko's self-sufficiency has as its unattractive side a persistent incomprehension of the sensations and capacities of his fellow slaves. He never outgrows this, but his proud mental isolation is ended by the discovery that his pregnant wife, Imoinda, is also a slave on the plantation. Though all the decisions open to him are equally fatal, the fatal decisions that he in fact takes are dictated by his love for her. At the end of the play, he is 'a Slave to Love!' (V. v. 1), longing to lose his identity in hers (V. v. 212–16), and prepared to accept servitude as the price of retaining Imoinda (V. v. 135–52). 'I lose my self' (V. v. 161), he exclaims, renouncing his imaginary autonomy. Along the path to his final predicament he has at crucial points allowed his self to be taken over and reshaped by others, being 'fashion'd' (III. ii. 217) by his friend Aboan to head the revolt and worked upon (IV. ii. 101) by his English friend Blanford to surrender when the revolt collapses.

Oroonoko's sequence of decisions thus ironically links an increasing sense of society to a diminishing sense of self; to this extent he is a tragic counterpart to a hollow social being such as Lord Malepert. At the same time, he undergoes a parallel yet strangely contrasting transformation in the eyes of his captors: from prince to slave. Yet even his princeliness is represented in the cultural terms of his captors. As in Behn, he is given the name Caesar, expressive of a culture and history which he does not know and about which his speculations are understandably erratic: 'Was *Cæsar* then a Slave?', he asks (I. ii.

245). It is while he bears the name of Caesar that he performs his noble exploit of rescuing the colonists from Indian attack and receives honour and preferential treatment appropriate to the perception of his role implicit in the name given to him. Not until he recognizes Imoinda as his wife (and thereby declares himself to be the Governor's sexual rival) does he name himself, the moment of self-naming being the moment at which his self-sufficiency ceases and his self-destruction commences. It is a moment that is recalled and reversed at the culmination of the tragedy, when the tortured and bloody Aboan enters and explicitly confronts Oroonoko with an image of the fate which is 'prepar'd for you' (V. v. 43):

> *I have no Name,*
> That can distinguish me from the vile Earth,
> To which I'm going: a poor, abject worm . . .

> (V. v. 23–5; italics added)

This transformation of the noble friend into an anonymous archetype of servility is followed by Oroonoko's own sensation of vanishing self, and by his willingness to embrace slavery could he thereby save Imoinda. His sense of self-sufficiency was articulated in the images of an alien and unknown culture; but his moment of self-naming leads to the obliteration of self represented by Aboan's self-unnaming.

Like *Oroonoko*, Congreve's *The Mourning Bride* (LIF, February 1697) deals with exile and with threats to the individual's power to define, and name, himself, but unlike *Oroonoko* it moves towards harmonious social reconstruction. Congreve had, indeed, been stimulated to write a tragedy by the success of Southerne's *The Fatal Marriage*, though another model is Dryden's *Love Triumphant*: a tyrannical Spanish king (Manuel) again opposes the marriage of his daughter (Almeria) to a rival king's son (Alphonso, as in Dryden), promoting her marriage to another (Garcia, as in Dryden), though here the rival king has been executed by the beginning of the play. Like the mature comedies, the play depicts an inflexible parental tyranny that denies autonomy of choice and desire, Manuel resembling Sir Sampson in *Love for Love* in viewing his subordinates as mere agents and projections of his will. Another point of contact with the comedies is the importance of the sea as an image of flux, counteracting the apparently fixed social orders which circumscribe the characters' lives. Shipwrecked on the African coast on their wedding day, Almeria and Alphonso have, far more literally than Mrs Fainall, been left 'to Sink or Swim' after the sudden dissolution of their accepted order of life. Surrendering nationality, faith, and name in the guise of the Moor Osmyn, Alphonso loses all the familiar signs of self, becoming 'that wretched thing, that was *Alphonso*' (II. ii. 35); restored by the wreck to the power of her father, Almeria is by contrast returned to the familiar world of her origins, but equally loses the power to determine her life. As so often, domesticity and estrangement turn out to be parallel conditions, and Almeria finds herself classified by a judicial language that ignores her individuality, defining her only as the property of her father-king: because she opposes his will, for example, she is termed a 'Parricide' (IV. i. 272, 284). Even the exiled Osmyn first reveals his true identity from the enclosure of his father's tomb: a tragic counterpart to the enclosures experienced by Ben and Sir Wilfull, similarly displaced amidst the confinements of ancestral territory.

Much of the imagery, therefore, emphasizes that the self is isolated and threatened. In her opening speech, Almeria feels herself 'more senseless grown | Than Trees, or Flint' (I. i. 6–7), and the image of petrifaction repeatedly returns to denote the oppression and negation of the self: the monumental tombs that overshadow much of the action become symbols of the characters' immurement within their own griefs and sensations, Osmyn at one point becoming 'a Statue amongst Statues' (II. ii. 233). The isolation is emphasized by the usual failures of language (mutes play a prominent role), sight, and manual contact (Almeria and Alphonso were shipwrecked and separated on the very day 'our Hands were joyn'd', I. i. 133), and in the virtually universal condition of captivity, which is ended only when the tyrant Manuel himself succumbs to it: helpless with love for the captured queen Zara, and jealous of her love for Osmyn, he disguises himself in Osmyn's robe and takes his place in the dungeon, where he is mistakenly murdered and beheaded. Only when the tyrant's autonomy and identity are erased can his subjects recover theirs. In the process, there is a movement away from isolation and partial communication to an order based on compassion, and reflecting the dispositions of Providence. Imprisoned, providentially, in a cell formerly occupied by his father, Osmyn discovers a prayer written by him, torn in one place, yet coherent enough to indicate that the missing word is 'Heav'n' (III. i. 20). The torn paper typifies the sign-systems which confront the characters: incomplete, yet reaching through their gaps towards disclosure of a celestial word. Indeed, Anselmo has been inspired to leave the prayer in this fortunate spot through access to the celestial 'Book of Prescience' (III. i. 133). This is strikingly different from the outlook of Congreve's own comedies: there, justice is attained, but likeness between earthly and heavenly designs is affirmed only by fools like Foresight, whose very name mocks the aspiration to 'Prescience'.

In the 1690s, tragedy was decreasingly a vehicle for a complex and fissured political vision and there is a distinctly alien feel to a 1670s piece which was belatedly premièred in this period: John Banks's *Cyrus the Great* (LIF, December 1695)[2] deals with a ruler traditionally viewed as a paragon of wisdom and justice, yet here his justice is flawed by a possessive love, which he

---

[2] Banks claims in the dedication that it was written before *The Unhappy Favourite* but was one of three plays (along with *The Innocent Usurper* and *The Island Queens*) that 'Through Spite and Envy were the Stage debarr'd' (sig. [A3ᵛ]). According to *A Comparison between the Two Stages*, however, it had simply been refused by the players (ed. Arthur Freeman (New York and London, 1973), 24).

conquers too late, and his militarism makes him both an agent of Providence and an indiscriminate destroyer, at once crushing the impious Belshazzar and devastating the land of innocent peasants (I, pp. 2–3). His equivocal character is conveyed in one laboured yet striking double image. The miracle of the writing hand at Belshazzar's feast is related, but it is not the only disembodied hand in the play: Abradatas, Cyrus's rival for the hand of the heroine Panthea, has been chopped into pieces by the wheel-knives of his own chariot, and in an aesthetically miscalculated scene we witness Panthea attempting to re-assemble the jigsaw of her lover's fragmented body, whereupon Cyrus enters and takes his dead adversary's hand, only to find that he is holding nothing else (V, pp. 53–4). The holding of the severed hand negates the conventional function of hand-holding as an image of human community, and recalls an earlier scene in which Panthea desperately clutches Abradatas' hand, willing to lose her own rather than release her hold (IV, p. 40). But it also recalls the disembodied hand at the feast: there is a troublesome symmetry between the hand that writes the designs of Providence and the hand that represents the annihilation of individual form amidst triumphant power (compare the breaking of the conspirators' bodies in *Venice Preserv'd*). Dealing as it does with the ambiguities of a warrior king, this play was far more topical in the reign of William III than in that of Charles II, when it was written. But drama of the 1690s rarely provides a ruler as divided in character and achievement as Cyrus: the age preferred tyrants and saviours.

There is, indeed, much partisan or patriotic drama about the deposition of tyrants or heroic resistance to the invader. The anonymous adaptation of Fletcher's *Bonduca* (PC, September 1695), published with a dedication by Powell, concerns noble, if doomed, British opposition to Rome. As Curtis Price has argued,[3] there is a crudely patriotic attempt to shift sympathy from the Romans to the British, which fails because the adapter does not sufficiently alter Fletcher to remove the Britons' flaws. An almost predictable addition is a rape attempt (though by an ally, not a Roman). Powell and Verbruggen's *A New Opera; called, Brutus of Alba* (PC, October 1696), with music composed or arranged by Daniel Purcell, shows the increasing dis-regard for artistic unity by cobbling together text, incident, and stage effects from a variety of sources (including *Albion and Albanius*, *The Virgin Martyr*, and *The Treacherous Brothers*) in order to compile a loose indictment of dis-affection during the King's absence on campaign. The work's most striking feature is its impudence in plundering *Albion and Albanius* in order to celeb-rate William III, who has called Astraea back to earth and guaranteed 'Liberties and Laws'.[4] With less effrontery, Settle toned down *Philaster* (PC,

---

[3] Price, *Henry Purcell and the London Stage*, 117–125.

[4] III, p. 25; V, p. 53. Price suggests that the use of *Albion and Albanius* creates subversive irony ('Political Allegory', 17–19), but this seems to me unlikely: what irony is there in the simultaneous use of *The Virgin Martyr*?

?December 1695), tactfully removing the King's status as usurper, and changing Philaster from a deposed king to a valiant stranger. The much altered final act greatly diminishes the importance of the popular revolt and instead emphasizes the exercise of royal justice, Philaster being cleared of the apparent murder of Arethusa. Restoration of the hereditary line is also excised from Thomas Scott's revision of *A Wife for a Month* as *The Unhappy Kindness* (PC, ?July 1696), where the just and rightful king is accidentally murdered by his mother, and his usurping brother at length meets justice at the hands of an injured subject (the husband of his prospective rape victim). The play vindicates a people, not a dynasty.

From mid-1696 onwards, indeed, there was an open season on rapist tyrants, perhaps stimulated by the increased support for William following the disclosure earlier in the year of the plot to assassinate him. The justly slain protagonist of Mary Pix's *Ibrahim the Thirteenth Emperour of the Turks* (PC, May 1696) plunders merchants' property to clothe his mistresses and rapes the daughter of the man who had saved his life (whereas Crowne's pre-Revolution *Darius* had stressed the subject's obligation to the King, Pix stresses the King's obligation to the subject). In Charles Gildon's *The Roman Brides Revenge* (PC, November 1696) a sexually oppressive tyrant is poisoned by his intended victim, whose brother assumes power (though she and her betrothed die). Rapist tyrants are dispatched in Crowne's *Caligula* (PC, February/March 1698), and in Cibber's *Xerxes* (LIF,[5] February 1699), in which 'No crown sits safe without the people's love', and 'the laws of nature' permit self-defence against irresponsible kings (II, p. 173). A notable feature of *Xerxes* is that the tyrant allies himself with the rabble, as had already happened in *Pausanias, the Betrayer of his Country* (PC, ?April 1696), probably by Richard Norton, in which Pausanias seeks absolute power with the aid of a helot revolt and Xerxes' (Louis XIV's) troops. The alliance of the monarch with the rabble rather than the nobility reverses traditional hierarchical patterns, perhaps in reaction to the shifting social basis of Jacobitism, and to the motley crew involved in the assassination plot.

There is a clear response to the assassination plot in the anonymous and possibly unperformed *Timoleon; or, the Revolution* (1697),[6] about a Syracusan attempt to murder the saviour who had liberated them from Dionysius' tyranny (when 'Astrea *to the Skies was fled*', II, p. 18) and who falls in love with Dionysius' daughter. Although this play does not express the disenchantment with William felt by radical Whigs, it espouses the discontents behind that disenchantment, combining enthusiasm for William with exasperation at the continuing influence of old Tories. Pharax, an enthusiastic minister of the

---

[5] Because the Patent Company would not have it.

[6] 'A first performance around February is likely, if the play was ever performed. . . . This may very well have been a "closet" tragi-comedy, written for obvious satirical purposes' (Danchin, *Prologues and Epilogues*, vi. 373).

banished tyrant who has clung to office in the new regime and nevertheless plots against it, presumably represents Sunderland, and the venal Alphonso, dominated by an ambitious wife, clearly represents Danby (now Duke of Leeds), who in 1694 had once more been (unsuccessfully) impeached, this time on the grounds of corruption. Libellously, the author associates both with the assassination plot, and has them torn to pieces by the people. There is emphasis on the unusual corruption of the period (Sir Keith Feiling has described William's reign as the most corrupt period in English politics),[7] and Timoleon's disgust eventually impels him to abdicate in order to gain 'the Throne of Love' (v, p. 79): an exaltation of the private man which would have been unthinkable in Orrery.[8] But, unlike the departure of Xantippus in Crowne's *Regulus*, the abdication of Timoleon is not unalloyed loss, for in departing he offers the Syracusans the vision of a functioning republican constitution, with power shared proportionately between the nobles and plebeians (v, p. 79): a civic equivalent to the intermittent pastoral scenes in which shepherds exist in a harmonious state of nature, without the contamination of power or money. Timoleon's supreme achievement would be to render himself dispensable. If Astraea had fled during Stuart tyranny, Timoleon brings a restoration, but a restoration profoundly different from that of 1660:

> Heav'n has *restor'd* you what Heav'n gives
> To all, till proud imperious Man invades
> His Fellow's Right. . . .
> The Rich no longer shall the Poor oppress,
> Whil'st Justice flows with an uninterrupted Stream.

> (v, p. 79; italics added)

Timoleon is a poor play, but its scope of political argument is exceptional. By contrast, in William Walker's amateurish *Victorious Love* (PC, May/June 1698), the overthrow of tyranny and the heroine's last-minute rescue from royal rape is merely a pretext for formulaic oriental melodrama. (Jamoan, Emperor of Tombat, lusts after Zaraida, a European shipwrecked in infancy and now betrothed to the captive king Barnagasso of Gualata. Meanwhile, Jamoan's villainous uncle plots against him. Virtue triumphs.) More substantial is William Philips's *The Revengeful Queen* (PC, June 1698), an interesting rejection of Carolean culture in which the libertinism and heroic individualism of a Dorimant and an Almanzor collide in mutual destructiveness, the womanizer Almachild being manœuvred because of his lusts into killing the heroic tyrant Alboino, and thereby ensuring his own death. The play simultaneously disowns rebellion and patrilineal kingship. Alboino has conquered Lombardy, killed its king, and married the king's daughter, whom he subsequently tricks into drinking from a goblet made from her father's skull. This

7 Dedication, sig. A2, 1, p. 9; Feiling, *A History of the Tory Party*, 275.
8 See Staves, *Players' Scepters*, 105–7.

trick inspires the conspiracy against him, but it does not justify it, for Alboino gained the kingdom by just conquest (a provocative thesis):⁹ the image of desecrated paternal authority has no moral potency, and the avenging daughter is destroyed by her own plot, thereby allowing further conquest to establish a juster order.

Obviously, tyrannicide is also the subject of Cibber's *The Tragical History of King Richard III* (PC, *c.* February 1700), a streamlined version of Shakespeare which draws on both *Richard III* and *3 Henry VI*, initially savagely censored through fear that the unfortunate Henry would remind the audience of James II. A noteworthy aspect of Cibber's adaptation is that he consistently cuts Shakespeare's interplay between human and transcendent language. Many of Richard's linguistic tricks are cut, but so is the supernatural linguistic power which triumphs over them. For example, the dropping of Queen Margaret excises most of Shakespeare's curses at a stroke, and the omission of King Edward's death scene excludes the perjured reconciliation of foes and the ironic curse which Buckingham brings on his head. The murder of the princes is, of course, retained (indeed, directly represented), but—in yet another demotion of the divine text—Forest is not moved by the sight of a prayer book. Nor does 'God say Amen' at the end. When Cibber adds an image of textual authority, the authority is purely human. Richard is not an unequivocal sign of hell but an illustration of the ambiguity of human potential; a man whose life might have been written differently:

> Had thy asp[ir]ing Soul but stir'd in Vertue,
> With half the Spirit it has dar'd in Evil,
> How might thy fame have grac'd our *English* Annals:
> But as thou art, how fair a Page thou'st blotted.

(V, p. 55)

The social reconstruction in *Love's Last Shift* had been accompanied by a sense of communion with celestial language, but here Cibber is more concerned to show man himself as the author of history.

Tyranny (associated, yet again, with sexual oppression) is also the subject of another Shakespearian adaptation, Gildon's *Measure for Measure; or, Beauty the Best Advocate* (LIF, February 1700), which uses both Shakespeare's play and Davenant's *The Law against Lovers* (unlike Davenant, Gildon retains the bedroom trick, here used to create an unproblematic harmony between sexuality and social order). Less expectedly, it also includes a performance of *Dido and Æneas* in four instalments, the two tales of betrayal and forbidden love mirroring and reversing each other in a variety of striking and

---

⁹ For accounts of attempts to justify the Revolution as conquest, see Straka, *Anglican Reaction to the Revolution of 1688*, 50–64; M. P. Thompson, 'The Idea of Conquest in Controversies over the 1688 Revolution', *Journal of the History of Ideas*, 38 (1977), 33–46. Charles Blount's *King William and Queen Mary Conquerors* (1693) was burned by the common hangman on the orders of Parliament.

satisfying ways. Inevitably, the play is much concerned with the definition and attainment of justice, and the absence of justice destroys a monarch's authority (V, p. '84' [48]).[10] Tyranny is also bloodlessly ended in John Oldmixon's opera *The Grove* (PC, February 1700), set to music by Daniel Purcell. Oldmixon's Whig principles are obvious ('Curst be him who wears | The marks of Bondage when he might be free', IV, p. 34), though, strangely, the play shows a despotic king reconciled with his son-in-law and daughter (Price sees an allusion to a rumoured reconciliation between James and Anne).[11] But perhaps the most notable aspect of this insignificant piece is Oldmixon's cheerful admission in the preface that he started the work as a pastoral but decided on a more elevated genre after two acts. Organic unity is again a low priority.

There is a more complex political vision in the three plays of the former Jacobite Charles Hopkins,[12] which increasingly expose conflicts between the male ethos of heroic conquest (a sensitive topic during an unpopular war) and feminine principles. In *Pyrrhus King of Epirus* (LIF, July/August 1695) the nobility of the valiant protagonist is amply stressed, and the narrative of his conquests is proclaimed by the ghost of Alexander. Yet the narrative is truncated, without climax or fulfilment, and the wars serve nothing beyond Pyrrhus' lust for power; his opponents are as noble as he, and women have different values; and, finally, the mighty conqueror falls 'by a Stone | Hurl'd by a Woman's hand' (V, p. 46). In Hopkins's successful *Boadicea* (LIF, ?November 1697), a morally complex account of the conflict between British autonomy and continental imperialism, the ruler of the threatened land is a woman, and one of Boadicea's daughters (Bracegirdle) is raped by a Roman soldier, who sees his act as expressing man's natural supremacy: 'Nature design'd your Sex to be controll'd' (III, p. 25). Significantly, the rapist is not a pure villain, but a person capable of acting nobly within the confines of the male military code. But man-created codes are clearly deficient, and Hopkins rejects the principle (unthinkingly accepted by Brady in *The Rape*) which dictates that victims of rape can purify themselves only in death. Camilla, the victim, does kill herself, but she is clearly submitting to an irrational and oppressive tradition, explicitly rejected by her fiancé.[13] In her suicidal ravings, she vows to take the 'Account' (V, p. 55) of the rape to the gods, fumbling towards the power of immortal narrative that in *Pyrrhus* had been the prerogative of the warrior Alexander. The clash of gender roles reaches extremes in Hopkins's

---

[10] In a debate with the Provost, Claudio has earlier persuasively argued that the oaths which subjects swear to their rulers are only valid if there is 'Justice, | In what shall be commanded' (IV, p. 33).

[11] Price, 'Political Allegory', 22.

[12] Hopkins had fought in Ireland in support of James II, but his first play, *Pyrrhus King of Epirus*, is dedicated to the Duke of Gloucester, with warm praise of William III. (The Duke was Princess Anne's young son, then the white hope of Protestant succession).

[13] Jacqueline Pearson thinks that the fact that she commits suicide constitutes an endorsement of the tradition which impels her to it (*The Prostituted Muse*, 99). This is unnecessary.

Friendship Improv'd (LIF, November 1699), which is daringly concerned with a militaristic usurper obsessed with foreign wars. Militarism and femininity are here in total opposition, for the usurper's daughter has been brought up as a man, since her father would certainly have murdered a daughter. Eventually, she resumes her true sex and marries the rightful king, creating a simultaneous release from political and sexual usurpation. The title refers to the conversion of friendship between two apparent males into marriage: a male code is expanded and enriched by its inclusion of the female.

Oppression of the woman also features in Southerne's *The Fate of Capua* (LIF, April 1700), though there is no final enlargement of male codes and no movement towards the benevolent polity that is now usual in political drama. Instead, Southerne again shows the inexorable disintegration of the household and the city. Capua's (?Ireland's) imprudent support for Hannibal (James II) leads to the total destruction of the community, with 'none permitted to inhabit here, | But Slaves made Free, *Strangers*, and meanest Trades' (V. iii. 84–5; italics added), and in the parallel domestic tragedy of the secondary plot communal disintegration is re-enacted in that of a single home. Virginius, a supporter of Hannibal, discovers that his friend Junius, a supporter of Rome, has been taken prisoner, and insists on keeping him in his own 'home' (V. ii. 74, 98). 'With your own hands you set it then on fire' (II. i. 332), murmurs Junius, for he and Virginius' home-loving[14] wife Favonia have a long suppressed passion for each other, and a single incautious kiss bestowed by Junius on his sleeping hostess (the standard Southerne violation of hospitality) initiates a fatal process of misunderstanding and jealousy. Both the city and the home are destroyed by the mistaken admission of an outsider.

But it requires an insider to admit him. Whereas the tragedies of tyrannicide assume that civilization can easily purge away its refractory elements, Southerne remains convinced that the stranger within is an intrinsic part of the social and familial web. As so often, he is a father: Pacuvius Calavius, the demagogic leader of the Hannibalian faction, who exercises calamitous influence both in national and sexual politics. His son opposes his political views, but Pacuvius unfortunately dissuades him from an attempt to assassinate Hannibal (to whom he feels himself bound by 'good rites of hospitality', III. i. 36), inducing him to prefer father to country (III. i. 1–101). Pacuvius is still more disastrous as father to Favonia, insisting on 'the Sword of *Justice*' (III. v. 42; italics added) when Virginius hands her over to paternal judgement after her apparent adultery. Though initially reluctant, Virginius soon decides on death and invests the punishment with the tokens of paternal authority: negating her home by turning it into a perpetual prison (she must 'live forlorn, immur'd within these Walls', IV. iv. 153), he leaves her with her father's bowl, filled with poison, and her father's dagger (IV. iv. 155–6).

---

[14] She longs only for 'private Peace at home' (I. iii. 26), and believes it 'most fit for me to stay at home' (II. i. 153).

Yet Pacuvius is neither a mere power-seeker nor a mere patriarchal tyrant, though he is certainly both to a large degree. Finally, he leads the Capuan senators in a noble act of suicide, movingly praising his chief antagonist, Decius Magius, and acknowledging Favonia's innocence. The collapse of community and family is here due not simply to the blind egocentricity of personal appetite but to the misinterpretations that are an inevitable part of human cognition, and which give a tragic fallibility to the trust (a recurrent term) which is the foundation of community. Pacuvius has misinterpreted both Hannibal and Favonia, placing excessive trust in the former (who readily leaves the Capuans to their fate) and too little trust in the latter. Virginius has misinterpreted Junius, who, despite his opposition to Hannibal, assumes a parallel role as a destructive intruder unworthy of the trust he receives. Though Capua is divided by faction, the portrayal of faction is neither that of *The Committee*, where the supporters of natural order oppose subversive upstarts, nor that of *The History and Fall of Caius Marius*, where both sides clothe base and destructive ambition with the fiction of a struggle between hierarchy and liberty. The obligations that bind Capua to Rome are clear, but those who break them are not unprincipled, and not all who observe them are devoid of frailty, only Decius Magius being wholly exemplary. Families, and friends of equal integrity, are divided by commitment to opposing causes, and both sides make moral decisions on the basis of fallible predictions and incomplete knowledge.

Such fallibility leads to the familiar failures of language and judicial ritual. Favonia, for example, resembles Dryden's Cleopatra in lacking a voice to counter the judicial processes arranged by her male proprietors: when her husband comes to impose 'Justice' (IV. iv. 51, 93), she laments 'that I must nothing say | In my Defence, to clear my Innocence' (IV. iv. 55–6). Language, tradition, and ceremony fail as principles of community, and life again declines into a chaos of disjunct manual actions. On being lodged in Virginius' house, Junius remarks that Virginius is burning his house with his 'own hands' (II. i. 332), the hand here explicitly causing domestic disintegration, as it also does when Junius brings suspicion upon Favonia by kissing her hand as she sleeps (III. v. 27b). Thereafter her husband's and father's hands execute the processes that deny her integrity and destroy her person.[15] Similar images mark the parallel failure of political community. Spies sent to Hannibal are captured by the Romans and returned with their hands cut off. Only when the Capuan factions bury their differences in a shared rite of suicide (following a feast—hospitality—at Pacuvius' house) is there, too late, a restoration of community: 'Let us unite our Hands, as well as Hearts' (V. iii. 40), says the former Hannibalian Vibius Virius. As in the main plot of *The Fatal Marriage*, the instinct for community is only restored with the destruction of community itself.

---

[15] IV. iv. 12, 34; V. ii. 2.

Durfey's two-part prose tragedy *The Famous History of the Rise and Fall of Massaniello* (DL, May 1699) portrays a brief plebeian seizure of power, and possibly has some topicality in portraying a population reacting against the unpopular taxes of a foreign dynasty. Order is restored, and Durfey pays his usual compliments to William III, but he also stresses the ruthlessness and blinkered self-interest that inevitably characterizes any power group. His dark portrayal of aristocratic pride forms a tragic counterpart to the comic satire provided by figures such as Lord Brainless in *The Marriage-Hater Match'd*, and it contrasts with the outlook of Henry Smith's almost contemporary *The Princess of Parma* (LIF, April 1699), which also concerns a popular uprising fomented by noble malcontents, but uncompromisingly supports the rights of the nobility to power, portraying a providential defeat of insurgency. Although Durfey's play follows the same outline, and ultimately provides the same message, it is far more ambivalent, emphasizing the rapacity and complacent arrogance of the nobles as well as the greed and violence of the mob. Massaniello is initially a man of selfless principle, whose administration of justice rectifies abuses of authority with an impartial wisdom that Durfey had denied to Sancho Panza. He also initially displays linguistic integrity. Although his antagonist, the Duke of Mataloni, finds that 'Language fails' (Part I, III, p. 22) when he wishes to define him, Massaniello can acutely criticize the '*Babel*' of Romish sophistry (Part I, IV, p. 40), and the climax of his first, and in some ways beneficent, rebellion is that his reforms are to be eternized in the language that regulates the community: 'Engraved like those of Old of *Charles* the Fifth and *Ferdinand*' (Part I, V, p. 52).

Intermittently, Durfey allows the briefly ennobled plebeians to supply both direct and implicit criticism of established nobility, as in Massaniello's contempt for the empty nobility of title and trappings. But Massaniello is the only plebeian of any moral worth, and Durfey more frequently works by suspending the expected distinctions between the nobles and the unwashed, treacherous mob, providing parallelism where we expect antithesis. For example, since both Mataloni and Massaniello have treacherous brothers, each faction identically demonstrates the hatred within the most ostensibly natural of communities, the family. An equally significant symmetry is that between the rantings of Massaniello when intoxicated with power (and wine) and those of the Vice-Queen Aurelia in her strident obsession with birth and class: both, for example, long to command the thunder (Part II, IV, pp. 38, 44). While the play explicitly portrays a providential restoration of order, it also recognizes the triumphant establishment's intolerant monopolization of power. If Massaniello abandons disinterested reform, it is because he is corrupted by a power-hunger which also corrupts the nobles, as Aurelia's rodomontades reveal. On both sides, justice degenerates into the ruthless protection of interest. Massaniello abandons his talionic punishment of oppression and becomes an irrational tyrant, seeking even to use the mechanisms of justice to rape the Duchess of Mataloni. But, for the nobles, justice is also an instrument of interest:

Revenge, why that shall be the dear twin-word;———Joyn'd with fair Justice, to begin the work . . .

> The hour comes on when the vile Herd shall Groan
> Beneath the wonted Yoke, and dread the Nobles Frown.

(Part II, III, p. 27)

These words are the more chilling for being spoken by the Cardinal Filomerino, the most moderate and compassionate of the nobles. An objective and universal conception of justice seems unattainable: it becomes a term redefined according to the convenience of the antagonists in the struggle for power.[16]

Personal and clashing notions of justice also run through Rowe's *The Ambitious Step-Mother* (LIF, *c*. December 1700), the limitation of comprehension affecting both virtuous and villainous. It is accentuated by imagery of darkness, and of light that fails to live up to its symbolism: the hero and heroine are captured in the Temple of the Sun, and lights are an important visual prop, though they rarely illuminate to much purpose, and towards the end are supplemented by the more effectual props of dagger and sword. The moral is tidier and more conventional than Durfey's: that personal injustice is redressed in another world, and that Providence only intervenes to secure justice for kingdoms (which do not have an afterlife).[17] But it is noteworthy that providential justice does not secure the succession of the heir to the throne of Persia: Artaxerxes attempts to recover the inheritance from which he has been excluded by the artifice of his villainous stepmother but commits suicide after his wife (Bracegirdle) has been murdered during the course of a rape attempt by the villainous politician Mirza. Artaxerxes is the chief focus of interest and in many ways is sympathetically viewed, though he is blinkered by his sense of unique prerogative. But Providence enthrones the rival claimant, his half-brother Artaban, who vows to exercise with *justice* the power entrusted by the gods (V, p. 91). The tragedy of the heir to the throne is a private tragedy, which produces no sympathetic convulsions in the larger fabric of the state. By a nice, if fortuitous, symmetry seventeenth-century tragedy ends with a reversal of the tragicomedy of Restoration, and also with a reversal of its horror of the mob (still, of course, an instinct with centuries of life in it). The crowd is here politically constructive, the agent of Astraea rather than her enemy; for its dismemberment of the villainous priest of the Sun, Magas, is strikingly

---

[16] For a good and informative reading of the play that has much in common with mine, see Christopher Wheatley, ' "Power like new Wine": The Appetites of Leviathan and Durfey's *Massaniello*', *Studies in Eighteenth-Century Culture*, 22 (1992), 231–51.

[17] This was a common argument. See Derek Hughes, 'Providential Justice and English Comedy 1660–1700: A Review of the External Evidence', *Modern Language Review*, 81 (1986), 273–92 (pp. 275–6).

represented not as an outburst of chaotic fury but as an act of measured and 'formal' justice:

> But all their Rage was ended in his Death:
> Like formal Justice that severely strikes,
> And in an instant is serene and calm.

(V, p. 90)

In restricting Artaxerxes' tragedy to one of private loss, Rowe reflects a general increase of interest in primarily private passions and experiences, often removed from any political context, even one as implicit and distant as had figured in Otway's *The Orphan*. In the anonymous tragicomedy *The Triumphs of Virtue* (PC, February/March 1697) the virtuous heroine pretends to be the mistress of a married nobleman in order to shock her dissolute brother into virtue, thereby converting both her brother and her alleged lover. (Pleasingly, her first and true love still wishes to marry her, even in her apparently fallen state.) But, more often, the emphasis is on tyranny within the private world, sometimes sustained by personal codes of honour that disregard the rule of law. In Robert Gould's *The Rival Sisters* (PC, ?October 1695) the heroine's father forbids her marriage to the hero and offers her elder sister to him instead, arguing that custom and justice decree that she should marry first (I, p. 3). There is an explicit, if artificial, conflict between the regulating rituals of society and the claims of individual desire, which reaches its climax when the hero unwittingly undergoes the ceremony of marriage to the wrong sister. Yet he uses his own authority with equal insensitivity, denying his sister the lover of her choice. The result is a bloodbath. Edward Filmer's *The Unnatural Brother* (LIF, December/January 1696/7) is yet another pale imitation of *Othello*, with some debts to an earlier *Othello* clone, Porter's *The Villain*. Here, the Iago-figure is the brother of the title. The play failed, but reappeared in boiled-down form as the fourth of the five contrasting playlets in Motteux's *The Novelty*. Motteux himself tried a similar theme in *Beauty in Distress* (LIF, April 1698), a play in which an evil younger brother (Ricardo) is the chief cause of many situations of dislocation and estrangement: exile, dispossession, dissolution of households, loss of social identity. For example, the virtuous elder brother, driven into exile by Ricardo's contrivance, returns from exile in the stereotypically alien disguise of a Moor, 'grown a Stranger to thy very self' (I, p. 1) (a situation complemented when Ricardo attempts to fly to Africa). Ricardo, however, turns out to be not a true brother at all, but a changeling of base birth: a social and biological outsider, who provides the most unqualified triumph of nature over nurture since the changelings in Durfey's *The Banditti*.

A bleaker view of family tyranny is given in Edward Ravenscroft's crude but interestingly experimental *The Italian Husband* (LIF, November 1697). This is preceded by a discussion between a poet, a critic, and an intelligent observer which both creates and analyses a situation of generic oddity: the tragedy is in three acts (a format more characteristic of farce), it dispenses with poeticisms such as similes in an unconvincing attempt to reproduce everyday speech, and it attempts to arouse sympathy for a 'guilty' woman (sig. [A3]). That is, it attempts to separate human particulars from the constraints of literary and judicial formulas. In the play itself, an Italian nobleman is led by outraged honour to inflict a terrible vengeance on his adulterous but penitent wife, in the process violating some primary institutions of social existence, the lover being murdered at a feast and the wife in her marriage-bed.

At the feast, the lover is entertained with a masque representing the punishment of Ixion for his attempted rape of Juno—one of the short entertainments with which Betterton's company provided mini-alternatives to the Dorset Garden spectacular. At the beginning, the double standard is questioned: why should a wife be chaste with a husband as archetypally unfaithful as Jupiter (III, pp. 28–9)? But the masque concludes with the punishment of lust in 'a Poetical Hell' (III, p. 30). As Hume observes, there is an unusual degree of integration between masque and context,[18] but the effect is not merely one of tautological parallel. A primordial myth enshrining the fundamental images and impulses of male sexual authority—the supreme and promiscuous patriarch, the intangibly chaste woman whom it is death to approach—is juxtaposed with an explicit exercise in complex realism which the ancient myth is insufficient to contain or interpret. The interplay of experience and text is repeated towards the end, when the doomed adulteress reads another drama couched as classical myth and offering an absolute polarization of chastity and lust: Guarini's *Il Pastor Fido* (III, pp. 36–7). But, unlike Guarini's heroine, Ravenscroft's is not accused falsely, and here there is no averting of sacrifice, and indeed no sacrifice: merely insensate murder, stripped of the support of myth and ritual and validated only by a murderous code of honour that clashes both with religion (the deed is condemned by a Friar) and with the rational, civilized principles of law. But reason and civilization remain hazy and theoretical standards. In an oddly inconsequential *coup de théâtre*, it is discovered that the erring wife is the daughter of the Great Duke: the ruler. Conventionally, such discoveries are socially redemptive: in *Beauty in Distress*, clarification of birth was to restore the community to its natural moral order. Here, however, it achieves nothing: the heroine is not saved, and the Great Duke's verdict on her fate is never pronounced. Hounded by a sense of personal remorse, the husband retires to a convent, nevertheless confident that the father's sense of honour will excuse his daughter's death (III, p. 43). But, like Caesar in *All for Love*, the Great Duke arrives immediately after the end of the play. The verdict of patriarchal authority remains uncertain and unspoken, and we are left with a tangle of private agonies, unresolved by any ordering public judgement.

---

[18] Hume, 'Opera in London, 1695–1706', 69.

Whereas Ravenscroft criticizes male codes that deny female desire, such codes are upheld in *The Fatal Discovery* (PC, February 1698), brought to the stage by George Powell, which shows how insubordinate female lust can reduce patrilineal order to chaos and Babel. In the main plot, Beringaria has years ago sought to revive her husband's flagging desires by means of a bedroom trick, but in the darkness sleeps with her son. Ignorant of the original incest, the son refines it by marrying the daughter whom he fathered on his mother. The moral is that wives should allow their desires to decline in company with those of their husbands, and the bedroom trick here simply emphasizes the social disruptiveness of desire. So does the bedroom trick in the comic plot, in which the old, ugly husband of a lively young wife (Susanna Verbruggen) is cured of jealousy by a complex ruse in which both he and a would-be cuckolder are tricked into joining each other in bed in female disguise, the object of the ruse being to prove that his wife could have cuckolded him but chose not to do so. After this thoroughly asexual parody of Beringaria's tragic bedroom trick, the vigorous young woman and impotent dotard settle down to a happy marriage. Female dominance is here assured, but through the sacrifice of female sexuality.

It is hazardous to see any cultural significance in the extraordinarily amateurish *The Unnatural Mother*, 'Written by a Young Lady' (LIF, *c.* September 1697), a tale of Siamese private life which features a mother and son who cannot behold a relative without attempting murder or incest. Providence, however, protects and unites Munzuffer and Bebbemeah, the virtuous hero and heroine, guiding the former with supernatural voices and even at one point rendering him usefully invisible. Equally amateurish is another anonymous play, *Neglected Virtue* (PC, March 1696),[19] loosely based on the Artaban–Elisa plot from La Calprenède's *Cléopâtre*, though events are here brought to a tragic conclusion through the schemes of the heroine's lustful stepmother, who is intent on gaining Artaban for herself. Artaban had provided Dryden with the inspiration for the young Montezuma and Almanzor, through whom he had studied the relationship between authority and naked power. Here, despite the royal setting, and despite an act of regicide, we have an apolitical play about a father who obstructs his daughter's love, the concentration on familial structures being emphasized by a comic secondary plot which also portrays the abuse of paternal authority. Descent from the heroic into domesticity is more purposefully contemplated in George Granville's *Heroick Love* (LIF, January 1698), also loosely based on a work which had helped to mould Dryden's early heroic supermen: the *Iliad*. But Granville

---

[19] The play was brought to the stage by the actor Hildebrand Horden, and published with a dedication by him. W. C. Hazlitt and others (including Wing) have attributed it to Charles Hopkins, but there is no contemporary evidence for the attribution (see Milhous and Hume, 'Attribution Problems', 25), and the play is inferior in quality to Hopkins's acknowledged work, and quite different from it in outlook.

follows his predecessors at some distance, showing Agamemnon and Chruseis suffering from pangs of love found too late that resemble less those of Almanzor and Almahide than of Lady Sullen and Archer (Agamemnon actually offers to divorce Clytemnestra, II, p. 21). Although public duty prevails, the heroic enterprise of the war is deeply tainted, whereas love is noble, and Agamemnon's tragedy is that he is not 'a private Man' (V, p. 69).[20]

A diluted version of the same tendency is apparent in Peter Motteux's *The Island Princess . . . Made into an Opera* (PC, February 1699), a successful counterblast to the modestly successful *Rinaldo and Armida*,[21] revising two earlier Restoration adaptations of the Fletcher play. In a typically sprawling Fletcherian plot, the Portuguese Armusia rescues an Indian king from captivity to the Governor of a neighbouring island, and thereby displaces another Portuguese, Ruy Dias, in the affections of the king's sister, Quisara. Armusia converts Quisara to Christianity, and a false priest (the villainous Governor in disguise) persuades a reluctant king to sentence his rescuer and his sister to death. The couple are, however, rescued by Ruy Dias, now transformed into a noble rival, and the Governor is exposed and punished. Unsurprisingly, the play gains different political overtones in each of its incarnations, for it has a very variable potential for topicality: there is restoration, but also royal ingratitude and royal persecution of the true religion. The first version (King's, November 1668) emphasizes the glory of restoration: '*A private Person to Redeem a King*,' Armusia reflects in an added speech, '*Will to thy Name, and Nation honor bring*' (I, p. 15). Nahum Tate's version, however, produced in the middle of James II's reign (April 1687), significantly modifies the conclusion, emphasizing that the king's intolerant idolatry is disgracing a providential act of restoration (IV, p. 41). But Motteux portrays a king bound by the will of his people, his natural inclination to mercy reinforced by the realization that this is what his people wish (V, p. 36). With the changing representations of the king go corresponding changes in the representation of the private person. For the 1668 Armusia, the ultimate self-fulfilment of the 'private Person', and the ultimate ratification of his 'Name', is to be an agent in the re-establishment of a monarch. By the time of Motteux's version, however, private experience is central, and there is an Otwayesque emphasis on interior agony: for example, when Quisara tests Armusia by asking him to renounce Christianity as a condition of marriage, there is a far stronger conflict between

[20] At the end of the published edition, Agamemnon rushes to seek death in battle (V, p. 72). After the first night, according to Granville's preface, he was simply left in a swoon, since Granville judged that the audience would find it unconvincing that he should run towards battle rather than after Chruseis. Granville indicates that he himself would have done the latter (sig. A2).

[21] For the dating of *Rinaldo and Armida* and *The Island Princess*, see Milhous and Hume, 'Dating Play Premières', 400–2, where they correct the statement in *A Comparison between the Two Stages* that *The Island Princess* came first (pp. 34–5). Whereas they see *The Island Princess* as a direct response to *Rinaldo and Armida*, Danchin speculates that the latter may have been hastily put together and mounted while *The Island Princess* was in preparation (vi. 543).

the demands of his culture and of his heart than in the previous versions. By contrast, Dennis's *Rinaldo and Armida* (November/December 1698), the rival operatic attraction at Lincoln's Inn Fields, sternly insists on the superiority of public duty to personal passion: Rinaldo recovers his identity— 'begins to be once more *Rinaldo*' (III, p. 29)—by renouncing Armida, who commits suicide (whereas in Tasso Rinaldo finally calms and converts her).

Dennis enforced a similar morality when, like Granville but in different vein, he turned to the House of Atreus for his *Iphigenia* (LIF, December 1699), a ploddingly moralistic adaptation of Euripides' *Iphigenia in Tauris*. Initially compelled by custom to the sacrifice of strangers, the Scythians transcend the primitive barbarity of their culture, discovering the virtues of sociability and the benevolence of Providence (the divine will being audibly communicated through a supernatural voice). Dennis emphasizes the ideal, selfless friendship of Orestes and Pilades and resurrects an equally well-tried topos of altruism when Iphigenia—herself formerly shipwrecked in Scythia—stands watching the storm-tossed boat of Orestes and Pilades with a quite un-Lucretian compassion. The play clearly foreshadows Dennis's later diatribes against priestcraft, in which he denounces religious cruelty and intolerance, singles out priestly pride as the mainstay of tyranny, declares the essence of religion to be charity and fellowship, and pronounces pagan Greece to have attained greater virtue than any Christian culture. This elaborately political transformation of Euripides was rivalled by Abel Boyer's hack translation of Racine's *Iphigénie* as *Achilles; or, Iphigenia in Aulis* (PC, December 1699), with the final narration replaced by a spectacular onstage sacrifice scene. Neither play did well.

Dennis's shipwreck has no precedent in Euripides, and was perhaps inspired by a slightly earlier Euripidean adaptation, Charles Gildon's *Phaeton* (PC, March/April 1698), whose action originates in the heroine's pity for a shipwrecked stranger. Gildon had started by adapting Quinault's *Phaéton* but decided in midstream to follow Euripides' *Medea* instead, thereby providing yet more evidence of the dwindling status of artistic unity. The resulting product is distinctly slapdash, and almost the only unifying element (apart from condemnation of the 'Arbitrary Pow'r' of man over woman, III, p. 14) is emphasis on the plight of the stranger. Althea, Princess of Samos, had rescued and married the shipwrecked Phaeton after he and his crew had been attacked by a mrb, commanded by a divine voice to drive the strangers from the shore. Having rejected family and country to follow Phaeton in a vagabond existence, she finds herself in the 'strange Land' (III, p. 15) of Egypt, where Phaeton seeks to establish security and refuge by marrying the Princess. After exacting Euripidean vengeance upon her rival, she in turn experiences the fury of the mob, who dismember her children, and are only prevented by her suicide from dismembering her. (Medea, of course, kills her children herself, as part of her vengeance.) Both plays are the works of religious radicals who stress the delusive, restrictive power of local cult and custom (Gildon was a deist, feminist, and anti-racist, who in his essay on *Othello* praised Shakespeare's distaste for the 'customary Barbarity, of confining Nations, without regard to their Virtue, and Merits, to slavery, and contempt for the meer Accident of their Complexion'.[22]) But, in Dennis, the arrival of the stranger-brother brings a savage, confined culture to an expanded sense of humanity and community; here, there are simply closed circles of local culture, separated by a reciprocal mistrust of the alien.

Plays such as *Phaeton*, *The Italian Husband*, and *The Fatal Discovery* show a continuing debate about the social and marital rights of women. Women tragedians, however, are on the whole surprisingly unadventurous, though Trotter and Manley are more inclined than men to derive oppression from ordinarily fallible kings rather than monstrous, and therefore anomalous, tyrants. In *Ibrahim* Mary Pix had followed Charles Hopkins in both portraying and condemning the woman's atonement of rape by suicide, but there is no sympathetic complexity in the portrayal of her ambitious villainess, Sheker Para. And, although women are oppressed by unwanted and powerful suitors in her *Queen Catharine; or, The Ruines of Love* (LIF, June 1698), the primary emphasis is more generally on the suppression of the personal by militarism and ambition. The play is set during the Wars of the Roses, the heroine being Henry V's widow (given—like Shakespeare's Queen Margaret—an unhistorical longevity), but the play focuses entirely on the amorous miseries of its central quartet of lovers. The longing to flee from public life to one of private autonomy is widespread, the lovesick Clarence, for example, wishing to retire 'from the bustling Crowd' (II, p. 11), and his beloved Isabella to elope with him to a French cottage (IV, p. 31). Like Orrery's *Henry the Fifth*, *Queen Catharine* depicts rivalry between Owen Tudor and a king (Edward IV in this case) for the hand of Katherine de Valois, but the contrast of outlook is significant: whereas Orrery's Henry has the superior claim because of his superior rank, in Pix the social inferior has the superior claim of shared love, though he is killed by the arbitrary oppression of superior power. In one particularly potent elevation of the private, Owen Tudor recalls longing for Catharine on a barren mountain top and filling 'the ambient | Air with your dear name' (III, p. 20). Whereas the name in Orrery evokes the network of public and social obligations that shape individual identity, naming here becomes an entirely private process, totally removed from the social prescription of identity. The only use of the name to denote public obligation occurs in a plainly disingenuous reference by Richard of Gloucester to King Edward's 'Sacred name' (II, p. 16). Crushed in their personal lives by power and ambition, the lovers complain of dislocation[23] and injustice, as when Clarence laments the death of his beloved Isabella:

[22] [Charles Gildon *et al.*], *Miscellaneous Letters and Essays, on Several Subjects* (London, 1694), 98.
[23] III, p. 23; IV, p. 33.

> but can Astrea, can Justice restore
> Her back again? No, 'tis impossible:
> Therefore to Wilds and Seas I will remove,
> And taste no comfort since I've lost my love.

(V, p. 49)

It is notable that *Astrea* occurs as subject of the verb *restore*: but the restoration is private, not political, and is in any case beyond the goddess's power. Her return is no longer the issue. Were she to descend from the heavens amidst these ruined personal lives, her arrival would be a tactless impertinence. No political dispensation can repair '*The Ruines of Love*'.

In general, however, the tyranny of authority over desire interested Mrs Pix far less than the subordination of desire to legitimate authority, and *The False Friend; or, The Fate of Disobedience* (LIF, May/June 1699) resembles her comedies in its abject affirmation of patriarchal authority. The father of the play is both literally and figuratively a Viceroy (substitute for the king), and the disobedience of his son and daughter in contracting secret marriages fittingly results in general massacre, engineered by a female Iago, the Viceroy's jealous and embittered foster-daughter. The concluding moral is that children should obey their parents, and that parents should not love their children too much.

There is a more painful and morally sensitive affirmation of authority in Trotter's *Agnes de Castro* (PC, December 1695), a considerable modification and simplification of Behn's novel of the same name. In both, the Prince of Portugal is trapped in marriage to a virtuous and unloved Princess and pines with nobly unconsummated love for Agnes. In Behn, the Princess dies through grief at her husband's love for another, whereas in Trotter she is murdered by a jealous rival. In Behn, the King is a tyrant who (unsuccessfully) authorizes a repulsive favourite to rape Agnes and who eventually has her murdered, causing his son to take up arms against him. In Trotter, the King mistakenly condemns Agnes for the murder of the Princess but discovers her innocence in time, Agnes here being killed by a rejected lover: not by a synthesis of male violence and institutionalized authority but by a simple criminal act. In Behn, there is the usual intolerable tension between the terms in which individuals seek to order their existence and those imposed by external systems of authority. The final rebellion of the son against the father provides yet another illustration of the division and hostility intrinsic to even the most apparently natural and intimate of social bonds, whereas Trotter shows social prohibitions to be fully internalized: unlike Behn's heroine, hers does not marry the Prince, and, although she has the chance of escape, she insists on obedience to authority, returning to face the King's justice. Even the wicked Elvira, who kills the Princess, is forced by the consciousness of her crime into delirium and confession. Justice is repeatedly desired and denied throughout the play, but it is not institutionally impossible: whereas the problem of Behn's heroine is (in words used of the rape attempt) 'unjust Authority' (p. 235), Trotter's heroine is merely persecuted by criminals. Constantly, Trotter works against Behn's emphasis on the fragility of a civilization that is constantly disrupted by the rebellious appetites of both subjects and rulers. Although she does allude to the flight of Astraea, the allusion is used by the villain in an attempt to obscure the cause of the villainess's penitent madness (IV, sig. F2ᵛ). It does not describe the true condition of society.

A cruder expression of the same outlook occurs in Trotter's *Fatal Friendship* (LIF, May/June 1698), though she here concentrates more on the male misuse of authority. The hero (Gramont) has a tyrannical father and the heroine an insensitive brother, who commands her to marry Gramont's father rather than Gramont himself, Gramont and his friend Castalio are persecuted by an unjust general, and the King is for much of the play badly advised. The play reverses the procedure of Hopkins's *Friendship Improv'd*, for Hopkins had transformed male friendship into love and respect between the sexes, whereas Trotter, as her title indicates, places conventionally ideal male codes in (desperately contrived) circumstances which give them destructive implications. For example, having secretly married the heroine, Gramont subsequently commits bigamy in order to save the imprisoned Castalio, unaware that he is marrying the woman Castalio loves. The constant oppression of the personal by blind institutional power leads to the usual expressions of disintegrating civilization: Otwayesque images of estrangement and of wandering in unknown lands, complaints of injustice, and a labyrinth of private and competing schemes of vengeance and justice (including, ominously, 'Manly Justice,' with its 'avenging Hand', III, p. 29), during the course of which Gramont accidentally kills Castalio and then commits suicide. But the descent into anarchy no longer reveals inevitable flaws in civilization. Too late, news comes that the King has pardoned Castalio and Gramont and restored them to fortune. Had Gramont delayed his bigamous marriage for a day, trusting in providential and royal justice, he would have been happy and prosperous (there is a clear parallel with Southerne's *The Fatal Marriage*): the tragedy has resulted not from the imperfection of civilization but from the folly of those who failed to trust in it.

Authority is not even temporarily problematic in Susanna Centlivre's first play, *The Perjur'd Husband* (PC, October 1700). Here, a comic plot in which the wife of an old, repulsive husband learns the practical dangers of attempted infidelity is juxtaposed with a tragic one in which the breaking of oaths within sexual relationships leads to disaster. As the title suggests, there is repeated emphasis on the socially and morally binding power of language: 'I urg'd my wretched Fate with impious Language,' a dying and perjured woman confesses (V, p. 38). Perhaps the most striking feature of the play is its carnival setting, here used to emphasize the dangerous threat which the flesh poses to the values enforced by the social instrument of language. There is none of the moral ambiguity of Vanbrugh's carnivals, still less any of the moral anarchism of the 1668 carnival in Dryden's *An Evening's Love*.

The only female tragedian to retain some of the moral subtlety and scepticism of Behn is Mrs Manley. In *The Royal Mischief* (LIF, April 1696) desire is violently and almost universally at odds with the order enforced by public power, even the virtuous hero and heroine sharing an indomitable passion that leaves them indifferent to their legal spouses. Marital rights convey arbitrary and destructive power over individuals incapable by nature of honouring them, and sexual passion is regularly defined as a grasping obsession with external form that is blind to the essence of the desired object (clutching or grasping is a characteristic expression of sexual desire).[24] When Prince Levan Dadian enters a liaison with Homais, his uncle's wife, the passion which prompts such a comprehensive subversion of social and familial imperatives has, on each side, been excited by a picture. Their first act of adultery is also their first meeting: a meeting, as Levan stresses, of 'Strangers' (III, p. 22). A complementary determination to possess external form is displayed by Homais' husband, the Prince of Libardian, who commences the play as her gaoler and ends it as her killer, fascinated by the 'Form' (V, p. 38) of a woman he cannot enjoy, and whose character he finally despises.

Neither in earth nor in heaven is there a just and visible order with authority to regulate the demands of passion. Reflecting on the agonies of her forbidden love for the Vizier Osman, and believing her passions to have been mercilessly and inexorably determined by serene and passionless gods, Levan's virtuous wife, Bassima, questions divine justice and defines man as an isolated creature, with no analogy to the divine inscribed within him: 'we're like our selves alone' (III, p. 24). There is no correspondence between human nature and the cosmic laws to which it is subject, for these impose on man a servitude to the senses that forever separates him from the condition of the beings who doom him. Earthly laws are not framed by the passionless and serene but, as we have seen, they are equally remote from the urgent and unruly passions that shape the general pattern of human existence; for law enforces the possessive rights of the few, the powerful, and the male. When Levan Dadian begins his incestuous liaison with Homais, he allows himself to be persuaded that his uncle's age and impotence remove all wrong from the act (II, p. 18), and exults that 'Honour and Justice are low sounds, can scarce | Be heard, when Love is named' (III, p. 26). Yet, on the same page, wrongly believing that Bassima has consummated her love for Osman, he is promised proof of her 'Injustice,' and when the adultery is apparently confirmed he becomes single-mindedly intent on bringing the offenders to 'Justice'.[25] Conversely the cuckolded Prince of Libardian uses his military authority (a male prerogative) to rebel and turn his castle into a self-sufficient realm, in

[24] II, p. 15; IV, p. 28.   [25] IV, p. 32; V, p. 44. Cf. IV, p. 31.

which he menaces and eventually executes 'Justice' on his faithless wife, while vainly (and inconsistently) promising Osman and Bassima protection from Levan's injustice.[26]

When Levan's version of justice is executed upon Osman, the sentence is that he be shot from the mouth of a cannon. Perhaps Jacqueline Pearson is on this occasion right to see a phallic image,[27] since the enforcement of justice is throughout the play associated with the exercise of male sexual aggression, but just as important is the annihilation of the victim's body achieved by the mode of execution: a fragmentation of individual form, reflecting the oppressive indifference of authority to personal desires. (Such an image had also occurred in Banks's *Cyrus the Great*, but that had been a relic from another reign; *The Royal Mischief* is unusual among new plays in its pessimistic view of civilization.) After Osman's execution his wife Selima, who has jealously incensed Levan against the lovers, gathers the fragments of the husband she has helped to destroy, groups them together, and stretches herself out upon them, merging sexual possession with the absolute annulment of the partner's individuality. The repeated clutching of the partner's 'Form' here receives its purest manifestation, and its extreme of self-negating destructiveness.

Justice in this play is exclusively concerned with imposing the sexual will of the powerful, legitimizing in them desires that it condemns in the weak. The pervasive waywardness of sexual desire is a rebellion less against immutable and abstract principles of law than against principles which themselves originate in the rival desires of those with authority. The result is to create an unusual moral standpoint for assessing the lustful villainess Homais, the embodiment of sexual waywardness, whose soul 'loaths the beaten path, and starts aside, | To seek new Regions out, disgusted with the old' (I, p. 3). There is no doubt about Homais' ruthlessness and malevolence, but she is not as simply set apart from her antagonists and victims as Sheker Para was in Pix's slightly later *Ibrahim*. At the beginning of the play, Manley stresses that Homais is oppressively imprisoned by her husband, treated as a possession to be guarded from 'Robber hands' (I, p. 6) and denied self-representation: 'What signifies the Crown upon my head,' she complains, 'When none can see how well the Circle sits' (I, p. 9). Nor is she unique in her sexual destructiveness, which is more exceptional in degree than in kind, being one manifestation of a general impulse variously displayed by the young, neglected wife, the elderly cuckold, and the adulterer determined to deny his wife the freedom that he himself takes. Even the two spouses who actually love their partners are motivated by a blind urge for possession that leads them to destroy what they cannot own: like Southerne in his treatment of the Pilgrim and Sir Anthony, Manley suggests that actions are judged as much according to the role of the actor as according to the essence of the act.

---

[26] IV, p. 36; V, pp. 37–8. [27] Pearson, *The Prostituted Muse*, 195.

One can claim no more for *The Royal Mischief* than that it handles tritely formulaic situations from an unconventional standpoint, occasionally expressed through striking (if never entirely original) symbols; Mrs Manley gives fuller meaning than Banks to the symbol of the lover's fragmented body, but Banks got there first.[28] Nevertheless, the play is a reminder of what is missing from most tragedy of the late 1690s. Alone with Southerne (and Ravenscroft in *The Italian Husband*), Mrs Manley retained a comprehensive sense of the incompleteness and dangerous incoherence of civilization; of tragedy not as the artifice of an unnatural brother or mother but as something intrinsic to political and familial relationships. In an endless contradiction, desire formulates laws for the suppression of desire, and love is most fittingly expressed as the solitary, egocentric reconstitution of the loved one's shattered and lost identity.

The Royal Mischief was the chief target of the unidentified W. M.'s *The Female Wits* (PC, September 1696), in which Marsilia (Mrs Manley) superintends the rehearsal of a parody of the tragedy, with unsisterly cameo appearances from Mrs Wellfed (Pix) and Calista (Trotter), who is portrayed as a vain, pretty bluestocking. The consistent, crude point is that the women are creatures of the flesh, to be judged—a recurrent term—by their appeal to the flesh. A poet visits Calista (i.e. 'most beautiful') daily under the pretext of seeing her verses, but 'Poets and *Judges*' (I, p. 6; italics added) never visit the unattractive Mrs Wellfed; and the final verdict on Marsilia is not condemnation by a critic but rejection by a disillusioned suitor (III, p. 67). Whereas Smith and Johnson, the commentators in *The Rehearsal*, are men of sense who apply genuine linguistic and cultural criteria to Bayes's play, the commentators in *The Female Wits* are at the rehearsal largely because they want to bed Marsilia, and the women themselves repeatedly confirm the association of female art with the female body: according to Marsilia, Wellfed's 'Heroicks want Beautiful Uniformity as much as her Person' (I, p. 11). Marsilia herself is matter in motion, absurdly and incessantly preoccupied with the adornment of her person, an art of the body which confirms that her physical and artistic vanity are one and the same impulse. Although she commences the play longing for her spirit to mount to the sky (a longing reflected in the journey to the moon in her tragedy), her impatient arrogance repeatedly vents itself in physical agitation and violence, which moves towards a climactic exaltation of body over text when, enraged because the actors' bodies cannot stand the strain of her proposed dance on all fours, she '*Throws down the Book, and stamps upon it*' (III, p. 65). As her increasingly dismayed suitor Awdwell has already said, 'Poetry ought to be for the use of the Mind . . . but to you, sure Madam, it proves only a Fatigue and Toyl' (II, p. 28).

[28] Eric Rothstein points out a common source in Seneca's *Hippolytus* 1256–7 (*Restoration Tragedy*, 155). Both incidents also have faint precedent in Jonson's *Sejanus*, where the mob who have torn Sejanus apart wish they could put him together again (V. 885–7).

Marsilia's play itself is a mere expression of her insubordinate sexuality (no wonder she wishes to act in it herself),[29] and her characters talk about little but physical sex. Although it is easy to be overzealous in the search for phallic imagery, it is difficult not to see it in the '*Two Men with Whiskers, large Truncheons, Drest strangely*' who speak Marsilia's prologue (II, p. 27), especially when we hear her keen disappointment with them: 'What shall I do for a larger sort of Men? . . . The Devil take thee, for a squeaking Treble' (II, pp. 27–8). Bayes in *The Rehearsal* had been implicitly judged against the standard of Jonson, and in this play the same standard is both more overtly and more crudely applied, for Marsilia's other literary project is an adaptation of Jonson's *Catiline*—an adaptation in which only the first speech of Jonson's original will remain. Her two explicitly proposed revisions are favourable treatments both of Fulvia (I, p. 10), Jonson's ambitious 'base | And common strumpet' (III. 450–1), and of Catiline himself (II, p. 23), one of the archetypal subversives of European history. Bayes's crime was to lack the genius and authority of Jonson; Marsilia's is to desire them, and her planned perversion of *Catiline* convicts her of a depressing synthesis of political, literary, and sexual insubordination. Finally, the play restores to her proper state the woman who mistook the female body for the male mind, and made it both source and medium of her art. Still in a state of violent bodily agitation,

The wrathful Lady has run over a Chair, shatter'd the Glasses to pieces: The Chair-Men, to save it, fell pell-mell in with her. She has lost part of her Tail, broke her Fan, tore her Ruffles, and pull'd off half my Lord *Whiffle's* Wigg, with trying to rise by it: So they are, with a Shagreen Air, and tatter'd Dress, gone into the Coach: Mr *Praisall* thrust in after'em, with the bundle of Fragments, his Care had pick'd up from under the Fellows Feet. (III, p. 66)

All the artifice with which Marsilia has covered her corporeal form is defiled and shattered. It is poetic justice for the woman who had conspired to 'pull' Aristotle 'in pieces' (I, p. 8), and of course it parodies the mangling of Osman in *The Royal Mischief* (alluded to in III, p. 54), with the fatuous Praiseall gathering the fragments of his loved one's dress as Selima had gathered those of her husband's body. In her deranged efforts to piece together an artifice of flesh, Selima is interpreted as a symbol of both Manley/Marsilia and her art, so that Marsilia here gains what she has so long desired: total identification with her creation. The woman writer still had many battles to fight.

[29] II, p. 39; III, p. 60.

Conclusion

'Remember me! remember me!' The most universally known, and most universally moving, moment of Restoration theatre is the climax of Dido's Lament. The desperate perpetuation of the self is sustained over, and in the face of, a descending, dissolving chromatic pattern in the bass, but this is counteracted by the strong, ascending direction of Dido's phrases: dominant, finally rising to tonic.[1] This is not the 'Remember me' of Hamlet's father: the voice of archaic social codes threatening the individual choice and consciousness of the son. Nor is it the appeal to memory that forms the turning-point of *Aeneid*: Mercury's 'regni rerumque oblite tuarum'[2] (also, as it happens, reinforced by a paternal ghost). This is a pure appeal to the personal. After all, Tate and Purcell's Mercury, with his call to public duty, is a demonic illusion. And the storm does not drive Dido and Aeneas into the Virgilian cave, that symbolic antithesis of the public spheres of city and culture; rather it drives them back from the healthful openness of the country to the oppressive snares of the court. Virgil's civic order has become Tate's chaos, and the sensations of the self emerge as the true criterion of value.

Dido's 'Remember me' is a beguilingly telling moment, and of course one that it is easy to overplay. The *Aeneid* itself still had a great future as the handbook of self-disciplined imperialism; and, despite Berlioz's intense interest in abandoned or oppressed heroines, Italy in *Les Troyens* has a teleological importance which is quite absent from Tate. The point is not that *Dido and Æneas* marks a total and irreversible shift in the evaluation of the public person, but that it reveals a significant and frequently apparent tilting of the balance. Tate himself affords many parallels, perhaps the most telling being the way in which Coriolanus, lost in grief for his dead child, reverses the image of Aeneas bearing Anchises from Troy. The agonies of Granville's Agamemnon represent a comparable reconstitution of classical epic into a narrative of private experience.

The isolation and exaltation of the personal is one of the best-known features of post-Revolution drama,[3] though it was not universal (as Southerne generally reveals), and it permitted widely contrasting interpretations of the relationship between individual and society. If personal fulfilment and social

---

[1] The Lament is finely analysed in Price, *Henry Purcell and the London Stage*, 258–9.

[2] *Aeneid*, iv. 267 ('Forgetful of the kingdom and your affairs').

[3] The transition is documented in various ways in Rothstein, *Restoration Tragedy*; Staves, *Players' Scepters*; Brown, *English Dramatic Form*; Rose A. Zimbardo, *A Mirror to Nature: Transformations in Drama and Aesthetics 1660–1732* (Lexington, Ky., 1986).

codes often conflict (Dido's successors include Lady Brute), the luxuriant exploration of personal sensation is more frequently combined with a belief that these sensations are intrinsically sociable in character. Man is once again a naturally political animal. If *Love's Last Shift* emphasizes the sensuous delights of virtue, it also depicts a recovery of name and rank that is structurally similar to the naming and social reassimilation of Edgar in *King Lear*. There is, however, a notable contraction in the social hierarchy that is invoked: the rank of gentleman does not mirror or imply any political or natural hierarchy greater than its own, and, whereas Edgar's name is clearly the link that binds him to the total social order (it was given by the king, his god-father), the authority of Loveless's name is far more private, since it gains force by being displayed on Amanda's arm. Perhaps a more appropriate analogy is with the naming not of Shakespeare's Edgar but of Tate's. A greater change is evident in *The Beaux Stratagem*, which also culminates in a significant confirmation of the hero's title, of Viscount Aimwell: but this is a title which he has hitherto possessed only by fraud, and which he genuinely gains only when he has earned it. Whereas Cibber portrays the hero's return to a moral character that is implicit in his social origins, Farquhar's preferred society is one where moral character precedes social rank. We are on our way to the total reversal of the Shakespearian pattern which Dickens achieved in *Our Mutual Friend*. There, Bella's self-discovery is marked by occasions on which she almost ritually pronounces the name of John Rokesmith, the man she loves and marries. They are occasions as solemnly marked out as the self-naming of Edgar in *King Lear*. But, of course, Rokesmith is not her lover's real name, but a pseudonym assumed in order to conceal his wealth: who he is is distinct from what he is, and what he is called, and the pronunciation of the false name is the guarantee that he is loved solely for his true nature, just as much as the pronunciation of Edgar's real name guarantees that his true nature has been recognized. There is, indeed, a very close anticipation of the Rokesmith plot in *She Ventures, and He Wins*, where Charlot divests herself of her name and rank in order to test the man she loves.

Some scholars have seen in Restoration drama a disappearance of the hierarchical cosmos of the Renaissance, in which individual, state, and visible universe are linked in an ascending chain of analogy, each level a structural replica of the others.[4] Such an approach has some merit, but it needs careful and considerable qualification. For one thing, scholars who take it tend to exaggerate the conservatism of Elizabethan and Jacobean drama. And, if Descartes and Hobbes offered a cosmos more empty and impersonal than that of Shakespeare's time, it was also more empty and impersonal than those which succeeded it. Ulysses' speech on degree notwithstanding, *Troilus and Cressida* depicts a universe far more hostile and chaotic than does *An Essay*

4 Norman N. Holland, *The First Modern Comedies*; Weber, *The Restoration Rake-Hero* (e.g. pp. 16–18); Gewirtz, *Restoration Adaptations of Early 17th Century Comedies*, 111–43.

on Man.[5] Nevertheless, large patterns of fluctuation may contain steady and linear changes. In Shirley's *Hyde Park*, the reform of the rakish Lord Bonvile (an obvious precursor of Cibber's Loveless) restores a moral character to an aristocratic rank whose power and value are still deeply felt. 'I am now myself' (V, p. 541), he announces, with a seamless identification of self and hierarchical status. Except in the very earliest years of the Restoration, there is no comparable sense that nobility carries a moral mystique, derived from its imaging of greater hierarchies; and, as has been noted, by the 1690s the aristocracy is frequently treated with contempt. Similarly, while the repeated failures of judicial ritual that pervade Carolean drama have plenty of counterparts in plays of Shakespeare and his contemporaries, the earlier plays far more often confront an assumed analogy between the human rituals of justice and their divine archetypes. The trial of Vittoria Corombona in Webster's *The White Devil* is as notable a Babel as anything in *The Plain-Dealer*, but the presence of Cardinal Monticelso brings to the fore memories of a possible bond between human ritual and divine dispensation. There are, obviously, no such memories in Wycherley. Similarly, the trial by combat in *Richard II* displays and breaks the analogy between royal judge and divine judge, whereas that in *The Conquest of Granada* evokes no such analogy: it is governed by a spurious text (the Koran), and its function is rather to show (like the mimic combat which celebrates Boabdelin's betrothal) that the governing rituals of civilization are essentially transmutations and attenuations of raw violence. Yet even here the line doubles back on itself: justice makes a partial but pronounced return in the 1690s, rarely with a sense of immediate divine agency, but frequently with a sense of overall and mysterious divine control.

The late seventeenth century encourages oversimplification. The special circumstances of the early Restoration produced a drama that was unusually hierarchical and reactionary (far more so than most Jacobean drama), produced by amateurs of exceptionally exalted social standing, whose prominence was in part due simply to the dearth of trained professionals after the long closure of the theatres; at the other end of the period, the constraints of theatrical writing in (once again) the aftermath of an initially precarious revolution encouraged a drama of Whig wish-fulfilment, which signally simplifies both the national and parliamentary perception of the King and his policies. Each is a significant and interesting historical phenomenon, but each stands in a different, though similarly incomplete, relationship to its time, and one cannot simply put both on the same graph and draw a line between them.

Nor, in the quest for symmetry, should one ignore the sheer untidiness of much of the particular evidence. There could scarcely be two more contrasting

---

5 'The ordered, providentially guided, mathematically regulated universe of Newton gave a model for a stable and prosperous polity, ruled by the self-interest of men' (Jacob, *The Newtonians and the English Revolution*, 18).

developments from 1660s carnival comedy than *The Country-Wife* and *Love in the Dark*; yet both were King's Company plays of 1675. And, while Dryden, Wycherley, and Crowne were wrapping the sign in ever more complex enigma, Ravenscroft was emphasizing its potential for pellucid clarity. When one turns from cross-section to sequence, one finds fashions (such as gay couple comedy) taking off and developing, but one also finds action and re-action, false starts, and sudden halts or periods of hibernation. The gay couple comedy which emerged in the mid-1660s certainly initiates the move towards the full-blown sex comedy of a decade later (though adaptations of Tuke's model were initially just as common). But the progress towards sexual abandon was interrupted by four years of only peripherally bawdy experi-mentation with Molière, and sex comedy itself was a rapidly changing phe-nomenon. *The Country-Wife* is anything but an archetypal Restoration comedy; rather, it shows what had become possible in 1675. Two years earlier, the time for such a play had not come; two years later, it had passed. *The Man of Mode* is a similarly unique product of a particular moment. Though vastly more influential than *The Country-Wife*, it produced reaction rather than direct imitation: a drama largely hostile to the predatory rake and sympath-etic to his victims. Audience taste see-sawed, too. As Hume has observed, four sex comedies failed in 1678, and only one comedy was staged in the 1678–9 season. When comedy resumed, it was dominated by politics, and in the lean period of the mid-1680s farce proved a safer bet than the exploration of sex. Although the modern theatrical repertoire of Restoration plays seems to show an uninterrupted progress of sex comedy from the 1670s to the 1690s, the successful sex comedies of the 1690s are sporadic exceptions to the gen-eral trend, and are often deeply engaged with the predominant enforcement of sexual morality. Durfey's *The Campaigners* moves from adultery to re-form, while confronting the imaginative limitations of the reformist outlook. *The Relapse* reacts against reform, yet portrays it, and yet again hints at the emotional blight that Amanda's triumphant virtue may bring. In *The Way of the World*, Mrs Fainall's sexual transgression is in the past, yet its con-sequences live on, and the public moral consensus of censoriousness means that personal scandal can destructively engulf a whole family in a way that is unimaginable in *The Country-Wife* and *The Man of Mode*. Despite its de-served reputation for polished and precious elegance, no other late seven-teenth-century play comes closer to Ibsen.

Yet it is restrictive to categorize comedy according to its sexual laxity (or liberalism) and probity (or repressiveness). On a simple bed-count, *An Evening's Love* is thoroughly chaste, and quite undeserving of Pepys's and Evelyn's outrage, yet it treats Christian eschatology with a blasphemous lev-ity that Wycherley never attempted and Etherege never equalled. While not a sex comedy, it fully displays the intellectual conditions that made sex comedy possible; for a decision to portray adultery sympathetically requires a number of antecedent and perhaps more fundamental departures from orthodoxy. Thus, years before Horner amassed his mistresses and cuckolds, we find dramatists portraying a universe of chance, where the social artefact of language cannot touch or convey the transcendent, where social systems themselves lack divine sanction, and where the claim of social systems on individual life, while inescapable, is also partial, ambiguous, and morally neutral. Equally, the changed emphasis in post-Revolution comedy involves far more than a renewed popularization of sexual reform and human benevolence. What is most noticeable is the widespread (though by no means unanimous) affirmation that the individual can find an appropriate and congruent social place: the renewed interest in the resurrection of the home, escape from dislocation, and attainment of justice; and, along with a renewed confidence in the capacity of place to symbolize fixed and agreed social values, a renewed use of the literal stranger to represent threats to those values. Even so, there is a continuing interest in dislocation which crosses political boundaries, from Dryden to Vanbrugh. But it is never the same as the dislocation of the 1670s. The warring fusion of savage and citizen, the shared postulate of all the major tragedies and comedies of the 1670s, has simply gone. The rekindled interest in the home brings a more relaxed definition of where it might be. The first post-Revolution celebration of the restored home, Shadwell's *Bury-Fair*, is situated in Suffolk (where Shadwell had spent part of his childhood), and the 1690s witness a weakening in the hold of London, which reaches a mini-peak with the three rural comedies of 1696. Farquhar is certainly the first great playwright to move into the provinces, and the first who knew what to do with the natives, but he was not the first playwright of the period to make the move, countless programme-notes notwithstanding.

Tragedy has been less subject to catch-all generalization than comedy, though the heroic play has been greatly oversimplified and misunderstood. The earliest heroic plays, *The Siege of Rhodes* and the tragedies of Orrery, are aristocratic and hierarchical, treating the individual as the mere sum of his social obligations, and endorsing Stuart monarchy, *The Siege of Rhodes* with politic indirectness, *The Generall* with equally politic ostentation (though for both men art disguised their own conduct as political beings at least as much as it expressed it). But exasperation with Charles II's conduct infiltrated even this stage of the heroic play, and *Mustapha* in particular combines the standard motif of Restoration with dark musings upon villainous counsellors, amorous kings, and an imperilled succession. And, as soon as Dryden made the heroic play his own, he reacted vigorously against the Orrery model, emphasizing the incompleteness of reason, language, and social instinct, and the fallibility of rigidly ordered codes amidst the tangled ambiguities of life. After 1670, the predominant theme of tragedy was tyranny, the fragmentation of authority, and the difficulties of succession. Heroic plays proliferated in this period, but they were inspired by Dryden's model, not Orrery's, and it is a grave mistake to treat two radically contradictory forms of drama as if they represented a single, uniform genre. It is also a mistake to attach too much ideological significance to the persistence of heroic drama into the 1670s. However it may strike us now, *The Conquest of Granada* was the most impressive serious play to appear between 1660 and the mid-1670s, and the ensuing wave of often feeble and short-lived Siege, Conquest, and Destruction plays reveals little more than that minor dramatists are unoriginal beings with a strong disposition to imitate the successes of their betters. When two new dramatists of talent, Otway and Lee, appear, they strike new paths, initially treating traditional heroic subjects with extremes of irony and distortion, and quickly moving beyond them altogether to expose the voluble agonies of individual minds trapped in inescapable yet imaginatively unacceptable networks of power and internalized duty.[6]

In their paradoxically linked rebelliousness and submissiveness, tragic heroes such as Polydore, Jaffeir, and Lee's Titus clearly recall the comic heroes—Horner, Manly, and many others—who are inescapably drawn into complicity with the social codes they reject, and the close intellectual links between tragedy and comedy discredit the hardy misconception that the Carolean audience was peculiarily split in its personality, turning into Mr Hyde to watch *The Country-Wife* and reverting to Dr Jekyll in order to demand more and more heroism. Idealistic and libertine plays were staged alongside each other (*The Valiant Cid* and, probably, *Mustapha* were staged in 1675),[7] but the new drama of the 1670s does not reveal a market for the ideal. The striking thing about Horner is not that he was contemporary with Clorimun and Mustapha—plainly he was not—but that he was contemporary with Lee's Nero and Augustus. The mores of Charles II's court took a long time to reach the stage, but I see no reason to doubt the view of Dryden and others that the stage was touched by the court's example. But it was touched in two ways, the progress towards the cheerful and essentially harmless bedhopper being shadowed and anticipated by that towards the tyrannical and Sardanapalian rapist. And, almost as soon as the innocuous bed-hopper had arrived, he disappeared in a puff of smoke to leave Dorimant, Goodvile, Thomas Frollick, and Nemours.

The ideology of drama during the Exclusion Crisis is unstable and (particularly in the case of tragedy) often shamelessly attendant upon the twists and turns of events; one cannot here look for organic development of form or philosophy. Clearly the greatest, and most influential, plays of the Crisis were *The Orphan* and *Venice Preserv'd*, for Otway's naked portrayal of volcanic and tormented desire provided the impetus for the lavish exposure of personal sensation in post-Revolution plays, both tragic (e.g. *Queen Catharine*) and comic: in Craufurd's *Courtship A-la-Mode*, for example, a fallen woman

---

[6] The diversity of drama in the mid-1670s is well analysed in Cannan, 'New Directions in Serious Drama'.   [7] *The London Stage*, ed. Van Lennep, i. 221, 261.

repents the wild roaming of her past and, in Otwayesque verse, imagines herself naked upon a sea-shore (II, pp. 17–18). Such plays, however, imitate manner rather than substance, spinning out desire and sorrow with none of the psychological depth and confusion that mark the outpourings of Otway's characters: outpourings which lay bare dark, inarticulate regions of the self that lie outside the compass of reason. The lovers in *Queen Catharine* suffer because legitimate desire is oppressed by unjust authority; Craufurd's heroine suffers because unsanctioned desire has transgressed a just code. Rarely are tragic victims in the 1690s engulfed by conflicts and impasses inextricably present in attempts at civilized existence: destruction comes rather from particular miscalculation, or particular villainy.

Thomas Southerne, the most important tragedian of the 1690s, was also the one who retained the fullest sense of fatal flaws in the fabric of civilization itself, perhaps because he most directly addresses the decisive social changes that were gathering pace in the period. *The Fatal Marriage* is certainly not a bourgeois tragedy (Baldwin is a count, and his oppressiveness is clearly linked to the system of power which he represents), but both this play and *Oroonoko* show the power of money to dissolve orders based on faith and the word. *Venice Preserv'd* is the first post-Restoration tragedy in which the practical and imaginative power of money is represented, but Southerne was the first post-Restoration tragedian to renew exploration of the clash between aristocratic and monetary power. Yet his tragedies are frustrating disappointments. While it is difficult to see how Congreve's *The Mourning Bride* could ever have been great, it is perfectly possible to imagine great tragedy being fashioned out of Behn's *Oroonoko*, and one can only feel disappointment at the simple and overblown way in which Southerne handled so promising a subject, especially when one thinks not only of the quality of his best comedies but of their near-tragic dimensions. In a recent seminar, the actor Philip Voss remarked on the spur of the moment that no comedies were currently (1994–5) running at the Swan in Stratford; yet the Swan repertoire includes a triumphant revival of *The Wives' Excuse*. One can see his point, for the primary subject of the play is unresolvable distress and doubt. The play ingeniously multiplies the endless, sometimes petty, yet always intolerable distresses which blight marriage between an intelligent, sensitive woman and a foolish and selfish social charlatan, and it emphasizes that life is a constant state of ambiguity, in which actions and motives are generally double and self-contradictory: Wittwoud's attempt to betray Sightly to Wilding, one of the basest actions in the play, also has a perverse dimension of principle, since it springs from her desire to rescue her cousin Fanny from him. At the end, confronted with the meaningless choice between a philandering husband and a philandering lover, Mrs Friendall preserves her integrity by rejecting both. But the permanence with which she rejects adultery is unclear, the play's given ending contradicts its title, and Southerne carries the principle of doubleness so far as to have a character within the play busily engaged in writing '*The Wives Excuse*, or, *Cuckolds make themselves*' (III. ii. 234). Who knows how the *doppelgänger* play will end?

Such ambiguities are now unknown in tragedy, and no tragic heroine endures the subtle, inventively particularized humiliations and temptations of Mrs Friendall (or Lady Brute); for love and lust in post-Revolution tragedies are generally simple, repetitive conditions, opposing polarities of requited and unrequited, permitted and forbidden, pure and impure. Some plays, such as Granville's *Heroick Love*, do provide tragic equivalents to the comedy of marital discord, but there is nothing subtle, inventive, or particularized about the sufferings of Agamemnon and Chruseis: there is simply a long, sub-Otwayesque moan. In comparison with the choices facing Mrs Friendall, those even of Southerne's own Isabella are formulated with a stark and polarized symmetry: survival, or suicidal fidelity to a probably dead husband. The choice is misleading, since she is not to know that her first husband is about to walk through the door, but even this misleadingness presents a simple polarity of truth and error, quite different from the ambiguities of Mrs Friendall's life: for Mrs Friendall, there is no such thing as a right choice, and there is nothing that could be saved by anything as simple as a day's delay. Even the comic plots in *The Fatal Marriage* and *Oroonoko* lack the bleak unresolvedness of *The Wives' Excuse* and *The Maid's Last Prayer*, cultivating instead the safer and simpler style of *Sir Anthony Love*. Southerne would scarcely, of course, have continued to exploit a comic style that had brought him so little success; nevertheless, the simpler form of comedy corresponds more satisfactorily to the shape of the tragedies. Yet it is *The Wives' Excuse* and *The Way of the World*, not *The Fatal Marriage* and *The Mourning Bride*, which constitute the best serious drama of the decade, and the ones which handle situations which we could now easily class as tragic. If it is idle to look in Restoration drama for precursors of Halvard Solness, and if Captain Lassen in his straitjacket has no closer precursor than Sir Paul Plyant, we can in the 1690s dimly begin to see the frustrations and obstacles that were to blight Hedda Gabler and Paula Tanqueray; but we see them most convincingly in comedy.

Bibliography of Non-Dramatic Texts

PRIMARY SOURCES

ALLESTREE, RICHARD, *The Gentlemans Calling* (London, 1660).

—— *The Art of Contentment. By the Author of the Whole Duty of Man* (Oxford, 1675).

An Antidote against the Present Fears and Jealousies of the Nation (London, 1679).

ARIOSTO, LODOVICO, *Orlando Furioso* (4 vols., Milan, 1955).

ARISTOTLE, *De Interpretatione*, tr. E. M. Edghill, in *The Works of Aristotle*, ed. J. A. Smith and W. D. Ross (12 vols., Oxford, 1908–52), i.

ASSHETON, WILLIAM, *A Discourse against Blasphemy*, 3rd edn. (London, 1694).

ASTELL, MARY, *A Serious Proposal to the Ladies, for the Advancement of their True and Greatest Interest* (London, 1694).

AUBREY, JOHN, *'Brief Lives', Chiefly of Contemporaries*, ed. Andrew Clark (2 vols., Oxford, 1898).

BENTLEY, RICHARD, *The Correspondence of Richard Bentley, D. D.*, ed. Christopher Wordsworth (2 vols., London, 1842).

BEVERIDGE, WILLIAM, *The Theological Works of William Beveridge, D. D.*, Library of Anglo-Catholic Theology (12 vols., Oxford, 1842–8).

BLOUNT, CHARLES, *Great is Diana of the Ephesians* (London, 1680).

—— *The Two First Books, of Philostratus. Concerning the Life of Apollonius Tyaneus* (London, 1680).

——, GILDON, CHARLES, et al., *The Oracles of Reason* (London, 1693).

BOYLE, ROBERT, *Some Considerations about the Reconcileableness of Reason and Religion* (London, 1675).

—— *Some Physico-Theological Considerations about the Possibility of the Resurrection* (London, 1675).

—— *A Free Enquiry into the Vulgarly Receiv'd Notion of Nature* (London, 1685/6).

BRADY, NICHOLAS, *A Sermon Preach'd . . . at the Cathedral Church of St. Paul on Monday the Twenty Ninth Day of May, 1738* (London, 1738).

BRATHWAIT, RICHARD, *The English Gentleman; and the English Gentlewoman*, 3rd edn. (London, 1641).

CHARRON, PIERRE, *De la sagesse, trois livres*, ed. Amaury Duval (3 vols., Paris, 1824; repr. Geneva, 1968).

CLIFFORD, ARTHUR (ed.), *Tixall Poetry* (Edinburgh, 1813).

COLLIER, JEREMY, *A Short View of the Immorality, and Profaneness of the English Stage* (London, 1698).

—— *A Defence of the Short View of the Profaneness and Immorality of the English Stage* (London, 1699).

COMBER, THOMAS, *The Nature and Usefulness of Solemn Judicial Swearing* (London, 1682).

CORDEMOY, LOUIS GÉRAUD DE, *A Philosophicall Discourse concerning Speech* (London, 1668).

CRANLEY, THOMAS, *Amanda; or, The Reformed Whore* (London, 1635).

CROWNE, JOHN, DRYDEN, JOHN, and SHADWELL, THOMAS, *Notes and Observations on The Empress of Morocco* (London, 1674).

CULVERWEL [*for* CULVERWELL], NATHANAEL, *An Elegant and Learned Discourse Of the Light of Nature, With several other Treatises* (London, 1654).

DANCHIN, PIERRE (ed.), *The Prologues and Epilogues of the Restoration, 1660–1700* (4 parts in 7 vols., Nancy, 1981–8).

DENNIS, JOHN, *The Danger of Priestcraft to Religion and Government* (London, 1702).

—— *Priestcraft Distinguish'd from Christianity* (London, 1715).

—— *The Critical Works of John Dennis*, ed. Edward Niles Hooker (2 vols., Baltimore, 1939–43).

DESCARTES, RENÉ, *Œuvres de Descartes*, ed. Charles Adam and Paul Tannery (11 vols., Paris, 1897–1909; repr. 1964–74).

DOWNES, JOHN, *Roscius Anglicanus*, ed. Judith Milhous and Robert D. Hume (London, 1987).

DRYDEN, JOHN, *The Vindication; or, the Parallel of the French Holy-League, and the English League and Covenant, Turn'd into a Seditious Libell against the* King *and his* Royal Highness, *By Thomas Hunt and the Authors of the Reflections upon the Pretended Parallel in the Play called The Duke of Guise* (London, 1683).

—— *The Works of John Dryden*, ed. Walter Scott (18 vols., London, 1808).

—— *The Letters of John Dryden*, ed. Charles E. Ward (Durham, NC, 1942).

—— *The Works of John Dryden* (20 vols., 1956–   ), i, ed. Edward Niles Hooker *et al.* (Berkeley and Los Angeles, 1956); iii, ed. Earl Miner *et al.* (Berkeley and Los Angeles, 1969).

EVELYN, JOHN, *The Diary of John Evelyn*, ed. E. S. de Beer (6 vols., Oxford, 1955).

FONTENELLE, BERNARD LE BOVIER DE, *The History of Oracles and the Cheats of the Pagan Priests*, tr. Aphra Behn (London, 1688).

FREEMAN, ARTHUR (ed.), *A Comparison between the Two Stages* (New York and London, 1973).

GAILHARD, JEAN, *The Compleat Gentleman; or, Directions for the Education of Youth* (London, 1678).

GASSENDI, PIERRE, *Disquisitio Metaphysica*, ed. Bernard Rochot (Paris, 1962).

GAYA, LOUIS DE, *Matrimonial Customs; or, the Various Ceremonies, and Divers Ways of Celebrating Weddings, Practised amongst all the Nations, in the whole World* (London, 1687).

GENEST, JOHN, *Some Account of the English Stage from the Restoration in 1660 to 1830* (10 vols., Bath, 1832).

GILDON, CHARLES, *The Deist's Manual; or, a Rational Enquiry into the Christian Religion* (London, 1705).

—— *et al.*, *Miscellaneous Letters and Essays, on Several Subjects* (London, 1694).

GRAHAM, RICHARD, VISCOUNT PRESTON, *Angliæ Speculum Morale: The Moral State of England* (London, 1670).

GRAZIANI, GIROLAMO, *Il Conquisto di Granata* (Parnaso Italiano, 38–9; 2 vols., Venice, 1789).

HICKES, GEORGE, *The True Notion of Persecution Stated* (London, 1681).

—— *A Discourse of the Soveraign Power, in a Sermon Preached at St. Mary Le Bow, Nov. 28. 1682* (London, 1682).

—— *The Judgment of an Anonymous Writer Concerning These following Particulars*, 2nd edn. (London, 1684).

HICKMAN, CHARLES, *A Sermon Preached . . . Octob. 2. 1692* (London, 1692).

—— *Fourteen Sermons Preach'd, at St. James's Church in Westminster* (London, 1700).

HOBBES, THOMAS, *The English Works of Thomas Hobbes of Malmesbury*, ed. Sir William Molesworth (11 vols., London, 1839–45; repr. Aalen, 1966).

—— *Leviathan*, ed. C. B. Macpherson (Harmondsworth, 1968).

—— *Computatio sive Logica*, translation and commentary by Aloysius Martinich, ed. and introd. by Isabel C. Hungerland and George R. Vick (New York, 1981).

HOMER, *Iliad*, ed. D. B. Monro (2 vols., Oxford, 1888).

HORACE, *Q. Horati Flacci Opera*, ed. Thomas Ethelbert Page, Arthur Palmer, and A. S. Wilkins (London, 1910).

HOWARD, SIR ROBERT, *The History of Religion* (London, 1694).

HYDE, EDWARD, EARL OF CLARENDON, *The Life of Edward Earl of Clarendon* (3 vols., Oxford, 1759).

—— *The History of the Rebellion and Civil Wars in England, Begun in the Year 1641*, ed. W. Dunn Macray (6 vols., Oxford, 1888).

JEKILL [*for* JEKYLL], THOMAS, *A Sermon Preach'd . . . June 27. 1698* (London, 1698).

JOHNSON, SAMUEL, *Lives of the English Poets*, ed. George Birkbeck Hill (3 vols., Oxford, 1905).

KNOLLES, RICHARD, *The Turkish History*, 6th edn. (London, 1687).

L'ESTRANGE, ROGER, *Citt and Bumpkin, in a Dialogue Over a Pot of Ale*, 4th edn. (London, 1680).

LA MOTHE LE VAYER, FRANÇOIS DE, ['ORATIUS TUBERO'], *Cincq dialogues, faits à l'imitation des Anciens* (2 vols., Frankfurt am Main, 1716).

LANGBAINE, GERARD, *An Account of the English Dramatick Poets* (Oxford, 1691; repr. Hildesheim, 1968).

LA ROCHEFOUCAULD, FRANÇOIS DE, *Maximes*, ed. Jacques Truchet (Paris, 1967).

LAWRENCE, WILLIAM, *Marriage by the Morall Law of God Vindicated against All Ceremonial Laws* (London, 1680).

—— *The Right of Primogeniture, in Succession to the Kingdoms of England, Scotland, and Ireland* (London, 1681).

LESLIE, CHARLES, *The Charge of Socinianism against Dr. Tillotson Considered* (Edinburgh, 1695).

LETSOME, SAMPSON, and NICHOLL, JOHN (eds.), *A Defence of Natural and Revealed Religion: Being a Collection of the Sermons Preached at the Lecture Founded by the Honourable Robert Boyle, Esq; (From the Year 1691 to the Year 1732)* (3 vols., London, 1739).

LOCKE, JOHN, *An Essay Concerning Human Understanding*, ed. Peter H. Nidditch (Oxford, 1975).

LORD, GEORGE DEF. (gen. ed.), *Poems on Affairs of State: Augustan Satirical Verse, 1660–1714*, (7 vols., New Haven and London, 1963–75).

LUCAS, RICHARD, *Sixteen Sermons, The Eight Last of which were Preach'd upon Particular Occasions* (London, 1716).

LUCRETIUS, *Titi Lucreti Cari, De Rerum Natura Libri Sex*, ed. Cyril Bailey (3 vols., Oxford, 1947).

M., A., *The Reformed Gentleman; or, The Old English Morals Rescued from the Immoralities of the Present Age* (London, 1693).

MACKENZIE, SIR GEORGE, *Moral Gallantry* (Edinburgh, 1667).

MILTON, JOHN, *Poetical Works*, ed. Douglas Bush (London, 1966).

MONTAIGNE, MICHEL EYQUEM DE, *Montaigne's Essays*, tr. John Florio, Everyman's Library (3 vols., London and New York, 1910).

MOORE, JOHN, *A Sermon Preach'd . . . 28th of May, 1682* (London, 1682).

NEVILLE, HENRY, *Plato Redivivus; or, A Dialogue Concerning Government, in Two English Republican Tracts*, ed. Caroline Robbins (Cambridge, 1969).

OGILBY, JOHN, *The Entertainment of His Most Excellent Majestie Charles II . . . A Facsimile*, introd. Ronald Knowles (Binghamton, NY, 1988).

PANTON, EDWARD, *Speculum Juventutis; or, a True Mirror; where Errors in Breeding Noble and Generous Youth . . . are clearly made manifest* (London, 1671).

PARKER, SAMUEL, *A Discourse of Ecclesiastical Politie*, 3rd edn. (London, 1671).

PARSONS, ROBERT, *A Sermon Preached at the Funeral of the Right Honourable John Earl of Rochester*, in Gilbert Burnet, *Some Passages in the Life and Death of John, Earl of Rochester* (London, 1810).

PATRICK, SIMON, *A Sermon Preached . . . Novemb. 13.* (London, 1678).

PEACHAM, HENRY, *Peacham's Compleat Gentleman 1634*, ed. G. S. Gordon (Oxford, 1906).

PEPYS, SAMUEL, *The Diary of Samuel Pepys*, ed. Robert Latham and William Matthews (11 vols., London, 1970–83).

RAMESAY, WILLIAM, *The Gentlemans Companion; or, A Character of True Nobility, and Gentility* (London, 1672).

RERESBY, SIR JOHN, *Memoirs & Travels of Sir John Reresby Bart.* (London, 1904).

SAWYER, THOMAS, *Antigamus; or, A Satyr against Marriage* (Oxford, 1681).

SCOTT, JOHN, *The Christian Life*, Part ii, 2nd edn. (London, 1686).

SCUDÉRY, GEORGES DE, *Alaric; ou, Rome vaincue* (Paris, 1654).

SCUDÉRY, MADELEINE DE, *Artamenes; or, the Grand Cyrus*, tr. F. G. (London, 1653). [Published under the name of Monsieur—i.e., Georges—de Scudéry.]

—— *Clelia, An Excellent New Romance* (London, 1678). [Published under the name of Monsieur de Scudéry].

SENECA, *Seneca's Tragedies*, tr. Frank Justus Miller, Loeb Classical Library (2 vols., London and New York, 1917).

SETTLE, ELKANAH, *Notes and Observations on The Empress of Morocco Revised* (London, '1674' [?1675]).

—— *The Character of a Popish Successour, and what England May Expect from Such a One*, 3rd edn. (London, 1681).

SHIPMAN, THOMAS, *Carolina; or, Loyal Poems* (London, 1683).

SMITH, JOHN, *Select Discourses*, 2nd edn. (Cambridge, 1673).

SOUTH, ROBERT, *Sermons Preached upon Several Occasions* (7 vols., Oxford, 1823).

SPINOZA, BENEDICT DE, *The Chief Works of Benedict de Spinoza*, tr. R. H. M. Elwes (2 vols., London, 1883; repr. New York, 1951).

SPRAT, THOMAS, *History of the Royal Society*, ed. Jackson I. Cope and Harold Whitmore Jones (St Louis and London, 1959).

STILLINGFLEET, EDWARD, *Six Sermons* (London, 1669).

TILLOTSON, JOHN, *The Works of the Most Reverend Dr. John Tillotson* (12 vols., London, 1757).

VIRGIL, P. *Vergili Maronis Opera*, ed. Fredericus Arturus Hirtzel (Oxford, 1900).

WALLER, EDMUND, *The Poems of Edmund Waller*, ed. G. Thorn Drury (2 vols., London, 1893).

WATTS, THOMAS, *The Christian Indeed, and Faithful Pastor* (London, 1714).

WILKINS, JOHN, *An Essay towards a Real Character, and a Philosophical Language* (London, 1668).

SECONDARY SOURCES

ARMISTEAD, J. M., *Nathaniel Lee*, Twayne's English Authors Series 270 (Boston, 1979).

ASHCRAFT, RICHARD, *Revolutionary Politics & Locke's 'Two Treatises of Government'* (Princeton, 1986).

BACON, JON LANCE, 'Wives, Widows, and Writings in Restoration Comedy', *Studies in English Literature*, 31 (1991), 427–43.

BARBOUR, FRANCES, 'The Unconventional Heroic Plays of Nathaniel Lee', *University of Texas Studies in English*, 20 (1940), 109–16.

BAZELY, L., *The Family of Boothby* (London, 1915), repr. from *Miscellanea Genealogica et Heraldica*, 5th ser., i (1914), 7–56, 115–18, 179–94.

BELL, MAUREEN, PARFITT, GEORGE, and SHEPHERD, SIMON, *A Biographical Dictionary of English Women Writers 1580–1720* (New York, London, Toronto, Sydney, Tokyo, and Singapore, 1990).

BERMAN, DAVID, 'Deism, Immortality, and the Art of Theological Lying', in *Deism, Masonry, and the Enlightenment: Essays Honoring Alfred Owen Aldridge*, ed. J. A. Leo Lemay (Newark, London, and Toronto, 1987).

—— *A History of Atheism in Britain: From Hobbes to Russell* (London, New York, and Sydney, 1988).

BIRDSALL, VIRGINIA OGDEN, *Wild Civility: The English Comic Spirit on the Restoration Stage* (Bloomington, Ind. and London, 1970).

BOTICA, ALLAN RICHARD, 'Audience, Playhouse and Play in Restoration Theatre, 1660–1710', D.Phil. thesis (Oxford, 1985).

BREDVOLD, LOUIS I., 'Dryden, Hobbes, and the Royal Society', *Modern Philology*, 25 (1927–8), 417–38, repr. in *Essential Articles for the Study of John Dryden*, ed. Swedenberg, pp. 314–40.

—— *The Intellectual Milieu of John Dryden: Studies in Some Aspects of Seventeenth-Century Thought* (Ann Arbor, 1934).

BROWN, LAURA, *English Dramatic Form, 1660–1700* (New Haven and London, 1981).

—— 'The Defenseless Woman and the Development of English Tragedy', *Studies in English Literature*, 22 (1982), 429–43.

BROWN, RICHARD E., 'Nathaniel Lee's Political Dramas, 1679–1683', *Restoration*, 10 (1986), 41–52.

BURKE, HELEN M., 'Wycherley's "Tendentious Joke": The Discourse of Alterity in *The Country Wife*', *The Eighteenth Century: Theory and Interpretation*, 29 (1988), 227–41.

BYWATERS, DAVID, 'Venice, Its Senate, and Its Plot in Otway's *Venice Preserv'd'*, *Modern Philology*, 80 (1982–3), 256–63.

—— *Dryden in Revolutionary England* (Berkeley, Los Angeles, and Oxford, 1991).

CANFIELD, J. DOUGLAS, 'The Authorship of *Emilia*: Richard Flecknoe's Revision of *Erminia*', *Restoration*, 3 (1979), 3–7.

—— 'Royalism's Last Dramatic Stand: English Political Tragedy, 1679–89', *Studies in Philology*, 82 (1985), 234–63.

—— '*Regulus* and *Cleomenes* and 1688: From Royalism to Self-Reliance', *Eighteenth-Century Life*, 12 (1988), 67–75.

—— *Word as Bond in English Literature from the Middle Ages to the Restoration* (Philadelphia, 1989).

—— 'Dramatic Shifts: Writing an Ideological History of Late Stuart Drama', *Restoration and 18th Century Theatre Research*, 2nd ser., 6/1 (1991), 1–9.

CANNAN, PAUL D., 'New Directions in Serious Drama on the London Stage, 1675–1678', *Philological Quarterly*, 73 (1994), 219–42.

CLARK, J. C. D., *English Society 1688–1832: Ideology, Social Structure and Political Practice during the Ancien Regime* (Cambridge, 1985).

COLEMAN, ANTONY, and HAMMOND, ANTONY (eds.), *Poetry and Drama 1570–1700: Essays in Honour of Harold F. Brooks*, (London, 1981).

COOKE, A. L., and STROUP, THOMAS B., 'The Political Implications in Lee's *Constantine the Great*', *Journal of English and Germanic Philology*, 49 (1950), 506–15.

COPELAND, NANCY, ' "Who Can . . . Her Own Wish Deny?": Female Conduct and Politics in Aphra Behn's *The City Heiress*', *Restoration and 18th Century Theatre Research*, 2nd ser., 8/1 (1993), 27–49.

CORDNER, MICHAEL, 'Time, the Churches, and Vanbrugh's Lord Foppington', *Durham University Journal*, 77 (1984–5), 11–17.

—— 'Marriage Comedy after the 1688 Revolution: Southerne to Vanbrugh', *Modern Language Review*, 85 (1990), 273–89.

DANCHIN, PIERRE, 'The Foundation of the Royal Academy of Music in 1674 and Pierre Perrin's *Ariane*', *Theatre Survey*, 25 (1984), 55–67.

DAVIES, H. NEVILLE, '*All for Love*: Texts and Contexts', *Cahiers Élisabéthains*, 36 (1989), 49–71.

DIAMOND, ELIN, '*Gestus* and Signature in Aphra Behn's *The Rover*', *ELH* 56 (1989), 519–41.

DOBSON, MICHAEL, *The Making of the National Poet: Shakespeare, Adaptation and Authorship, 1660–1769* (Oxford, 1992).

DROUGGE, HELGA, 'Colley Cibber's "Genteel Comedy": *Love's Last Shift* and *The Careless Husband*', *Studia Neophilologica*, 54 (1982), 61–79.

—— 'Love, Death, and Mrs. Barry in Thomas Southerne's Plays', *Comparative Drama*, 27 (1993), 408–25.

EDMUNDS, JOHN, ' "Timon of Athens" blended with "Le Misanthrope": Shadwell's Recipe for Satirical Tragedy', *Modern Language Review*, 64 (1969), 500–7.

EMPSON, WILLIAM, 'Dryden's Apparent Scepticism', *Essays in Criticism*, 20 (1970), 172–81.

—— 'A Deist Tract by Dryden', *Essays in Criticism*, 25 (1975), 74–100.

FEILING, KEITH, *A History of the Tory Party 1640–1714* (Oxford, 1924).

FERRY, ANNE DAVIDSON, *Milton and the Miltonic Dryden* (Cambridge, Mass., 1968).

FISHER, ALAN S., 'The Significance of Thomas Shadwell', *Studies in Philology*, 71 (1974), 225–46.

FOUCAULT, MICHEL, *The Order of Things: An Archaeology of the Human Sciences* (London, 1970).

FREEHAFER, JOHN, 'The Formation of the London Patent Companies in 1660', *Theatre Notebook*, 20 (1965–6), 6–30.

GAGEN, JEAN, 'The Design of the High Plot in Etherege's *The Comical Revenge*', *Restoration and 18th Century Theatre Research*, 2nd ser., 1/2 (1986), 1–15.

GARDINER, ANNE BARBEAU, 'A Conflict of Laws: Consequences of the King's Inaction in *The Duke of Guise*', *English Language Notes*, 19 (1981–2), 109–15.

—— 'Dryden's *Cleomenes* (1692) and Contemporary Jacobite Verse', *Restoration*, 12 (1988), 87–95.

—— 'John Dryden's *Love Triumphant* and English Hostility to Foreigners 1688–1693', *Clio*, 18 (1989), 153–70.

GARRETT, JANE, *The Triumphs of Providence: The Assassination Plot, 1696* (Cambridge, 1980).

GEWIRTZ, ARTHUR, *Restoration Adaptations of Early 17th Century Comedies* (Washington, DC, 1982).

GILL, JAMES E., 'Character, Plot, and the Language of Love in *The Relapse*: A Reappraisal', *Restoration*, 16 (1992), 110–25.

GRANSDEN, K. W., 'Milton, Dryden, and the Comedy of the Fall', *Essays in Criticism*, 26 (1976), 116–33.

GREGORY, TULLIO, 'Pierre Charron's "Scandalous Book" ', in *Atheism from the Reformation to the Enlightenment*, ed. Hunter and Wootton, pp. 87–109.

HALEY, K. H. D., *The First Earl of Shaftesbury* (Oxford, 1968).

HAMMOND, ANTONY, 'John Wilson and the Andronicus Plays: A Re-consideration', *Yearbook of English Studies*, 4 (1974), 112–19.

—— 'The "Greatest Action": Lee's *Lucius Junius Brutus*', in *Poetry and Drama 1570–1770*, ed. Coleman and Hammond, pp. 173–85.

HAMMOND, PAUL, 'Dryden's *Albion and Albanius*: The Apotheosis of Charles II', in *The Court Masque*, ed. David Lindley (Manchester, 1984), 169–83.

HARBAGE, ALFRED, 'Elizabethan-Restoration Palimpsest', *Modern Language Review*, 35 (1940), 287–319.

HARTH, PHILLIP, *Contexts of Dryden's Thought* (Chicago and London, 1968).

—— 'Dryden in 1678–1681: The Literary and Historical Perspectives', in *The Golden & The Brazen World: Papers in Literature and History, 1650–1800*, ed. John M. Wallace (Berkeley, Los Angeles, and London, 1985), 55–77.

—— 'Political Interpretations of *Venice Preserv'd*', *Modern Philology*, 85 (1987–8), 345–62.

—— *Pen for a Party: Dryden's Tory Propaganda in its Contexts* (Princeton, 1993).

HARTSOCK, MILDRED E., 'Dryden's Plays: A Study in Ideas', in *Seventeenth Century Studies (Second Series)*, ed. Robert Shafer (Princeton and London, 1937), 69–176.

HARWOOD, JOHN T., *Critics, Values, and Restoration Comedy* (Carbondale and Edwardsville, 1982).

HAUSER, DAVID R., 'Otway Preserved: Theme and Form in *Venice Preserv'd*', *Studies in Philology*, 55 (1958), 481–93.

HOBBY, ELAINE, *Virtue of Necessity: English Women's Writing 1649–88* (London, 1988).

HOLLAND, NORMAN N., *The First Modern Comedies: The Significance of Etherege, Wycherley and Congreve* (Cambridge, Mass., 1959).

HOLLAND, PETER, 'Durfey's Revisions of *The Richmond Heiress* (1693)', *Archiv für das Studium der neueren Sprachen und Literaturen*, 216 (1979), 116–20.

HORDERN, JOHN, and VANDER MOTTEN, J. P., '*Five New Playes*: Sir William Killigrew's Two Annotated Copies', *Library*, 6th ser., 11 (1989), 253–71.

HOTSON, LESLIE, *The Commonwealth and Restoration Stage* (Cambridge, Mass., 1928; repr. New York, 1962).

HOWE, ELIZABETH, *The First English Actresses: Women and Drama 1660–1700* (Cambridge, 1992).

HUGHES, DEREK, 'The Significance of *All for Love*', *ELH* 37 (1970), 540–63.

——'A New Look at *Venice Preserv'd*', *Studies in English Literature*, 11 (1971), 437–57.

—— '*Aphrodite katadyomene*: Dryden's Cleopatra on the Cydnos', *Comparative Drama*, 14 (1980), 35–45.

—— *Dryden's Heroic Plays* (London and Basingstoke, 1981).

—— 'Lee's *Lucius Junius Brutus* and Seneca's *Hercules Furens*', *American Notes and Queries*, 19 (1981), 103–4.

—— 'Dryden's *The Indian Emperour* and Georges de Scudéry's *Alaric*', *Review of English Studies*, NS 33 (1982), 47–51.

—— 'Art and Life in *All for Love*', *Studies in Philology*, 80 (1983), 84–107.

—— 'Providential Justice and English Comedy 1660–1700: A Review of the External Evidence', *Modern Language Review*, 81 (1986), 273–92.

HUME, ROBERT D., 'Dryden, James Howard, and the Date of *All Mistaken*', *Philological Quarterly*, 51 (1972), 422–9.

—— 'The Satiric Design of Nat. Lee's *The Princess of Cleve*', *Journal of English and Germanic Philology*, 75 (1976), 117–38, repr. in Hume, *The Rakish Stage*, 111–37.

—— *The Development of English Drama in the Late Seventeenth Century* (Oxford, 1976).

—— 'Marital Discord in English Comedy from Dryden to Fielding', *Modern Philology*, 74 (1976–7), 248–72, repr. in Hume, *The Rakish Stage*, 176–213.

—— (ed.), *The London Theatre World, 1660–1800* (Carbondale and Edwardsville, 1980).

—— 'Securing a Repertory: Plays on the London Stage 1660–5', in *Poetry and Drama 1570–1700*, ed. Coleman and Hammond, pp. 156–72.

—— 'The Nature of the Dorset Garden Theatre', *Theatre Notebook*, 36 (1982), 99–109.

—— ' "The Change in Comedy": Cynical Versus Exemplary Comedy on the London Stage, 1678–1693', *Essays in Theatre*, 1 (1982–3), 101–18.

—— *The Rakish Stage: Studies in English Drama, 1660–1800* (Carbondale and Edwardsville, Ill., 1983).

—— 'Opera in London, 1695–1706', in *British Theatre and the Other Arts, 1660–1800*, ed. Kenny, pp. 67–91.

—— and ZIMANSKY, CURT A., 'Thomas Shipman's *Henry the Third of France*: Some Questions of Date, Performance, and Publication', *Philological Quarterly*, 55 (1976), 436–44.

HUNTER, MICHAEL, ' "Aikenhead the Atheist": The Context and Consequences of Articulate Irreligion in the Late Seventeenth Century', in *Atheism from the Reformation to the Enlightenment*, ed. Hunter and Wootton, pp. 221–54.

—— and WOOTTON, David (eds.), *Atheism from the Reformation to the Enlightenment* (Oxford, 1992).

HUTTON, RONALD, *The Restoration: A Political and Religious History of England and Wales 1658–1667* (Oxford, 1985).

—— *Charles the Second: King of England, Scotland, and Ireland* (Oxford, 1989).

JACOB, MARGARET C., *The Newtonians and the English Revolution 1689–1720* (Hassocks, 1976).

JOHNSTON, JOSEPH S., JR., 'Sir William Killigrew's Revised Copy of his *Four New Plays*: Confirmation of His Claim to *The Imperial Tragedy*', *Modern Philology*, 74 (1976–7), 72–4.

JONES, J. R., *The Revolution of 1688 in England* (London, 1972).

—— *Country and Court: England, 1658–1714* (Cambridge, Mass., 1978).

JOSE, NICHOLAS, *Ideas of the Restoration in English Literature, 1660–71* (London and Basingstoke, 1984).

KASTAN, DAVID SCOTT, '*Nero* and the Politics of Nathaniel Lee', *Papers on Language and Literature*, 13 (1977), 125–35.

KENNY, SHIRLEY STRUM, 'Farquhar, Wilks, and Wildair; or, the Metamorphosis of the "Fine Gentleman"', *Philological Quarterly*, 57 (1978), 46–65.

—— 'The Publication of Plays', in *The London Theatre World*, ed. Hume, pp. 309–36.

—— (ed.), *British Theatre and the Other Arts, 1660–1800* (Washington, London, and Toronto, 1984).

KENYON, JOHN, *Revolution Principles: The Politics of Party 1689–1720* (Cambridge, 1977).

KING, BRUCE, *Dryden's Major Plays* (Edinburgh and London, 1966).

KROLL, RICHARD W. F., 'Discourse and Power in *The Way of the World*', *ELH* 53 (1986), 727–58.

LEVIN, RICHARD, 'Performance-Critics vs. Close Readers in the Study of English Renaissance Drama', *Modern Language Review*, 81 (1986), 545–59.

LOFTIS, JOHN, *The Spanish Plays of Neoclassical England* (New Haven and London, 1973).

LOVE, HAROLD, 'State Affairs on the Restoration Stage, 1660–1675', *Restoration and 18th Century Theatre Research*, 14/1 (1975), 1–9.

—— 'Who Were the Restoration Audience?', *Yearbook of English Studies*, 10 (1980), 21–44.

McBURNEY, WILLIAM H., 'Otway's Tragic Muse Debauched: Sensuality in *Venice Preserv'd*', *Journal of English and Germanic Philology*, 58 (1959), 380–99.

McFADDEN, GEORGE, 'Political Satire in *The Rehearsal*', *Yearbook of English Studies*, 4 (1974), 120–8.

MAGUIRE, NANCY KLEIN, 'Nahum Tate's *King Lear*: "the king's blest restoration" ', in *The Appropriation of Shakespeare: Post-Renaissance Reconstructions of the Works and the Myth*, ed. Jean I. Marsden (London, 1991), 29–42.

—— 'Regicide and Reparation: The Autobiographical Drama of Roger Boyle, Earl of Orrery', *English Literary Renaissance*, 21 (1991), 257–82.

—— *Regicide and Restoration: English Tragicomedy, 1660–1671* (Cambridge, 1992).

MARKLEY, ROBERT, *Two-Edg'd Weapons: Style and Ideology in the Comedies of Etherege, Wycherley, and Congreve* (Oxford, 1988).

MASON, JOHN E., *Gentlefolk in the Making: Studies in the History of English Courtesy Literature and Related Topics from 1531 to 1774* (Philadelphia, 1935; repr. New York, 1971).

MAUS, KATHARINE EISAMAN, '"Playhouse Flesh and Blood": Sexual Ideology and the Restoration Actress', *ELH* 46 (1979), 595–617.

MILHOUS, JUDITH, *Thomas Betterton and the Management of Lincoln's Inn Fields 1695–1708* (Carbondale, Edwardsville, London, and Amsterdam, 1979).

—— 'Company Management', in *The London Theatre World*, ed. Hume, pp. 1–34.

—— 'The Multimedia Spectacular on the Restoration Stage', in *British Theatre and the Other Arts, 1660–1800*, ed. Kenny, pp. 41–66.

—— and HUME, ROBERT D., 'Dating Play Premières from Publication Data, 1660–1700', *Harvard Library Bulletin*, 22 (1974), 374–405.

——and—— 'Attribution Problems in English Drama, 1660–1700', *Harvard Library Bulletin*, 31 (1983), 5–39.

——and—— *Producible Interpretation: Eight English Plays 1675–1707* (Carbondale and Edwardsville, 1985).

——and—— 'New Light on English Acting Companies in 1646, 1648, and 1660', *Review of English Studies*, NS 42 (1991), 487–509.

MILLER, JOHN, *James II: A Study in Kingship*, rev. edn. (London, 1989).

—— *Charles II* (London, 1991).

MILLER, RACHEL A., 'Political Satire in the Malicorne–Melanax Scenes of *The Duke of Guise*', *English Language Notes*, 16 (1978–9), 212–18.

MILLS, LAURENS J., *One Soul in Bodies Twain: Friendship in Tudor Literature and Stuart Drama* (Bloomington, Ind., 1937).

MINTZ, SAMUEL I., *The Hunting of Leviathan: Seventeenth-Century Reactions to the Materialism and Moral Philosophy of Thomas Hobbes* (Cambridge, 1962).

MUNNS, JESSICA, 'Thomas Otway's *Titus and Berenice* and Racine's *Berenice*', *Restoration*, 7 (1983), 58–67.

—— ' "The Dark Disorders of a Divided State": Otway and Shakespeare's *Romeo and Juliet*', *Comparative Drama*, 19 (1985), 347–62.

MURRAY, BARBARA A., 'The Butt of Otway's Political Moral in *The History and Fall of Caius Marius* (1680)', *Notes and Queries*, 234 (1989), 48–50.

NEILL, MICHAEL, 'Horned Beasts and China Oranges: Reading the Signs in *The Country Wife*', *Eighteenth-Century Life*, 12 (1988), 3–17.

NEMAN, BETH S., 'Setting the Record Straight on John Crowne', *Restoration and 18th Century Theatre Research*, 2nd ser., 8/1 (1993), 1–26.

NOVAK, MAXIMILLIAN E., 'The Closing of Lincoln's Inn Fields Theatre in 1695', *Restoration and 18th Century Theatre Research*, 14/1 (1975), 51–2.

—— 'Margery Pinchwife's "London Disease": Restoration Comedy and the Libertine Offensive of the 1670's', *Studies in the Literary Imagination*, 10 (1977), 1–23.

OGG, DAVID, *England in the Reign of Charles II*, 2nd edn. (2 vols., Oxford, 1955).

—— *England in the Reigns of James II and William III*, corrected edn. (Oxford, 1957), 5.

OLIVER, H. J., *Sir Robert Howard (1626–1698): A Critical Biography* (Durham, NC, 1963).

Owen, Susan Jane, ' "Partial tyrants" and "Freeborn People" in *Lucius Junius Brutus*', *Studies in English Literature*, 31 (1991), 463–82.

—— 'Drama and Politics in the Exclusion Crisis: 1678–83', Ph.D. thesis (Leeds, 1992).

—— 'Interpreting the Politics of Restoration Drama', *The Seventeenth Century*, 8 (1993), 67–97.

—— 'The Politics of John Dryden's *The Spanish Fryar; or, The Double Discovery*', *English*, 43 (1994), 97–113.

Parker, Gerald D., ' "History as Nightmare" in Nevil Payne's *The Siege of Constantinople* and Nathaniel Lee's *Lucius Junius Brutus*', *Papers on Language and Literature*, 21 (1985), 3–18.

Parnell, Paul E., 'Equivocation in Cibber's *Love's Last Shift*', *Studies in Philology*, 57 (1960), 519–34.

Patterson, Annabel, '*The Country Gentleman*: Howard, Marvell, and Dryden in the Theater of Politics', *Studies in English Literature*, 25 (1985), 491–509.

Payne, Deborah C., 'Reading the Signs in *The Country Wife*', *Studies in English Literature*, 26 (1986), 403–19.

—— 'Patronage and the Dramatic Marketplace under Charles I and II', *Yearbook of English Studies*, 21 (1991), 137–52.

Pearson, Jacqueline, *The Prostituted Muse: Images of Women & Women Dramatists 1642–1737* (New York, London, Toronto, Sydney, and Tokyo, 1988).

—— 'Gender and Narrative in the Fiction of Aphra Behn', *Review of English Studies*, NS 42 (1991), 40–56, 179–90.

Peters, Julie Stone, *Congreve, the Drama, and the Printed Word* (Stanford, Calif., 1990).

Pintard, René, *Le Libertinage érudit dans la première moitié du XVIIᵉ siècle* (Paris, 1943).

Popkin, Richard H., *The History of Scepticism from Erasmus to Spinoza* (Berkeley, Los Angeles, and London, 1979).

Price, Curtis A., *Henry Purcell and the London Stage* (Cambridge, 1984).

—— 'Political Allegory in Late-seventeenth-century Opera', in *Music and Theatre: Essays in Honour of Winton Dean*, ed. Nigel Fortune (Cambridge, 1987), 1–29.

Rawson, C. J., *Henry Fielding and the Augustan Ideal under Stress: 'Nature's Dance of Death' and other Studies* (London, 1972).

Redwood, John, *Reason, Ridicule and Religion: The Age of Enlightenment in England 1660–1750* (London, 1976).

Rich, Julia A., 'Heroic Tragedy in Southerne's *Oroonoko* (1695): An Approach to a Split-plot Tragicomedy', *Philological Quarterly*, 62 (1983), 187–200.

Rigaud, N. J., *George Etherege: dramaturge de la Restauration anglaise* (2 vols., Paris, 1980).

—— 'Les Faiblesses d'un héros: Dorimant dans *The Man of Mode*', *Études Anglaises*, 41 (1988), 24–36.

Robinson, K. E., 'A Glance at Rochester in Thomas Durfey's "Madam Fickle" ', *Notes and Queries*, 220 (1975), 264–5.

—— 'Two Cast Lists for Buckingham's "The Chances" ', *Notes and Queries*, 224 (1979), 436–7.

ROOT, ROBERT L., JR., *Thomas Southerne*, Twayne's English Authors Series 315 (Boston, 1981).

ROPER, ALAN, 'Language and Action in *The Way of the World, Love's Last Shift*, and *The Relapse*', *ELH* 40 (1973), 44–69.

ROTHSTEIN, ERIC, *Restoration Tragedy: Form and the Process of Change* (Madison, 1967).

—— and KAVENIK, FRANCES M., *The Designs of Carolean Comedy* (Carbondale and Edwardsville, 1988).

RUNDLE, JAMES URVIN, 'Wycherley and Calderón: A Source for *Love in a Wood*', *PMLA* 64 (1949), 701–7.

SCHILLE, CANDY B. K., 'Reappraising "Pathetic" Tragedies: *Venice Preserved* and *The Massacre of Paris*', *Restoration*, 12 (1988), 33–45.

SCOUTEN, ARTHUR H., 'The Premiere of Dryden's *Secret Love*', *Restoration*, 9 (1985), 9–11.

SIMMONS, EVA, ' "Virtue Intire": Aphra Behn's Contribution, in her Comedies, to the Marriage Debates of the Seventeenth Century', Ph.D. thesis (London, 1990).

SKRINE, PETER N., 'Blood, Bombast, and Deaf Gods: The Tragedies of Lee and Lohenstein', *German Life and Letters*, 24 (1971), 14–30.

SLAGLE, JUDITH B., 'Thomas Shadwell's Censored Comedy, *The Lancashire-Witches*: An Attack on Religious Ritual or Divine Right?', *Restoration and 18th Century Theatre Research*, 2nd ser., 7/1 (1992), 54–63.

SMITH, JOHN HARRINGTON, *The Gay Couple in Restoration Comedy* (Cambridge, Mass., 1948).

—— 'Shadwell, the Ladies, and the Change in Comedy', *Modern Philology*, 46 (1948–9), 22–33.

SOLOMON, HARRY M., 'The Rhetoric of "Redressing Grievances": Court Propaganda as the Hermeneutical Key to *Venice Preserv'd*', *ELH* 53 (1986), 289–310.

SORELIUS, GUNNAR, 'Shadwell Deviating into Sense: *Timon of Athens* and the Duke of Buckingham', *Studia Neophilologica*, 36 (1964), 232–44.

—— 'The Rights of the Restoration Theatrical Companies in the Older Drama', *Studia Neophilologica*, 37 (1965), 174–89.

SPURR, JOHN, 'Perjury, Profanity and Politics', *The Seventeenth Century*, 8 (1993), 29–50.

STAVES, SUSAN, 'Why Was Dryden's *Mr. Limberham* Banned?: A Problem in Restoration Theatre History', *Restoration and 18th Century Theatre Research*, 13/1 (1974), 1–11.

—— *Players' Scepters: Fictions of Authority in the Restoration* (Lincoln, Nebr. and London, 1979).

—— 'A Few Kind Words for the Fop', *Studies in English Literature*, 22 (1982), 413–28.

STOCKER, MARGARITA, 'Political Allusion in *The Rehearsal*', *Philological Quarterly*, 67 (1988), 11–35.

STONE, LAWRENCE, *The Crisis of the Aristocracy 1558–1641* (Oxford, 1965).

—— and STONE, JEANNE C. FAWTIER, *An Open Elite? England 1540–1880* (Oxford, 1984).

STRAKA, GERALD M., *Anglican Reaction to the Revolution of 1688* (Madison, 1962).

SUTHERLAND, JAMES, 'The Date of James Howard's "All Mistaken, or The Mad Couple" ', *Notes and Queries*, 209 (1964), 339–40.

SWEDENBERG, H. T., JR., (ed.) *Essential Articles for the Study of John Dryden* (Hamden, Conn., 1966).

TEETER, LOUIS, 'The Dramatic Use of Hobbes's Political Ideas', *ELH* 3 (1936), 140–169, repr. in *Essential Articles for the Study of John Dryden*, ed. Swedenberg, pp. 341–73.

THOMPSON, M. P., 'The Idea of Conquest in Controversies over the 1688 Revolution', *Journal of the History of Ideas*, 38 (1977), 33–46.

TUCK, RICHARD, 'The "Christian Atheism" of Thomas Hobbes', in *Atheism from the Reformation to the Enlightenment*, ed. Hunter and Wootton, pp. 111–30.

VANDER MOTTEN, J. P., *Sir William Killigrew (1605–1695): His Life and Dramatic Works* (Ghent, 1980).

—— 'Some Unpublished Restoration Prologues and Epilogues: New Light on the Stage History of Sir William Killigrew's Plays', *Modern Philology*, 77 (1979–80), 159–63.

VAN LENNEP, WILLIAM (ed.), *The London Stage 1660–1800* (5 parts in 11 vols., Carbondale, Ill., 1960–8, 1660–1700, introd. Emmett L. Avery and Arthur H. Scouten (1965).

VERNON, P. F., 'Wycherley's First Comedy and its Spanish Source', *Comparative Literature*, 18 (1966), 132–44.

VERRALL, A. W., *Lectures on Dryden*, ed. Margaret de G. Verrall (Cambridge, 1914; repr. New York, 1963).

VIATOR, TIMOTHY J., 'Nahum Tate's *Richard II*', *Theatre Notebook*, 42 (1988), 109–17.

VIETH, DAVID M., 'Psychological Myth as Tragedy: Nathaniel Lee's *Lucius Junius Brutus*', *Huntington Library Quarterly*, 39 (1975–6), 57–76.

—— 'The Discovery of the Date of *Mac Flecknoe*', in *Evidence in Literary Scholarship: Essays in Memory of James Marshall Osborn*, ed. René Wellek and Alvaro Ribeiro (Oxford, 1979), 63–87.

WALLACE, JOHN M., 'Otway's *Caius Marius* and the Exclusion Crisis', *Modern Philology*, 85 (1987–8), 363–72.

WALSH, MARTIN W., 'The Significance of William Mountfort's *Greenwich-Park*', *Restoration and 18th Century Theatre Research*, 12/1 (1973), 35–40.

WEBER, HAROLD M., *The Restoration Rake-Hero: Transformations in Sexual Understanding in Seventeenth-Century England* (Madison, 1986).

WHEATLEY, CHRISTOPHER J., ' "Power like new Wine": The Appetites of Leviathan and Durfey's *Massaniello*', *Studies in Eighteenth-Century Culture*, 22 (1992), 231–51.

—— 'Thomas Durfey's *A Fond Husband*, Sex Comedies of the Late 1670s and Early 1680s, and the Comic Sublime', *Studies in Philology*, 90 (1993), 371–90.

—— 'Thomas Shadwell's *The Volunteers* and the Rhetoric of Honor and Patriotism', *ELH* 60 (1993), 397–418.

WIKANDER, MATTHEW H., 'The Spitted Infant: Scenic Emblem and Exclusionist Politics in Restoration Adaptations of Shakespeare', *Shakespeare Quarterly*, 37 (1986), 340–58.

WINN, JAMES ANDERSON, *John Dryden and his World* (New Haven and London, 1987).

WINTERBOTTOM, JOHN A., 'The Place of Hobbesian Ideas in Dryden's Tragedies',

Journal of English and Germanic Philology, 57 (1958), 665–83, repr. in *Essential Articles for the Study of John Dryden*, ed. Swedenberg, pp. 374–94.

YOTS, MICHAEL A., 'Dryden's *All for Love* on the Restoration Stage', *Restoration and 18th Century Theatre Research*, 16/1 (1977), 1–10.

ZIMBARDO, ROSE A., *A Mirror to Nature: Transformations in Drama and Aesthetics 1660–1732* (Lexington, Ky., 1986).

Index of Plays

The following bibliographical list includes all editions of plays cited, with the exception of seventeenth-century quartos. These are identified in the index by a parenthetical date of publication. The other editions are identified by an appropriate short title or editor's name (e.g. *Works* or Cordner), accompanied where necessary by a volume number. One exceptional case is *Mr. Turbulent; or, The Melanchollicks* (London, 1682), which has been read in its second printing, under the title of *The Factious Citizen; or, The Melancholy Visioner* (London, 1685).

I. COLLECTED EDITIONS

The Dramatic Works in the Beaumont and Fletcher Canon, ed. Fredson Bowers (10 vols., Cambridge, 1966–   ).

The Works of Aphra Behn, ed. Montague Summers (6 vols., London and Stratford-upon-Avon, 1915; repr. New York, 1967).

The Dramatic Works of Roger Boyle Earl of Orrery, ed. William Smith Clark, II (2 vols; Cambridge, Mass., 1937).

The Dramatic Works of William Burnaby, ed. F. E. Budd (London, 1931).

The Dramatic Works of Colley Cibber, Esq. (5 vols., London, 1777; repr. New York, 1966).

The Complete Plays of William Congreve, ed. Herbert Davis (Chicago and London, 1967).

The Works of Sir William D'avenant K^t (London, 1673).

The Dramatic Works of Thomas Dekker, ed. Fredson Bowers (4 vols., Cambridge, 1953–61).

The Dramatick Works of John Dryden, Esq. (6 vols., London, 1735).

The Works of John Dryden (20 vols., 1956–   ), viii, ed. John Harrington Smith *et al.* (Berkeley and Los Angeles, 1967); ix, ed. John Loftis and Vinton A. Dearing (Berkeley, Los Angeles, and London, 1966); x, ed. Maximillian E. Novak and George Robert Guffey (Berkeley, Los Angeles, and London, 1970); xi, ed. John Loftis *et al.* (Berkeley, Los Angeles, and London, 1978); xiii, ed. Maximillian E. Novak, George R. Guffey, and Alan Roper (Berkeley, Los Angeles, and London, 1984); xiv, ed. Vinton A. Dearing and Alan Roper (Berkeley, Los Angeles, and London, 1992); xv, ed. Earl Miner, George R. Guffey, and Franklin B. Zimmerman (Berkeley, Los Angeles, and London, 1976).

The Dramatic Works of Sir George Etherege, ed. H. F. B. Brett-Smith (2 vols., Oxford, 1927).

The Works of George Farquhar, ed. Shirley Strum Kenny (2 vols., Oxford, 1988).

Poems and Dramas of Fulke Greville First Lord Brooke, ed. Geoffrey Bullough (2 vols., Edinburgh and London [1939]).

Ben Jonson, ed. C. H. Herford, Percy and Evelyn Simpson (11 vols., Oxford, 1925–52).

The Works of Nathaniel Lee, ed. Thomas B. Stroup and Arthur L. Cooke (2 vols., New Brunswick, NJ, 1954–5).

The Plays and Poems of Philip Massinger, ed. Philip Edwards and Colin Gibson (5 vols., Oxford, 1976).

The Works of Thomas Middleton, ed. A. H. Bullen (8 vols., London, 1885–6).

Œuvres complètes de Molière, ed. Robert Jouanny (2 vols., Paris, 1962).

The Works of Thomas Otway, ed. J. C. Ghosh (2 vols., Oxford, 1932).

The Works of Henry Purcell, 2nd edn. (32 vols. London, 1961–   ), xix, *The Indian Queen*, ed. Margaret Laurie and Andrew Pinnock (1994).

Racine, *Œuvres complètes*, préface de Pierre Clarac (Paris, 1962).

The Dramatick Works of Nicholas Rowe, Esq. (2 vols., London, 1720; repr. Farnborough, 1971).

The Poetical and Dramatic Works of Sir Charles Sedley, ed. V. de Sola Pinto (2 vols., London, 1928).

The Complete Works of Thomas Shadwell, ed. Montague Summers (5 vols., London, 1927; repr. New York, 1968).

The Dramatic Works and Poems of James Shirley, ed. William Gifford (6 vols., London, 1833).

The Works of Thomas Southerne, ed. Robert Jordan and Harold Love (2 vols., Oxford, 1988).

The Complete Works of Sir John Vanbrugh, ed. Bonamy Dobrée and Geoffrey Webb (4 vols., Bloomsbury, 1927–8).

The Works of His Grace, George Villiers, Late Duke of Buckingham (2 vols., London, 1715).

Collected Works of John Wilmot Earl of Rochester, ed. John Hayward (London, 1926).

The Plays of William Wycherley, ed. Arthur Friedman (Oxford, 1979).

II. INDIVIDUAL EDITIONS AND ANTHOLOGIES

Anon., *The Tragedy of Nero*, ed. Elliott M. Hill (New York and London, 1979).

John Banks, *The Unhappy Favourite*, in *Restoration Tragedies*, ed. James Sutherland (London, Oxford, and New York, 1977).

Chef-d'œuvres dramatiques de Boursault (2 vols., Paris, 1791).

[Margaret Cavendish, Marchioness of Newcastle], *Playes Written by the Thrice Noble, Illustrious and Excellent Princess, the Lady Marchioness of Newcastle* (London, 1662).

George Chapman, *The Gentleman Usher*, ed. John Hazel Smith, Regents Renaissance Drama Series (London, 1970).

Colley Cibber: Three Sentimental Comedies, ed. Maureen Sullivan (New Haven and London, 1973).

Antonio Coello y Ochoa, *Los Empeños de seis horas*, in Sir Samuel Tuke, *The Adventures of Five Hours*, ed. A. E. H. Swaen (Amsterdam, 1927).

John Crowne, *City Politiques*, ed. John Harold Wilson, Regents Restoration Drama Series (London, 1967).

Davenant's 'Macbeth' from the Yale Manuscript, ed. Christopher Spencer (New Haven, 1961).

Sir William Davenant, *The Siege of Rhodes: A Critical Edition*, ed. Ann-Mari Hedbäck, Acta Universitatis Upsaliensis, Studia Anglistica Upsaliensia 14 (Uppsala, 1973).

John Dryden: Four Tragedies, ed. L. A. Beaurline and Fredson Bowers (Chicago and London, 1967).

John Dryden, *All for Love*, ed. N. J. Andrew, New Mermaids (London and Tonbridge, 1975).

Three Burlesque Plays of Thomas Duffett, ed. Ronald Eugene DiLorenzo (Iowa City, 1972).

Two Comedies by Thomas D'Urfey, ed. Jack A. Vaughn (Rutherford, Madison, Teaneck, and London, 1976).

Sir George Etherege, *The Man of Mode*, ed. W. B. Carnochan, Regents Restoration Drama Series (London, 1967).

—— *She Would If She Could*, ed. Charlene M. Taylor, Regents Restoration Drama Series (London, 1973).

Edward Howard, *The Change of Crownes*, ed. Frederick S. Boas (London, 1949).

Sir Robert Howard, *Four New Plays* (London, 1665).

—— *Five New Plays* (London, 1692).

—— and George Villiers, Duke of Buckingham, *The Country Gentleman*, ed. Arthur H. Scouten and Robert D. Hume (London, 1976).

Sir William Killigrew, *Three Playes* (London, 1665).

—— *Four New Playes* (London, 1666).

Peter Anthony Motteux and John Eccles, *The Rape of Europa by Jupiter (1694) and Acis and Galatea (1701)*, introd. Lucyle Hook, Augustan Reprint Society 208 (Los Angeles, 1981).

Elizabeth Polwhele, *The Faithfull Virgins*, in Bodleian MS Rawl. Poet. 195, fos. 49–78.

—— *The Frolicks; or, The Lawyer Cheated (1671)*, ed. Judith Milhous and Robert D. Hume (Ithaca, NY and London, 1977), p. 36.

Sir Charles Sedley, *The Mulberry Garden*, in *Restoration Comedies*, ed. Dennis Davison (London, Oxford, and New York, 1970).

Elkanah Settle, *The Empress of Morocco*, in *Five Heroic Plays*, ed. Bonamy Dobrée (Oxford, 1960).

Thomas Shadwell, *The Virtuoso*, ed. Marjorie Hope Nicolson and David Stuart Rodes, Regents Restoration Drama Series (London, 1966).

The Humorists by Thomas Shadwell 1670, ed. Richard Perkin (Dublin, 1975).

William Shakespeare, in the Arden editions: *Coriolanus*, ed. Philip Brockbank (London, 1976); *Cymbeline*, ed. J. M. Nosworthy (London, 1955); *The Second Part of King Henry VI*, ed. Andrew S. Cairncross, corrected edn. (London, 1962); *King Lear*, ed. Kenneth Muir, corrected edn. (London, 1963); *King Richard III*, ed. Antony Hammond (London and New York, 1981); *The Merchant of Venice*, ed. John Russell Brown, corrected edn. (London, 1959); *Much Ado About Nothing*, ed. A. R. Humphreys (London, 1981); *Romeo and Juliet*, ed. Brian Gibbons (London and New York, 1980); *The Tempest*, ed. Frank Kermode (London, 1954); *Titus Andronicus*, ed. J. C. Maxwell, (London and New York, 1953); *Troilus and Cressida*, ed. Kenneth Palmer (London and New York, 1982); *Twelfth Night*, ed. J. M. Lothian and T. W. Craik (London and New York, 1975).

Thomas Southerne, *Oroonoko*, ed. Maximillian E. Novak and David Stuart Rodes, Regents Restoration Drama Series (London, 1977).

Nahum Tate, *The History of King Lear*, ed. James Black, Regents Restoration Drama Series (London, 1976).

A Critical Old-Spelling Edition of Nahum Tate's Brutus of Alba, ed. Robert Russell Craven (New York and London, 1987).

[Nahum Tate and] Henry Purcell, *Dido and Æneas*, ed. Margaret Laurie and Thurston Dart, revised edn. (Sevenoaks, 1974).

Sir Samuel Tuke, *The Adventures of Five Hours*, ed. A. E. H. Swaen (Amsterdam, 1927).

Sir John Vanbrugh, *The Relapse*, ed. Curt A. Zimansky, Regents Restoration Drama Series (London, 1970).

Sir John Vanbrugh: Four Comedies, ed. Michael Cordner (London, 1989).

George Villiers, Duke of Buckingham, *The Rehearsal*, ed. D. E. L. Crane (Durham, 1976).

John Wilson's The Cheats, ed. Milton C. Nahm (Oxford, 1935).

References to plays are not duplicated under the name of the author unless they occur in a general discussion of his or her work. Thematic sub-entries would have inflated the index unreasonably, but I have tried to orientate the reader by indicating when one play is discussed in relation to another. In the case of simple adaptations, the fact of adaptation is noted only in the entry for the source play, but comparisons and discussions of influence are indexed under all the plays involved. I have noted even very brief comparisons where they bear some critical weight, and whenever possible have indicated the topic of comparison. When a play is discussed more than once, a principal discussion is indicated by bold-face type.

Abdelazer (Summers ii) 111–12
  affinities with *The Empress of Morocco*
    111–12
Achilles; or, Iphigenia in Aulis (1700) 442
Adelphi, influences:
  The City Heiress 232
  The Mulberry Garden 74, 324, 325
  The Spanish Wives 419
  The Squire of Alsatia 325
Adventures of Five Hours, The (Swaen) **38–40**,
    45, 58, 77, 113, 453
  compared with: *The Amorous Old-woman*
    113 (male power); *The Carnival* 40 (male
    power); *Elvira* 41 (role of heroine); *Flora's
    Vagaries* 40 (male power); *The Generous
    Enemies* 113 (male power); *Guzman* 116
    (male power); *The Mulberry Garden* 74
    (male power); *The Rival Ladies* 41–3;
    Squire Oldsapp 201 (power of women)
Agnes de Castro [Trotter] (1696) 444–5
Albion and Albanius (California Dryden xv)
    240, 266 n., 311, **312–13**, 318, 369,
    371
  adapted in *A New Opera; called, Brutus of
    Alba* 429
  compared with *Don Sebastian* 364, 365
    (symbol of Eden)
Alcibiades (Ghosh i) **103–4**, 109, 317

compared with *Don Carlos* (libertine char-
    acters) 110–11
All for Love (California Dryden xiii) 79, 143,
    189, 239, 242, 245, **249–55**, 258, 264 n.,
    296, 338, 439
  casting of female roles 6
  compared with: *Antony and Cleopatra*
    [Shakespeare] 253 (Cydnos voyage);
    Aureng-Zebe 252 (language), 253 (trial
    of heroine); *The Country-Wife* 143
    (truth), 252 (morality/language), 253
    (Truth); *Don Sebastian* 365 (concluding
    speeches); *The Fate of Capua* 435 (female
    self-representation); *The Man of Mode*
    251 (language); *The Miseries of Inforst
    Mariage* 252 (power of titles); *Troilus and
    Cressida* [Dryden] 266 (female self-repres-
    entation)
  influenced by *The Merchant of Venice* and
    Much Ado about Nothing 250
  influences *Romulus and Hersilia* 255
All Mistaken (1672) **63–4**, 67, 68, 151
  compared with: *The Country-Wife, The
    Countrey Wit*, and *Love in the Dark* 150
    (extravagant hero); *Secret Love* 64–5 (split
    plots)
  influences *The Frolicks* 116
All's Well that Ends Well 28

Alphonso King of Naples (1691) 358–9
borrows from *Fatal Love* 289
compared with *The Injur'd Lovers* 358–9 (unjust king)
Altemera 32 n.
see also *The Generall.*
Amant indiscret, L', adapted in *Sir Martin Marall* 67
Ambitious Slave, The (1694) 86, **362**
Ambitious Statesman, The (1679) **263–5**, 273, 277, 330, 361
imitates *Othello* 263–4, 330
Ambitious Step-Mother, The (Works i) 437–8
Amboyna (Works (1735) iii) 91–2
compared with: *An Evening's Love* 92 (carnality; Hell); *Henry the Third of France* 91 (Dutch War); *The Indian Queen, The Indian Emperour*, and *The Conquest of Granada* 91 (noble savage); *King Richard III* 92 (power of writing); *The Wild Gallant* 92 (carnality)
Aminta (Tasso), adapted by Oldmixon 390
Amintas (1698) 390
Amour à la Mode, L' [Thomas Corneille], adapted as *Amorous Orontus* 64
Amour médecin, L', adapted:
in *The Dumb Lady* 117–18
in *Sir Patient Fancy* 214
Amorous Bigotte, The (Summers v) 335
compared with *The Rover*, Part I 335 (the prostitute)
influence on *Greenwich-Park* 337
Amorous Old-woman, The (1674) 113–14
compared with *The Adventures of Five Hours* 113 (male power)
Amorous Orontus 64 (1665)
Amorous Prince, The (Summers iv) 161, **166–7**, 177, 243
compared with: *The Conquest of Granada* 167 (female self-representation); *The Feign'd Curtezans* 216 (prostitute disguise)
Amorous Widow, The (1710) 120
Amphitryon (California Dryden xv) 340, **342–3**, 346, 350, 404 n.
compared with: *Cleomenes* 366, 368 (identity); *The Injur'd Lovers* 342 (bedroom trick); *King Arthur* 370–1 (identity); *Love Triumphant* 368, 369 (identity); *Marriage A-la-Mode* 343 (identity)
Anatomist, The (1697) 385
incorporates *The Loves of Mars and Venus* 378
Andromache [Crowne] (1675) 96
Andromaque (Œuvres) adapted as *Andromache*, 96
Andronicus (1661) 56 n.
Andronicus Comnenius (1664) 56

Antony and Cleopatra [Sedley] (Pinto i) 245, **246**, 249–50, 264 n.
compared with *The Mulberry Garden* 246 (political outlook)
Antony and Cleopatra [Shakespeare] 255
compared with *All for Love* 253 (Cydnos voyage)
Ariadne [translation of *Ariane*] (1673/4) 178
Æsop (Dobrée and Webb ii) 401–2
satirizes tax evasion, 332
Æsop, Part II (Dobrée and Webb ii) 402
Assignation, The (California Dryden xi) **126–30**, 137
compared with *An Evening's Love* 127–8 (carnival)
failure 91, 134
quoted in *The Woman Turn'd Bully* 134
Atheist, The (Ghosh ii), 229, 283, 296, 307, **314–17**, 323
compared with *The Woman-Captain* 316 (women's rights)
Aureng-Zebe (Four Tragedies) 46, **104–6**, 180
compared with: *All for Love* 252 (language), 253 (trial of heroine); *The Country-Wife* 143 (truth/innocence); *The Plain-Dealer* 191 (words/things); *The State of Innocence* 182 (language)
influences *Ibrahim* and *Don Carlos* 110
prologue praises Shakespeare 104

Banditti, The (1686) 31 n., **319**, 340, 438
Beau Defeated, The (1700) 19–20, **420–1**
Beauty in Distress (1698) 31 n., **438**, 439
Beaux Stratagem, The (Kenny ii) 408, 409, 412–13
compared with: *The Committee* 412–13 (master/servant); *Juliana* 168 (portable property); *Love and a Bottle* 410 (law); *Love's Last Shift* 451 (recovery of name)
echoes *Sir Hercules Buffoon* 317
foreshadowed in *The Triumphant Widow* 115
Bellamira (Pinto ii) 307, 322, **324–5**
Belphegor (1691) 332
Bérénice, adapted as *Titus and Berenice* 198
Birthday Party, The 3
Black Prince, The (Clark i) 33, 43
compared with *Ibrahim* [Settle] 110 (father as rival)
Bloody Brother, The 6
Boadicea (1697) 433
Bonduca [Fletcher], anonymously adapted 429
Bonduca (1696) 429
Bourgeois gentilhomme, Le, adapted as *The Citizen Turn'd Gentleman* 121–2, 319

Britannicus 96

Brutus of Alba [Tate] (Craven) 245–6

Bury-Fair (Summers iv) 218, 331 n., **333–5**, 389, 454
  compared with: *Love for Money* 338 (the Stranger); *The Man of Mode* 334 (Francophile characters); *The Squire of Alsatia* 334 (character of hero; step-parents); *The Treacherous Brothers* 358 (the Stranger)
  dedication 235 n., 325

Bussy D'Ambois [Chapman], adapted by Durfey 373

Bussy D'Ambois [Durfey] (1691) 373

Caesar Borgia (Stroup and Cooke ii) 246 n. **268–9**
  imitates *Othello* 268–9
  quotes *King Henry VI, Part II* 268 n.

Caligula (1698) 361 n., 430
  preface 241

Calisto (1675) 148, 178

Cambyses King of Persia (1671) **85–8**, 93, 176, 281

Campaigners, The (1698) **404–8**, 453
  influenced by *The Wives' Excuse* 405

Canterbury Guests, The (1695) **349**, 389
  recycles *The Careless Lovers* and *King Edgar and Alfreda* 349

Careless Lovers, The (1673) 23, **132–4**
  imitates *Secret Love* 132, 206
  prologue mocks Dryden as plagiarist 132
  quoted in *The Revenge* 287
  reused in *The Canterbury Guests* 349

Carnival, The (1664) 40

Catiline (Herford and Simpson v) 6
  mentioned in *The Female Wits* 449

Chances, The [Buckingham] (1682) 64, **66–7**
  compared with *The Comical Revenge* 67 (doubling of name)

Chances, The [Fletcher] adapted by Buckingham 66–7

Change of Crownes, The (Boas) **36**
  compared with *The Tempest* [Shakespeare] 36 (usurpation)

Charles the Eighth of France, see *The History of Charles the Eighth of France*

Cheats, The (Nahm) 55–6
  compared with *The Committee* 55–6 (satire of Puritans)
  imitated in *Mr. Turbulent* 231

Cheats of Scapin, The (Ghosh i) 198

Cid, Le 37, 96

Cinthia and Endimion, see *A New Opera, call'd Cinthia and Endimion*

Circe (1677) 240
  imitates *Iphigenia in Tauris* and *The Indian Queen* 240

Citizen Turn'd Gentleman, The (1672) **121–2**, 133, 319
  compared with *The City Lady* 386 (parvenu)

City Bride, The (1696) 391

City Heiress, The (Summers ii) 209, **232–5**
  compared with: *The Committee* 234 (master/servant); *The Man of Mode* 232 (rake-hero); *The Souldiers Fortune* 234 (qualified Toryism)

City Lady, The (1697) **386–7**
  compared with: *The Citizen Turn'd Gentleman* 386 (parvenu); *The City Madam* 387 (parvenu)

City Madam, The (Edwards and Gibson iv)
  compared with *The City Lady* 387 (parvenu)

City Politiques (Wilson) **308–10**, 320
  temporarily banned 308

City Wit, The, adapted in *A Very Good Wife* 341–2

Cleomenes (Works (1735) vi) **365–8**, 404 n.
  banned 365
  compared with: *Amphitryon* 366, 368 (identity); *Don Sebastian* 368 (signs, identity); *Love Triumphant* 368 (self-representation)
  imitated in *Oroonoko* (Southerne) 366

Comical History of Don Quixote, The (three parts, 1694, 1696) **340**, 387, 436

Comical Revenge, The (Brett-Smith i) 43, 58, **60–3**, 64, 68, 77, 127, 190, 240, 386
  compared with: *The Chances* 67 (doubling of name); *The Committee* 63 (social upstarts); *The Man of Mode* 151 (festive characters); *The Mulberry Garden* 74 (heroic ideals); *Secret Love* 64–5 (split plots), 66 (female self-representation); *She Would If She Could* 70 (festive characters); *Trick for Trick* 202 (festive characters); *The Virtuous Wife* 204–5 (festive characters)
  influences: *The Humorous Lovers* 68; *The Morning Ramble* 117, 130; *The Mulberry Garden* 74; *The Revenge* 286
  reacts against Orrery's plays 60–3

Committee, The (Four New Plays) 22, **31–2**, 38, 43, 44, 55, 60, 114
  compared with: *The Beaux Stratagem* 412–13 (master/servant); *The Cheats* 55–6 (satire of Puritans); *The City Heiress* 234 (master/servant); *The Comical Revenge* 63 (social upstarts); *The Country Gentleman* 114–15 (reassessment of Restoration); *The Fate of Capua* 435 (civil disorder); *The Kind Keeper* 221 (gentlewoman adopted by Puritan); *King Lear* 32 (recovery of name); *Love's Last Shift* 388 (master/servant); *The Marriage-Hater Match'd* 339

(Irish servant); *Secret Love* 66 (rebellion); *Sir Martin Mar-all* 67 (impoverished Royalist; inverted order); *The Slighted Maid* 35 (master/servant); Southerne's plays 344 (service); *The Spanish Rogue* 113 (master/servant); *The Twin-Rivals* 22, 412 (Irish servant); *The Way of the World* 381 (social structure)
hierarchical outlook 7, 23, 34, 38, 57, 60, 113, 115
imitated in: *The Mulberry Garden* 74; *The Royalist* and *Mr. Turbulent* 231
theme of service 46, 54, 425
Common-Wealth of Women, A (1686) 319
Confederacy, The (Dobrée and Webb iii) 401
Conquest of China by the Tartars, The (1676) 86 n., **98–100**
Conquest of Granada, The (California Dryden xi) 46, 49, 51, 58, **79–84**, 104, 112, 440, 455
'a Pris'ner of the Mind' 27, 48, 83, 170
compared with: *Amboyna* 91 (heroic ideals; noble savage); *The Amorous Prince* 167 (female self-representation); *The Country-Wife* 144 (trial of heroine); *An Evening's Love* 82 (festivity); *The History of Charles the Eighth of France* 88–9 (views of heroism); *King Richard II* 452 (trial by combat); *The Rival Ladies* 84 (materialist psychology); *The Siege of Constantinople* 96–7; *Sophonisba* [Lee] 101
influences: *The Destruction of Jerusalem* 240; *Gloriana* 107; *The Siege of Memphis* 109–10
preface discusses genesis of heroic play 2
quoted in *Love and a Bottle* 409
satirized in *The Rehearsal* 83 n., 84–5
uncivilized hero 47, 50
Conspiracy, The (1680) 261, **275–6**
Constant Couple, The (Kenny i) 408–9, **410–12**
influenced by *Madam Fickle* 189, 408 n., 411
influences *Love at a Loss* 421
Constantine the Great (Stroup and Cooke ii) 282 n., 307, **308**, 328
compared with *Theodosius*, 308 (vision of Constantine)
Constant Nymph, The (1678) 199
Coriolanus (Arden) 26, 49, 66
adapted as *The Ingratitude of a Common-Wealth* 279–80
Cornish Comedy, The (1696) 388, **391**
Counterfeit Bridegroom, The (1677) 206–7
adapted in *A Very Good Wife* 341–2
influenced by *The Plain-Dealer* 206
Counterfeits, The (1679) 197, 207
compared with *Tom Essence* 197 (seduced heroine)
Countrey Wit, The (1675) 6, **148–50**, 241, 264

compared with: *All Mistaken* and *Secret Love* 150 (extravagant hero); *The Country-Wife* 148, 149 (signs)
Countrie Girle, The, adapted as *The Country Innocence* 196–7
Country Gentleman, The (Scouten and Hume) 55, **114–15**, 122, 123
compared with *The Committee* 114–15 (re-assessment of Restoration)
influences *Mr. Anthony* 116
Country House, The (Dobrée and Webb ii) 402
Country Innocence, The (1677) **196–7**, 207
Country-Wake, The (1696) 388, **390–1**
Country-Wife, The (Friedman) 4, 6, 13, 24–5, 27–8, 102, 106, 115, 117, 122, 126, 134, **137–45**, 148, 155, 228, 323, 385, 453
character of Horner 6, 64, 150, 294
China scene discussed in *The Plain-Dealer* 192, 367
compared with: *All for Love* 252 (morality/language), 253 (truth); *All Mistaken* and *Secret Love* 150 (extravagant hero); *Aureng-Zebe* 143 (truth/innocence); Carolean tragedy 455; *The Conquest of Granada* 144 (trial of heroine); *The Countrey Wit* 148, 149 (signs); *An Evening's Love* 145 (festivity); *A Fond Husband* 200 (fear of cuckoldom); *The Husband his Own Cuckold* 389 (woman as text); *Love in the Dark* 146 (signs); *The Plain-Dealer* 194–5 (Alithea and Fidelia), 195 (sexual difference); *Sir Courtly Nice* 321 (language); *The State of Innocence* 182 (language); *Troilus and Cressida* [Dryden] 143, 268 (Truth); *The Virtuoso* 156–7 (civility); *The Wrangling Lovers* 147 (signs)
influences *A Fond Husband* and *The London Cuckolds* 147
limited influence on subsequent comedy 147–8
not a typical Restoration comedy 453
production at Swan, Stratford, 1993–4 25
symbolic use of door 5
Courtship A-la-Mode (1700) 235 n., **390**
influenced by Otway, 455–6
Cruelty of the Spaniards in Peru, The (Works) 38
Cuckolds-Haven (1685) 318
Cure for a Cuckold, A, adapted in *The City Bride* 391
Cure for Jealousie, A (1701) 390
Custom of the Country, The, adapted in *Love Makes a Man* 389
Cutter of Coleman-Street (1663) 30–1
imitated in *Mr. Turbulent* 231
Cymbeline (Arden) 18
adapted as *The Injured Princess* 22, 23, 280

Cymbeline (Arden) (*cont.*)
   compared with *The Relapse* 398 (language and the sacred)
Cyrus the Great (1696) 282 n., **428–9**
   compared with *The Royal Mischief* 447, 448 (dismemberment)

Dame Dobson (1684) 313
Damoiselles a la Mode, The (1667) **117**, 118, 218
Darius King of Persia (1688) 307, **329–30**, 361
   compared with: *Ibrahim* [Pix] 430 (kingship and obligation); *Otway* 330 (the Stranger)
   imitates *Othello* 330
Debauchee, The (1677) 196
   compared with *Love's Last Shift* 196 (reformed rake)
Deceiver Deceived, The (1698) 420
   plagiarized in *Imposture Defeated* 420
Dépit amoureux, used in *An Evening's Love* 72 n.
Destruction of Jerusalem, The (2 parts, 1677) 4, 149, **240–2**, 245
   influenced by *The Conquest of Granada* 240
Destruction of Troy, The (1679) 242
Devil is an Ass, The 332
Devil of a Wife, The (1686) **318**, 332
Dido and Æneas (Laurie and Dart) 246, 371, **450**
   compared with *Hamlet* 450 ('Remember me')
   conflated with *Measure for Measure* 378
Disappointment, The (Jordan and Love i) **317**, 343, 346
Distress'd Innocence (1691) 86 n., 361–2
   compared with: *King Edward the Third* and *Henry the Second* 362 (hereditary right); *Tamerlane the Great*, 361–2 (power of heredity)
Doctor Faustus [Marlowe], adapted as *The Life and Death of Doctor Faustus* 318
Don Carlos Prince of Spain (Ghosh i) **110–11**, 263, 282
   compared with *Alcibiades* 110–11 (libertine characters)
   imitates *Othello* 111
   influenced by *Aureng-Zebe* 110
Don Sebastian (California Dryden xv) 192 n., **362–5**, 404 n.
   compared with: *Albion and Albanius* 364, 365 (symbol of Eden); *All for Love* 365 (concluding speeches); *Cleomenes* 368 (signs; identity); *King Lear* 364 (recovery of name)
Double-Dealer, The (Davis) 73 n., 333, 352, **354–7**, 379, 382, 404 n., 416, 457
   compared with Durfey and Shadwell 357 (justice)

Double Gallant, The (*Dramatic Works* iii) 415, 416
Duchess of Malfi, The 6
Duke and No Duke, A (1685) **318**, 332
Duke of Guise, The (*Works* (1735) v) 307–8
   compared with *Henry the Third of France Stabb'd by a Fryer* 89
   temporarily banned 307
   The Vindication of the Duke of Guise 261 n., 307 n.
Dumb Lady, The (1672) 117–18
Dutch Courtezan, The:
   adapted as *The Revenge* 286–8
   used in *The Town-Fop* 286
Dutch Lover, The (Summers i) 127, **176–8**
   compared with *The Feign'd Curtezans* 216 (prostitute disguise)

Eastward Ho (Herford and Simpson iv), adapted as *Cuckolds-Haven* 318
Ecclesiazusae, imitated in *The Six Days Adventure* 165
École des femmes, L' 6
   adapted in: *The Country-Wife* 117, 122; *The Damoiselles a la Mode* 117; *Sir Salomon* 6, 118–19
École des maris, L' 6
   adapted in: *The Country-Wife* 117, 122; *The Damoiselles a la Mode* 117; *Sir Salomon* 6, 118–19
Edgar (1677) 243
Elder Brother, The, adapted in *Love Makes a Man* 389
Elvira (1667) 41
   compared with *King Lear* 41 (recovery of name)
Empeños de seis horas, Los (Swaen), adapted as *The Adventures of Five Hours* 38–40
Emperor of the Moon, The (Summers iii) 318
Empress of Morocco, The [Duffett] (DiLorenzo) 134–5
Empress of Morocco, The [Settle] (Dobrée) 86, **92–5**, 97, 98, 109, 178
   affinities with *Abdelazer* 111–12
   parodied in *The Empress of Morocco* [Duffett] 134–5
   scenic spectacle in 5
English Frier, The (1690) 234 n., 331 n., 333, **336–7**, 338, 361 n.
   dedication 274 n.
   influences *Womans Wit* 389
English Lawyer, The (1678) 199, 216
English Mounsieur, The (1674) **59–60**, 64
   influences *The Humorous Lovers* 68
English Princess, The (1667) 34, 35, 119
Epicoene, influences *The Woman-Captain* 222, 223

Epsom-Wells (Summers ii) 121, **131–2**, 133
  compared with *An Evening's Love* 132
    (justice)
  influenced by *She Would If She Could* 68, 75,
    117, 130, 131
Erminia (1661) 36
Étourdi, L', adapted in *Sir Martin Mar-all* 67
Eunuchus, source of *Bellamira* 324
Evening's Love, An (California Dryden x) 18,
  71–3, 113, 116
  compared with: *Amboyna* 92 (carnality;
    Hell); *The Assignation* 127–8 (carnival);
    The Conquest of Granada 82 (festivity);
    The Country-Wife 145 (festivity), 146
    (signs); *Epsom-Wells* 132 (justice); *Love in
    the Dark* 145–6 (carnival); *The Man of
    Mode* 154 (carnival), 155 (carnality/law);
    The Mulberry Garden 74 (paternal
    authority); *The Perjur'd Husband* 446 (car-
    nival); *The Provoked Wife* 397 (carnival);
    The Rover, Part I 213 (rape/justice); *She
    Would If She Could* 71–2 (splitting of
    self)
  influences *The French Conjurer* 199
  religious levity 453–4
  satirizes gentlemanly ideals 57–8

Fables d'Ésope, Les (*Chef-d'oeuvres*), adapted
  in *Æsop* 401–2
Fâcheux, Les, adapted in: *The Humorists* 120;
  The Sullen Lovers 120
Factious Citizen, The, see *Mr. Turbulent*
Fairy-Queen, The (1692) 371
Faithful Shepherdess, The, mentioned in *Love in
  a Wood* 124
'Faithful Virgins, The' (Bodleian MS Rawl.
  Poet. 195) 79
False Count, The (Summers iii) 215–16,
  218–19, 372, 393
  compared with *The Spanish Wives* 419 (male
    authority)
False Friend, The [Pix] (1699) 444
*Famous History of the Rise and Fall of
  Massaniello, The* (2 parts, 1700) 280 n.,
  332, **436–7**
Fatal Contract, The (1653) adapted as *Love and
  Revenge* 97–8
Fatal Discovery, The (1698) **440**, 443
Fatal Friendship (1698) 445
  compared with *Friendship Improv'd* 445
    (male codes)
  recalls *The Fatal Marriage* 445
Fatal Jealousie, The (1673) **89–91**, 97, 338
  imitates *Othello* 89–91
  uses *Much Ado about Nothing* 90
Fatal Love (1680) 288–9
  echoed in *Alphonso King of Naples* 289

Fatal Marriage, The (Jordan and Love ii) 288,
  344, **373–6**, 404 n., 425, 456, 457
  compared with: *The Fate of Capua* 435 (so-
    cial disintegration); *The Loyal Brother* 374
    (dislocation)
  influences *The Mourning Bride* 427
  recalled in *Fatal Friendship* 445
Fate of Capua, The (Jordan and Love ii) **434–5**
  compared with: *All for Love* 435 (female self-
    representation); *The Committee* 435 (civil
    disorder); *The Fatal Marriage* 435 (social
    disintegration); *The History and Fall of
    Caius Marius* 435 (civil disorder)
Father, The 457
Feign'd Curtezans, The (Summers ii) 215,
  216–17, 231 n.
  compared with *The Amorous Prince* and *The
    Dutch Lover* 216 (prostitute disguise)
Feign'd Friendship (?1699) 386
Female Prelate, The (1680) 86, 261, 269 n.,
  276–7
Female Vertuoso's, The (1693) 213, **341–2**
Female Wits, The (1704) 333, **448–9**
  compared with *The Rehearsal* 448–9
  satirizes *The Royal Mischief* 448–9
Femmes savantes, Les, adapted in: *The Female
  Vertuoso's* 213, 341–2; *Sir Patient Fancy*
  213
Flora's Vagaries (1670) 40
Fond Husband, A (1677) 187–8, 189, 196,
  199–201, 202, 393
  compared with: *The Country-Wife* 200 (fear
    of cuckoldom); *The Souldiers Fortune*
    200–1 (women/language)
  influenced by *The Country-Wife* 147
  influences *The Kind Keeper* 219
  mentioned in *The Relapse* 394
  satirized in *A True Widow* 221
Fool's Preferment, A (1688) 319
Fool Turn'd Critick, The (1678) 187, **189–90**,
  196, 205 n.
  influenced by *The Gamester* [Shirley] 187 n.
Forc'd Marriage, The (Summers iii) **164–5**, 243
  compared with *The Royal Shepherdess* (hero-
    ine's obscure birth) 164
  imitates: *The Indian Queen* 164; *Much Ado
    about Nothing* 165; *Othello* 163, 164, 165
Fortune-Hunters, The (1689) 331 n., **333**
  influence on *Greenwich-Park* 337
Fourberies de Scapin, Les (*Œuvres* ii), adapted
  as *The Cheats of Scapin* and *Scaramouch a
  Philosopher* 198–9
French Conjurer, The (1678) 199
  compared with *The Villain* 199 (male viol-
    ence)
  influenced by *An Evening's Love* 199
Friendship Improv'd (1700) 433–4

Friendship Improv'd (1700) (*cont.*)
  compared with *Fatal Friendship* 445 (male codes)
Friendship in Fashion (Ghosh i) 187, **225–7**, 228, 231 n., 455
  compared with: *The Man of Mode* 225; *A Midsummer Night's Dream* 226 (buffoonish playwright); *The Virtuous Wife* 205 (neglected wife); *The Woman-Captain* 225 (image of the Fool), 227 (class structure)
Frolicks, The (Milhous and Hume) 116, 234 n.
  influenced by *All Mistaken* 116

Gamester, The [Shirley] 162
  influences *The Fool Turn'd Critick* 187 n.
Generall, The (Clark i) **32–3**, 35, 43, 454, 455
Generous Choice, The (1700) 390
Generous Enemies, The (1672) 113
  compared with *The Adventures of Five Hours* 113 (male power)
Gentleman Dancing-Master, The (Friedman) 2–3, 117, **125–6**, 353 n.
Gentleman Usher, The (Hazel Smith) 26
George Dandin, adapted in *The Amorous Widow* 120
Gloriana (Stroup and Cooke i) **106–9**, 246, 247, 308, 455
  influenced by *The Conquest of Granada* 107
Great Favourite, The (*Five New Plays*) 44–5, 114
Greenwich-Park (1691) **337–8**, 404 n.
  ?influences *Win Her and Take Her* 338
  influenced by *The Amorous Bigotte* and *The Fortune-Hunters* 337
Grove, The (1700) 433
Guardian, The [Cowley], revised as *Cutter of Coleman-Street* 30
Guardian, The [Massinger], adapted in *The City Heiress* 232
Guzman (Clark i) 116
  compared with *The Adventures of Five Hours* 116 (male power)

Hamlet (Arden) 247, 282
  compared with *Dido and Æneas* 450 ('Remember me')
Hedda Gabler 457
Heir of Morocco, The (1682) 261, **281**
Henry IV, see *King Henry IV*
Henry the Fifth [Orrery], see *The History of Henry the Fifth*
Henry the Second (1693) 359–60
  compared with *Distress'd Innocence* 362 (hereditary right)
Henry the Sixth, The First Part [Crowne] (1681) **274–5**, 336 n.
  banned 274

Henry the Third of France Stabb'd by a Fryer (1678) 89
  compared with: *Amboyna* 91 (Dutch War); *The Duke of Guise* 89
Henry V, see *King Henry V*
Henry VI, see *King Henry VI*
Héraclius 37, 96
Heraclius, Emperour of the East [Carlell] (1664) 37
Hercules Furens [Seneca]:
  alluded to in *Theodosius* 291
  quoted in *Lucius Junius Brutus* 293–4, 298
Herod and Mariamne (1673) 88
Herod the Great (Clark ii) 38 n.
Heroick Love (1698) **440–1**, 450, 457
  ending altered after first night 441 n.
History and Fall of Caius Marius, The (Ghosh i) 270–3
  compared with *The Fate of Capua* 435 (civil disorder)
  influenced by *King Lear* 271
History of Charles the Eighth of France, The (1672) 88–9
  compared with *The Indian Emperour* and *The Conquest of Granada* (views of heroism), 88–9
History of Henry the Fifth, The [Orrery] (Clark i) 32, 33
  compared with: *The Comical Revenge* 62 (love between social unequals); *Queen Catharine* 443 (power of names)
History of King Lear, The [Tate] (James Black) 181, **277–8**, 279, 322
  compared with: *Love's Last Shift* 451 (recovery of name); *Troilus and Cressida* [Dryden] 278
History of King Richard the Second, The [Tate] (1680) 278
  banned 278
History of Sir Francis Drake, The (Works) 38
History of Timon of Athens, The [Shadwell] (Summers iii) 20, 223, **256**
  influenced by *The Plain-Dealer* 256
Horace [Corneille] 37–8
Horace [Philips-Denham] (1671) 37–8
Humorists, The (Summers i) 120–1
  preface 75–6
  preface praises *She Would If She Could* 75
Humorous Lovers, The (1677) 68
  influenced by *The English Mounsieur* and *The Comical Revenge* 68
Husband his Own Cuckold, The (1696) **389**, 390
  compared with *The Country-Wife* 389 (woman as text)
Hyde Park (Gifford ii)
  adapted in *A Very Good Wife* 341–2

compared with *Love's Last Shift* 452 (re-formed rake)
Hypocrite, The (lost) 120

Ibrahim the Illustrious Bassa (1677) 85–6, 94, 110
compared with *The Black Prince* 110 (father as rival)
influenced by *Aureng-Zebe* 110
Ibrahim the Thirteenth Emperour of the Turks (1696) **430**, 443, 447
compared with *Darius King of Persia* 430 (kingship and obligation)
Ignoramus 199
Imperial Tragedy, The (1669) 78
Imposture Defeated (1698) 420
plagiarizes *The Deceiver Deceived* 420
Inconstant, The (Kenny i) 409
Indian Emperour, The (California Dryden ix) 16, 46, **47–9**, 51, 60, 80, 83, 383, 440
compared with: *Amboyna* 91 (noble savage); *The History of Charles the Eighth of France* 88–9 (views of heroism); *The Sullen Lovers* 76 (retreat to wilderness)
Indian Queen, The (California Dryden viii) 46, 48, 50
compared with *Amboyna* 91 (heroic ideals; noble savage)
imitated in: *Circe* 240; *The Forc'd Marriage* 164
uncivilized hero 47, 50
Indian Queen, The [Operatic] (*Works of Purcell* xix) 424
Ingratitude of a Common-Wealth, The (1682) **279–80**, 450
imitates *Othello* 279
Injur'd Lovers, The (1688) 307, **328–9**, 346
compared with: *Alphonso King of Naples* 358–9 (unjust king); *Amphitryon* 342 (bedroom trick)
Injured Princess, The (1682) 18, 22, 23, **280**
influenced by *King Lear* 280
Innocent Mistress, The (1697) 419–20
Innocent Usurper, The (1694) **281–2**, 428 n.
Intrigues at Versailles, The (1697) 403–4
compared with: *Love and a Bottle* 409 (playwright within the play); *The Wives' Excuse* 403 (playwright within the play)
Iolanthe 87
Iphigenia (1700) 240, **442**, 443
Iphigenia in Tauris, imitated in: *Circe* 240; *Iphigenia* [Dennis] 240, 442
Iphigénie, adapted as *Achilles; or, Iphigenia in Aulis* 442
Irena (1664) 43, 97
Irene 43 n.
Island Princess, The [Fletcher]

adapted by Tate 318–19
compared with the three post-1660 adaptations 441
Island Princess, The [1668 adaptation] (1669) 441
Island Princess, The [Motteux] (1699) 441–2
Island-Princess, The [Tate] (1687) 318–19, 441
Island Queens, The (1684) **281–2** n., 428 n.
Italian Husband, The (1698) **438–39**, 443, 448

Juliana (1671) 127, **167–8**
compared with *The Beaux Stratagem* 168 (portable property)
Justice Busy (lost) 341 n.

Kind Keeper, The (*Works* (1735) iv) 126, **219–21**, 231 n.
compared with: *The Committee* 221 (gentlewoman adopted by Puritan); *The Man of Mode* 220 (amorous judge); *The Spanish Fryar* 236 (long-lost son)
influenced by *A Fond Husband* 219
King Arthur (*Works* (1735) vi) 369–71
compared with: *Amphitryon* 370–1 (identity); *The State of Innocence* 370–1 (doubling of self)
King Edgar and Alfreda (1677) 242–3
reused in *The Canterbury Guests* 349
King Edward the Third (1691) 359–60
compared with *Distress'd Innocence* 362 (hereditary right)
quoted in epigraph to Chapter Ten 358
King Henry IV, Falstaff mentioned in *Amboyna* 92
King Henry V 229
King Henry VI (Arden):
Part II adapted in *Henry the Sixth, The First Part* [Crowne] 274–5
Part II quoted in *Caesar Borgia* 268 n.
Part III adapted as *The Misery of Civil-War* 274
Part III used in *The Tragical History of King Richard III* 432
King Lear [Shakespeare] (Arden) 26
adapted as *The History of King Lear* 181, 277–8
compared with: *The Committee* 32 (recovery of name); *Don Sebastian* 364 (recovery of name); *Elvira* 41 (recovery of name); *Love's Last Shift* 451 (recovery of name); *Our Mutual Friend* 451 (recovery of name); *Tamerlane the Great* 278 (villainous brother)
influences: *The History and Fall of Caius Marius* 271; *The Injured Princess* 280
King Lear [Tate] see *The History of King Lear*

King Richard II:
   adapted as *The History of King Richard the
      Second* 278
   compared with *The Conquest of Granada*
      452 (trial by combat)
King Richard III (Arden):
   adapted as *The Tragical History of King
      Richard III* 18–19, 432
   compared with *Amboyna* 92 (power of
      writing)

Ladies Visiting-Day, The (Budd) 413, 414,
   415–16
   adapted in *The Double Gallant* 415, 416
Lancashire Witches, The (Summers iv) 5,
   235–6, 325, 335
Law against Lovers, The (Works) 34, 35
   used in Gildon's *Measure for Measure* 432
Libertine, The (Summers iii) 20, **102–3**, 160
   influenced by *The Tempest* 102–3
Life and Death of Doctor Faustus, The (1697)
   318
Limberham, see *The Kind Keeper*
London Cuckolds, The (1682) 199, **230**, 313, 314
   influenced by *The Country-Wife* 147
Lost Lover, The (1696) 421
Love and a Bottle (Kenny i) 408–10
   compared with: *The Beaux Stratagem* 410
      (law); *The Intrigues at Versailles* and *The
      Wives' Excuse* 409 (playwright within the
      play)
   quotes Dryden's heroic plays 409
Love and Revenge (1675) 97–8
Love at a Loss (1701) 421–3
   compared with *The Rover*, Part I 210 n. (vote
      on heroine's future)
   influenced by *The Constant Couple* 421
Love Betray'd (Budd) 413–14
Love for Love (Davis) 242, 333, 350, 351–2, 353,
   354–5, **378–85**, 387, 404 n., 418
   compared with: *The Mourning Bride* 427
      (tyrannical patriarchs); *She Ventures, and
      He Wins* 385 (trial of lover)
   first production of Lincoln's Inn Fields com-
      pany 378
   quoted in epigraph to Chapter Eleven 377
Love for Money (1691) **338–9**, 340
   compared with: *Bury-Fair* 338 (the Stranger);
      The Man of Mode 339 (justice); Shadwell
      338 (oppressive guardian)
   influenced by *Sir Hercules Buffoon* 317
   rejects libertine comedy 339
Love in a Wood (Friedman) 4, **122–5**
Love in the Dark (1675) **145–7**, 148, 453
   compared with: *An Evening's Love* 145–6
      (carnival); *The Man of Mode* 154 (carni-
      val); *The Wrangling Lovers* 147 (signs)

relationship to *All Mistaken* and *Secret Love*
   150
Love Makes a Man (1701) 389
Lover's Luck, The (1696) 386, 387
Love's a Jest (1696) 388, **391**
Love's a Lottery (1699) 391
Love's Dominion (1654) 34
Love's Kingdom (1664) 34
Love's Last Shift (Sullivan) 26, 28, **387–8**
   compared with: *The Beaux Stratagem* 451
      (recovery of name); *The Committee* 388
      (master/servant); *The Debauchee* 196 (re-
      formed rake); *Hyde Park* 452 (reformed
      rake); *King Lear* and *The History of King
      Lear* 451 (recovery of name); *The Pilgrim*
      [Vanbrugh] 402 (moral reform); *The
      Relapse* 393, 395, 396; *The Tragical
      History of King Richard III* 432 (language)
Loves of Mars and Venus, The (1696) 385, 390
   incorporated in *The Anatomist* 378
Loves Victory, adapted as *Wits Led by the Nose*
   243
Love Triumphant (Works (1735) vi) **368–9**
   compared with: *Amphitryon* 368, 369 (ident-
      ity); *Cleomenes* 368 (self-representation);
      Marriage A-la-Mode 368 (royal changel-
      ings); *The Wild Gallant* 369 (ancestry)
   influences *The Mourning Bride* 427
Love Without Interest (1699) 390
Loving Enemies, The (1680) 229–30
Loyal Brother, The (Jordan and Love i) 265,
   280, 317, 343
   compared with *The Fatal Marriage* 374 (dis-
      location)
Loyal General, The (1680) 260, 265, **273**, 278
   imitated in *The Injur'd Lovers* 358
   used in *The History of King Lear* 277
Lucius Junius Brutus (Stroup and Cooke ii)
   261, 282, **293–300**
   banned 295
   intellectual affinities with comedy 455
Lucky Chance, The (Summers iii) 3, 214, 307,
   317, 318, **322–4**, 372, 393
   compared with: *The Rover*, Part I 323 (hero
      becomes prostitute); *Sir Patient Fancy* 323
      (bedroom trick)
   prologue quoted as epigraph to Chapter
      Eight, 307
Lust's Dominion (Bowers iv), adapted as
   Abdelazer 111–12
Lysistrata, imitated in *The Six Days Adventure*
   165

Macbeth [Davenant] (Spencer) 34, 35, 178, 246
Macbeth [Shakespeare] 330
Madam Fickle (Vaughn) **187–9**, 190, 191, 205,
   316

compared with *The Siege of Memphis* 188 (dominant heroine)

influences: *The Constant Couple* 189, 408 n., 411; *The Plain-Dealer* 340

Mad Couple Well Match'd, A 67

adapted as *The Debauchee* 196

Mad World My Masters, A, adapted in *The City Heiress* 232

Maestro de danzar, El, source of *The Gentleman Dancing-Master* 122 n.

Maid's Last Prayer, The (Jordan and Love i) 333, 343, 344, 345, 346, **348–9**, 404 n., 425, 457

compared with *Oroonoko* 426 (identity)

Maison de campagne, La, adapted as *The Country House* 402

Malade imaginaire, Le, adapted in: *Sir Patient Fancy* 120, 213–14

Mall, The (1674) **136–7**, 145, 190 n.

compared with: *Sir Salomon* 136 (menacing fool); *Sir Salomon* and *The Town-Fop* 186 (menacing fool)

Mañanas de abril y mayo, source of *Love in a Wood* 122 n.

Man of Mode, The (Carnochan) 6, 9, 60, 64, 70 n., 112, 148, **150–5**, 186, 317, 384, 385, 453, 455

changes course of comedy 6, 147–8, 161, 185, 190

compared with: *All for Love* 251 (nature of language); *Bury-Fair* 334 (Francophile characters); *The City Heiress* 232 (rake-hero); *The Comical Revenge* 151 (festive characters); *An Evening's Love* 155 (carnality/law); *An Evening's Love* and *Love in the Dark* 154 (carnival); *Friendship in Fashion* 225; *The Kind Keeper* 220 (amorous judge); *Love for Money* 339 (justice); *The Morning Ramble* 155 (carnality/law); *The Relapse* 396 (Bellinda/Berinthia); *The Rover*, Part I 208 (rake-hero), 210 (male perjury), 213 (rape/justice); *The Town-Fop* 186 (vows); *Trick for Trick* 202–4; *A True Widow* 222 (gay couple); *Venice Preserv'd* 306 (cursing)

influenced by Hobbes 14

its exceptional nature 453

quoted in epigraph to Chapter Four 113

satirizes gentlemanly ideals 22–3

use of public and private space 4

Man of Newmarket, The (1678) 197–8

criticizes *The Plain-Dealer* 197–8

mentioned in *The Rambling Justice* 197 n.

Man's the Master, The (Works) 68

Marcelia (1670) 163–4

imitates *Othello* 163

Mariage Night, The (1664) **36–7**, 353 n.

Marriage-Hater Match'd, The (1692) 333, **339**, 340, 404 n., 436

commendatory letter from Gildon criticizes *The Wives' Excuse* 403

compared with *The Committee* 339 (Irish servant)

Marriage A-la-Mode (California Dryden xi) 10, 16, 27, 126, **168–76**

compared with: *Amphitryon* 343 (identity); *Love Triumphant* 368 (royal changelings); *The Spanish Fryar* 238 (usurper's daughter); *The State of Innocence* 184 (language)

quoted in *The Woman Turn'd Bully* 134

satirized in *The Reformation* 134

Married Beau, The (1694) 341

Massacre of Paris, The (Stroup and Cooke ii) 246, **269**, 276, 358

banned 269

compared with *The Rival Queens* 269 (corporealism)

Massaniello, see *The Famous History of the Rise and Fall of Massaniello*

Master Builder, The 457

Mayor of Queenborough, The 353

Measure for Measure [Gildon] (1700) 378, **432–3**

Measure for Measure [Shakespeare] 28

conflated with: *Dido and Æneas* 378, 432–3; *Much Ado about Nothing* (in *The Law against Lovers*) 34, 35

Medea [Euripides], used in *Phaeton* 442

Médecin malgré lui, Le, adapted as: *The Dumb Lady* 117–18

The Physician Against his Will 118 n.

Merchant of Venice, The (Arden) 26, 55

influences *All for Love* 250

Mère coquette, La ?influences *The Humorists* 120

Michaelmas Term 120

Midsummer Night's Dream, A 4

adapted as *The Fairy-Queen* 371

compared with *Friendship in Fashion* 226 (buffoonish playwright)

Misanthrope, Le (Œuvres i):

adapted in *The Plain-Dealer* 122, 194 n., 195, 256 n.

influences *The Sullen Lovers* 76

Miser, The (Summers ii) 120, 121

Miseries of Inforst Mariage, The (1607) 187

adapted as *The Town-Fop* 186–7

compared with *All for Love* 252 (power of titles)

Misery of Civil-War, The (1680) 274

Mistaken Husband, The (1675) 136

Mistakes, The (1691) 358

imitates *Othello* 358

Mithridates (Stroup and Cooke i) **256–9**, 308

Mock-Duellist, The (1675) 116, 145, 148

Mock-Marriage, The (1696) 387

Mock-Tempest, The (DiLorenzo) 134–6

Modish Husband, The (Budd) 413, 414

Monsieur de Pourceaugnac:
  used in: *The Careless Lovers* 132; *The Citizen Turn'd Gentleman* 122; *Scaramouch a Philosopher* 199

Monsieur Thomas (Bowers iv), adapted as *Trick for Trick* 202–4, 319

More Dissemblers Besides Women, used in *The Rambling Justice* 207–8

Morning Ramble, The (1673) **130–1**, 132, 133, 134
  alludes to Descartes 180 n.
  compared with *The Man of Mode* 155 (carnality/law)
  influenced by *The Comical Revenge* 117

Mort de Pompée, La 37, 38

Mourning Bride, The (Davis) 350, **427–8**, 456, 457
  compared with: Congreve's comedies 427–8; *Love for Love* 427 (tyrannical patriarchs); *Oroonoko*, 427 (exile self-definition)
  influenced by *The Fatal Marriage* and *Love Triumphant* 427

Mr. Anthony (Clark ii) 116–17
  influenced by *The Country Gentleman* 116

Mr. Turbulent (reprinted as *The Factious Citizen*, 1685) 230, **231–2**
  imitates *Cutter of Coleman-Street, The Cheats*, and *The Committee* 231

Much Ado about Nothing (Arden)
  conflated with *Measure for Measure* (in *The Law against Lovers*) 34, 35
  used in: *All for Love* 250; *The Fatal Jealousie* 90; *The Forc'd Marriage* 165

Mulberry Garden, The (Davison) 38, 69, **74–5**, 324
  compared with: *The Adventures of Five Hours* 74 (male power); *Antony and Cleopatra* [Sedley] 246 (political outlook); *The Comical Revenge* 74 (heroic ideals); *An Evening's Love* 74 (paternal authority)
  influenced by: *Adelphi* 74, 324, 325; *The Committee, The Comical Revenge*, and *She Would If She Could* 74

Murder in the Cathedral 3

Mustapha [Greville] (Bullough ii) 12

Mustapha [Orrery] (Clark i) 32, 33, **43–4**, 45, 77, 247, 455
  betrays exasperation with Charles II 454

Neglected Virtue (1696) 440

Nero (1624), see *The Tragedy of Nero*

Nero [Lee], see *The Tragedy of Nero, Emperour of Rome*

New Opera, call'd Cinthia and Endimion, A (1697) 402–3

New Opera; called, Brutus of Alba, A (1697) 429
  adapts *Albion and Albanius, The Treacherous Brothers*, and *The Virgin Martyr* 429

New Way to Pay Old Debts, A 26, 120

Noble Gentleman, The, adapted as *A Fool's Preferment* 319

No puede ser, adapted as: *Sir Courtly Nice* 40, 320; *Tarugo's Wiles* 40–1, 320

No siempre lo peor es cierto, adapted as *Elvira* 41

Novelty, The (1697) 378, 389, 438

No Wit, No Help Like a Woman's (Bullen iv), adapted as *The Counterfeit Bridegroom* 206–7

Ocásion hace al ladrón, La, adapted as *The Counterfeits* 197

Oedipus (California Dryden xiii) 261–2
  compared with *The Spanish Fryar* 237

Old Batchelour, The (Davis) 340, 345, **350–1**, 352, 353, 354, 356
  attacked by Henry Higden 340
  influences *The Canterbury Guests* 349

Old Troop, The (1672) 56–7

Ormasdes (Three Playes) 34

Oroonoko [Southerne] (Jordan and Love ii) 344, 346, 374, 375, 387, **424–7**, 456, 457
  compared with: *The Maid's Last Prayer* 426 (identity); *The Mourning Bride* 427 (exile; self-definition)
  imitates *Cleomenes* 366

Orphan, The (Ghosh ii) 13, 28, 261, 282, **283–6**, 293, 294, 315, 346, 438, 455
  compared with *The Plain-Dealer* (bedroom trick) 283–4
  intellectual affinities with comedy 455

Othello 317
  analysed by Gildon 443
  imitated in: *The Ambitious Statesman* 263–4, 330; *Caesar Borgia* 268–9; *Darius King of Persia* 330; *Don Carlos* 111; *The Fatal Jealousie* 89–91; *The Forc'd Marriage* 163, 164, 165; *The Ingratitude of a Common-Wealth* 279; *Marcelia* 163; *The Mistakes* 358; *The Treacherous Brothers* 358; *The Unnatural Brother* 438; *The Villain* 45, 89
  Pepys prefers *The Adventures of Five Hours* 39

Pandora (Three Playes) 75

Pastor Fido, Il [Guarini]

adapted by Settle 199
mentioned in *The Italian Husband* 439
Pastor Fido [Settle] (1677) 199
Pausanias, the Betrayer of his Country (1696) 430
Pericles 31, 50
Perjur'd Husband, The (1700) 445–6
compared with *An Evening's Love* and Vanbrugh (carnival) 445–6
Phaéton, used in *Phaeton* 442
Phaeton (1698) 442–3
Philaster [Beaumont and Fletcher], adapted:
as *The Restauration* 310–11
by Settle 429–30
Philaster [Settle] (1695) 429–30
Physician Against his Will, The (lost) 118 n.
Pilgrim, The [Fletcher] (Bowers vi) adapted by Vanbrugh 402
Pilgrim, The [Vanbrugh] (Dobrée and Webb ii) 402
compared with *Love's Last Shift* (moral reform) 402
Piso's Conspiracy (1676) 96
Plain-Dealer, The (Friedman) 6, 28, 122, 125, 143, 150, **190–6**, 250, 350
1988 production at the Swan, Stratford 191 n.
alludes to: *The Country-Wife* 192, 367; *Twelfth Night* 190, 224 n.
compared with: *Aureng-Zebe* 191 (words/things); *The Country-Wife* 194–5 (Alithea and Fidelia); *The Orphan* 283–4 (bedroom trick); *The Rover*, Part I 213 (rape/justice); *The White Devil* 452 (law); *The Woman-Captain* 223 (women/law)
criticized in *The Man of Newmarket* 197–8
influences: *The Counterfeit Bridegroom* 206; *The History of Timon of Athens* 256; *The Richmond Heiress* 339–40; *The Virtuous Wife* 206; *Womans Wit* 389
intellectual affinities with tragedy 455
used in *The Younger Brother* 392–3
Play-house to be Let, The (Works) 38
Plot and No Plot, A (1697) 390
Poetaster (Herford and Simpson iv) 26, 36, 310
Pompey [Philips] (1663) 37
parodied in *The Play-house to be Let* 38
Pompey the Great (1664) 37
Précieuses ridicules, Les, adapted in: *Bury-Fair* 218, 334; *The Damoiselles a la Mode* 117, 218; *The False Count* 218
Pretenders, The (1698) 386
satirizes tax evasion 332–3
Princess of Cleve, The (Stroup and Cooke ii) 246 n., 307, **313–14**, 323, 455
Princess of Parma, The (1699) 436

epilogue quoted in epigraph to Chapter Twelve 424
Prophetess, The (Bowers ix) 371
Prophetess, The [Betterton] (1690) 371
Provoked Wife, The (Cordner) **396–401**, 451, 457
compared with *An Evening's Love* (carnival) 397
Psyché [Molière-Corneille-Quinault] (*Œuvres* ii), adapted by Shadwell 178–9
Psyche [Shadwell] (Summers ii) 3, **178–9**, 181, 371
parodied in *Psyche Debauch'd* 134–5
scenic effects 4
Psyche Debauch'd (DiLorenzo) **134–5**, 148
Pyrrhus King of Epirus (1695) 433

Queen Catharine (1698) 443–4
compared with *The History of Henry the Fifth* 443 (power of names)
influenced by Otway 455–6

Rambling Justice, The (1678) 197 n., **207–8**
Rape, The (1692) **373**, 374, 433
Rape of Europa by Jupiter, The (Hook) 373
Recruiting Officer, The (Kenny ii), influenced by *The Royalist* 231, 408 n.
Reformation, The (1673) 134
Reform'd Wife, The (Budd) 413, 414, 415–16
adapted in *The Double Gallant* 415, 416
Regulus (1694) 332, **360–1**
compared with *Timoleon* 431 (foreign saviour)
Rehearsal, The (Crane) 84–5
compared with *The Female Wits* 448–9
satirizes: *Cambyses* 86; *The Conquest of Granada* 83 n., 84–5
Relapse, The (Zimansky) 28, 332, 333, 350, **393–6**, 453
compared with: Congreve's comedies 350 (dislocation); *Cymbeline* 398 (language and the sacred); *Love's Last Shift* 393, 395, 396; *The Man of Mode* 396 (Bellinda/Berinthia)
induces resurgence of sex comedy 388
Restauration, The (Works i) 310–11
Revenge, The (1680) **286–8**, 392
uses *The Careless Lovers* and *The Comical Revenge* 287
Revengeful Queen, The (1698) 431–2
Rewards of Vertue, The (1661), adapted as *The Royal Shepherdess* 162
Richard II, see *King Richard II*
Richard III, see *King Richard III*
Richard the Second [Tate], see *The History of King Richard the Second*

Richmond Heiress, The (1693) 189, 332, **339–40**, 389
    influenced by *The Plain-Dealer* 339–40
Rinaldo and Armida (1699) 441, **442**
Rival Fools, The (*Dramatic Works* ii) 353 n.
Rival Kings, The (1677) 242
    influenced by *The Rival Queens* 242
Rival Ladies, The (California Dryden viii) **41–3**, 180
    compared with *The Conquest of Granada* 83, 84 (materialist psychology)
    reacts against Orrery 42–3
Rival Queens, The (Stroup and Cooke i) 245, **246–9**, 257
    compared with: *The Massacre of Paris* 269 (corporealism); *Venice Preserv'd* 306 (laceration of the body)
    influences *The Rival Kings* and *The Siege of Babylon* 242
    quoted in epigraph to Chapter Seven 240
    quoted in epigraph to Chapter Six 185
Rivals, The (1668) 35
Rival Sisters, The (1696) 438
Roman Brides Revenge, The (1697) 430
Roman Empress, The (1671) **78–9**, 83, 90
Romeo and Juliet [James Howard] (lost) 44
Romeo and Juliet [Shakespeare] (Arden):
    adapted: as *The History and Fall of Caius Marius* 270–3; by James Howard 44
Romulus and Hersilia (1683) 255
    influenced by *All for Love* 255
Roundheads, The (Summers i) 230, **232**, 215–17
    adapts *The Rump* 231, 232
Rover, The, Part I (Summers i) 176, **208–13**, 215–17
    compared with: *The Amorous Bigotte* 335 (the prostitute); *An Evening's Love* 213 (rape/justice); *Love at a Loss* 210 n. (vote on heroine's future); *The Lucky Chance* 323 (hero becomes prostitute); *The Man of Mode* 208 (rake-hero), 210 (male perjury), 213 (rape/justice); *The Plain-Dealer* 213 (rape/justice)
Rover, The, Part II (Summers i) 215–16, **217–18**, 278
Royalist, The (1682) 205 n., 230, **231**
    imitates *The Committee* 231
    influences *The Recruiting Officer* 231, 408 n.
Royal Mischief, The (1696) 446–8
    compared with *Cyrus the Great* 447, 448 (dismemberment)
    satirized in *The Female Wits* 448–9
Royal Shepherdess, The (Summers i) 162
    compared with *The Forc'd Marriage* 164 (heroine's obscure birth)
Rump, The (1660) **30–1**, 38, 55
    adapted as *The Roundheads* 231, 232

Sauny the Scot (1698) 67
Scaramouch a Philosopher (1677) **198–9**, 216
Scornful Lady, The 217
Scowrers, The (Summers v) 334, **335–6**
    compared with *The Squire of Alsatia* 335 (hero's conduct)
Sea Voyage, The, adapted as *A Common-Wealth of Women* 319
Second Mrs. Tanqueray, The 457
Second Part of Loves Adventures, The (*Playes* (1662)) 74 n.
Secret Love (California Dryden ix) **64–6**, 126
    compared with: *All Mistaken* 64–5 (split plots); *The Comical Revenge* 64–5 (split plots), 66 (female self-representation); *The Committee* 66 (rebellion); *The Country-Wife, The Countrey Wit*, and *Love in the Dark* 150 (extravagant hero)
    imitated in: *The Careless Lovers* 132, 206; *The Virtuous Wife* 206
Seege of Urbin, The (*Four New Plays*) 40, 74 n.
Sejanus (Herford and Simpson iv) 448 n.
Selindra (*Three Playes*) 35
Sganarelle:
    adapted in *Tom Essence* 160
    included in *The Play-house to be Let* 38
Sham-Lawyer, The (1697) 389–90
She-Gallants, The (1696) **385–6**, 387
She Ventures, and He Wins (1696) **385**, 387, 451
    compared with *Love for Love* 385 (trial of lover)
She Would If She Could (Taylor) **68–71**, 77, 113, 126, 127, 141, 152
    compared with: *The Comical Revenge* 70 (festive characters); *An Evening's Love* 71–2 (splitting of self)
    influences: *Epsom-Wells* 68, 75, 117, 130, 131; *The Mulberry Garden* 74; *The Virtuoso* 75, 155–6
    praised in preface to *The Humorists* 75
    satirizes gentlemanly ideals 23, 57–8
Sicilian Usurper, The, retitling of *The History of King Richard the Second* 278
Sicilien, Le, adapted in *The Countrey Wit* 149
Siege of Babylon, The (1678) 242
    influenced by *The Rival Queens* 242
Siege of Constantinople, The (1675) 43 n., 90, **96–7**, 108, 189, 282 n., 338
    compared with *The Conquest of Granada* 96–7
Siege of Memphis, The (1676) **109–10**, 187
    compared with *Madam Fickle* 188 (dominant heroine)
    influenced by *The Conquest of Granada* 109
Siege of Rhodes, The (Hedbäck) 1, 2, 34, 88, 454

Sir Anthony Love (Jordan and Love i) 340, 343, 344, 345–8, 424, 426, 447, 457
  compared with: Congreve's comedies 350 (dislocation); *The Woman-Captain* 347 (heroine in male disguise)
Sir Barnaby Whigg (1681) 230, **231**, 266
Sir Courtly Nice (1685) 40, **320–2**, 329
  compared with *The Country-Wife* 321 (language)
Sir Hercules Buffoon (1684) 317
  influences *The Beaux Stratagem* and *Love for Money* 317
Sir Martin Mar-all (California Dryden ix) 67–8, 70 n., 117, 127, 133
  compared with *The Committee* 67 (inverted order; impoverished Royalist)
Sir Patient Fancy (Summers iv) 120, 186, **213–15**, 218, 230, 231 n.
  compared with: *The Lucky Chance* 323 (bedroom trick); *The Woman-Captain* 214 (women/language)
Sir Popular Wisdom (lost) 230
Sir Salomon (1671) 6, **118–19**
  compared with: *The Mall*, 136, 186 (menacing fool); *The Town-Fop* 186 (menacing fool)
Six Days Adventure, The (1671) 23–4, 117, **165–6**
Slighted Maid, The (1663) 31 n., **35–6**, 40, 75
  compared with *The Committee* 35 (master/servant)
Sophonisba [Lee] (Stroup and Cooke i) **100–1**, 108, 248
  compared with *The Conquest of Granada* 101
Souldiers Fortune, The (Ghosh ii) **227–9**, 230, 255, 260, 282, 296, 314, 405
  compared with: *The City Heiress* 234 (qualified Toryism); *A Fond Husband* 200–1 (women/language); *The Way of the World* 417 (women/language)
Spanish Curate, The, adapted in *The Sham Lawyer* 389–90
Spanish Fryar, The (Works (1735) v) 127, **236–9**, 260, 274
  compared with: *The Kind Keeper* 236 (long-lost son); *Marriage A-la-Mode* 238 (usurper's daughter); *Oedipus* 237
Spanish Rogue, The (1674) **113**, 134
  compared with *The Committee* 113 (master/servant)
Spanish Wives, The (1696) 419
  compared with *The False Count* 419 (male authority)
  influenced by *Adelphi* 419
Squire of Alsatia, The (Summers iv) **325–8**, 331 n., 333, 404 n.
  compared with: *Bury-Fair* 334 (moral hero;

step-parent); Cibber 328 (reform comedy); *The Scowrers* 335 (hero's conduct); *The Virtuous Wife* 328 (reform comedy)
  quotes *Twelfth Night* 224 n.
Squire Oldsapp (1679) 196, 199, **201**, 202, 205 n.
  compared with *The Adventures of Five Hours* 201 (power of women)
State of Innocence, The (Works (1735) iv) 8, **179–84**
  compared with: *Aureng-Zebe* 182 (language); *The Country-Wife* 182 (language); *King Arthur* 370–1 (doubling of self); *Marriage A-la-Mode* 184 (language)
  quoted in the epigraph to Chapter Five 162
Step-Mother, The (1664) **36**, 56
Successful Straingers, The (1690) **333**, 335
Sullen Lovers, The (Summers i) **76–7**, 117, 120
  compared with *The Indian Emperour* 76 (retreat to wilderness)
  preface attacks gay couple comedy 75
Surprisal, The (Four New Plays) **31**, 32, 44

Tamburlaine 278 n., 249
Tamerlane the Great (1681) 31 n., **278**
  compared with: *Distress'd Innocence* 361–2 (power of heredity); *King Lear* 278 (villainous brother)
Taming of the Shrew, The 381
  adapted as *Sauny the Scot* 67
Tartuffe [Medbourne] (1670) 119–20
Tartuffe, Le [Molière]
  adapted: ?as *The Hypocrite* 120; by Matthew Medbourne 119–20; in *The English Frier* 336
Tarugo's Wiles (1668) **40–1**, 320
Tempest The [Dryden-Davenant] (California Dryden x) 18, 26, 35, **49–55**, 71, 73, 77, 135
  influences *The Libertine* 102–3
  revised by Shadwell 102
Tempest The [Operatic] (Summers ii) 3, 102, 178, 371
  parodied in *The Mock Tempest* 134–6
  scenic effects 4
Tempest The [Shakespeare] (Arden) 18, 47
  adapted by Dryden and Davenant 26, **49–55**, 77
  compared with: with *The Change of Crownes* 36 (usurpation); with *The Libertine* 102–3
  influences *The Sea Voyage* 319
Theodosius (Stroup and Cooke ii) **289–93**, 294, 297, 315
  compared with *Constantine the Great* 308 (vision of Constantine)
Thyestes [Crowne] (1681) **275**, 310
Timoleon (1697) 332, **430–1**
  compared with *Regulus* 431 (foreign saviour)

Timon of Athens [Shadwell], see *The History of Timon of Athens*

Timon of Athens [Shakespeare]:
adapted as *The History of Timon of Athens* 20, 160 n., 223, 256
influences *The Virtuoso* and *The Woman-Captain* 160 n., 223

Titus and Berenice (Ghosh i) 198, 245, 246

Titus Andronicus [Ravenscroft] (1687) **262–3**, 276

Titus Andronicus [Shakespeare] (Arden) 26, 55, 263, 276
adapted by Ravenscroft 262–3

Tom Essence (1677) 160–1
compared with *The Counterfeits* 197 (seduced heroine)

Town-Fop, The (Summers iii) **185–7**, 286
compared with: *The Man of Mode* 186 (vows); *Sir Salomon* and *The Mall* 186 (menacing fool)
uses *The Dutch Courtezan* 286

Town-Shifts, The (1671) 116, 117

Tragedy of Nero, The [Anon., 1624] (Hill) 96

Tragedy of Nero, Emperour of Rome, The (Stroup and Cooke i) 6, **95–6**, 108, 247, 455
quoted in epigraph to Chapter Three 78

Tragedy of Sertorius, The (1679) **263**, 359

Tragedy of Valentinian, The [Rochester] (Hayward) 307, **311–12**, 328 n, 373

Tragical History of King Richard III, The [Cibber] (1700) 18–19, 92, **432**
censored 432
compared with *Love's Last Shift* 432 (language)

Trappolin Creduto Principe, adapted as *A Duke and No Duke* 318

Treacherous Brothers, The (1690) 358
used in *A New Opera; called, Brutus of Alba* 429
imitates *Othello* 358

Trick for Trick (1678) 6, 188, **201–4**, 205, 319, 455
compared with: *The Comical Revenge* 202 (festive characters); *The Man of Mode* 202–4

Triumphant Widow, The (1677) 115

Triumphs of Virtue, The (1697) 438

Troilus and Cressida [Dryden] (California Dryden xiii) 23, **265–8**, 236 n., 273
compared with: *All for Love* 266 (female self-representation); *The Country-Wife* 143, 268 (Truth); *The History of King Lear* 278

Troilus and Cressida [Shakespeare] (Arden) 19, 21, 73, 76, 394, 451–2
adapted by Dryden 23, 265–8

Troyens, Les 450

True Widow, A (Summers iii) 20, **221–2**, 231 n.

compared with *The Man of Mode* 222 (gay couple)
satirizes *A Fond Husband* 221

Tryphon (Clark i) 32, 33, 38, 78

Tunbridge-Wells (1678) 197, **198**

Twelfth Night (Arden):
adapted as *Love Betray'd* 413, 414
allusion to in: *The Plain-Dealer* 190, 224 n., 392; *The Woman-Captain* 224; *The Younger Brother* 224 n., 392
quoted in *The Squire of Alsatia* 224 n.

Twin-Rivals, The (Kenny i) 408, 409
compared with *The Committee* 22, 412 (Irish servant)

Two Noble Kinsmen, The adapted as *The Rivals* 35

Tyrannick Love (California Dryden x) 46, 47, 49, 50, 78, 86, 88
preface 8 n.
quoted in *Love and a Bottle* 409

Unfortunate Usurper, The (1663) 56 n.

Unhappy Favourite, The (Sutherland) **278–9**, 282 n., 428 n.

Unhappy Kindness, The (1697) 430

Unnatural Brother, The (1697) 438
imitates *Othello* and *The Villain* 438
shortened version included in *The Novelty* 389 n.

Unnatural Mother, The (1698) 440

Usurper, The (1668) 35

Valentinian [Fletcher], adapted by Rochester 307, 311–12

Valentinian [Rochester], see *The Tragedy of Valentinian*

Valiant Cid, The [Rutter] 37, 455

Venice Preserv'd (Ghosh ii) 10, 13, 271, 282, 283, **300–6**, 429, 455
compared with: *The Man of Mode* 306 (cursing); *The Rival Queens* 306 (laceration of the body)
intellectual affinities with comedy 455
portrays power of money 456

Vertue Betray'd (1682) 281

Very Good Wife, A (1693) 341–2

Vestal Virgin, The (Five New Plays) **44**, 45

Victorious Love (1698) 431

Vida es sueño, La, adapted in *The Young King* 243

Villain, The (1663) **45–6**, 77, 164
compared with *The French Conjurer* 199 (male violence)
imitated in *The Unnatural Brother* 438
imitates *Othello* 45, 89

Virgin Martyr, The, adapted in *A New Opera; called, Brutus of Alba* (1697) 429

Virtuoso, The (Nicolson and Rodes) 20–1, 22, 121, **155–60**, 179, 221
  compared with *The Country-Wife* 156–7 (civility)
  influenced by: *She Would If She Could* 155–6; *Timon of Athens* 160 n., 223
Virtuous Wife, The (1680) 204–6
  compared with: *The Comical Revenge* 204–5 (festive characters); *Friendship in Fashion* 205 (neglected wife); *The Squire of Alsatia* 328 (reform comedy)
  imitates *Secret Love* and *The Plain-Dealer* 206
Volunteers, The (Summers v) 334, **336**, 339

Wary Widdow, The (1693) 340–1
  quoted in epigraph to Chapter Nine 331
Way of the World, The (Davis) 10, 235 n., 350, 351, **352–3**, 379–80, 380–1, 382, 383, **416–19**, 427, 453, 457
  compared with: *The Committee* 381 (social structure); *The Souldiers Fortune* 417 (women/language)
White Devil, The, compared with *The Plain-Dealer* 452 (law)
Widow Ranter, The (Summers iv) 186–7, 244, **372–3**
  compared with *The Young King* 372–3 (Amazonian heroine)
Wife for a Month, A, adapted as *The Unhappy Kindness* 430
Wild Gallant, The (California Dryden viii) 41, 43, **58–9**, 67
  compared with: *Amboyna* 92 (carnality); *Love Triumphant* 369 (ancestry)
Win Her and Take Her (1691) 338
  ?influenced by *Greenwich-Park* and *The English Frier* 338
Winter's Tale, The 50, 369
Wit at Severall Weapons (Bowers vii) 353 n.
Wits Led by the Nose (1678) 243
Witty Combat, A (1663) 40

Wit Without Money, adapted in *The Sham-Lawyer* 389–90
Wives' Excuse, The (Jordan and Love i) 343, 344–5, 346, **348**, 349, 404 n., **456–7**
  compared with: *The Intrigues at Versailles* 403 (playwright within the play); *Love and a Bottle* 409 (playwright within the play)
  criticized by Charles Gildon 403
  influences *The Campaigners* 405
  revived at the Swan, Stratford, 1994–5 456
Woman-Captain, The (Summers iv) 121, 130, 207, **222–4**, 230–1, 235, 325
  alludes to *Twelfth Night* 224
  compared with: *The Atheist* 316 (women's rights); *Friendship in Fashion* 225 (image of the Fool), 227 (class structure); *The Plain-Dealer* 223 (women/law); *Sir Anthony Love* 347 (heroine in male disguise); *Sir Patient Fancy* 214 (women/language)
  dedication, 20
  influenced by: *Epicoene*, 222, 223; *Timon of Athens* 160 n., 223
Womans Wit (1697) 389
  influenced by *The English Frier* and *The Plain-Dealer* 389
Woman Turn'd Bully, The (1675) 130, **134**, 148
Womens Conquest, The (1671) 117, **165**
World in the Moon, The (1697) 378, 386
Wrangling Lovers, The (1677) **147**, 242
  compared with *The Country-Wife* and *Love in the Dark* 147 (signs)

Xerxes (*Dramatic Works* v) 192 n., 430

Younger Brother, The (Summers iv) 389, **391–3**
  alludes to: *The Plain-Dealer* 392–3; *Twelfth Night* 224 n., 392
Young King, The (Summers ii) 164 n., **243–5**
  compared with *The Widow Ranter* 372–3 (Amazonian heroine)

Zeno; sive, Ambitio Infelix 78

General Index

Some incidental references have been omitted. Topics are indexed when they are narrowly defined and manageable in extent, but some (such as language or the stranger) are too multi-faceted, or too pervasive, to be satisfactorily indexed.

Addison, Joseph, on the imagination 27
Aikenhead, Thomas 7 n.
Ailesbury, Earl of, *see* Bruce, Thomas
Allestree, Richard 19, 57
  on duties of gentry 21
  The Whole Duty of Man, satirized in *The Woman Turn'd Bully* 134
Andrew, N. J. 246 n., 264 n.
Anne, Princess, afterwards Queen:
  acts in *Calisto* 178
  ?represented in *The Grove* 433
Antidote against the Present Fears and Jealousies of the Nation, An 308 n.
Ariosto, Lodovico, *Orlando Furioso* 109
aristocracy and gentry 6–7, 115–17, 266
  changing role and standing of aristocracy 7, 19–20, 23, 452
  complaints about degenerate gentry 20–2
  criticized by Shadwell 75–7, 102, 121, 156–7, 162, 223–4
  economic difficulties of minor gentry 333
  hereditary excellence of upper classes:
    affirmed 19, 21, 30, 35, 36, 278, 319, 368; denied 14, 22, 380, 411–13
  ideals of conduct 20–2, 136
  ideals of conduct mocked 57–8, 130
  satire of aristocracy 133, 150, 221, 256, 320–1, 333, 336–7, 339, 344, 413
  satire of gentry 360, 412, 414–15
Aristotle, 13, 14, 106 n.
Arlington, Earl of, *see* Bennet, Henry
Armistead, J. M. 95 n., 269 n., 293 n., 295 n.
Arran, Earl of, *see* Douglas, James
Arundell, Henry, Lord Arundell of Wardour, dedicatee of Ravenscroft's *Titus Andronicus* 263
Ashcraft, Richard 19 n., 260 n., 359 n.
Assheton, William 9
Astell, Mary 412
Astraea 28, 30, 55, 78, 82, 95, 312, 373, 376, 414, 429, 430, 431, 444, 445
atheism 7–11, 240–1
Aubrey, John 42
Avery, Emmett L. 30 n.

Bacon, Jon Lance 141 n., 191 n.
Bailey, Cyril 50 n.

Bancroft, John 359
Banks, John 283, 288
Banquet of the Senses 205
Barbour, Frances 95 n.
Barry, Elizabeth:
  specialisms 404 n.
  unusual casting in *The Intrigues at Versailles* 403–4
Basset, Elizabeth 163 n.
Bazely, L. 163 n.
bedroom trick 28, 35, 36, 75, 102, 136–7, 160, 162, 167, 193, 206, 207, 214–15, 216–17, 220, 225, 242–3, 277, 283–4, 313, 314, 315, 316, 317, 323–4, 329, 342, 346, 352, 386, 388, 389, 391, 425, 432, 440
Beer, E. S. de 71 n.
Beeston, William 30 n.
Behn, Aphra 2, 23, 24, 28, 46, 126–7, 130, 185, 223, 227, 255, 283, 325, 372, 373, 377, 406, 408, 446
  non-dramatic works: *Agnes de Castro*, adapted by Catherine Trotter 444–5; *The Dumb Virgin* 176; *The History of the Nun*, adapted in *The Fatal Marriage* 373–4; *The Lucky Mistake*, adapted in *Sir Anthony Love* 373–4; *Lycidus; or, The Lover in Fashion* 215; *Oroonoko* 187, 426, adapted by Southerne 374, 456; *The Unfortunate Happy Lady* 177
  suggested author of: *The Counterfeit Bridegroom* 206; *The Debauchee* 196; *The Revenge* 286
  translates Fontenelle 8
Bell, Maureen 163 n.
Bennet, Henry, Earl of Arlington 114 n.
  represented in *The Rehearsal* 85 n.
Bentley, Richard 9–10
Berlioz, Hector 450
Berman, David 7 n.
Bernard, Edward 9–10
Betterton, Mary 250
Betterton, Thomas 6, 225, 232
  leads actors' rebellion 377
  stages operatic spectaculars 178, 179
Beveridge, William 18 n.
Birdsall, Virginia Ogden 61 n., 194 n.
Blount, Charles 7, 8, 10 n., 11, 12, 17, 432 n.

Blue Posts Tavern, used in William III assassination plot 397
Boothby, Sir Brooke 163 n.
Boothby, Catherine 163 n.
Boothby, Frances (née Milward) 163 n.
Boothby, Frances 163 n.
Boothby, Frances, of Tottenham, later Mrs Brewester 163 n.
Boothby, Walter 163 n.
Boothby, Sir William 163 n.
Botica, Allan Richard 3 n.
bourgeois characters:
   favourably portrayed 205, 218, 223, 230, 231, 325, 337, 342, 386–7, 412, 420–1
   satirized 318, 341–2, 360, 369, 401–2
Bowman, Elizabeth 403
Bowman, John 390 n., 403
Bowtell, Elizabeth 6, 250, 253
Boyle, Robert 8, 12, 13 n., 27
Boyle, Roger, Lord Broghill and Earl of Orrery 43, 240
   dedicatee of *The Rival Ladies* 42
   his outlook rejected: in *The Comical Revenge* 60–3; by Dryden 34, 42–3, 46–7, 72, 81, 82–3, 129, 454–5; by Lee 268, 289–90; by Mountfort 329; by Otway 104, 283; by Settle 86, 110, 362; in *Timoleon* 431; by Wycherley 194
   interest in the noble rival 32–3, 42, 43, 72, 75, 81, 82, 86, 110, 160, 194, 255, 280, 283, 289–90, 362
   writes drama of aristocratic and public values 6–7, 25, 26, 29, 32–4, 48, 454
Bracegirdle, Anne 5–6, 327, 331, 339, 358, 360, 361, 373, 433, 437
   rarely plays unchaste characters 404 n.
   unusual casting in *The Intrigues at Versailles* 403–4
Brady, Nicholas 7
Bramhall, John, debate with Hobbes 181
Brathwait, Richard 22–3
Bredvold, Louis I. 10 n., 42, 181 n.
Bristol, Earl of, *see* Digby, George
Brome, Richard 58 n.
Brown, Laura 23 n., 247 n., 450 n.
Brown, Richard E. 308 n.
Bruce, Thomas, Earl of Ailesbury 338 n.
Brutus, Lucius Junius, as republican hero 263, 293, 308, 312
Buckhurst, Lord, *see* Sackville, Charles
Buckingham, second Duke of, *see* Villiers, George
Burke, Helen M. 137 n.
Burnaby, William 413
   compared with Etherege 415 (duties of gentry)
   plays 413–16

satirizes aristocracy 333
Burnet, Gilbert 7 n.
Butler, Charlotte 6 n.
Butler, James, second Duke of Ormonde 9
Bywaters, David 283 n., 342 n., 363 n., 366 n., 369 n.

Cambert, Robert 178
Camoëns, Luis de, *The Lusiads* 80 n.
Canfield, J. Douglas 36 n., 82 n., 185 n., 361 n., 420 n.
Cannan, Paul D. 240 n., 455 n.
Capel, Algernon, Earl of Essex, dedicatee of *Greenwich-Park* 333 n.
Capel, Arthur, Earl of Essex 333 n.
Carlell, Lodowick 37
Carmarthen, Marquess of, *see* Osborne, Thomas
carnival 28, 40, 58, 71, 72, 74, 82, 127–9, 130, 132, 134–6, 145, 147, 154, 155, 202, 205, 208–13, 318, 345, 396, 397, 445–6, 453
Cartwright, William (actor) 92
Cary, Henry, fourth Viscount Falkland 36
Castlemaine, Countess of, *see* Villiers, Barbara
Catherine of Braganza, Queen of England 242
Catullus 213
Cavendish, Henry, Lord Ogle, dedicatee of *The Woman-Captain* 20
Cavendish, Margaret, Marchioness, afterwards Duchess, of Newcastle 23
Cavendish, William, Earl, afterwards Duke, of Devonshire, dedicatee of *The English Frier* 336 n.
Cavendish, William, Marquess, afterwards Duke, of Newcastle 20, 163 n.
   dedicatee of *Love's Kingdom* 34 n.
Centlivre, Susanna 377
Cervantes Saavedra, Miguel De, *Don Quixote*:
   dramatized by Durfey 340
   'The Curious Impertinent' used in *The Married Beau* 341
Charles I, King of England, ?represented in *The Siege of Rhodes* 1
Charles II, King of England 89 n., 95, 179, 260, 273, 308 n., 429, 455
   death necessitates revision of *Albion and Albanius* 313
   Flanders campaign 202 n.
   likes *A Fond Husband* 199, 219
   likes *The Old Troop* 57
   pardons Danby 265
   praised by Settle 276
   represented or alluded to in: *Albion and Albanius* 312–13; *Antony and Cleopatra* [Sedley] 246; *The Black Prince* 43; *Caesar Borgia* 268; *The Change of Crownes* 36; *The Conspiracy* 275; *Constantine the*

Charles II, King of England (*cont.*)
Great 308; ? *The Duke of Guise* 307 n.;
The English Princess 35; ? 'The Faithful
Virgins' 79; *Henry the Second* 360; *The
Indian Emperour* 47; *Irena* 43; *Macbeth*
[Davenant] 35; *The Massacre of Paris*
276; *The Misery of Civil-War* 274;
Mustapha [Orrery] 44; prologue to *The
History and Fall of Caius Marius* 273; *The
Souldiers Fortune* 227–8; ? *Theodosius*
293 n.; *The Tragedy of Valentinian*
[Rochester] 311; *The Usurper* 35
satirized by John Lacy 97
sees *Tamerlane the Great* 278
suggests source play to: Crowne 320; Tuke 38
Charron, Pierre 10 n., 11, 47, 204
Cibber, Colley 29, 377, 388, 389, 390
compared with: Congreve 417
(individual/society); Farquhar 408 (he-
roes); Jonson and Shadwell 387; Vanbrugh
395 (language and the sacred)
his reform comedies compared with *The
Squire of Alsatia* 328
Cicero, quoted in *Lucius Junius Brutus* 299
Clarendon, Earl of, *see* Hyde, Edward
Clark, Andrew 42 n.
Clark, J. C. D. 359 n.
Clarke, Jeremiah 378 n.
Clarke, Samuel 260 n.
Cleveland, Duchess of, *see* Villiers, Barbara
Clifford, Arthur 163 n.
Clun, Walter 66 n.
Coleman, Antony 2 n.
College, Stephen, represented in *City Politiques*
310
Collier, Jeremy:
*A Defence of the Short View of the
Profaneness and Immorality of the English
Stage* 357
*A Short View of the Immorality, and
Profaneness of the English Stage* 357;
answered by Durfey 404–5; mentioned in
The Constant Couple 411
Columbus, Christopher, treatment by Dryden
and Graziani 80 n.
Comber, Thomas 18
Comparison between the Two Stages, A 428 n.,
441 n.
Congreve, William 8, 29, 331, 340, 370, 377,
386, 391, 423
characteristics of his plays 350–2
compared with: Cibber 417 (individual/soci-
ety); Durfey, Shadwell, and Vanbrugh 380
(individual/society); Pix 419
(individual/society); Southerne, Vanbrugh,
and Wycherley 350 (dislocation);
Vanbrugh 396 (individual/society)

debt to *An Evening's Love* 73 n.
persistence with sex comedy 387
Constantine I, Emperor of Rome 308
Cooke, A. L. 308 n.
Cooke, Sarah 6 n.
Cooper, Anthony Ashley, Lord Ashley and Earl
of Shaftesbury 89, 112 n., 185, 230 n., 256,
264, 265
mocked in epilogue to *The Restauration* 311
quarrel with Buckingham 310–11
represented in: *The City Heiress* 232;
Constantine the Great 282 n., 308; ? *The
Duke of Guise* 308; *The History and Fall
of Caius Marius* 272–3; *The History of
King Richard the Second* 278; *The Loyal
Brother* 280; *Sir Popular Wisdom* 230;
The Siege of Constantinople 96, 282 n.;
Tamerlane the Great 278; *Troilus and
Cressida* [Dryden] 236 n., 266; *Venice
Preserv'd* 282
Cope, Jackson I. 16 n.
Copeland, Nancy 233 n.
Cordemoy, Géraud de 106
Cordner, Michael 344 n., 393 n., 397 n., 399
Corey, Katherine 6, 191 n., 197, 250
Corneille, Pierre, translations of 37
Coventry, Sir William:
challenges Buckingham 114
represented in *The Country Gentleman* 114
Cranley, Thomas, *Amanda; or, The Reformed
Whore* 211
Cromwell, Oliver, represented in *The History of
King Richard the Second* 278
Crowne, John 2, 85, 106, 242, 283, 377, 453
attitude to monarchy 150, 329–30, 360–1
collaborates in attack on *The Empress of
Morocco* 93
influenced by Dryden 85
political sympathies: during the Exclusion
Crisis 236 n., 260, 274–5, 277; during the
Tory Reaction, 308–10; after the
Revolution 336, 360–1
Culverwell, Nathanael 183
Cutts, John, Lord Cutts of Gowran, dedicatee
of *Distress'd Innocence* 361

D'Urfé, Honoré, *L'Astrée* 64, 280
Danby, Earl of, *see* Osborne, Thomas
Danchin, Pierre 118 n., 148 n., 178 n., 197 n.,
202 n., 221 n., 230 n., 265 n., 282 n., 311 n.,
430 n., 441 n.
Davenant, Alexander 377 n.
Davenant, Sir William 32 n., 34, 43, 77
adaptations of Shakespeare 34–5
conduct and legacy as manager of Duke's
company 1–3
in Interregnum 1

Davies, H. Neville 250 n.
deism 7–11
  in *Oroonoko* [Behn] 187
  in *The State of Innocence* 181
Democritus, the laughing philosopher 194
Dennis, John:
  on composition of *Sir Courtly Nice* 320 n.
  *The Danger of Priestcraft to Religion and
    Government* 8, 442
  Priestcraft Distinguish'd from Christianity 8,
    442
Descartes, René 27, 451
  influences Dryden 41–2, 105–6, 180, 183
  mentioned in *The Morning Ramble* 180 n.
Devonshire, Duke of, *see* Cavendish, William
Diamond, Elin 211 n.
Dickens, Charles, *Our Mutual Friend* 451
Digby, George, Earl of Bristol 41
Dilke, Thomas:
  plays 386–7
  rejects comedy based on metropolitan values
    386, 390
Dobson, Michael 278 n.
Dorset, Earl of, *see* Sackville, Charles
double standard 78, 132, 136, 162, 201, 205,
  207, 217–18, 231, 337, 403–4, 405–7, 414,
  421, 439, 446–8
Douglas, James, Earl of Arran and Duke of
  Hamilton, dedicatee of *The Injur'd Lovers*
  333 n.
Downes, John 44 n. 385 n.
Drougge, Helga 387 n., 404 n.
Drury, G. Thorn 4 n.
Dryden, John 126, 201, 332, 366, 372, 377, 455
  at King's Company 2, 3, 77, 91
  attacked by: Ravenscroft 132; Shadwell 75
  brings *The Mistaken Husband* to the stage
    136
  collaborates in attack on *The Empress of
    Morocco* 93
  compared with: Etherege and Wycherley
    (identity) 175; Farquhar 410 (justice)
  contributes 'The Secular Masque' to
    Vanbrugh's *The Pilgrim* 402
  comedies 68, 77, 117, 130, 185
  heroic plays: characteristics 46–9; cited in
    Love and a Bottle 409; discusses their
    genesis 2; incantation scenes 4; influence
    85, 95
  intellectual outlook: Cartesianism 41–2,
    105–6, 180; deism 8–9, 181; determinism
    42–3; linguistics and epistemology 16, 27,
    29, 33, 103, 146, 453
  low view of *The Husband his Own Cuckold*
    389
  on casting of *All for Love* 6 n
  on composition of *The Kind Keeper* 219

poems: *Absalom and Achitophel* 104, 230,
  236, 281; *Astraea Redux* 28, 30, 72; epilogues to *Tamerlane the Great* 278; *The
  Hind and the Panther* 8–9; *Mac Flecknoe*
  156 n.; 'Prologue . . . Spoken at the
  Opening of the New House' 2; prologue
  and epilogue to *The Unhappy Favourite*
  278; *Religio Laici* 181
  polishes *Tamerlane the Great* 278
  political views during the Exclusion Crisis
    236, 277, 283, 310
  post-Revolution preoccupation with exile 29,
    331, 365, 454
  reacts against *The Adventures of Five Hours*
    39, 41
  reacts against Orrery's plays 34, 46–7, 240,
    454–5
  represented in: *The History of Timon of
    Athens* 256; ? *The Humorists* 120; *The
    Reformation* 134; *The Rehearsal* 84–5
  satirized in *The Virtuoso* 156
  satirizes gentlemanly ideals 57–8, 130
  share in composition: of *The Duke of Guise*
    307 n.; of *Oedipus* 261 n.
Duffett, Thomas 113 n., 134–6
Duke's Company:
  absorbs King's 307
  foundation and history 1–3
  repertory 77, 133–4
Duncombe, Sir John, represented in *The
  Country Gentleman* 114
Durfey, Thomas 2, 210, 223, 225–6, 227, 377,
  380
  answers Jeremy Collier 404–5
  caricatured in *A True Widow* 221, 231
  compared with: Congreve, 357 (justice), 380
    (individual/society); Vanbrugh 397
    (justice)
  influences Farquhar 408
  plays of the mid-1680s 319
  post-Revolution plays and allegiances 331–2,
    338
  prologue to *Sir Hercules Buffoon* 317
  return to sex comedy after *The Relapse* 402
Duval, Amaury 47 n.
Duval, Claude (highwayman), represented in
  Psyche Debauch'd 135

Eccles, John 378 n.
  music for: *The Loves of Mars and Venus* 378;
    The Rape of Europa by Jupiter 373
Edghill, E. M. 106
Edmunds, John 256 n.
Elizabeth I, heroine of Whigs 89, 235, 279
Elwes, R. H. M. 17 n.
Empson, William 8 n.
Epicureanism 8, 240–1, 268

Essex, Earl of, *see* Capel, Algernon, and Capel, Arthur
Etherege, Sir George 68, 71, 103, 117, 130, 377, 453
    compared with: Burnaby, 415 (duties of gentry); Dryden 175 (identity); Farquhar 410 (justice); Shadwell 156 (Epicureanism; language and the sacred), 328 (man as savage); Southerne 344; Vanbrugh 395 (language and the sacred), 397 (justice)
    Epicureanism 23, 156, 205
    satirizes gentlemanly ideals, 22–3, 57–8
Evelyn, John, condemns *An Evening's Love* 71, 453
Exclusion Crisis 104, 112, 185, 227, 228, **230–9, 259–311,** 336

Falkland, fourth Viscount, see Cary, Henry
fallen woman 155, 197, 227, 234–5, 256, 317, 337, 340–1, 390, 409, 419, 420, 421–2, 438, 439, 455–6
Farquhar, George 115, 377, 408, 454
    compared with Cibber, Southerne, and Vanbrugh 408 (dislocated heroes)
    distinctive characteristics 408–9, 410
    influenced by Durfey 408
Feiling, Sir Keith 265 n., 431
felt-makers, social status of 353
Fenwick, Lady (Mary) 338 n.
Fenwick, Sir John 338 n.
Ferry, Anne Davidson 252 n.
festivity 62, 63, 74, 82, 85, 92, 131, 134–6, 145, 150, 151, 203, 205, 222–4, 225–6, 233, 318, 349, 396
Filmer, Edward 37 n.
Filmer, Sir Robert 220, 259
Finger, Gottfried 378 n.
    music for *The Loves of Mars and Venus* 378
Fisher, Alan S. 256 n.
Fletcher, John 9 n.
Fontenelle, Bernard Le Bovier de 8
Fortune, Nigel 1 n.
Foucault, Michel 304 n.
Frazer, John 7 n.
Freehafer, John 1 n., 30 n.
Freeman, Arthur 428 n.

Gage family 163 n.
Gagen, Jean 60 n.
Gailhard, Jean 21–2
Gardiner, Anne Barbeau 307–8 n., 365, 367 n., 368 n.
Garrett, Jane 397 n.
Gassendi, Pierre 27, 180, 183
gay couple 6, 40, 59, 64, 66, 67, 74, 75, 77, 116, 132, 164, 196, 197, 199, 222, 228, 229, 337, 349, 453

Gaya, Louis de 11
Genest, John 206
gentry, *see* aristocracy and gentry
Gewirtz, Arthur 207 n., 451 n.
Gildon, Charles 7, 12 n., 443
    analyses *Othello* 443
    brings *The Younger Brother* to the stage 392
    criticizes *The Wives' Excuse* 403
Gill, James E. 393 n.
Glanvill, Joseph 235
Gloucester, William Henry, Duke of, dedicatee of *Pyrrhus King of Epirus* 433 n.
Godfrey, Sir Edmund Berry, alluded to in:
    Caesar Borgia 268
    Henry the Sixth, The First Part [Crowne] 274–5
Godolphin, Sidney 37 n.
Gordon, G. S. 20 n.
Grabu, Luis 178
Graham, Anne, Lady Preston 338 n.
Graham, Richard, Viscount Preston 338 n.
    on women 24
Gransden, K. W. 181 n.
Gratian (canon lawyer), 315
Gray, Thomas 21
Graziani, Girolamo, *Il Conquisto di Granata* 79, 80
Gregory, Tullio 10 n.
Gwyn, Nell 59, 64, 66, 148 n.
    partnership with Charles Hart 2, 6, 64, 71, 77, 190

Haley, K. H. D. 89 n., 112, 265 n.
Hammond, Antony 2 n., 56 n., 269 n., 295
Hammond, Paul 5 n., 266 n.
Harbage, Alfred 58 n.
Harris, Henry 70 n., 130, 151
Harris, John 14 n.
Hart, Charles 6, 64, 190
    partnership with Nell Gwyn 2, 6, 64, 71, 77, 190
    rarely plays villains 6, 150
    takes darker roles in late 1670s 6, 190, 202
Harth, Phillip 8 n., 236 n., 278 n., 283 n.
Hartsock, Mildred E. 42 n.
Harwood, John T. 327 n.
Haughton, Lord, *see* Holles, John
Hauser, David R. 305 n.
Haynes, Jo 6, 127
Hazlitt, W. C. 440 n.
Henrietta Maria, Queen of England, ?represented in *The Siege of Rhodes* 1
Heraclitus, the weeping philosopher 194
Herbert, Sir Henry, censors 'The Faithfull Virgins' 79
heroic drama:
    in the mid-1670s 240–2

its Orrerian and Drydenesque phases distinguished 454–5
parodied in: *Epsom-Wells* 121, 131; *The Rehearsal* 84–5; *The Virtuoso* 121
Hickeringill, Edmund 8
Hickes, George 259, 308 n.
   on women 24
Hickman, Charles 17–18, 91
Higden, Henry, attacks *The Old Batchelour* 340
Hill, George Birkbeck 50 n.
Hobbes, Thomas 8, 10, **12–17**, 22, 23, 27, 51, 135, 251, 451
   compared with Montaigne 12–13
   debate with Bramhall 181
   influences Dryden 42–3
   on signs and language 14–17, 139, 143, 192, 194, 253
   state of nature 52, 54–5, 93, 137, 179, 192, 286, 324
Hobby, Elaine 163 n.
Hodgetts, Michael 163 n.
Holland, Norman N. 61 n., 451 n.
Holland, Peter 332 n., 339 n.
Holles, John, Lord Haughton, dedicatee of *The Spanish Fryar* 236
Homer 156
   Iliad 192 n., 213–14, 440
Hook, Lucyle 373 n.
Hooker, Edward Niles 2 n., 320 n.
Hopkins, Charles 332
   on conflict of masculine and feminine 433–4
   political allegiances 433 n.
   suggested author of *Neglected Virtue* 440 n.
Horace 21, 22, 280, 327, 368
Horden, Hildebrand, brings *Neglected Virtue* to the stage 440 n.
Hordern, John 78 n.
hospitality 102, 103, 115, 138, 235, 256, 344, 374, 395, 424–5, 434, 435, 439
Hotson, Leslie 1 n.
Howard, Charles, Earl of Carlisle 338 n.
Howard, Edward 7
   on women 23–4
   quarrel with John Lacy 36, 76
   represented in *The Sullen Lovers* 76
Howard, James 7, 77
Howard, Sir Robert 7, 34, 43
   attacked by Charles Leslie 8 n.
   The History of Religion 8
   political allegiances in 1660s 38, 44–5, 114
   represented in *The Sullen Lovers* 76
Howard, Thomas, Earl of Berkshire 7
Howard, William, Viscount Stafford 260
Howard family 7, 43, 163 n.
Howe, Elizabeth 64, 404 n.
Howe, Sir Scrope 89

Hughes, Derek 46 n., 47 n., 50 n., 78 n., 251 n., 252 n., 253 n., 294 n., 301 n., 303 n., 437 n.
Hume, Robert D. 1 n., 3 n., 25 n., 36 n., 44 n., 63 n., 79 n., 85 n., 89 n., 113 n., 114, 116 n., 127 n., 134 n., 148 n., 160 n., 178 n., 196 n., 197 n., 221 n., 230–1 n., 269 n., 278 n., 286 n., 311, 313 n., 327 n., 332 n., 343–4 n., 385 n., 439, 440 n., 441 n.
   on failure of sex comedies in 1678 453
   on formation of early Restoration repertory 2 n.
Hungerland, Isabel C. 16 n.
Hunter, Michael 7 n., 8 n.
Hutton, Ronald 38 n., 41 n.
Hyde, Anne, Duchess of York, possible allusions to her marriage in:
   'The Faithful Virgins' 79
   Marcelia 163
   The Rewards of Vertue 162
Hyde, Edward, Earl of Clarendon 31, 38 n., 41 n., 114 n., 242, 353 n.
   represented in: *The Great Favourite* 44–5, 114; ? *Mustapha* [Orrery] 44

Ibsen, Henrik 453
Invisible Mistress 28, 71–2, 129, 145, 147, 201, 211, 216–17, 313, 316, 323, 340, 386, 388, 391

Jacob, Margaret C. 259–60, 452 n.
James, Duke of York and Albany, afterwards King James II of England 76 n., 114, 273, 360 n., 369, 395, 432, 433 n.
   conversion to Catholicism 89, 96
   dedicatee of *Don Carlos* 282
   during the Exclusion Crisis 185, 259, 273–4, 277, 279
   marriage to Mary of Modena 95, 178
   relationship with Danby 264–5
   represented or alluded to in: *Albion and Albanius* 313; *Alphonso King of Naples* 359; *Aureng-Zebe* 104; *Cleomenes* 365; *The Conspiracy* 275; *Constantine the Great* 308; *Darius King of Persia* 329; *Don Sebastian* 362, 365; *The Duke of Guise* 307–8; 'The Faithfull Virgins' 79; *The Fate of Capua* 434; *The Grove* 433; *Henry the Second* 360; *The History of King Lear* 277; *The Ingratitude of a Common-Wealth* 279; *King Arthur* 369–70; *King Edward the Third* 360; *Love for Money* 338; *Love Triumphant* 368; *The Loyal Brother* 265, 280; ? *Marcelia* 163; ? *Oroonoko* 425; ? *The Rewards of Vertue* 162; Shadwell's late comedies 360
Jeffreys, Sir George 359
   represented in *King Edward the Third* 360

Jekyll, Thomas 18
Jenkins, George 372 n.
Jermyn, Henry, ?represented in the original version of *The Humorists* 121 n.
Johnson, Samuel 50 n., 369
Johnston, Joseph S., Jr 78 n.
Jones, Harold Whitmore 16 n.
Jones, J. R. 19 n., 360 n.
Jonson, Ben 9 n., 18
    compared with Cibber 387
    'To Penshurst' 75
Jordan, Robert 331 n., 343 n.
Jose, Nicholas 30 n., 37 n., 56 n.

Kastan, David Scott 95 n.
Kavenik, Frances M. 67 n., 113 n., 134 n.
Kenny, Shirley Strum 3 n., 421 n.
Kenyon, John 359 n.
Kéroualle, Louise Renée de, Duchess of
    Portsmouth, dedicatee of *The Destruction
    of Jerusalem* 241
Killigrew, Thomas 1–2
King, Bruce 84 n., 181 n.
King's Company:
    foundation and history 1–3
    merges with Duke's 307
    repertory 77, 113–14, 134, 136, 137
Knepp, Elizabeth 150
Knolles, Richard 43 n.
Knowles, Ronald 312 n.
Kroll, Richard W. F. 384 n.

L'Estrange, Sir Roger 295 n.
La Calprenède, Gauthier de Costes de:
    Cassandre: influences *The Rival Queens, The
        Rival Kings*, and *The Siege of Babylon*
        242; mentioned in *The Constant Couple*
        409, 411
    Cléopâtre, adapted in: *Herod and Mariamne*
        and *Tyrannick love* 88; *The Indian Queen*
        and *The Conquest of Granada* 440; *Neg-
        lected Virtue* 440; *The Young King* 243
La Fayette, Marie-Madeleine, Comtesse de, *La
    Princesse de Clèves* adapted by Lee 313–14
La Mothe Le Vayer, François de 10 n., 11
La Rochefoucauld, François, Duc de 169 n.
Lacy, John 136, 317 n.
    provides dance interlude in *Horace* 38
    quarrel with Edward Howard 36, 76
    satirizes Charles II 97
Langbaine, Gerard 38, 78, 113 n., 160 n., 196
    n., 197 n., 207 n.
Latham, Robert 33 n.
Lawrence, William 11, 17
Le Brun, Charles 4
Leanerd, John 196–7
Lee, Elinor 213

Lee, Mary 250, 255
Lee, Nathaniel 2, 3, 16, 104, 251, 283, 310, 358,
    377
    influenced by Dryden 85
    reacts against Orrery's plays 240
    share in composition of: *The Duke of Guise*
        307 n.; *Oedipus* 261 n.
    use of spectacle 5
Leeds, Duke of, *see* Osborne, Thomas
Leigh, Anthony 227, 232–3, 236, 338 n., 360
Lemay, J. A. Leo 7 n.
Lennep, William Van 30 n.
Leslie, Charles, attacks:
    Sir Robert Howard 8 n.
    Tillotson 9
Letsome, Sampson 14 n.
Leveridge, Richard 378 n.
Levin, Richard 3 n.
Lincoln's Inn Fields company 377, 378, 439
    satirized in *Æsop*, Part II 402
Lindley, David 5 n.
Livy 299
Locke, John 22, 27, 301
Loftis, John 122 n., 197 n.
London Stage 1660–1800, The 30 n., 79 n., 197
    n., 243 n., 278 n., 295 n., 311 n., 338 n.,
    455 n.
Lord, George DeF. 97 n.
Louis XIV, King of France 43, 179, 273
    mentioned or alluded to in: *Bury-Fair* 334;
        Love for Money 338; *Pausanias, the
        Betrayer of his Country* 430; *The Relapse*
        397; *The Scowrers* 336
Love, Harold 3 n., 30 n., 88 n., 96 n., 331 n.,
    343 n.
Lucas, Richard 18 n.
Lucretia, as dramatic character or icon 229,
    254–5, 296–8, 312, 315
Lucretius 304
    influence on Shadwell 156, 179
    Lucretian spectator 50, 51, 53, 54, 103, 204,
        442

M., A., of the Church of England 22
Machiavelli, Niccolò 332
    influences: English republicanism 268 n.;
        Lucius Junius Brutus 268n.
Mackenzie, Sir George 19
Macpherson C. B. 13 n.
Macray, W. Dunn 353 n.
Maguire, Nancy Klein 5 n., 32 n., 277 n.
Manley, Mary de La Rivière 443
    represented in *The Female Wits* 448–9
Marius, Gaius 270 n.
Markley, Robert 61 n., 124 n.
Marsden, Jean I. 277 n.
Marshall, Rebecca 150

Martinich, Aloysius 16 n.
Marvell, Andrew, *An Account of the Growth of Popery and Arbitrary Government in England* 91
Mary, Princess, afterwards Queen Mary III 260, 332, 363 n.
acts in *Calisto* 178
Mary of Modena, Duchess of York, afterwards Queen of England 95, 178
dedicatee of: *The Orphan* 282; *The State of Innocence* 104 n.
Mason, John E. 22
Matthews, William 33 n.
Maus, Katharine Eisaman 23 n.
McBurney, William H. 305 n.
McFadden, George 85 n.
Milhous, Judith 1 n., 3 n., 4 n., 25 n., 36 n., 44 n., 79 n., 113 n., 116 n., 134 n., 160 n., 196 n., 197 n., 221 n., 286 n., 318 n., 377 n., 440 n., 441 n.
Miller, Frank Justus 294 n.
Miller, John 95, 273–4
Miller, Rachel A. 308 n.
Mills, Laurens J. 33 n.
Milton, John 94
Paradise Lost 365; adapted by Dryden 179–84; quoted in *Caesar Borgia* 268
Miner, Earl 9 n.
Mintz, Samuel I. 7–8 n.
Moders, Mary, represented in *A Witty Combat* 40
Molesworth, Sir William 13 n.
Molière (Jean-Baptiste Poquelin) 199, 453
early Restoration adaptations of 117
Monck, George, Duke of Albemarle, represented in:
The Generall 32
The Rump 30
The Usurper 35
Monmouth, Duchess of, *see* Scott, Anne
Monmouth, Duke of, *see* Scott, James
Montaigne, Michel Eyquem de 50 n., 171
compared with Hobbes 12–13
influence on drama and free thought 10–11
influences Dryden 105
moral systems as little cells and municipal laws 10, 12, 17, 50 n., 55, 61, 103, 123, 138, 151, 158, 292, 310, 354, 378
Moore, John 11, 259–60
Motteux, Peter 373
Mountfort, Susanna 345, 440
Mountfort, William 6 n., 345 n.
post-Revolution Whig views 359
Moyle, Walter 8
Mulgrave, Earl of, *see* Sheffield, John
Munns, Jessica 246, 270 n.
Murray, Barbara A. 272–3 n.

Neill, Michael 139 n.
Neman, Beth S. 88 n.
Neville, Henry 19
translates Machiavelli 268 n.
Newcastle, Duchess of, *see* Cavendish, Margaret
Newcastle, Duke of, *see* Cavendish, William
Nicholl, John 14 n.
noble rival 32–3, 34, 42–3, 72, 75, 79, 81, 82, 86, 110, 113, 136, 179, 194, 242–3, 268, 280, 283, 289–90, 315, 362, 421–2, 441
North, Sir Thomas 253
Novak, Maximillian E. 12 n., 344 n., 385 n.

Oates, Titus 185, 256, 259, 260, 263
represented in: *City Politiques* 309; *Lucius Junius Brutus* 295–6
Ogg, David 89 n., 339 n., 359 n.
Ogilby, John 312 n.
Ogle, Lord, *see* Cavendish, Henry
Oldmixon, John, contribution to *The Novelty* 389 n.
Oliver, H. J. 38 n., 44 n.
Ormonde, second Duke of, *see* Butler, James
Orrery, Earl of, *see* Boyle, Roger
Osborne, Thomas, Earl of Danby, Marquess of Carmarthen, and Duke of Leeds:
dedicatee of *All for Love* 264 n.
represented in: *The Ambitious Statesman* 264–5; ? *Antony and Cleopatra* [Sedley] 264 n.; *The Loyal General* 260, 273; *Timoleon* 431
Otway, Thomas 2, 104, 106, 185, 207, 288, 314, 377, 394
as innovator 455
bedroom tricks 28, 102, 277
compared with: Crowne 330 (the Stranger); Settle and Wycherley 277 (bedroom tricks); Shadwell and Wycherley 102 (bedroom tricks)
influence 455–6
influenced by Dryden 85
The Poet's Complaint of his Muse 282
political views during Exclusion Crisis 282–3
portrays dislocation 238, 280
reacts against Orrery's plays 240
Owen, Susan J. 185 n., 236 n., 260 n., 295 n.

Page, Thomas Ethelbert 21
Palmer, Arthur 21
Panton, Edward 21
Parfitt, George 163 n.
Parker, Gerald D. 97 n.
Parker, Samuel 9
Parnell, Paul E. 387 n.
Parsons, Robert 7 n.
Patrick, Simon 10 n.

Patterson, Annabel 114 n.
Payne, Deborah C. 1 n., 139 n.
Payne, Henry Neville 2, 106, 130, 254
Peacham, Henry 20–1, 22, 156, 157, 325–6
Pearson, Jacqueline 163 n., 167 n., 421 n., 433
    n., 447
Pepys, Samuel 33 n., 36 n., 37, 38 n., 46 n., 76
    n., 106
    admires *The Adventures of Five Hours* 39
    condemns *An Evening's Love* 71, 453
Perkin, Richard 121 n.
Peters, Julie Stone 148 n.
Philips, Katherine 37 n.
Philostratus, translated by Charles Blount 11
Pintard, René 10 n.
Pix, Mary 419, 443
    compared with Congreve 419 (individual/
        society)
    represented in *The Female Wits* 448
Plato 179–80
    influences *Love in the Dark* 146
Plutarch 253
Pope, Alexander, *An Essay on Man* 451–2
Popish Plot 89, 256, 262–3, 264–5, 268, 269,
    276, 286
Popkin, Richard 10 n.
Porter, Thomas 46
Portia (wife of the younger Brutus) 315
Portsmouth, Duchess of, *see* Kéroualle, Louise
    Renée de
Powell, George:
    brings *The Fatal Discovery* to the stage 440
    plagiarizes Pix's *The Deceiver Deceived* 420
    writes dedication to *Bonduca* (1696) 429
Price, Curtis A. 1 n., 36 n., 178 n., 371, 385 n.,
    424 n., 429, 433, 450 n.
Purcell, Daniel 378 n., 429, 433
Purcell, Henry 369, 371, 378, 424

Quin, Ann 213

Rabelais, François 135, 222 n.
Ramesay, William 22
rape 20, 32, 35, 46, 79, 81, 90, 92, 98, 102–3,
    107, 128, 176, 190–6, 201, 203–4, 206,
    208–9, 213, 214–15, 228, 233–4, 244, 245,
    255, 257, 263, 275, 279, 280, 296–8, 300,
    301, 311–12, 323, 324–5, 328–9, 331, 337,
    356, 358, 359–60, 361, 366, 373, 387, 405,
    429, 430, 431, 433, 437
Ravenscroft, Edward 2, 23, 199, 453
    prologue and epilogue to *The Conspiracy* 276
'Rawlins' 160 n., 197 n.
Rawson, C. J. 125 n.
Redwood, John 7 n.
Reresby, Sir John 265
Ribeiro, Alvaro 156 n.

Rich, Christopher 377, 378
Rich, Julia A. 344 n.
Rigaud, Nadia-J. 153 n.
Robbins, Caroline 19 n.
Robinson, K. E. 66 n., 188 n.
Rochester, Earl of, *see* Wilmot, John
Rochot, Bernard 180 n.
Rodes, David Stuart 344 n.
Root, Robert L. 344 n.
Roper, Alan 261 n., 393 n.
Ross, W. D. 106 n.
Rothstein, Eric 67 n., 95 n., 113 n., 134 n., 448
    n., 450 n.
Rouse, Francis 230 n.
Rowe, Nicholas 377
Royal Society 16
Rundle, James Urvin 122 n.
Rye House Plot 308

Sackville, Charles, Lord Buckhurst and Earl of
    Dorset 37 n.
Sandford, Samuel 372 n.
Sawyer, Thomas 11–12
Scargill, Daniel 7 n.
Scarron, Paul 68
    Le Roman comique 28; adapted in *The
        Atheist* 316
Schille, Candy B. K. 269 n.
Schomberg, Frederick Herman, Duke of, repres-
    ented in *The Siege of Constantinople* 96
Scott, Anne, Duchess of Monmouth and
    Buccleuch, acts in *Horace* 37
Scott (or Crofts), James, Duke of Monmouth
    and Buccleuch 11, 185
    attacked in epilogue to *Romulus and Hersilia*
        255
    conduct in 1678–9 273 n.
    dedicatee of Shipman's *Henry the Third of
        France* 89
    his invasion causes the failure of *Albion and
        Albanius* 313
    represented in: *The Duke of Guise* 307; *The
        Heir of Morocco* 281; *The History of
        King Lear* 277; *The Loyal General* 260,
        265, 273, 277; ? *The Massacre of Paris* 269;
        ? *The Unhappy Favourite* 279
Scott, John 9
Scott, Sir Walter 8 n.
Scouten, Arthur H. 30 n., 64 n., 66 n., 114
Scudéry, Georges de, *Alaric*, adapted in *The
    Indian Emperour* 47–8
Scudéry, Madeleine de:
    Artamenes; or, The Grand Cyrus [*Artamène;
        ou, Le Grand Cyrus*] 28 n.; source of
        Marriage A-la-Mode 168 n., 171
    Clelia [*Clélie*], source of *Lucius Junius Brutus*
        296 n., 299

Sedley, Sir Charles 37 n.
dedicatee of *Henry the Sixth, The First Part*
[Crowne] 274
service 46, 54, 56, 58, 113, 134, 138, 163, 197,
224, 234, 319, 344, 356, 374, 412, 425
Settle, Elkanah 2, 104, 128, 166, 363
becomes Tory pamphleteer (1683) 261
brings Pordage's *Herod and Mariamne* to the
stage 88
characteristics of his plays 86
The Character of a Popish Successour 261,
276 n.
compared with Otway and Wycherley 277
(bedroom tricks)
influenced by Dryden 85
organizes 1680 Pope-burning 261
rejects Orrery's outlook 86
responds to attack on *The Empress of
Morocco* 93
Sextus Empiricus 11, 14 n.
Shadwell, Anne 155–6
Shadwell, Thomas 2, 197, 228, 331, 377, 454
admires and imitates Etherege 75
assists Duke of Newcastle in *The Triumphant
Widow* 115
silenced for political views 325
collaborates in attack on *The Empress of
Morocco* 93
compared with: Cibber 387; Congreve 357
(justice), 380 (individual/society); Durfey
338 (oppressive step-parent); Etherege 156
(Epicureanism; language and the sacred),
328 (man as savage); Otway and Wycherley
102 (bedroom tricks); Vanbrugh 397
(justice)
Epicureanism and religious scepticism 4, 8,
156
on aristocracy and gentry 20–1, 75–6, 221,
223–4; on their decay and duties 22, 23,
76–7, 102, 121, 156–7, 162, 256
post-Revolution outlook 29, 338, 380
praises Charles II 276 n.
represented in *Sir Barnaby Whigg* 231, 266
Shafer, Robert 42 n.
Shaftesbury, Earl of, *see* Cooper, Anthony Ashley
Shakespeare, William 10, 94, 185 n., 255–6,
451, 452
praised in prologue to *Aureng-Zebe* 104
Sheffield, John, Earl of Mulgrave, afterwards
Marquess of Normanby, afterwards Duke
of Buckingham and Normanby, dedicatee
of *Aureng-Zebe* 104 n.
Shepherd, Simon 163 n.
Shipman, Thomas:
Carolina; or Loyal Poems, 89
dedicates *Henry the Third of France* to Duke
of Monmouth 89

Sidney, Algernon 333 n., 359
Sidney, Henry, Viscount Sheppey and Earl of
Romney, dedicatee of *King Edward the
Third* 333 n., 359
Simmons, Eva 211 n.
Simons, Joseph 78
Skipwith, Thomas 377 n.
Skrine, Peter N. 101 n.
Slagle, Judith B. 235 n.
Smith, J. A. 106 n.
Smith, John 13
Smith, John Harrington 6, 331 n., 390 n.
Smith, William 6
Solomon, Harry M. 283 n.
Somerset, Anne 163 n.
Sorelius, Gunnar 1 n., 256 n.
South, Robert 12, 18, 19, 181
Southerne, Thomas 28, 115, 283, 331, 377, 394,
448, 450, 456–7
assists Dryden in completion of *Cleomenes*
365
characteristics of his mature plays 343–9
compared with: Congreve and Vanbrugh 350
(dislocation); Etherege and Wycherley 344
(man as savage); Farquhar 408 (dislocation)
outlook after Revolution 343
portrays clash between aristocratic and com-
mercial systems 456
preoccupied with dislocation 280, 331
satirizes aristocracy 333
Spencer, Robert, Earl of Sunderland, ?repres-
ented in *Timoleon* 430–1
Spinoza, Benedict de 17
Sprat, Thomas 16
Spurr, John 18 n.
Stapylton, Sir Robert 34, 43
Staves, Susan 18 n., 24 n., 40 n., 67 n., 85 n.,
219 n., 341 n., 431 n., 450 n.
Stillingfleet, Edward 8
Stocker, Margarita 85 n.
Stone, Jeanne C. Fawtier 19 n., 339 n.
Stone, Lawrence 19 n., 20 n., 116 n., 339 n.
Straka, Gerald M. 359 n., 432 n.
Stroup, Thomas B. 308 n.
Suetonius 10 n.
Sulla, Lucius Cornelius 270 n.
Summers, Montague 121 n., 176 n.
Sunderland, Earl of, *see* Spencer, Robert
Sutherland, James 63 n.
Swaen, A. E. H. 39 n.
Swedenberg, H. T., Jr 42 n.

Tasso, Torquato, *Gerusalemme Liberata*
213–14
adapted in *Rinaldo and Armida* 442
Tate, Nahum:
political views in Exclusion Crisis 260

Tate, Nahum: (*cont.*)
  The Second Part of Absalom and Achitophel
  260
Teeter, Louis 42 n.
Theodoret (church historian) 315
Thompson, M. P. 432 n.
Tillotson, John 7, 12
  attacked by Charles Leslie 9
  quoted in epigraph to Chapter One 1
Trotter, Catherine 443
  represented in *The Female Wits* 448
Tuck, Richard 13 n.
Tuke, Sir Samuel 43

Underhill, Cave:
  indisposition causes failure of *The City Lady*
  386
  unusual casting in *The Intrigues at Versailles*
  404
United Company:
  initial reluctance to stage new plays 3, 307
  taken over by Christopher Rich 377

Vanbrugh, Sir John 29, 377
  compared with: Centlivre 445–6 (carnival);
    Congreve 350 (dislocation), 380, 396 (indi-
    vidual/society); Durfey 397 (justice);
    Etherege 395 (language and the sacred),
    397 (justice); Farquhar 408 (dislocation),
    410 (justice); Shadwell 397 (justice);
    Southerne 350 (dislocation); Wycherley
    397 (justice)
  portrays dislocation 331, 454
Vander Motten, J. P. 34 n., 75 n., 78 n.
Verbruggen, John 345 n.
Verbruggen, Susanna, *see* Mountfort, Susanna
Vernon, P. F. 122 n.
Verrall, A. W. 8–9
Verrall, Margaret de G. 8 n.
Vespasian 10
Viator, Timothy J. 278 n.
Vick, George R. 16 n.
Vieth, David M. 156 n., 295 n.
Villiers, Barbara, Countess of Castlemaine
    and Duchess of Cleveland, acts in *Horace*
    37
  ?represented in the original version of *The
    Humorists* 121 n.
Villiers, George, second Duke of Buckingham
    38 n.
  challenged by Sir William Coventry 114
  dedicatee of *The History of Timon of
    Athens*, and represented in the character of
    Alcibiades 256
  imprisoned in 1677 256
  political alliance with Sir Robert Howard 114
  quarrel with Shaftesbury 310–11

represented in *Troilus and Cressida* [Dryden],
    236 n., 265–6
  satirizes Arlington in *The Rehearsal* 85 n.
Virgil, *Aeneid* 56 n., 280, 312, 414 n.
  compared with: *Dido and Æneas* 450;
    The Ingratitude of a Common-Wealth
    450
Voss, Philip 456

Wallace, John M. 236 n., 272 n.
Waller, Edmund 37 n.
  quoted in *The Man of Mode* 4
Walsh, Martin W. 337 n.
Ward, Charles E. 6 n.
Watts, Thomas 9
Weber, Harold M. 205 n., 346–7, 380, 451 n.
Wellek, René 156 n.
Wentworth, Lady Henrietta, dedicatee of *The
    Heir of Morocco* 281
Wharton, Thomas, Marquess of Wharton,
    dedicatee of *The Successful Straingers*
    333 n.
Wheatley, Christopher J. 200 n., 336 n.,
    437 n.
Wikander, Matthew H. 185 n., 275 n.
Wilkins, A. S. 21
Wilkins, John 16–17
Wilks, Robert 421 n.
William III, King of England 369, 429, 430
  assassination plot 332, 397, 430, 431
  praised in: *The Famous History of the Rise
    and Fall of Massaniello* 436; *A New
    Opera; called, Brutus of Alba* 429; *A
    New Opera, call'd Cinthia and Endimion*
    402–3; dedication of *Pyrrhus King of
    Epirus* 433 n.; *The Successful Straingers*
    333
  represented in: ? *Don Sebastian* 362, 363 n.;
    King Arthur 369–70; *Love Triumphant*
    368; *Regulus* 361; *Timoleon* 430–1
Wilmot, John, Earl of Rochester 7, 311 n.
  allusion to in *Madam Fickle* 188 n.
  represented in *The Princess of Cleve* 313
  writes epilogue for *Love in the Dark* 145
Wing, Donald 440 n.
Winn, James Anderson 38 n., 104 n., 120 n.,
    230 n., 365 n., 389 n.
Winterbottom, John A. 42 n.
women, discussions of their rights and status 7,
    11, 14, 166
Wootton, David 7 n.
Wordsworth, Christopher 10 n.
Wycherley, William 2–3, 68, 122, 152, 197, 201,
    328, 377, 423
  compared with: Congreve 350 (dislocation);
    Dryden 175 (identity); Farquhar 410
    (justice); Otway and Settle 277 (bedroom

tricks); Otway and Shadwell 102
(bedroom tricks); Southerne 344 (man as
savage); Vanbrugh 397 (justice)
linguistics and epistemology 33, 106, 146,
152, 453

Yate, Lady (Mary), dedicatee of Marcelia 163 n.

York, Duchess of, *see* Hyde, Anne, and Mary of
Modena
York, Duke of, *see* James, Duke of York
Yots, Michael A. 6 n.

Zimansky, Curt A. 89
Zimbardo, Rose A. 450 n.